EXPERT DATA STRUCTURES WITH C++

SECOND EDITION

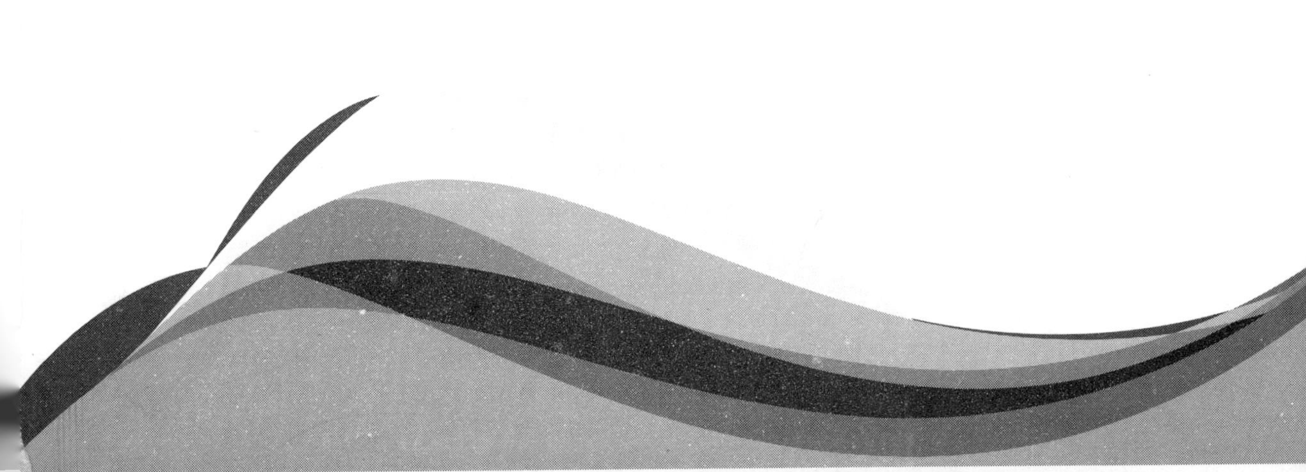

OTHER BOOKS BY THE SAME AUTHOR

- Expert Data Structure with C
- Computer Concepts and Programming in C
- Theory of Computation (With Formal Languages)
- Fundamentals of Computers & Programming in C

EXPERT DATA STRUCTURES WITH C++

SECOND EDITION

DR. R.B. PATEL
Deptt. Of Computer Science & Engg.
M.M. Engineering College, M.M. University,
Mullana, Ambala (Haryana)

KHANNA BOOK PUBLISHING CO. (P) LTD.

Publisher of Engineering and Computer Books

4C/4344, Ansari Road, Darya Ganj, New Delhi-110002
Phone : 011-23244447-48 **Mobile:** +91-9910909320
E-mail : contact@khannabooks.com
Website : www.khannabooks.com

Dear Readers,

To prevent the piracy, this book is secured with HIGH SECURITY HOLOGRAM on the front title cover. In case you don't find the hologram on the front cover title, please write us to at contact@ khannabooks.com or whatsapp us at +91-99109 09320 and avail special gift voucher for yourself.

Specimen of Hologram on front Cover title:

Moreover, there is a SPECIAL DISCOUNT COUPON for you with EVERY HOLOGRAM.

How to avail this SPECIAL DISCOUNT:

Step 1: Scratch the hologram
Step 2: Under the scratch area, your "coupon code" is available
Step 3: Logon to www.khannabooks.com
Step 4: Use your "coupon code" in the shopping cart and get your copy at a special discount
Step 5: Enjoy your reading!

Thanks,

Khanna Publishing House

Price: ₹ 495.00

Expert Data Structures With C++

Dr. R.B. Patel

ISBN: 978-81-87522-03-4

First Edition: 2011

Reprint: 2021

Published by:

Khanna Book Publishing Co. (P) Ltd.

4C/4344, Ansari Road, Darya Ganj, New Delhi-110 002

Phone: 011-23244447-48 **Mobile:** +91-9910909320

E-mail: contact@khannabooks.com

Printed by: SPS Printers

Acknowledgement

Sitting on the seashore we had thought that it was an easy task to dine but it was only when we dined into one ocean of data structures and brought for you the pearl "EXPERT DATA STRUCTURES WITH C++". We realize how much helpful were so many people to us. Without these people this exploration could never have materialized. We now realize that the acknowledgment is some thing that really comes from the bottom of the heart of every writer.

Our primary obligation is to Dr. L.N. Paliwal, Ex-principal G.B. Pant Engineering College Pauri-Garhwal, presently serving as Professor (Electrical Engineering) in Moti Lal Nehru Regional Engineering College Allahabad. For those who knew him, no words are necessary and for those who do not know him, no words will suffice.

Our Principal Dr. Satya Sheel aided ourselves immensely at all stages in the development and production of this book and without his guidance this book would not have seen the light of the day.

We are deeply indebted to the contribution to our faculty members and friends Professor M.L. Dewel, Mr. Rajeev Srivastava, Mr. Ashish Negi, Mr. D.K. Yadav, Mr. B.C. Sharma, Dr. B. Rai, Dr. H Goel and Dr. V. N. Kala whose moral boosting and support motivated us to work efficiently in odd hours.

We are also deeply indebted to the contribution offered by Dr. R. Kumar, Professor, & Head (Computer Science & Engineering) M.M.M. Engineering College, Gorakhpur to us.

Our big thanks, to Khanna Publishing Company, Delhi, for providing ourselves a platform for which we proud ourselves.

Special thanks are due to Mr. V.K. Srivastava, Mr. Guman Singh, Mr. Kamlesh Joshi, Mr. Ashok Kumar Raiwani, Ms. Geeta Rawat, Ms. Vijaya Chandola, Mr. Vinod Kumar and Mr. Suresh Kumar whose co-operation was always with us.

Our sincere thanks are due to our wives Mrs. Kanchan Lata and Mrs. Sushma Rauthan and our daughters lovely Rachita and Misthi for their co-operation in the development of this book.

Last but not the least, the contribution of our students Mr. Praveen Lakhera, Mr. Shanker Narayan Srivastava, Mr. Anant Narain, Mr. Nimesh Bhadoria, Mr Manish Vajpai and Mr Vigant Maheswari can not be overlooked for their pain staking efforts and finding even the minutest bugs that had creeped into the manuscript and deserve sincere appreciation.

Suggestions and queries are most welcome through publisher.

R.B. Patel

Preface To First Edition

"A picture does work of thousand words and a memory of thousand pictures"- We have done the first thousand, the second thousand is left for you. The primary objective of writing this book is to give "an easy to understand" –pictorial treatment to such a subject of theoretical complexities as Data Structures. The book turns out to be voluminous owing to its pictorial nature. Don't get frightened the number of pages, just take a glance at the figures and you would find the monster of Data Structures being tamed within no time. Just go through the book once and after that you'll just need to turn the pages over and its back again.

This book starts with the fundamentals of Data Structures and finally leading to the much-detailed discussion of the subject. The very first chapter introduces the readers with **C++** elementary concepts as type conversions, structures, pointers, dynamic memory management, functions and function overloading, class and objects and files and streams.

The next step deals with recursion and involves factorials, various forms of exponential power, Fibonacci numbers, greatest common divisor of two integer numbers, much popular Towers of Hanoi problem and finally divide-and-conquer technique.

Chapter third is the concepts of "String Manipulation and Pattern matching" incorporating structures of string storage, string functions and Markov algorithm.

Arrays an elementary subject of Data Structures is dealt next, covering the basic one-dimensional, two-dimensional and multidimensional arrays with special emphasis on matrices and a detailed treatment to various operations related to matrices as addition of two matrices, subtraction, multiplication, transpose, inverse and rank of a matrix etc.

After getting firm hold on fundamentals we come to more specialized linked list, which introduces the readers with linear linked list and doubly linked lists. The operations such as traversal, insertions, deletions are performed on them for giving the in-depth knowledge on linked list. Further, the header-linked list, circular linked list and polynomials have also been discussed.

Chapter sixth deals with "Stacks and Queues" another building block of Data Structures. The portion covers stack representations, stack operations- traversal, insertion, deletion, peep and update. Stack applications are also introduced in detail. The latter portion of the chapter conceptualizes queues- their implementation and types like circular queues, double ended queues and priority queues with adequate illustrations.

Exploring further we come across "Trees" their representation as sequential & linked list. The binary tree and complete binary trees form the striking note to the chapter. Traversal of the binary tree pre-order, in-order and post-order are covered in detail. Another important concept of Huffman tree is discussed next leading to applications of the binary trees. Search trees and deletion in binary search tree is discussed adequately. Balanced binary trees, AVL tree, B-trees and threaded binary trees have been covered in detail.

Chapter eighth on "Graphs" gives its basic concepts, path; representation including sequential representation, shortest path algorithms such as Warshall's algorithms, Dijkstra, Floyd, adjacency lists and graph traversal is discussed next. Depth and Breadth first searches and topological sorting mark the end of the chapter.

The last chapter "Sorting and Searching" has been given special attention in which efficiency factor has been kept in mind. This chapter searches (linear and binary) and covers different types of sorting techniques such as Bubble sort, Insertion sort, Quick sort, Selection sort, Donald Shell sort, Merge sort, Heap sort and Radix sort.

This textbook covers the syllabus of Semester College course on data structures. It provides both a strong theoretical basis in data structures and an advanced approach to their representation in **C++**. The text is useful to **C++** professionals and programmers as well as students of any branch of Engineering of graduate and postgraduate courses. The data structures are presented with in the context of complete working programs that have been tested both on a **UNIX** system and a personal computer using **Turbo-C++ 3.0** Compiler. The code is developed in a top-down fashion, typically with the low-level data structures implementation following the high-level application code. This approach foster good programming habits and makes subject matter more interesting.

The book has three-goals- to develop a consistent programming methodology, to develop data structures access techniques and to introduce algorithms. The bulk of the text is developed to make a strong hold on data structures. Programming style and development methodology are introduced and its applications are presented. This has the advantage of allowing the reader to concentrate on the data structures, while illustrating how good practices make programming easier.

Final words of advice to readers is that, in case you find hard to grasp through words, go to figures and again come back to the text. This would reinforce the idea expressed and I am sure you will never find anything as easy as data structures.

Enhanced Features Of Second Edition

Heading in the direction, "Easy Þ Easier Þ Easiest", some modifications and amendments are done in this second edition.

- *To further strengthen the base of readers some new bricks are added to the foundation, viz. Flowcharts, Algorithms and Basics of Data Structures in* ***Introduction.***

- ***Function Overhead*** *is a tool added in Recursion techniques (second chapter). "Algebra of matrices is now equipped with information about* ***sparse matrix*** *(chapter four).*

- *Further, to make the "Linked List" (chapter five) easy for your gray matter to compile, it is implemented with the help of index values rather than the conventional and complex method of memory address used in the first edition. Although in programs it is demonstrated with the help of memory address. While dealing with insertion and deletion routed arrows are used to show the insertion, deletion & resulting displacements which will further reduce the complexity understanding this method.*

- *Another step towards betterment is the "Implementation of Polish Notation (i.e. conversion of Infix to Postfix Notation)" introduced in chapter six dealing with "Stack and Queues".*

- *In chapter seven dealing with "Trees", stress in given on practicality. Thus implementation of "Deletion in Binary Search Tree" and "Insertion in AVL Tree" is added in this chapter.*

- *In chapter nine (Sorting and Searching), Two-way merge sort, techniques of Radix Exchange sort and Hashing are introduced to enhance the skills in field of Sorting and Searching.*

Along with these new features this edition is backup by more examples, programs, exercises and of course sincere efforts to develop this book as an efficient learning tool in the field of Data Structures.

CONTENTS

CHAPTER 1 INTRODUCTION

1.1 CONSTANTS 1
1.1.1 ESCAPE SEQUENCES 3
1.1.2 ENUMERATION CONSTANTS 4
1.2 TYPE CONVERSION 6
1.3 ARITHMETIC OPERATOR WITH ASSIGNMENT 8
1.4 PRECEDENCE AND ASSOCIATIVITY 9
1.5 CONDITIONAL EXPRESSIONS 11
1.6 HOW THE OVERFLOW ARISE 11
1.7 STRUCTURES 12
1.8 UNION 18
1.9 POINTERS 19
1.9.1 ARRAYS OF POINTERS 24
1.9.2 POINTER TO STRUCTURES 28
1.10 DYNAMIC MEMORY ALLOCATION 32
1.10.1 The new and delete 38
1.11 FUNCTION 40
1.11.1 FUNCTION INVOCATION 41
1.11.2 TERMINATION OF FUNCTION 43
1.11.3 PARAMETER PASSING TECHNIQUES 45
1.11.3.1 PASS BY VALUE 45
1.11.3.2 PASS BY REFERENCE 46
1.11.4 PROTOTYPES 47
1.11.5 FUNCTION OVERLOADING 49
1.11.6 FUNCTION AND STRUCTURES 52
1.12 The class 54
1.12.1 STRUCTURE AND CLASS 57
1.12.2 CONSTRUCTORS AND DESTRUCTORS 59
1.13 FILES AND STREAMS 62
1.14 FLOWCHART 74
1.15 ALGORITHMS 78
1.15.1 ANALYSIS OF ALGORITHMS 79
1.15.1.1 RATE OF GROWTH 79
1.15.1.2 TIME ANALYSIS 80
1.15.1.3 BIG O-NOTATION 82
1.16 DATA STRUCTURE 83
1.16.1 LINEAR DATA STRUCTURES 83
1.16.1.1 ARRAYS 84
1.16.1.2 LINKED LIST 84
1.16.1.3 STACK AND QUEUES 85
1.16.2 NONLINEAR DATA STRUCTURES 85
1.16.2.1 TREE 85
1.16.2.2 GRAPH 86

1.17 DATA STRCUTURE OPERATIONS 87
EXERCISE 87

CHAPTER 2 RECURSION

2.1 RECURSION 91
2.2 TYPES OF RECURSION 93
2.3 EXPONENTIAL POWER 97
2.4 FIBONACCI NUMBERS 102
2.5 GEATEST COMMON DIVISOR 104
2.6 THE TOWERS OF HANOI 105
2.7 DIVIDE AND CONQUER 115
2.8 FUNCTION OVERHEAD 120
EXERCISE 121

CHAPTER 3 STRING MANIPULATION AND PATTERN MATCHING

3.1 STRUCTURE OF STRING STORAGE 127
3.1.1 FIXED LENGTH 127
3.1.2 VARIABLE LENGTH FIXED MAXIMUM 133
3.1.3 LINKED LIST STORAGE 139
3.2 STRING OPERATIONS 139
3.2.1 INDEXING (Pattern Matching) 141
3.2.2 CONCATENATION 148
3.2.3 LENGTH 149
3.3 APPLICATION OF STRING OR TEXT PROCESSING 150
3.3.1 TEXT EDITING 151
3.3.1.1 INSERTION 151
3.3.1.2 DELETION 153
3.3.1.3 PATTERN MATCHING (REPLACEMENT) 158
3.3.2 TEXT FORMATTING 165
3.4 MARKOV ALGORITHM 166
3.4.1 BASIC CONCEPT 166
3.4.2 IDENTITY PROPERTY 167
3.4.3 ASSOCIATIVE PROPERTY 167
3.4.4 PRODUCTION 167
3.4.5 TERMINATION 168
3.4.6 ALGORITHM 168
EXERCISE 173

CHAPTER 4 ARRAYS

4.1 INTRODUCTION 176
4.2 ONE DIMENSIONAL ARRAYS 177
4.3 ONE DIMENSIONAL ARRAYS IN MEMORY 179
4.4 TRAVERSING ONE DIMENSIONAL ARRAY 180
4.5 INSERTION IN ONE DIMENSIONAL ARRAY 183

4.6 DELETION FROM ONE DIMENSIONAL ARRAY 190
4.7 SEARCHING 201
4.8 MULTI DIMENSIONAL ARRAYS 206
4.8.1 TWO DIMENSIONAL ARRAYS 207
4.8.2 REPRESENTATION OF TWO DIMENSIONAL ARRAYS IN MEMORY 210
4.8.3 TRAVERSING TWO DIMENSIONAL ARRAYS 211
4.9 ALGEBRA OF MATRICES 216
4.9.1 ADDITION OF MATRICES 218
4.9.2 SUBTRACTION OF MATRICES 220
4.9.3 MULTIPLICATION OF TWO MATRICES 224
4.9.4 TRANSPOSE OF A MATRIX 230
4.9.5 ORTHOGONAL OF A MATRIX 233
4.9.6. SINGULAR MATRIX 238
4.9.7 INVERSE OF A MATRIX 242
4.9.8 SYMMETRIC MATRIX 248
4.9.9 RANK OF A MATRIX 251
4.10 GENERAL MUTLIDIMENSIONAL ARRAYS 257
4.11 SPARSE MATRICES 262
EXERCISE 265

CHAPTER 5 LINKED LIST

5.1 LINKED LIST 269
5.2 BUILDING A LINKED LIST 271
5.3 TRAVERSING A LINKED LIST 279
5.4 INSERTION IN A LINKED LIST 282
5.4.1 INSERTION AS A FIRST NODE 284
5.4.2 INSERTION AS A LAST NODE 288
5.4.3 INSERTION OF A NODE AT SPECIFIC LOCATION 293
5.5 DELETION IN A LINKED LIST 304
5.5.1 Deletion of First Node 305
5.5.2 Deletion of Last Node 310
5.5.3 Deletion of A Desired Node 316
5.6 Searching A Linked List 327
5.7 Sorting A Linked List 332
5.8 Doubly Linked List 342
5.9 Traversing A Doubly Linked List 347
5.10 Insertion in A Doubly Linked List 351
5.10.1 Inserting First Node (LEFT OF THE LEFT MOST NODE IN A LIST) 352
5.10.2 Inserting A Node At The End 358
5.10.3 Inserting A Node At Desired Place 365
5.11 Deletion In A Doubly Linked List 367
5.11.1 Deletion of Left Most Node 368
5.11.2 Deletion Of Right Most Node 373
5.11.3 Deletion of A Desired Node 380
5.12 Merging Two Lists 387
5.13 Header Linked List 394
5.13.1 Grounded Header Linked List 394

5.13.2 Circular Header Linked List 401
5.14 Application of Header Linked List 409
5.14.1 Polynomials 409
5.14.2 Addition of Polynomials 412
EXERCISE 415

CHAPTER 6 STACKS AND QUEUES

6.1 STACK 421
6.2 REPRESENTATION OF STACK 423
6.3 IMPLEMENTATION OF STACK 424
6.3.1 ARRAY'S IMPLEMENTATION 424
6.3.1.1 PUSH OPERATION 425
6.3.1.2 POP OPERATION 425
6.3.1.3 PEEP OPERATION 434
6.3.1.4 UPDATE OPERATION 438
6.4 POLISH NOTATION 443
6.4.1 USES OF STACK 444
6.4.1.1 EVALUATION OF THE POSTFIX EXPRESSION 452
6.5 QUEUES 452
6.5.1 IMPLEMENTATION OF QUEUES 453
6.6 CIRCULAR QUEUES 461
6.7 DOUBLE ENDED QUEUE 470
6.8 PRIORITY QUEUES 472
EXERCISE 475

CHAPTER 7 TREES

7.1 INTRODUCTION 479
7.2 BINARY TREE 482
7.3 COMPLETE BINARY TREE 495
7.4 EXTENDED BINARY TREE OR 2-TREE 500
7.5 REPRESENTATION OF BINARY TREE 500
7.5.1 SEQUENTIAL REPRESENTATION 501
7.5.2 LINKED LIST REPRESENTATION 504
7.6 TRAVERSING BINARY TREE 506
7.6.1 PREORDER 506
7.6.2 INORDER 509
7.6.3 POST ORDER 510
7.7 MINIMUM WEIGHTED PATH LENGTH ALGORITHMS 514
7.8 APPLICATION OF BINARY TREE 526
7.9 SEARCH TREE 528
7.9.1 DELETION IN A BINARY SEARCH TREE 532
7.10 BALANCED BINARY TREE 540
7.10.1 HEIGHT BALANCED 540
7.10.2 INSERTION IN AVL TREE 545
7.10.2.1 RIGHT HIGH (height of the right sub-tree is greater than left sub-tree) 551
7.10.3 THE HEIGHT OF AN AVL TREE 555

7.11 B-TREE (Balanced Multi-Way Tree) 568
7.12 THREADED BINARY TREES 577
EXERCISE 579

CHAPTER **8** **GRAPHS**

8.1 BASIC CONCEPTS AND DEFINITIONS 587
8.2 PATH 593
8.3 REPRESENTATION OF GRAPH 594
  8.3.1 SEQUENTIAL REPRESENTATION 594
8.4 SHORTEST PATH ALGORITHMS 600
  8.4.1 WARSHALL'S ALGORITHM 600
  8.4.2 WARSHALL'S MODIFIED ALGORITHM 607
  8.4.3 DIJKSTRA' S TECHNIQUE 615
  8.4.4 FLOYD'S TECHNIQUE 622
8.5 ADJACENCY LIST 629
8.6 GRAPH TRAVERSAL 630
  8.6.1 DEPTH FIRST SEARCH (DFS) 630
  8.6.2 BREADTH FIRST SEARCH (BFS) 636
8.7 TOPOLOGICAL SORTING 646
EXERCISE 647

CHAPTER **9** **SEARCHING AND SORTING**

9.1 LINEAR SEARCH 652
9.2 BINARY SEARCH 657
9.3 BUBBLE SORT 662
9.4 INSERTION SORT 668
9.5 QUICK SORT 673
9.6 SELECTION SORT 681
9.7 SHELL SORT 686
9.8 MERGE SORT 691
9.9 HEAP SORT 706
9.10 RADIX SORT 719
9.11 RADIX EXCHANGE SORT 731
9.12 HASHING 732
  9.12.1 COLLISIONS 735
  9.12.2 LINEAR PROBING 735
  9.12.3 DELETION 737
  9.12.4 CLUSTERING 738
  9.12.5 REHASHING 738
  9.12.6 BUCKET AND CHAINING 740
  9.12.7 SELECTING GOOD HASH FUNCTION 742
EXERCISE 744

INDEX 748

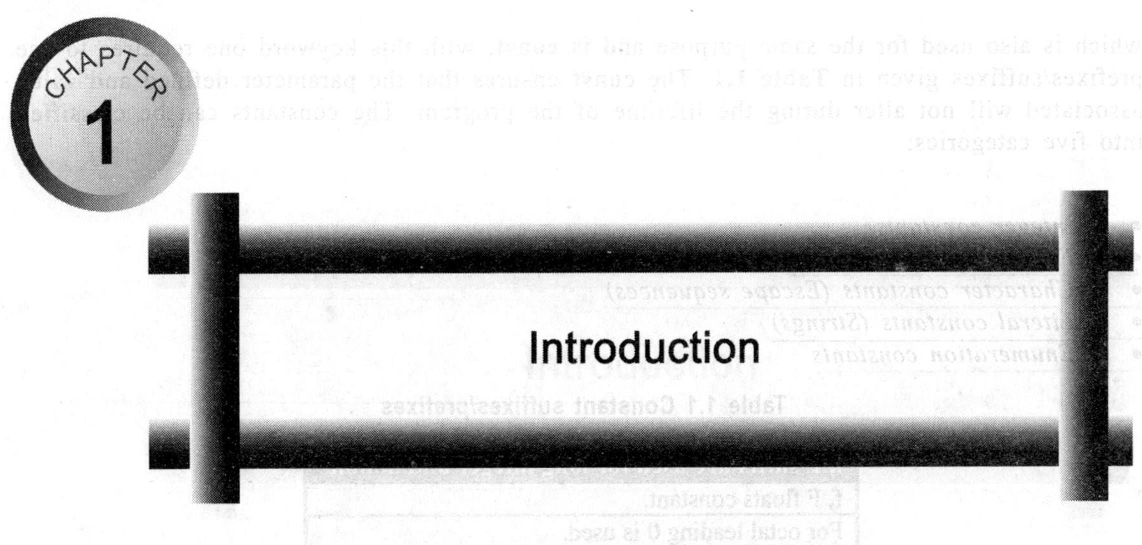

The early version of **C++** language was known as **"C with Classes"**, has been in use since **1980**. The language was invented because the author of the language wanted to write some event driven simulations for which **Simula67** would have been ideal, except for efficiency considerations. **"C with Classes"** was used for major simulation projects facilitating major simulation projects in which the facilities for writing programs that use minimal time and space were severely tested. **"C with Classes"** lacked operator overloading, references, virtual functions, and other details. **C++** was first installed outside the author's research group in July' 1983.

Rick Mascitti coined the name **C++** in the summer of **1983**. Primarily designed **C++** did not support assembly language. The explosive growth of **C++** was during **1987**. However, the actual scope of the language came into the software industry on **25th January' 1994.**

This chapter illustrates the basic concepts of **C++**, and it is assumed that the readers are well familiar with the language **C** and **C++**.

1.1 CONSTANTS

Constant is a name **C++** compiler associates with a value that does not change. To create a constant we use the **define** directive. For example, the following directive creates a constant named **Size** and assigns to the constant the value 256.

```
# define Size 256
```

When **C++** preprocessor later encounters the **Size** constant name in the program, the preprocessor will replace the constant name with its value. For example:

```
int List [Size];
```

This statement defines an array of 256 elements. There is a keyword available in **C++**, which is also used for the same purpose and is **const,** with this keyword one requires to use prefixes/suffixes given in **Table 1.1**. The **const** ensures that the parameter defined and value associated will not alter during the lifetime of the program. The constants can be classified into five categories:

- *Integer constants*
- *Floating point constants*
- *Character constants (Escape sequences)*
- *Literal constants (Strings)*
- *Enumeration constants*

Table 1.1 Constant suffixes/prefixes

l, L suffix are used for long integer and double
f, F floats constant.
For octal leading 0 is used.
For hexadecimal 0x is written in leading.
For unsigned numbers u, U suffix is used
Character constant quoted in single quote.

For example, the program segment **CONSTANT.C** discusses the constant declarations with help of keyword **const**.

```
// Constant
// CONSTANT.C
# include<iostream.h>
# include<stdio.h>

void main()
{
    const int I = 12345;
    const long int L =99999L;
    const float F = 123456.345f;
    const int O = 01234;
    const int H = 0x1abc;
    const int U = 123u;
    cout<<"\n Integer "<<I;
    cout<<"\n Long integer "<<L;
    cout<<"\n Float "<<F;
    printf("\n Octal %o", O);
    printf("\n Hexadecimal %X",H);
    cout<<"\n Unsigned integer "<<U;
}
```

```
Integer 12345
Long integer 99999
Float 123456.34375
Octal 1234
Hexadecimal 1ABC
Unsigned integer 123
```

1.1.1 ESCAPE SEQUENCES

The new line character is an example of something called an escape sequence, so called because the backslash symbol '\' is considered an escape character: it causes an escape from the normal interpretation of a character/string so that the next character is recognized as having a special meaning. For example, consider the following segment that uses the new line character and a new escape sequence, '\t' which means tab.

```
#include <stdio.h>

void main(void)
{
    printf("\nEach\tword\tis\ntabbed\tover\tonce");
}
```

```
Each   word   is
tabbed        over   once
```

Some of the escape sequences are defined as octal values with the help of backslash character. For example, consider the following examples of escape sequence representation:

```
# define VTAB '\013'     /* ASCII VERTICAL TAB */
# define BELL '\007'     /* ASCII BELL */
```

Table 1.2 Escape sequences characters

Escape Character	Meaning	Short Notation
\a	Bell	BEL
\b	Backspace	BS
\f	Form Feed	FF
\n	New Line	NL
\r	Carriage Return	CR
\t	Horizontal Tab	HT
\v	Vertical Tab	VT
\\	Backslash	BAS
\?	Question Mark	QM
\'	Single Quote	SQ
\"	Double Quotes	DQ
\onnn	Octal Number	ON
\xhhh	Hexadecimal Number	HN
'\0'	Null Character	NC

The above definitions can be also defined in hexadecimal. The hexadecimal definition of the above octal definition is as follows:

```
# define VTAB '\xd' /* ASCII VERTICAL TAB */
# define BELL '\x7  /* ASCII BELL CHARACTER */
```

An escape sequence can also be denoted a backslash followed by maximum three digits (no leading zero is needed). For example, character **A** has the **ASCII** value 65, which is 101 in octal, so the escape sequence for it would be '\101'. Usually octal escape sequences are used to represent non-printing characters. For example bell, null character and other characters are illustrated in the **Table 1.2**

1.1.2 ENUMERATION CONSTANTS

The enumerated data type gives one the opportunity to invent his/her own data type and specify what values it can take on. This can help make listings more readable, which can be an advantage when a program gets complicated or when more than one programmer will be working on it. Using enumerated types can also help reduce programming errors.

The keyword **enum** is used to specify an enumerated data type. The format of the **enum** definition is similar to that of structure. An enumeration is a list of constant integer values as:

```
enum Boolean {sparrow, robin, eagle, egret};
enum Boolean Flag1, Flag2; /* defines variable */
```

The first statement declares the data type itself-type **enum Boolean** and specifies its possible values, which are called enumerators. The second statement defines one or more variables- **Flag1** and **Flag2** - to be of this type. Now we will assign values to these variables.

```
Flag1 = sparrow;
Flag2 = egret;
```

It is not possible to use values that are not in the original list. For example, consider the expression

```
Flag1 = magpie;
```

would cause an error.

Internally, the compiler treats enumerated variables as integers. Each value on the list of permissible values corresponds to an integer, starting with 0. Thus, in the **Boolean** example, **sparrow** is stored as 0, **robin** as 1, **eagle** as 2 and **egret** as 3.

Thus, we can say that first has value 0 and second has value 1 and so on, unless explicit values are specified. If all the values are not specified, unspecified values continue the progression from the last specified value. The programmer cam override this way of assigning numbers by initializing the enumerated to different integers values. For example, consider the following declaration of **escape** and **months:**

```
enum escape { BELL = '\a', BACKSPACE = '\b', TAB='\t', NEWLINE ='\n', VTAB = '\v', RETURN = '\r' };
enum months { JAN = 1, FEB, MAR, APR, MAY, JUN, JUL, AUG, SEP, OCT, NOV, DEC};
```

In the above example: FEB = 2, MAR = 3 and so on. Thus, we can say that the enumeration provides a convenient way to associate constant (character or integer) values with names. For example, consider the following program segment that shows the implementation of enumeration data type.

```
// ENUMS.C
// Demonstrates enumerated variables
#include <stdio.h>
#include <string.h>
void main(void)
{                                       // declare new type and values
    enum empcats {Principal, Professor, Lecturer, Clerical};
    struct      // declare structure
    {
        char name[30];
        float salary;
        enum empcats category; /* use new type for member */
    } employee;

    strcpy(employee.name, "R.B. Patel");
    employee.salary = 16298.50;
    employee.category = Professor;  /* assign value to member */

    printf("Name = %s\n", employee.name);
```

```
    printf("Salary = %8.2f\n", employee.salary);
    printf("Category = %d\n", employee.category);

    if(employee.category== Professor)
        printf("Employee category is Professor. \n");
    else
        printf("Employee category is not Professor. \n");
}
```

1.2 TYPE CONVERSION

When the variables of one type are mixed with variables of another type, a type conversion is required. In an assignment statement the type conversion rules are easy. The value of the right hand side of the assignment is converted to the type of the left-hand side. For example, consider the following code slice:

```
int i;
char ch;
float f;
void conversion ()
{
    ch = i;
    i = f;
    f = ch;
    f = i;
}
```

In **ch** = **i**; the left high order bits of the integer variable **i** are lopped off, leaving **ch** with the lower 8 bits. If **i** is between 256 and 0, **i** and **ch** will have identical values. Otherwise, the value of **ch** will reflect only lower order of bits of **i**. In **i** = **f**; **i** will receive the non-fractional part of the **f**. In **f** = **ch**; **f** will convert the 8 bits integer value stored in **ch** to the same value in the floating point format. This is also happening in **f** = **i**; except that **f** will convert an integer value into floating point format.

When converting from integers to characters and long integers to integers, the appropriate amount of high order bits will be removed. In many environments, this means that 8 bits will be lost when going from an integer to character and 16 bits will be lost when going from a long integer to an integer. For assignment type conversion consider the **Table 1.3**.

Table 1.3 type conversion on 16-bit word machine

Target type	Expression	Possible information loss
singed char	char	If value > 127 target is negative
char	short int	High order 8 bits
char	int	High order 8 bits
char	long int	High order 24 bits
int	long int	High order 16 bits
int	float	Fractional part possibly more
float	double	Precision result rounded
double	long double	Precision result rounded

Sometimes it requires converting string of numeric characters into integer value. If one defines **s [i] - '0'**, it gives the numeric value of the character stored in **s [i]**, because the values of **'0'** and **'1'**, etc form a contiguous increasing sequence. For example, consider the following program segment that converts "12345" string into its integer equivalent:

```
# include<iostream.h>
# include<conio.h>

long int atoi1(char *);

void main()
{
     long int result ;
     result = atoi1("12345" );
     cout<<"\n"<<result;
     getchar();
}

long int atoi1( char *s)
{
     int i ;
     long int n = 0L ;

     for( i = 0 ; (s[i] >= '0' && s[i] <= '9') ; i++)
     {
          n = n*10 + ( s[i] - '0');
          cout<<"\n "<<n;
     }
     return (n) ;
}
```

1.3 ARITHMETIC OPERATOR WITH ASSIGNMENT

If we compare a **C++** program with a program with a similar purpose written in another language, we may well find that **C++** source file is shorter. One reason for this is that *C++ has several operators that* can compress often used programming statements. For example, consider the following code slice:

Total = Total + Number;

Here the value of **Number** is added to the value in **Total** and result is placed in **Total**. In **C++** this statement can be written as **Total += Number;** The effect is same; but the expression is more compact, as shown in **Fig. 1.1.**

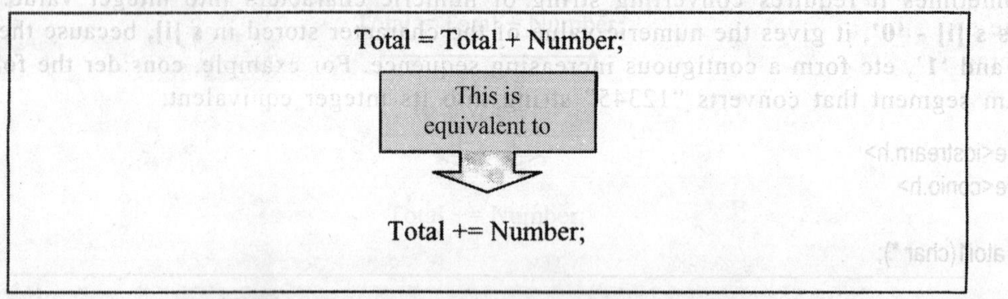

Fig. 1.1 The arithmetic assignment operator

For example, consider the following program segment that implements the above discussion (ASSIGN.C):

```
// ASSIGN.C

#include <stdio.h>

void main(void)
{
     int total = 0;
     int count = 10;

     printf("\nTotal = %d\n", total);
     total += count;
     printf("Total = %d\n", total);
     total += count;
     printf("Total=%d\n", total);
}
```

The expressions such as **Total = Total + Number;** in which the variable on the left-hand side is repeated on the right, can be written as **Total += Number;** The operator += is called an assignment operator. Most binary operators have a corresponding assignment **op=**, where **op** is one of + - * / << & ^ |. For example, if **Total += Number;** then operator pair += tells the compiler to assign **Total,** the value of **Tota!** plus **Number**. If $\mathbf{exp_1}$ and $\mathbf{exp_2}$ are expressions, then $\mathbf{exp_1}$ **op** = $\mathbf{exp_2}$; is equivalent to $\mathbf{exp_1}$=($\mathbf{exp_1}$) **op** ($\mathbf{exp_2}$); except that $\mathbf{exp_1}$ is computed only once. For example: **a* = b +1;** means **a = a * (b + 1);** rather than **a = a * b + 1;** . See another example, which counts 1's in an integer number interpreting integer number as binary.

```
bc ( unsigned a) /* Counts number of 1's in a given number */
{
    int b = 0;
    for ( b; a!=0; a>>1)
    if (a &1)
    b += 1;
    return(b);
}
```

The parentheses are used '( )' and bracket '[ ]' to increase the precedence of expressions. The details of the assignment operators are given in **Table 1.4.**

Table 1.4 assignment operators

Symbol	Operator	Example
=	Equal	a = b
+=	Addition	a += b (same as a = a + b)
-=	Subtraction	a -= b (same as a = a – b)
*=	Multiplication	a *= b (same as a = a * b)
/=	Division	a /= b (same as a = a / b)
%=	Remainder	a %= b (same as a = a %b)
&=	Bitwise AND	a &= b (same as a = a & b)
|=	Bitwise OR	a |= b (same as a = a | b)
^=	Bitwise exclusive OR	a ^= b (same as a = a ^ b)
<<=	Left shift	a <<= 2 (same as a = a << 2)
>>=	Right shift	a >>= 3 (same as a = a >> 3)

1.4 PRECEDENCE AND ASSOCIATIVITY

What will be printed if one executes the following program? Remember that true is the integer 1 and false is the integer 0. These values can be used just like any other integer values as shown by the following program segment:

```
#include <stdio.h>
void main(void)
{
    printf("\n Answer is %d", 2+1 < 4 );
}
```

If one guessed the **Answer is 1**, one is right. First 2 + 1 is evaluated to yield 3, then this is compared with 4. It's less, so the expression:

2 + 1 <4

is true. True is 1 so that's what's printed?

Now watch closely! We are going to try something a little trickily. What will the following program segment print?

```
#include <stdio.h>
void main(void)
{
    printf("\nAnswer is %d", 1<2 + 4 );
}
```

Did one can guess **Answer is 5**? If so, one probably decided that 1<2 would evaluate to true or 1 and 1 added to 4 would give 5. Sorry this is plausible but in correct. We misled one with the use of spaces in the expression 1< 2 + 4. Here's how we should have written it.

1< 2 + 4

There are two things to discuss here. First, as we mentioned before, the compiler doesn't care where one puts spaces; both forms of the expression compile into the same program. Second, arithmetic operators have higher precedence than relational operators. That is, in absence of parentheses the arithmetic operators are evaluated before the relational operators. In the expression above, the arithmetic operator '+' is evaluated first, yielding a value of 6 from the expression 2+4. Then the relational operator (<) is evaluated. Because the 1 is less than 6, the value of the entire expression is true. Thus, the output of this program will be **Answer is 1.**

Table 1.5 Associativity of operators

<table>
<tr><th>Operators</th><th>Type</th><th>Associativity</th></tr>
<tr><td>( ) [ ] . →</td><td>Groups, membership</td><td>LTR</td></tr>
<tr><td>- ! ~ | * &</td><td>Unary</td><td>RTL</td></tr>
<tr><td>++ -- sizeof casts</td><td>Unary</td><td>RTL</td></tr>
<tr><td>* / %</td><td>Multiplicative</td><td>LTR</td></tr>
<tr><td>+ -</td><td>Additive</td><td>LTR</td></tr>
<tr><td><< >></td><td>Shift</td><td>LTR</td></tr>
<tr><td>< > <= >=</td><td>Relational</td><td>LTR</td></tr>
<tr><td>= = !=</td><td>Equality</td><td>LTR</td></tr>
<tr><td>&</td><td>Bitwise AND</td><td>LTR</td></tr>
<tr><td>^</td><td>Bitwise Exclusive OR</td><td>LTR</td></tr>
<tr><td>|</td><td>Bitwise OR</td><td>LTR</td></tr>
<tr><td>&&</td><td>Logical AND</td><td>LTR</td></tr>
<tr><td>?:</td><td>Ternary (Conditional)</td><td>RTL</td></tr>
<tr><td>= *= /= %= += -= <<= >>= &= ^= |=</td><td>Arithmetic assignment</td><td>RTL</td></tr>
<tr><td>,</td><td>Comma</td><td>LTR</td></tr>
</table>

where: LTR => Left To Right
RTL => Right To Left

All operators in **C++** are ranked according to their precedence. Precedence is a more important issue in **C++** than it is in some languages because of the complexity of the expressions that are routinely created.

The unary operators and assignment operators are right associative and the remaining operators are left associative. For example: **a = b = c**; means **a = (b = c), a + b – c** means **(a + b) – c** and **p++** means * **(p++)** not **(*p) ++**. The associativity of different type of operators are given in **Table 1.5**

1.5 CONDITIONAL EXPRESSIONS

In the conditional expressions ternary operator **(? :)** is used. The Syntax for conditional expression is

```
exp1 ? exp2 : exp3 ;
```

For example:

```
a = 20 ;
b = 19 ;
z = (a>b) ? a + b : a - b ;
```

In the above example, the value of **a** is greater than the value of **b,** which means condition is true, so that the value of **z** will be the value of **a + b**. If the condition is false then the value of **z** will be the value of **a - b**.

1.6 HOW THE OVERFLOW ARISE

C++ language uses 16 bit to represent variable type **int**. Most significant bit is used to **Table 1.6** Discuss of overflow condition represent the sign. If the most significant bit is zero then the value is treated as positive, if it is **1** then negative. For example, consider the 16-bit integer number representation which is illustrated in **Table 1.6.**

Table 1.6 Discuss of overflow condition

Binary number	Decimal equivalent
0000 0000 0000 0000	0
0000 0000 0000 0001	1
0000 0000 0000 0010	2
...	...
...	...
...	...
0111 1111 1111 1101	32,765
0111 1111 1111 1110	32,766
0111 1111 1111 1111	32,767
If we add 1 to 32,767, we would expect the result to be 32,768. However, to C++, the value becomes -32,768, as follows:	
0111 1111 1111 1111	32,767
0000 0000 0000 0001	1
1000 0000 0000 0000	-32,768

For example, consider the following program segment.

```
// OVERFLOW.C
#include <stdio.h>
void main (void)
{
    int positive = 32767;
    int negative = -32768;

    printf("%d + 1 is %d\n", positive, positive+1);
    printf("%d - 1 is %d\n", negative, negative-1);
}
```

```
32767 + 1 is –32768
-32768 – 1 is 32767
```

1.7 STRUCTURES

A structure is a collection of fields in which the fields may be same or of different types. A structure declaration forms a template that can be used to create structures. The fields that *make up the structure are called members of the structure.*

Generally all the member of a structure are logically related. For example, we consider the mailing list of all of the employees of GBPEC Company. The list contains the following information about the employees:

- *Name*
- *Date of joining*
- *Grade*
- *Department*
- *Address*

The list can be represented with the help of structure for the above details of the employees. The keyword **struct** is used to declare a structure. The syntax is

```
struct Tag name
{
    data type1 field1;
    data type2 field2;
    data type3 field3;
        ...
        ...
        ...
    data typen fieldn;
};
```

For example, the list of employees of GBPEC Company can be declared as:

```
struct Mailing_List
{
    char Name[20];
    char Join_Date [8];
    char Grade;
    char Department [30];
    char Address [120];
};
Maling_List List; // List is a variable of type Mailing_List
```

Fig. 1.2 illustrates the above structure of employees in memory. If one wants to access individual member of the structure then one requires to use a period (.) operator. The syntax is

```
Process (Structure_namemember_name) ; or
Process (Structure_name.field_name);
```

Name	Joining Date	Grade	Department	Address
20 bytes	8 bytes	1 byte	30 bytes	120 bytes

Fig. 1.2 List structure in the memory

For example, if one wants to input **Name** from an input device then it is possible with the help of input functions such as **gets(), scanf (), fread (), fscanf ()**, etc.

```
gets (List.Name);
```

Most common use of structures is found in the case of arrays of structures. To declare an array of structures, we must define a structure and then declare an array variable of that type. For example, if GBPEC Company has 1000 employees and company manager wants to maintain a record of each employee in the computer, then one can maintain it with the help of an array. The following declaration defines array of 1000 records:

```
Mailing_List List [1000];
```

When a structure variable is defined as a pointer type then individual fields can be processed with the help of arrow (→) operator. The pointer type declaration of structures can be implemented with the help of following syntax:

```
Mailing_List *List [1000];
```

If one wants to process **Name** field then it is possible with the help of following syntax:

```
Process (List [i]->Name);
```

For example, if we want to maintain customer bank account for the following information:

- *Name*
- *Account number*
- *Profession*
- *Address*
- *Street*
- *City*
- *State*
- *Pin code*

Then the above information can be maintained with the help of following declarations:

```
// Structure declaration for address
struct Addr{    char Street[30];       char City [30];
    char State[20];
    long int Pin_Code;
};

// Nested structure declaration

struct Customer
{
    char Name[20];
    char Account_No [10];
    char Profession[30];
    Addr Address;
};
Customer *List [100];
```

To access information about individual field in the **List** one can do **List [index]->field name.** The program segment **STRUCT.C** illustrates the above discussion in detail.

```
// Definition of structure
// STRUCT.C

# include<iostream.h>
# include<stdio.h>

// Structure declaration for address
struct Addr
{
        char Street[30];
        char City [30];
        char State[20];
        long int Pin_Code;
};

// Nested structure declaration

struct Customer
{
        char Name[20];
        char Account_No [10];
        char Profession[30];
        Addr Address;
};

// Function main

void main()
{
        Customer *List[100];
        int n;

        cout<<"\n Input number of record you want to process: ";
        cin>>n;
        cout<<"\n Input the information of customer \n";

        for(int i=0; i< n; i++)
        {
            cout<<"\n Name: ";
            cin>>List[i]->Name;
            cout<<"\n Account Number:";
            cin>>List[i]->Account_No;
            cout<<"\n Profession:";
```

```
        cin>>List[i]->Profession;
        cout<<"\n*** Address ***";
        cout<<"\n**************\n";
        cout<<"\n Street:";
        cin>>List[i]->Address.Street;
        cout<<"\n City:";
        cin>>List[i]->Address.City;
        cout<<"\n State:";
        cin>>List[i]->Address.State;
        cout<<"\n Pin Code:";
        cin>>List[i]->Address.Pin_Code;
    }

    cout<<"\n List of the customer";
    cout<<"\n *********************\n";
    for(i= 0; i< n; i++)
    {
        cout<<"\n Name: ";
        cout<<List[i]->Name;
        cout<<"\n Account Number:";
        cout<<List[i]->Account_No;
        cout<<"\n Profession:";
        cout<<List[i]->Profession;
        cout<<"\n *** Address ***\n";
        cout<<"\n ***************\n";
        cout<<"\n Street:";
        cout<<List[i]->Address.Street;
        cout<<"\n City:";
        cout<<List[i]->Address.City;
        cout<<"\n State:";
        cout<<List[i]->Address.State;
        cout<<"\n Pin Code:";
        cout<<List[i]->Address.Pin_Code;
    }
}
```

```
Input the information of customer

Name: R.B.PATEL
Account Number: T2/254
Profession: SERVICE
*** Address***
**************

Street: B-23
City: JAUNPUR
State: U.P.
Pin Code: 222136
Name: M.M.S.RAUTHAN
Account Number: T1/456
Profession: SERVICE

*** Address***
**************

Street: 34 DONG
City: SRINAGAR
State: U.P.
Pin Code: 246010

List of the customer
********************

Name: R.B.PATEL
Account Number: T2/254
Profession: SERVICE
*** Address ***
***************
Street:B-23
City: JAUNPUR
State: U.P.
Pin Code: 222136

Name: M.M.S.RAUTHAN
Account Number: T1/456
Profession: SERVICE

*** Address ***
***************
Street: 34 DONG
City: SRINAGAR
State: U.P.
Pin Code: 246010
```

1.8 UNION

A union is a memory location that is shared by two or more different type of variables, generally these variables can be used for different data types at different times. The syntax is:

```
union tag name
{
    Datatype1 field1; Datatype2 field2; Datatype3 field3;   ...
        ...
        ...

    Datatypen fieldn;
};
```

For example, consider the following declaration of union:

```
union Data_Types
{
    char Ch;
    int Integer_Number;
    long int Int_Long_Number;
    float Float_Number;
    double Double_Number;
};
```

The above declaration does not create any variables. We can declare a variable by either placing its name at the end of the declaration or by using a separate declaration statement. To declare a **union** variable data of type **Data_Types** we use the definition such that:

```
Data_Types Data;
```

In **Data**, charactêr **Ch**, integer **Integer_Number**, long integer **Integer_Long_Number**, floating point number **Float_Number** and double **Double_Number** share the same memory locations. **Fig. 1.3** illustrates the concepts of sharing memory. To access a member of **union**, same syntax is used as for structures. The dot (.), arrow (→), pointer (*) and dot (.) operators will work in the case of union. If we want to operate direct on the union then we use dot operator, if the union is accessed through a pointer we use arrow operator or use pointer and dot operators. For example, assign **char 'c'** to the field variable **Ch** of **Data** we use:

```
Data.Ch = 'c';
```

If a pointer to **Data** is passed to a function them we use:

```
Data_Types Fun (Data_Types *Member)
{
 Member->Ch = 'c';
 Member->Integer_Number= 100;
 Member->Float_Number = 20.50;
 (*Member).Double_Number = 30.5;
```

```
return (Member);
}
```

Using a union helps in the production of machine independent (portable) code. Because the compiler keeps track of the actual size of the union members, no machine dependencies are produced, which mean that one should not be worry about the size of an **int, long; char, float, double** or whatever.

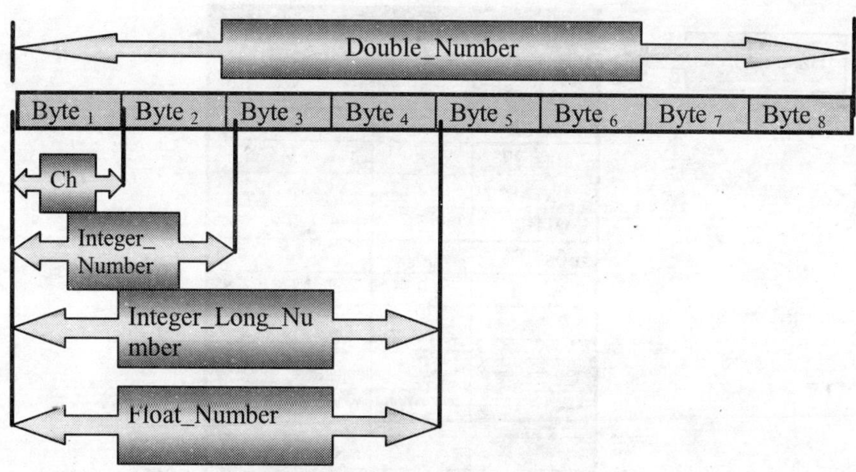

Fig. 1.3 Data in memory

1.9 POINTERS

Pointer variable P

0xff02 →

Address	Information
0xff02	11
0xff04	22
0xff06	33
0xff08	44
0xff0a	55

Fig. 1.4 Pointer

A pointer stores nothing but a memory address, this is its object value. It does not store a string, an integer, a double, etc. However, it may point to a storage location for such object value types. A pointer points to a memory location, and through the use of proper operators (& for address, * for value), the object value at the address to which it points can be retrieved or written. For example, **Fig. 1.4** illustrates a pointer attached with some location in memory. If one is interested fetching the information, then one can easily obtain the information by using operator (*) with the pointer variable.

Base address →

Address	Index	Information
0xff04	0	E
0xff05	1	X
0xff06	2	P
0xff07	3	E
0xff08	4	R
0xff09	5	T
0xff0a	6	
...	7	D
...	8	A
...	9	T
	10	A
	11	
	12	S
	13	T
	14	R
	15	U
	16	C
	17	T
	18	U
	19	R
	20	E
	21	S
	22	
	23	W
	24	I
	25	T
	26	H
...	27	
...	28	C
...	29	+
0xff22	30	+
0xff23	31	
0xff24	32	
0xff25	33	

Fig. 1.5 Pointer and base address

For example, consider the following code slice:

```
INFORMATION = *P;
```

where **P** contains the address 0xf f02 and the information stored at this location is 11, after this assignment we will get 11 in **INFORMATION**.

A pointer does not point to any single memory location. It can point to even through out **RAM** locations. For example, if **P** is a pointer (character) type variable then the following assignment is correct:

```
char *P;
P = "Expert Data Structures With C++";
```

The initial value of **P** is called the base address. In the above example the base address holds '**E**', base address plus 1 holds '**x**', base address plus 2 holds '**p**' and base address +30 holds '**+**'. Above discussion can be illustrated with the help of **Fig. 1.5.**

Some times it is also required to declare a pointer variable to another pointer (pointer to pointer to variable). The syntax is:

```
Data type **variable name;
```

For example:

```
int ** Pointer_To_Pointer_Integer;
```

The actual representation of this declaration is a two-dimensional array of infinite length and is illustrated in **Fig. 1.5.**

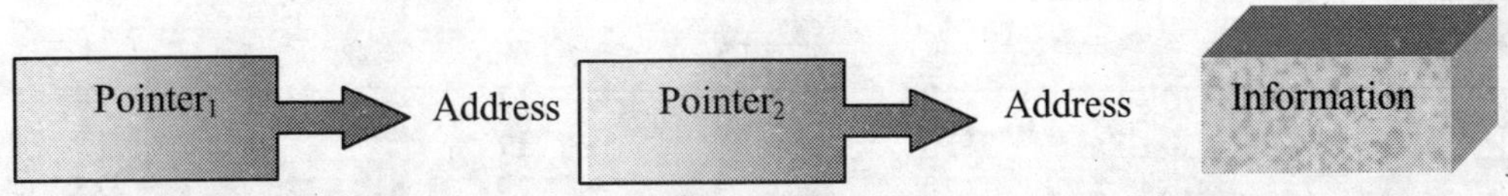

Fig. 1.6 Double pointer

	Column 0	Column 1	Column 2	Column 3	Column 4
Row 0	10	11	12	13	14
Row 1	15	16	17	18	19
Row 2	20	21	22	23	24
Row 3	25	26	26	27	28
Row 4	30	31	32	33	34

Array Table [5][5]

Row 0	10	11	12	13	14

Array Table [0][5]

Row 1	15	16	17	18	19

Array Table [1][5]

Row 2	20	21	22	23	24

Array Table [2][5]

Row 3	25	26	26	27	28

Array Table [3][5]

Row 4	30	31	32	33	34

Array Table [4][5]

Fig. 1.7 Array and rows of array

Table + 1 = 0xff0a **Table = 0xff00**

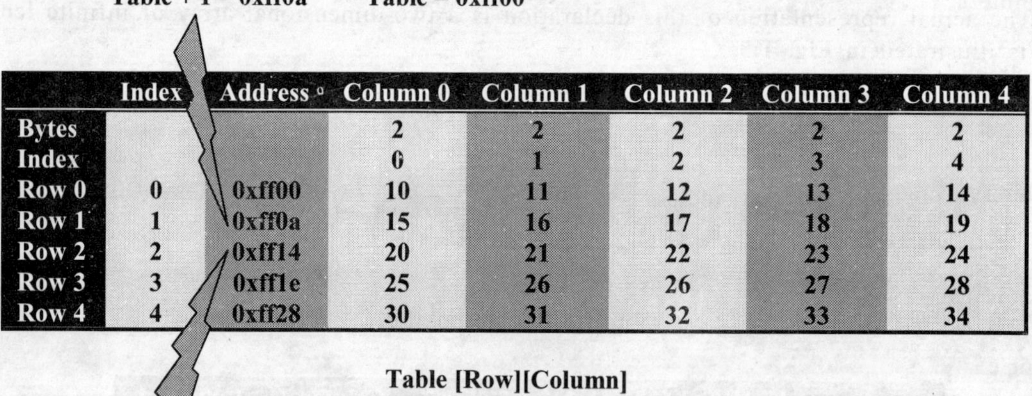

	Index	Address	Column 0	Column 1	Column 2	Column 3	Column 4
Bytes			2	2	2	2	2
Index			0	1	2	3	4
Row 0	0	0xff00	10	11	12	13	14
Row 1	1	0xff0a	15	16	17	18	19
Row 2	2	0xff14	20	21	22	23	24
Row 3	3	0xff1e	25	26	26	27	28
Row 4	4	0xff28	30	31	32	33	34

Table [Row][Column]

Table + 2 = 0xff14

Address	0xff00	0xff02	0xff04	0xff06	0xff8
Row 0	10	11	12	13	14

Array Table [0][5]

Address	0xff0a	0xff0c	0xff0e	0xff10	0xff12
Row 1	15	16	17	18	19

*(Table+2)

(*Table+2) + 2

Address	0xff14	0xff16	0xff18	0xff1a	0xff1c
Row 2	20	21	22	23	24

((Table+2)+2)

Address	0xff1e	0xff20	0xff22	0xff24	0xff26
Row 3	25	26	26	27	28

Address	0xff28	0xff2a	0xff2c	0xff2e	0xff30
Row 4	30	31	32	33	34

Fig. 1.8 Pointing to element in two-dimensional Array

For example, suppose we have an array as illustrated in **Fig. 1.7**. Let's figure out how to use pointers with reference to the third element in the third row of the array or **Table [2][2],** which is 22. First, the base address of the entire array is **Table**. Let's assume that the array starts at address **0xff00** in the memory, so **Table = 0xff00**. It is an integer array so each element will take two bytes. There are five elements in each row, so each row takes 10 bytes. Thus, each row starts 10 bytes further. Because row is a one-dimensional array, each of these one-dimensional arrays starts 10 bytes further along than the last one. **Fig. 1.8** illustrates that the address of the third element is ***(Table+2)+2** and content of this location is ***(*(Table+2)+2),** whose value is **22**. Simply we can say that

Table [i][j] = *(*Table +i)+ j);

For example, if we will execute the program segment **POINTER.C** we will get the desired result.

```
// Definition of Pointer and arrays
// POINTER.C

# include<iostream.h>
# include<stdio.h>
# define rows 5
# define cols 5

void main()
```

```
{
    int Table[rows][cols] = {
                            {10,11,12,13,14},
                            {15,16,17,18,19},
                            {20,21,22,23,24},
                            {25,26,27,28,29},
                            {30,31,32,33,34}    };

    for (int i = 0; i < 5; i++)
    {
        for (int j = 0; j < 5; j++)
        {
            printf(" 0x%x",*(Table+i)+j);
            cout<<" "<< *(*(Table+i)+j);
        }
        cout<<"\n";
    }
}
```

1.9.1 ARRAYS OF POINTERS

An array of pointers is similar to an array of any predefined data types. As a pointer variable contains an address, an array of pointers is a collection of addresses. These can be addresses of ordinary isolated variables or addresses of an array elements. The elements of an array of pointers are stored in the memory just like the elements of other kinds of array. The syntax for defining an array of pointer is the same as an array, except that pointer operator (*) precedes the array name. The syntax is

```
Data type * array_ name [size of array];
```

An array of pointer is useful for holding a pointer, pointing to a list of string. They can be utilized in implementing algorithms involving excessive information movements, we provide an example, where the use of pointer to pointer seems to be effective. The simplest way is to sort information by information movement. This method of sorting incurs many overheads in terms of both the time and space complexity, as it requires temporary space for exchanging the information between the records and has excessive information movement. This is especially large if the size of information is large. Pointers can be utilized to perform the same with much flexibility and less overhead. In this method, instead of information exchange, pointers are exchanged to accomplish the same task. The program segment **POINTSRT.C** illustrates the above discussion. In this program segment we have used **string [n] = new char(48);** statement that allocates 48 bytes to the **n**th element and stores its memory address in the array of pointers to strings indexed by **n**. The sorting procedure through the pointers is illustrated in **Fig. 1.9**.

```
sort (string, n);
```

The above statement invokes the sorting function by passing the array of pointers and information count as actual parameters.

```
// Pointer and Array
// POINTSRT.C

# include<iostream.h>
# include<string.h>
# include<ctype.h>

// PROTOTYPE

void sort(char **, int );

// Definition of function

void sort(char **str, int n)
{
    int i,j, flag;
    char *temp = new char(50);
    for(i =0; i < n; i++)
    {
        flag = 1;
        for (j=0; j <(n-i-1); j++)
        {
            if (strcmp (str[j], str[j+1])>0)
            {
                flag = 0;
                temp = str[j];
                str[j] = str[j+1];
                str[j+1] = temp;
            }
        }
        if (flag)
            break;
    }
}

// Function main

void main()
{
    char choice;
    int i, n = 0;
    char *string[100];
    do
    {
        string[n] = new char(50);
        cout<<"Input string: ";
```

```
        cin>>string[n];
        n++;
        cout<<"\n Input another Y/N? ";
        cin>>choice;
    }while(toupper(choice) == 'Y');
    cout<<"Unsorted list \n";
    cout<<"\n************\n";
    for (i =0; i < n ; i++)
    {
        cout<<&string[i];
        cout<<" ";
        cout<<string[i];
        cout<<"\n";
    }
    sort(string, n);
    cout<<"\n Sorted list";
    cout<<"\n************\n";
    for (i =0; i < n ; i++)
    {
        cout<<&string[i];
        cout<<" ";
        cout<<string[i];
        cout<<"\n";
    }
}
```

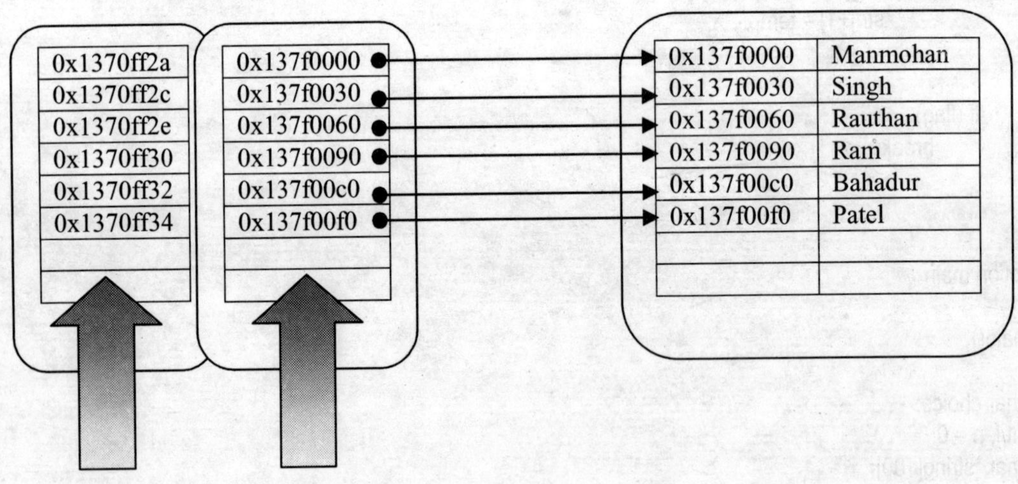

Fig. 1.9 (a) Sorting using pointers

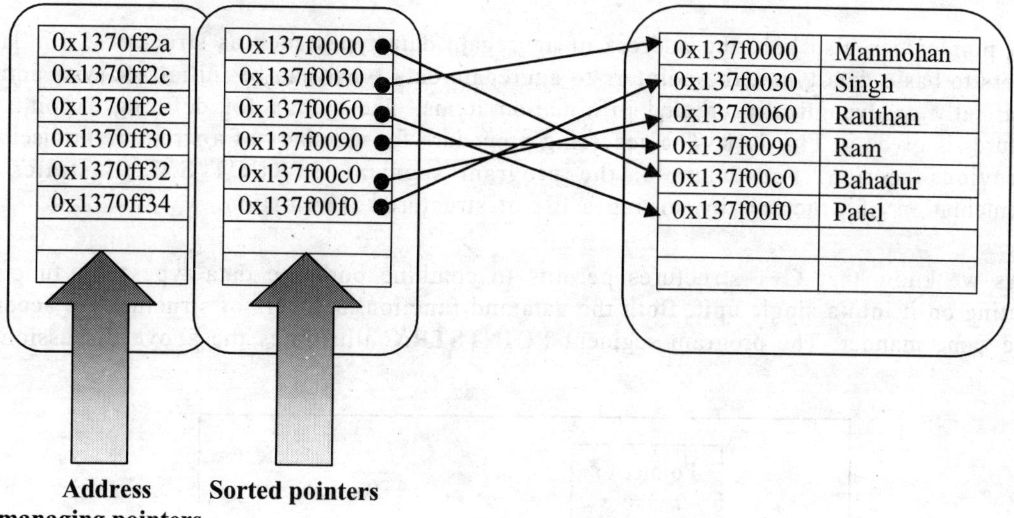

Fig. 1.9(b) Sorting using pointers

```
Input string: Manmohan
Input another Y/N? y
Input string: Singh
Input another Y/N? y
Input string: Rauthan
Input another Y/N? y
Input string: Ram
Input another Y/N? y
Input string: Bahadur
Input another Y/N? y
Input string: Patel
Input another Y/N? n

Unsorted list

************
0x1370ff2a Manmohan
0x1370ff2c Singh
0x1370ff2e Rauthan
0x1370ff30 Ram
0x1370ff32 Bahadur
0x1370ff34 Patel

Sorted list
************
0x1370ff2a Bahadur
0x1370ff2c Manmohan
0x1370ff2e Patel
0x1370ff30 Ram
0x1370ff32 Rauthan
0x1370ff34 Singh
```

1.9.2 POINTER TO STRUCTURES

A pointer can also hold the address of aggregate data types such as structures. Similar to pointers to basic data types, the pointers to aggregate data types can be initialized with address of statically or dynamically created information items. The syntax for defining a pointer to structures is given in **Fig. 1.10**. The accessing procedure for members of a structure is discussed in previous section. For example, the program segment **STRUCT_S.C** illustrates the implementation of structures by sorting a list of structured information.

As we know that **C++** structures permits to combine both the data types and functions operating on it into a single unit. Both the data and function members of structure are accessed in the same manner. The program segment **POINTSTR.C** illustrates the above discussion.

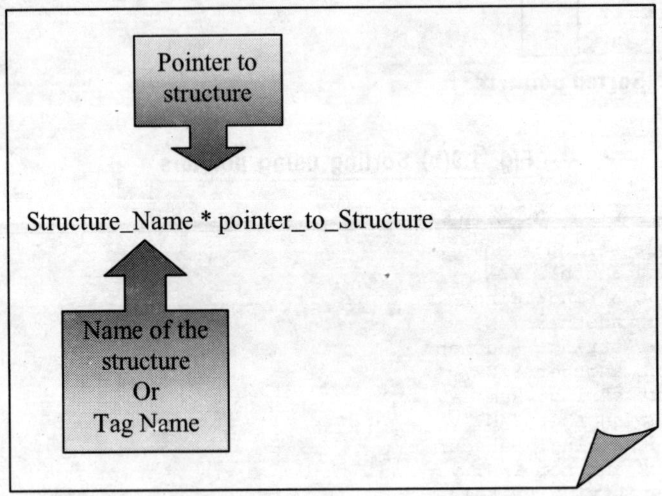

Fig. 1.10 Pointer to structures

```
// Pointer and structures

// STRUCT_S.C

# include<iostream.h>
# include<string.h>
# include<stdio.h>

struct Record
{
      char *name;
      char *address;
      long Pin_code;
};
```

```
// PROTOTYPE

void sort(Record * , int );

void sort(Record *str, int n)
{
    int i,j, flag;
    Record temp;
    for(i =0; i <n-1; i++)
    {
        flag = 1;
        for (j=0; j <(n-i-1); j++)
        {
            if (strcmp (str[j].name, str[j+1].name)>0)
            {
                flag = 0;
                temp = str[j];
                str[j] = str[j+1];
                str[j+1] = temp;
            }
        }
        if (flag)
            break;
    }
}

// Function main

void main()
{
    char choice;
    int i, n = 0;
    Record string[10];
    cout<<"Input The List\n ";
    cout<<"\n**************\n";

    do
    {
        string[n].name = new char(50);
        string[n].address=new char(100);

        cout<<"Name: ";
        cin>>string[n].name;
        cout<<"Address: ";
```

```
            cin>>string[n].address;
            cout<<"Postal index number: ";
            cin>>string[n].Pin_code;
            n++;
            cout<<"\n Input another y/n? ";
            cin>>choice;
        }while(choice == 'y');
        cout<<"Unsorted list \n";
        cout<<"\n********************\n";
        for (i =0; i < n ; i++)
        {
            cout<<"\n"<<string[i].name;
            cout<<"\n"<<string[i].address;
            cout<<"\n"<<string[i].Pin_code;
            cout<<"\n********************\n";
        }
        getchar();
        sort(string, n);
        cout<<"\n Sorted list";
        cout<<"\n********************\n";
        for (i =0; i < n ; i++)
        {
            cout<<"\n"<<string[i].name;
            cout<<"\n"<<string[i].address;
            cout<<"\n"<<string[i].Pin_code;
            cout<<"\n********************\n";
        }
        getchar();
}
```

```
Input The List
**************
Name: TOM
Address: NEWYORK
Postal index number: 96111
Input another y/n? y
Name: KRIS
Address: DELHI
Postal index number: 110001
Input another y/n? y
Name: ALTER
Address: BOMBAY
Postal index number: 220001
Input another y/n? n

    Unsorted list
********************
TOM
NEWYORK
96111
********************
KRIS
DELHI
110001
********************
ALTER
BOMBAY
220001
********************
 Sorted list
********************
ALTER
BOMBAY
220001
********************
KRIS
DELHI
110001
********************
TOM
NEWYORK
96111
********************
```

```
// Pointer to Structure
// Structure with data types and function in itself
// POINTSTR.C

# include<iostream.h>
# include<stdio.h>
```

```
struct rec
{
    char *string;
    void display()
    {
        while(*string)
            putchar(*string++);
    }
};

// Function main

void main()
{
    rec Record;
    Record.string = new char(200);
    Record.string ="There is no alternative of hard work";
    Record.display();
}
```

1.10 DYNAMIC MEMORY ALLOCATION

When we declare an array in our program, the compiler allocates memory to hold the array prior to providing it. Some times it is required to change the size of the array and in that case it is required to edit and compile the program. To reduce the number of changes, it is required to allocate required memory during the runtime. For example, suppose we want to read a file into memory from the disk, which contains information about students of a University. If we have prior information about the number of students and information associated with each student, then we can simply allocate required memory to an array and size of array is equal to the size of file. If the size of file is not known and we have to load it into memory and defining very large array, so that file can fit into the array. If the size of the array is larger than that of file then the space is wasted. If the size of file is larger then it is not possible to load the complete file into the array, leading to a need for dynamic memory allocation. In the dynamic memory allocation we use a pointer variable and it's size is allocated during the execution of the program. There are two principal functions in **C++**, which are used to allocate required memory to pointer variable.

- ***malloc ()***
- ***calloc ()***

Both the **malloc ()** and **calloc ()** functions perform the operations and checks memory availability, based on the memory block size requested. When a suitable segment of memory is located, a pointer to the address of the allocated block is returned by the function.

The **malloc ()** function simply finds a free block in memory and then returns a pointer to it. The **calloc ()** function works in similar fashion, except that it is more convenient when allocating memory for storage units of more than one byte. Also, **calloc ()** clears all memory blocks as a part of its operation. This means that a block of pointer to block whose bytes have been set to **NULL**. For example, the program segment **CALLOC.C** illustrates the operation performed by **calloc ()** function. In this program segment **calloc ()** allocates 800*2 = 1600 bytes long block. The number of storage units is 800, but the size of each storage unit is 2 bytes. This program segment can safely address from 0 to 799 units in this block without overwriting memory. This means ***(p+799)** will access the 1599th and 1600th bytes in the allocated block. **Fig. 1.11** illustrates the memory allocation by **calloc()** function and **Fig. 1.12** shows the values written into allocated block.

```
// Calloc function
// CALLOC.C

# include<iostream.h>
# include<malloc.h>
# include<stdlib.h>
# include<stdio.h>

void main()
{
    int *p;
    if((p =(int *) calloc(800, 2)) == NULL)
    {
        cout<<"\n Out of Memory \n";
        exit(0);
    }
    for (int i = 0; i < 800; i++)
    {
        cout<<" "<<(p+i);
        cout<<" "<< *(p+i);
        cout<<"\n";
    }

    getchar();

    for (i = 0; i < 800; i++)
    {
        *(p+i) = 77;
    }

    for (i = 0; i < 800; i++)
    {
```

```
        cout<<" "<<(p+i);
        cout<<" "<< *(p+i);
        cout<<"\n";

    }
    getchar();
}
```

```
0x13580f0a 0
0x13580f0c 0
0x13580f0e 0
0x13580f10 0
0x13580f12 0
0x13580f14 0
0x13580f16 0
0x13580f18 0
0x13580f1a 0
0x13580f1c 0
...
...
...
0x1358153e 0
0x13581540 0
0x13581542 0
0x13581544 0
0x13581546 0
0x13581548 0
```

```
0x13580f0a 77
0x13580f0c 77
0x13580f0e 77
0x13580f10 77
0x13580f12 77
0x13580f14 77
0x13580f16 77
0x13580f18 77
0x13580f1a 77
0x13580f1c 77
...
...
...
0x1358153e 77
0x13581540 77
0x13581542 77
0x13581544 77
0x13581546 77
0x13581548 77
```

Address	Information
0x13580f0a	0
0x13580f0c	0
0x13580f0e	0
0x13580f10	0
0x13580f12	0
0x13580f14	0
0x13580f16	0
0x13580f18	0
0x13580f1a	0
0x13580f1c	0
...	...
...	...
...	...
0x1358153e	0
0x13581540	0
0x13581542	0
0x13581544	0
0x13581546	0
0x13581548	0

Fig. 1.11 Before writing information calloc (800, 2)

Address	Information
0x13580f0a	77
0x13580f0c	77
0x13580f0e	77
0x13580f10	77
0x13580f12	77
0x13580f14	77
0x13580f16	77
0x13580f18	77
0x13580f1a	77
0x13580f1c	77
...	...
...	...
...	...
0x1358153e	77
0x13581540	77
0x13581542	77
0x13581544	77
0x13581546	77
0x13581548	77

Fig. 1.12 After writing information calloc (800, 2)

Address	Information
0x13450ef2	88
0x13450ef4	88
0x13450ef6	88
0x13450ef8	88
0x13450efa	88
0x13450efc	88
0x13450efe	88
...	...
...	...
...	...
...	...
0x13451076	88
0x13451078	88
0x1345107a	88
0x1345107c	88
0x1345107e	88
0x13451080	88

Fig. 1.13 malloc (200* sizeof (int))

The **malloc ()** function returns a pointer of type **void**, which means that we can assign it to any type of pointer. After a successful call **malloc ()** returns a pointer to the first byte of the block of memory which is allocated. If there is not enough available memory to satisfy the **malloc ()** request, an allocation failure occurs and **malloc ()** returns a **NULL**. For example:

```
int *p;
p = malloc (200*2);
```

After the assignment, **p** points to the 200*2 bytes of free memory. As we know that **malloc ()** returns a void pointer so a **cast operator** is required to change the returned pointer type according to need. The above statement can be written as:

```
int *p;
p = (int ) mallc(200*sizeof(int));
```

The allocated memory by **malloc ()** and **calloc ()** function are not free automatically and it is required to free the allocated space after the completion of the job. For this purpose **C++** has **free()** function that frees the allocated space. For example, the program segment **MALLOC.C** first of all allocates 400 bytes of memory space and frees these bytes. **Fig. 1.13** illustrates operation performed by **malloc ()** function.

```
// Malloc function
// MALLOC.C
# include<iostream.h>
# include<malloc.h>
# include<stdlib.h>
# include<stdio.h>

void main()
{
    int *p;
    p = (int *) malloc(200* sizeof(int));

    for (int i = 0; i < 200; i++)
    {
        *(p+i) = 88;
    }

    for (i = 0; i < 200; i++)

    {
        cout<<" "<<(p+i);
        cout<<" "<< *(p+i);
        cout<<"\n";

    }
    getchar();
}
```

```
0x13450ef2 88
0x13450ef4 88
0x13450ef6 88
0x13450ef8 88
0x13450efa 88
0x13450efc 88
0x13450efe 88
0x13450f00 88
0x13450f02 88
0x13450f04 88
0x13450f06 88
0x13450f08 88
...
...
...
0x13451076 88
0x13451078 88
0x1345107a 88
0x1345107c 88
0x1345107e 88
0x13451080 88
```

1.10.1 THE NEW AND DELETE

In **C++ malloc ()** and **free ()** functions are replaced by **new** and **delete.** These operators are the part of the language. These unary operators (**new** and **delete)** are available to manipulate free store. Free store is a system, which provides memory pool for objects whose lifetime is directly managed by the programmer. The programmer creates the object by using **new** and destroys the object by using **delete**. These operators are generally used for dynamic data structures like **linked list, trees** and **graphs**. The syntax for **new** operator is

```
new data type name;
new data type initializer;
```

In each case there are two effects:

(i) *An appropriate amount of store is allocated from free pool to contain the named data type.*
(ii) *The base address of the object is returned as the value of the new expression. The expression is of type* ***void **** *and can be assigned to any pointer type variable. The operator* ***new*** *returns the value* ***NULL*** *when memory is unavailable. For example:*

```
int *pointer_integer;
pointer_integer = new int (5);
```

Here, the pointer to integer variable **pointer_integer** is assigned the address of the store obtained by allocating an object of type **int**. The location pointed by **pointer_integer** is initialized to the value 5. This use is not usual for a simple type such as **int**, in which it is far more convenient and natural to automatically allocate an integer variable on the stack or globally.

The operator **delete** destroys an object created by **new**, in effect returns its allocated storage free store for reuse. The syntax for **delete** is

delete expression;

This is used when the corresponding new expression did not allocate an array.

delete [ ] expression;

The brackets indicating that the original allocation was an array of objects. The operator **delete** does not return a value and one can say its return type is **void.**

Here, the pointer variable **data** is used as the base addresses of a dynamically allocated array **size** of elements. The user is prompted for the integer-valued **size**. The **new** operator is used to allocate storage from the free space capable of storing an object of type **int (size)** on a system where integers take two bytes, this would allocate **2*size** bytes. At this point, **data** is assigned the base address of this space.

If one accesses free space again then there is no need to initialize the **data** array. The same memory just returned to free space is used, with the old values re-appearing. However, no one can guarantee about the values that will appear in the objects allocated from free space.

```
// new and delete operators
// NEWDEL.C

# include<iostream.h>

void main()
{
    int *data;
    int size;
    cout<<"\n Input size of array: ";
    cin >> size;
    data = new int (size); // allocates an array of integers
    for (int j = 0; j < size; j++)
    {
        data[j]= j;
        cout<<data[j]<<"\t";
    }
    cout<<"\n";
    delete [] data; // De-allocate an array again allocating array but not assigning data
    cout<<"\n Without assigning second time data to \n";
```

```
    cout<<"the array we are getting output approximate same \n";
    data = new int (size);
    for (j = 0; j < size; j++)
        cout<< data[j]<<"\t";
}
```

```
Input size of array: 100
0    1    2    3    4    5    6    7    8    9
10   11   12   13   14   15   16   17   18   19
20   21   22   23   24   25   26   27   28   29
30   31   32   33   34   35   36   37   38   39
40   41   42   43   44   45   46   47   48   49
50   51   52   53   54   55   56   57   58   59
60   61   62   63   64   65   66   67   68   69
70   71   72   73   74   75   76   77   78   79
80   81   82   83   84   85   86   87   88   89
90   91   92   93   94   95   96   97   98   99
```

```
      Without assigning second time data to
  The array we are getting output approximate same

100  1    2    3    4    5    6    7    8    9
10   11   12   13   14   15   16   17   18   19
20   21   22   23   24   25   26   27   28   29
30   31   32   33   34   35   36   37   38   39
40   41   42   43   44   45   46   47   48   49
50   51   52   53   54   55   56   57   58   59
60   61   62   63   64   65   66   67   68   69
70   71   72   73   74   75   76   77   78   79
80   81   82   83   84   85   86   87   88   89
90   91   92   93   94   95   96   97   98   99
```

1.11 FUNCTION

We are familiar with several types of functions like **square, square root, exponential** and **trigonometric** functions. These functions and other functions are available to **C++** programmer through libraries that are provided by **C++** compiler developer. **C++** also allows us to define and write our own functions. There are facilities in **C++**, to modify the standard libraries or to incorporate new functions in the libraries. In either case function provide facilities to transfer a prewritten block of code to perform a specific task. This is very convenient when the same task is to be repeated several times or at different places in a program. The functions relieve us of writing the code for routine tasks, also different users can share functions written by one user. This saves time and money. The functions are main building blocks of **C++** Language. The syntax for function is:

```
Datatype specified name of function (Data types specified list of parameters)
{
    Data type specifies list of parameters;

        Statement 1;
        Statement 2;
            ...
            ...
            ...
        Statement n ;
}
```

The attached list of parameters to functions name has a type specified. For example, the function **summation ()** has its type integer and parameter passed to it is also of integer type. The function returns integer value.

```
// FUNCT.C
int summation( int n )
{
    int sum = 0;

    for (int i = 0 ; i <= n ; i++)
    {
        sum += i ;
    }
    return (sum) ;
}
```

1.11.1 FUNCTION INVOCATION

The syntax to activate a function is:

```
Name of function (list of arguments) ;
```

where name of the function is any valid variable name and the argument list is to be passed to function subprogram. The argument list may be **variables, subscripted variable names, array names, constant values, expressions** or **function names**. The value of the function is returned through the name of functions acting as a variable.

We know that function can return one and only one value at a time also it can participate in arithmetic operations. For example, consider the program segment **FUN_ARTH.C** that illustrates the above discussion.

```
// FUN_ARTH.C

# include<iostream.h>

int fun (int, int);

// Function main

void main()
{
      int x , y ;
      int result ;
      x = 20 ;
      y = 30 ;
      result = fun (x, y) * x / y ;
      cout<<" Value = "<<result ;
}

// Definition of the function fun ()

fun(int a , int b )
{
      int result ;
      result = a*b ;

      return (result) ;
}
```

When we call a function in function main or else where, in any function then the called function is invoked. For example, consider the program segment **FACT.C** that illustrates the above discussion.

```
// FACT.C

// FIND FACTORIAL OF AN INTEGER NUMBER

# include<iostream.h>

factorial (int );

void main()
{
      int n ;
      long int result ;
      cout<<"\n Input a number = ";
      cin>>n;
      result = factorial(n) ; // invocation of function
```

```
    cout<<"\n Factorial = "<<result;
}

// Definition of the function factorial()

factorial(int m)
{
    int fact ;
    if ( m == 0 )
        return ( 1 );
    else
        fact = m * factorial(m-1) ;
    return (fact);
}
```

Here, in this program segment when we have called the function **fact ()** in the main function then it is invoked. Here, type of function is integer and the value passed to it is also an integer.**1.11.2**

1.11.2 TERMINATION OF FUNCTION

A function is terminated in two ways:

- *When we define a function* ***void*** *type then when the last closing brace of that function is encountered the function is terminated. For example, consider the function* ***fun ().***

```
void fun ( int n , char *s )
{
    int i ;
    for( i = n ; i ; —i)
    {
        cout<<"\n "<<s ;
    }
}
```

Here, the above function starts from opening brace '{' and terminates at closing brace '}'.

- *Second way of termination of function is by return statement. When* ***return*** *statement is encountered, control of execution of program exits immediately from currently executing function to the calling routine, optionally returning a value. For example, consider the* ***find () function*** *in the* ***FIND.C*** *program segment.*

```
// FIND.C
find ( int a[3] , int b )
{
```

```
        int i ;
        for( i = 0 ; i < 3 ; i++)
            if(a[i] == 'B' )
            return (i) ;
        else
            return (-1);
}
```

Here, in the above program segment the function **find()** can be terminated at two places first at **return (i)** and second at statement **return (-1)** depending on the value of the conditions. If the condition is false then it will terminate at return **(-1)** otherwise at **return (i)** statement.

We do not specify function's type, it is treated as an integer type. So, we should define function type according to our requirement. We should define function types, before constructing its body. Another way to define a function is:

Data type specified name of function (no arguments)

```
{
    Data type specifies list of parameters;
        Statement 1;
        Statement 2 ;
            ...
            ...
            ...
        Statement n ;
}
```

For example, consider the program segment **FUNC_WP.C** that illustrates the above discussion in a better fashion.

```
// FUNT_WP.C

# include<iostream.h>
# include<math.h>

int x , y ; /* global variable */
float xy_power(void) ; /* prototype */

void main()
{

    cout<<"\n Input values of x , y =>";
    cin>>x;
    cin>>y;
    cout<<"\n y power x is = "<<xy_power();
}
```

```
// Definition of the function xy_power()

float xy_power(void)
{
    float result ;
    int a , b ;
    a = x ;
    b = y ;
    result = pow(b,a) ;
    return(result) ;
}
```

Here, in the above program segment no arguments were passed to the function **xy_power ().** We have declared the data type global and assign values to them. The values assigned to them always remain in the program. In other words we can say that scope of variables equals is to the total time needed to execute the program.

1.11.3 PARAMETER PASSING TECHNIQUES

In addition to parameters, functions usually use variables. Every variable has a scope- the region of the program in which it is visible. A variable is visible in a region if it can be referenced in that region.

1.11.3.1 PASS BY VALUE

C++ language supports mainly passes by value technique for parameter passing. In this method copying the value of an argument into formal parameter of the subprogram is done. When we make changes in the parameter of the subprogram, it produces no effect on the variables used to call it. For example, consider program segment **FUNC_VAL.C** that illustrates pass by this technique.

```
// FUNC_VAL.C

# include<iostream.h>
# include<math.h>

float m_payment(float , float , int ) ; // prototype

void main()
{
    float A , I ; // mortgage amount A , I interest rate
    int D ;     // Duration is D

    cout<<"\n Input mortgage Amount = ";
```

```
    cin>>A;
    cout<<"\n Input interest rate = ";
    cin>>I;
    cout<<"\n Input Duration = ";
    cin>>D;
    cout<<"\n Monthly Payment = "<<m_payment(A,I,D);
}

// Definition of function

float m_payment( float a , float i , int d )
{
    float num ;
    float deno ;
    float payment ;
    num = ( a * i /12 ) ;
    deno = pow( (1/(1+i/12)),d*12);
    payment = num / ( 1 - deno ) ;
    return(payment);
}
```

In the above program segment when function **m_payment()** is called the value of **A, I** and **D** are copied into **a, i** and **d.**

1.11.3.2 PASS BY REFERENCE

Second method, which is used to communicate between arguments via function, is known as pass by reference. This operation is implemented with the help of pointers. For example, consider the following program segment that illustrates the parameter passing by reference. // Definition of functionvoid exchange (float *x , float *y)

```
{
    float t ;
    t = *x ; // copy x into t
    *x = *y ; // copy y into x
    *y = t ; // copy x into y
}
```

The pointer operator '*' is used to access the variable pointed to by its operands as illustrated in the following program segment.

```
// FUNCT_REF.C

# include<iostream.h>

void exchange (float *x , float *y )
{
```

```
    float t ;
    t = *x ;  // copy x into t
    *x = *y ; // copy y into x
    *y = t ;  // copy x into y
}
# include<stdio.h>

void exchange(float * , float * ) ; // prototype
void main()
{
    float x , y ;
    printf("\n Input value for x and y : ");
    cin>>x;
    cin>>y;

    exchange(&x, &y);
    cout<<"\n Value of x = "<<x;
    cout<<"\n Value of y = "<<y;
}
```

Let x = **0.5** and **y** = **20.5**. The **exchange ()** function is called with the address of **x** and **y**. The operator (&) is used to produce the addresses of the variables. Hence, the addresses of **x** and **y** are passed to the function **exchange ().**

```
Input value for x and y : 0.5 20.5

Value of x ->20.500000
Value of y->0.500000
```

1.11.4 PROTOTYPES

When a function is declared before its use, it is known as prototype declaration and the name is known as prototype name. Prototype has two advantages:

- *For identifiers, the return type of the function so that compiler can generate the correct code for the return data.*
- *It specifies the type and number of arguments used by function.*

The syntax to define prototype is:

Data type name of function (Data type $_1$, Data type $_2$, Data type$_3$ ... Data type$_n$);

Generally, the name is placed near the top of the program. In other words, it must appear before any call is made to the function. The prototype allows compiler to find and report any illegal type conversion among the type of arguments used to call the function and the type in the function definition and its parameters.

When we define prototype(s), the information about the function(s) is stored into the stack during the compilation, starting from the beginning of the program. In the subsequent programs the compiler compares the function(s) with the stack name of the function. If there is a match then there no errors will be generated, otherwise errors will be generated. The possible error messages are:

- *To few arguments.*
- *Too many arguments.*
- *Type mismatch between function prototype and function definition name.*
- *Type mismatch between parameters called in function, etc.*

```
// PROTO.C
// RADIX FUNCTION DISCUSSES ABOUT PROTOTYPE DECLARATION

# include<iostream.h>

int radix(int ) ; // prototype

void main()
{
      int x ;
      int r ;

      x = 20 ;
      r = radix(x) ;
      cout<<"\n"<<r;
}

// Definition of function

float radix(float n )
{
      int r ;
      r = n * 10 ;
      return(r) ;
}
```

While compiling the above program segment errors will be generated because in prototype, **radix ()** is type integer and the parameter passed to it is also of integer type. But in function definition its type is **float** and parameter used with it is also **float**. Hence, when we compile this program segment following errors will be flashed.

- *Undefined symbol radix (int) linker error.*

The remedy of above problem is function overloading. Consider the next section that will discuss about function overloading. The corrected code of **PROTO.C** is:

```
// PROTO.C (CORRECTED CODE)
// RADIX FUNCTION DISCUSSES ABOUT PROTOTYPE DECLARATION

# include <iostream.h>

// Definition of function

float radix(float n )
{
    int r ;
    r = n * 10 ;
    return(r) ;
}

void main()
{
    int x ;
    int r ;

    x = 20 ;
    r = radix(x) ;
    cout<<"\n"<<r;
}
```

1.11.5 FUNCTION OVERLOADING

Overloading is a process of assigning two or more functions with the same name. During the compilation, C++ compiler determines, which function to call, based on the number and type of arguments or parameters passed. For example, the program segment **OVERLOAD.C** creates three functions named **sum ()** that returns the summation of the number of elements in an array. The first function supports arrays of type **int**, second supports arrays of type **float** and third one support arrays of type **double**.

```
// OVERLOAD.C

// DISCUSSION OF OVERLOADING OF FUNCTION
```

```
#include <iostream.h>

// Function sum() when returned value is integer

int sum(int *array, int element_count)
{
    int result = 0;
    int count;

    for (count = 0; count < element_count; count++)
        result += array[count];

    return(result);
}

// Function sum() when returned value is float

float sum(float *array, int element_count)
{
    float result = 0;
    int count;

    for (count = 0; count < element_count; count++)
        result += array[count];

    return(result);
}

// Function sum() when returned value is double

double sum(double *array, int element_count)
{
    float result = 0;
    int count;

    for (count = 0; count < element_count; count++)
        result += array[count];

    return(result);
}

// Function main
void main(void)
{
    int i[5] = {1, 2, 3, 4, 5};
```

```
    float f[4] = {1.11, 2.22, 3.33, 4.44 };
    double d[5] = {11.111, 22.222, 33.333, 44.444, 55.555};

    cout << "Sum of integer values: " << sum(i, 5) << '\n';
    cout << "Sum of float values: " << sum(f, 4) << '\n';
    cout << "Sum of double values: " << sum(d, 5) << '\n';
}
```

Another example of function overloading is **swap ()** function. The first function swaps the two values while the second function swaps four values. For example, the program segment **USEPARAM.C** illustrates function overloading.

```
// USEPARAM.C

#include <iostream.h>

// The swap() function enterchnage two elements

void swap(int *a, int *b)
{
    int temp = *a;
    *a = *b;
    *b = temp;
}

// The swap() function interchange four elements

void swap(int *a, int *b, int *c, int *d)
{
    int temp = *a;
    *a = *b;
    *b = temp;
    temp = *c;
    *c = *d;
    *d = temp;
}

void main(void)
{
    int a = 1, b = 2 , c = 3, d = 4;

    cout<<"\n a = "<< a;
    cout<<"\n b = "<< b;
    cout<<"\n c = "<< c;
    cout<<"\n d = "<< d;
```

```
    swap(&a, &b); // Invoking function swap()

    cout << "\n Swapped a and b " <<" "<< a <<" "<< b << '\n';
    a = 1;
    b = 2;
    c = 3;
    d = 4;

    cout<<"\n a = "<< a;
    cout<<"\n b = "<< b;
    cout<<"\n c = "<< c;
    cout<<"\n d = "<< d;

    swap(&a, &b, &c, &d);
    cout << "\n Swapped four " << a <<" "<< b <<" "<< c << " "<<d << '\n';
}
```

1.11.6 FUNCTION AND STRUCTURES

When a function is used as member of structure the syntax is:

```
struct Tag Name
{
    // Data type declarations

    Data type 1 field 1;
    Data type 2 Field 2;
    Data type 3 Field 3;
        ...
        ...
        ...
    Data type n Field n;

    // Member function declarations

    Data type 1 function 1 (List of parameters);
    Data type 2 Function 2 (List of parameters);
    Data type 3 Function 3 (List of parameters);
        ...
        ...
        ...
    Data type n Function n (List of parameters);
};
```

When we want to define functions within structures, we have two options: either we define code of the functions body within the structure or prototype in structure keeping definition of the function is given outside of the structure. To invoke the function the program simply refers to the structure member. The syntax is:

Name of the Structure.Member function (List of the actual parameters);

The program segment **FUNC_MBR.C** illustrates that a member function within the structure with its associated body codes and program segment **FUNC_TWO.C** defines the function outside of the structure. The function communicates by using scope resolution operator (::) with **Message** structure. The program segment precedes the function name with the structure name followed by two colons (::).

```
// FUNC_MBR.C
// Member function when body of the function defined within the structure

#include <iostream.h>

struct Message
{
      char *message;

      // Member function

      void show_message()
      {
            cout << message;
      }
};

// Function main

void main(void)
{
      Message Display;
      Display.message = "C++ is a powerful language";
      Display.show_message();
}

// FUNC_TWO.C
// Member function when body of the function defined within the structure

#include <iostream.h>

struct Message
{
```

```
    char *message;

    // Prototype

    void show_message();
};

// Member function

void Message :: show_message()
{
    cout << message;
}

// Function main

void main(void)
{
    Message Display;
    Display.message = "C++ is a powerful language";
    Display.show_message();
}
```

1.12 THE CLASS

A class is defined as a collection of **data** and **functions**. Classes are created using the keyword **class**. A class declaration defines a new type that links data and functions. The new type is then used to declare objects of that class. Thus, a class is a logical abstraction, but an object has physical existence. In other words, an object is an instance of a class. A class is defined as structures. The syntax is:

```
class Class Name
{

    Access specifier:
        Data and functions
    Access specifier:
        Data and functions
    Access specifier:
        Data and functions
            ...
            ...
            ...
    Access specifier:
        Data and functions
} List of objects;
```

The list of objects is optional. If it is present, it declares objects of the class. The **Access-specifier** may be one of the following:

- *public*
- *private*
- *protected*

By default, functions and data declared within a class are private to that class and may be accessed only by the member functions of the class. However, by using the **public** access specifier, we allow functions or data to be accessible to other parts of the program segment. Once an access specifier has been used, it remains in effect until either another access specifier is encountered or the end of the class declaration is reached. The protected access specifier is needed only when inheritance is involved. There is option to change specification whenever it is required. For example, the program segment **CLASS.C** illustrates the definition of the class when the member functions are defined within the class with their associated code. The program segment **CLASS_OS.C** defines class when the prototypes of the functions are defined within the class but their definitions are defined outside of the class.

```
// CLASS.C

#include <iostream.h>
#include <iomanip.h>
#Include <strlng.h>

class Def_Class
{
public:
     char title[256];
     char author[64];
     float price;
     void show_title(void)
     {
          cout << title << '\n';

     }
     void show_author()
     {
          cout << author<< '\n';

     }

     float get_price()
     {
          return(price);
     }
};
void main(void)
```

```
{
     Def_Class Data_strcutures;

     strcpy(Data_strcutures.title, "EXPERT DATA STRUCTURES WITH C++");
     strcpy(Data_strcutures.author, "R.B.Patel and M.M. Singh Rauthan");
     Data_strcutures.price = 250.00;

     Data_strcutures.show_title();
     Data_strcutures.show_author();
     cout << "The book's price is " << setprecision(2) << Data_strcutures.get_price();
}
```

```
EXPERT DATA STRUCTURES WITH C++
R.B.Patel and M.M. Singh Rauthan
The book's price is 250.00
```

```
// CLASS_OS.C
// Class when function's body is defined outside of the class

#include <iostream.h>
#include <iomanip.h>
#include <string.h>

class Def_Class
{
  public: char title[256];
          char author[64];
     float price;

// Prototypes of member functions

 void show_title(void);
 void show_author();
 float get_price();
};

// Function's definitions

void Def_Class :: show_title(void)
{
     cout <<"\n "<< title;

}
```

```
void Def_Class :: show_author()
{
    cout <<"\n "<< author<< '\n';
}

float Def_Class :: get_price()
{
    return(price);
}

// Function main

void main(void)
{
    Def_Class Data_strcutures;

    strcpy(Data_strcutures.title, "EXPERT DATA STRUCTURES WITH C++");
    strcpy(Data_strcutures.author, "R.B.Patel and M.M. Singh Rauthan");
    Data_strcutures.price = 250.00;

    Data_strcutures.show_title();
    Data_strcutures.show_author();
    cout << "The book's price is " << setprecision(2) << Data_strcutures.get_price();
}
```

```
EXPERT DATA STRUCTURES WITH C++
R.B.Patel and M.M. Singh Rauthan
The book's price is 250.00
```

1.12.1 STRUCTURE AND CLASS

The classes and structures in **C++** are same except that the data types in the structures are always being **public** types. The data types of the class have been defined in the previous section. If one considers data types **public** in the class then the classes are equivalent to the structures. In declaration of both structure and class keyword is required, for structure **struct** and for class keyword **class** is required. The program segment **CLASS_ST.C** is equivalent to the program segment **CLASS_OS.C**. If we define in the program segment **CLASS_ST.C,** data types as **private** or **protected** we commit too many errors.

```
// CLASS_ST.C
// Structure equivalent to the class when function's body is defined outside of the class

#include <iostream.h>
#include <iomanip.h>
```

```
#include <string.h>

struct Def_Class
{
  public:  char title[256];
           char author[64];
           float price;

// Prototypes of member functions

  void show_title(void);
  void show_author();
  float get_price();
  };

// Function's definitions

void Def_Class :: show_title(void)
{
      cout <<"\n "<< title;
}

void Def_Class :: show_author()
{
      cout <<"\n "<< author<< '\n';
}

float Def_Class :: get_price()
{
      return(price);
}

// Function main

void main(void)
{
      Def_Class Data_strcutures;

      strcpy(Data_strcutures.title, "EXPERT DATA STRUCTURES WITH C++");
      strcpy(Data_strcutures.author, "R.B.Patel and M.M. Singh Rauthan");
      Data_strcutures.price = 250.00;

      Data_strcutures.show_title();
      Data_strcutures.show_author();
      cout << "The book's price is " << setprecision(2) << Data_strcutures.get_price();
}
```

```
EXPERT DATA STRUCTURES WITH C++
R.B.Patel and M.M. Singh Rauthan
The book's price is 250.00
```

1.12.2 CONSTRUCTORS AND DESTRUCTORS

Sometimes it is required to initialize an object before using. A constructor is a special member function whose main operation is to allocate the required resources such as memory and initialize the objects of its class. A constructor is distinct from other member functions of the class, and it has the same name as its class. It is executed automatically when a class is initiated that is when the object is created. The constructor has no return specification. The constructor is the first member function, which is executed first automatically. For example, consider the program segment **CONSTR.C** which illustrates a constructor.

```
// CONSTR.C
// Constructor
# include<iostream.h>

class Count
{
    private:
    int c;

    public:

    Count ()  // Constructor
    {
        c= 0;
        cout<<"\n Constructor";
    }
    void Increment ()
    {
        c++;
    }
    int Input ()
    {
        return (c);
    }
};

void main()
{
    Count c1, c2;
    cout<<"\n c1 = "<<c1.Input ();
```

```
        cout<<"\n c2 = "<<c2.Input ();
        c1.Increment ();
        c1.Increment ();
        c2.Increment ();
        c2.Increment ();
        c2.Increment ();
        cout<<"\n c1 = "<<c1.Input ();
        cout<<"\n c2 = "<<c2.Input ();
}
```

```
Constructor
Constructor
c1 = 0
c2 = 0
c1 = 2
```

A class has one more special member function called destructor, which is invoked when an object is destroyed. This function compliments the operation performed by any of the destructors, in the sense that, it is invoked when an object ceases to exist. For objects, which are local non-static variables, the destructor is called when the function in which the object is defined is about to terminate. For static or global variables, the destructor is called before the program terminates. As constructor is executed automatically, so is the case with destructor. A destructor has the same syntax as the constructor, but is preceded by a tilde (~). For example:

```
Class Count
{
    private: int c;
    public:
        Count ()
        {
            c = 0;
            cout<<"\n Counstructor";
        }
        ~Count ()
        {}
};
```

Like constructors, destructors do not have a return value and take no arguments. The most common use of destructor is to de-allocate memory that was allocated for the object by the constructor. For example, the program segment **DESTR.C** illustrates destructor in which **String** is the name of the class. The function **String ()** is defined as constructor in which we allocate some memory to variable **str**, again we define a destructur function **~String ()**, and this function is executed when we leave the execution of the member function and release the allocated memory.

```
// DESTR.C
```

```
// Destructor

# include<iostream.h>
# include<string.h>

class String
{
      private:
      char *str;
      public:
      String (char *s)       // Constructor
      {
            int length = strlen (s);
            str = new char [length +1];
            strcpy(str, s);
      }

      ~String()  // Destructor
      {
            cout<<"\n Destructor";
            delete str;
      }
      void Output ()
      {
            cout<<"\n"<<str;
      }
};

// Function main

void main ()
{
      String S1 = "Expert Data Structures With C++";
      cout<<"\n";
      S1.Output ();
}
```

Expert Data Structures With C++
Destructor

1.13 FILES AND STREAMS

A stream is a general name given to a flow of information. Different streams are used to represent different kinds of information flow. Each stream is associated with a particular class, which contains member functions and definitions for dealing with that particular kind of information flow. For example, the **ofstream** represents output disk files. **Fig. 1.14** illustrates different types of streams available in **C++** with their destination.

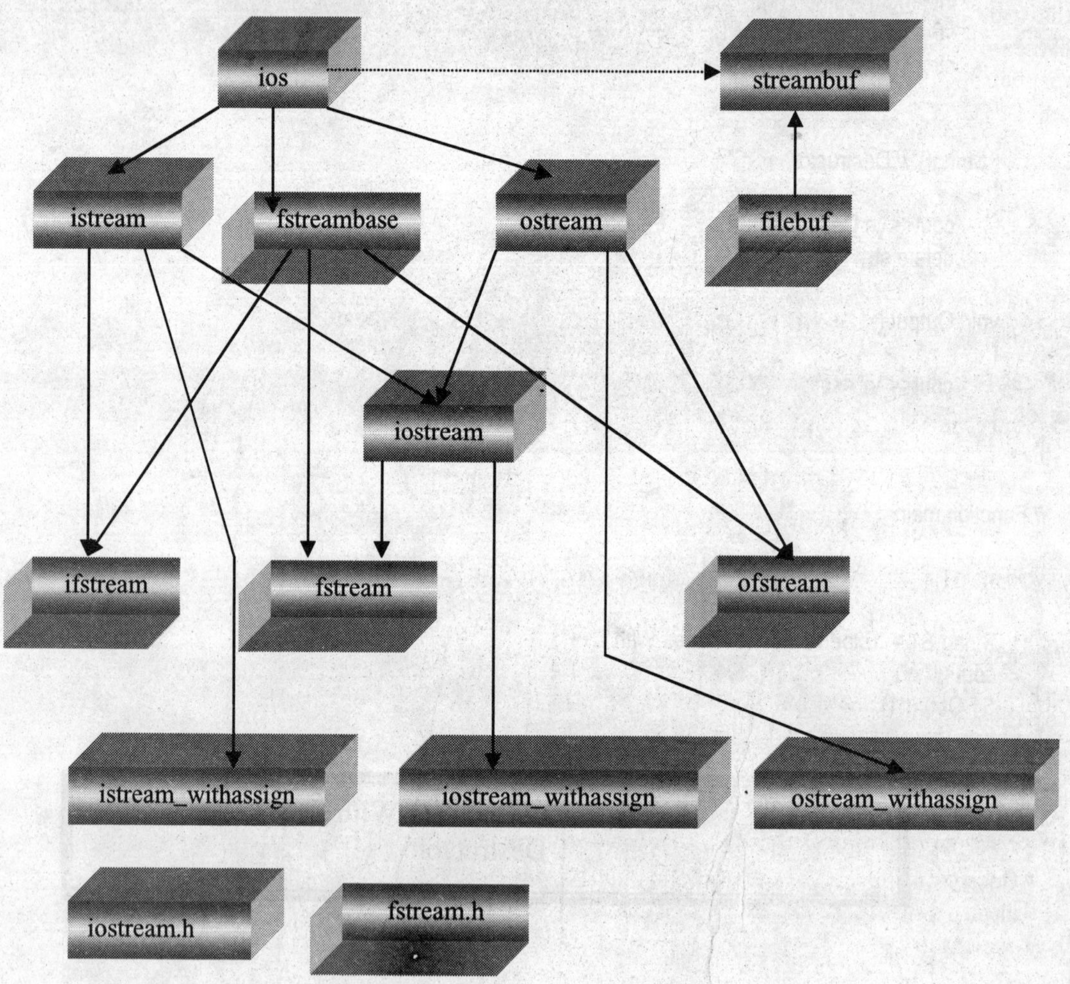

Fig. 1.14 Stream class hierarchy

The **istream** and **ostream** classes are derived from **ios** and are dedicated to input and output, respectively. The **istream** contains the **cin** and **ostream** used for output to **cout, cerr** and **clog**. The following are input functions, which are used with input streams:

- *get ()*
- *getline ()*
- *read ()*

and following are the output stream functions:

- *put ()*
- *write ()*

The **iostream** class is derived from both **istream** and **ostream** by multiple inheritance, so that other classes can inherit both of these classes from it. Three classes **istream_withassign, ostream_withassign** and **iostream_withassign** are inherited from **istream, ostream** and **iostream**, respectively.

The classes, which we want to discuss here for file input and output operations are **ifstream** for input files, **ofstream** for output files and **fstream** for files that will be used for both input and output. These classes are derived from **istream, ostream** and **iostream,** respectively and also from **fstreambase.** The syntax for **ifstream** and **ofstream** are:

```
ifstream file pointer name (file to open);
ofstream file pointer name (file to open);
```

For example, the program segment **IFOFST.C** first of all creates **TEST** file puts some information into it and then read information from it.

```
// IFOFST.C

# include<iostream.h>
# include<fstream.h>
# include<stdio.h>

// Prototype

void Output ();
void Input();

void main()
{
    Output();
    Input();
}

// Opening file TEST in write mode

void Output()
```

```
{
    ofstream output_file("TEST");
    // Creates a file TEST

    output_file<<"Expert Data Structures With C++ \n";
    output_file<<"Written by R.B.Patel and Manmohan Sing Rauthan \n";
    output_file<<"Published by Khanna Publishing Company \n";
}

// Opening file TEST in read mode

void Input()
{
    ifstream input_file ("TEST");
    // Open file TEST in read mode
    const int size = 80;
    char buffer [size];

    while(input_file)
    {
        input_file.getline(buffer, size);
        cout<<"\n "<<buffer;
    }
}
```

In the simplest sense we can say that an output stream is a destination for bytes. Mainly there are three output streams and these are:

- ***ostream*** *used to perform output to* ***cout, cerr and clog***
- ***ofstream*** *used to perform file output to* ***disk***
- ***ostrstream*** *used to perform buffered output to a* ***stream***

Table 1.7 file class (handling modes)

Mode name	Meaning
ios::app	Open the stream in append mode
ios::ate	Opens a file for either input or output, move the file pointer to the end of the file when one wants to append information into the file and move file pointer to the beginning of the file when one wants read information from the file.
ios::in	Opens a file for input
ios::out	Opens a file for output
ios::nocreate	Opens a file only if it already exists
ios::noreplace	Opens a file only if it does not already exist
ios::trunc	Truncates an existing file
ios::binary	Opens a file in binary mode (available in DOS/WINDOWS based compiler)

In the simplest way one can say, an input stream is simply byte source, which is used to perform input operations on standard input devices such as **keyboard, disk**, etc, mainly there are three input streams which are popular. These are:

- ***istream*** *used for input from* ***cin*** *object*
- ***ifstream*** *used for file input from disk*
- ***istrstream*** *used to read buffered input from a* ***strieam***

These input and output streams are defined in **iostream.h, fstream.h**, and **strstream.h** header files. Other type of syntax for **ifstream** and **ofstream** is:

```
ofstream input_file (file name, ios::mode);
ofstream output_file(file name, ios::mode);
```

The different file open modes of **ifstream** and **ofstream** are illustrated in **Table 1.7**.

Table 1.8 status returned by file handling function

MEMBER	TEST	OPERATION PERFORMED
bad ()	File_pointer.bad ()	Returns true if an unrecoverable error was encountered
fail ()	File_pointer.fail ()	Returns true if an unrecoverable or expected error such as a file not found was encountered
eof ()	File_pointer.eof ()	Returns true if an end of file was encountered
clear ()	File_pointer.clear ()	Clears the status flag
rdstate ()	File_pointer.rdstate()	Returns the current error state
good ()	File_pointer.good()	Returns true if the operation was successful

The status of the file **I/O** operations using the **ifstream** and **ofstream** class streams, the program segment in which these are used can determine the success of an open, read or write operation using the member illustrated in **Table 1.8.**

For example, consider the program segment **FILECP.C** that demonstrates **ifstream** and **ofstream** with the help of command line argument **argc** and **argv**. The program segment **FILEBIN.C** demonstrates the said operations on the binary files. To close an opened file we use **close ()** function with file pointer. To check the end of the file we use the **eof ()** function with the help of file pointer, some times it is also required to check the status of the **I/O** operation performed. The program segment **FILESTAT.C** illustrates how one can check the status of a file. The stream status bit is a one byte long and different bits are set according to the status of the **I/O** operations **Fig. 1.15** illustrates the status bit.

Unused	Unused	Unused	Unused	Hard fail 0x08	Bad bit 0x04	Fail bit 0x02	Eof bit 0x01
7	6	5	4	3	2	1	0

Fig. 1.15 Stream status bits

The status word can be read with **rdstate ()**, a member function of **ios**. Several other member functions are illustrated in the program segment **FILESTAT.C** and also illustrate in **Table 1.8**. The values of stream status bits are shown in **Table 1.9.**

Table 1.9 Stream status bits values

Bit	Meaning
0x00	No bit set, no errors
0x01	At end of file (EOF)
0x02	Read or write failed
0x04	Invalid operation (opening nonexistent file)
0x08	Hard error

```
// FILECP.C
#include <iostream.h>
#include <stdlib.h>
#include <fstream.h>
void main(int argc, char *argv[])
{
    char buffer[1];

ifstream input(argv[1], ios::in);

    if (argc != 3)
    {
        cout<<"\n Missing destination file";
        return ;
    }
    if (input.fail())
    {
        cout << "Error opening the file " << argv[1];
        exit(1);
    }
ofstream output(argv[2], ios::out);

    if (output.fail())
    {
        cout << "Error opening the file " << argv[2];
        exit(1);
    }
```

```
    do {
        input.read(buffer, sizeof(buffer));
        if (input.good())
            output.write(buffer, sizeof(buffer));
    } while (! input.eof());

    input.close();
    output.close();
}

// FILEBIN.C
#include <iostream.h>
#include <stdlib.h>
#include <fstream.h>
void main(int argc, char *argv[])
{
    char buffer[1];

    ifstream input(argv[1], ios::in|ios::binary);

    if (argc != 3)
    {
        cout<<"\n Missing destination file";
        return ;
    }

    if (input.fail())
    {
        cout << "Error opening the file " << argv[1];
        exit(1);
    }

    ofstream output(argv[2], ios::out|ios::binary);

    if (output.fail())
    {
        cout << "Error opening the file " << argv[2];
        exit(1);
    }

    do {
        input.read(buffer, sizeof(buffer));
        if (input.good())
            output.write(buffer, sizeof(buffer));
    } while (!input.eof());
```

```
        input.close();
        output.close();
}

// FILESTAT.C
 # include<iostream.h>
 # include<fstream.h>
 # include<stdio.h>

void main()
{
        char ch;
        ifstream file;
        file.open("TEST", ios::nocreate);
        if(!file)
        {
                cout<<"\n File TEST does not exist \n";
                perror("\n Error:");
//return ;
        }
        else
                cout<<"\n File TEST opened successfully \n";
                while(!file.eof())
                {
                        file.get(ch);
                cout<<ch;
                }


// Different status associated with a file

        cout<<"\n Status associated with a file \n";
        cout<<"\n Error status rdstate () = "<<file.rdstate ();
        cout<<"\n Good status good () = "<<file.good ();
        cout<<"\n End of file eof () = "<<file.eof ();
        cout<<"\n Failed status fail () = "<<file.fail ();
        cout<<"\n Bad status bad () = "<<file.bad ();
        cout<<"\n Clear status clear () = ";
        file.clear ();
}
```

```
File TEST does not exist

Status associated with a file

Error status rdstate () = 4
Good status good () = 0
End of file eof () = 0
Failed status fail () = 4
Bad status bad () = 4
Clear status clear ()
File TEST opened successfully
Expert Data Structures With C++
Written by R.B.Patel and Manmohan Sing Rauthan
Published by Khanna Publishing Company

Status associated with a file

Error status rdstate () = 3
Good status good () = 0
End of file eof () = 1
Failed status fail () = 2
Bad status bad () = 0
Clear status clear ()
```

When one plans to a design database or wants to develop an application software then it is required to read or write the complete information about some objects for which he is developing the software. For example, consider the program segment **FILECLAS.C** and **FILECLA1.C** that read or writes one complete record from/into the file **TEST**.

```
// FILECLAS.C

# include<iostream.h>
# include<fstream.h>
# include<stdlib.h>
# include<stdio.h>

class Student
{
    protected:
    char Name[20];
    char RollNo[10];
    char Father[20];
    int age;
```

```
    char Date_Of_Birth[10];

    public:
    void Input ()
    {
        cout << "\n Input the following information of a student";
        cout << "\n Name: ";
        cin>>Name;
        cout << "\n Roll Number: ";
        cin >> RollNo;
        cout << "\n Father' Name: ";
        cin >> Father;
        cout << "\n Age: ";
        cin >> age;
        cout << "\n Date of birth: ";
        cin >> Date_Of_Birth;
    }
    void Output ()
    {
        cout << "\n Information of a student";
        cout <<"\n Name: ";
        cout << Name;
        cout << "\n Roll Number: ";
        cout << RollNo;
        cout << "\n Father' Name: ";
        cout << Father;
        cout << "\n Age: ";
        cout <<age;
        cout <<"\n Date of birth: ";
        cout << Date_Of_Birth;
    }
};

// Function main

void main()
{
    char choice;
    Student std;
ofstream file("TEST", ios::app);
    cout<<"\n Want to add records y/n: ";
    cin>>choice;

    while(choice == 'Y' || choice == 'y')
    {
        std.Input();
```

```
        cout<<"\n Want to add more record y/n: ";
        cin >> choice;
        file.write((char *)&std, sizeof(std));
    }
    file.close();

    ifstream file1("TEST");
    file1.read((char *)&std, sizeof(std));

    cout<<"\n Want to list the records y/n: ";
    cin>>choice;
    if (choice == 'y')

        while (!file1.eof())
        {
            cout<<"\n ******************************* ";
            std.Output();
            cout<<"\n ******************************* \n";

            cout<<"\n\n Want to list more records y/n: ";
            cin>>choice;
            if (choice != 'y')
                break;

            file1.read((char *)&std, sizeof(std));
        }

    file1.close();
}

// FILECLA1.C

# include<iostream.h>
# include<fstream.h>
# include<stdlib.h>
# include<stdio.h>

class Student
{
    protected:
    char choice;
    char Name[20];
    char RollNo[10];
    char Father[20];
    int age;
    char Date_Of_Birth[10];
```

```
    public:
    void Input();
    void Output();
    void Random_file();
    void Write_file();
    void Display();
};

void Student :: Input ()
{
    cout << "\n Input the following information of a student";
    cout << "\n Name: ";
    cin>>Name;
    cout << "\n Roll Number: ";
    cin >> RollNo;
    cout << "\n Father' Name: ";
    cin >> Father;
    cout << "\n Age: ";
    cin >> age;
    cout << "\n Date of birth: ";
    cin >> Date_Of_Birth;
}

void Student :: Output ()
{
    cout << "\n Information of a student";
    cout <<"\n Name: ";
    cout << Name;
    cout << "\n Roll Number: ";
    cout << RollNo;
    cout << "\n Father' Name: ";
    cout << Father;
    cout << "\n Age: ";
    cout <<age;
    cout <<"\n Date of birth: ";
    cout << Date_Of_Birth;
}

void Student :: Random_file()
{
    int n;
    Student std;
    ifstream file2;
    file2.open("TEST");
    file2.seekg(0,ios::end); // Go to 0 byte from the end
```

```
    int end_file;
    end_file = file2.tellg();
    int Number_record = end_file/sizeof(Student);
    cout<<"\n Number of records in the file are: "<<Number_record;
    cout<<"\n Input the record number want list: ";
    cin>>n;
    int position;
    position = n*sizeof(Student);
    file2.seekg(position);
    file2.read((char *)&std, sizeof(std));
    Output();
    file2.close();
}

void Student :: Write_file()
{
    Student std;
    ofstream file("TEST", ios::app);
    cout<<"\n Want to add records y/n: ";
    cin>>choice;

    while(choice == 'Y' || choice == 'y')
    {
        Input();
        file.write((char *)&std, sizeof(std));
        cout<<"\n Want to add more record y/n: ";
        cin >> choice;

    }
    file.close();
}

void Student :: Display()
{
    Student std;
    ifstream file1("TEST");
    file1.read((char *)&std, sizeof(std));

    cout<<"\n Want to list the records y/n: ";
    cin>>choice;
    if (choice == 'y')

        while (!file1.eof())
        {
            cout<<"\n ****************************** ";
            Output();
```

```
        cout<<"\n ***************************** \n";

        cout<<"\n\n Want to list more records y/n: ";
        cin>>choice;
        if (choice != 'y')
            break;

        file1.read((char *)&std, sizeof(std));
    }

    file1.close();
}

// Function main

void main()
{
    Student std;
    std.Write_file();
    std.Display();
    std.Random_file();
}
```

1.14 FLOWCHART

Table 1.10 Decision table

Conditions	Rule1	Rule2	Rule3	Rule4	Rule5	Else
Main marks %age	≥50	≥40	≥60	≥40	≥40	
Ancillary marks %age	≥40	≥50	< 40	≥40	< 40	
Special status	No	No	No	Yes	Yes	
Actions						
Pass	x	x	-	x	-	-
Repeat	-	-	x	-	x	-
Fail	-	-	-	-	-	x

A flowchart depicts pictorial sequence in which instructions are carried out in an algorithm. Flowchart is used not only as an aid in developing algorithms but also to document algorithms. For example, consider **Fig. 1.16,** which is equivalent to the algorithm shown in **Fig. 1.19.** Another algorithm development and documentation aid is the decision table. A decision table depicts in a tabular form the set of conditions to be tested and the sequence of actions to be performed for solving a problem. This aid is useful in solving the problems, which require a large number of decisions. For example, suppose three numbers are given and we have to find out the largest one. Let **x, y** and **z** are three numbers. Algorithm can be constructed such as:

- *Compare **x** with **y** if **x** is larger. Then compare it with z. If **x** is found larger than z then **x** is the largest; otherwise z is the largest.*
- *If in the first step **x** is smaller than or equal to **y** then **y** is compared with z. if **y** is larger than z then it is the largest number else z is the largest.*

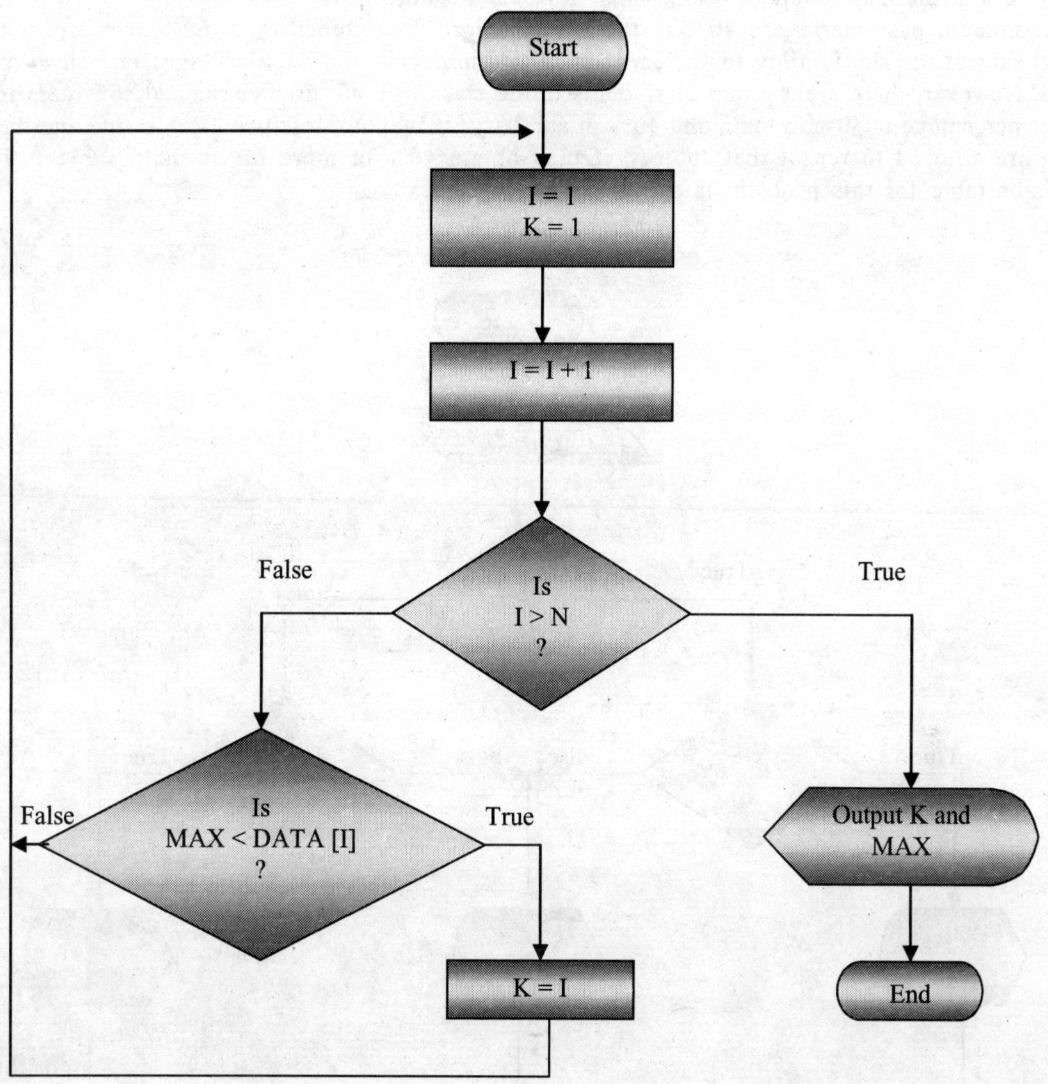

Fig. 1.16 Flowchart for algorithm discussed in Fig. 1.19

The flowchart of this algorithm is illustrated in **Fig. 1.17.** Different symbols used in flowchart are shown in **Fig. 1.18.**

To explain algorithms and flowcharts further we take another example; Student results are declared using the following rules:

There are two subjects in the examination called main and ancillary. If a student gets 50 % or more in the main subject and 40% in the ancillary he/she is passed. If he/she gets less than 50% in the main subject, he/she must get 50% or more in the ancillary to pass. However, the minimum pass marks are 40% in the main subject. If a student gets 60% or more in the main subject, he/she is allowed to repeat ancillary subject if the ancillary subject is less than 40%. However, there are a group of students in the class who are granted special consideration. Their percentage is 40% in main and 40% in ancillary. If they get less than 40% in the ancillary, they are allowed to repeat that subject, if they obtain 40% or more in the main subject. The decision table for this problem is shown in **Table 1.10.**

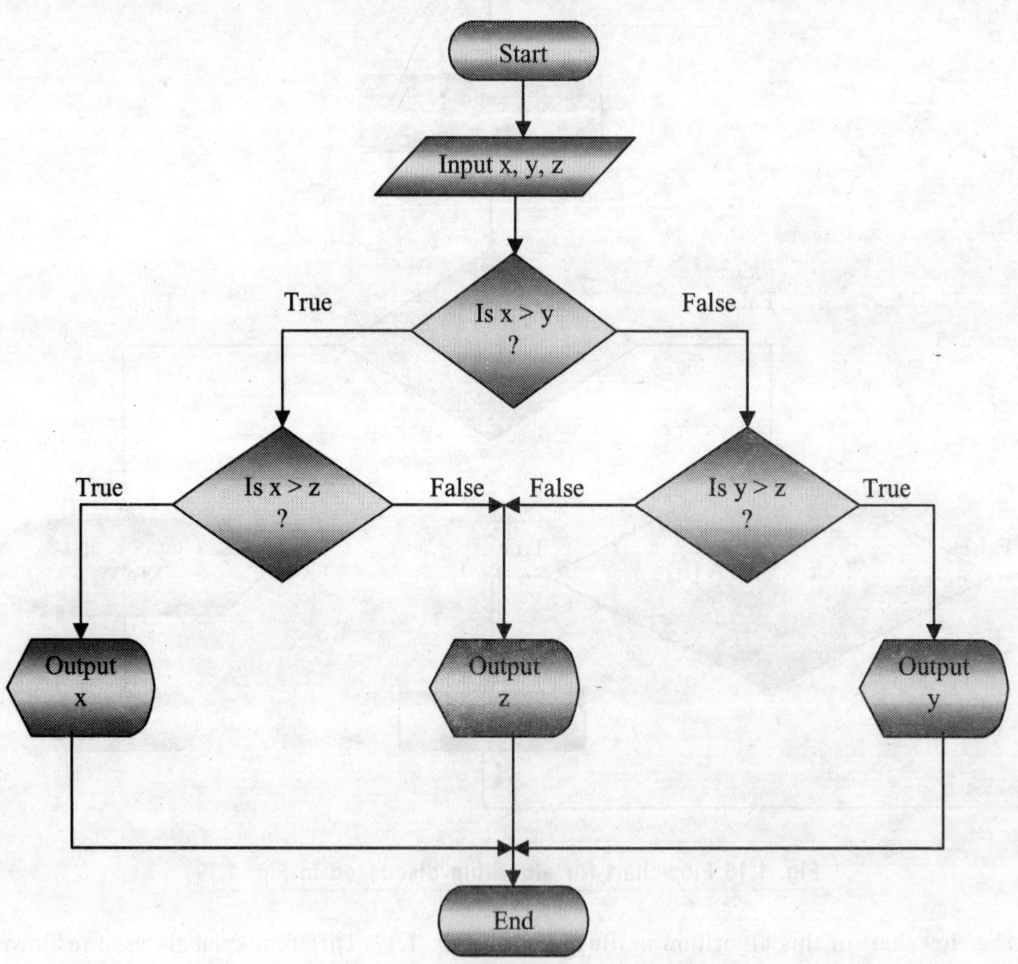

Fig. 1.17 Largest of 3-numbers

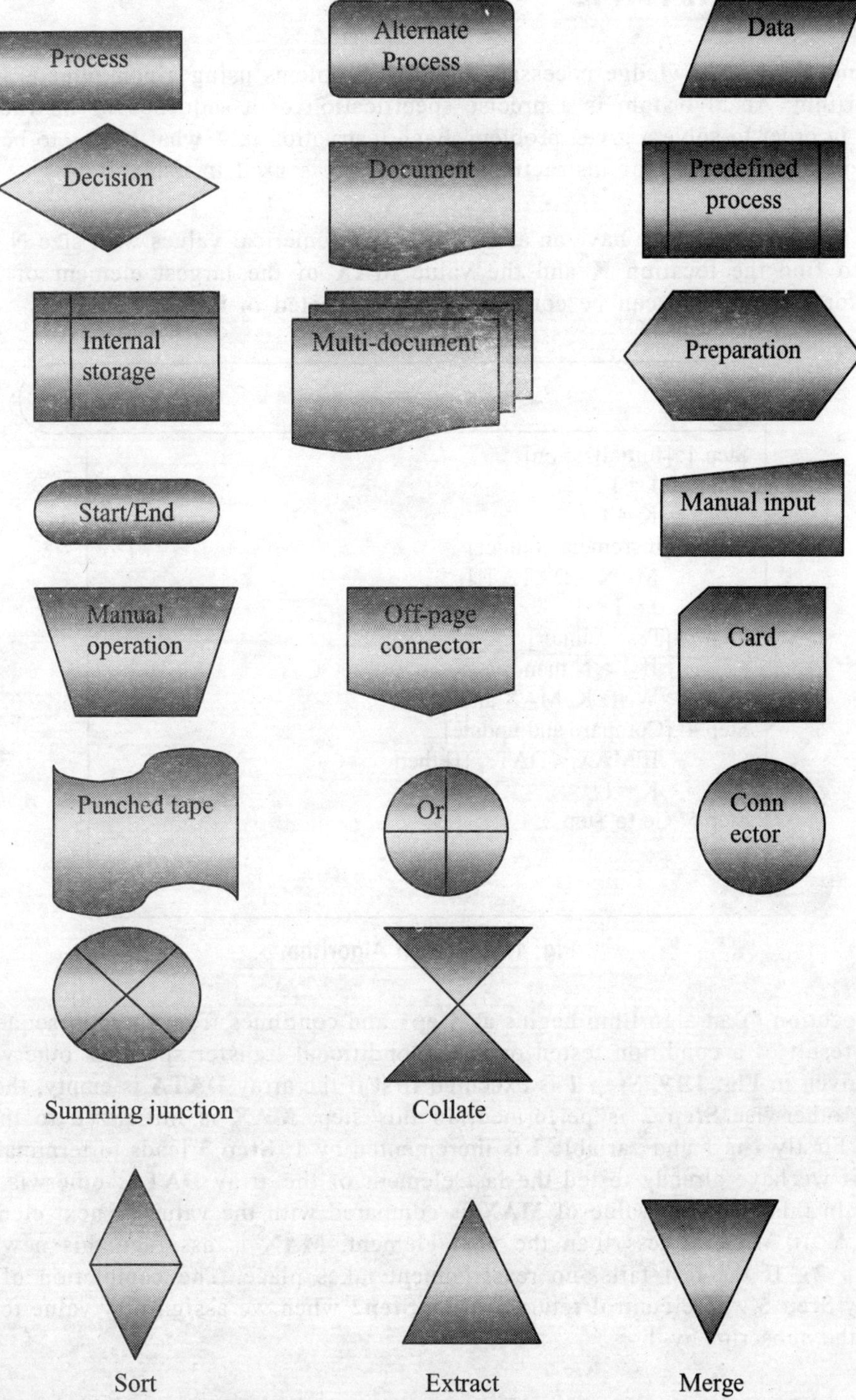

Fig. 1.18 Symbols for flowchart

1.15 ALGORITHMS

The fundamental knowledge necessary to solve problems using a computer is the notation of an algorithm. An algorithm is a precise specification of a sequence of instructions to be carried out in order to solve a given problem. Each instruction tells what task is to be performed. Specification of a sequence of instructions to do a job is used in many fields.

For example, suppose we have an array **DATA** of numerical values with size **N** in memory. We want to find the location **K** and the value **MAX** of the largest element of **DATA**. An algorithm for this problem can be constructed as illustrated in **Fig. 1.19.**

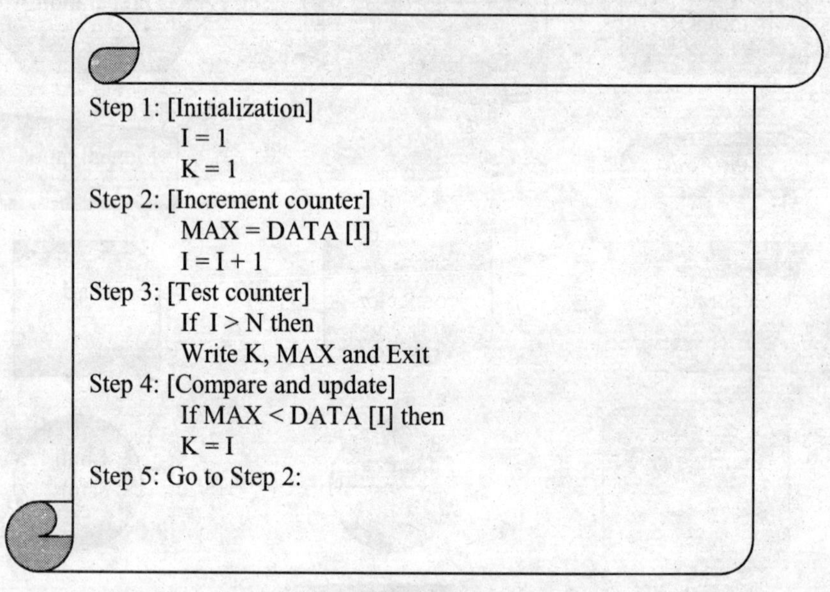

```
Step 1: [Initialization]
        I = 1
        K = 1
Step 2: [Increment counter]
        MAX = DATA [I]
        I = I + 1
Step 3: [Test counter]
        If I > N then
        Write K, MAX and Exit
Step 4: [Compare and update]
        If MAX < DATA [I] then
        K = I
Step 5: Go to Step 2:
```

Fig. 1.19 Search Algorithm

The execution of an algorithm begins at **Step1** and continues from there in sequential order unless the result of a condition tested or an unconditional transfer specifies otherwise. In the algorithm given in **Fig. 1.19, Step 1** is executed first if the array **DATA** is empty, the algorithm terminates; otherwise **Step 2** is performed. In this step, **MAX** is initialized to the value of **DATA [I].** Firstly **I** is 1 and variable **I** is incremented by 1. **Step 3** leads to termination of this algorithm if we have already tested the last element of the array **DATA**; otherwise **Step 4** is performed. In this step, the value of **MAX** is compared with the value of next element of the array **DATA**. If **MAX** is less than the next element, **MAX** is assigned this new value (by calling Step 2). If the test fails, no reassignment takes place. The completion of **Step 4** is followed by **Step 5** where control returns to the **Step2** when we assign new value to **MAX** and increment the subscript by 1.

An algorithm can be classified as a finite sequence of instructions, which has the following basic properties:

- *A number of quantities provided to an algorithm initially before the algorithm begins. These quantities are the inputs, which are processed by the algorithm.*
- *The processing rules specified in the algorithm must be precise and unambiguous and lead to a specific action.*
- *Each instruction must be sufficiently basic so that a person using paper and pencil can in principle carry it out in a finite time.*
- *The total time to carry out all the steps in the algorithm must be finite. As algorithms may contain instructions to repetitively carry out a group of instructions, this requirement implies that the total number of repetitions must be finite.*
- *An algorithm must have one or more outputs.*

1.15.1 ANALYSIS OF ALGORITHMS

As soon as one can write an algorithm, it is necessary to learn how to analyze an algorithm. The first type of analysis that one encounters is of the correctness of an algorithm. Tracing the algorithm, reading the algorithm for logical correctness, implementing the algorithm and testing it on some data or using mathematical techniques to prove it correct can do this analysis. Another type of analysis is of the simplicity of the algorithm. Perhaps the algorithm can be expressed in a simpler way, so that it is easier to implement and perform other analyses on the algorithm. However, the simplest and most straightforward way of solving a problem is sometimes not the best one. Usually this occurs when the simplest approach involves the use of too much computer time or space. Thus, it is important to be able to analyze the time and space requirements of an algorithm to see if it is within acceptable limits. For example, if an algorithm to control the trajectory of a rocket required several seconds for each trajectory adjustment, it would be unacceptable. Time and space analysis are also important for comparisons of algorithm to determine the best one.

1.15.1.1 RATE OF GROWTH

Unfortunately it is generally not possible to perform a simple analysis of an algorithm to determine the exact amount of time required by it. The first complication is that the exact amount of time will depend on the implementation of the algorithm on the actual machine. Another complication arises in doing time analysis in that the time requirements will normally depend on the amount of input data. For example, an algorithm that sums the values in an array can be expected to require more time for a array of size 10000 values that for one of size 100. As a result the estimate for the time required by an algorithm is usually expressed as a function of the size of the input data. Thus, if input has size **n**, as in the above example, where there are **n** values in the array, then the time is expressed as **T (n)** and space as **S (n),** where **T** and **S** are functions of the amount of data.

Before starting analysis of algorithms it is beneficial to recall the rates of growth for some functions that are often used to express **T** and **S**. In **Fig. 1.20** we have plotted several functions. The functions that involve **n** as an exponent, $\mathbf{2^n}$, $\mathbf{n^n}$ and $\mathbf{n! \sim (n/2.56)^n}$ are called exponential functions. Any algorithm whose execution time grows proportionally to an exponential function is too slow for some constant **c**, for example, $\mathbf{n^3}$, $\mathbf{n^2}$, **n** $\mathbf{\log_2 n}$, **n** and $\mathbf{\log_2 n}$ are said to be polynomial. Algorithms with polynomial time can solve rescannable sized problems if the constant in the exponent is small. For problems involving large amounts of data, it is necessary to find an algorithm whose execution time grows linearly, proportional to **n** or sub-linearly, for instance, proportional to $\mathbf{\log_2 n}$.

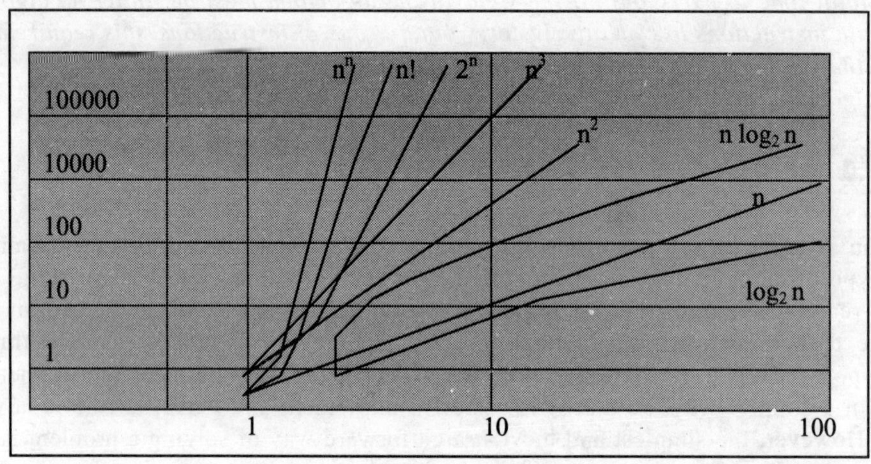

Fig. 1.20 Rate of growth

1.15.1.2 TIME ANALYSIS

For example, consider the algorithm **Summation** that finds summation of an array containing **n** values, given in **Fig. 1.21.**

As we have already discussed that calculation of exact amount of time required by an algorithm is very difficult, so we want an estimate of it. Usually this is most easily done by isolating a particular operation, sometimes called active operation, that is central to the algorithm and that is executed essentially as often as any other. In the algorithm given in **Fig. 1.21,** a good operation to isolate is the addition that occurs when another array value is added to the partial sum. The other operations in the algorithm, the assignments, the manipulations of index **I** and the accessing of a value in the array, occur no more often than the addition of the array values. These other operations are collectively called bookkeeping operations and are not generally counted. It is very important that none of the bookkeeping operations are executed significantly more often than the active operation. After the active operation is isolated, the number of times that it is executed is counted. If we follow this approach in the summation algorithm shown in **Fig. 1.21,** the number of additions of values is **n.** As long as the active operation occurs at least as often as the others, then the execution time will increase in proportion to the number of times the active operation is executed. Thus, the above algorithm has execution time proportional to **n**.

```
Summation (A, n)
Step 1: [Initialization]
        Sum = 0
Step 2: [Sum the values in array A]
        Repeat while (I ≤ n)
        Sum = Sum + A[I]
Step 3: [Finish]
        Exit
```

Fig. 1.21 Summation of values lie in an array

Consider another example, matrix multiplication of two **n x n** matrix **M** and **N,** to form a **n x n** matrix **R.** The matrix multiplication algorithm is given in **Fig. 1.22**.

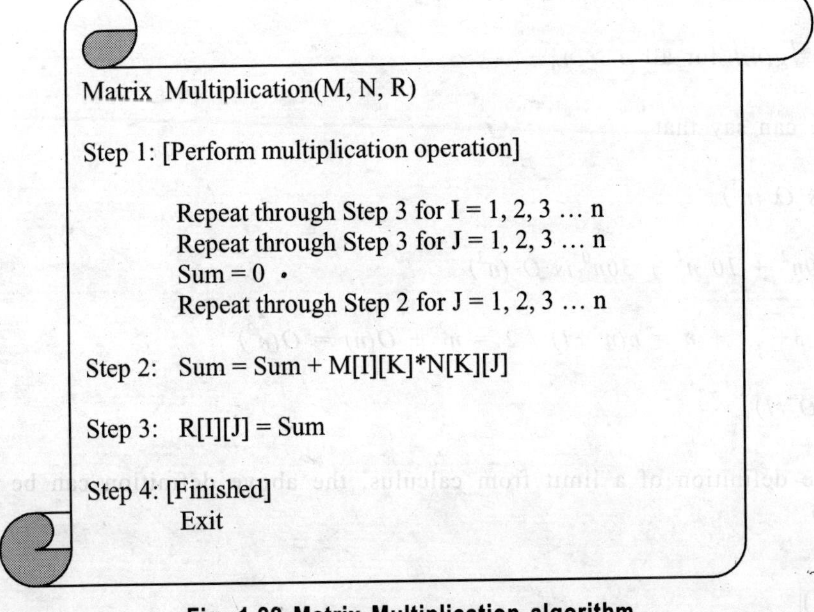

```
Matrix Multiplication(M, N, R)

Step 1: [Perform multiplication operation]

         Repeat through Step 3 for I = 1, 2, 3 … n
         Repeat through Step 3 for J = 1, 2, 3 … n
         Sum = 0
         Repeat through Step 2 for J = 1, 2, 3 … n

Step 2:  Sum = Sum + M[I][K]*N[K][J]

Step 3:  R[I][J] = Sum

Step 4: [Finished]
         Exit
```

Fig. 1.22 Matrix Multiplication algorithm

The actual size of the input for this algorithm is $\mathbf{2n^2}$, but it is convenient to use **n** as our measure of the size of the input in orders to simplify the calculations. For the active operations, we can select either the multiplication of **M [I][K]** and **N [I][K]** or addition of the above product to **Sum**. This follows since both are central operations and essentially occur as often as any other does. It is easy to see that either of these operations is executed $\mathbf{n^3}$ times, so that the time for the algorithm is proportional to $\mathbf{n^3}$.

Note that there are actually more assignments than multiplication or additions. There are **n** assignment to **I**, n^2 assignments to **J** and **R**, n^3 assignments to **K** and n^2+n^3 assignments to **Sum**. This yields a total of $n + 3n^2 + 2n^3$ assignments. Certainly assignment could have been selected as our active operation, although it is questionable whether it is as central to the problem as either multiplication or addition. If it were used as the active operation, we would conclude that the time was proportional to $n + 3n^2 + 2n^3$. Fortunately we are normally only interested in the order of magnitude of the time required. The order only considers the term that grows the fastest, $2n^3$ and ignores the constant 2, associated with it. Thus, we obtain that the order of magnitude for the time required in n^3, independent of which operation is chosen as active, but that just happens in this problem. In other cases, may be assignments would have to be active.

1.15.1.3 BIG O-NOTATION

A notation has been developed to facilitate the handling of order of magnitude functions. A function **f(n)** is defined to be **O(g(n))**, i.e., **f(n) = O(g(n))** and is said to be of order **g(n)**, if there exists positive constants n_0 and **c**, such that

$|f(n)| \le c * |g(n)|$ for all $n > n_0$

Thus, we can say that

$400\, n^5$ *is* $O(n^5)$

$100n^3+50n^2 + 10\, n^1 + 30n^0$ *is* $O(n^3)$

$1 + 2 + 3 + \ldots + n = n(n+1) / 2 = n^2 + O(n) = O(n^2)$

2402 is $O(1)$

Using the definition of a limit from calculus, the above definition can be shown to be equivalent to

$$\lim_{n\to 0} \frac{|f(n)|}{|g(n)|} = c$$

For some constant **c**. in this form, ***L. Hospital's*** rule is often useful for computing the limit. It states that if

$$\lim_{n\to\infty} f(n) = \infty \text{ and } \lim_{n\to\infty} g(n) = \infty$$

then

$$\lim_{n\to\infty}\frac{|f(n)|}{|g(n)|} = \lim_{n\to\infty}\frac{|f'(n)|}{|g'(n)|}$$

where **f'** and **g'** are derivatives of **f** and **g.**

For example:

$$\lim_{n\to\infty}\frac{|ln(n)|}{n} = \lim_{n\to\infty}\frac{1/n}{1} = \lim_{n\to\infty}\frac{1/n}{1} = 0 \text{ so } ln(n) = 0(n)$$

where **ln(n)** is the natural logarithm of **n**. Using this notation we have

T_s **(n) = O (n)** and T_M **= O (n^3)**, are the time analysis for summation of array and multiplication algorithm, respectively.

1.16 DATA STRUCTURE

Data may be organized in many different ways; the logical or mathematical model of a particular organization of data is called data structures. Choice of a particular data model depends on two considerations: it must be rich enough in structure to mirror the actual relationships of the data in the real world. On the other hand, the structure should be simple enough that one can effectively process the data when necessary. In other words data structure is a collection of data elements whose organization is characterized by assessing operations that are used to store and retrieve the individual data elements; the implementation of the composite data members in an abstract data type. A abstract data type can be defined as a data type whose properties are specified independently of any particular implementation. The data structures are classified in the following two categories

- *Linear data structures*
- *Nonlinear data structures*

1.16.1 LINEAR DATA STRUCTURES

In the linear data structures processing of data items is possible in linear fashion, i.e., data can be processed one by one sequentially. Linear data structures includes the following types of data structures:

- *Array*
- *Linked list*
- *Stack and Queues*

1.16.1.1 ARRAYS

This is the simplest type of data structure, is a linear (one-dimensional) array. By a linear array, we mean a list of finite number **n** of similar data elements referenced respectively by a set of **n** consecutive numbers, usually **1, 2, 3 ... n.** If we choose the name **V** for the array, then the elements of **V** are denoted by parenthesis notation

V(1), V(2), V(3) ... V(N)

or by bracket notation

V[1], V[2], V[3] ... V[n]

or by subscript notation

$V_1, V_2, V_3 \ldots V_n$

1.16.1.2 LINKED LIST

A linked list can be defined as collection of nodes. A node has two fields, information and address field that contains the address of the next node, i.e., pointer to the next node. For example, **Fig. 1.23** represents a linked list in memory.

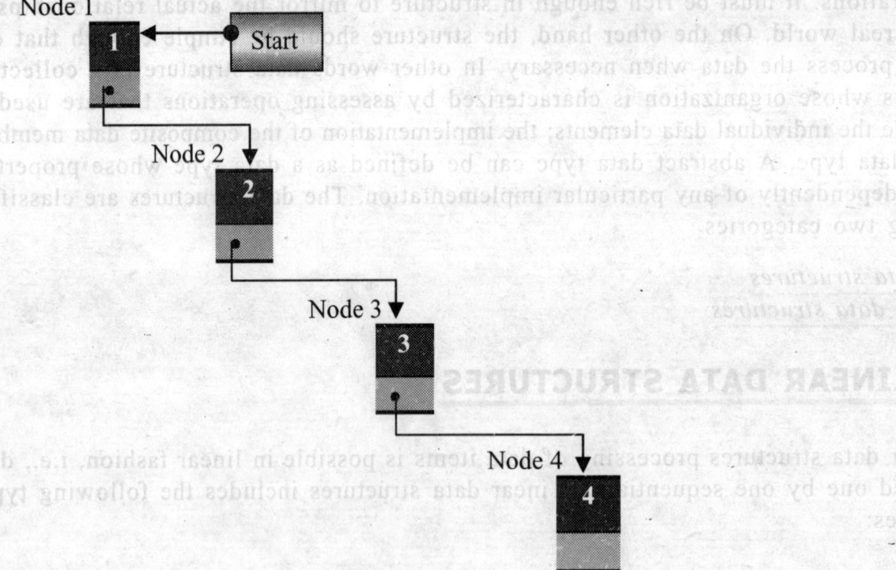

Fig. 1.23 Linked list

1.16.1.3 STACK AND QUEUES

A stack, also called a last-in first-out (LIFO) system, is a linear list in which insertions and deletions can take place at one end, called the **TOP**. This structure is similar in its operation to a stack of dishes on a peg system shown in **Fig. 1.24.**

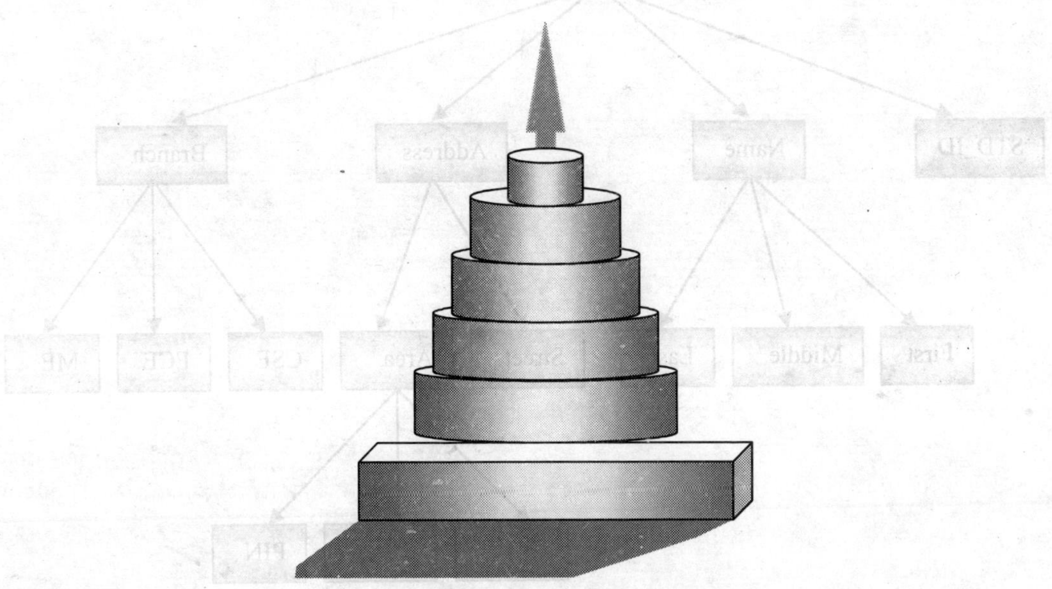

Fig. 1.24 Stack of dishes on a peg

A queue, also called a first-in first-out (FIFO) system, is linear list in which deletions can take place at one end of the list, the **front** of the list and insertions can take place only at the other end of the list, the **rear** of the list. This structure operates in much same way as a line of people waiting for railway reservation ticket at booking window.

1.16.2 NONLINEAR DATA STRUCTURES

A data structure in which insertion and deletion is not possible in a linear fashion is called nonlinear data structure. In this category of data structure, we will discuss the following:

- *Tree*
- *Graph*

1.16.2.1 TREE

Data frequently contain a hierarchical relationship between various elements. The data structure, which reflects this relationship, is called a rooted tree graph or simply a tree. We will discuss trees in detail in **Chapter 7**. For example, **Fig. 1.25** discusses a tree structure of student personnel record.

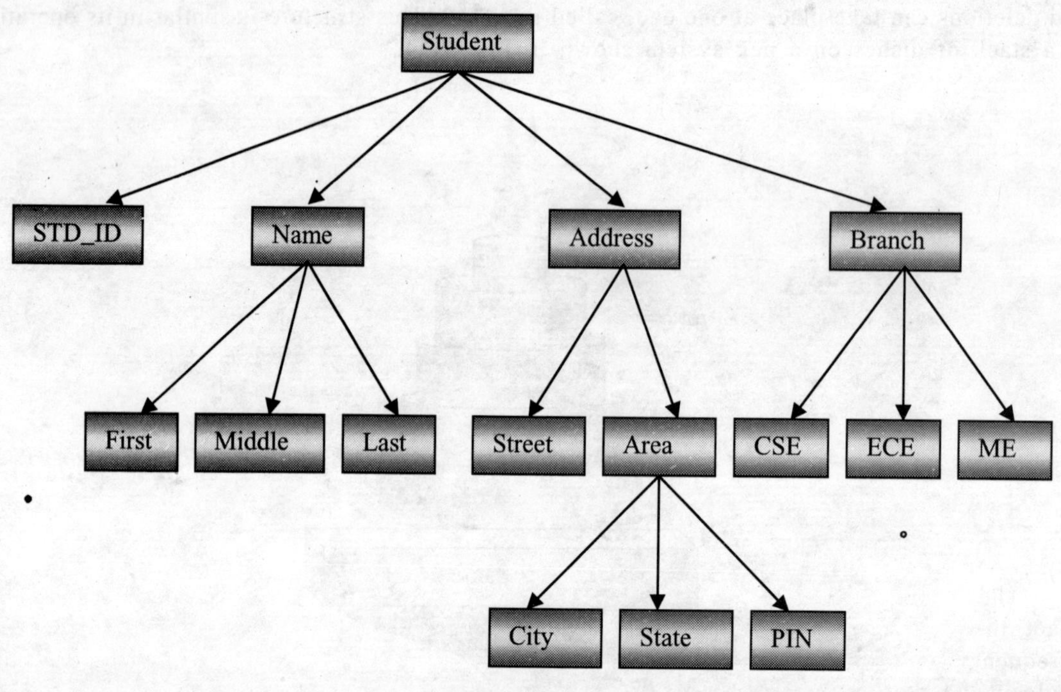

Fig. 1.25 Tree

1.16.2.2 GRAPH

This is a data structure that some times contain a relationship between pairs of elements, which is not necessarily hierarchical in nature. For example, suppose airline flies only between the cities connected by line in **Fig. 1.26.** The data structure graph is discussed in detail in **chapter 8**.

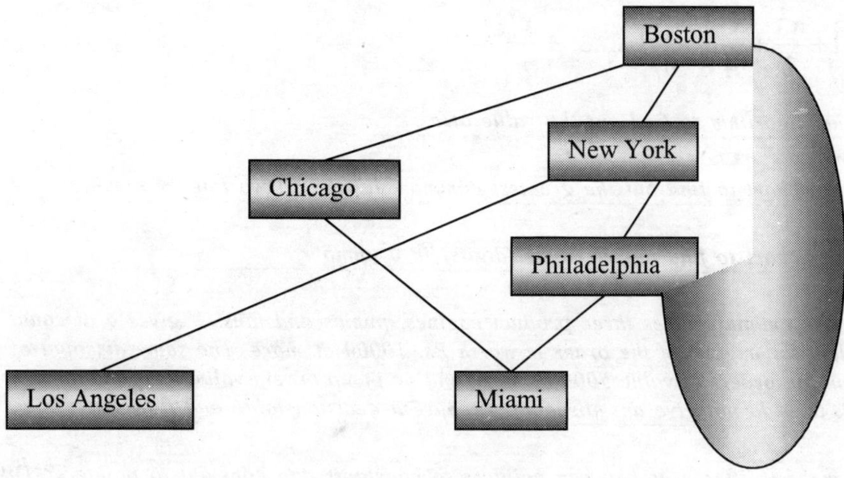

Fig. 1.26 Airline flights

1.17 DATA STRCUTURE OPERATIONS

The data appearing in our data structures are processes by means of certain operation. In fact, the particular data structures that one chooses for a given situation depends largely on the frequency with which specific operations are performed. The following operations play major role in the processing of data:

(a) *Traversing*
(b) *Searching*
(c) *Inserting*
(d) *Deleting*
(e) *Sorting*
(f) *Merging*

The details of these operations are given in subsequent chapters.

EXERCISE

1.1 *Design an algorithm to find the summation of following series.*

$$F(x) = \sum_{r=1}^{r=n} x^r$$

1.2 *Construct flowchart to find out summation of following series:*

$$F(x) = 1 + \frac{x^2}{2} + \frac{x^4}{4} + \frac{x^6}{6} + \ldots\ldots + \frac{x^n}{n}$$

1.3 *Write an algorithm to find out the value of* a^b.

1.4 *Draw flowchart to find out the greatest common divisor of two integer numbers.*

1.5 *Draw flowchart to find out elements (digits) in a number.*

1.6 *A Company manufactures three product engines, pumps and fans. It gives a discount of 20 percent on orders for engines if the order is worth Rs. 10000 or more. The same discount of 20 percent or more on fan orders of value 5000 or more and on pump orders value Rs. 7000 or more. On all other orders, they do not give any discount. Prepare a decision table and flowchart.*

1.7 *What are :he differences between pointers to constants and constant to pointers? Discuss with the help of suitable examples.*

1.8 *Write a function that counts number of vowels in a given text.*

1.9 *Write a function that works like petrol pump counter, it increases character counter by one when a key is pressed, when finds a blank it increases the word counter by one and when it finds a dot after that a blank then it increases the sentence counter by one.*

1.10 *Write a function that counts number of words in a given text and also counts the words of different types.*

1.11 *Write a function that inserts a sub-string in a string some where in the middle.*

1.12 *Write a complete program to access number of students in a class using pointers to structure.*

1.13 *Write a complete program to implement a structure for the following fields:*

- *Name*
- *Father's Name*
- *Enrollment Number*
- *Roll Number*
- *Date of Birth*
- *Date of joining the college*
- *Address*

And also provide the provision to sort the list on any desired field e.g. on Name, Enrollmen Number, etc.

1.14 *Write a function, which reads a string and transfers its reverse to another pointer variable.*

1.15 *Write a program for inventory control, which should contain the following options:*

- *Add record*
- *Delete record*
- *Update record*
- *Print record*
- *List record (Random access)*

You can choose different fields by your won.

1.16 *The following is the list entries with level number in a student's record*

1 Student 2 Number 2 Name 3 Last 3 First 3 Middle 2 Sex 2 Birth Day 3 Day 3 Month 3 Year 2 SAT 3 C-Programming 3 Viva Voce

(a) *Draw the corresponding hierarchical structure*
(b) *Which of the items are elementary items?*
(c) *Write a function that implements*

1.17 *Write a complete program to access number of students in a class using pointers to object members.*

1.18 *Discuss the function overloading with the help of suitable examples. Write a overloaded functions that compute values of* $\mathbf{ApR}^3/4$ *where parameters are used as:*

- *Integer*
- *Float*
- *Double*

1.19 *What do you understand by aggregate data types? Discuss with the help of suitable examples.*

1.20 *The harmonic mean defined by*

$$h = \frac{n}{\sum_{i=1}^{n} 1/a_i}$$

is some times used as a mean of central tendency. Develop a program that computes the harmonic mean of ***n*** *data values.*

1.21 *Write a program that works like a binary calculator for the flowing operations:*

(a) *Addition*
(b) *Subtraction*
(c) *Multiplication*
(d) *Division*

(e) *Modulo operation*
(f) *Remainder*

1.22 ***Design an algorithm that reads in n single digits and converts them into a single integer. For example, the algorithm should convert the set of 5 digits {2, 7, 4, 9 and 3} to the integer 27493. Finally implement the designed algorithm.***

1.23 ***The binomial theorem of basic algebra indicates that the coefficient ^nC_r of the rth power of x in the expansion of $(1+x)^n$ is given by***

$$^nC_r = \frac{n!}{r!(n-r)}$$

Draw flowchart that evaluates all coefficient of x for a given value of n. Also design an algorithm and implement the designed algorithm.

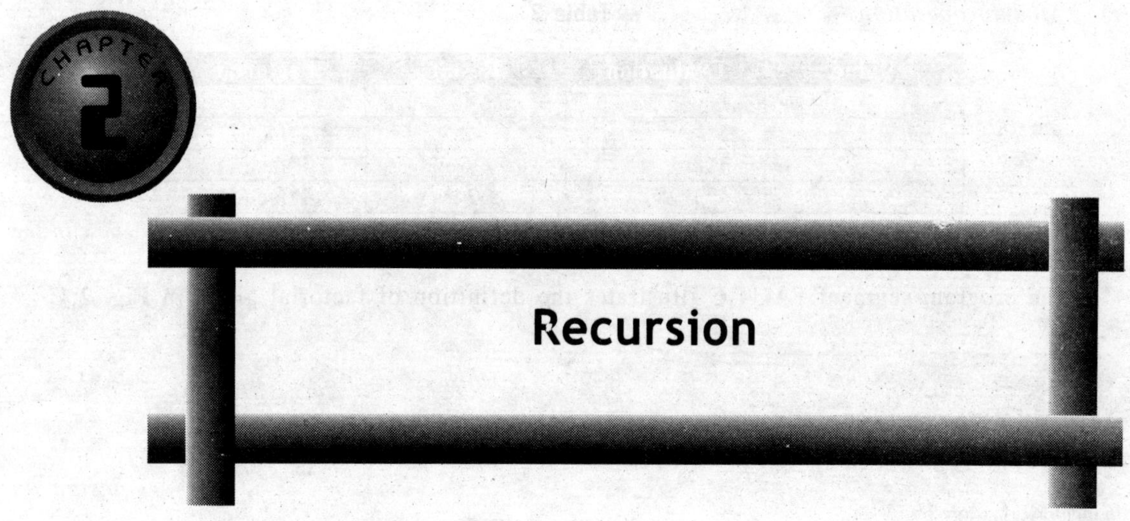

2.1 RECURSION

C++ language supports recursion. With the help of recursion, the process of execution is not speeded; rather it defines the process in a simple way to understand. Recursion is the name given to a technique for defining a function in terms of itself. For example, recursive definition of factorial of a natural number is:

$$Factorial\_num(n) = \begin{cases} 1 & \text{if } n = 1 \\ n * Factorial\_.num(n-1) & \text{if } n > 1 \end{cases}$$

Fig. 2.1 Factorial algorithm

Here, **Factorial_num(n)** is defined in terms of **Factorial_num(n - 1),** which is again defined in terms of **Factorial_num(n-2)** and so on, until **Factorial_num(0)** is reached. The value of **Factorial_num(0)** is defined as 1.

The factorial of 0 is 1. The factorial of 1 is 1. The factorial of 2 is 2*1. The factorial of 3 is 3*2*1. Likewise, the factorial of 4 is 4*3*2*1. This process will continue. If we take a close look on the processing of the factorial, we will find that factorial of 4 is actually 4 times the factorial of 3, i.e., 3*2*1. Likewise, the factorial of 3 is 3 times the factorial of 2, i.e., 2*1. The factorial of 2 is 2 times the factorial of 1. The actual operation of the definition given in **Fig. 2.1** is shown in **Table 2.1.**

Table 2.1

Value	Evaluation	Result	Factorial
1	1	1	1
2	2*1	2	2*fact(1)
3	3*2*1	6	3*fact(2)
4	4*3*2*1	24	4*fact(3)

The program segment **FACT.C** illustrates the definition of factorial given in **Fig. 2.1.**

```
// Factorial of integer number
// FACT.C

# include<iostream.h>

class Factorial
{
    private :
            int n;
    public :
            long int Factorial_num( int );
            void Display( int);
};

// The definition of the Factorial_num() function

long int Factorial :: Factorial_num( int n)
{
    if( n == 0)
        return(1);
    else
        return(n * Factorial_num( n -1 ));
}

// Output Function

void Factorial :: Display(int n)
{
    cout<<"\n Factorial of : "<< n<<" = "<< Factorial_num(n);
}

// main function
```

```
void main()
{
	Factorial Cal_Fact;
	int n ;
	cout<<"\n Input the number of which you want to find factorial:";
	cin>>n;
	Cal_Fact.Factorial_num( n );
	Cal_Fact.Display( n );
}
```

```
Input the number of which you want to find factorial: 5
 Factorial of : 5 = 120
```

Here, the function **Factorial_num()** is called with argument 0 value. Then function returns 1, otherwise it returns **n*Factorial_num(n-1)**. To calculate the value of the expression, the **Factorial_num()** is called with **n-1.** This process continues until **n** equals to 0. **Fig. 2.2** illustrates how the recursive function is invoked.

2.2 TYPES OF RECURSION

Recursion is of two types:

- *Preemptive recursive function for example, factorial algorithm (discussed above).*
- *Non-preemptive recursive function for example,* **Ackermann**'*s function, a function with two arguments which can be assigned any positive integer such as 0, 1, 2, 3 ..., etc. The function is defined as:*

$$Ack\_fun(M,N)=\begin{cases} N+1 & \text{if } M=0 \\ Ack\_fun(M-1,1) & \text{if } N=0 \\ Ack\_fun(M-1, Ack\_fun(M,N-1)) & Otherwise \end{cases}$$

Fig. 2.3 Ackermann's recursive algorithm

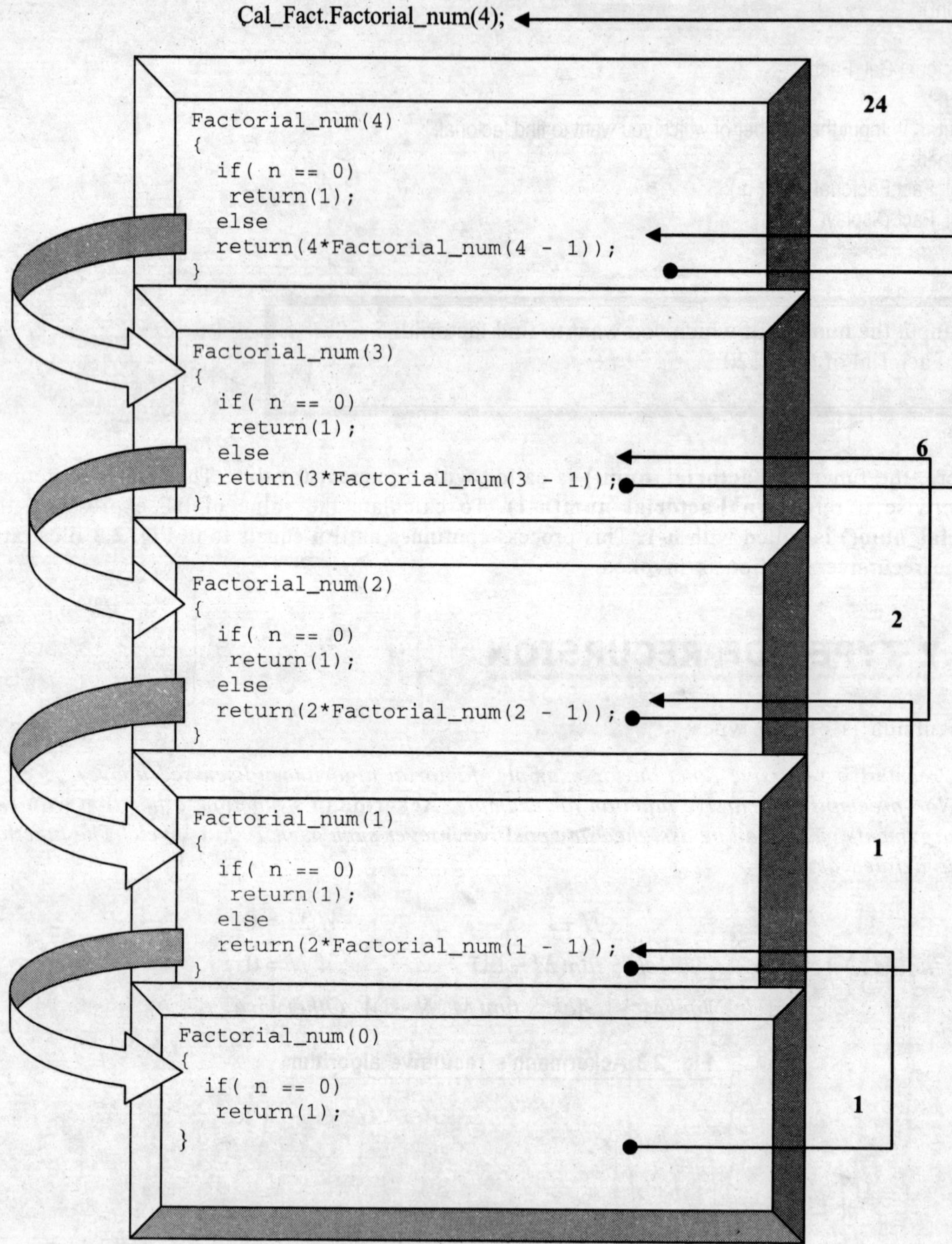

Fig. 2.2 Sequence of function calls and the value returned

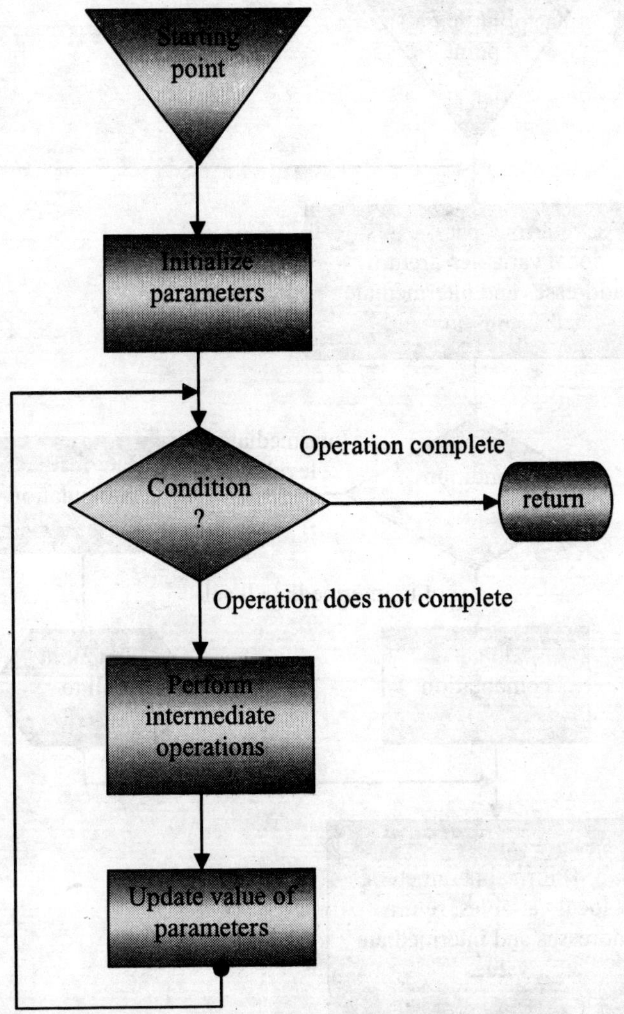

Fig. 2.4 Iterative method

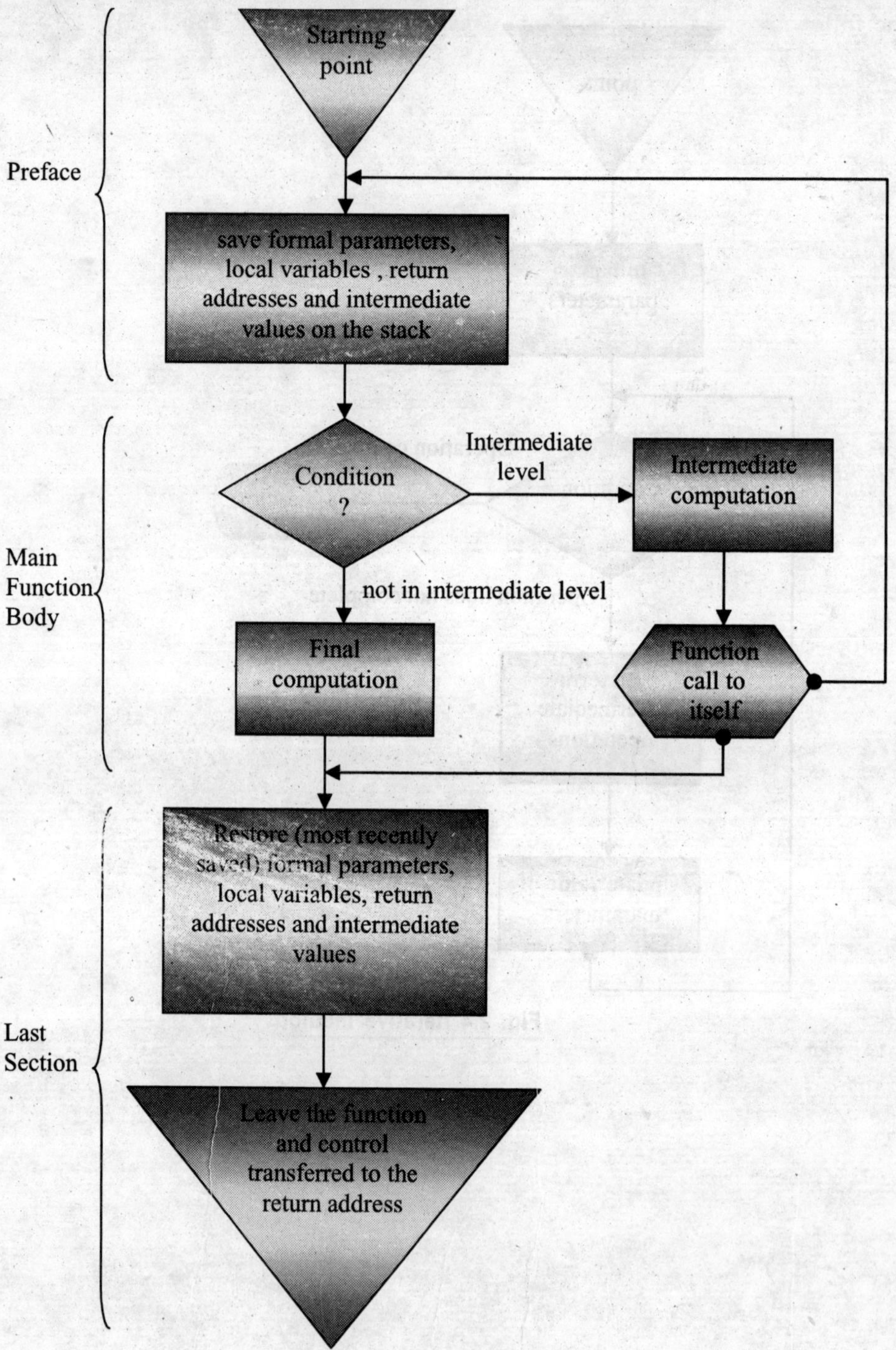

Fig. 2.5 Recursive process

The following steps show, how one can find the value **Ack_fun(1, 3)?**

(i) Ack_fun(1,3) = Ack_fun(1-1,Ack_fun(1,3-1)) = Ack_fun(0,Ack_fun(1,2))
(ii) Ack_fun(1,2) = Ack_fun(1-1,Ack_fun(1,2-1)) = Ack_fun(0,Ack_fun(1,1))
(iii) Ack_fun(1,1) = Ack_fun(1-1,Ack_fun(1,1-1)) = Ack_fun(0,Ack_fun(1,0))
(iv) Ack_fun(1,0) = Ack_fun(1-1,1) = Ack_fun(0,1)
(v) Ack_fun(0,1) = N+1 = 1 + 1 = 2 ***Here value of N is 1***
(vi) Ack_fun(1,0) = 2
(vii) Ack_fun(1,1) = (0,2) Consider step 3 to 6
(viii) Ack_fun(0,2) = 2 + 1 = 3 ***Here value of N is 2***
(ix) Ack_fun(1,1) = Ack_fun(0,2) Consider step 3 to 8
(x) Ack_fun(1,2) = Ack_fun(0,3)
(xi) Ack_fun(0,3) = 3 + 1 = 4 ***Here value of N is 3***
(xii) Ack_fun(1,2) = 4
(xiii) Ack_fun(1,3) = Ack_fun(0,4)
(xiv) Ack_fun(0,4_ = 4 + 1 = 5 ***Here value of N is 4***
(xv) Ack_fun(1,3) = 5 Result

Recursion occurs in ***Ackermann's*** function, because the function **Ack_fun()** becomes an argument in a call of function **Ack_fun()**. This is a very typical case of recursion. Preemptive recursive algorithm can be easily implemented with the help of iterative method {Fig. 2.4}. The pictorial representation of recursive algorithm is given in **Fig. 2.5**.

2.3 EXPONENTIAL POWER

In the similar way one can easily compute the positive (integer) exponential power of a number, i.e., a^b. The recursive definition is:

$$power\_f(a,b) = \begin{cases} 1 & \text{if } b = 0 \\ a * power\_f(a,b-1) & \text{if } b > 0 \end{cases}$$

Fig. 2.6 Recursive definition of a^b

In the similar way one can easily compute the negative (integer) exponential power of a number, i.e., $\mathbf{a}^{-b}$. The recursive definition is:

$$power\_f(a,b) = \begin{cases} 1 & \text{if } b = 0 \\ a * power\_f(a,-b+1) & \text{if } b < 0 \end{cases}$$

Fig. 2.7 Recursive definition of a^{-b}

Here, we have taken **mantissa = a** and **exponent = - b**. The power is negative so the returned value of the function is taken as inverse of the **returned value of the function.**

The recursive program for the two definitions shown in **Fig. 2.6** and **Fig. 2.7** is illustrated in the program segment **POWER.C**.

```
// Power Function
// POWER.C

# include<iostream.h>

class Power_Fun
    {
        public:
        double power_f(double, float );
    };

// Definition of the function power_f()

double Power_Fun :: power_f(double a, float b)
    {
        if( b == 0)
    {
        return 1;
    }
        else if ( b< 0)
    {
        return( (a * power_f(a,b+1)));
    }

    else
        return( a* power_f(a,b-1));
}

// Function main

void main()
    {
        Power_Fun pow1;

    double mantissa;
    float exponent;

    cout<<"\n Input the Mantissa:";
    cin>> mantissa;
```

```
    cout<<"\n Input the exponent:";
    cin>>exponent;
    if( exponent < 0)
        cout<<" maintissa ^ exponent:"<< 1/pow1.power_f(mantissa,exponent);
    else cout<<" maintissa ^ exponent:"<<pow1.power_f(mantissa,exponent);
}
```

```
Input the Mantissa: 12.34
Input the exponent: 4

mantissa ^ exponent = 23187.858355
```

In the similar way one can easily compute the positive (fractional) exponential power of a number, i.e., $\mathbf{a}^b$. The recursive definition is:

$$power\_f(a,b) = \begin{cases} 1 & \text{if } b = 0.0 \\ a * power\_f(a, b-i+1) & \text{if } b > 0.0 \end{cases}$$

Fig. 2.8 Recursive definition of a^b

For computing the negative (fractional) exponential power of a number, i.e., $\mathbf{a}^{-b}$, the following recursive definition can be used:

$$power\_f(a,b) = \begin{cases} 1 & \text{if } b = 0.0 \\ a * power\_f(a, -b+i, i) & \text{if } b < 0.0 \end{cases}$$

Fig. 2.9 Recursive definition of a^b

To see, how the definitions shown in **Fig. 2.8** and **Fig. 2.9** work, consider the following program segment **(POWER1.C).**

In this program segment, **i** has been taken as a counter and its value is calculated by passing 10 as **mantissa**. The number of digits after the decimal point is passed as **exponent**. For example, if the digits after the decimal point are four then we pass 4 to the recursion function for calculating the value of **i**. After getting the value of **i,** the exponential power of the number is calculated. If the exponent is positive then returned value of the function will be the value of the exponential power the number else we take the inverse of the returned value of the function as the exponential power of the number. Here, in this function we input exponent. parameter value as a string because it is easier to find the number of digits before and after the decimal point by using string.

```
// Power Function
// POWER1.C
```

```
# include<iostream.h>
# include<math.h>
# include<stdio.h>

class Power_Fun
{
    public:
        double power_fract(double, float, float );
        void expo();
};

// The definition of the power_fract() function

double Power_Fun :: power_fract(double a, float b, float i)
{
    if( b == 0)
    {
        return 1;
    }
        else if ( b< 0)
    {
        return( (a * power_fract(a,b + i,i)));
    }

    else
        return( a* power_fract(a,b - i,i));
}

// The definition of the expo() function

void Power_Fun :: expo()
{
    char str[50];
    char *pstr;
    char temp;
    int count = 0;
    char ch;
    float exponent;
    float mantissa;
    cout<<"\n Input the Mantissa:";
    cin>> mantissa;
    cout<<" Input the Exponent:";
    ch = getchar();
    int i = 0;
    while( ch != '\n')
```

```
    {
        if((ch == '-') || (ch == '+'))
            count--;
        if( ch == '.')
            temp = ch;
        str[i] = ch;
            ch = getchar();
        i ++;
        count ++;
    }
    str[i]='\0';
        cout<<"\n\n Number of digits including '.' = "<<count;
    count = i;
    if (temp == '.')
 {
        i = 1;
        pstr = &str[0];
        while(*pstr != '.')
        {
            pstr++;
            i ++;
        }
    }
    cout<<"\n Number of digits including sign & period(.) character = "<<i;
    count = count - i;
    cout<<"\n Number of digits after decimal point = "<<count;
    exponent = atof(str);
    float counter = 1/power_fract(10, -count,1);
    cout<<"\n Increment/Decrement counter = "<<counter;
    cout<<"\n\n Mantissa = "<<mantissa;
    cout<<"\n Exponent = "<<exponent;

    if(exponent < 0)
        cout<<"\n\n mantissa ^ exponent = "<< 1/power_fract(mantissa,exponent,counter);
    else
        cout<<"\n\n mantissa ^ exponent = "<< power_fract(mantissa,exponent,counter);
}
// Function main

void main()
{
    Power_Fun pow1;
    pow1.expo();
}
```

```
Input the Mantissa: 12
Input the Exponent: 4

Number of digits including '.' = 1
Number of digits including sign & period(.) character = 1
Number of digits after decimal point = 0
Increment/Decrement counter = 1.000000

Mantissa = 12.000000
Exponent = 4.000000

mantissa ^ exponent = 20736.000000
```

2.4 FIBONACCI NUMBERS

This is another problem, which can be easily solved with the help of recursion. The recursive definition of the Fibonacci number generator function is:

$$fibo\_number(n) = \begin{cases} 0 & \text{if } n = 0 \text{ or } n = 1 \\ 1 & \text{if } n = 2 \\ fibo\_number(n-1) + fibo\_number(n-2) & \text{if } n > 2 \end{cases}$$

Fig. 2.10 Recursive definition of Fibonacci generator function

The fibonacci sequence is as follows, which is generated from the definition shown in **Fig. 2.10.**

0, 1, 1, 2, 3, 5, 8, 13, 21, 21, 34, 55, etc.

If we consider $\mathbf{F_0 = 0}$ and $\mathbf{F_1 = 1}$, then $\mathbf{F_2 = F_1 + F_0 = 1 + 0 = 1}$, similarly $\mathbf{F_3 = F_2 + F_1 = 1 + 1 = 2}$, $\mathbf{F_4 = F_3 + F_2 = 2 + 1 = 3}$ and so on. Thus it is clear that each succeeding term is the sum of the two preceding terms. The **fibo_number ()** function generates one Fibonacci number at a time. So in the main program a **while** loop is implemented, which calls the **fibo_number ()** function until the value of **i** becomes less than the value of **n.** The program segment **FIBO.C** illustrates this idea.

```
// Fibonacci Numbers
// FIBO.C

# include<iostream.h>

class Fibonacci
```

```
{
public:
      long fibo_number(int );
};

// Definition of the function Fibonacci number generator

long Fibonacci :: fibo_number( int n)
{
      int r;
      if(( n == 1) || ( n == 0))
            return 0;
      else
            if(n == 2)
                  return 1;
            else
                  return (fibo_number(n-1) + fibo_number(n-2));
}

// main function

void main()
{
      Fibonacci F_generator;
      int n;
      cout<<"\n Input the number for Fibonacci series, you want to generate:";
      cin>>n;
      cout<<"\n Fibonacci Series is as follows:\n";
      int i =0;
      while(i < n)
 {
            ++i;
            cout << " " <<F_generator.fibo_number(i);
 }
}
```

```
Input the number for Fibonacci series, you want to generate: 10
Fibonacci Series is as follows:
0 1 i 2 3 5 8 13 21 34
```

2.5 GEATEST COMMON DIVISOR

A more complex recursive example is to find the greatest common divisor of two positive integers with the help of **Euclid**'s algorithm. The definition of **Euclid**'s algorithm is as follows:

$$Greatest\_Comm\_Div(n,m) = \begin{cases} Greatest\_Comm\_Div(m,n) & \text{if } n < m \\ m & \text{if } n^3 m \text{ and } n \bmod m = 2 \\ Greatest\_Comm\_Div(m, n \bmod m) & Otherwise \end{cases}$$

Fig. 2.11 Greatest common divisor algorithm

The greatest common divisor algorithm is implemented in the program segment **GCD.C.**

```
// Greatest Common Divisor
// GCD.C

# include<iostream.h>

class Greatest_Comman_Div
{
      public:
      int Greatest_Comm_Div(int , int);
};

// Definition of the Greatest Common Divisor Function
int Greatest_Comman_Div :: Greatest_Comm_Div( int n, int m)
{
      if(( n >= m) && (( n % m) == 0))
            return(m);
      else
            Greatest_Comm_Div(m,(n % m));
}

// main function
void main()
{
      Greatest_Comman_Div G_C_D;
      int n,m;

      cout<<"\n Input The First integer number:";
      cin>>n;

      cout<<"\n Input the Second integer number:";
      cin>>m;
```

```
int result = G_C_D.Greatest_Comm_Div(n, m);
cout<<"\n Greatest Common Divisor of : "<<n <<" and "<<m <<" is = "<<result;
}
```

```
Input the first integer number: 120
Input the second integer number: 9
Greatest Common Divisor of: 120 and 9 is = 3
```

2.6 THE TOWERS OF HANOI

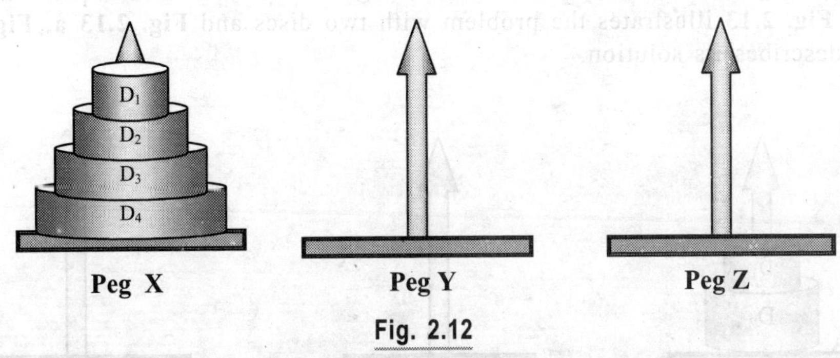

Fig. 2.12

Table 2.2 Tower of Hanoi for n=4

```
Input the number of disc : 4
Tower of Hanoi for 4 DISC
Move Disk from X to Y
Move Disk from X to Z
Move Disk from Y to Z
Move Disk from X to Y
Move Disk from Z to X
Move Disk from Z to Y
Move Disk from X to Y
Move Disk from X to Z
Move Disk from Y to Z
Move Disk from Y to X
Move Disk from Z to X
Move Disk from Y to Z
Move Disk from X to Y
Move Disk from X to Z
Move Disk from Y to Z
```

The Tower of Hanoi is a famous recursive problem, which is based on three pegs and a set of discs of graduated sizes. Suppose three pegs, labeled **X, Y** and **Z** are given and on peg **X** there are finite number of discs **n** in increasing (size) order, i.e., biggest one at the bottom and smallest one at the top. The problem is to move discs from peg **X** to peg **Z** using peg **Y** whenever it is required. The rules, which we have to take into account before moving a disc, are:

(i) Only one disc may be moved at a time.
(ii) Only the top disc on any peg may be moved to any other peg.
(iii) A larger disc can not be placed on a smaller one.

Pictorial view of Tower of Hanoi is given in **Fig. 2.12. Fig. 2.12** shows that there are 4 discs on peg **X**. The solution of the Tower of Hanoi for **n** = **4** discs are shown in **Table 2.2.**

The solution of this problem is very simple, if there are only two discs to move. First disc $\mathbf{D_1}$ is moved to peg **Y**, then disc $\mathbf{D_2}$ is moved to peg **Z**. Finally the disc $\mathbf{D_1}$ is moved from peg **Y** to peg **Z**. **Fig. 2.13** illustrates the problem with two discs and **Fig. 2.13 a, Fig. 2.13 b** and **Fig. 2.13 c** describes its solution.

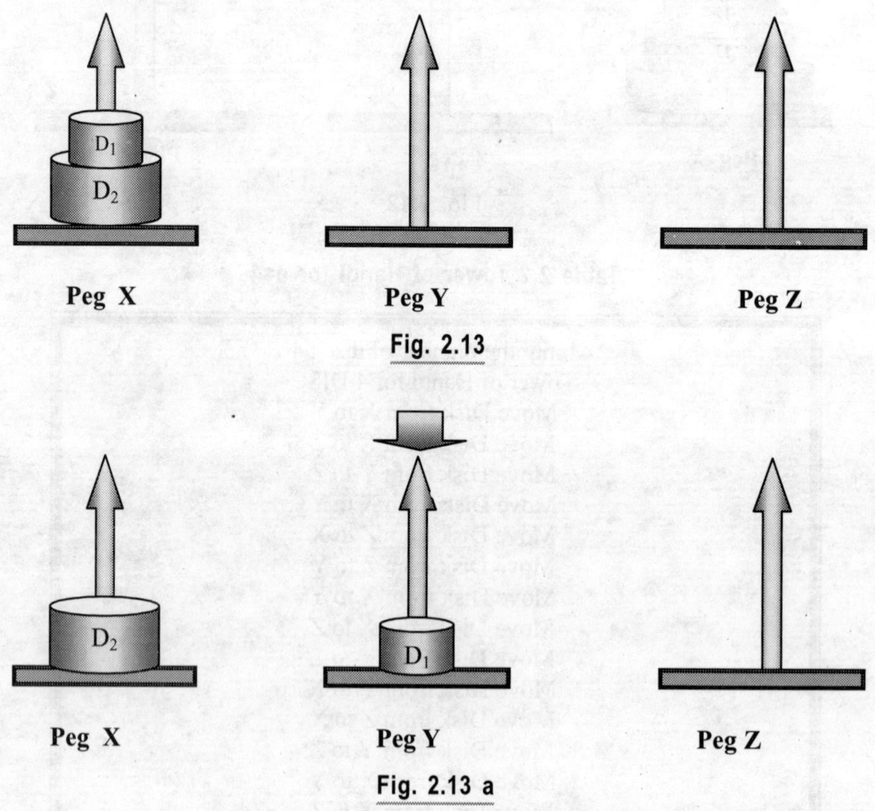

Fig. 2.13

Fig. 2.13 a

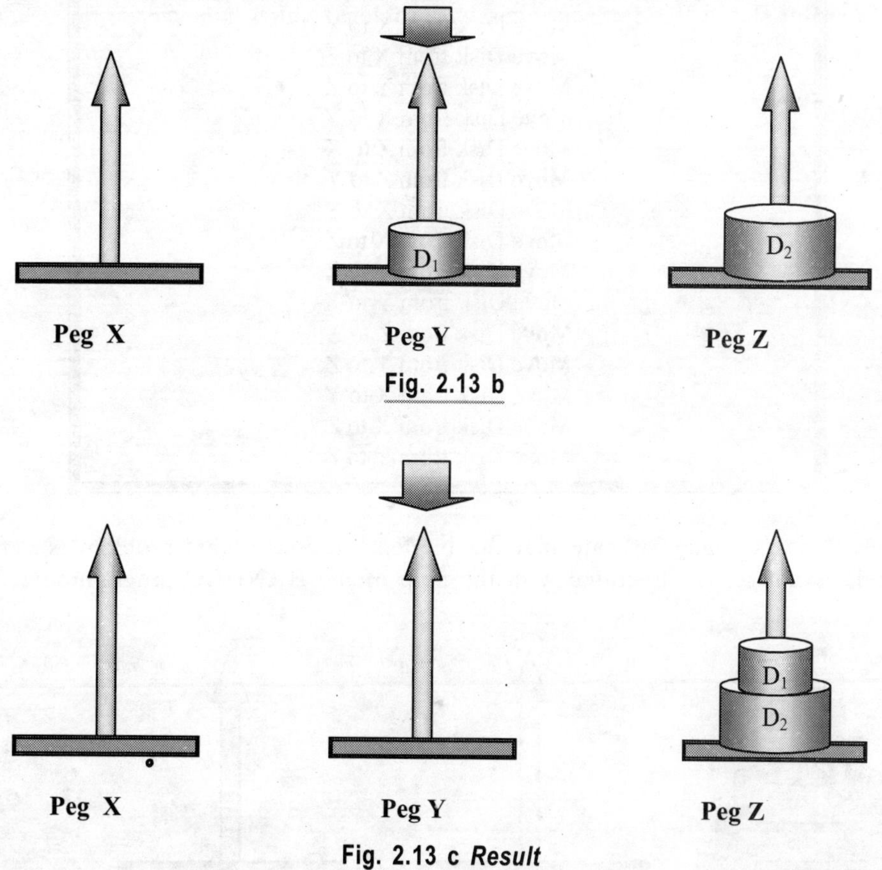

Fig. 2.13 b

Fig. 2.13 c *Result*

With four discs the problem becomes more complex and complicated. After analyzing the problem it is found that in order to move the largest disc from peg **X** to peg **Z**, we must do the following:

If n = 1 then move the disc from the peg X to peg Z

If n > 1 then the following moves are to be performed:

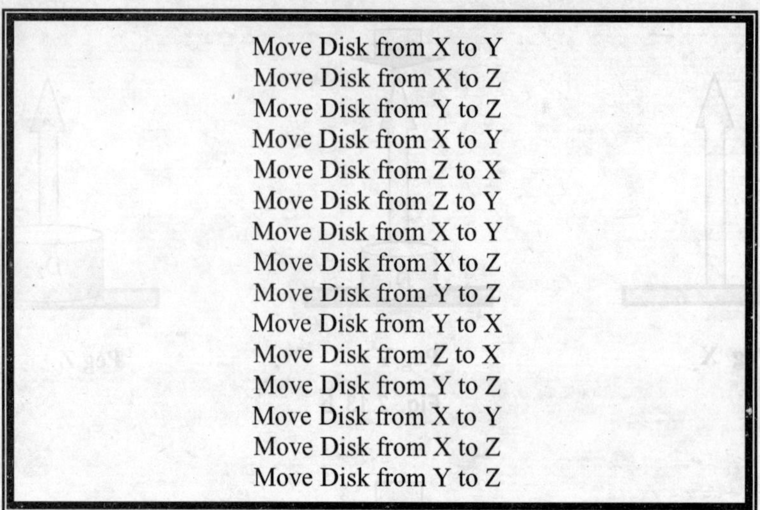

Move Disk from X to Y
Move Disk from X to Z
Move Disk from Y to Z
Move Disk from X to Y
Move Disk from Z to X
Move Disk from Z to Y
Move Disk from X to Y
Move Disk from X to Z
Move Disk from Y to Z
Move Disk from Y to X
Move Disk from Z to X
Move Disk from Y to Z
Move Disk from X to Y
Move Disk from X to Z
Move Disk from Y to Z

The above analysis may indicate that the implementation of this problem is very typical. However, this is not so as illustrated with the help of the **HANOI.C** programming.

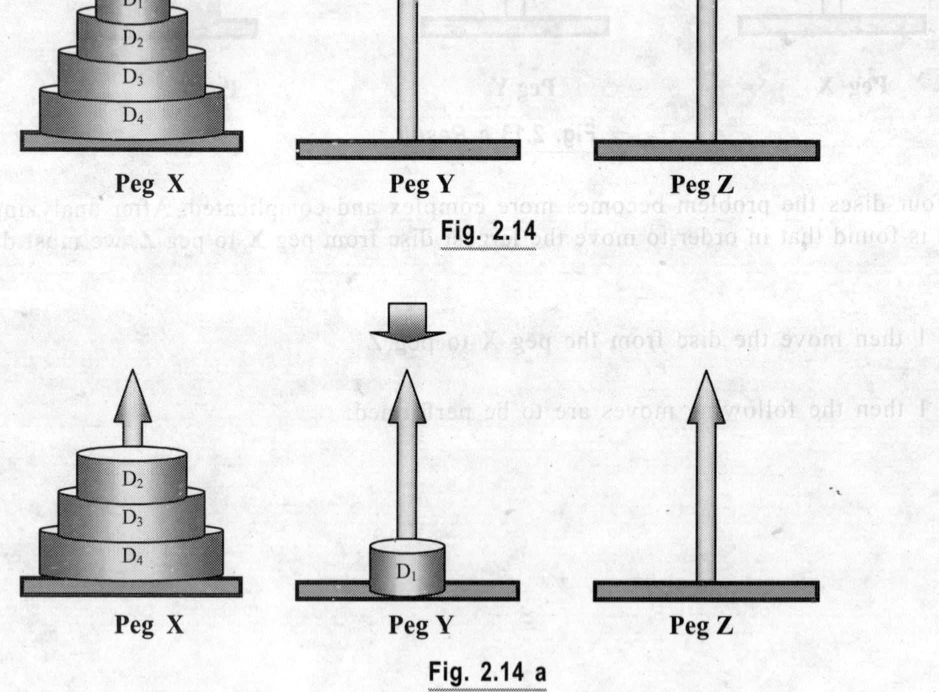

Fig. 2.14

Fig. 2.14 a

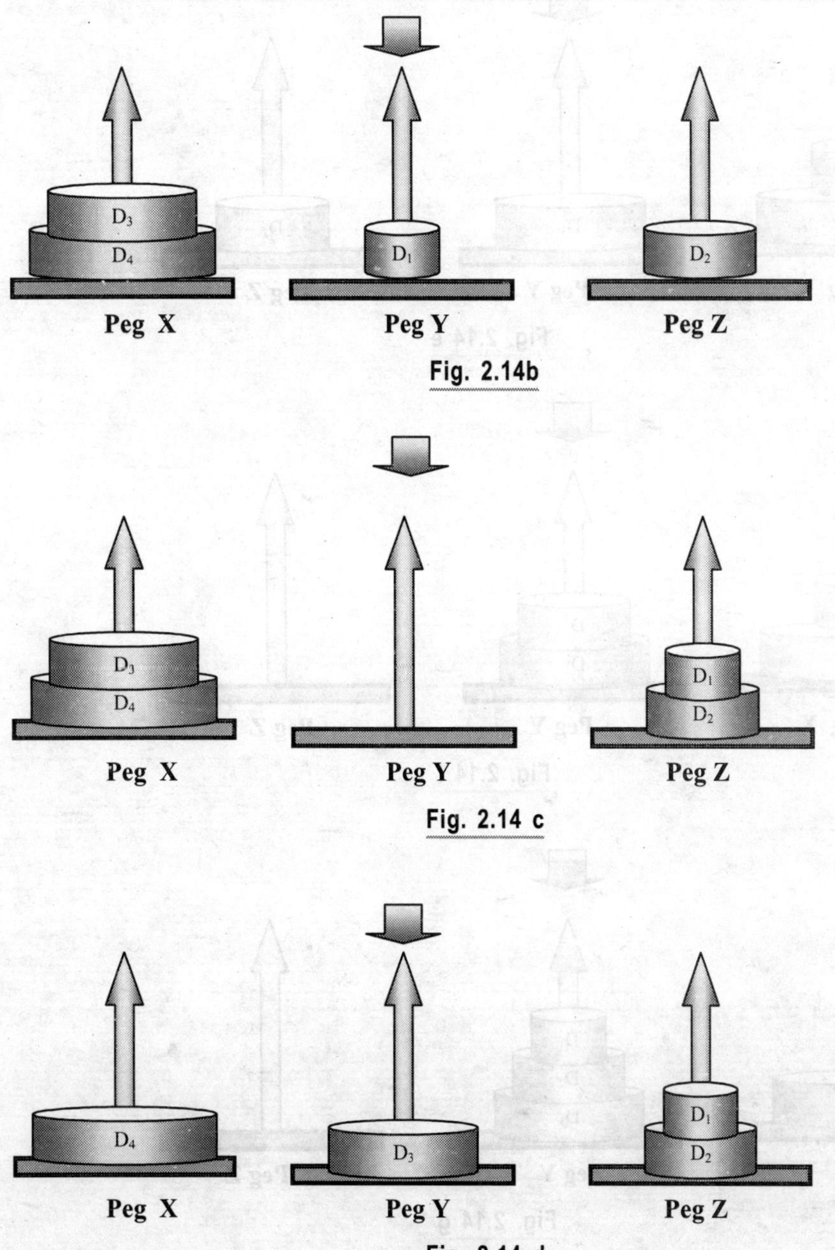

Fig. 2.14b

Fig. 2.14 c

Fig. 2.14 d

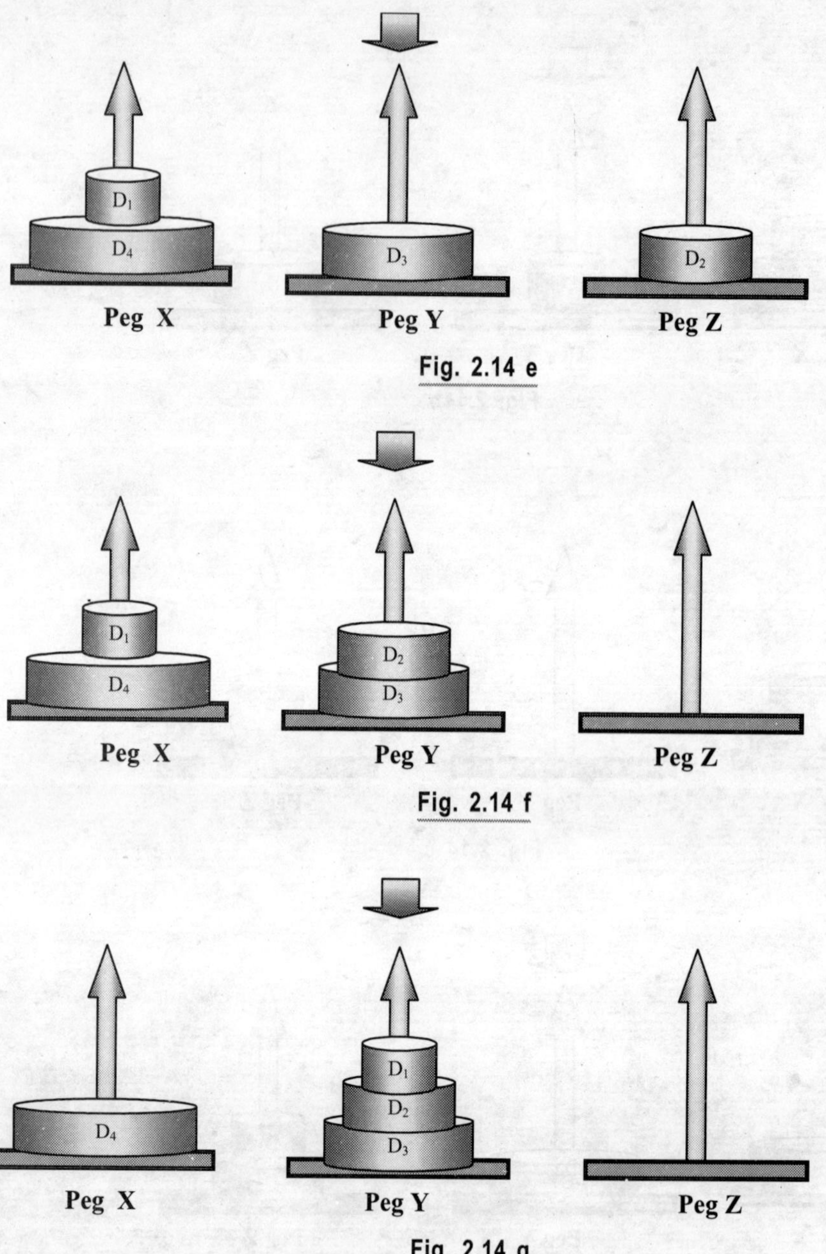

Fig. 2.14 e

Fig. 2.14 f

Fig. 2.14 g

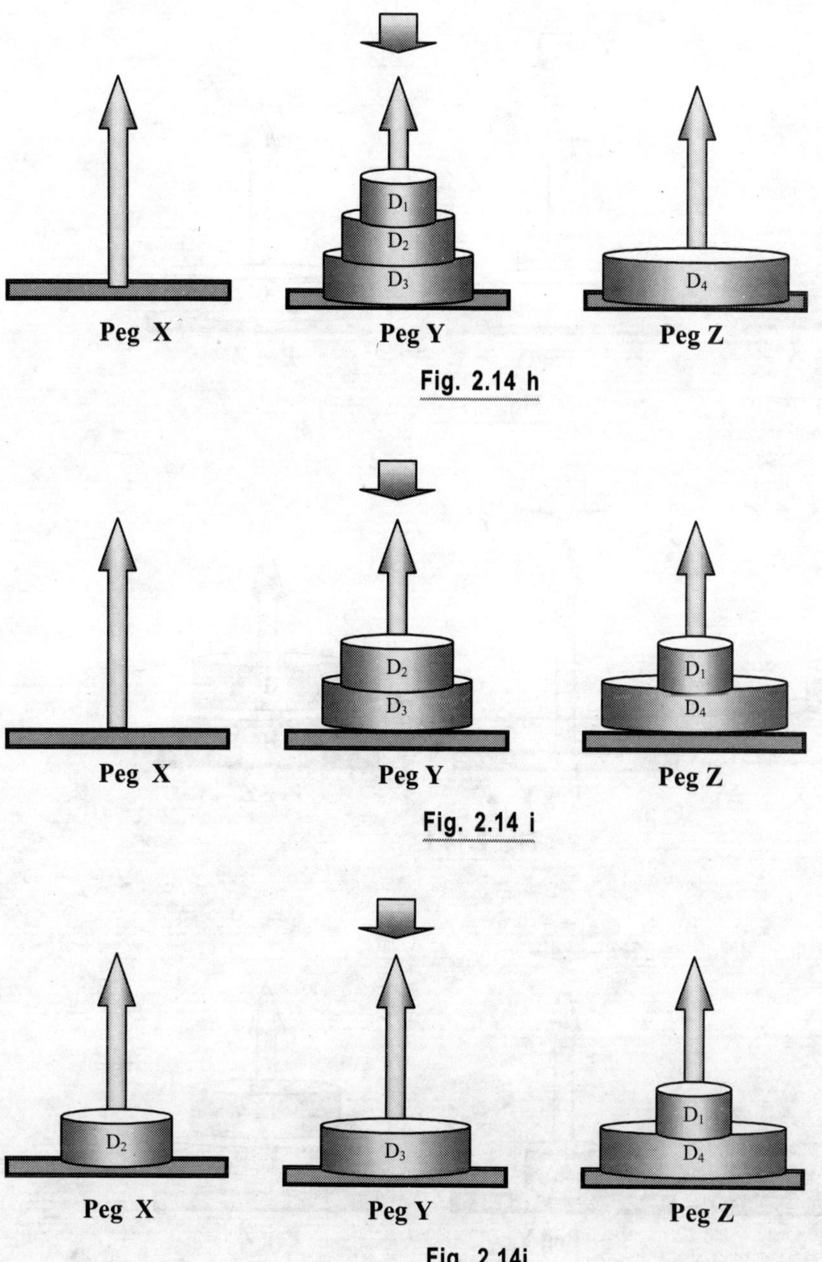

Fig. 2.14 h

Fig. 2.14 i

Fig. 2.14j

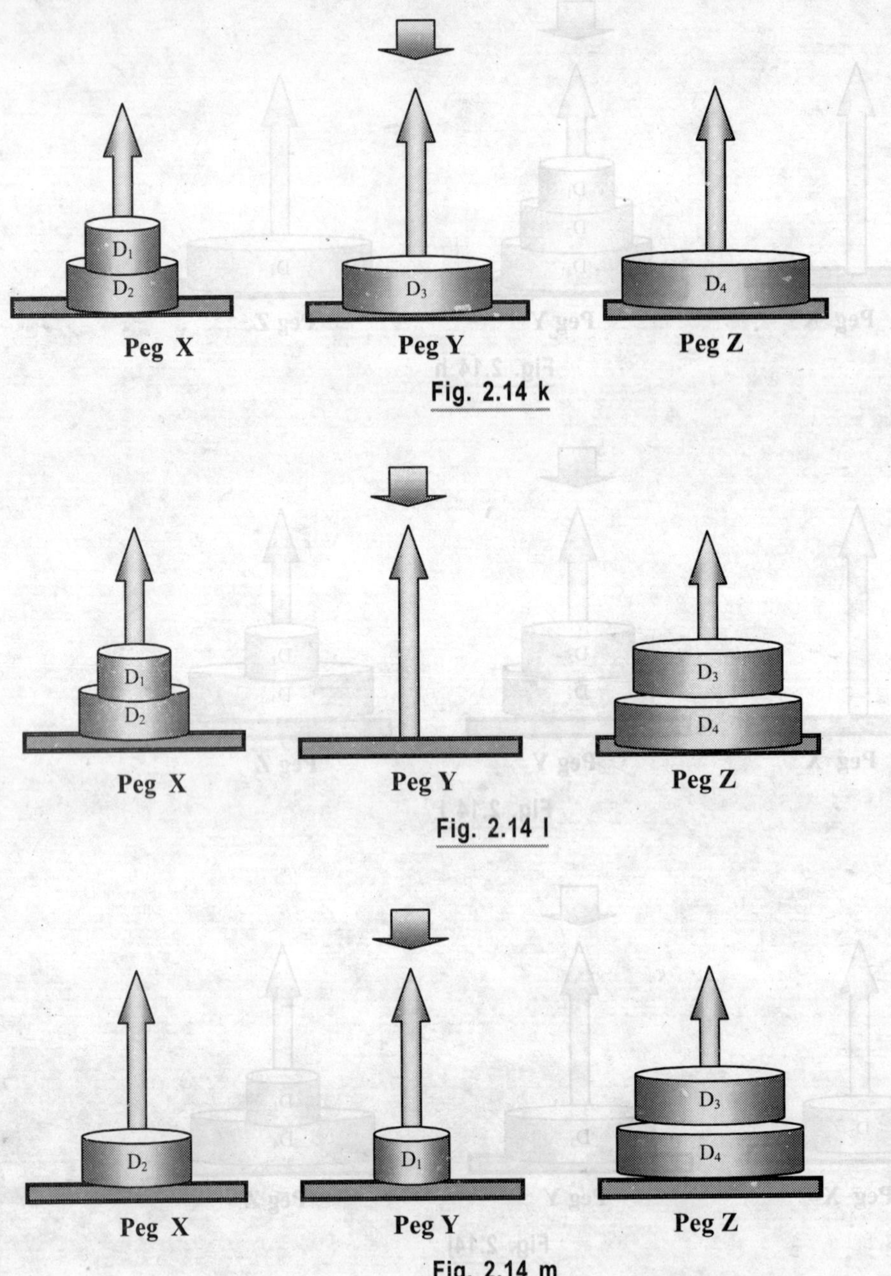

Fig. 2.14 k

Fig. 2.14 l

Fig. 2.14 m

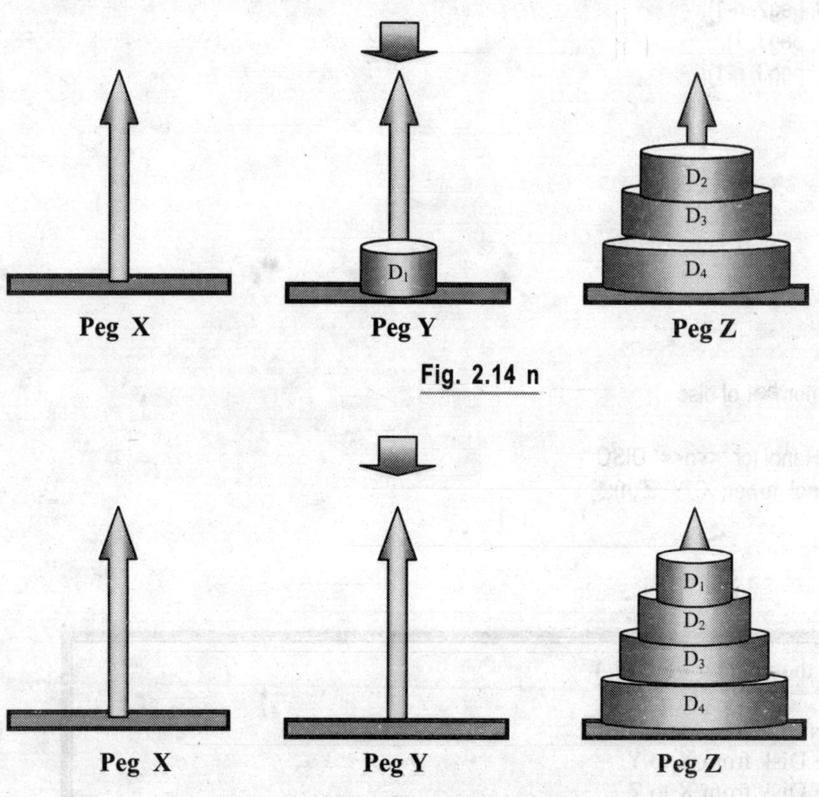

Fig. 2.14 n

Fig. 2.14 o Result

```
// Tower of Hanoi
// HANOI.C

 # include<iostream.h>

class Tower
{
      public: void hanoi_tower(char peg1, char peg2, char peg3, int n);
};

// Definition of the Tower Of Hanoi generator function

void Tower :: hanoi_tower(char peg1, char peg2, char peg3, int n)
{
      if( n <= 0)
            cout<<"\n Illegal entry";
      if(n ==1)
            cout<<"\n Move Disk from "<<peg1<<" to "<<peg3;
      else
  {
```

```
hanoi_tower(peg1, peg3, peg2, n-1);
hanoi_tower(peg1, peg2, peg3, 1);
hanoi_tower(peg2, peg1, peg3, n-1);
}
}

// main function

void main()
{
	Tower Tower_of_Hanoi;
	int n;
	cout<<"\n Input the number of disc : ";
	cin>> n;
	cout<<"\n Tower of Hanoi for "<<n<<" DISC ";
	Tower_of_Hanoi.hanoi_tower('X','Y','Z',n);
}
```

```
Input the number of disc: 4

Tower of Hanoi for 4 DISC
Move Disk from X to Y
Move Disk from X to Z
Move Disk from Y to Z
Move Disk from X to Y
Move Disk from Z to X
Move Disk from Z to Y
Move Disk from X to Y
Move Disk from X to Z
Move Disk from Y to Z
Move Disk from Y to X
Move Disk from Z to X
Move Disk from Y to Z
Move Disk from X to Y
Move Disk from X to Z
Move Disk from Y to Z
```

The pictorial view of this result is shown in **Fig. 2.14** to **Fig. 2.14 o.**

2.7 DIVIDE AND CONQUER

In general divide-and-conquer algorithms involve doing some work to split the input into two pieces or to merge the results of processing two independent "solved" portions of the input or to help things along after half of the input has been processed. That is, there may be code before, after or in between the two-recursive calls. For example, **quicksort** is a **divide-and-conquer** method for sorting. It works by partitioning a file into two parts, then sorting the parts independently. As we will see, the exact position of the portion depends on the file, so the algorithm has following recursive structure:

```
Quicksort(int a[], int l, int r)
{
    int i;
    if (r > l)
    {
        i = partition(l, r);
        Quicksort(a, l, i-1);
        Quicksort (a, i+1, r);
    }
}
```

The parameters **l** and **r** the sub-file within the original file that is to be sorted; the call **Quicksort(1, n)** sorts the whole file.

The crux of the method is the partition procedure, which rearrange the array to make the following three considerations hold:

*(i) the element **a[i]** is in its final place are less than or equal to some **i**.*
*(ii) all the elements in **a[1] ... a[i-1]** are less than or equal to **a[i]**.*
*(iii) all the elements in **a[i+1] ... a[r]** are greater than or equal to **a[i]**.*

This can be simply and easily implemented through the general strategy. First, arbitrarily choose **a[r]** to be the element that will go into its final position, next, scan from the left end of the array until an element greater than **a[r]** is found and scan from right end of the elements which stopped the scans are obviously out of place in the partitioned array, so exchange them. Continuing in this way ensures that all array elements to the left of the left pointer are less than **a[r]** and all array elements to the right of the right pointer are greater than **a[r]**. When nearly complete all that remains is to exchange **a[r]** with the leftmost element of the right sub-file. **Fig. 2.15a** shows how our sample file of keys is partitioned with this method. The rightmost element, E, is chosen as the partitioning element. First, the scan from the left stops at the S, then the scan from the right stops at A, see **Fig. 2.15b** and then these two are exchanged. Next, the scan from left stops at the O, then the scan from the right stops at E, see **Fig. 2.15c,** then these two are exchanged. Next, the pointers cross. The scan from the left stops at the R and the scan from the right stops at the E. The proper move at this point is to exchanged the E at the right with the R, leaving the partitioned file as shown in **Fig. 2.15e.**

Sorting the two sub-files on either side of the partitioning element (recursively) finishes the sort. Consider the following program that gives full implementation of the method:

```
Quicksort( int a[], int l, int r)
{
    int v, i, j, t;
    if(r > l)
    {
        v = a[r];
        i = l-1;
        j = r;
        for(; ;)
        {
            while (a[++i] < v);
            while(a[--j] > v);
            if(i >= j)
                break;
            t = a[i];
            a[i] = a[j];
            a[j] = t;
        }
        t = a[i];
        a[i] = a[r];
        a[r] = t;
        Quicksort(a, l, i-1);
        Quicksort(a, i+1, r);
    }
}
```

In this implementation, the variable v holds the current value of the partitioning element, a[r] and i and j are the left and right scans pointers, respectively. The partitioning loop is implemented as an infinite loop, with a break out when the pointer cross.

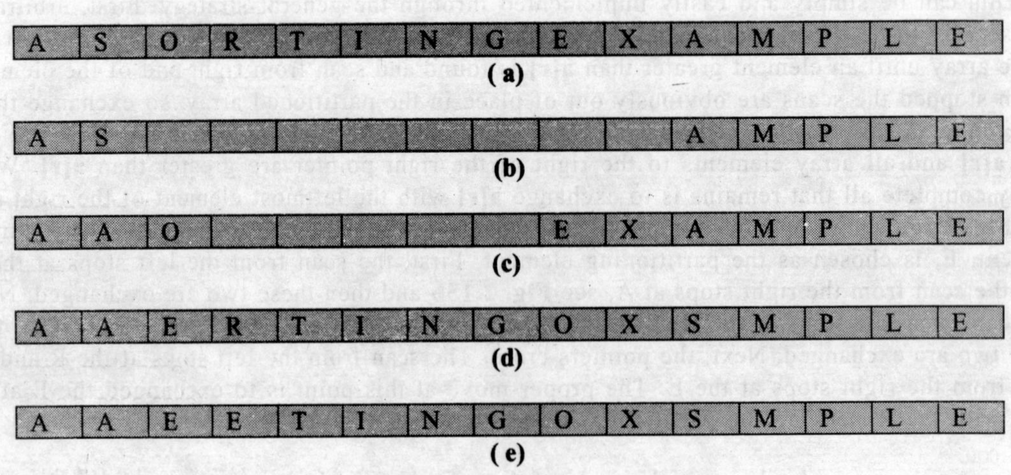

Fig. 2.15 Partitioning

A problem that can be separated into two sub-problems that can be handled separately is more than half solved by that separation. This simple principle can be applied in an amazing variety of ways. The divide and conquer is one of them.

For example, consider the problem of finding maximum and minimum of a list of integers simultaneously. The solution of the problem is implemented below **(DIV_ITER.C)**:

```
// Find maximum and minimum using iterative method
// DIV_ITER.C

# include<iostream.h>

class maximum
{
    public :
        void max_min(int *, int, int , int );
};

// Definition of the function max_min()

void maximum :: max_min(int l[], int n, int max, int min)
{
    max = min = l[0];
    for( int i = 1; i < n; i++)
    {
        if(l[i] > max)
            max = l[i];
        if(l[i] < min)
            min = l[i];
    }
    cout<<"\n Maxmum = "<< max;
    cout<<"\n Minimum = "<< min;
}

// main function

void main()
{
    maximum minimum;
    int l[100],n,max,min;

    cout<<"\n Number of elements in the list :";
    cin>> n;

    cout<<"\n Input elements of the list:";
    for( int i =0; i < n; i++)
```

```
      cin>> l[i];
   minimum.max_min(l, n, max, min);
}
```

```
Number of elements in the list: 8
Input elements of the list:
1
66
656
99
44
66
88
99

Maximum = 656
Minimum = 1
```

div_con(l, n, max, min)

where l → Represents the list of elements
n → Represents the number of elements in the list
max → It has to found
min → It has to found

Step 1: If n = 1 do Step 2
Step 2: min = max = l[0]
Step 3: If n = 2 then
(i) max = l[0]
(ii) min = l[1]
Else
(iii) max = l[1]
(iv) min = l[0]

Else

Divide the list in two sections and find recursively the min and max of each half. Assign min the smaller of two **mins** and max the larger of the two **maxs**.

Fig. 2.16 Algorithm for Divide and Conquer

In the above program segment, the function **max_min ()** performs **2*(n –1)** comparisons. The recursive definition for **divide and conquer** for the above problem is given in **Fig. 2.16.** Following program segment illustrates the implementation of the algorithm given in **Fig. 2.16 (DIV_CON.C):**

```
// Divide and Conquer
// Find minimum and maximum from a given series of numbers
// by using above said policy

// DIV_CON.C

# include<iostream.h>
# define size 100

class Divide_Conquer
{
	private:
		int min1, max1;
	public:
		void div_con(int *, int, int *, int *);
};

// Definition of the function div_con()
void Divide_Conquer :: div_con( int list[], int n, int *min, int *max)
{
	if( n == 1)
		*min = *max = list[0];
	else
		if( n == 2)
		{
			if(list[0] < list[1])
			{
				*min = list[0];
				*max = list[1];
			}
			else
			{
				*min = list[1];
				*max = list[0];
			}
		}
		else
		{
			div_con(list, n/2, min, max);
			div_con(list+ n/2, n - n/2, &min1, &max1);
			if( min1 < *min)
```

```
                *min = min1;
        if( max1 > *max)
                *max = max1;
        }
}

// Function main

void main()
{
    Divide_Conquer div_Con;
    int *min, *max;
    int list[size];
    int number;
    cout<<"\n Input the number of elements in the list :";
    cin >> number;

    cout<<"\n Input the list elements:\n";
    for( int i = 0; i < number; i++)
    {
        cin>>list[i];
    };

    cout<<"\n Min and Max are :";
    div_Con.div_con( list, number, min, max);
    cout<<"\n Mimimum ="<<*min;
    cout<<"\n";
    cout<<"\n Maximum ="<<*max;
}
```

2.8 FUNCTION OVERHEAD

When we define functions in a program, **C++** pushes the return address, parameters and local variables onto the stack. When the function completes, **C++** discards (pops) the stack space that contained the local variables then uses the return value to resume the program's execution at the correct location. The use of the stack lets the program invoke and pass information to the functions consuming processing time. The amount of time required pushing and popping stack information is function overhead. For example, go through the program segment **FUNCTOVR.C**, in this first for loop requires approximately 8 seconds to sum 1 to 1,00, 000, 000. The second loop for the same range of data with the help of function takes approximately 54 seconds on 133 MHz machine **SCO UNIX** machine for same number of running processes.

```
// FUNCTOVR.C
# include<iostream.h>
#include <stdio.h>
#include <time.h>
```

```
float add_em(long int a, float b)
{
    float result;
    result = a + b;
    return(result);
}

// Function main
void main(void)
{
    long int i;
    float result = 0;
    time_t start_time, stop_time;
    cout<<"Working...\n";
    time(&start_time);

    for (i = 1; i <= 100000000L; i++)
    result += i;
    time(&stop_time);
    printf("Using loop: %d seconds\n", stop_time - start_time);

    cout<<"Working...\n";
    time(&start_time);

    for (i = 1; i <= 100000000L; i++)
        result = add_em(i, result);

    time(&stop_time);
    printf("Using function: %d seconds\n", stop_time - start_time);
}
```

```
Working…
Using loop: 8 seconds
Working…
Using function: 54 seconds
```

EXERCISE

2.1 *What will be the output of the following program segment, if one gives input GARHWAL.*

```
// RECURSION TO REVERSE A STRING
// STRING_R.C
```

```
# include<stdio.h>

void recurs_string(char * );

// Definition of the recurs_string() function

void recurs_string(char *string)
{
      if (*string)
      {
            recurs_string(string+1);
            putchar(*string);
      }
}

void main(void)
{
      char str[100];
      cout<<"\n Input a string: ";
      gets(str);
      cout<<"\n Reverse of the string: " << str;
      cout<<"\n Reverse string is: ";
      recurs_string(str);
}
```

2.2 *What does the following function represent? Implement the function in* **C++**.

$$F(n)=\frac{1}{\sqrt{5}}x\left[\left[\frac{1+\sqrt{5}}{2}\right]^{n-1}-\left[\frac{1-\sqrt{5}}{2}\right]^{n-1}\right]$$

2.3 *The function* ***F(n, r)*** *can be defined recursively as* ***F(n-1, r) + F(n-1, r-1).*** *Write a recursive program to compute* ***F(n, r).*** *What is the base case?*

2.4 *Design an algorithm, which concatenates two strings using recursion.*

2.5 *Write a recursive function, which takes a floating number as input and displays real and integer part separately.*

2.6 *Compute the value of* ***A (4, 3)*** *using* **Ackermann's** *function.*

2.7 *Write a program, which takes an integer number as input and displays reverse of the number on the screen. Use recursion to implement the problem.*

2.8 *Suppose* **x** *and* **y** *represent positive integer numbers and a function* **F** *is defined as*

$$F(x,y)=\begin{cases}0 & \text{if } x<y\\ F(x-y,y)+1 & \text{if } x\leq y\end{cases}$$

(i) Find the value of ***F (4, 5).***
(ii) Explain the working of this function.

2.9 *Suppose* **n** *is a positive integer number and a function* **Lambda(n)** *is defined as*

$$Lambda(n)=\begin{cases}0 & \text{if } n=1\\ Lambda(n/2)+1 & \text{if } n>1\end{cases}$$

(i) Find the value of ***Lambda (50).***
(ii) Explain the working of this function.

2.10 *Suppose* **LIST** *is an integer array with* **m** *elements and let* **F** *is an integer function defined by*

$$F(j)=F(\text{List},m,j)=\begin{cases}0 & \text{if } j=0\\ F(j-1)+\text{LIST}[j] & \text{if } 0<\text{j}\leq \text{m}\\ F(j-1) & \text{if } j>m\end{cases}$$

Find **F (5)** for each of the following list

(i) m = 8 LIST: 3,7, -2, 5, 6, -4, 2, 7
(ii) m = 3 LIST: 8, 7, 10

2.11 *Let* **m** *be an integer and suppose* **L(m)** *is defined as*

$$L(m)=\begin{cases}3\times m & \text{if } m<1\\ 2*L(m-1)+7 & \text{otherwise}\end{cases}$$

Discuss for **m = 10**.

Consider the problem of calculating a ***binomial coefficient*** *(BC). The binomial coefficient refers to the kth coefficient of the polynomial resulting from the expansion of a binomial term of the form* ***A+B*** *raised to the nth power.*

$$(A+B)^n = \frac{A^n}{0!} + \frac{n*A^{n-1}B}{1!} + \frac{n*(n\text{-}1)*A^{n-2}*B^2}{2!} + \frac{n*(n*\text{-}1)*(n\text{-}2)*A^{n-3}*B^3}{3!} +$$

An explicit formula for the coefficient of the kth term of that nth term degree polynomials is

$$BC(n,k) = \frac{n*(n\text{-}1)*(n-2)*..............*(n-k+1)}{k!}$$

or

$$BC(n,k) = \frac{n!}{K!(n-k)!}$$

Note that we can expand this formula to

$$BC(n,k) = \frac{(n\text{-}1)*(n-2)*..............*(n-k)}{k!} + \frac{(n\text{-}1)*(n-2)*..............*(n-k+1)}{(k-1)!}$$

Equivalently, *BC(n, k) = BC(n-1, k) +BC(n-1, k-1)*

Note that when **n = k BC(k, k) = 1** and that **BC(n , 0) = 1** for any value of **n**.

(i) *Write a recursive function based on the above identities for calculating the kth binomial coefficient of the polynomial of degree **n** given by **(A+B)^n**.*

(ii) *Illustrate how the contents of the run-time stack change as program for calculating **BC(n, k)** computes **BC(4, 3).***

2.12 *What is need of stack in implementing a recursive function?*

2.13 *Write a recursive function that trims all blanks from the front and rear of a string of text.*

2.14 *Write a recursive function to convert decimal integers to their radix **r** representation by successive divisions.*

Write a recursive function to compute the square root of a number.

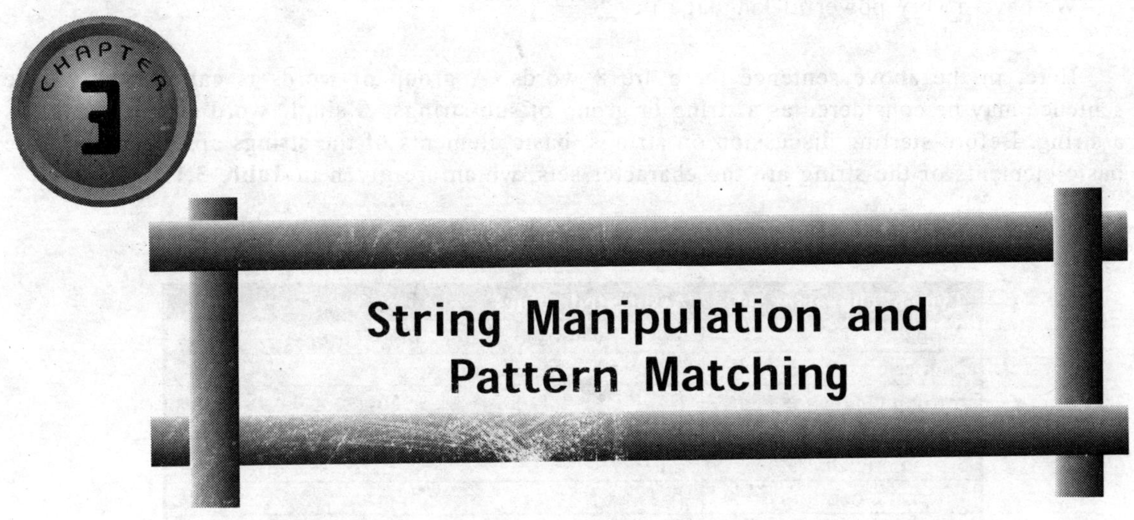

String Manipulation and Pattern Matching

Today computers are being frequently used in processing numbers character data, records, arithmetic calculations, etc. In small organizations as well as in multinational companies word processing is widely used. Small shops to big one use the word processing. In word processing pattern matching is required to finding a word in a given text. For example:

```
TWINKLE, TWINKLE LITTLE STAR
HOW I WONDER WHAT YOU ARE
UP ABOVE THE WORLD SO HIGH
LIKE A DIAMOND IN THE SKY
WHEN THE BURNING SUN IS SET
AND THE GRASS WITH DUE IS WET
THEN YOU SHOW YOUR LITTLE LIGHT
```

Suppose one wants to search word **"TWINKLE"** in the above text. Each word in the text is compared or matched with **"TWINKLE"**. If a match is found then the counter may be incremented else next word is read from the text to match with **"TWINKLE"**. This process is repeated until end of the text is reached. In the above text we find that **"TWINKLE"** word appears at four places. Pattern matching algorithms are discussed latter on. For the time being we define some of the terms, which are commonly used in word processing:

- *String processing.*
- *String manipulation.*
- *Text editing, etc.*

The above terminologies are used in word processing. ***Word*** is defined as a collection of characters. In other words one can define a word as concatenation of characters. For example:

We have a very powerful language i.e. "C++".

Here, in the above sentence there are 8 words. A group of words is called **string**. The sentence may be considered as a string or group of sub-strings. A single word is also treated as a string. Before starting discussion on strings, basic elements of the strings are discussed. The basic elements of the string are the character sets, which are given in **Table 3.1.**

Table 3.1 Character set

Type of character set	Associated values
Alphabets	a to z lower case, A to Z upper case
Numeric	0 to 9
Special characters	{ } ( ) [ ] " ' , . < > _ (underscore) & $? : ; # NULL ('\0')
Arithmetic Operator	+ - * / ++ --
Logical Operators	|| && !
Relational Operators	< <= > >= == !=
Bitwise Operators		& ^ ~ >> <<

The significance of NULL character or the blank character varies from language to language. In **C++** language it is represented as '\0' and called NULL string marker or terminator of string. In other words a string is defined as a finite sequence of zero, one or more characters. The number of characters in a string is called its length. For example:

"C++ language is very powerful."

This string contains five words and its size is thirty characters long. Generally, a word or group of words or a sentence is put with in double quotes ("") to represent a string. A string of zero length is called NULL string. For example, " " is a NULL string of zero length. For the above discussion consider the program segment **STRING1.C.**

```
// STRING1.C
# include<iostream.h>
void main()
{
    char null_string[] = "\0";
    char blank_string[] = " ";
    char string[] = "The C++ is a powerful language";
    cout<<"\n"<<null_string;
    cout<<"\n"<<blank_string;
    cout<<"\n"<<string;
}
```

The C++ is a powerful language

From the above result it is clear that the two strings are not printed indicating that those are blank.

3.1 STRUCTURE OF STRING STORAGE

The strings are stored in three ways:

- *Fixed length (Array type structure).*
- *Variable length but maximum size is fixed during running time (Pointer type structure).*
- *Linked list structure.*

3.1.1 FIXED LENGTH

In this structure each record is of fixed size, *i.e.*, each record contains the same number of characters. Consider the monitor of a computer or **TURBO-C/C++/vi** editor. In the case of monitor and **vi** editor its size is 80 columns where as in the case of **Turbo/C/C++** editor its size is 256 characters. If one inputs the information with the help of keyboard using **TURBO-C/C++** editor then the editor contains standard size 256 characters. Suppose one defines an array in the following format:

```
char screen[256];
```

Here, it is possible to input a string of 256 characters into the array screen. This type of storage of strings is of fixed length. If one wants to store 128 strings of each having 128 characters then the program segment **STRING2.C** can be used to implement the same:

```
// STRING2.C

# include<iostream.h>
# include<stdio.h>

void main()
{
    char s[128][128];
    int i, j;
    char ch;
    int n,m;
    j = 0;
    i = 0;
    cout<<"Enter size of information in line : ";
    cin>>n;
    while(n)
```

```
{
        ch = getchar();
        s[i][j] = ch ;
        j++;
        if(ch == '\n')
        {
                s[i][j]='\0';
                cout<<"\n";
                j = 0;
                i++;
                n - - ;
        }
}
s[i][j]='\0';
m = i;
cout<<"\nm--> "<<m;
// Display section

cout<<"\n";
for(i = 0 ; i < m ; i++)
{
        cout<<"\n "<<s[i];
}
}
```

S[0][]			...	
S[1][]			...	
S[2][]			...	
...				
...				
...				
...				
S[126][]			...	
S[128][]			...	

Fig. 3.1 Fixed length string storage

Fig. 3.1 discusses how the strings are stored in the computer memory. The major advantages of using fixed length storage techniques are:

- *Easy to access information*
- *Easy to update records or information*
- *Easy to insert new additional information*

The main problems associated with fixed storage techniques are:

- *When one wants to update a record of larger size than the room fixed for storage (Update operation not possible).*
- *If one wants to update a record, which is longer than that of new one, then the record may be misspelled, if care is not taken properly.*
- *If most of the space of a record is blank then more time is required to update/access the records.*

Consider the following program segment, which illustrates the above discussion.

```
// STRING3.C

# include<iostream.h>
# include<stdio.h>
# include<iomanip.h>

class update
{
    private:
        int i, choice;
        char ch;

    public:
        void display (int, char day[7][20]);
        void update_fun (int, char day[7][20]);
        void draw_back ( int, char day[7][20]);
};

// Output function

void update :: display (int n, char weak_days[7][20])
{
    cout<<"\n **************************";
    cout<<"\n RECORD No. INFORMATION";
    cout<<"\n **************************";
    for(i = 0 ; i < n ; i++)
    {
        cout<<"\n "<<setw(5)<<i<<setw(20)<<weak_days[i];
    }
```

```
	cout<<"\n **************************";
	cout<<"\nPress a key";
	getchar();
}

// Update function

void update :: update_fun(int n, char weak_days[7][20])
{
	cout<<"\nInput the record number to which want to update: ";
	cin>>choice;

	cout<<"\nYou want to update it : "<<weak_days[choice];
	cout<<"\n Input the new value : ";
	cin>>weak_days[choice];
}

// Draw back function

void update :: draw_back(int n, char weak_days[7][20])
{
	cout<<"\n Draw back section Update";
	cout<<"\n ************************";
	cout<<"\nInput the record number to which want to update: ";
	cin>>choice;
	cout<<"\n You want to update it :"<<weak_days[choice];
	cout<<"\nInput the new value : ";
	ch = getchar();
	i = 0 ;

	while(ch != '\n')
	{
		weak_days[choice][i++] = ch ;
		ch = getchar();
	}
}

// Function main

void main()
{
	update update_rec;

	char weak_days[7][20]= {
				"MONDAY",
				"TUESDAY",
```

```
                        "WEDNESDAY",
                        "THURSDAY",
                        "FRIDAY",
                        "SATURDAY",
                        "SUNDAY"
                        };

    int n = 7;
    cout<<"\n Information List ";

    update_rec.display(n, weak_days);
    update_rec.update_fun(n, weak_days);

    cout<<"\n List after update operation\n";
    update_rec.display(n, weak_days);
    update_rec.draw_back (n, weak_days);

    cout<<"\n List after Draw back operation\n";
    update_rec.display(n, weak_days);
}
```

```
 Information List
 **************************
 RECORD No. INFORMATION
 **************************
     0              MONDAY
     1             TUESDAY
     2            WEDNESDAY
     3            THURSDAY
     4              FRIDAY
     5            SATURDAY
     6              SUNDAY
 **************************
Press a key
Input the record number to which want to update: 4
You want to update it : FRIDAY
 Input the new value : Friday
 List after update operation

 **************************
 RECORD No. INFORMATION
 **************************
     0              MONDAY
     1             TUESDAY
     2            WEDNESDAY
     3            THURSDAY
     4              Friday
     5            SATURDAY
     6              SUNDAY
 **************************
Press a key
 Draw back section Update
 ************************
Input the record number to which want to update: 0
You want to update it : MONDAY
Input the new value : Mon
List after Draw back operation

 **************************
 RECORD No. INFORMATION
 **************************
     0              MonDAY
     1             TUESDAY
     2            WEDNESDAY
     3            THURSDAY
     4              Friday
     5            SATURDAY
     6              SUNDAY
 **************************
Press a key
```

3.1.2 VARIABLE LENGTH FIXED MAXIMUM

When size of a string is known, according that size the space for the string is fixed into computer memory. The strings occupy space in the memory from beginning that is from the base address of the array on word. Here, the space occupies by string, assigned according to its size, so that the updating is being easy. This implementation varies from language to language. Suppose, we want to implement it through **C++**, then the pointers are used, we define it as:

```
char *string[128];
```

This definition declares a group of 128 strings of variable length. In other words we can say that the string variable reserves space for 128 strings and size of each string being infinite. The actual size of the string depends upon the type of computer being used. It is required to input the size of the string first before starting to input the string itself. It ensures that the required storage space for the string is properly allocated. In **TURBO C/C++** and **UNIX C/C++** storage space is automatically allocated as we start inputting the information. Pressing return key marks end of string. For the above discussion consider the following example **(STRING4.C)**:

```
// STRING4.C

# include<iostream.h>
# include<stdio.h>
# include<malloc.h>

class fix
{

    public:
        void gets1 (char **, int );
        void display ( char **);
        void input (char **);
};

// gets1() function to read a string

void fix :: gets1(char **s, int i)
{
    int j;
    char ch;
    ch = getchar();
    while(ch != '\n')
    {
        s[i][j] = ch ;
        ch = getchar();
        j++;
```

```
	}
	s[i][j]='\0';
}

// Output funtion

void fix :: display(char **str)
{
	cout<<"\nEntered strings are follows";
	cout<<"\n***************************";
	for(int i = 0 ; i < 2 ; i++)
	{
		cout<<"\n";
		cout<< str[i];
		//printf("\n %s",str[i]);
	}
	cout<<"\n Press a key";
	getchar();
}

// Input function


void fix :: input( char **str)
{
	int i;
	int size;

	for ( i = 0 ; i < 2 ; i++ )
	{
		cout<<"\n Enter Approximate size of string->";
		cin>>size;
		str[i] = (char *) malloc(size);
		cout<<"\n Input the string: ";
		gets1(str,i);
	}
}

// Function main

void main()
{
	fix fixed;
	char *str[5];

	fixed.input(str);
	fixed.display(str);
}
```

Fig. 3.2 illustrates how the strings are attached to the pointers.

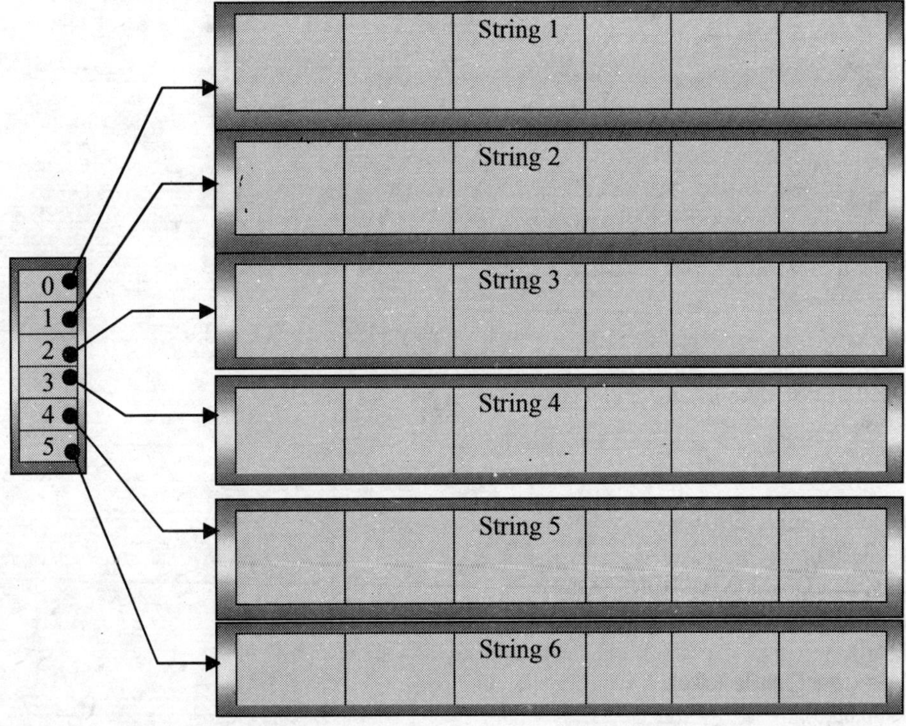

Fig. 3.2 Pointer attachment to the strings

The update operation on these types of stored strings is also simple. In this case string may shrink or expand, but the programmer does these operations (shrink/expand) because allocation of memory spaces is done on the request of the programmer. For this discussion consider the following example (**STRING5.C**).

```
// STRING5.C

# include<stdio.h>
# include<iostream.h>
# include<string.h>
# include<malloc.h>
# include<stdlib.h>

void main()
{
    char *buffer;
```

```
char string[] = "language";
char *s;
char s1[8];
int size ;
int i, j;
int length;
int l ;
int position ;
int back1, back2 ;
FILE *fp ;

fp = fopen("TEST","r");
if( fp == NULL )
{
    cout<<" FILE \n";
    perror("ERROR : ");
    exit(0);
}

fseek(fp, 0L, SEEK_END);
size = ftell(fp);
cout<<"SIZE OF INFORMATION: "<<size;
cout<<"\n Press a key";
getchar();
buffer = (char *) malloc(size);
fseek(fp,0L,0);
fread(buffer, size, 1, fp) ;
cout<<"\n";
buffer[size]='\0';
cout<<buffer;
fclose(fp);

cout<<"\n Input the Pattern: ";
cin>>string;

length = strlen(string);
s = ( char *) malloc(length);
cout<<"Length => "<<length;
back1 = length ;
back2 = size ;
getchar();

i = 0 ;
j = 0 ;
l = 0 ;
position = 0 ;
```

```
while(size)
{
    size --;
    while(length)
    {
        position ++ ;

        if ( buffer[i] == string[j])
        {
            if ((position >= back2) || (position < 0))
                exit(0);
            s[j] = buffer[i];
            l ++ ;
            i ++ ;
            size --;
            j ++ ;
            length --;
            if( l == back1)
            {
                s[j] = '\0';
                cout<<"\n Pattern is found\n";
                cout<<" Length of pattern: "<<l <<" and Pattern is : "<<s;
                cout<<"\n Starting Position -> "<<(position-l);
                cout<<"\n Press a key";
                getchar();
                l= 0 ;
                j = 0 ;
                for(i = (position - back1); i < position ; i++)
                {
                    s1[j] = buffer[i] ;
                    j++;
                }
                cout<<"\n";
                s1[j] = '\0';
                cout<<"\nThe old pattern is as follows ";
                cout<<"\n******************************\n";
                puts(s1);
                cout<<"\n Enter New Pattern : ";
                cin>>s1;
                cout<<"\nThe pattern replacement in progress";
                cout<<"\n************************************\n";
                j = 0 ;
                for(i = (position - strlen(s1)); i < position ; i++)
                {
                    buffer[i] = s1[j];
```

```
                    putchar(buffer[i]);
                    getchar();
                    j++;
                }
                cout<<"\n After replacing the pattern";
                cout<<"\n ****************************\n";
                cout<<buffer;
            }
        }

        else
        {
            i++;
            j = 0;
            l = 0;
            size -- ;
            length = back1;
        }

    }
    length = back1 ;
}
fclose(fp);
}
```

Fig. 3.3 shows the above implementation.

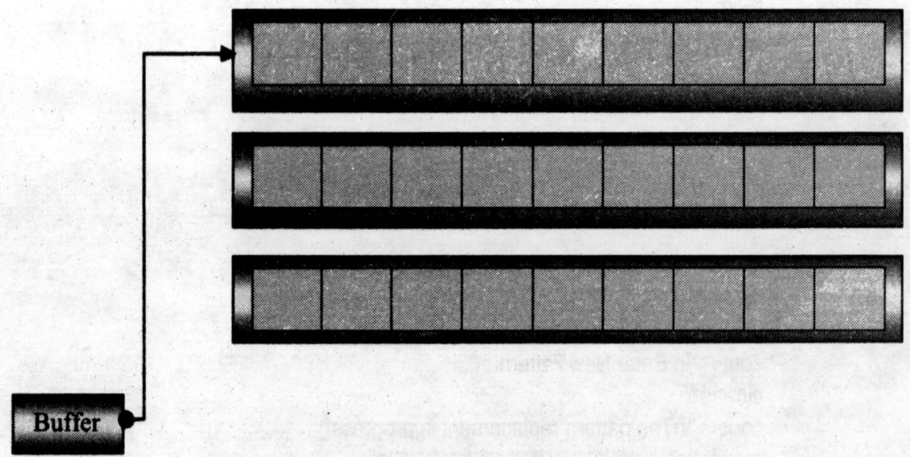

Fig. 3.3 Representation of strings in memory

3.1.3 LINKED LIST STORAGE

The major use of the computers is in data/information processing. Towards this word processing is one of the task performed by many organizations. Computers in word processing, perform the following operations.

- *Deletion (Word, sentence, line, string, sub-string, block, paragraphs, etc.).*
- *Insertion (Word, sentence, line, paragraph, etc.).*
- *Changing spelling of word (Updating).*
- *Formatting paragraph (Text).*

If we use fixed length memory storage (arrays) to perform the above operations, it is not always possible. For this purpose linked list type of storage structure is used.

3.2 STRING OPERATIONS

A string is simply a linear array of characters but there is a basic difference between linear array and string. A linear array may be treated as a continuous stream of characters where as a string can be defined as a collection of sub-strings for example:

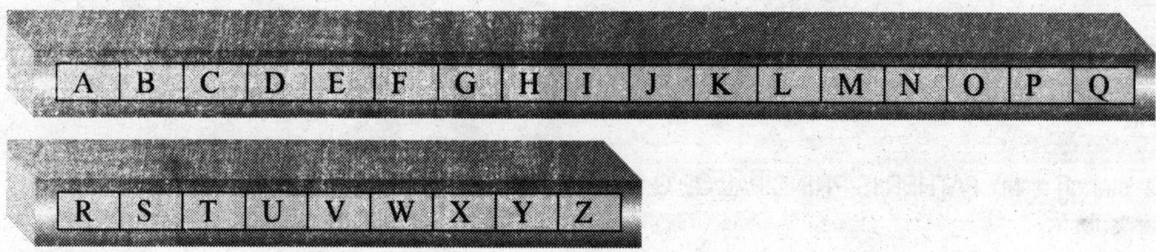

Fig. 3.4 Linear array of alphabets

Fig. 3.4 represents a linear array of 26 characters. This array may be treated as a single string of 26 character, where size of the array is 26 characters. Consider the following example:

Fig. 3.5 Array of integers

This array represents a linear array of 17 integers. This is a linear array but it is not a string. **Fig. 3.4** and **Fig. 3.5** illustrate the linear representation of the array. Consider the following example:

"Drastic change in environment"

This is a string of 29 characters or in other words we can say that this is a string formed by four sub-strings. The sub-strings are as follows:

"Drastic"

"change"

"in"

"environment"

From the above discussion of linear array, it is clear that if one wants to update the array, it can be updated one character at a time. But if one wants to update the string, one can change a word (sub-string) or complete sentence according to the requirements.

For finding a sub-string in a string, a function, which takes input string, starting position of the sub-string and the size of the sub-string can be easily written as follows:

```
// STRING6.C

# include<iostream.h>
# include<stdio.h>
# include<malloc.h>

char *sub_string(char *, int , int );

void main()
{
    char string[] = "MY FATHER IS PRINCIPAL OF G.B.P.E.C";
    char *substr;

    substr = ( char *) malloc(9);

    cout<<"\n INPUT PATTERN IS ";
    cout<<"\n **************** \n";
    cout<<string;

    cout<<"\n\n PATTERN FOUND ";
    cout<<"\n ************* \n";
    substr = sub_string(string, 13, 9);
    cout<<substr;
    cout<<"\n Press a key";
    getchar();
}

// This function finds the pattern
char *sub_string(char *string, int strpos, int size )
{
```

```
    char *substring;
    int i = 0 ;
    substring = ( char *) malloc(size);
    while(size)
{
        substring[i] = string[strpos];
        strpos ++;
        i ++;
        size --;
}
    substring[i] = '\0';
    return(substring);
}
```

```
INPUT PATTERN IS
****************
PRINCIPAL

PATTERN FOUND
****************
PRINCIPAL

Press a key
```

3.2.1 INDEXING (Pattern Matching)

Finding the position where a string pattern first appears in a given string text is called **indexing**. The syntax for indexing operation is as follows:

index(text, pattern)

If a pattern does not appear in the text, the function **index()** returns the value 0. For example, if a text contains the text (string)

"MY FATHER IS PRINCIPAL OF G.B.P.E.C."

then

index (text,"THE") has value 0.
index(text,"MY") has value 1.
index(text,"TO") has value 0.
index(text,"PRINCIPAL") has value 14.

How can **index()** be function written? For example, the program segment **STRING7.C** illustrates the development procedure.

```
// STRING7.C

// In this program segment the text provided through file

# include<iostream.h>
# include<stdio.h>
# include<string.h>
# include<malloc.h>
# include<stdlib.h>

class indexing
{
    public:
        index(char *buffer, char *string);
};

// Global Parameters

char *buffer;
char string[] = "language";
char *s;
char s1[8];
int size ;
int i, j;
int length;
int l ;
int position ;
int back1, back2 ;

// End

void main()
{
    indexing INDEX;
    FILE *fp;
    char file[13];

    cout<<"\nEnter Text File ";
    cin>>file;
    fp = fopen(file,"r");
    if( fp == NULL )
    {
        cout<<file;
        perror("ERROR : ");
        exit(0);
    }
```

```
    fseek(fp, 0L, SEEK_END);
    size = ftell(fp);
    cout<<"\n SIZE OF FILE : "<<size;
    cout<<"\n Press a key";
    getchar();
    buffer = (char *) malloc(size+1);
    fseek(fp,0L,0);
    fread(buffer, size, 1, fp) ;
    buffer[size+1] = '\0';
    cout<<"\n Enter The Pattern ";
    cin>>string;

    cout<<"TEXT PROVIDED IS AS FOLLOWS \n";
    cout<<"****************************\n\n";
    cout<<buffer;
    cout<<"\n Press a key";
    getchar();
    fclose(fp);
    cout<<"\n Index value :"<<INDEX.index(buffer, string);
}

// Index function

indexing :: index(char *buffer, char *string)
{
    length = strlen(string);
    s = ( char *) malloc(length);
    cout<<"Length : "<<length;
    back1 = length ;
    back2 = size ;

    i = 0 ;
    j = 0 ;
    l = 0 ;

    position = 0 ;

    while(size!= 0)
    {
        size --;
        while(length)
        {
            position ++ ;
            if ( buffer[i] == string[j])
            {
```

```
                s[j] = buffer[i];
                l ++ ;
                i ++ ;
                j ++ ;
                length --;
                if( l == back1)
                {
                    s[j] = '\0';
                    cout<<"\nPattern is found";
                    cout<<"\nSize of Pattern: "<<l;
                    cout<<"\n Pattern is : ";
                    cout<<s;
                    cout<<"\n Pattern Found at "<<position-back1;

                    free(s);

                    return(position-back1);
                }
            }
            else
            {
                i++;
                j = 0;
                l = 0;
                length = back1;
            }
        }
    }
    free(buffer);
}
```

```
Enter text file: TEST

SIZE OF FILE : 344

Press a key

Enter pattern: LITTLE

TEXT PROVIDED IS AS FOLLOWS
***************************

TWINKLE, TWINKLE LITTLE STAR
HOW I WONDER WHAT YOU ARE
UP ABOVE THE WORLD SO HIGH
LIKE A DIAMOND IN THE SKY
WHEN THE BURNING SUN IS SET
AND THE GRASS WITH DUE IS WET
THEN YOU SHOW YOUR LITTLE LIGHT
TWINKLE, TWINKLE ALL THE NIGHT

Press a key

Length => 6

Pattern is found
Size of Pattern: 6
Pattern is : LITTLE

Pattern Found at  29

Press a key
```

```
// Find locations of a sub-string in a string
// LO_NO.C

# include<iostream.h>
# include<stdio.h>
# include<string.h>

class Location
{
	public:
		int index_str1,index_str2,k;
		int c[100];
```

```
	public:
		int str(char *, char *, int *);
		Number_occ(char *, char *, int *);
};

// Function str that finds locations of the sub-string

int Location :: str(char *s1, char *s2, int c[])
{
	int count = 0;
	int l =0;
	for(index_str1 = 0; s1[index_str1]; index_str1++)
		for( int index_str2=index_str1, k = 0; s1[index_str2] == s2[k]&&s1[index_str1]; index_str2++, k++)
			if( !s2[k+1])
			{
				count ++;
				c[l++] = index_str1;
			}

	return(count);
}

// Function main

void main()
{
	Location Locat;
	char *s;
	int c[100];
	int location ;
	char s1[]="Ram Bahadur Bahadur Patel";
	char s2[] ="Baha";
	int i, loc;
	int count;

	count = Locat.str (s1, s2,c);

	cout<<"\n Number of occurences = "<<count;

	for(i = 0;i < count; i++)
	{
		location = c[i];
		s = &s2[0];
		cout<<"\n Starting location = "<<location+1<< " : ";
		while(*(s++))
```

```
            {
                putchar(s1[location++]);
            }
        }

}

// Find location of a sub-string first start in a string
// LOCAT.C

# include<iostream.h>
# include<stdio.h>

class Location
{
    private:
        int index_str1,index_str2,k;
    public:
        int str(char *, char *);
};

// Function str that finds first location of the sub-string

int Location :: str(char *s1, char *s2)
{
    for(index_str1 = 0; s1[index_str1]; index_str1++)
        for( int index_str2=index_str1, k =0; s1[index_str2] == s2[k]; index_str2++, k++)
            if( !s2[k+1])
            {
                return(index_str1);
            }
    return(NULL);
}

// Function main

void main()
{
    Location Locat;
    char *s;
    char s1[]="Ram Bahadur Patel";
    char s2[] ="Baha";
    int location = Locat.str (s1, s2);
    s = s2;
    cout<<"\n Location =" <<location<< " ";
    while(*(s++))
```

```
    {
        putchar(s1[location++]);
    }
}
```

3.2.2 CONCATENATION

Suppose we have two-string s_1 and s_2 then concatenation of s_1 and s_2 denoted by s_1+s_2, is linking together two strings. The concatenation function varies from language to language. In **C** language it is **strcat ()**, in **BASIC** s_1+s_2 and in **SNOBOL** it is s_1 s_2.

If s_1 = "RAM"
s_2 = "LAKHAN"
then $s_1 + s_2$ = "RAMLAKHAN"

The above discussion can be implemented as follows (**STRING8.C**):

```
// STRING8.C

# include<iostream.h>
# include<stdio.h>
# include<string.h>
# include<malloc.h>

class cat
{
    public:
        void concatenate( char *, char *, char *);
};

void main()
{
    cat cat_string;
    char str1[128];
    char str2[128];
    char *output_str;

    cout<<" Input the first string : ";
    cin>>str1;
    cout<<"\nInput the second string : ";
    cin>>str2;
    output_str = (char *) malloc(strlen(str1)+strlen(str2)+1);
    cat_string.concatenate(str1, str2, output_str);
    while(*output_str)
    {
        cout<<*output_str++;
```

```
    }
}

// This function concatenates two strings

void cat :: concatenate( char *s1, char *s2, char *rs)
{
    while(*s1)
    {
        *rs++ = *s1++ ;
    }

    while(*s2)
    {
        *rs++ = *s2++ ;
    }
    *rs = '\0';
}
```

3.2.3 LENGTH

The number of characters in a string represent its length. For example, the string "**ENGINEERING**" has length 11. The function **length ()** is given below to find the length of a string.

```
int length(char *p)
{
    int len = 0 ;
    while(*p++)
{
    len ++;
}
return (len) ;
}
```

In the above function a string is passed. The function **length ()** processes the string character by character and finds the length of the string. The program segment **STRING9.C** illustrates the idea.

```
// STRING9.C

// Length function

# include<iostream.h>
# include<stdio.h>
# include<string.h>
```

```
class Length
{
    public:
        int length(char *p);

};

// Definition of the length function

int Length :: length(char *p)
{
    int len = 0 ;
    while(*p++)
    {
        len ++;
    }
    return (len) ;
}

// Function main

void main()
{
    Length len;
    char string[60];
    cout<<" Input the string : ";
    cin>>string;
    cout<<"Length of Input String = "<<len.length(string);
    getchar();
}
```

```
Input the string : NO ALTERNATIVE OF HARD WORK
Length of Input String = 27
```

3.3 APPLICATION OF STRING OR TEXT PROCESSING

There are many applications of the string processing, but there are two main areas where the string processing is widely used. These are:

- *TEXT EDITING*
- *TEXT FORMATTING*

3.3.1 TEXT EDITING

General functions that are required in text editor are as follows:

- *Insertion (Insert a string, word and paragraph in a given text).*
- *Deletion (Delete a string, word, a line and paragraph from a given text).*
- *Update (a word, sub-string, string and a line, etc.).*
- *Replacement (Replacing a string, sub-string, line, paragraph, etc. by another in the text).*

3.3.1.1 INSERTION

Suppose in a given text one is interested in insertion of a string at some location (position). Then the syntax of insertion function will be:

insertion (text , position, string)

For example, if there is a text “**COMPUTER ENGINEERING**” and one wants to insert string “**SCIENCE**” in between “**COMPUTER**” and “**ENGINEERING**” then it can be written as:

insertion(“COMPUTER ENGINEERING”, 10, “SCIENCE”)

The output produced by this function is:

“**COMPUTER SCIENCE ENGINEERING**”

Similarly, one can insert “**AND**” between “**SCIENCE**” and “**ENGINEERING**”.

insertion(“COMPUTER SCIENCE ENGINEERING”, 18 , “AND”)

The output comes as:

“**COMPUTER SCIENCE AND ENGINEERING**”

The program segment **STRING10.C** illustrates the procedure.

```
// STRING10.C

# include<iostream.h>
# include<stdio.h>
# include<string.h>
# include<malloc.h>
# include<ctype.h>

class insert
```

```
{
    public:
        void insertion ( char *, int , char *, char *);
};

// Function insert

void insert:: insertion ( char *text , int position, char *s, char *p)
{
    char ch ;
    while(position)
    {
        *p++ = *text++ ;
        position--;
    }
    while(*s)
    {
        *p++ = *s++ ;
    }
    cout<<"\n After insertion of the pattern\n ";
    cout<<"there needs blank at right side of the pattern(y) : ";
    ch = getchar() ;
    ch = toupper(ch);

    if (ch == 'Y')
        *p++ = ' ';
    while(*text)
    {
        *p++ = *text++ ;
    }
    *p = '\0';
}

// Function main

void main()
{
    insert ins;
    char *point ;
    char text[128]="COMPUTER SCIENCE ENGINEERING";
    char s[4] ="AND";
    int position = 17 ;
    point =(char*) malloc(128);
    cout<<"\n********************************\n";
    cout<<" TEXT AND PATTERN ARE AS FOLLOWS\n";
    cout<<"\n********************************\n";
```

```
    cout<<text<<"\n";
    cout<<s;
    cout<<"\n********************************\n";
    ins.insertion ( text, position, s, point);
    cout<<"\n********************************\n";
    cout<<"\n";
    cout<<point;
    cout<<"\n********************************\n";
    cout<<"\n Press a key";
    getchar();
}
```

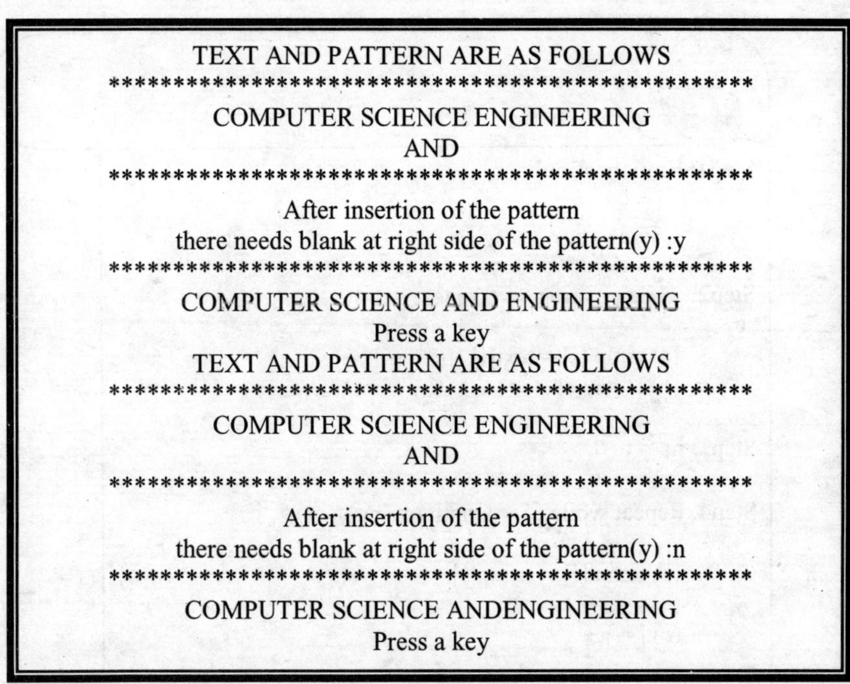

TEXT AND PATTERN ARE AS FOLLOWS
****
COMPUTER SCIENCE ENGINEERING
AND
****
After insertion of the pattern
there needs blank at right side of the pattern(y) :y
****
COMPUTER SCIENCE AND ENGINEERING
Press a key
TEXT AND PATTERN ARE AS FOLLOWS
****
COMPUTER SCIENCE ENGINEERING
AND
****
After insertion of the pattern
there needs blank at right side of the pattern(y) :n
****
COMPUTER SCIENCE ANDENGINEERING
Press a key

The above program segment creates a temporary array in the memory. Copy the content of the text up to the position where we want to insert the sub-string, then copy sub-string into temporary array. In the last rest of the text is copied into the temporary array. The algorithm is shown in the **Fig. 3.6.**

3.3.1.2 DELETION

Suppose in a given text one wants to delete a sub-string **S,** which begins from position **K** and has a length **L** that is possible with the help of following syntax.

```
deletion(text, position, length)
```

For example, if there is a text

"COMPUTER SCIENCE AND ENGINEERING"

and one wants to remove sub-string "AND" then

deletion("COMPUTER SCIENCE AND ENGINEERING", 18, 3)

will produce the following output

"COMPUTER SCIENCE ENGINEERING"

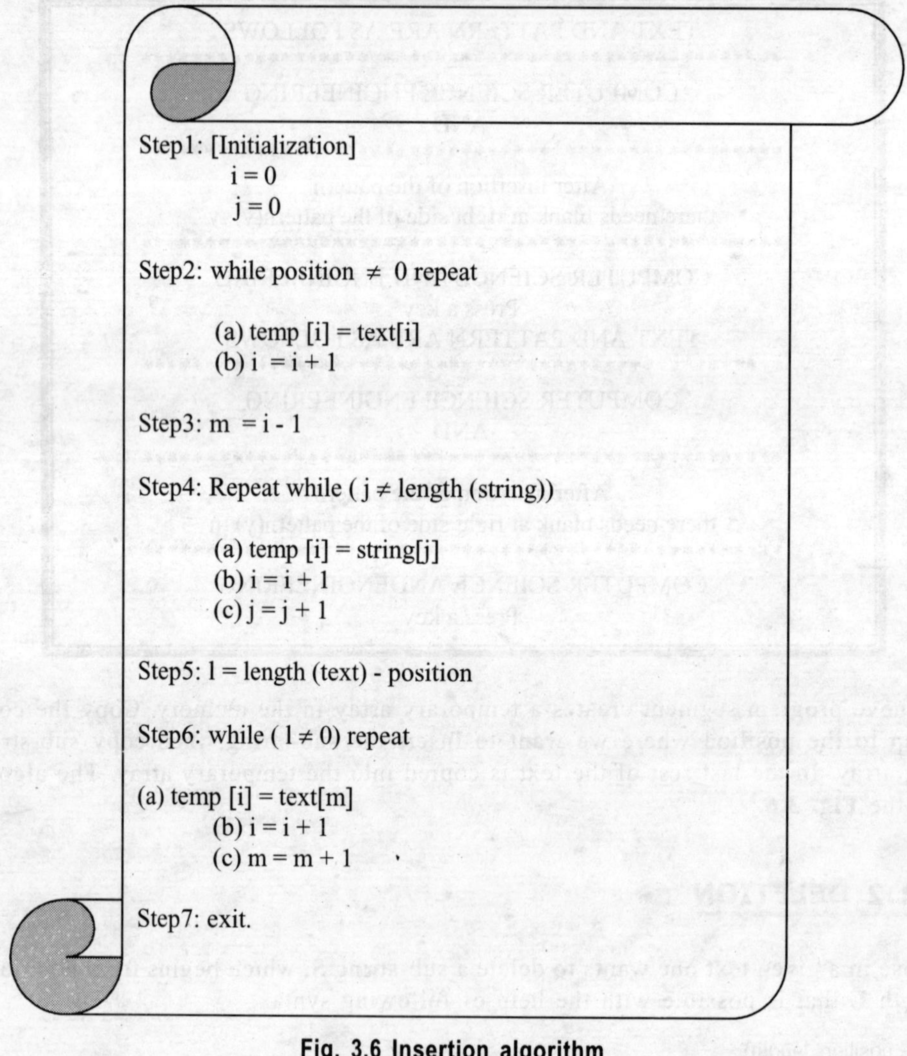

Fig. 3.6 Insertion algorithm

The following steps are required to implement the deletion operation:

- *Copy from starting position of the text to the given position into **temp** string variable.*
- *Copy text from the **(length (text) - position -length (string) + 1)** until end of the text, into **temp** string variable.*

The deletion function can be developed as illustrated in the program segment **STRING11.C**.

```
// STRING11.C

# include<iostream.h>
# include<stdio.h>
# include<string.h>
# include<malloc.h>

class Delete
{
	public:
		void deletion ( char *, int , int , char * );
};

// Function delete

void Delete :: deletion (char *text, int position, int length, char *p)
{
	while(position)
	{
		*p++ = *text++ ; // copying the pattern
		position--;
	}

	while(length)
	{
		*text++; // skipping the pattern
		length --;
	}

	*p++ = ' ';
	while(*text)
	{
		*p++ = *text++ ; // copying the rest of text
	}
	*p = '\0';
}
```

```
// Function main

void main()
{
    Delete Delet;
    char *point ;
    char text[128]="COMPUTER SCIENCE AND ENGINEERING";
    int length = 3 ;
    int position = 17 ;

    point = (char *) malloc(128);

    cout<<"\n TEXT IS AS FOLLOWS  ";
    cout<<"\n**********************************\n";
    cout<<text;
    cout<<"\n**********************************\n";
    Delet.deletion (text, position, length , point);
    cout<<"\nOUTPUT AFTER DELETION OF PATTERN";
    cout<<"\n**********************************\n";
    cout<<point;
    cout<<"\n**********************************\n";
    cout<<"\n Press a key";
    getchar();
}
```

```
TEXT IS AS FOLLOWS
**************************************
COMPUTER SCIENCE AND ENGINEERING

OUTPUT AFTER DELETION OF PATTERN
*************************************
COMPUTER SCIENCE   ENGINEERING

Press a key
```

The program **DELET.C** also shows the above discussion in different way. The algorithm is shown in **Fig. 3.7.**

```
// Delete a sub-string from a string

// DELET.C

# include<iostream.h>
# include<stdio.h>
```

```
# include<string.h>

class Deletion
{
      public:
            int index_str1,index_str2,k;
            int c[100];

      public:
            int str_del_loc(char *, char *, int *);
};

// Function str_del_loc that finds location of the sub-string and delete.

int Deletion :: str_del_loc(char *s1, char *s2, int c[])
{
      int count = 0;
      int l =0;

      for(index_str1 = 0; s1[index_str1]; index_str1++)
            for( int index_str2=index_str1, k = 0; s1[index_str2] == s2[k]&&s1[index_str1]; index_str2++, k++)
                  if( !s2[k+1])
                  {
                        count ++;
                        c[l++] = index_str1;
                        for(int j = index_str1, i = strlen(s2)+index_str1; s1[i]; j++, i++)
                              s1[j] = s1[i];
                        s1[j] = NULL;
                        cout<<"\n After delete operation the output";
                        cout<<"\n "<<s1;
                  }

      return(count);
}

// Function main

void main()
{
      Deletion Delet;
      char *s;
      int c[100];
      char s1[]="Ram Bahadur Bahadur Patel";
      char s2[] ="Baha";
      int count;
      count = Delet.str_del_loc (s1, s2,c);
```

```
    cout<<"\n Number of occurrences ="<< count;
}
```

```
After delete operation the output
Ram dur Bahadur Patel
After delete operation the output
Ram dur dur Patel
Number of occurrences =2
```

If one wants to delete first occurrence of a pattern in a given text then the same can be achieved with one modification in the above algorithm. The modification involves the replacement of $\textbf{length}_1$ by **length(pattern)** if the $\textbf{length}_1$ is not equal to **length(pattern).**

If one wants to delete every occurrences of a pattern in a given text then **index()** function can be used to find the different occurrences of a pattern. After finding the position **delete()** function is called to delete the pattern.

3.3.1.3 PATTERN MATCHING (REPLACEMENT)

Suppose one wants to replace the first occurrence of a $\textbf{pattern}_1$ by $\textbf{pattern}_2$ in a given text then it is possible with the help of following syntax:

replacement(text, $pattern_1$, $pattern_2$)

For example, suppose one wants to replace "**and**" pattern by "**AND**" in the given text.

"COMPUTER SCIENCE and ENGINEERING"

replacement("COMPUTER SCIENCE and ENGINEERING", "and", "AND")
deletion(text, position, $length_1$)

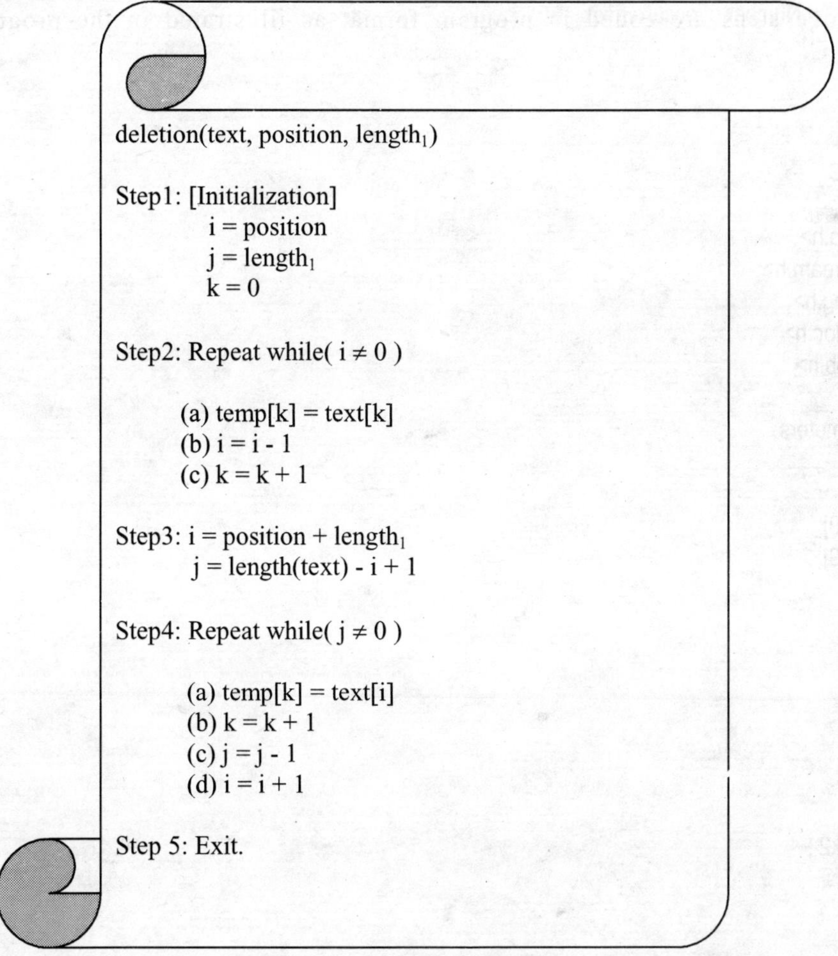

deletion(text, position, $length_1$)

Step1: [Initialization]
 i = position
 j = $length_1$
 k = 0

Step2: Repeat while(i ≠ 0)

 (a) temp[k] = text[k]
 (b) i = i - 1
 (c) k = k + 1

Step3: i = position + $length_1$
 j = length(text) - i + 1

Step4: Repeat while(j ≠ 0)

 (a) temp[k] = text[i]
 (b) k = k + 1
 (c) j = j - 1
 (d) i = i + 1

Step 5: Exit.

Fig. 3.7 Deletion algorithm

The output of the above function is

"COMPUTER SCIENCE AND ENGINEERING"

This operation can be implemented with the help of following steps:

- *Index the text for* ***$pattern_1$*** *and record the position.*
- *Delete the* ***$pattern_1$***
- *Copy content of text from beginning to the position (recorded in step 1) into the* ***temp*** *string variable.*
- *Add* ***$pattern_2$*** *to* ***temp.***
- *Copy contents of the text from the* ***position + 1*** *into the* ***temp***.

The above steps are coded in program format as illustrated in the program segment **STRING12.C.**

```
// STRING12.C

# include<stdio.h>
# include<iostream.h>
# include<string.h>
# include<malloc.h>
# include<stdlib.h>

// Global parameters

char *buffer;
char pattern1[9];
char pattern2[9];

char *s;
char s1[8];
int size ;
int i, j;
int length;
int l ;
int position ;
int back1, back2 ;

class replace
{
    public:
        void replacement(char *, char *, char * );
};

void replace :: replacement(char *buffer, char *pattern1, char *pattern2 )
{
    length = strlen(pattern1);
    s = ( char *) malloc(length);
    printf("Length => %d", length);
    back1 = length ;
    back2 = size ;
    getchar();

    i = 0 ;
    j = 0 ;
    l = 0 ;
```

```
position = 0 ;

while(size)
{
      size --;
      while(length)
      {
            position ++ ;
            if ( buffer[i] == pattern1[j])
            {
                  if ((position >= back2) || (position < 0))
                        exit(0);
                  s[j] = buffer[i];
                  l ++ ;
                  i ++ ;
                  size --;
                  j ++ ;
                  length --;
                  if( l == back1)
                  {
                        s[j] = '\0';
                        cout<<"\nPATTERN IS FOUND";
                        cout<<"\n*****************\n";
                        cout<<" LENGTH OF PATTERN : "<<l;
                        cout<<"\n PATTERN IS : ";
                        cout<<s;
                        cout<<"\n Starting Position = "<< (position-l);
                        cout<<"\n Press a key";
                        getchar();
                        l= 0 ;
                        j = 0 ;
                        cout<<"\nPATTERN REPLACEMENT IN PROGRESS";
                        cout<<"\n*******************************\n";

                        for(i = (position - strlen(pattern2)); i < position ; i++)
                        {
                              buffer[i] = pattern2[j];
                              putchar(buffer[i]);
                              j++;
                              getchar();
                        }

                        cout<<"\nSEE AFTER FIRST PATTERN REPLACEMENT ";
                        cout<<"\n**********************************\n";

                        cout<<buffer;
```

```
                        cout<<"\n Press a key";
                        getchar();

                    } // end of if
                } // end of if

                else
                {
                    i++;
                    j = 0;
                    l = 0;
                    size -- ;
                    length = back1;
                }

            } // end first while

            length = back1 ;
        } // end of second while
}

// Function main

void main()
{
        replace rec;
        FILE *fp ;
        fp = fopen("TEST","r");
        if( fp == NULL )
        {
            cout<<" FILE \n";
            perror("ERROR : ");
            exit(0);
        }
        fseek(fp, 0L, SEEK_END);
        size = ftell(fp);
        cout<<"SIZE OF FILE : "<<size;
        cout<<"\n Press a key";
        getchar();
        buffer = (char *) malloc(size);
        fseek(fp,0L,0);
        fread(buffer, size, 1, fp) ;
        buffer[size+1] = '\0';
        cout<<buffer;
        cout<<"\nPress a key";
        getchar();
```

```
    fclose(fp);
    cout<<"\n ENTER PATTERN TO WHICH WANT TO REPLACE: ";
    cin>>pattern1;
    cout<<"\n ENTER NEW PATTERN : ";
    cin>>pattern2;
    rec.replacement(buffer, pattern1, pattern2);
    cout<<buffer;
    cout<<"\nPress a key";
    getchar();
}
```

```
SIZE OF FILE : 344
Press a key

TWINKLE, TWINKLE LITTLE STAR
HOW I WONDER WHAT YOU ARE
UP ABOVE THE WORLD SO HIGH
LIKE A DIAMOND IN THE SKY
WHEN THE BURNING SUN IS SET
AND THE GRASS WITH DUE IS WET
THEN YOU SHOW YOUR LITTLE LIGHT
TWINKLE, TWINKLE ALL THE NIGHT
Press a key
ENTER PATTERN TO WHICH WANT TO REPLACE: LITTLE
ENTER NEW PATTERN : little
Length => 6
PATTERN IS FOUND
******************
LENGTH OF PATTERN: 6
PATTERN IS : LITTLE
Starting Position = 29
Press a key
PATTERN REPLACEMENT IN PROGRESS
***************************************
little
SEE AFTER FIRST PATTERN REPLACEMENT
****************************************
TWINKLE, TWINKLE little STAR
HOW I WONDER WHAT YOU ARE
UP ABOVE THE WORLD SO HIGH
LIKE A DIAMOND IN THE SKY
WHEN THE BURNING SUN IS SET
AND THE GRASS WITH DUE IS WET
THEN YOU SHOW YOUR LITTLE LIGHT
TWINKLE, TWINKLE ALL THE NIGHT
Press a key
```

```
PATTERN IS FOUND
*******************
LENGTH OF PATTERN : 6
PATTERN IS : LITTLE

Starting Position -> 274
Press a key

PATTERN REPLACEMENT IN PROGRESS
*************************************
SEE AFTER FIRST PATTERN REPLACEMENT
***************************************

TWINKLE, TWINKLE little STAR
HOW I WONDER WHAT YOU ARE
UP ABOVE THE WORLD SO HIGH
LIKE A DIAMOND IN THE SKY
WHEN THE BURNING SUN IS SET
AND THE GRASS WITH DUE IS WET
THEN YOU SHOW YOUR little LIGHT
TWINKLE, TWINKLE ALL THE NIGHT
Press a key
```

The program segment **REPLACE.C** also shows the above discussion in some different way.

```
// Replace a sub-string in a string
// REPLACE.C

# include<iostream.h>
# include<string.h>


class Replace_str
{
    public:
        int index_str1,index_str2,k;
        int c[100];

    public:
        int str_rep(char *, char *, int *);
};

// Function str that finds first location of the sub-string
```

```
int Replace_str :: str_rep(char *s1, char *s2, int c[])
{
     int count = 0;
     int l =0;
     char s3[]= "Jaunpur";
     for(index_str1 = 0; s1[index_str1]; index_str1++)
          for( int index_str2=index_str1, k = 0; s1[index_str2] == s2[k]&&s1[index_str1];
index_str2++, k++)
               if( !s2[k+1])
               {
                    count ++;
                    c[l++] = index_str1;
                    int i = 0;
                    for(int j = index_str1; j < strlen(s3)+index_str1; j++)
                         s1[j] = s3[i++];
                    cout<<"\n "<<s1;
               }

     return(count);
}

// Function main

void main()
{
     Replace_str rep;
     char *s;
     int c[100];
     char s1[]="Ram Bahadur Bahadur Patel";
     char s2[] ="Bahadur";
     int count;
     rep.str_rep(s1, s2,c);
}
```

3.3.2 TEXT FORMATTING

Text formatting comprises of many related functions. These functions vary from word processor (editor) to word processor. The objectives of these functions are same in the every word processor. The common text formatting functions are listed below:

- *Formatting a paragraph.*
- *Setting left margin.*
- *Setting right margin.*
- *Left justified.*
- *Right justified etc.*

3.4 MARKOV ALGORITHM

The ***Markov*** algorithm named after the Russian mathematician ***A. Markov***, is a formal system for string manipulation that was originally developed to support a theory of computation. First language to support string-processing concept was **COMIT.** After this language another language **SNOBOL** used this concept. At present **C, PASCAL** and **C++** all are supporting ***Markov*** algorithm for string processing.

The main strategy in a ***Markov*** algorithm is that it takes an input string **x** and through a number of production rules in the algorithm it transforms **x** to an output string **y**. When we pass **s** string through a number of production rules, the string may shrink or expand in length. For example, the following program segment produces an output string **"STRING MANIPULATION AND PATTERN MATCHING"**.

```
# include<iostream.h>

void main()
{
    cout<<"STRING MANIPULATION AND PATTERN MATCHING";
}
```

The size of this source code is 108 bytes when we compile this source code through **C++** compiler the size of output object code becomes 454 bytes.

3.4.1 BASIC CONCEPT

Let **A** is a finite nonempty set of symbols, i.e.,

A = {a, b, c, ..., z}

The concatenation of two alphabetic characters form a sequence of characters for example, if **a** and **b** are two characters, then their concatenation will produce **ab,** a sequence of characters. The concatenation operation is also possible on sequence of characters. The concatenation of **ab** with **ab** will produce **abab**. If we consider **o** as a concatenation operator then the concatenation of **ab** to **ab** can be written as **ab o ab** and it produces **abab** as an output.

Thus we can define a string over an alphabet set **A** as a

- *A letter from the alphabet set **A**.*
- *A sequence of letters derived from the concatenations from the alphabet set **A**.*

For example, consider the alphabet set A = {a, b, c}

The string derived from this alphabet set is as follows:

"abc" string of 3 characters.
"aaaaaa" string of 6 characters.
"aabbcc" string of 6 characters.
"a" string of 1 character.
"b" string of 1 character.
"c" string of 1 character.

similarly,

$A \circ A = A^2$ *represents all strings length two.*
$A \circ A \circ A = A^3$ *represents all strings of length three.*
$A \circ A \circ A \circ \ldots \circ A = A^n$ *represents all strings of length* ***n.***

Closure of **A** denoted by $\mathbf{A}^+$ and is defined as follows:

$$A^+ = A^1 U A^2\ U\ A^3 U\ A^4\ U\ldots$$

If L is empty string or **NULL** string then

$$A^* = LUA^1 U\ A^2\ U\ A^3\ U\ A^4\ U\ \ldots$$
$$= L\ U\ A^+$$

L is called the identify elements in the algebra formed by the set $\mathbf{A}^*$.

The followings are some properties of strings, for any string **y**

3.4.2 IDENTITY PROPERTY

y o L = L o y = y

3.4.3 ASSOCIATIVE PROPERTY

(x o y) o z = x o (y o z) = x o y o z where **x, y, z** belongs to A^*

3.4.4 PRODUCTION

The production is a statement of the form **a ® b**, where **a** and **b** represents string in $\mathbf{A}^*$, where **A** does not contain the symbol arrow (®) and period (.). In the above production **a** is called antecedent and **b** is called consequent. A production **a ® b** is applicable to a string **c**, if **c** belongs to **A*** and there is at least one occurrence of **a** in **c**, otherwise production is not applicable. If production is applicable then the first occurrence of **a** in **c** is replaced by **b**. For example, let "**abababbcabbc**" is a input string and **bc ® c** is production rule. If we apply this production rule on the above input string, the output comes like:

abababcabbc First Step
ababacabbc Second Step
ababacabc Third Step
ababacac Fourth Step

If we consider the production rule **bd ® a,** it is not applicable to the above input string.

3.4.5 TERMINATION

Markov algorithm terminates in one of the following ways:

- *Last production is not applicable.*
- *A terminal production is applicable.*

A terminal production is a statement of the form **a ® b**, where **a** and **b** represents string in **A*** and the period operator immediately follows the consequent. For example:

P_1: $bc \rightarrow c$
P_2: $ba \rightarrow a$
P_3: $aa \rightarrow a$
P_4: $ac \rightarrow a$
P_5: $ad \rightarrow d$

On the alphabet set **A** = {a, b, c } and input string is "abababbcabbcd".

Applying the above production rules on the input string provided in the problem the discussion is given in **Table 3.1.**

Table 3.1

Let w = abababbcabbcd	
=> aababbcabbcd	By P_2
=> aaabbcabbcd	By P_2
=> aabbcabbcd	By P_3
=> abbcabbcd	By P_3
=> abcabbcd	By P_1
=> acabbcd	By P_1
=> acabcd	By P_1
=> acacd	By P_1
=> aacd	By P_4
=> aad	By P_4
=> ad	By P_3
=> a	By P_5

3.4.6 ALGORITHM

Markov algorithm is illustrated in **Fig. 3.8).** Let $\mathbf{P_1}$, $\mathbf{P_2}$, $\mathbf{P_3}$ ... $\mathbf{P_n}$ are production rules that are applicable to input string **u** which belongs to **A***. The variable k and l are indices and $\mathbf{u_k}$ denotes the result after application of the $\mathbf{k}^{th}$ transformation or production rule to the input string

u. The algorithm illustrated in **Fig. 3.8** is discussed in the program segment **STRING13.C**

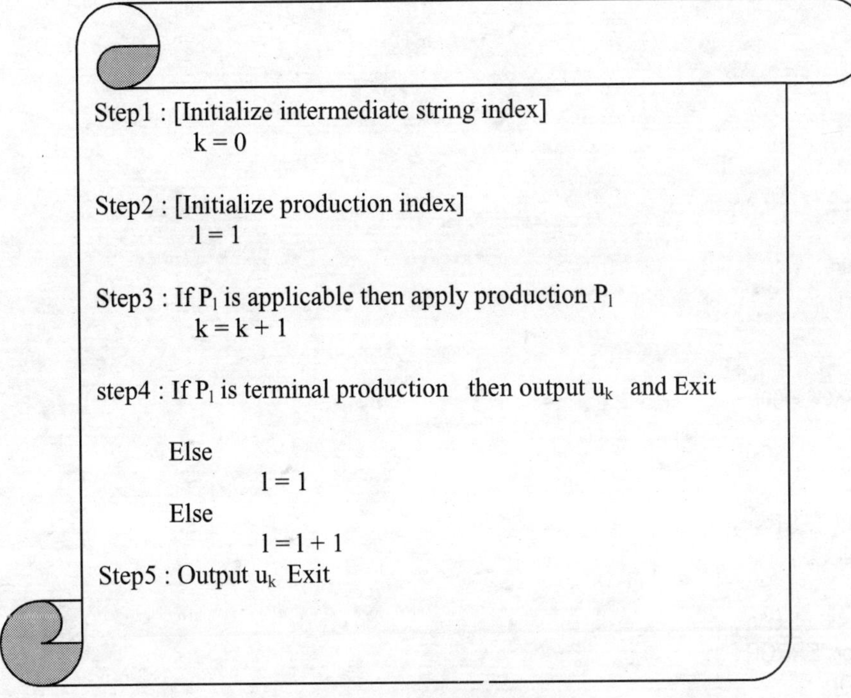

Fig. 3.8 Markov lagorithm

```
// STRING13.C

# include<iostream.h>
# include<stdio.h>
# include<string.h>
# include<malloc.h>
# include<stdlib.h>

class mark
{
	public:
		void markov(char *, char *, char * );
};

// Global parameters

char *buffer;
char ch;
char pattern1[9];
char pattern2[9];
```

```
char *s;
char s1[8];
int size ;
int i, j;
int length;
int l ;
int position ;
int back1, back2 ;

// Function main

void main()
{
      mark markov_algo;

      FILE *fp ;

      fp = fopen("TEST","r");
      if( fp == NULL )
      {
            cout<<" FILE \n";
            perror("ERROR : ");
            exit(0);
      }
      fseek(fp, 0L, SEEK_END);
      size = ftell(fp);
      cout<<"SIZE OF FILE : "<<size;
      cout<<"\n Press a key\n";
      getchar();
      buffer = (char *) malloc(size+1);
      fseek(fp,0L,0);
      fread(buffer, size, 1, fp) ;
      buffer[size] = '\0' ;
      cout<<buffer;
      getchar();
      fclose(fp);

      do
      {
            cout<<"Enter choice n for break ";
            ch = getchar();
            cout<<"\n ENTER PATTERN TO WHICH WANT TO REPLACE: ";
            cin>>pattern1;

            cout<<"\n ENTER NEW PATTERN : ";
```

```
        cin>>pattern2;

        markov_algo.markov(buffer, pattern1, pattern2 );
    } while( ch !='n');
}

void mark :: markov(char *buffer, char *pattern1, char *pattern2 )
{
    int k, b;
    char *temp ;

    length = strlen(pattern1);
    s = ( char *) malloc(length);
    cout<<"Length = "<< length;
    back1 = length ;
    back2 = size ;
    getchar();

    i = 0 ;
    j = 0 ;
    l = 0 ;
    position = 0 ;

    while(size)
    {
        size --;
        while(length)
        {
            position ++ ;
            if ( buffer[i] == pattern1[j])
            {
                if ((position >= back2) || (position < 0))
                    exit(0);
                s[j] = buffer[i];
                l ++ ;
                i ++ ;
                size --;
                j ++ ;
                length --;
                if( l == back1)
                {
                    s[j] = '\0';
                    cout<<"\nPATTERN IS FOUND";
                    cout<<"\n****************\n";
                    cout<<" LENGTH OF PATTERN = "<< l;
                    cout<<"\n PATTERN IS : ";
```

```
        cout<<s;
        cout<<"\n Starting Position = "<<(position-l);

        // REPLACEMENT SECTION

        k = 0;
        for( k = 0 ; k < (position-l) ; k++ )
        {
            temp[k] = buffer[k] ;
        }
        j = 0 ;
        b = (k+ strlen(pattern2));

        for ( ; k < b ; k ++)
        {
            temp[k] = pattern2[j] ;
            j++ ;
        }
        temp[k] = '\0';
        getchar();

        b = k ;
        k = position + 1;

        for (; k < back2 ; k ++)
        {
            temp[b] = buffer[k] ;
            b++ ;
        }
        temp[b] = '\0';
        buffer = temp ;

        // END OF REPLACEMENT SECTION

        l= 0 ;
        j = 0 ;
        cout<< "\nPATTERN REPLACEMENT IN PROGRESS";
        cout<< "\n*********************************\n";
        cout<< "\nSEE AFTER FIRST PATTERN REPLACEMENT ";
        cout<< "\n*************************************\n";
        cout<<buffer;

    } // end of if
} // end of if

else
```

```
            {
                i++;
                j = 0;
                l = 0;
                size -- ;
                length = back1;
            }

        } // end first while

        length = back1 ;
    } // end of second while
}
```

EXERCISE

3.1 *Design a general* **Markov** *algorithm, which takes an input the following text:*

"Cobbler, Cobbler Mend My Shoe"

and produces output

"My Shoe Cobbler, Cobbler Mend"

Write ***C++*** *program to implement the designed algorithm.*

3.2 *Write an algorithm and* **C++** *program to implement right justifies text-processing function.*

3.3 *Consider the integer numbers* ***1 2 3 4 5 6 7 8 ... n*** *develop an algorithm to find the output*

1 2 3 4 5 6.... n-2 n-1 n n-1 n-2 ... 6 5 4 3 2 1.

3.4 *Design an algorithm, which trims off all the blank characters except the single one between two words for example, if the input string or text is as follows:*

" TOM ALTER HAS TWO APPLES"

then the output must come:

"TOM ALTER HAS TWO APPLES"

Implement this algorithm in ***C++.***

3.5 *Design an algorithm, which finds number of words, lines and characters in a given text. Implement the algorithm in* ***C++.***

3.6 *Design an algorithm which counts different types of words occurred in a given text. Implement the algorithm in* ***C++.*** *The output is to be displayed in tabular form.*

3.7 *Design an algorithm, which searches a word in a given text and replaces the word by another word if it is found.*

3.8 *Design an algorithm, which will generate all possible words of four characters, formed from alphabet set*

A = {a, b, c ... z}

Implement it in ***C++.***

3.9 *Implement the* ***lexical analyzer*** *phase of any compiler.*

3.10 *Design an algorithm that counts the number of paragraphs in a short story. Implement the designed algorithm.*

3.11 *Find the string stored in* ***Fig. 3.9.***

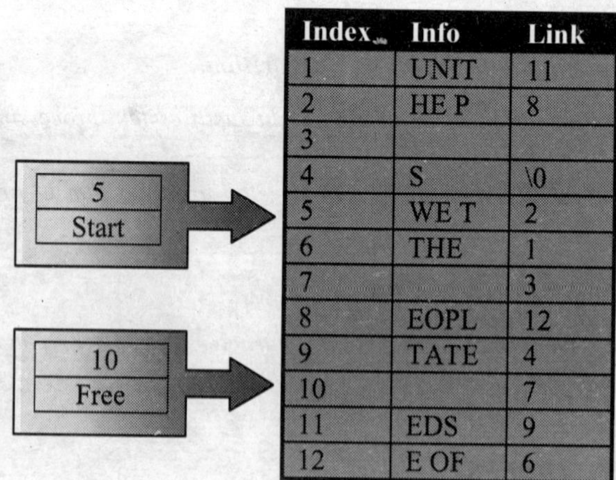

Index	Info	Link
1	UNIT	11
2	HE P	8
3		
4	S	\0
5	WE T	2
6	THE	1
7		3
8	EOPL	12
9	TATE	4
10		7
11	EDS	9
12	E OF	6

Fig. 3.9 List in memory

3.9 *Write a program, which reads a word and then counts the number of times the word in a given paragraph.*

3.10 *Write a program, which interchanges the jth and k^{th} paragraphs.*

3.11 *Write a sub-program* ***insert (Text, New, k),*** *which inserts a string* ***New*** *into* ***Text*** *beginning at* ***Text [k].***

3.12 *Write a sub-program* ***output(Text, k),*** *which prints the character string* ***Text*** *in lines with at most* ***k*** *characters. No words should be divided in the middle and appear on two lines, so some lines may contain trailing blank spaces. Each paragraph should begin with its own line and be indented using 6 blank spaces.*

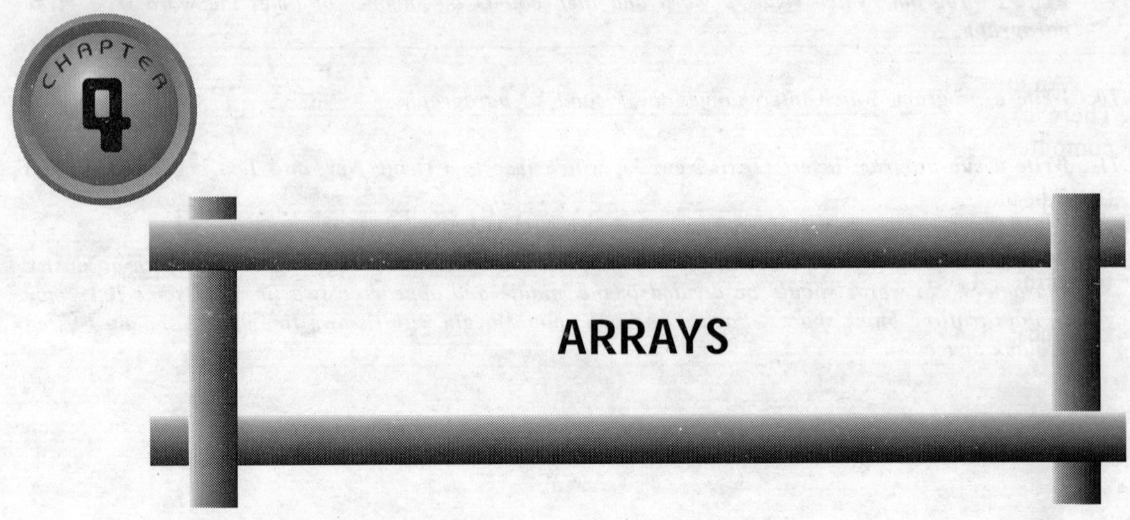

In this chapter we will discuss about linear data structure arrays. The operations possible on arrays like insertion, deletion, searching, sorting, matrix operations, multidimensional arrays, sparse matrix, etc.

4.1 INTRODUCTION

Data structures are classified into two categories:

- *Linear, and*
- *Non-linear*

A data structure is said to be linear if its elements form a linear sequence. There are two ways to represent a linear information in memory.

- *By contiguous memory locations*
- *By pointers and links*

The possible operations on the linear data structures are:

- *Traversal*
- *Insertion*
- *Deletion*
- *Searching*
- *Sorting*
- *Merging*
- *Updating*

4.2 ONE DIMENSIONAL ARRAYS

An array is a collection of similar data elements. An array is also called linear data structure. There exists a linear relationship between the array elements. The array elements lie in the computer memory in a linear fashion. The syntax to define an array is:

```
Data type array name [size];
```

The above syntax is equivalent to **C, C++ Visual C** and **Visual C++.** For example, if we want to define an array, which has 100 elements then the declaration will be:

```
int Number [100];
```

INDEX	INFO
1	11
2	22
3	33
4	44
5	55
6	66
7	77
8	88
9	99
10	00
11	
12	
13	
14	

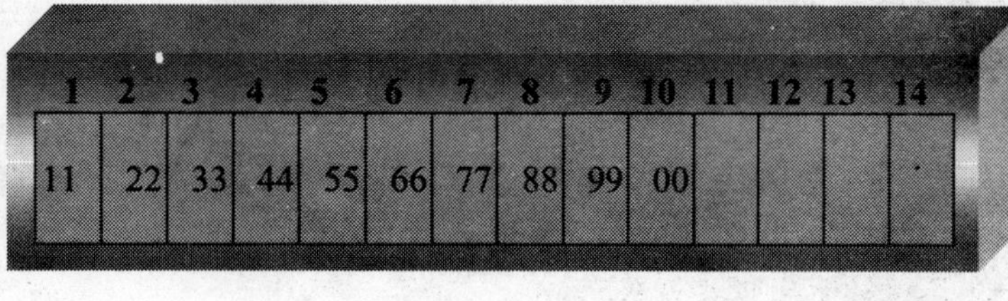

(a) Vertical representation of an array (Safe type)

(b) Horizontal representation of an array

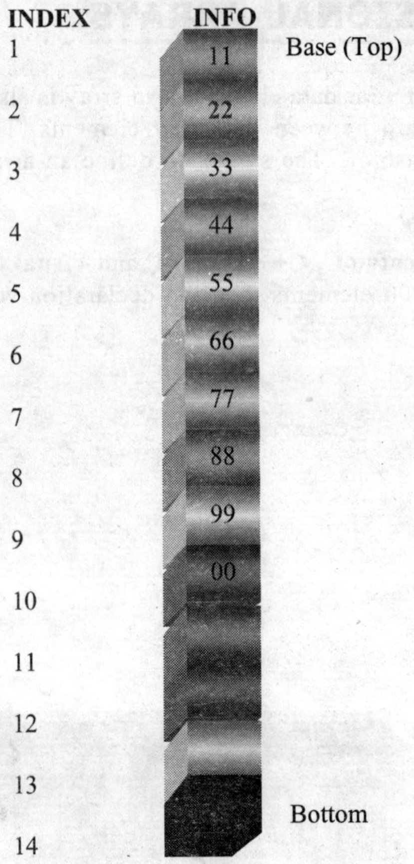

(c) Building representation of an array

Fig. 4.1 Array's representation

In the above example **Number** is an array name with size 100. The data type that is used to declare **Number** is integer type. The array **Number** can store maximum of 100 integer data. The size of an array is also called its length. The subscripts of an array are also called index. The index set consists of integers **0, 1, 2, 3 ... n - 1**, if we are using the language said above. The index set **1, 2, 3 ... n** is used by **PASCAL, FORTRAN, BASIC** and **PL/I.** The elements of the array **Number** may be denoted by the subscripted variables as:

$Number_1$, $Number_2$, $Number_3$ ... $Number_n$

In **FORTRAN, BASIC** and **PL/I** languages the elements can be represented as:

Number (1), Number (2), Number (3) ... Number (n)

But in **C, C++, Visual C/C++** and **PASCAL** language the above notations are written as:

Number [1], Number [2], Number [3] ... Number [n]

For example, if we have an array **N** with storage capacity of 14 elements and having 10 elements that is:

N [14] ={11, 22, 33, 44, 55, 66, 77, 88, 99, 00}

The illustration of array **N** is shown in **Fig. 4.1.**

The length of an array can be evaluated as:

Length = Upper limit – Lower limit + 1

That is

Length = UL – LL + 1

For an array **N [100]** the length of the array can be evaluated as:

UL = 99
LL = 0
Length = UL – LL + 1
⇨ 99 – 0 + 1
⇨ 100

From the above example, it is clear that **N** will store maximum of 100 elements only.

4.3 ONE DIMENSIONAL ARRAYS IN MEMORY

There is very simple way to find the address or location of an array element by using pointer operator (&) in **C, C++** and **Visual C/C++.**

If one is interested in address of array's elements, one can evaluate in the following fashion. The base address or starting address of an array is denoted by **Base (A).** Thus, the address of an element of an array **A** evaluated by:

Loc (A[k]) = Base(A) +w*(k - Lower limit)

Where, **w** represents number of words per memory cell for the array **A**. If capacity of **A** is 14 elements then they can represented as:

A[14] = {99,88,77,66,55,44,33,22,11,100,200,300,400,500}

The memory representation of the array **A** is illustrated in **Fig. 4.2.**

Address	Info
0x1334ff dc	99
0x1334ffde	88
0x1334ffe0	77
0x1334ffe2	66
0x1334ffe4	55
0x1334ffe6	44
0x1334ffe8	33
0x1334ffea	22
0x1334ffec	11
0x1334ffee	100
0x1334fff0	200
0x1334fff2	300
0x1334fff4	400
0x1334fff6	500

Fig. 4.2 Array in memory

4.4 TRAVERSING ONE DIMENSIONAL ARRAY

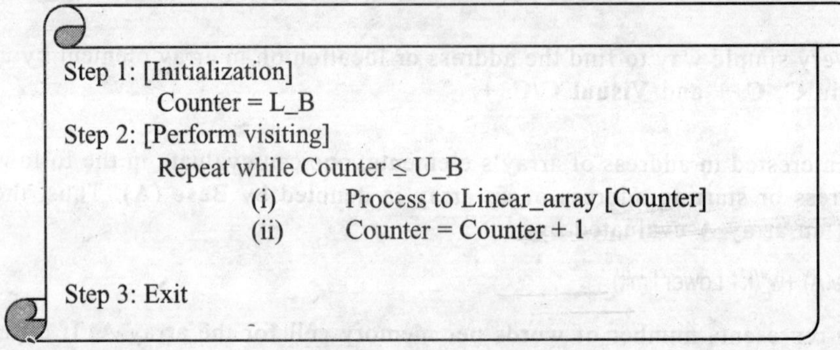

Step 1: [Initialization]
Counter = L_B
Step 2: [Perform visiting]
Repeat while Counter ≤ U_B
(i) Process to Linear_array [Counter]
(ii) Counter = Counter + 1
Step 3: Exit

Fig. 4.3 Traversing algorithm

Suppose we have an array **M** that is a collection of integer data type in the computer memory. If we visit each and every element in **M** then this visiting process is called traversing. The traversing algorithm is illustrated in **Fig. 4.3.** Suppose we have an array as illustrated in **Fig. 4.4.** If we look into **Fig. 4.4** then find that

L_B = 0 (Lower bound)
U_B = 12 (Upper bound)
Counter = L_B = 0
Linear_array [Counter] = 100
Counter = Counter +1 = 0+1 = 1
Linear_array [Counter] = 200

Index	Info
0	100
1	200
2	300
3	400
4	500
5	600
6	700
7	800
8	900
9	11
10	22
11	33
12	44

Fig. 4.4 Array in memory

This process continues and stops when the value 44 and **Counter** becomes 12. If one wants to find number of elements in an array, the following algorithm illustrates the idea:

(i) [Initialization]
    Number = 0
(ii) [Count information in the array]
    Repeat for Counter = L_B, L_B+1 ... U_B
    Process Linear_array [Counter]
    Number = Number +1
(iii) Exit

The program segment **ARRAY_T.C** implements the traversing algorithm shown in **Fig. 4.3.**

```
// Traversing a linear array
// ARRAY_T.C

# include<iostream.h>

class array_T
{
    public:
        void traversing_array(int *, int, int);
        void input(int *, int, int);
};
```

```
// Definition of the function

void array_T :: traversing_array(int linear_array[], int l_b, int u_b)
{

    for( int counter = l_b; counter<=u_b; counter++)
    {
        cout<<"\n Element at position : " << counter<< " is : "<<linear_array[counter];
    }
}

// Defintion of the function

void array_T :: input(int array[], int l_b, int u_b)
{
    for(int counter = l_b; counter<= u_b; counter++)
    {
        cout<<"\n Input value for the :" <<counter << " : ";
        cin>>array[counter];
    }
}

// Definition of the function

void main()
{
    array_T array;
    int a[100];
    int lb, ub;

    cout<<"\n Lower limit of the array:";
    cin>>lb;
    cout<<"\n Upper limit of the array:";
    cin>>ub;
    array.input(a, lb, ub);
    array.traversing_array(a,lb,ub);
}
```

```
Lower limit of the array: 0
Upper limit of the array: 12
Input value for the: 0: 100
Input value for the: 1: 200
Input value for the: 2: 300
Input value for the: 3: 400
Input value for the: 4: 500
Input value for the: 5: 600
Input value for the: 6: 700
Input value for the: 7: 800
Input value for the: 8: 900
Input value for the: 9: 11
Input value for the: 10: 22
Input value for the: 11: 33
Input value for the: 12: 44

Element at position: 0 is: 100
Element at position: 1 is: 200
Element at position: 2 is: 300
Element at position: 3 is: 400
Element at position: 4 is: 500
Element at position: 5 is: 600
Element at position: 6 is: 700
Element at position: 7 is: 800
Element at position: 8 is: 900
Element at position: 9 is: 11
Element at position: 10 is: 22
Element at position: 11 is: 33
Element at position: 12 is: 44
```

4.5 INSERTION IN ONE DIMENSIONAL ARRAY

It can be visualized that for inserting an element in one-dimensional array, one has to shift all the elements one position down, for example, if we have an array of items as illustrated in **Fig. 4.5,** where the array represents **"COMPTER SCIENCE"**. But the actual information, which is to be stored is **"COMPUTER SCIENCE"**. Now we have to insert '**U**' in the array at the proper place so that we get the desired string. By inspecting the array we find that '**U**' is missing at position 5. Before inserting '**U**' in the array we have to move each element of the array from position 5 to 12 one position down. The operations performed are:

Temp = 15 [Represents number of elements in the array]
Array [15] = Array [14] = E
Temp = Temp – 1 = 14 – 1
Array [14] = Array [13] = C
Temp = 14 – 1 = 13

Array [13] = Array [12] = N
Temp = 13 – 1 = 12
Array [12] = Array [11] = E
Temp = 12 – 1 = 11
Array [11] = Array [10] = I
Temp = 11 – 1 = 10
Array [10] = Array [9] = C
Temp = 10 – 1 = 9
Array [9] = Array [8] = S
Temp = 9 – 1 = 8
Array [8] = Array [7] = ' '
Temp = 8 – 1 = 7
Array [7] = Array [6] = R
Temp = 7 – 1 = 6
Array [6] = Array [5] = E
Temp = 6 – 1 = 5 [This is proper, one position down, insert new element here]
Array [5] = Array [4] = T
Array [4] = U [Newly inserted element]

Index	Info
0	C
1	O
2	M
3	P
4	T
5	E
6	R
7	
8	S
9	C
10	I
11	E
12	N
13	C
14	E
15	
16	
17	

Fig. 4.5 Array before insertion

The size of the array is also changed from 15 to 16. After insertion the array becomes like **Fig. 4.6.** Consider another example, suppose we have an array **LIST** with 15 rooms as illustrated in **Fig. 4.7.** Suppose we want to insert integer 255 in the list at position 10. The insertion is not possible because there is no free room in **LIST**. Thus before making an insertion into an array one should first of all check for the available room in the array. For it, there is very simple way subtracting occupied space from maximum size of an array one can get the number of available rooms.

Index	Info
0	C
1	O
2	M
3	P
4	U
5	T
6	E
7	R
8	
9	S
10	C
11	I
12	E
13	N
14	C
15	E
16	
17	

Fig. 4.6 Array after inserting U

Index	Info
0	11
1	22
2	33
3	44
4	55
5	66
6	77
7	88
8	99
9	100
10	111
11	122
12	133
13	144
14	155

Fig. 4.7 Array with no free room

The insertion algorithm is illustrated in **Fig. 4.8** and its implementation is illustrated by **ARRAY_I.C** program segment.

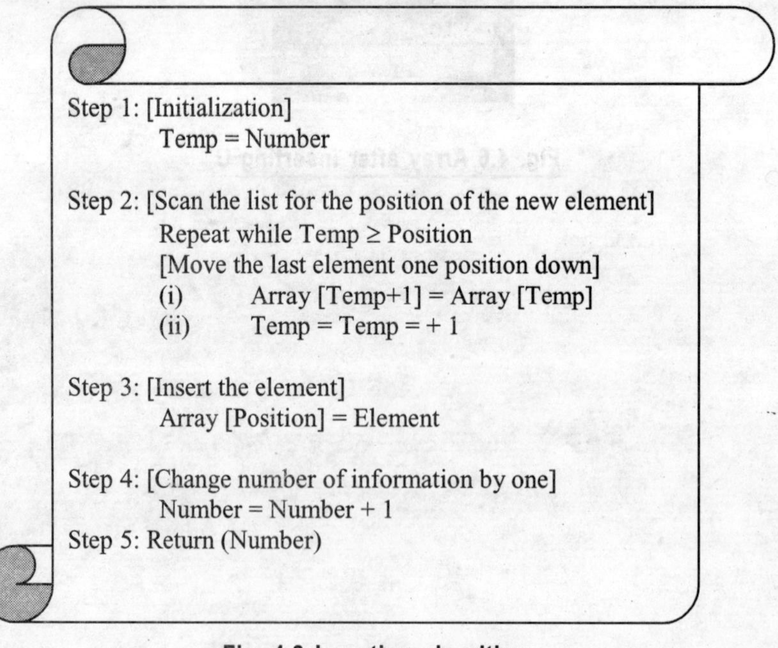

Step 1: [Initialization]
Temp = Number

Step 2: [Scan the list for the position of the new element]
Repeat while Temp ≥ Position
[Move the last element one position down]
(i) Array [Temp+1] = Array [Temp]
(ii) Temp = Temp = + 1

Step 3: [Insert the element]
Array [Position] = Element

Step 4: [Change number of information by one]
Number = Number + 1

Step 5: Return (Number)

Fig. 4.8 Insertion algorithm

```
// Inserting an element into linear array at specified position
// ARRAY_I.C

# include<iostream.h>

class insertion
{
    public:
        int insert_array(char *, int, int, char);
        void input(char *, int );
        void display(char *, int );
};

// Definition of the function

int insertion :: insert_array(char array[], int number, int position, char element)
{
    int temp = number;
    while( temp >= position)
    {
        array[temp+1] = array[temp];
        temp --;
    }

    array[position] = element;
    number = number +1 ;
    return(number);
}

// Input function to read data

void insertion :: input(char array[], int number)
{
    for(int i = 1; i<= number ; i++)
    {
        cout<<"\n Input value for : "<<i<<" : ";
        cin>>array[i];
    }
}

// OUTPUT FUNCTION TO PRINT ON THE CONSOLE

void insertion :: display(char array[], int number)
{
    for(int i = 1; i<= number; i++)
    {
```

```
        cout<<"\n Value at the position: "<<i<<" : "<<array[i];
    }
}

// main function

void main()
{
    insertion insert;
    int number;
    char array[100];
    int position;
    char element;
    cout<<"\n Input the number of element into the LIST:";
    cin>>number;
    insert.input(array, number);
    cout<<"\n Entered list as follows:\n";
    insert.display(array, number);
    cout<<"\n Input the position where you want add a new data:";
    cin>>position;
    cout<<"\n Input the value for the position:";
    cin>>element;
    number = insert.insert_array(array, number, position, element);
    insert.display(array, number);
}
```

```
Input the number of element into the LIST: 15
Input value for : 0 : C
Input value for : 1 : O
Input value for : 2 : M
Input value for : 3 : P
Input value for : 4 : T
Input value for : 5 : E
Input value for : 6 : R
Input value for : 7 :
Input value for : 8 : S
Input value for : 9 : C
Input value for : 10 : I
Input value for : 11 : E
Input value for : 12 : N
Input value for : 13 : C
Input value for : 14 : E
Entered list is as follows:
Value at the position: 1 : C
Value at the position: 2 : O
Value at the position: 3 : M
Value at the position: 4 : P
Value at the position: 5 : T
Value at the position: 6 : E
Value at the position: 7 : R
Value at the position: 8 :
Value at the position: 9 : S
Value at the position: 10 : C
Value at the position: 11 : I
Value at the position: 12 : E
Value at the position: 13 : N
Value at the position: 14 : C
Value at the position: 15 : E
Input the position where you want add a new data: 4 ( That is from 0 to 4 means 5)
Input the value for the position: U
Value at the position: 1 : C
Value at the position: 2 : O
Value at the position: 3 : M
Value at the position: 4 : P
Value at the position: 5 : U
Value at the position: 6 : T
Value at the position: 7 : E
Value at the position: 8 : R
Value at the position: 9 :
Value at the position: 10 : S
Value at the position: 11 : C
Value at the position: 12 : I
Value at the position: 13 : E
Value at the position: 14 : N
Value at the position: 15 : C
Value at the position: 16 : E
```

4.6 DELETION FROM ONE DIMENSIONAL ARRAY

Deleting an element or information from the end of an array is simple but deleting an element from some other position is difficult and requires moving all the element up-word to fill-up the gap into the array. Before deleting an element from an array one should go through the following points:

- *Delete an element if it is known then find whether it is in the array or not.*
- *Delete an element if its value is known. The value is searched in the array.*
- *Update the array.*

Index	Info
0	DON
1	TOM
2	HITLER
3	CHARLES
4	JONES
5	CHAIPPEL
6	BOTHOM
7	DESMOND
8	LARA
9	RACHITA

Fig. 4.9 List of employes EMPLOY

Index	Info
0	DON
1	TOM
2	HITLER
3	CHARLES
4	CHAIPPEL
5	BOTHOM
6	DESMOND
7	LARA
8	RACHITA
9	

Fig. 4.10 List of employes after leaving JONES EMPLOY

For example, suppose we have list of 10 employes **EMPLOY** as illustrated in **Fig. 4.9**. If **Mr. JONES** leaves the organization, so it is required to update the employee list. To update the employee list following steps are made:

Position of Mr. JONES in the list is 5

EMPLOY [4] = EMPLOY [5] = CHAIPPEL
EMPLOY [5] = EMPLOY [6] = BOTHOM
EMPLOY [6] = EMPLOY [7] = DESMOND
EMPLOY [7] = EMPLOY [8] = LARA
EMPLOY [8] = EMPLOY [9] = RACHITA
EMPLOY [10] = NULL

The resulting employee list is illustrated in **Fig. 4.10.** The deletion algorithm illustrated in **Fig. 4.11** and implemented as **ARRAY_D.C.**

Step 1: [Initialization]
  Element = Array [Position] [Keep information of deleted item]
Step 2: [Make copy of the position]
  Temp = Position
Step 3: [Update the list, Number represents number of items in the list]
  Repeat while Temp ≤ Number – 1
    (i) Array [Temp] = Array [Temp + 1]
    (ii) Temp = Temp + 1

Step 4: [Decrease size of information in the list by one]
  Number = Number + 1

Step 5: Return (Number)

Fig. 4.11 Deletion algorithm

```
// Deleting from a linear array at specified position
// ARRAY_D.C

# include<iostream.h>
# define s 20
char employ[s][s];

class deletion
{
    public:
        int delete_array(char employ[s][s], int, int, char *);
        void input(char emply[s][s], int );
        void display(char employ[s][s], int );
};

// Definition of the function
```

```
int deletion :: delete_array(char employ[s][s], int number, int position, char element[])
{
      element = employ[position];
      cout<<"\n Information which we have to delete:"<<element;
      int temp = position;
      while( temp <= number -1
      {
          *employ [temp] = *employ[temp+1];
          temp ++;
      }

      number = number - 1 ;
      return(number);
}

void deletion :: input(char employ[s][s], int number)
{
      for(int i = 1; i<= number ; i++)
      {
          cout<<"\n Input value for : "<<i<<" : ";
          cin>>employ[i];
      }
}

void deletion :: display(char employ[s][s], int number)
{
      for(int i = 1; i<= number; i++)
      {
          cout<<"\n Value at the position: "<<i<<" : "<<employ[i];
      }
}

// main function

void main()
{
      deletion deleting;
      int number;

      int position;
      char element[s];

      cout<<"\n Input the number of elements in the array:";
      cin>>number;
```

```
    deleting.input(employ, number);
    cout<<"\n Entered list is as follows:\n";

    deleting.display(employ,number);

    cout<<"\n !nput the position from where you want to delete an element:";
    cin>>position;

    number = deleting.delete_array(employ, number, position, element);
    deleting.display(employ, number);
}
```

```
Input the number of elements in the array: 10
Input value for: 1: DON
Input value for: 2: TOM
Input value for: 3: HITLER
Input value for: 4: CHARLES
Input value for: 5: JONES
Input value for: 6: CHAIPPEL
Input value for: 7: BOTHOM
Input value for: 8: DESMOND
Input value for: 9: LARA
Input value for: 10: RACHITA
Entered list is as follows:

Value at the position: 1: DON
Value at the position: 2: TOM
Value at the position: 3: HITLER
Value at the position: 4: CHARLES
Value at the position: 5: JONES
Value at the position: 6: CHAIPPEL
Value at the position: 7: BOTHOM
Value at the position: 8: DEMOND
Value at the position: 9: LARA
Value at the position: 10: RACHITA
Input the position from where you want to delete an element: 9

Value at the position: 1: DON
Value at the position: 2: TOM
Value at the position: 3: HITLER
Value at the position: 4: CHARLES
Value at the position: 5: JONES
Value at the position: 6: CHAIPPEL
Value at the position: 7: BOTHOM
Value at the position: 8: DEMOND
Value at the position: 9: LARA
```

If in a list same information happens to be more than one place then the repeated information is called duplicate. The removal of such duplicates is very necessary in some applications. Because if some one is accessing an information from a list but does not know about its duplication and modifying such an information in one place can cause inconsistency.

For example, suppose we have a list of 15 elements as illustrated in **Fig. 4.12.** It is clear that 11 exists at 4 places, 77 at 3 and 88 at 2 places. Suppose, we want to remove duplicates from the list. First of all we consider the first element in the list and start scanning for the next occurrences of it. It is found at position 8. Now from position 8 move, one position up-word each element of the array. In **Fig. 4.12** first element is 11 and it is repeated at position 8 that is

Position = 8 [FROM 0 TO 7]
LIST [7] = LIST [8] = 100
LIST [8] = LIST [9] = 22
LIST [9] = LIST [10] = 11
LIST [10] LIST [11] = 77
LIST [11] = LIST [12] = 88
LIST [12] = LIST [13] = 77
LIST [13] = LIST [14] = 11
LIST [14] = NULL

Index	Info
0	11
1	13
2	14
3	44
4	99
5	88
6	77
7	11
8	100
9	22
10	11
11	77
12	88
13	77
14	11
15	

Fig. 4.12 List of information

After first iteration the list becomes as shown in **Fig. 4.13**. Again we start scanning for the next occurrence of 11 in the list. By scanning the list, we find the next occurrence of 11 at position 10.

LIST [9] = LIST [10] = 77
LIST [10] = LIST [11] = 88
LIST [11] = LIST [12] = 77

LIST [12] = LIST [13] = 11

After second iteration the resulting list is as shown in **Fig. 4.14.** After third iteration resulting list is shown as in **Fig. 4.15.**

Index	Info
0	11
1	13
2	14
3	44
4	99
5	88
6	77
7	100
8	22
9	11
10	77
11	88
12	77
13	11
14	
15	

Fig. 4.13 List after eliminating 11 at position 8

Index	Info
0	11
1	13
2	14
3	44
4	99
5	88
6	77
7	100
8	22
9	77
10	88
11	77
12	11
13	
14	
15	

Fig. 4.14 List after eliminating 11 at position 10

Index	Info
0	11
1	13
2	14
3	44
4	99
5	88
6	77
7	100
8	22
9	77
10	88
11	77
12	
13	
14	
15	

Fig. 4.15 List after eliminating 11 at position 13

Index	Info
0	11
1	13
2	14
3	44
4	99
5	88
6	77
7	100
8	22
9	
10	
11	
12	
13	
14	
15	

Fig. 4.16 List after eliminating all the duplicates

Now choose second element in the list and repeat the above process and it is continued till all the duplicates are removed from the list. Final list after elimination of all the duplicates is illustrated in **Fig. 4.16.** The algorithm to remove duplicates from a list is given in **Fig. 4.17.** The program segment **DUPL_A.C** implements the duplicate removal algorithm.

Step 1: [Initialization]
    Duplicate = Number [Number of elements in the list]
Step 2: [Set flag]
    Status = 0
Step 3: [Check and remove duplicates]
    Repeat through Step 8 for I = 0, 1, 2 ...N – 2
Step 4: Repeat through Step 8 for J = I+1, I+2 ...N – 1
Step 5: If Array [I] = Array [J]
    N = N – 1
Step 6: Repeat for K = J, J+1 ... N – 1
    Array [K] = Array [K+1]
Step 7: [Set flag]
    Status = 1
Step 8: J = J – 1
Step 9: If Status = 0
    Output "No duplicate is found"
Step 10: [Find total duplicates in the list]
    Duplicate = Duplicate – Number
Step 11: [Return the total duplicates in the list]
    Return (Duplicate)

Fig. 4.17 Duplicate removal algorithm

```
// Deleting duplicates from a linear array
// DUPL_A.C

# include<iostream.h>
# include<stdio.h>

class duplicate
{
	private:
		int status ;
		int dup;
```

```
    public:
        int duplicate_array(int *, int);
        void input(int *, int );
        void display(int *, int );
};

// Definition of the function

int duplicate :: duplicate_array(int array[], int number)
{
    status = 0;
    dup = number;
    for(int i = 0; i< number-1; i++)
        for(int j = i+1; j< number; j++)
        {
            if(array[i] == array[j])
            {
                number = number - 1 ;
                for(int k = j; k<number; k++)
                    array[k] = array[k+1];
                status = 1;
                j = j - 1;
            }
        }
    if( status ==0)
        cout<<"\n No duplicate is found";
    return(dup-number);
}

// Input function to read data

void duplicate :: input(int array[], int number)
{
    for(int i = 0; i< number ; i++)
    {
        cout<<"Input value for : "<<i+1<<" : ";
        cin>>array[i];
    }
}

// Output function

void duplicate :: display(int array[], int number)
{
    for(int i = 0; i< number; i++)
    {
```

```
        cout<<"\n Value at the position: "<<i+1<<" : "<<array[i];
    }
}

// main function

void main()
{
    duplicate dup;
    int number;
    int array[100];
    int n;
    cout<<"\n Input the number of elements in the list:";
    cin>>number;
    dup.input(array, number);
    cout<<"\n Entered list is as follows: \n";

    dup.display(array,number);

    n = dup.duplicate_array(array, number);
    cout<<"\n Number of duplicate elements in the list are :"<< n;
    cout<<"\n After removing duplicates from the list, the list is as follows:";
    dup.display(array, number-n);
}
```

```
Input the number of elements in the list: 15
Input value for: 1: 11
Input value for: 2: 13
Input value for: 3: 14
Input value for: 4: 44
Input value for: 5: 99
Input value for: 6: 88
Input value for: 7: 77
Input value for: 8: 11
Input value for: 9: 100
Input value for: 10: 22
Input value for: 11: 11
Input value for: 12: 77
Input value for: 13: 88
Input value for: 14: 77
Input value for: 15: 11
Entered list is as follows:

Value at the position: 1: 11
Value at the position: 2: 13
Value at the position: 3: 14
Value at the position: 4: 44
Value at the position: 5: 99
Value at the position: 6: 88
Value at the position: 7: 77
Value at the position: 8: 11
Value at the position: 9: 100
Value at the position: 10: 22
Value at the position: 11: 11
Value at the position: 12: 77
Value at the position: 13: 88
Value at the position: 14: 77
Value at the position: 15: 11
Number of duplicate elements in the list is: 6
After removing duplicates from the list, the list is as follows:
Value at the position: 1: 11
Value at the position: 2: 13
Value at the position: 3: 14
Value at the position: 4: 44
Value at the position: 5: 99
Value at the position: 6: 88
Value at the position: 7: 77
Value at the position: 8: 100
Value at the position: 9: 22
```

4.7 SEARCHING

Index	Info
0	MORE
1	DAVID
2	TOM
3	THOMPSON
4	ARVIND
5	SANATH
6	MAJID
7	KIRAN
8	DEEPAK
9	MISHTHU
10	
11	
12	
13	
14	
15	

Fig. 4.18 List employee EMPLOY

Index	Info
0	MORE
1	DAVID
2	TOM
3	THOMPSON
4	ARVIND
5	SANATH
6	MAJID
7	KIRAN
8	DEEPAK
9	MISHTHU
10	JONES
11	
12	
13	
14	
15	

Fig. 4.19 List employee EMPLOY after adding Mr. JONES

Suppose a specific **INFO** information is given in an array. Searching refers to the operation of finding the location of the **INFO** in an array or output some message if **INFO** does not exist in the array. The search is said to be successful if **INFO** appears in the array else it is called unsuccessful. Sometimes it is required to add **INFO** in the array if it does not exist.

For example, suppose we have a list of employees **EMPLOY** as illustrated in **Fig. 4.18**. Mr. **JONES** joins the institute and it is required to update the database **EMPLOY**. Before any insertion into the list, it is required to scan the list of employees to find some other employee with similar name. If in the list there is no other employee with name **JONES**, insert the name Mr. **JONES** into the list. After inserting Mr. **JONES** in the employee list the new list is illustrated in **Fig. 4.19.**

Index	Info
0	22
1	99
2	10
3	1
4	100
5	200
6	999
7	88
8	77
9	
10	
11	
12	
13	
14	
15	

Fig. 4.20 List of integers in memory

We shall have more discussion on sorting, searching, and merging, in **Chapter 9.**

Sometimes it is required to find maximum and minimum elements in a list. For example, if we have a list of 9 elements as illustrated in **Fig. 4.20,** then by inspection one can easily say 999 is maximum and is minimum element in the list. When a list becomes very large it is very difficult to perform such type of operation by inspection. By inspection one can say that 7th element is the largest and 4th element is the smallest in the given list. But the actual operation that is performed by a computer is quite different and can be described as follows:

Big = Small = List [0] = 22
List [1] > Big that is 99 > 22. The value of **Big** requires to be change.

Big = List [1] = 99
List [1] > Small that is 99 > 22. The value of **Small** will remain unchanged.
List [2] < Big that is 10 < 99. The value of **Big** will remain unchanged.
List [2] < Small that is 10 < 22. The value of **Small** requires to be change.
Small = List [2] = 10

```
Step 1: [Initialization]
        Temp = 0
Step 2: [Consider the first element of the list as Big and Small]
        Big = Small = List [0]

Step 3: [Check whether the size of the list is 1]
        If N = 1
                Then
                        Big = Small = List [0]

Step 4: [Check whether the size of the list is 2]
        If N = 2
            Then
                If List [0] < List [1]
                    Then
                        Big = List [1]
                        Small = List [0]
                    Else
                        Big = List [0]
                        Small = List [1]

Step 5: [This step is performed if the number of elements in the
list is more than 2]
        Big = Small = List [0]
        Repeat while Temp ≤ N
            If List [Temp] > Big
                Big = List [Temp]
            Else if List [Temp] < Small
                Small = List [Temp]
Step 6: Temp = Temp + 1
Step 7: Output Small and Big
Step 8: Exit
```

Fig. 4.21 Algorithm to find smallest and largest element

List [3] < Big that is 1 < 99. The value of **Big** will remain unchanged.
List [3] < Small that is 1 < 10. The value of **Small** requires to change.
Small = List [3] = 1

If we will continue this process at the end of process we will get

Small = 1 Smallest element in the list
Big = 999 Largest element in the list

The algorithm to find out smallest and largest in a list is illustrated in **Fig. 4.21.** The program segment **S_L_S_A.C** implements the above discussion.

```
// Searching for largest and smallest elements in a linear array
// S_L_S_A.C

# include<iostream.h>

int s;
class search
{
    private:
        int small,big,temp;

    public:
        int search_array(int *, int);
        void input(int *, int );
        void display(int *, int );
};

// Definition of the function

int search:: search_array(int array[], int number)
{
    big = small = array[0];
    temp = 0;

    while( temp < number)
    {
        if(array[temp] > big)
        {
            big = array[temp] ;
        }
        else if( array[temp] < small)
        {
            small = array[temp];
        }
```

```
            temp ++;
        }
        s = small;
        return(big);
}

// Input function

void search :: input(int array[], int number)
{
        for(int i = 0; i< number ; i++)
        {
            cout<<"Input value for : "<<i+1<<" : ";
            cin>>array[i];
        }
}

// Output function

void search :: display(int array[], int number)
{
        for(int i = 0; i< number; i++)
        {
            cout<<"\n Value at the position: "<<i+1<<" : "<<array[i];
        }
}

// main function

void main()
{
        search searching;
        int number, big;
        int array[100];

        cout<<"\n Input the number of elements in the list:";
        cin>>number;
        searching.input(array, number);
        cout<<"\n Entered list is as follows: \n";

        searching.display(array, number);

        big = searching.search_array(array, number);
        cout<<"\n Largest number in the array is :"<<big;
        cout<<"\n Smallest number in the array is :"<<s;
}
```

```
Input the number of elements in the list:9
 Input value for : 1 :22
 Input value for : 2 :99
 Input value for : 3 :10
 Input value for : 4 :1
 Input value for : 5 :100
 Input value for : 6 :200
 Input value for : 7 :99
 Input value for : 8 :88
 Input value for : 9 :77
 Entered list is as follows:

 Value at the position: 1 : 22
 Value at the position: 2 : 99
 Value at the position: 3 : 10
 Value at the position: 4 : 1
 Value at the position: 5 : 100
 Value at the position: 6 : 200
 Value at the position: 7 : 999
 Value at the position: 8 : 88
 Value at the position: 9 : 77
Largest number in the array is :999
Smallest number in the array is :1
```

4.8 MULTI DIMENSIONAL ARRAYS

Most of the programming languages permit two, three, four, five and more dimensional arrays whereas an element is referenced by more than one subscript. If an array is two-dimensional then two subscripts are used to reference an element in the array. Similarly, if the array is a three-dimensional then three subscripts are used to reference an element of the array. **C, C++** and **Visual C/C++** languages permit 1, 2, 3, 4 or more dimensional arrays, whereas **BASIC** language permits only 1, 2 and 3 dimensional arrays. The advanced versions of **BASIC, Visual BASIC** permit arrays as permitted by **C, C++** and **Visual C/C++** languages.

ROW COLUMN

	0	1	2
0	11	33	22
1	22	44	11
2	33	55	99
3	44	66	88
4	55	66	77

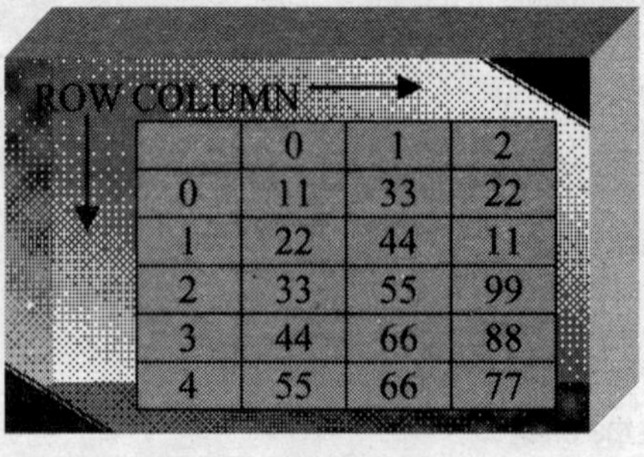

Fig. 4.22 Two dimensional array

Table 4.1 represents array in different languages. **Fig. 4.22** illustrates a two-dimensional array, one can also implement 3-D, 4-D, 5-D or more dimensional matrices according to applications requirement and limitation of a language.

Table 4.1 Different types of arrays in different languages

Dimension	Basic	Fortran	Pascal	C, C++ And Visual C/C++
1-D	MAT(5)	MAT(5)	MAT[1..5]	MAT[5]
2-D	MAT(5,5)	MAT(5,5)	MAT[1..5,1..5]	MAT[5][5]
3-D	MAT(5,5,5)	MAT(5,5,5)	MAT[1..5,1..5,1..5]	MAT[5][5][5]

4.8.1 TWO DIMENSIONAL ARRAYS

Suppose **Mat** is a two dimensional array with **Row** number of rows and **Col** number of columns. Then one may define array **Mat** as a collection of **Row x Col** information. Each element of the array **Mat** is accessed by specified pairs of integers called subscripts. If **I** and **J** are integers and are used to access information from a two-dimensional array **Mat**, then there should be following relations among subscript variable **I** and **J**, and rows and columns maximum limit:

$$\left.\begin{array}{l} 0 \le I < Row \\ 0 \le J < Col \end{array}\right\} \text{For C, C++ and Visual C/C++ languages.}$$

$$\left.\begin{array}{l} 1 \le I \le Row \\ 1 \le J \le Col \end{array}\right\} \text{For other popular languages e.g. FORTAN, etc.}$$

Two-dimensional arrays are called matrices in mathematics and tables in business applications. There is a standard way for drawing a two dimensional **Row x Col** array **Mat**. The elements of **Mat** form a rectangular array with **Row** rows and **Col** columns. The element **Mat [I][J]** appears in row **I** and column **J**. A row is a horizontal list of elements and a column is a vertical list of elements. In the field of database a row is called a tupple. **Fig. 4.23** illustrates a two-dimensional array **Mat** with 6 rows and 5 columns.

Suppose GBPEC Company decides to purchase some high speed computing machines and calls quotations from 10 reputed companies of market. GBPEC calls quotations for the Main Frame computers, Mini Computers, Pentium Systems, Dumb Nodes and Printers. The company quotes unit price for each said system. After collecting quotations the purchase assistant is asked to make comparative chart for the systems. It is assumed that highly reputed company should be at top of the list. The chart prepared by purchase assistant is illustrated in **Fig. 4.24.** From **Fig. 4.24** it is clear that the chart prepared by the purchase assistant is a two dimensional array **Purchase [10][5],** where row number represents company and columns represents price quoted in **Lac** against items. If we consider third row that represents XYZ Company then we can say that

COLUMN →

ROW ↓

Mat [0][0]	Mat [0][1]	Mat [0][2]	Mat [0][3]	Mat [0][4]
Mat [1][0]	Mat [1][1]	Mat [1][2]	Mat [1][3]	Mat [1][4]
Mat [2][0]	Mat [2][1]	Mat [2][2]	Mat [2][3]	Mat [2][4]
Mat [3][0]	Mat [3][1]	Mat [3][2]	Mat [3][3]	Mat [3][4]
Mat [4][0]	Mat [4][1]	Mat [4][2]	Mat [4][3]	Mat [4][4]
Mat [5][0]	Mat [5][1]	Mat [5][2]	Mat [5][3]	Mat [5][4]

Fig. 4.23 Two dimensional representation of an array

COMPARATIVE CHART FOR NEW PURCHASE OF SYSTEMS

Company	Main Frame	Mini System	Pentium System	Dumb Node	Printer
1	26.10	5.0	0.70	0.11	2.00
2	26.50	5.2	0.80	0.125	1.99
3	26.10	5.4	0.75	0.127	2.10
4	27.01	5.5	0.80	0.11	1.75
5	26.40	4.9	0.75	0.120	1.80
6	25.95	4.8	0.76	0.115	1.81
7	24.56	4.98	0.77	0.14	1.99
8	28.09	5.01	0.80	0.13	2.0
9	26.75	5.2	0.84	0.12	2.10
10	26.50	5.0	0.72	0.115	1.90

Note: All prices are in Lac

Fig. 4.24 Two dimensional Table

Purchase [3][1] = 26.10 Lacs for Main Frame
Purchase [3][2] = 5.40 Lacs for Mini System
Purchase [3][3] = 0.75Lacs for Pentium System
Purchase [3][4] = 0.127Lacs for Dumb Node
Purchase [3][5] = 2.10 Lacs for Printer

Suppose **Mat** is a two dimensional **Row x Col** array. The first dimension of **Mat** contains the index set **0, 1, 2 ... Row-1** with lower bound **0** and upper bound **Row – 1** and the second dimension contains the index set **0, 1, 2 ... Col - 1** with lower bound **0** and upper bound **Col – 1**. This array is **Row x Col.**

Some programming languages allow one to define multidimensional arrays in which the lower bounds is 1 and rather than 0. However, the index set for each dimension still consists of the consecutive integers from lower bound to the upper bound of the dimension. The length of a given dimension can be obtained by

Length = Upper bound – Lower bound + 1

Column → / Row ↓	10	11	12	13	14	15
6	1	2	3	4	5	6
7	7	8	9	10	11	12
8	13	14	15	16	17	18
9	19	20	21	22	23	24
10	25	26	27	28	29	30

Fig. 4.25 Two dimensional array in memory

For example, suppose we have an array as illustrated in **Fig. 4.25.** The length of each dimension may be

Row = Upper bound – Lower bound + 1

⇨ 10 – 6 + 1

⇨ 5

Col = Upper bound – Lower bound – 1

⇨ 15 – 10 + 1

⇨ 6

The size of the array shown in **Fig. 4.25** will be

⇨ Row * Col

⇨ 5 * 6
⇨ 30

4.8.2 REPRESENTATION OF TWO DIMENSIONAL ARRAYS IN MEMORY

Let **Mat** be a two-dimensional **Row x Col** array. Although **Mat** is represented as a rectangular array of elements with **Row** rows and **Col** columns, the array will be represented in the memory by a block of **Row x Col** sequential memory locations. The **Mat** array may be stored in the memory in one of the following way:

(i) Column by column that is in column major order
(ii) Row by row that is in row major order

Mat

Row	Column	Info
0	0	11
1	0	12
2	0	13
3	0	14
0	1	21
1	1	22
2	1	23
3	1	24
0	2	31
1	2	32
2	2	33
3	2	34
0	3	41
1	3	42
2	3	43
3	3	44
0	4	51
1	4	52
2	4	53
3	4	54
0	5	61
1	5	62
2	5	63
3	5	64

Represents column number

(a) Column major order

Mat

Row	Column	Info
0	0	11
0	1	21
0	2	31
0	3	41
0	4	51
0	5	61
1	0	12
1	1	22
1	2	32
1	3	42
1	4	52
1	5	62
2	0	13
2	1	23
2	2	33
2	3	43
2	4	53
2	5	63
3	0	14
3	1	24
3	2	34
3	3	44
3	4	54
3	5	64

Represents row number

(b) Row major order

Fig. 4.26 Two dimensional array in memory

Fig. 4.26 illustrates the different memory representation of a two-dimensional array **Mat.** **Fig. 4.27** illustrates two-dimensional array in memory.

Mat

Column	Address	Info
0	0x1884fe 62	1
	0x1884fe8a	5
	0x1884feb2	9
1	0x1884fe66	2
	0x1884fe8e	6
	0x1884feb6	10
2	0x1884fe6a	3
	0x1884fe92	7
	0x1884feba	11
3	0x1884fe6e	4
	0x1884fe96	8
	0x1884febe	12

Represents column number

(a) Column major order

Mat

Row	Address	Info
0	0x1884fe62	1
	0x1884fe66	2
	0x1884fe6a	3
	0x1884fe6e	4
1	0x1884fe8a	5
	0x1884fe8e	6
	0x1884fe92	7
	0x1884fe96	8
2	0x1884feb2	9
	0x1884feb6	10
	0x1884feba	11
	0x1884febe	12

Represents row number

(b) Row major order

Fig. 4.27 Two dimensional array in memory

4.8.3 TRAVERSING TWO DIMENSIONAL ARRAYS

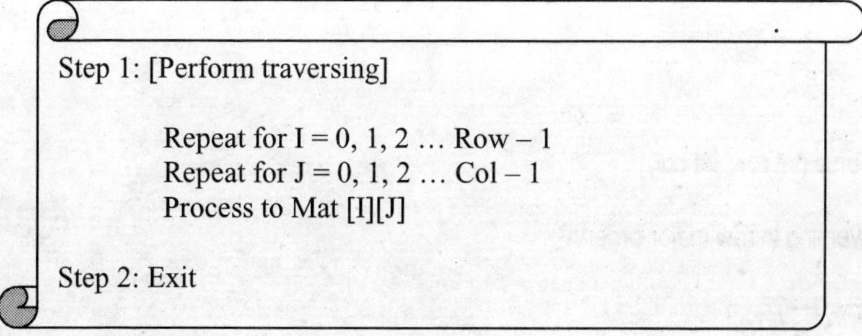
Step 1: [Perform traversing]

Repeat for I = 0, 1, 2 … Row – 1
Repeat for J = 0, 1, 2 … Col – 1
Process to Mat [I][J]

Step 2: Exit

Fig. 4.28 Algorithm to traverse a two-dimensional array in row major order

Traversing of a two-dimensional array can be classified into two categories, depending upon the two types of representation:

(i) Column major order
(ii) Row major order

Note that the traversing in above two techniques is different. The program segment **TWO_D_A_.C** illustrates the two traversing algorithms.

Step 1: [Perform traversing]

Repeat for J = 0, 1, 2 … Col – 1
Repeat for I = 0, 1, 2 … Row – 1
Process to Mat [I][J]

Step 2: Exit

Fig. 4.29 Algorithm to traverse a two dimensional array in column major order

```
// Traversing a two dimensional array

// TWO_D_A_.C

# include<iostream.h>
# include<iomanip.h>

class Two_D
{
      private:
            int i, j;
            float mat[10][10];

      public:
            void Traverse ( int, int);
            void input( int, int);
};

// Display function

void Two_D :: Traverse (int row, int col)
{
      cout<<"\n Traversing in row major order\n";

      for( i = 0; i < row; i++)
      {
            for( j = 0; j < col; j++)
            {
                  cout<<"\n"<<&mat[i][j];
                  cout<<" "<<mat[i][j];
            }
```

```
        cout<<"\n";
    }

    cout<<"\n Traversing in column major order\n";

    for( j = 0; j < col; j++)
    {
        for( i = 0; i < row; i++)
        {
            cout<<" \n"<<&mat[i][j];
            cout<<" "<<mat[i][j];
        }
        cout<<"\n";
    }
    cout<<"\n Traversing in row major order\n";

    for( i = 0; i < row; i++)
    {
        for( j = 0; j < col; j++)
        {
            cout<<" mat["<<i<<"]"<<"["<<j<<"] = ";
            cout<<" "<<mat[i][j];
        }
        cout<<"\n";
    }

    cout<<"\n Traversing in column major order\n";

    for( j = 0; j < col; j++)
    {
        for( i = 0; i < row; i++)
        {
            cout<<" mat["<<i<<"]"<<"["<<j<<"] = ";
            cout<<" "<<mat[i][j];
        }
        cout<<"\n";
    }
}

// Input function

void Two_D :: input( int row, int col)
{

    for( i = 0 ; i< row; i++)
    {
```

```
        for( j = 0 ; j<col; j++)
        {
            cout<<"\nInput Value for : "<< i+1 <<" : "<<j+1<<" : " ;
            cin>>mat[i][j];
        }
    }
}

// main function

void main()
{
    Two_D Trav;
    int r,c;
    cout<<"\n Input the number of rows:";
    cin>>r;
    cout<<" Input the number of cols:";
    cin>>c;
    Trav.input(r,c);
    Trav.Traverse(r, c);
}
```

```
Traversing in row major order

mat[0][0] =  1 mat[0][1] =  2 mat[0][2] =  3 mat[0][3] =  4
mat[1][0] =  5 mat[1][1] =  6 mat[1][2] =  7 mat[1][3] =  8
mat[2][0] =  9 mat[2][1] =  10 mat[2][2] =  11 mat[2][3] = 12

Traversing in column major order

mat[0][0] =  1 mat[1][0] =  5 mat[2][0] =  9
mat[0][1] =  2 mat[1][1] =  6 mat[2][1] =  10
mat[0][2] =  3 mat[1][2] =  7 mat[2][2] =  11
mat[0][3] =  4 mat[1][3] =  8 mat[2][3] =  12
```

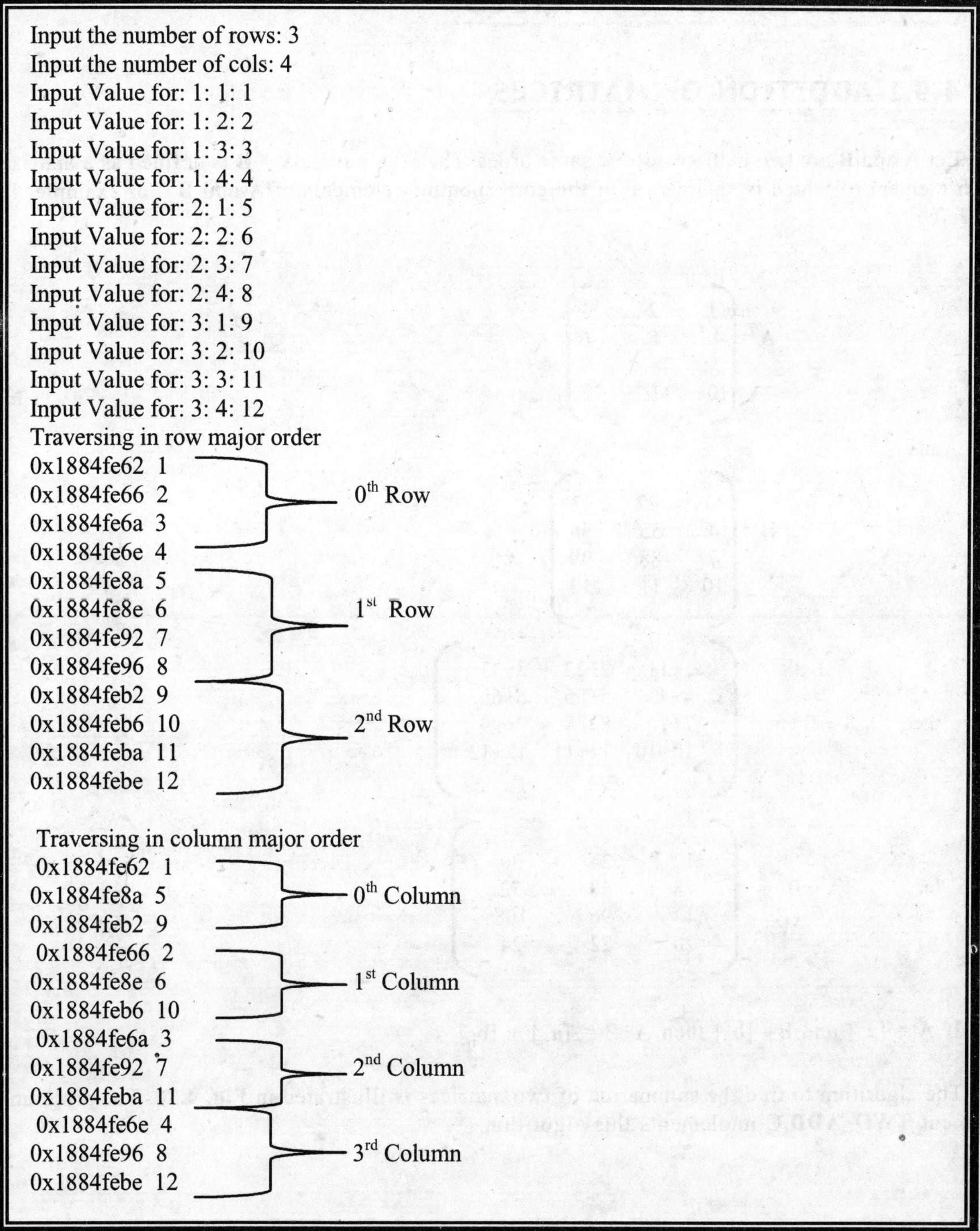

```
Input the number of rows: 3
Input the number of cols: 4
Input Value for: 1: 1: 1
Input Value for: 1: 2: 2
Input Value for: 1: 3: 3
Input Value for: 1: 4: 4
Input Value for: 2: 1: 5
Input Value for: 2: 2: 6
Input Value for: 2: 3: 7
Input Value for: 2: 4: 8
Input Value for: 3: 1: 9
Input Value for: 3: 2: 10
Input Value for: 3: 3: 11
Input Value for: 3: 4: 12
Traversing in row major order
0x1884fe62 1
0x1884fe66 2
0x1884fe6a 3
0x1884fe6e 4
0x1884fe8a 5
0x1884fe8e 6
0x1884fe92 7
0x1884fe96 8
0x1884feb2 9
0x1884feb6 10
0x1884feba 11
0x1884febe 12

Traversing in column major order
0x1884fe62 1
0x1884fe8a 5
0x1884feb2 9
0x1884fe66 2
0x1884fe8e 6
0x1884feb6 10
0x1884fe6a 3
0x1884fe92 7
0x1884feba 11
0x1884fe6e 4
0x1884fe96 8
0x1884febe 12
```

4.9 ALGEBRA OF MATRICES

4.9.1 ADDITION OF MATRICES

Let **A** and **B** are two matrices of the same order. Then their sum, **A + B** is defined as a matrix, each element of which is summation of the corresponding elements of **A** and **B**. For example, if we have

$$A = \begin{pmatrix} 1 & 2 & 3 \\ 4 & 5 & 6 \\ 7 & 8 & 9 \\ 10 & 11 & 12 \end{pmatrix}$$

and

$$B = \begin{pmatrix} 11 & 22 & 33 \\ 4 & 55 & 66 \\ 7 & 88 & 99 \\ 10 & 11 & 12 \end{pmatrix}$$

then $$A + B = \begin{pmatrix} 1+11 & 2+22 & 3+33 \\ 4+4 & 5+55 & 6+66 \\ 7+7 & 8+88 & 9+99 \\ 10+10 & 11+11 & 12+12 \end{pmatrix}$$

or $$A + B = \begin{pmatrix} 12 & 24 & 36 \\ 8 & 60 & 72 \\ 14 & 96 & 108 \\ 20 & 22 & 24 \end{pmatrix}$$

If $A = [a_{ij}]$ and $B= [b_{ij}]$ then $A+B = [a_{ij}] + [b_{ij}]$

The algorithm to find the summation of two matrices is illustrated in **Fig. 4.30.** The program segment **TWO_ADD.C** implements this algorithm.

Step 1: [Check possibility of addition]
If $Row_1 = Row_2$ and Col_1 to Col_2
Output "Addition is Possible"
Else
Output "Addition is not possible" and Exit

Step 2: Repeat for I = 0, 1, 2 … Row – 1
Repeat for J = 0, 1, 2 … Col – 1
Mat_Res [I][J] = Mat_1 [I][J]+Mat_2 [I][J]
Step 3: Exit

Fig. 4.30 Algorithm to add two matrices

```
// Add Tow Matrices
// TWO_ADD.C

# include<iostream.h>
# include<iomanip.h>
# include<stdlib.h>
# define row 10
# define col 10

class Two_D
{
    public:
        int i, j;
        int row1, col1);
        int row2, col2);
        float mat1[row][col];
        float mat2[row][col];
        float mat_res[row][col];
    public:
        void mat_add( float mat1[row][col], int, int,
        float mat2[row][col], int, int,
        float mat_res[row][col]);
        void display(float mat[row][col], int, int);
        void input(float mat[row][col], int , int);
};
// Function mat_add
void Two_D :: mat_add( float mat1[row][col], int row1, int col1, float mat2[row][col],
int row2, int col2, float mat_res[row][col])
```

```
{
    if(( row1 == row2 && (col1 == col2))
    {
        cout<<"\n Addition is possible and Result is as follows\n";

        for( int i =0; i<row1; i++)
            for(int j=0; j<col1); j++)
                mat_res[i][j] = mat1[i][j]+mat2[i][j];
        display(mat_res,row1,col1);
    }
    else
        cout<<"\n Addition is not possible";
    exit(0);
}

// Output function

void Two_D :: display(float mat[row][col], int r, int c )
{
    for( i = 0; i < r; i++)
    {
        for( j = 0; j < c; j++)
        {
            cout <<setw(8)<<mat[i][j];
        }
        cout<<"\n";
    }
}

// Input function

void Two_D :: input(float mat[row][col], int r, int c)
{

    for( i = 0 ; i< r; i++)
    {
        for( j = 0 ; j<c; j++)
        {
            cout<<"Input Value for : "<< i+1 <<" : "<<j+1<<" : ";
            cin>>mat[i][j];
        }
    }
}

// main function
void main()
```

```
{
    Two_D add_mat;

    int row1, col1);
    int row2, col2);
    float mat1[row][col];
    float mat2[row][col];
    float mat_res[row][col];

    cout<<"\n Input the row of the matrix->1:";
    cin>>row1;
    cout<<" Input the col of the matrix->1:";
    cin>>col1);
    cout<<"\n Input data for matrix-> 1\n";

    add_mat.input(mat1, row1, col1);
    cout<<"\n Input the row of the matrix ->2:";
    cin>>row2;
    cout<<"\n Input the col of the matrix->2:";
    cin>>col2);

    cout<<"\n Input data for matrix-> 2\n";
    add_mat.input(mat2, row2, col2);
    cout<<"\n Entered Matrix First is as follows:\n";
    add_mat.display(mat1,row1,col1);
    cout<<"\n Entered Matrix Two is as follows:\n";
    add_mat.display(mat2,row2,col2);
    add_mat.mat_add(mat1, row1, col1, mat2, row2, col2, mat_res);
}
```

```
Input the row  of the matrix->1: 3
Input the col  of the matrix->1: 3
Input data for matrix-> 1
Input Value for : 1 : 1 : 11
Input Value for : 1 : 2 : 22
Input Value for : 1 : 3 : 33
Input Value for : 2 : 1 : 44
Input Value for : 2 : 2 : 55
Input Value for : 2 : 3 : 66
Input Value for : 3 : 1 : 77
Input Value for : 3 : 2 : 88
Input Value for : 3 : 3 : 99
```

```
Input the row  of the matrix->2: 3
Input the col  of the matrix->2: 3
Input data for matrix-> 2
Input Value for : 1 : 1 : 1
Input Value for : 1 : 2 : 2
Input Value for : 1 : 3 : 3
Input Value for : 2 : 1 : 4
Input Value for : 2 : 2 : 5
Input Value for : 2 : 3 : 6
Input Value for : 3 : 1 : 7
Input Value for : 3 : 2 : 8
Input Value for : 3 : 3 : 9

Entered Matrix First is as follows:
   11    22    33
   44    55    66
   77    88    99
Entered Matrix Two is as follows:
    1     2     3
    4     5     6
    7     8     9

Addition is possible and Result is as follows
   12    24    36
   48    60    72
   84    96   108
```

4.9.2 SUBTRACTION OF MATRICES

The difference of two matrices is a matrix, each element of which is obtained by subtracting the elements of the second matrix from the corresponding element of the first matrix. If **A** and **B** are two matrices then the difference of **B** and **A** is noted by **B – A** will be defined by:

$B - A = [b_{ij} - a_{ij}]$

For example, if

$$A = \begin{pmatrix} 11 & 12 & 3 \\ 41 & 15 & 6 \\ 71 & 8 & 19 \\ 10 & 11 & 12 \end{pmatrix}$$

and

$$B = \begin{pmatrix} 11 & 22 & 33 \\ 4 & 55 & 6 \\ 7 & 88 & 9 \\ 100 & 11 & 12 \end{pmatrix}$$

$$\text{then} \quad B - A = \begin{pmatrix} 11-11 & 22-12 & 33-3 \\ 4-41 & 55-15 & 6-6 \\ 7-71 & 88-8 & 9-19 \\ 100-10 & 11-11 & 12-12 \end{pmatrix}$$

$$B - A = \begin{pmatrix} 0 & 10 & 30 \\ -37 & 40 & 0 \\ -64 & 80 & -10 \\ 90 & 0 & 0 \end{pmatrix}$$

Step 1: [Check possibility of addition]
If $Row_1 = Row_2$ and Col_1 to Col_2
Output "Subtraction is Possible"
Else
Output "Subtraction is not possible" and Exit

Step 2: Repeat for I = 0, 1, 2 …, Row – 1
Repeat for J = 0, 1, 2 … Col – 1
Mat_Res [I][J] = Mat_1 [I][J] - Mat_2 [I][J]

Step 3: Exit

Fig. 4.31 Algorithm to subtract two matrices

Algorithm to find difference of two matrices is shown in **Fig. 4.31.** The following program segment implements the algorithm.

```
// Subtraction of two Matrices
// TWO_SUB.C
# include<iostream.h>
# include<iomanip.h>
# include<stdlib.h>
```

```
# define row 10
# define col 10
class Two_D
{
    public:
        int i, j;
        int row1, col1);
        int row2, col2);
        float mat1[row][col];
        float mat2[row][col];
        float mat_res[row][col];
    public:
        void mat_sub( float mat1[row][col], int, int,
        float mat2[row][col], int, int,
        float mat_res[row][col]);
        void display(float mat[row][col], int, int);
        void input(float mat[row][col], int , int);
};
// Function mat_sub
void Two_D :: mat_sub( float mat1[row][col], int row1, int col1,
float mat2[row][col], int row2, int col2,
float mat_res[row][col])
{
    if(( row1 == row2 && (col1 == col2))
    {
        cout<<"\n Subtraction is possible and Result is as follows\n";

        for( int i =0; i<row1; i++)
            for(int j=0; j<col1); j++)
                mat_res[i][j] = mat1[i][j] - mat2[i][j];
        display(mat_res,row1,col1);
    }
    else
        cout<<"\n Subtraction is not possible";
    exit(0);
}
// Output Function
void Two_D :: display(float mat[row][col], int r, int c )
{
    for( i = 0; i < r; i++)
    {
        for( j = 0; j < c; j++)
        {
            cout <<setw(8)<<mat[i][j];
        }
        cout<<"\n";
```

```
    }
}
// Input function
void Two_D :: input(float mat[row][col], int r, int c)
{
    for( i = 0 ; i< r; i++)
    {
        for( j = 0 ; j<c; j++)
        {
            cout<<"Input Value for : "<< i+1 <<" : "<<j+1<<" : " ;
            cin>>mat[i][j];
        }
    }
}
// main function
void main()
{
    Two_D sub_mat;

    int row1, col1);
    int row2, col2);
    float mat1[row][col];
    float mat2[row][col];
    float mat_res[row][col];

    cout<<"\n Input the row of the matrix->1:";
    cin>>row1;
    cout<<"\n Input the col of the matrix->1:";
    cin>>col1);
    cout<<" Input data for matrix-> 1\n";

    sub_mat.input(mat1, row1, col1);
    cout<<" Input the row of the matrix ->2:";
    cin>>row2;
    cout<<" Input the col of the matrix->2:";
    cin>>col2);
    cout<<" Input data for matrix-> 2\n";

    sub_mat.input(mat2, row2, col2);
    cout<<"\n Entered Matrix First is as follows:\n";
    sub_mat.display(mat1,row1,col1);
    cout<<"\n Entered Matrix Two is as follows:\n";
    sub_mat.display(mat2,row2,col2);
    sub_mat.mat_sub(mat1,row1,col1,mat2,row1,col2,mat_res);
    sub_mat.display(mat_res,row2,col2);
}
```

```
Input the row  of the matrix->1: 3
Input the col  of the matrix->1: 3
Input data for matrix-> 1
Input Value for : 1 : 1 : 1
Input Value for : 1 : 2 : 2
Input Value for : 1 : 3 : 3
Input Value for : 2 : 1 : 4
Input Value for : 2 : 2 : 5
Input Value for : 2 : 3 : 6
Input Value for : 3 : 1 : 7
Input Value for : 3 : 2 : 8
Input Value for : 3 : 3 : 9
Input the row  of the matrix ->2: 3
Input the col  of the matrix->2: 3
Input data for matrix-> 2
Input Value for : 1 : 1 : 99
Input Value for : 1 : 2 : 88
Input Value for : 1 : 3 : 7
Input Value for : 2 : 1 : 5
Input Value for : 2 : 2 : 4
Input Value for : 2 : 3 : 34
Input Value for : 3 : 1 : 23
Input Value for : 3 : 2 : 12
Input Value for : 3 : 3 : 11

Entered Matrix First is as follows:
   1    2    3
   4    5    6
   7    8    9

Entered Matrix Two is as follows:
  99   88    7
   5    4   34
  23   12   11

Subtraction is possible and Result is as follows

 -98  -86   -4
  -1    1  -28
 -16   -4   -2
```

4.9.3 MULTIPLICATION OF TWO MATRICES

The product of two matrices **A** and **B** is possible if the number of columns in **A** is equal to the number of rows in **B** or number of rows in **A** is equal to the number of columns in **B**. Let **A** = $[a_{ij}]$ be an **m x n** matrix and **B** = $[b_{jk}]$ be an **n x p** matrix. Then the product **A.B** of these matrices is of the order of **m x p** say **C = [c_{ik}]**, where

$$c_{ik} = a_{i1}.b_{1k}+a_{i2}.b_{2k}+\ldots + a_{in}.b_{nk}$$

$$c_{ik} = \sum_{k=1}^{n} a_{ij}b_{jk})$$

For example, suppose we two matrices **A** and **B** then by multiplying row of first matrix and column of second matrix we will get

$$A = \begin{pmatrix} 1 & -2 & 3 \\ 2 & 3 & -1 \\ -3 & 1 & 2 \end{pmatrix} \quad B = \begin{pmatrix} 1 & 0 & 2 \\ 0 & 1 & 2 \\ 1 & 2 & 0 \end{pmatrix}$$

$$A.B = \begin{pmatrix} 1*1+ -2*0 + 3*1 & 1*0+-2*1+3*2 & 1*2+-2*2+3*0 \\ 2*1+3*0+-1*1 & 2*0+3*1+-1*2 & 2*2+3*2+-1*0 \\ -3*1+1*0+2*1 & -3*0+1*1+2*2 & -3*2+1*2+2*0 \end{pmatrix}$$

Step 1: [Check condition of multiplicity]

If Col_1 = Row_2 [When we are taking column of first matrix and multiplying it with rows of second matrix]

Repeat for I = 0, 1, 2 … Row_1 – 1
Repeat for J = 0, 1, 2 … Col_2 – 1
Mat_res[I][J] = 0
Repeat for K= 0, 1, 2 … Col_1 – 1
Mat_res[I][J] = Mat_res[I][J]+Mat_1[I][K]*Mat_2[K][J]

Else if Row_1 = Col_2 [When we are taking rows of first matrix and multiplying it with the columns of the second matrix]

Repeat for I = 0, 1, 2 … Col_1 – 1
Repeat for J = 0, 1, 2 … Row_2 – 1
Mat_res[I][J] = 0
Repeat for K= 0, 1, 2 … Col_2 – 1
Mat_res[I][J] = Mat_res[I][J]+Mat_1[I][K]*Mat_2[K][J]

Else
Output "Multiplication is not possible" and Exit

Step 2: Exit

Fig. 4.32 Algorithm to multiply two matrices

$$A.B = \begin{pmatrix} 1-0+3 & 0-2+6 & 2-4+0 \\ 2+0-1 & 0+3-2 & 4+6-0 \\ -3+0+2 & -0+1+4 & -6+2+0 \end{pmatrix}$$

$$A.B = \begin{pmatrix} 4 & 4 & -2 \\ 1 & 1 & 10 \\ -1 & 5 & -4 \end{pmatrix}$$

The program segment **MULT_MAT.C** implements the algorithm shown In **Fig. 4.32,** i.e., multiplication performed on two matrices.

```
// Multiply Two Matrices
// MULT_MAT.C

# include<iostream.h>
# include<iomanip.h>
# include<stdlib.h>
# include<stdio.h>

# define row 10
# define col 10

class Two_D
{
    public:
        int i, j;
        int row1, col1);
        int row2, col2);
        float mat1[row][col];
        float mat2[row][col];
        float mat_res[row][col];

    public:
        void mat_mult( float mat1[row][col], int, int,
        float mat2[row][col], int, int,
        float mat_res[row][col]);

        void display(float mat[row][col], int, int);
        void input(float mat[row][col], int , int);
};

// Function to multiply two matrices

void Two_D :: mat_mult( float mat1[row][col], int row1, int col1,
float mat2[row][col], int row2, int col2,
float mat_res[row][col])
```

```
{
    if(col1 == row2)
    {
        cout<<"\n Multiplication is possible and Result is as follows\n";

        for( int i =0; i<row1; i++)
            for(int j=0; j<col2); j++)
            {
                mat_res[i][j] = 0;
                for(int k = 0; k < col1); k ++)
                {
                    mat_res[i][j] += mat1[i][k] * mat2[k][j];

                }
            }
        display(mat_res,row1,col2);
    }

    else
        cout<<"\n Multiplication is not possible";
    exit(0);
}

// Output function

void Two_D :: display(float mat[row][col], int r, int c )
{
    for( i = 0; i < r; i++)
    {
        for( j = 0; j < c; j++)
        {
            cout <<setw(8)<<mat[i][j];
        }
        cout<<"\n";
    }
}

// Input function

void Two_D :: input(float mat[row][col], int r, int c)
{
    for( i = 0 ; i< r; i++)
    {
        for( j = 0 ; j<c; j++)
        {
            cout<<"Input Value for : "<< i+1 <<" : "<<j+1<<" : " ;
```

```
                cin>>mat[i][j];
            }
        }
}

// main function

void main()
{
        Two_D mult_matrices;

        int row1, col1);
        int row2, col2);
        float mat1[row][col];
        float mat2[row][col];
        float mat_res[row][col];

        cout<<"\n Input the row of the matrix->1:";
        cin>>row1;

        cout<<"\n Input the col of the matrix->1:";
        cin>>col1);

        cout<<"\n Input data for matrix-> 1\n";
        mult_matrices.input(mat1, row1, col1);

        cout<<"\n Input the row of the matrix ->2:";
        cin>>row2;

        cout<<"\n Input the col of the matrix->2:";
        cin>>col2);

        cout<<"\n Input data for matrix-> 2\n";
        mult_matrices.input(mat2, row2, col2);

        cout<<"\n Entered Matrix First is as follows:\n";
        mult_matrices.display(mat1,row1,col1);

        cout<<"\n Entered Matrix Two is as follows:\n";
        mult_matrices.display(mat2,row2,col2);

        mult_matrices.mat_mult(mat1 ,row1 ,col1, mat2, row2, col2, mat_res);
}
```

```
Input the row  of the matrix->1: 3
Input the col  of the matrix->1: 3
Input data for matrix-> 1
Input Value for : 1 : 1 : 1
Input Value.for : 1 : 2 : 2
Input Value for : 1 : 3 : 3
Input Value for : 2 : 1 : 4
Input Value for : 2 : 2 : 5
Input Value for : 2 : 3 : 6
Input Value for : 3 : 1 : 7
Input Value for : 3 : 2 : 8
Input Value for : 3 : 3 : 9

Input the row  of the matrix->2: 3
Input the col  of the matrix->2: 3
Input data for matrix-> 2
Input Value for : 1 : 1 : 8
Input Value for : 1 : 2 : 9
Input Value for : 1 : 3 : 7
Input Value for : 2 : 1 : 6
Input Value for : 2 : 2 : 5
Input Value for : 2 : 3 : 4
Input Value for : 3 : 1 : 3
Input Value for : 3 : 2 : 2
Input Value for : 3 : 3 : 1

Entered Matrix First is as follows:
     1     2     3
     4     5     6
     7     8     9

Entered Matrix Two is as follows:
     8     9     7
     6     5     4
     3     2     1

Multiplication is possible and Result is as follows
    29    25    18
    80    73    54
   131   121    90
```

4.9.4 TRANSPOSE OF A MATRIX

Transpose of a matrix is obtained by interchanging the rows with corresponding columns of a given matrix. The transpose of matrix **A** is generally denoted by $\mathbf{A}^T$. If matrix **A** is an **m x n** then after transposing it we will get an **n x m** matrix $\mathbf{A}^T$. If $\mathbf{A} = [\mathbf{a}_{ij}]$ then $\mathbf{A}^T = [\mathbf{a}_{ji}]$. For example, if

$$A = \begin{pmatrix} 1 & 2 & 3 & 4 & 5 \\ 6 & 7 & 8 & 9 & 10 \\ 11 & 12 & 13 & 14 & 15 \end{pmatrix}$$

Then transpose of matrix **A** is:

$$A^T = \begin{pmatrix} 1 & 6 & 11 \\ 2 & 7 & 12 \\ 3 & 8 & 13 \\ 4 & 9 & 14 \\ 5 & 6 & 15 \end{pmatrix}$$

Step 1: [Transpose the matrix]

Repeat for I = 0, 1, 2 … Row – 1
Repeat for J = 0, 1, 2 … Col – 1
Transpose [I][J] = Mat [J][I]

Step 2: Exit

Fig. 4.33 Algorithm to transpose a matrix

The program segment **TRANS_M.C** implements the transpose algorithm illustrated in **Fig. 4.33.**

```
// Transpose of a matrix

// TRANS_M.C

# include<iostream.h>
# include<iomanip.h>

class Two_D
{
    public:
```

```
        int i, j;
        int value;
        int mat[10][10];
    public:
        void display( int transp[10][10],int, int);
        void display_o( int transp[10][10],int, int);
        void input( int transp[10][10],int, int);
        void transpose( int transp[10][10],int, int);
};

// Transpose function

void Two_D :: transpose( int transp[10][10],int row, int col)
{

    for( i = 0; i< row; i++)
    {
        for( j = 0; j < col; j++)
        {
            mat[i][j] = transp[j][i] ;
        }
    }
}

// Output function

void Two_D :: display( int transp[10][10],int row, int col)
{

    for( i = 0; i < row; i++)
    {
        for( j = 0; j < col; j++)
        {
            cout <<setw(8)<<mat[i][j];
        }
        cout<<"\n";
    }
}

// Output function

void Two_D :: display_o( int transp[10][10],int row, int col)
{
    for( i = 0; i < row; i++)
    {
        for( j = 0; j < col; j++)
```

```
            {
                  cout <<setw(8)<<transp[i][j];
            }
            cout<<"\n";
      }
}

// Input function
void Two_D :: input( int transp[10][10],int row, int col)
{
      for( i = 0 ; i< row; i++)
      {
            for( j = 0 ; j<col; j++)
            {
                  cout<<"Input Value for : "<< i+1 <<" : "<<j+1<<" : " ;
                  cin>>value;
                  transp[i][j] = value;
            }
      }
}

// main function
void main()
{
      Two_D trans;
      int row,col;
      int transp[10][10];
      cout<<"\n Input the number of rows:";
      cin>>row;
      cout<<" Input number of cols:";
      cin>>col;
      trans.input(transp,row,col);
      cout<<"\n Entered Matrix is as follows:\n";
      trans.display_o(transp, row, col);
      trans.transpose(transp, col, row);
      cout<<"\n Transpose of above matrix is as follows:\n";
      trans.display(transp, col, row);
}
```

```
Input the number of rows: 3
Input number of cols: 4
Input Value for : 1 : 1 : 1
Input Value for : 1 : 2 : 2
Input Value for : 1 : 3 : 3
Input Value for : 1 : 4 : 4
Input Value for : 2 : 1 : 5
Input Value for : 2 : 2 : 6
Input Value for : 2 : 3 : 7
Input Value for : 2 : 4 : 8
Input Value for : 3 : 1 : 9
Input Value for : 3 : 2 : 10
Input Value for : 3 : 3 : 11
Input Value for : 3 : 4 : 12

Entered Matrix is as follows:
    1    2    3    4
    5    6    7    8
    9   10   11   12

Transpose of above matrix is as follows:
    1    5    9
    2    6   10
    3    7   11
    4    8   12
```

4.9.5 ORTHOGONAL OF A MATRIX

A square matrix **A** is called an orthogonal matrix if the product of the matrix **A** and the transpose matrix $\mathbf{A}^T$ is an identity matrix. A square matrix is called an identity matrix if all the diagonal elements are unity and non-diagonal elements are zero, that is, if

$$U = \begin{pmatrix} 1 & 0 & 0 & 0 \\ 0 & 1 & 0 & 0 \\ 0 & 0 & 1 & 0 \\ 0 & 0 & 0 & 1 \end{pmatrix}$$

then **U** is called the identity matrix. If matrix A is:

$$A = \begin{pmatrix} 1 & 0 & 0 & 0 \\ 0 & 1 & 0 & 0 \\ 0 & 0 & 1 & 0 \\ 0 & 0 & 0 & 1 \end{pmatrix}$$

Then A^T

$$A^T = \begin{pmatrix} 1 & 0 & 0 & 0 \\ 0 & 1 & 0 & 0 \\ 0 & 0 & 1 & 0 \\ 0 & 0 & 0 & 1 \end{pmatrix}$$

If we multiply the above two matrices **A** and $\mathbf{A}^T$ we will get an identity matrix, that is:

$$A * A^T = U$$

Hence, we can say that **A** is an orthogonal matrix. The program segment **ORTH_MAT.C** discusses orthogonal of two matrices.

```
// Find Orthogonality of a matrix

// ORTH_MAT.C

# include<iostream.h>
# include<iomanip.h>
# include<stdlib.h>
# include<stdio.h>

# define row 10
# define col 10

class Two_D
{
    public:
        int i, j;
        int row1, col1);
        float mat1[row][col];
        float mat2[row][col];
        float mat_res[row][col];

    public:
        void mat_mult( float mat1[row][col], int, int,
        float mat_res[row][col]);

        void transpose( float transp[row][col], int, int);
        void display(float mat[row][col], int, int);
        void input(float mat[row][col], int , int);
};
```

```
// function mat_mult

void Two_D :: mat_mult( float mat1[row][col], int row1, int col1,
float mat_res[row][col])
{
    int flag;
    if(col1 == row1)
    {
        cout<<"\n Multiplication is possible and Result is as follows\n";

        for(int i =0; i<row1; i++)
            for(int j=0; j<col1); j++)
            {
                mat_res[i][j] = 0;
                for(int k = 0; k < col1); k ++)
                {
                    mat_res[i][j] += mat1[i][k] * mat2[k][j];

                }
            }
        display(mat_res,row1,col1);
    }

    else
    {
        cout<<"\n Multiplication is not possible";
        exit(0);
    }

    for(i = 0; i< row1; i++)
    {
        for(j = 0; j < col1); j++)
        {
            if(((int)mat_res[i][i] == 1) && ((int ) mat_res[i][j] == 0))
                flag = 1;
        }
    }
    if(flag == 1)
    {
        cout<<"\n Matrix X * Transpose of X = Identity Matrix";
        cout<<"\n The given Matrix is Orthogonal";
    }
    else
    {
        cout<<"\n Matrix X * Transpose of X != Identity Matrix";
        cout<<"\n The given Matrix is not Orthogonal";
```

```
    }
}

// Output function

void Two_D :: display(float mat[row][col], int r, int c )
{
    for(i = 0; i < r; i++)
    {
        for(j = 0; j < c; j++)
        {
            cout <<setw(8)<<mat[i][j];
        }
        cout<<"\n";
    }
}

// Input function

void Two_D :: input(float mat[row][col], int r, int c)
{

    for(i = 0 ; i< r; i++)
    {
        for(j = 0 ; j<c; j++)
        {
            cout<<"Input Value for : "<< i+1 <<" : "<<j+1<<" : " ;
            cin>>mat[i][j];
        }
    }
}

// Transpose of a matrix

void Two_D :: transpose( float transp[10][10],int row1, int col1)
{
    for(i = 0; i< row1; i++)
    {
        for(j = 0; j < col1); j++)
        {
            mat2[i][j] = transp[j][i] ;
        }
    }
    display(mat2,row1,col1);
}
```

```
// main function

void main()
{
     Two_D mult_matrices;

     int row1, col1);
     int row2, col2);
     float mat1[row][col];
     float mat2[row][col];
     float mat_res[row][col];

     cout<<"\n Input the row of the matrix:";
     cin>>row1;

     cout<<" Input the col of the matrix:";
     cin>>col1);

     cout<<"\n Input data for matrix\n";
     mult_matrices.input(mat1, row1, col1);

     cout<<"\n Entered Matrix First is as follows:\n";
     mult_matrices.display(mat1,row1,col1);

     cout<<" \n Transpose of above matrix is as follows:\n";
     mult_matrices.transpose(mat1, col1, row1);

     mult_matrices.mat_mult(mat1 ,row1 ,col1, mat_res);
}
```

```
 Input the row  of the matrix: 4
 Input the col  of the matrix: 4
 Input data for matrix
Input Value for : 1 : 1 : 1
Input Value for : 1 : 2 : 0
Input Value for : 1 : 3 : 0
Input Value for : 1 : 4 : 0
Input Value for : 2 : 1 : 0
Input Value for : 2 : 2 : 1
Input Value for : 2 : 3 : 0
Input Value for : 2 : 4 : 0
```

```
Input Value for : 3 : 1 : 0
Input Value for : 3 : 2 : 0
Input Value for : 3 : 3 : 1
Input Value for : 3 : 4 : 0
Input Value for : 4 : 1 : 0
Input Value for : 4 : 2 : 0
Input Value for : 4 : 3 : 0
Input Value for : 4 : 4 : 1

Entered Matrix First is as follows:
    1   0   0   0
    0   1   0   0
    0   0   1   0
    0   0   0   1

Transpose of above matrix is as follows:
    1   0   0   0
    0   1   0   0
    0   0   1   0
    0   0   0   1

Multiplication is possible and Result is as follows
    1   0   0   0
    0   1   0   0
    0   0   1   0
    0   0   0   1

Matrix X * Transpose of X = Identity Matrix
The given Matrix is Orthogonal
```

4.9.6. SINGULAR MATRIX

Let **A** is an **m x n** matrix. Then the determinant formed by the elements of **A** is |**A**|. For example:

$$A = \begin{pmatrix} 2 & 0 & 3 & 8 \\ 3 & 11 & -4 & 99 \\ 7 & 9 & 11 & 13 \\ 6 & 2 & 5 & 8 \\ 24 & 16 & 23 & 22 \end{pmatrix}$$

then determinant of matrix **A** will be

$$|A| = \begin{vmatrix} 2 & 0 & 3 & 8 \\ 3 & 11 & -4 & 99 \\ 7 & 9 & 11 & 13 \\ 6 & 2 & 5 & 8 \\ 24 & 16 & 23 & 22 \end{vmatrix}$$

A square matrix **A** for which $|A| = 0$ is called a singular matrix. If $|A| \neq 0$ then matrix is called a non-singular matrix. The program segment illustrates the above discussion in detail. Crammer's rule is usually used to evaluate the matrix determinant value, which is implemented in the program segment **SINGULAR.C.**

```
// Test singularity of a given matrix using Cramer's rules to find determinant

// SINGULAR.C

# include<iostream.h>
# include<iomanip.h>

class Two_D
{
      private: int i, j;
            float mat[10][10];
            float mat1[10][10];

      public:
            void display( int, int);
            void input( int, int);
            float Singular_Matrix(int, int);
};

// Output function

void Two_D :: display( int row, int col)
{
      for( i = 0; i < row; i++)
      {
            for( j = 0; j < col; j++)
            {
            cout <<setw(8)<<mat[i][j];
            }
            cout<<"\n";
      }
}
```

```
// Input function

void Two_D :: input( int row, int col)
{
      for( i = 0 ; i< row; i++)
      {
      for( j = 0 ; j<col; j++)
      {
            cout<<"Input Value for : "<< i+1 <<" : "<<j+1<<" : " ;
            cin>>mat[i][j];
      }
      }

}

// Find Determinant using Cramer's rule

float Two_D :: Singular_Matrix( int row1, int col1)
{
      float sum=0, psum=0, partial=0, nsum=0;
      if( row1 == col1)
      {
            cout<<"\n Number rows = Number of cols";
            cout<<"\n Singular Test is possible\n";

            if(row1 < 3)
            {
                  sum = mat[0][0]*mat[1][1] - mat[0][1]*mat[1][0];
                  return(sum);
            }

            else
            {
                  for( int k = 0; k <row1; k++)
                   for( int j = 0; j < row1; j++)
                   mat1[k][j] = mat[k][j];

                  for( k = 0; k <row1; k++)
                   for( j = row1); j < (2*row1-1; j++)
                   mat1[k][j] = mat1[k][j-row1];

                   for( int l = 0; l <row1; l++)
                   {
                   partial = 1;
                         for( int i =0; i <row1; i++)
```

```
                {
                partial *= mat1[i][i+l];
                }
                psum += partial;
            }

            for( l = row1-1; l < ( 2*row1 -1); l++)
            {
                partial = 1;
                for( i =0; i < row1; i++)
                {
                 partial *=mat1[i][l-i];
                }
                nsum += partial;
            }
            sum = psum - nsum ;
            return(sum);
        }
    }

            else
                cout<<"\n Check about singularity is not possible";

            return 0;
}

// main function

 void main()
 {
     Two_D Singular_Mat;
     float Determinant;
     int r,c;
     cout<<"\n Input the number of rows:";
     cin>>r;
     cout<<" Input the number of cols:";
     cin>>c;
     Singular_Mat.input(r,c);
     cout<<"\n Entered Matrix is as follows:\n";
     Singular_Mat.display(r,c);
     Determinant = Singular_Mat.Singular_Matrix(r, c);
     cout<<"\n Determinant is :"<<Determinant;

     if(Determinant == 0)
     cout<<"\n The Above matrix is Singular";
     else
```

```
    cout<<"\n Above matrix is not singular";

}
```

```
Input the number of rows: 4
Input the number of cols: 4
Input Value for : 1 : 1 : 2
Input Value for : 1 : 2 : 2
Input Value for : 1 : 3 : 2
Input Value for : 1 : 4 : 2
Input Value for : 2 : 1 : 2
Input Value for : 2 : 2 : 2
Input Value for : 2 : 3 : 2
Input Value for : 2 : 4 : 2
Input Value for : 3 : 1 : 2
Input Value for : 3 : 2 : 2
Input Value for : 3 : 3 : 2
Input Value for : 3 : 4 : 2
Input Value for : 4 : 1 : 2
Input Value for : 4 : 2 : 2
Input Value for : 4 : 3 : 2
Input Value for : 4 : 4 : 2

Entered Matrix is as follows:
    2    2    2    2
    2    2    2    2
    2    2    2    2
    2    2    2    2

Number rows  = Number of cols
Singular Test is possible

Determinant is :0
Above matrix is Singular
```

4.9.7 INVERSE OF A MATRIX

If **A** and **B** are two matrices of the same order such that

A.B = **B.A** = **U** [Where **U** is a unity matrix]

then **B** is called the inverse of **A** and denoted as $\mathbf{B} = \mathbf{A}^{-1}$, to possesses an inverse of a matrix **A**, the matrix should be a nonsingular, that is

$|A| \neq 0$

If **A** is a matrix and **B** be it's inverse, then

A.B = U

Taking determinant of the both sides

| A.B| = | U|

| A| .| B| = | U|

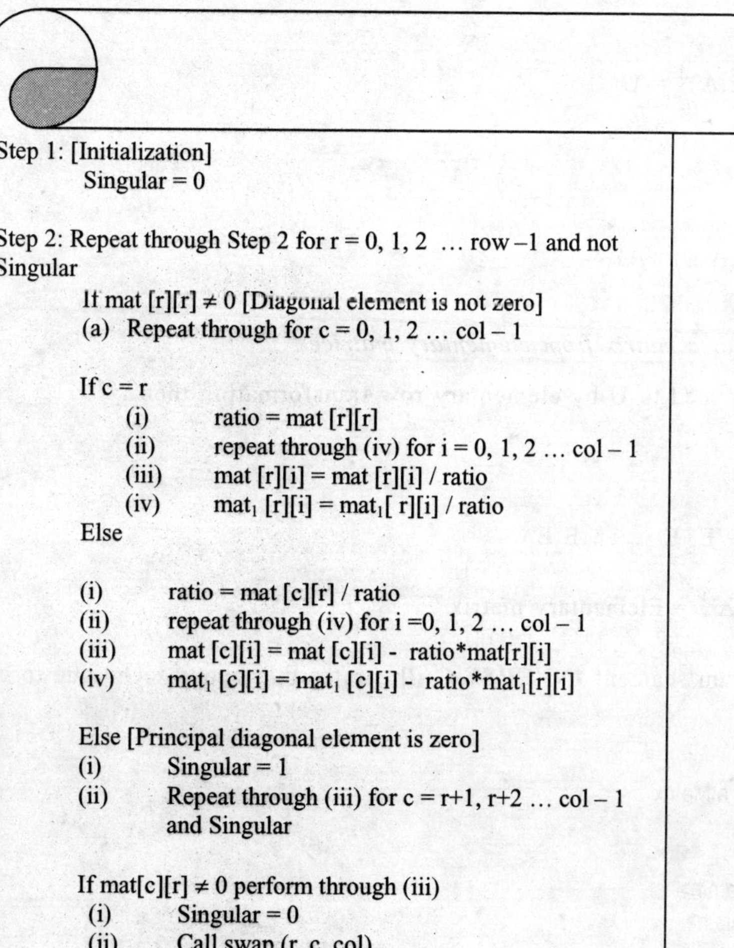

Fig. 4.34 Algorithm for inverse a matrix

From this relation it is clear that **|A| ≠ 0** that is matrix **A** is non-singular. There are two techniques to find inverse of a matrix

(i) Inverse of matrix with the help of adjoin matrix, that is

A.(Adjoin A) = | A| .U

Or

$$A.\frac{1}{|A|}.(\text{Adjoin } A) = U$$

and A.A^{-1} = U

that is

$$A^{-1} = \frac{1}{|A|}.(\text{Adjoin } A)$$

(ii) Inverse of a matrix from elementary matrices

If A is reduced to U by elementary row transformation then

E.A= U

where E = $E_n E_{n-1} \dots E_2E_1$

then E = A^{-1} = Elementary matrix

The program segment **INVERSE.C** illustrates the second technique to compute the inverse of a matrix.

```
// Find Inverse of a Matrix
// INVERSE.C

# include<iostream.h>
# include<iomanip.h>
# include<stdio.h>

int R,C;

class Two_D
{
```

```
        private: int i, j;
                float mat[10][10];
                float mat1[10][10];

        public:
                void display( int, int);
                void input( int, int);
                Inverse_Mat(int , int);
                void swap(int, int, int);
};

// This function exchange two rows of a matrix

void Two_D :: swap( int row1,int row2, int col)
{
        for( i = 0; i < col; i++)
        {
        float temp = mat[row1][i];
        mat[row1][i] = mat[row2][i];
        mat[row2][i] = temp;

        temp = mat1[row1][i];
        mat1[row1][i] = mat1[row2][i];
        mat1[row2][i] = temp;
        }
}

// This function finds inverse of matrix

int Two_D :: Inverse_Mat(int row1, int col1)
{
        int singular = 0;
        for( int r = 0;( r < row1)&& !singular; r++)
        {

        if( mat[r][r] ) // Diagonal element is not zero
        for( int c = 0; c < col1); c++)

                if( c == r)
                {

// Make all the elements above and below the current principal
// diagonal element zero

                        float ratio = mat[r][r];
                        for( i = 0; i < col1); i++)
```

```
                {
                    mat[r][i] /= ratio ;
                    mat1[r][i] /= ratio;
                }
            }
            else
            {
                float ratio = mat[c][r] / mat[r][r];
                for( i = 0; i < col1); i++)
                {
                    mat[c][i] -= ratio * mat[r][i];
                    mat1[c][i] -= ratio * mat1[r][i];
                }
            }

            else
            {
             // If principal diagonal element is zero
             singular = 1;

             for( int c = (r+1); (c < col1) && singular; ++c)

                if(mat[c][r])
                {
                singular = 0;
             // Find non zero elements in the same column
                swap(r,c,col1);
                --r;
                }
             }
            }
            return(!singular);
        }
// To print output this is used

void Two_D :: display( int row, int col)
{
// Output of inverse Matrix
    for( i = 0; i < row; i++)
    {
        for( j = 0; j < col; j++)
        {
        cout <<setw(15<<mat1[i][j];
        }
        cout<<"\n";
    }
```

```
}

// Input function

void Two_D :: input( int row, int col)
{
    for( i = 0 ; i< row; i++)
    {
    for( j = 0 ; j<col; j++)
    {
        cout<<"Input Value for : "<< i+1 <<" : "<<j+1<<" : " ;
        cin >>mat[i][j];
        mat1[i][j] = 0;
    }
        mat1[i][i] = 1;
    }
    cout<<"\n Entered Matrix is as follows:\n";
    for( i = 0; i < row; i++)
    {
        for( j = 0; j < col; j++)
        {
        cout <<setw(20)<<mat[i][j];
        }
        cout<<"\n";
    }
}

// main function

void main()
{
    Two_D Inverse_Matrix;
    int R, C;
    cout<<"\n Input number of rows:";
    cin>>R;
    cout<<" Input number of cols:";
    cin>>C;
    Inverse_Matrix.input(R,C);

    Inverse_Matrix.Inverse_Mat(R,C);
    cout<<"\n Inverse of above matrix is as follows:\n ";
    Inverse_Matrix.display(R,C);
}
```

```
Input number of rows: 3
Input number of cols: 3

Input Value for: 1: 1: 0
Input Value for: 1: 2: 1
Input Value for: 1: 3: 2
Input Value for: 2: 1: 1
Input Value for: 2: 2: 2
Input Value for: 2: 3: 3
Input Value for: 3: 1: 3
Input Value for: 3: 2: 1
Input Value for: 3: 3: 1

Entered Matrix is as follows:
        0    1    3
        1    2    1
        2    3    1

Inverse of above matrix is as follows:
        0.5   -4    2.5
       -0.5    3   -1.5
        0.5   -1    0.5
```

4.9.8 SYMMETRIC MATRIX

A square matrix is called symmetric if for all values of **i** and **j**, $\mathbf{a_{ij}} = \mathbf{a_{ji}}$. In other words if transpose of matrix is equal to the matrix then the matrix is called the symmetric matrix. If we have matrix **A** and transpose of it is denoted by $\mathbf{A^T}$ then symmetry condition will be:

$$A = A^T$$

The program segment **SYMMET.C** performs the symmetry operation.

```
// Test for symmetry of a matrix
// SYMMET.C
# include<iostream.h>
# include<iomanip.h>
# define r 10
# define c 10

class Two_D
{
    public:
```

```
        int i, j;
        int value;
        float mat[r][c];
    public:
        void display(int, int);
        void display_o( float transp[r][c],int, int);
        void input( float transp[r][c],int, int);
        void transpose( float transp[r][c],int, int);
        int Symmetry_Matrix(float transp[r][c], int , int );
};

// Transpose function

void Two_D :: transpose( float transp[r][c],int row, int col)
{
    for( i = 0; i< row; i++)
    {
        for( j = 0; j < col; j++)
        {
            mat[i][j] = transp[j][i] ;
        }
    }
}

// Output function
void Two_D :: display( int row, int col)
{
    for(i = 0; i < row; i++)
    {
        for( j = 0; j < col; j++)
        {
            cout <<setw(8)<<mat[i][j],
        }
        cout<<"\n";
    }
}

// Output function

void Two_D :: display_o( float transp[r][c],int row, int col)
{
    for(i = 0; i < row; i++)
    {
        for( j = 0; j < col; j++)
        {
            cout <<setw(8)<<transp[i][j];
```

```
        }
        cout<<"\n";
    }
}

// Input function
void Two_D :: input( float transp[r][c],int row, int col)
{
    for(i = 0 ; i< row; i++)
    {
        for(j = 0 ; j<col; j++)
        {
            cout<<"Input Value for : "<< i+1 <<" : "<<j+1<<" : " ;
            cin>>value;
            transp[i][j] = value;
        }
    }
}

// Test for Symmetry
int Two_D :: Symmetry_Matrix(float transp[r][c], int row, int col)
{
    int status = 0;
    for(i =0; i < row; i++)
    {
        for(j =0; j<col; j++)
            if(mat[i][j] != transp[i][j])
                status = 1;
    }
    return(status);
}

// main function
void main()
{
    Two_D trans;
    int status;
    int row,col;
    float transp[10][10];
    cout<<"\n Input number of rows:";
    cin>>row;
    cout<<"\n Input number of cols:";
    cin>>col;
    trans.input(transp,row,col);
    cout<<"\n Entered Matrix is as follows:\n";
    trans.display_o(transp,row,col);
```

```
    trans.transpose(transp,col,row);
    cout<<" \n Transpose of above matrix is as follows:\n";
    trans.display(col,row);
    status = trans.Symmetry_Matrix(transp, row, col);
    if( status)
        cout<<"\n Matrix is not symmetric ";
    else
        cout<<"\n Matrix is Symmetric ";
}
```

```
Input number of rows: 3
Input number of cols: 3
Input Value for : 1 : 1 : 1
Input Value for : 1 : 2 : 0
Input Value for : 1 : 3 : 0
Input Value for : 2 : 1 : 0
Input Value for : 2 : 2 : 1
Input Value for : 2 : 3 : 0
Input Value for : 3 : 1 : 0
Input Value for : 3 : 2 : 0
Input Value for : 3 : 3 : 1

Entered Matrix is as follows:
    1   0   0
    0   1   0
    0   0   1

Transpose of above matrix is as follows:
    1   0   0
    0   1   0
    0   0   1

Matrix is Symmetric
```

4.9.9 RANK OF A MATRIX

The rank of a matrix **r** is defined, if

(i) *It has at least one non-zero minor of order* ***r****.*
(ii) *Every minor of* ***A*** *of order higher than* ***r*** *is zero.*

To find the rank of a matrix reduce the given matrix to upper triangular form. Rank of the matrix is equal to the number of non-zero rows. A non-zero row must contain at least one non-zero element. The algorithm to find rank of a matrix is given in **Fig. 4.35.**

For example, suppose we have matrix **A**

$$A = \begin{pmatrix} 1 & 4 & 5 \\ 2 & 6 & 8 \\ 3 & 7 & 22 \end{pmatrix}$$

Step 1: Subtract **2** times of the first row from the second row that is $\mathbf{R_2 - 2*R_1}$ and **3** times of the first row from the third row that is $\mathbf{R_3 - 3*R_1}$.

$$=> \begin{pmatrix} 1 & 4 & 5 \\ 0 & -2 & -2 \\ 0 & -5 & 7 \end{pmatrix}$$

Taking **-2** common from the second row we get

$$=> \begin{pmatrix} 1 & 4 & 5 \\ 0 & 1 & 1 \\ 0 & -5 & 7 \end{pmatrix} \quad -1/2\, R_2$$

Adding **5** times the second row into the third row that is $\mathbf{R_3 + 5*R_2}$

$$=> \begin{pmatrix} 1 & 4 & 5 \\ 0 & 1 & 1 \\ 0 & 0 & 12 \end{pmatrix}$$

Thus from the above resulting matrix it is clear that there is no non-zero row in the matrix hence the rank of the matrix **A** is **3**. For example, **RANK.C** implements the above discussion.

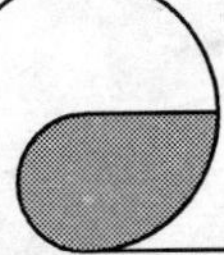

Step 1:[Find rank]
Repeat through for r = 0, 1, 2 … Col –1
Step 2: [Check whether the diagonal element is zero or not]
If mat [r][r] ≠ 0
Repeat through Step 3 for c = 0, 1, 2 … Col – 1
Step 3: [Check equality of row and column indices]
If r ≠ c
(i) ratio = mat [c][r] / mat [r][r]
(ii) repeat through (iii) for I =0, 1, 2 … Col – 1
(iii) mat [c][i] = mat [c][i] – ratio *mat [r][i]

Step 4: [Move execution forward]
Else
Output "Execution in progress"
Step 5: Else
Repeat through (ii) for c = r+1, r+2 … Row – 1
(i) if mat [c][r] ≠ 0 [Find non-zero element]
(ii) call swap (r,c, col)

Step 6: if c = row
(i) Col = Col – 1
(ii) Repeat through (iii) for c = 0, 1, 2 … Row – 1
(iii) mat [c][r] = mat [c][col]
(iv) r = r – 1

Sstep 7: Return (Col) [Last value of Col gives rank of matrix]

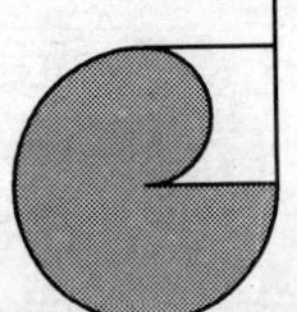

Fig. 4.35 Algorithm to find rank of a matrix

```
// Find Rank of a Matrix
// RANK.C

# include<iostream.h>
# include<iomanip.h>

int R,C;
class Two_D
```

```
{
        private: int i, j;
            int mat[10][10];

        public:
            void display( int, int);
            void input( int, int);
            Rank_Mat(int , int);
            void swap(int, int, int);
};

// This function exchanges two rows of a matrix

void Two_D :: swap( int row1,int row2, int col)
{
        for( i = 0; i < col; i++)
        {
        int temp = mat[row1][i];
        mat[row1][i] = mat[row2][i];
        mat[row2][i] = temp;
        }
}

// This function find rank of matrix

int Two_D :: Rank_Mat(int row1, int col1)
{
        for( int r = 0; r< col1); r++)
        {
        display(R,C);
        if( mat[r][r] ) // Diagonal element is not zero
            for( int c = 0; c < row1; c++)
            if( c != r)
            {

// Make all the elements above and below the current principal
// diagonal element zero

            float ratio = mat[c][r]/ mat[r][r];
            for( i = 0; i < col1); i++)
            mat[c][i] -= ratio * mat[r][i];
            }
                else
            cout<<"\n";

// Principal Diagonal elment is zero
```

```
        else
    {
    for( int c = r+1 ; c < row1; c++)
        if ( mat[c][r])
        {
        // Find non zero elements in the same column
        swap(r,c,col1);
        break ;
        }

    if( c == row1
    {
        -- col1);

        for( c= 0; c < row1; c ++)
            mat[c][r] = mat[c][col1];
    }
    --r;
}
}
    return col1);
}

// Output function

void Two_D :: display( int row, int col)
{
    for( i = 0; i < row; i++)
    {
        for( j = 0; j < col; j++)
        {
        cout <<setw(8)<<mat[i][j];
        }
        cout<<"\n";
    }
}

// Input function

void Two_D :: input( int row, int col)
{
    int value;
    for( i = 0 ; i< row; i++)
    {
    for( j = 0 ; j<col; j++)
```

```
        {
            cout<<"Input Value for : "<< i+1 <<" : "<<j+1<<" : " ;
            cin >> value;
            mat[i][j] = value;
        }
        }
}

// main function

void main()
{
        Two_D Rank_Matrix;

        int rank;
        cout<<"\n Input number of rows:";
        cin>>R;
        cout<<"\n Input number of cols:";
        cin>>C;
        Rank_Matrix.input(R,C);
        cout<<"\n Row is :"<<R;
        cout<<"\n Column is :"<<C;

        cout<<"\n Entered Two Dimensional array is as follows:\n";
        Rank_Matrix.display(R,C);
        cout<<"\n Row is :"<<R;
        cout<<"\n Column is :"<<C;

        rank = Rank_Matrix.Rank_Mat(R,C);
        cout<<"\n Rank of above matrix is : "<< rank;
}
```

```
Input number of rows: 3
 Input number of cols: 4
 Input Value for : 1 : 1 : 1
 Input Value for : 1 : 2 : 2
 Input Value for : 1 : 3 : -1
 Input Value for : 1 : 4 : 3
 Input Value for : 2 : 1 : 3
 Input Value for : 2 : 2 : 4
 Input Value for : 2 : 3 : 0
 Input Value for : 2 : 4 : -1
 Input Value for : 3 : 1 : -1
 Input Value for : 3 : 2 : 0
 Input Value for : 3 : 3 : -2
 Input Value for : 3 : 4 : 7

 Entered Two Dimensional array is as follows:
     1    2    -1     3
     3    4     0    -1
    -1    0    -2     7
            STEP 1
     1    2    -1     3
     3    4     0    -1
    -1    0    -2     7
            STEP 2
     1    2    -1     3
     0   -2     3   -10
     0    2    -3    10
            STEP 3
     1    0     2    -7
     0   -2     3   -10
     0    0     0     0
           STEP 4
     1    0    -7    -7
     0   -2   -10   -10
     0    0     0     0

 Rank of above matrix is : 2
```

4.10 GENERAL MUTLIDIMENSIONAL ARRAYS

General multidimensional arrays can be defined analogously. Suppose we want to define a n-dimensional $\mathbf{d_1 \ x \ d_2 \ x \ d_3 \ x...x \ d_n}$ array **M.** Then a collection of $\mathbf{d_1.d_2.d_3 \ ... \ d_n}$ information, in which each information specified by a list of **n** integers such as $\mathbf{I_1, I_2, I_3 \ ... \ I_n}$ are called subscripts, with the property that

$0 \le I_1 < d_1, 0 \le I_2 < d_2 \ldots\ 0 \le I_n < d_n$

The information of **M** with subscripts $I_1, I_2, I_3 \ldots I_n$ will be represented by

$M_{I1,\ I2,\ I3\ \ldots\ In}$ or $M[I_1][I_2][I_3]\ \cdots\ [I_n]$

The memory representation of multidimensional arrays is illustrated in **Fig. 4.36** and **Fig. 4.37.** The program segment **D9.C** illustrates a 9 subscript array.

```
// D9.C
# include<iostream.h>
# define r 2
 void main()
 {
 int m[r][r][r][r][r][r][r][r][r];

 // Input section
 for (int a = 0; a < r; a++)
       for (int b = 0; b < r; b++)
       for (int c = 0; c < r; c++)

 for (int d = 0; d < r; d++)
       for (int e = 0; e < r; e++)
       for (int f = 0; f < r; f++)
 for (int g = 0; g < r; g++)
       for (int h = 0; h < r; h++)
       for (int i = 0; i < r; i++)

         m[a][b][c][d][e][f][g][h][i] = a + b + c + d + e + f + g + h + i;

// Output section row major order
cout<<"\n ADDRESS        ARRAY M WITH INDEX VALUE \n";
 for (a = 0; a < r; a++)
       for (b = 0; b < r; b++)
       for (c = 0; c < r; c++)
 for (d = 0; d < r; d++)
       for (e = 0; e < r; e++)
       for (f = 0; f < r; f++)
 for (g = 0; g < r; g++)
       for (h = 0; h < r; h++)
       for (i = 0; i < r; i++)
       {
       cout<<"\n"<< &m[a][b][c][d][e][f][g][h][i];

       cout<<" m["<<a<<"]["<<b<<"]["<<c<<"]["<<d<<"]["<<e<<"]["<<f
```

```
<<"]["<<g<<"]["<<h<<"]["<<i<<"] = "<<m[a][b][c][d][e][f][g][h][i];
}

// Column major order
cout<<"\n ADDRESS     ARRAY M WITH INDEX VALUE \n";

for (i = 0; i < r; i++)
    for (h = 0; h < r; h++)
     for (g = 0; g < r; g++)
for (f = 0; f < r; f++)
    for (e = 0; e < r; e++)
     for (d = 0; d < r; d++)
for (c = 0; c < r; c++)
    for (b = 0; b < r; b++)
     for (a = 0; a < r; a++)
     {
     cout<<"\n"<< &m[a][b][c][d][e][f][g][h][i];

     cout<<" m["<<a<<"]["<<b<<"]["<<c<<"]["<<d<<"]["<<e<<"]["<<f
     <<"]["<<g<<"]["<<h<<"]["<<i<<"] = "<<m[a][b][c][d][e][f][g][h][i];
     }
}
```

If one runs the above program segment the output comes like:

ROW MAJOR ORDER

```
ADDRESS      ARRAY M WITH INDEX VALUE

0x1ebbfbe8   m[0][0][0][0][0][0][0][0][0] = 0
0x1ebbfbea   m[0][0][0][0][0][0][0][0][1] = 1
0x1ebbfbec   m[0][0][0][0][0][0][0][1][0] = 1
0x1ebbfbee   m[0][0][0][0][0][0][0][1][1] = 2
0x1ebbfbf0   m[0][0][0][0][0][0][1][0][0] = 1
0x1ebbfbf2   m[0][0][0][0][0][0][1][0][1] = 2
0x1ebbfbf4   m[0][0][0][0][0][0][1][1][0] = 2
0x1ebbfbf6   m[0][0][0][0][0][0][1][1][1] = 3
0x1ebbfbf8   m[0][0][0][0][0][1][0][0][0] = 1
0x1ebbfbfa   m[0][0][0][0][0][1][0][0][1] = 2
             ...
             ...
             ...
0x1ebbffb8   m[1][1][1][1][0][1][0][0][0] = 5
0x1ebbffba   m[1][1][1][1][0][1][0][0][1] = 6
0x1ebbffbc   m[1][1][1][1][0][1][0][1][0] = 6
0x1ebbffbe   m[1][1][1][1][0][1][0][1][1] = 7
0x1ebbffc0   m[1][1][1][1][0][1][1][0][0] = 6
```

```
0x1ebbffc2    m[1][1][1][1][0][1][1][0][1] = 7
0x1ebbffc4    m[1][1][1][1][0][1][1][1][0] = 7
0x1ebbffc6    m[1][1][1][1][0][1][1][1][1] = 8
0x1ebbffc8    m[1][1][1][1.][1][0][0][0][0] = 5
0x1ebbffca    m[1][1][1][1][1][0][0][0][1] = 6
0x1ebbffcc    m[1][1][1][1][1][0][0][1][0] = 6
0x1ebbffce    m[1][1][1][1][1][0][0][1][1] = 7
0x1ebbffd0    m[1][1][1][1][1][0][1][0][0] = 6
0x1ebbffd2    m[1][1][1][1][1][0][1][0][1] = 7
0x1ebbffd4    m[1][1][1][1][1][0][1][1][0] = 7
0x1ebbffd6    m[1][1][1][1][1][0][1][1][1] = 8
0x1ebbffd8    m[1][1][1][1][1][1][0][0][0] = 6
0x1ebbffda    m[1][1][1][1][1][1][0][0][1] = 7
0x1ebbffdc    m[1][1][1][1][1][1][0][1][0] = 7
0x1ebbffde    m[1][1][1][1][1][1][0][1][1] = 8
0x1ebbffe0    m[1][1][1][1][1][1][1][0][0] = 7
0x1ebbffe2    m[1][1][1][1][1][1][1][0][1] = 8
0x1ebbffe4    m[1][1][1][1][1][1][1][1][0] = 8
0x1ebbffe6    m[1][1][1][1][1][1][1][1][1] = 9
```

ADDRESS	INFO	m[a][b][c][d][e][f][g][h][i]
0x1ebbfbe8	0	m[0][0][0][0][0][0][0][0][0]
0x1ebbfbea	1	m[0][0][0][0][0][0][0][0][1]
0x1ebbfbec	1	m[0][0][0][0][0][0][0][1][0]
0x1ebbfbee	2	m[0][0][0][0][0][0][0][1][1]
0x1ebbfbf0	1	m[0][0][0][0][0][0][1][0][0]
0x1ebbffe0	7	m[1][1][1][1][1][1][1][0][0]
0x1ebbffe2	8	m[1][0][1][1][1][1][1][0][1]
0x1ebbffe4	8	m[1][1][1][1][1][1][1][1][0]
0x1ebbffe6	9	m[1][1][1][1][1][1][1][1][1]

Fig. 4.36 Row major order representation of a 9x9 array in memory

COLUMN MAJOR ORDER

```
ADDRESS       ARRAY M WITH INDEX VALUE
0x1ebbfbe8    m[0][0][0][0][0][0][0][0][0]=    0
0x1ebbfde8    m[1][0][0][0][0][0][0][0][0]=    1
0x1ebbfce8    m[0][1][0][0][0][0][0][0][0]=    1
```

```
0x1ebbfee8    m[1][1][0][0][0][0][0][0][0]=    2
0x1ebbfc68    m[0][0][1][0][0][0][0][0][0]=    1
0x1ebbfe68    m[1][0][1][0][0][0][0][0][0]=    2
0x1ebbfd68    m[0][1][1][0][0][0][0][0][0]=    2
0x1ebbff68    m[1][1][1][0][0][0][0][0][0]=    3
0x1ebbfc28    m[0][0][0][1][0][0][0][0][0]=    1
0x1ebbfe28    m[1][0][0][1][0][0][0][0][0]=    2
0x1ebbfd28    m[0][1][0][1][0][0][0][0][0]=    2
0x1ebbff28    m[1][1][0][1][0][0][0][0][0]=    3
0x1ebbfca8    m[0][0][1][1][0][0][0][0][0]=    2
0x1ebbfea8    m[1][0][1][1][0][0][0][0][0]=    3
0x1ebbfda8    m[0][1][1][1][0][0][0][0][0]=    3
0x1ebbffa8    m[1][1][1][1][0][0][0][0][0]=    4
0x1ebbfc08    m[0][0][0][0][1][0][0][0][0]=    1
              ...
              ...
              ...

0x1ebbfc26    m[0][0][0][0][1][1][1][1][1]=    5
0x1ebbfe26    m[1][0][0][0][1][1][1][1][1]=    6
0x1ebbfd26    m[0][1][0][0][1][1][1][1][1]=    6
0x1ebbff26    m[1][1][0][0][1][1][1][1][1]=    7
0x1ebbfca6    m[0][0][1][0][1][1][1][1][1]=    6
0x1ebbfea6    m[1][0][1][0][1][1][1][1][1]=    7
0x1ebbfda6    m[0][1][1][0][1][1][1][1][1]=    7
0x1ebbffa6    m[1][1][1][0][1][1][1][1][1]=    8
0x1ebbfc66    m[0][0][0][1][1][1][1][1][1]=    6
0x1ebbfe66    m[1][0][0][1][1][1][1][1][1]=    7
0x1ebbfd66    m[0][1][0][1][1][1][1][1][1]=    7
0x1ebbff66    m[1][1][0][1][1][1][1][1][1]=    8
0x1ebbfce6    m[0][0][1][1][1][1][1][1][1]=    7
0x1ebbfee6    m[1][0][1][1][1][1][1][1][1]=    8
0x1ebbfde6    m[0][1][1][1][1][1][1][1][1]=    8
0x1ebbffe6    m[1][1][1][1][1][1][1][1][1]=    9
```

ADDRESS	INFO	m[a][b][c][d][e][f][g][h][i]
0x1ebbfbe8	0	m[0][0][0][0][0][0][0][0][0]
0x1ebbfde8	1	m[1][0][0][0][0][0][0][0][0]
0x1ebbfce8	1	m[0][1][0][0][0][0][0][0][0]
0x1ebbfee8	2	m[1][1][0][0][0][0][0][0][0]
0x1ebbfc68	1	m[0][0][1][0][0][0][0][0][0]
0x1ebbfce6	7	m[0][0][1][1][1][1][1][1][1]
0x1ebbfee6	8	m[1][0][1][1][1][1][1][1][1]
0x1ebbfde6	8	m[0][1][1][1][1][1][1][1][1]
0x1ebbffe6	9	m[1][1][1][1][1][1][1][1][1]

Fig. 4.37 Column major order representation of a 9x9 array in memory

4.11 SPARSE MATRICES

Matrices with a relatively high proportion of zero entries are called sparse matrices. Two general types of n-square sparse matrices, which occur in various applications, are shown in **Fig. 4.38.** The second matrix where all entries above the main diagonal are zero or equivalently where nonzero entries can only occur on or below the main diagonal is called a lower triangular matrix. The first matrix where nonzero entries can only occur on the diagonal or on elements immediately above or below the diagonal is called a tri-diagonal matrix.

4	-3					
5	-5	6				
	0	6	-9			
		-4	3	-7		
			2	-8	0	
				5	-7	9
					8	10

(a) Tri-diagonal matrix

4						
3	-5					
1	0	6				
-7	8	-4	3			
5	-5	0	2	-8		
1	4	-9	-8	0	-7	
6	-8	4	-56	1	8	10

(b) Triangular matrix

Fig. 4.38 sparse matrices

The natural method of representing matrices in memory as two-dimensional arrays may not be suitable for sparse matrices. That is, one may save space by storing only those entries, which may be nonzero. This can be explained with the help of suitable example, consider the matrix given below:

M [6][7] =

0	0	6	0	9	0	0
2	0	0	7	8	0	4
10	0	0	0	0	0	0
0	0	12	0	0	0	0
0	0	0	0	0	0	0
0	0	0	3	0	0	5

of the 42 elements in this 6x7 matrix only 10 are nonzero. These are

M[1][3] = 6, M[1][5] = 9, M[2][1] = 2, M[2][4] = 7, M[2][5] = 8, M[2][7] = 4
M[3][1] = 10, M[4][3] = 12, M[6][4] = 3, M[6][7] = 5

Index	Row	Col	V
1	1	3	6
2	1	5	9
3	2	1	2
4	2	4	7
5	2	5	8
6	2	7	4
7	3	1	10
8	4	3	12
9	6	4	3
10	6	7	5

Fig. 4.39 sequential representation of sparse matrix

One of the basic methods for storing such a sparse matrix is to store nonzero elements in a one-dimensional array and to identify each array element with row and column indices as shown in **Fig. 4.39.**

The ith element of vector **V** is the matrix element with row and column indices **Row[i]** and **Col[i].** Note that the matrix elements are stored in row major order with zero elements removed. A more efficient representation in terms of storage requirements and access time to the rows of the matrix is shown in **Fig. 4.40.** The Row vector is changed so that its ith element is the index to the first of the column indices for the element in row **i** of the matrix. We assume that the **Row** and **Col** vectors consist of half words. The representations of matrix **M** in **Fig. 4.39** and **Fig. 4.40** have cut storage requirements by more than one half. For large matrices the conservation of storage is very significant. The sequential allocation scheme for sparse matrices is also of value, in that matrix operations can be executed faster than possible with a conventional two-dimensional array representation, particularly when matrices are large. A general algorithm for adding two sparse matrices is as follows:

1 *Repeat through step 8 until all rows have been processed*
2 *Obtain current row indices for matrix **M** and **N***
3 *Obtain starting position in vectors of next row in matrix **M** and **N***
4 *Repeat through step 6 until either the end of matrix **M's** or **N's** row is reached*
5 *If elements exist in the same column in matrix **M** and **N** then sum elements and move on the next column in matrix **M** and **N** else if matrix **M** column number is less than matrix **N's** column number then move on to the next column in matrix M else move on to next column of matrix **N***
6 *Add new element to matrix **R***
7 *If the end of matrix **M's** row has not been reached then add remaining elements in row to matrix **R***
8 *If the end of matrix N's row has not been reached then add remaining elements in row to matrix **R***

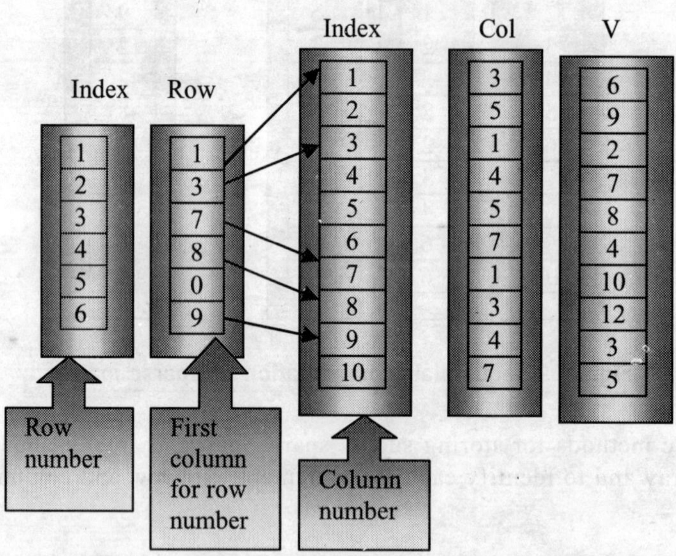

Fig. 4.40 Sequential representation of sparse matrix

EXERCISE

4.1 *Suppose we have an array **M** as illustrated in **Fig. 4.41.** If one deletes 11 and insert 22 at place of 11 then find the number of moves performed to complete operations. If final array required in sorted order then how many moves are required to complete the insertion and deletion operations.*

4.2 *Let **A** and **B** are two arrays and their size are 50 and 60 respectively. Suppose one wants to keep 100 data in these arrays. But in accessing the data problems are that when one makes a search for particular data if he/she does not find the data in array **A** then goes into array **B** in this fashion accessing of data being very slow. Suggest remedies for this problem.*

4.3 *Consider the following list of elements and generate PASCAL triangle.*

LIST: 0, 1, 2, 3, 4, 5, 6, 7, 8, 9, 10, 15, 20, 21, 28, 35, 36, 56, 70, 84, 126.

INDEX	INFO
0	99
1	88
2	77
3	66
4	55
5	11
6	10
7	11
8	22
9	100
10	33
11	44
12	
13	
14	

Fig. 4.41 Array M in memory

4.4 *Suppose one wants to create students record of a class with following information:*

- *Name*
- *Father's name*

- *Branch*
- *Class*
- *Roll number*
- *Enrollment number*

How will one maintain records of 20 students with the help of arrays?

4.5 *Evaluate the following polynomial with the help of* **Horner's** *method.*

$$P(x) = a_1x^{n} + a_2x^{n-1} + a_3x^{n-2} + \dots + a_{n+1}.$$

4.6 *Write an algorithm to concatenate two arrays **A** and **B**. Implement the designed algorithm.*

4.7 *Find inverse of the following matrices:*

(a)
$$A = \begin{pmatrix} 1 & 2 & 3 \\ 2 & 4 & \cdot 7 \\ 3 & 6 & 10 \end{pmatrix}$$

(b)
$$B = \begin{pmatrix} 1 & 2 & 1 \\ 1 & 0 & 2 \\ 2 & 1 & -3 \end{pmatrix}$$

4.8 *Find rank of the following matrices:*

(a)
$$A = \begin{pmatrix} 1 & 3 & 2 & 5 & 1 \\ 2 & 2 & -1 & 6 & 3 \\ 1 & 1 & 2 & 3 & -1 \\ 0 & 2 & 5 & 2 & -3 \end{pmatrix}$$

(b)
$$B = \begin{pmatrix} 1 & 2 & 3 & 4 & 5 \\ 6 & 7 & 8 & 9 & 10 \\ 3 & 3 & 3 & 3 & 3 \\ 2 & 2 & 2 & 2 & 2 \\ 1 & 1 & 1 & 1 & 1 \end{pmatrix}$$

4.9 *Consider the matrix*

$$A = \begin{pmatrix} 1 & 2 & 3 & 4 & 5 & 6 & 7 \\ 8 & 9 & 10 & 11 & 12 & 13 & 14 \\ 15 & 16 & 17 & 18 & 19 & 20 & 21 \end{pmatrix}$$

Write a program that finds upper and lower half of the matrix.

4.10 An input alphabet consists of the following twenty nine symbols:

ZERO, ONE, TWO, THREE, FOUR, FIVE, SIX, SEVEN, EIGHT, NINE, TEN, ELEVEN, TWELVE, THIRTEEN, FOURTEEN, FIFTEEN, SIXTEEN, SEVENTEEN, EIGHTEEN, NINTEEN, TWENTY, THIRTY, FORTY, FIFTY, SIXTY, SEVENTY, EIGHTY, NINETY, HUNDRED.

*Write an algorithm that accepts as input the English language representation for example "**ONE HUNDRED THIRTY**" of any number from 0 to 999 and outputs the equivalent decimal number (130 in this case). Implement the designed algorithm.*

4.11 What do you understand trace of a matrix? Design an algorithm.

*4.12 A dynamic declared array **A** is defined with row subscripts varying from **0** to **n-1** and column subscripts varying from 0 to 5. Show the storage mapping function to map **A** into memory assuming row-major order storage.*

*4.13 Assume that 8-byte of storage are required to hold each element of the following **A** array:*

```
int A[10][18];
```

*Assuming further that storage for the array begins at byte 4000 in memory, show the actual address of the element values **A [8][4]**.*

*4.14 Consider the three-dimensional array **D** whose subscript limits are*

$1 \leq i \leq 3,\ 1 \leq j \leq 3,\ 0 \leq k \leq 1$

*Give the addressing function for the element **D[i][j][k]** where the storage representation is in column major order.*

*4.15 Consider the linear array **A[5:100], B[-5:20]** and **C[20]***

(i) Find the number of elements in each array.
*(ii) Suppose **base(A) = 0x800** and **w = 4** per words per memory cell for **A**. Find the address of **A[10]** and **A[85]***

*4.16 Suppose a company keeps a linear array **year[1940:1985]** such that **year[k]** contains the number of employees born in year **k**. Write a function for each of the following tasks:*

(i) Find years in which no employee was born.
*(ii) To find the number of employees who will be at least **L** year old at the end of the year. Read the systems date for the current date; take care of **Y2K** problem.*

*4.17 Consider the alphabetized linear arrays List in **Fig. 4.42***

(i) *Find the number of elements that must be moved if Scotch, David and Sanath are inserted into List at the three different times.*
(ii) *How many elements are moved if three names are inserted at the same time?*
(iii) *How does the Telephone Company handle insertions in a telephone directory?*
(iv) *Write a function for each of the above tasks.*

4.18 *Let **M** is a **n x n** matrix. Write a function which finds*

(i) *The number of zero elements in **M***
(ii) *The summation of the diagonal elements*
(iii) *The products of the diagonal elements*

4.19 *An array contains 100 integers number. Write a module which*

(i) *Finds all pairs of elements whose sum is 50.*
(ii) *Finds even and odd, +ve and –ve numbers.*

Index	Name
1	Ajay Jadeja
2	Anil Kumble
3	Chndra Shekhar
4	Donald
5	Edwords
6	Gopal
7	Hunter
8	Imran
9	Klein
10	Lewis
11	More
12	Richards
13	Sachin
14	Vinod Kambli

Fig. 4.42 List in memory

The computers are used in data processing to perform operations like:

- *Deletion of information*
- *Insertion of information*
- *Updating information*
- *Report writing, etc.*

If we use fixed length memory storage (arrays) it is not always possible to perform above tasks. A linked list allocation storage method can result in efficient use of computer memory and computer time. Linked list are useful because:

- ***Unpredictable storage requirements**: The exact amount of data storage space required by a program in these areas often depends on the data being processed and consequently this requirement can not be easily determined at the time of writing the program.*

- ***Extensive manipulation of the stored data**: Programs in these areas require the operations such as insertion and deletion to perform frequent operations on the data.*

In this chapter we will discuss linear data structures **linked list: singly, doubly, circular, circular header**, application of linked list- **polynomial,** etc.

5.1 LINKED LIST

A linked list is defined as a collection of nodes. Each node has two parts:

- *Information*
- *Pointer to next node*

Information part may consist of one or more than one field. In other words a linked list consists of series of structures, which are not necessarily contiguous. Each structure contains one or more than one contiguous information fields and a pointer to a structure containing its successor. The last node of the list contains **NULL ('\0')** in the pointer field. The pointer contains the address of the location where next information is stored. For example, **Fig. 5.1** illustrates a linked list structure with 4 nodes, each node containing one information field. A linked list also contains a list pointer variable called **start**, which contains the address of the first node in the list. Hence, there is an arrow drawn from **start** to the first node in the linked list. If there is no node in the list, the list is called **NULL** list or empty list.

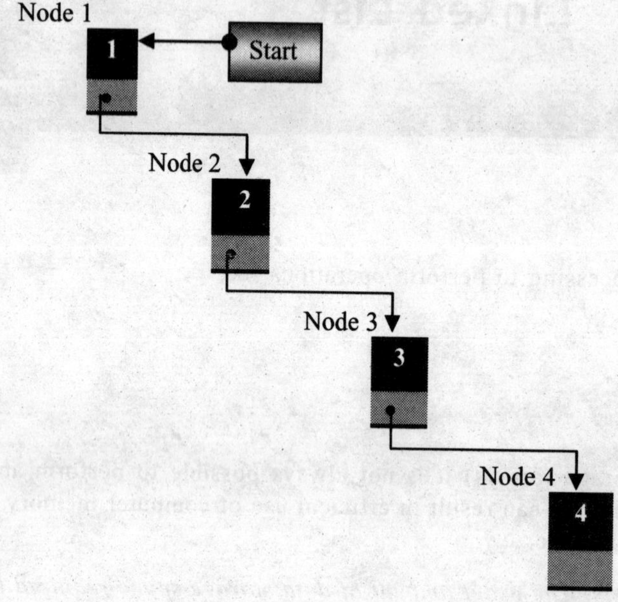

Fig. 5.1 Linked list

Suppose Indian Cricket coach decides to keep batting order according to past performance of players. Also, the first 6 positions are decided and rest four positions depend on the team performance. **Fig. 5.2** illustrates this policy. If we examine the list given in **Fig. 5.2**, we find that batting order-opened by Sachin then Saurabh at 2nd position, at 3rd position Azaharuddin, 4th position Jadeja, 5th position Kambli and at 6th position Kumble is placed.

Fig. 5.2 Alphabet arrangement of batting order

5.2 BUILDING A LINKED LIST

To create a linked list, following steps are required:

(a) *Declare the structure that defines the list entries.*

(b) *Declare the variables* ***start*** *and* ****node (or *start*** *and* ****node)***

(c) *Assign* ***start.next = NULL (or start = NULL*** *if* ***start*** *is* ****start)*** *to signify an empty list.*

(d) *Find each list entry*

  (i) *Find end of the list so that* ***node->next*** *is* ***NULL.***

  (ii) *Allocate memory for the new entry by assigning it to* ***node->next***.

  (iii) *Assign node the value of* ***node->next***.

  (iv) *Assign the member values to node.*

  (v) *Assign* ***node->next*** *the value* ***NULL*** *to indicate the end of the list.*

We have discussed that a linked list is a collection of the nodes (structure) of the same type and hence it can be defined as:

```
struct Node
{
    Data type Information;
    struct Node *Next ;
} start, *node;
```

The above definition of the structure (node) is equivalent to the following figure:

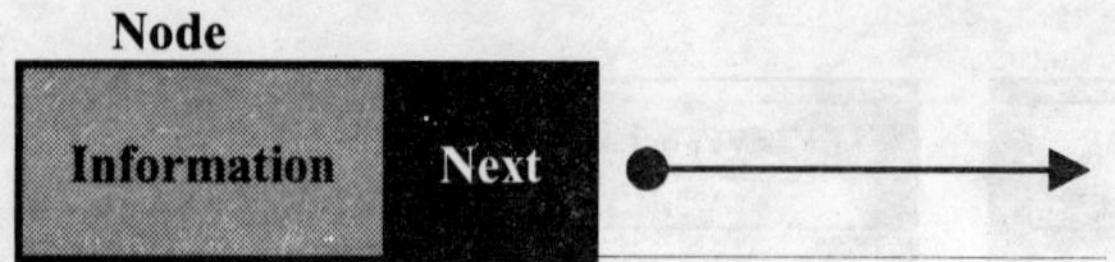

A node may contain any number of information fields. The general declaration of a node is:

```
struct Tag Name
{
    Data Type1 Field1 ;
    Data Type2 Field2 ;
    Data Type3 Field3 ;
        ...
        ...
        ...
    Data Type n Field n ;
    struct Tag Name *Next ;
};
```

The above syntax may be represented as:

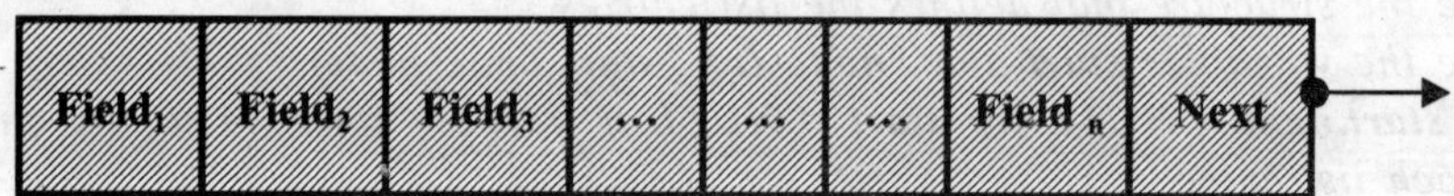

How can a linked list be created? To do this, let one has a node as follows:

```
struct List
{
    char Data ;
    struct List *Next ;
};
```

Let one wants to create a linked list that contains four nodes, the nodes are **Node$_1$**, **Node$_2$**, **Node$_3$** and **Node$_4$**. These nodes are defined as

```
struct List Node1, Node2, Node3, Node4;
```

Fig. 5.3 illustrates the allocation of memory spaces to the nodes **Node$_1$**, **Node$_2$**, **Node$_3$** and **Node$_4$**.

$Node_1$.Data
$Node_1$.Next

$Node_2$.Data
$Node_2$.Next

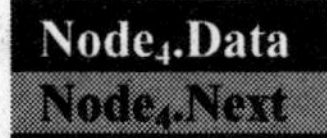

Fig. 5.3 Allocation of memory space to individual node

If one wants to create a link between these four nodes, the following arrangement is required.

- $Node_1.Next = \&Node_2$;

Assign the address of the **$Node_2$** to **$Node_1$.Next**, which establishes a link between **$Node_1$** and **$Node_2$**

- $Node_2.Next = \&Node_3$;

Assign the address of the **$Node_3$** to **$Node_2$.Next**, which establishes a link between **$Node_2$** and **$Node_3$**

- $Node_3.Next = \&Node_4$;

Assign the address of the **$Node_4$** to **$Node_3$.Next,** which establishes a link between **$Node_3$** and **$Node_4$**.

By repeating the above process, one can create a linked list of desired size. The program segment **LINK.C** implements the above discussion.

```
// LINK.C
// This program segment defines linked list having a character type data in node

# include<iostream.h>
# include<malloc.h>
struct list
{
    char data ;
```

```
        struct list *next ;
} ;

typedef struct list Linked;

void main()
{
        Linked *start, node1, node2 , node3 , node4;
        int i ;
        start = (struct list *) malloc(sizeof(Linked));
        start = &node1;

        node1.data = 'A' ;
        node1.next = &node2;

        node2.data = 'B' ;
        node2.next = &node3;

        node3.data = 'C' ;
        node3.next = &node4;
        node4.data = 'D' ;

       for( i = 0 ; i < 4 ; i++ )
       {
              cout<<"\n %c", start->data;
              start = start->next ;
              cout<<"\n Press a key";
              getchar();
       }
}
```

```
 A
Press a key
 B
Press a key
 C
Press a key
 D
Press a key
```

The program segment **LINK.C** illustrates that four nodes exist in the memory as illustrated in **Fig. 5.4.**

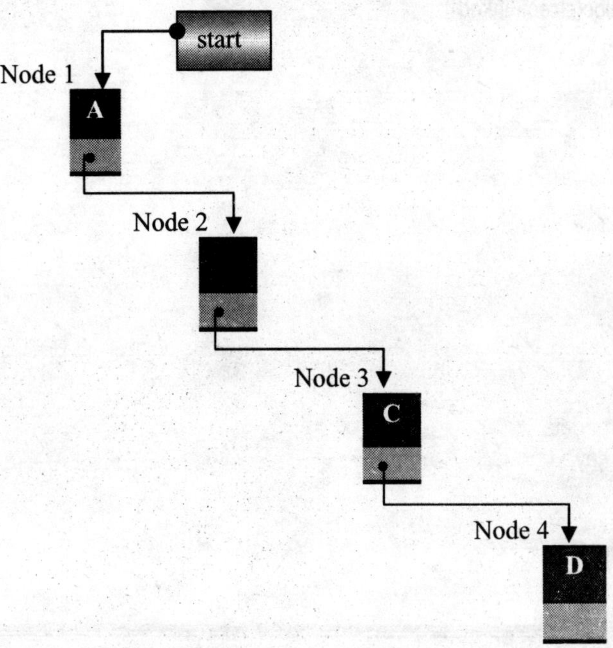

Fig. 5.4 Existence of nodes in memory

If one wants to supply string type information to information node, can do the same as illustrated in the following program segment:

```
// LINK_N.C
// This program segment define linked list having string type node

# include<iostream.h>
# include<malloc.h>

struct list
{
    char data[30];
    struct list *next ;
};

typedef struct list linked;

void main()
{
    linked *start, node1, node2 , node3 , node4;
    int i ;
```

```
    start = (struct list *) malloc(sizeof(linked));
    start = &node1;
    gets(node1.data);
    node1.next = &node2;
    gets(node2.data) ;
    node2.next = &node3;
    gets(node3.data) ;
    node3.next = &node4;
    gets(node4.data);
    node4.next = '\0' ;
    cout<<"\n Output is\n";
    do
    {
        cout<<"\n %s",start->data;
        cout<<"\n Press a key";
        getchar() ;
        start = start->next ;
    } while(start->next!='\0');
}
```

```
Input is

Ram
Bahadur
Patel
Jaunpur

Output is

Ram
Press a key
Bahadur
Press a key
Patel
Press a key
Jaunpur
Press a key
```

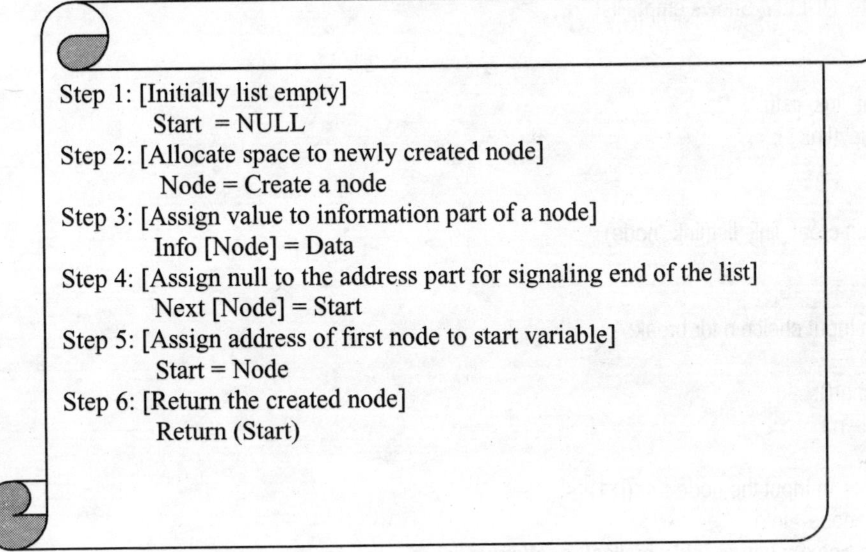

Fig. 5.5 Linked list creation algorithm

Algorithm for creating a linked list is illustrated in **Fig. 5.5.** The program segment **LINK_C.C** can be used to create a list of desired size.

```
// CREATING SIMPLE LINKED LIST
// LINK_C.C

# include <iostream.h>
# include <malloc.h>
# include <stdio.h>

struct link
{
    int info;
    link *next;
};

class creat_link
{
    private:
        int i;
        int number ;
        link *start;
    public:

    creat_link()
    {
```

```
            start = NULL; // Shows empty list
        }

        void creat_link_list(link *);
        void display(link *);
};

void creat_link :: creat_link_list(link *node)
{
        char ch;
        cout<<"\n Input choice n for break: ";
        i = 0;
        ch = getchar();
        while(ch !='n')
        {
            cout<<"\n Input the node :"<<(i+1)<<" : ";
            cin>>node->info;
            node->next = (struct link* ) malloc(sizeof(struct link));
            node = node->next;
            node->next = start;
            i++;
            cout<<"\n Input choice n for break: ";
            ch = getchar();
        }
}

// Display the list

void creat_link:: display(link *node)
{
        cout<<"\n Values of the entered nodes are as follows:\n";
        while (node->next)
        {
            cout<<" "<< node->info;
            node = node->next;
        }
}

// Function main
void main()
{
        creat_link link_c;
        link *node = (link *)malloc(sizeof(link));
        link_c.creat_link_list(node);
        link_c.display(node);
}
```

```
Input choice n for break:
Input the node: 1 : 11
Input choice n for break:
Input the node: 2 : 22
Input choice n for break:
Input the node: 3 : 33
Input choice n for break:
Input the node: 4 : 44
Input choice n for break:
Input the node: 5 : 55
Input choice n for break:
Input the node: 6 : 66
Input choice n for break:
Input the node: 7 : 77
Input choice n for break:
Input the node: 8 : 88
Input choice n for break:
Input the node: 9 : 99
Input choice n for break: n

Values of the entered nodes are as follows:
 11  22  33  44  55  66  77  88  99
```

5.3 TRAVERSING A LINKED LIST

Suppose we want to traverse a list in order to process each node exactly once. Let list be stored in memory as a linked list. Our aim is to traverse the list starting from the first node to the end of the list. Consider a pointer type variable **Current_node** that points to the node currently being processed. Accordingly, **Next [Current_node]** points to the next node that is to be processed. Thus the statement

Current_node = Next [Current_node];

moves the pointer to the next node in the list as illustrated in **Fig. 5.6**.

The variable **start.next** points to the first entry in the list. The code **node = strart.next** assigns the address of the first entry to **node**. Likewise, as we will recall, the end of the list is indicated by **NULL**; the loop simply tests the current value of **node** to see if it is **NULL**. If **node** is not **NULL**, the loop displays the entry's value and assigns **node** the address of the next list entry. For example, consider the list shown in **Fig. 5.7** and details of the processing is as follows:

Current_node = 2
Start.Next = 2
Info [2] = 11   Next [2] = 5

Info [5] = 55 Next [5] = 6
Info [6] = 44 Next [6] = 12
Info [12] = 80 Next [12] = 1
Info [1] = 22 Next [1] = 9
Info [9] = 33 Next [9] = 4
Info [4] = 66 Next [4] = 8
Info [8] = 99 Next [8] = 7
Info [7] = 88 Next [7] = '\0'

Thus the processed list is: 11, 55, 44, 80, 22, 33, 66, 99, 88

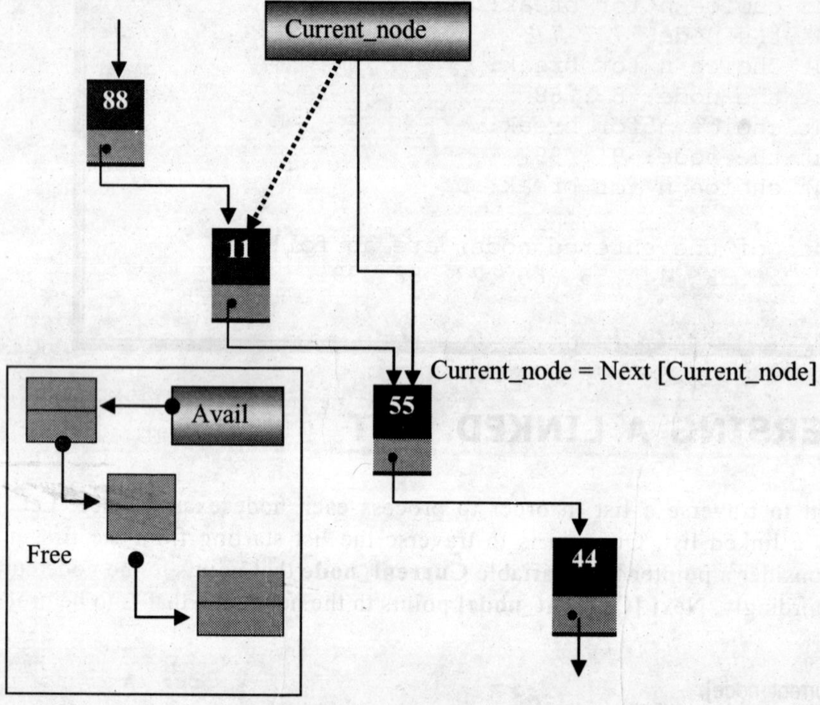

Fig. 5.6 Current_node = Next [Current_node]

```
// TRAVERSE.C

#include <iostream.h>
#include <malloc.h>

void main(void)
{
     int i;
```

```
    struct ListEntry
    {
        int number;
        struct ListEntry *next;
    } start, *node;

    start.next = NULL; /* Empty list */
    node = &start; /* Point to the start of the list */

    for (i = 1; i <= 10; i++)
    {
        node->next = (struct ListEntry *) malloc(sizeof(struct ListEntry));
        node = node->next;
        node->number = 50 + i;
        node->next = NULL;
    }

    // Display the list

    node = start.next;

    while (node)
    {
        cout<< node->number;
        node = node->next;
    }
}
```

In the above program, we have used the code segment which traverse the each node exactly once.

```
// Display the list

node = start.next;
while (node)
{
    cout<< node->number;
    node = node->next;
}
```

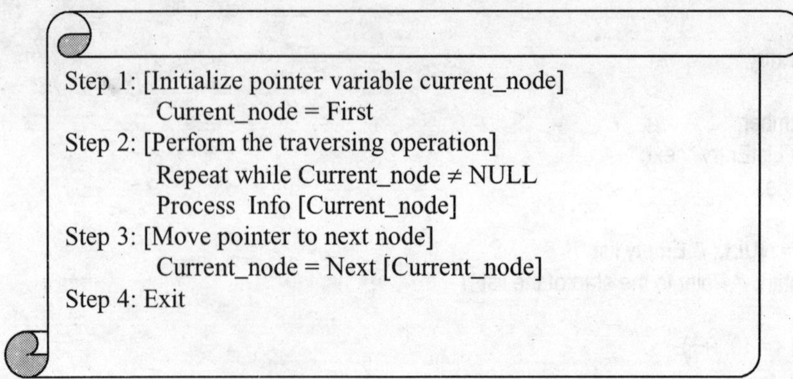

Step 1: [Initialize pointer variable current_node]
Current_node = First
Step 2: [Perform the traversing operation]
Repeat while Current_node ≠ NULL
Process Info [Current_node]
Step 3: [Move pointer to next node]
Current_node = Next [Current_node]
Step 4: Exit

Fig. 5.8 Algorithm to traverse nodes in a linked list

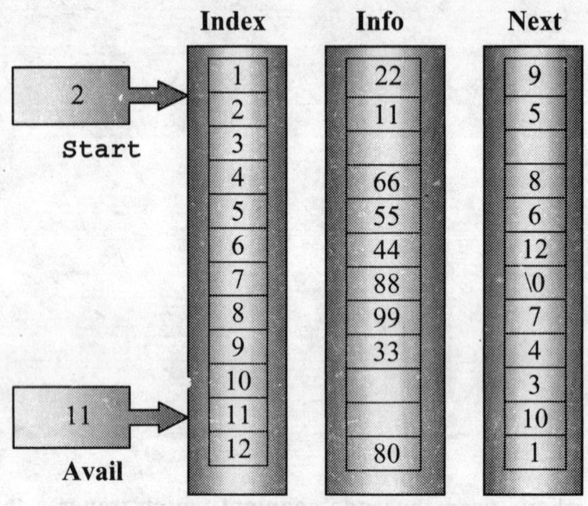

Fig. 5.7 Links of nodes

Suppose we have a list that contains **9** elements (integer) numbers. The links of each element are illustrated in **Fig. 5.7.** Algorithm for traversing a linked list is given in **Fig. 5.8.** The program segment **TRAVERSE.C** describes **Fig. 5.8.**

5.4 INSERTION IN A LINKED LIST

There are many applications where it is desirable to maintain an ordered linear list. The ordering may be in increasing or decreasing order of the information field. Such an ordering often results more efficient processes in many cases. If one wants to insert some information into linked list, following points must be remembered before performing the required operation:

1. *Create a new node or remove a node from the availability stack or free memory space.*
2. *Setting the field of the new node means allocating required memory space to newly created*

node.

3. *If the linked list is empty, return the address of a new node.*
4. *If the node precedes all others in the list, insert the node at front of the list and return its address.*
5. *Repeat the Step 6 while information contents of the new node.*
6. *Obtain the next node in the linked list.*
7. *Insert the new node in the linked list and return address of its first node.*

Suppose we have a list as illustrated in **Fig. 5.9** and want to perform insertion operation on the list. The insertion operation is classified into following three categories:

- *Insert as a first node*
- *Insert as a last node*
- *Insert as a node at any place in a list*

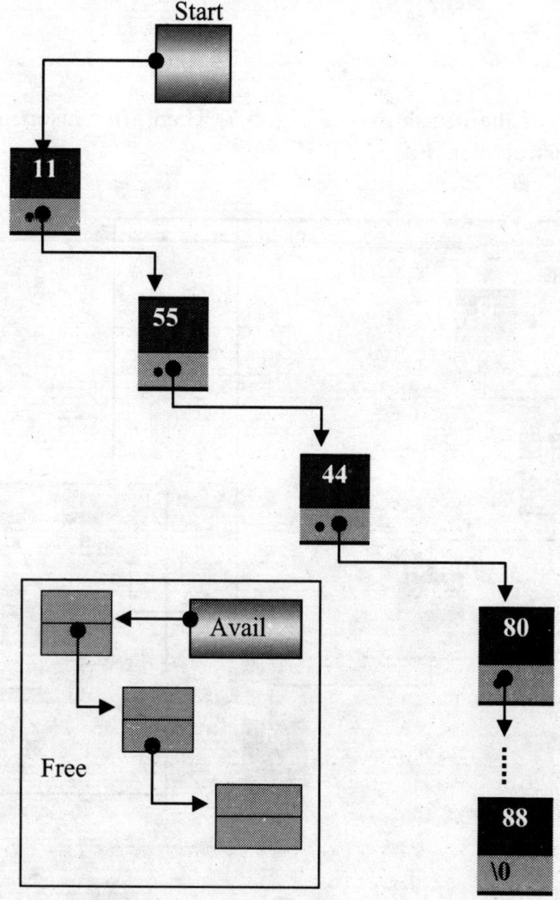

Fig. 5.9 List in memory

5.4.1 INSERTION AS A FIRST NODE

Let the **start** pointer hold the address of the first node and **previous** be a pointer type variable that holds the address of the **start**. The **new$_1$->next** variable holds the address of the first node of the list. Now **previous->next** variable holds the address of the **new$_1$** (Newly inserted node) into the list. Hence, the list becomes as illustrated in **Fig. 5.10. Fig. 5.9** illustrates a list before insertion operation.

In the statement form, above discussion can be written as:

```
node = start.next;
previous = &start;
new1 = (struct link *) malloc (sizeof (struct link));
new1->next = node;
previous->next = new1;
new1->data = some_value;
```

For example, consider the list shown in **Fig. 5.7**. Then after inserting 100 in this list as a first node, the list is as illustrated in **Fig. 5.11.**

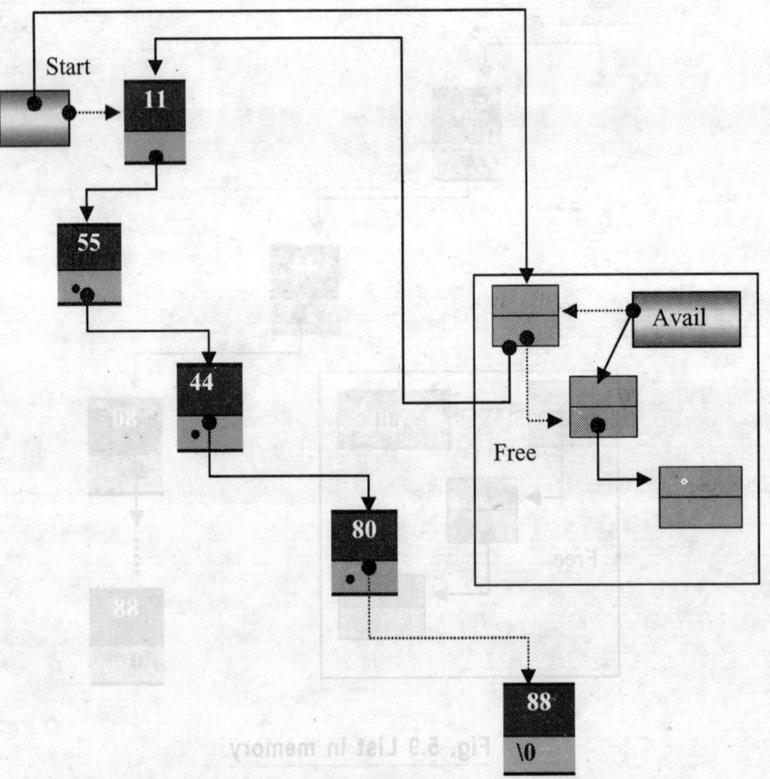

Fig. 5.10 Insertion as a first node

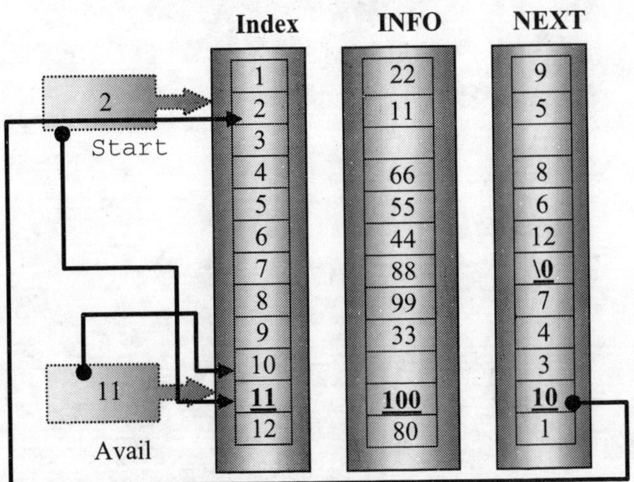

Fig. 5.11 Insertion as a first node

Step 1: [Allocate free space]
New_1= Create new node
Step 2: [Check for free space]
If New_1= NULL output "OVERFLOW" and Exit
Step 3: [Read value of information part of a new node]
Info [New_1] = Value
Step 4: [Link address part of the currently created node with the address of the first node in the list]
Next [New_1] = Start
Step 5: [Now assign address of newly created node to the start]
Start = New_1
Step 6: Exit

Fig. 5.12 Algorithm to insert a node at the begging of a list

The program segment **LINK_IF.C** implements the algorithm given in **Fig. 5.12.**

```
// INSERT A NODE INTO A SIMPLE LINKED LIST AT THE BEGINNING
// LINK_IF.C

# include <iostream.h>
# include <malloc.h>
```

```
# include<stdio.h>

struct link
{
    int info;
    struct link *next;
};

class insert
{
    private:
        int i;
        int number;
        link start, *previous, *new1;

    public:
        void insertion(link *);
        void create_list(link *);
        void display(link *);
};

// Function create a linked list

void insert :: create_list( link *node)
{
    start.next = NULL; // Empty list

    node = &start;  // Point to the start of the list
    i = 0;
    cout<<"\n Input choice n for break: ";
    char ch = getchar();
    while(ch != 'n')
    {
        node->next = (struct link* ) malloc(sizeof(struct link));
        node = node->next;
        cout<<"\n Input the node :"<<(i+1)<<" : ";
        cin>>node->info;
        node->next = NULL;
        cout<<"\n Input choice n for break: ";
        ch = getchar();
        i++;
    }
}

// Inserting a node
```

```
void insert :: insertion(link *node)
{
    node = start.next;
    previous = &start;

    new1 = (struct link* ) malloc(sizeof(struct link));
    new1->next = node ;
    previous->next = new1;
    cout<<"\n Input the fisrt node value: ";
    cin>>new1->info;
}

// Display the list

void insert :: display(link *node)
{
    node = start.next;
    cout<<"\n After Inserting a node list is as follows:\n";
    while (node)
    {
        cout<<"\n"<< node;
        cout<<" "<< node->info;
        node = node->next;
    }
}

// Function main
void main()
{
    insert i_mode;
    link *node = (link *) malloc(sizeof(link));

    i_mode.create_list(node);
    i_mode.insertion(node);
    i_mode.display(node);
}
```

```
Input choice n for break:
  Input the node :1 : 22
Input choice n for break:
  Input the node :2 : 11
Input choice n for break:
  Input the node :3 : 77
Input choice n for break:
  Input the node :4 : 66
Input choice n for break:
  Input the node :5 : 55
Input choice n for break:
  Input the node :6 : 44
Input choice n for break:
  Input the node :7 : 88
Input choice n for break:
  Input the node :8 : 99
Input choice n for break:
  Input the node :9 : 33
Input choice n for break:
  Input the node :10 : 100
Input choice n for break:n
Input the first node value: 1
After inserting a node list is as follows:
        Address     Value
        0x147211ac  1 inserted node
        0x1472115c  22
        0x14721164  11
        0x1472116c  77
        0x14721174  66
        0x1472117c  55
        0x14721184  44
        0x1472118c  88
        0x14721194  99
        0x1472119c  33
        0x147211a4  100
```

5.4.2 INSERTION AS A LAST NODE

The easiest way to add an entry is to append it. To append an item to a linked list, we loop through the list until find the element whose next member points to **NULL**. The code segment, which is used to perform this task, is:

```
node = &start;
while (node->next)
node = node->next;
```

When **node->next** points to **NULL**, it gives the end of the list. So we can allocate memory for the entry as given below:

```
node->next = malloc(required size);
```

Next we assign the desired entry values and assign the new entry's next field to point to **NULL**.

```
node = node->next;
node->member = some_value;
node->next = NULL;
```

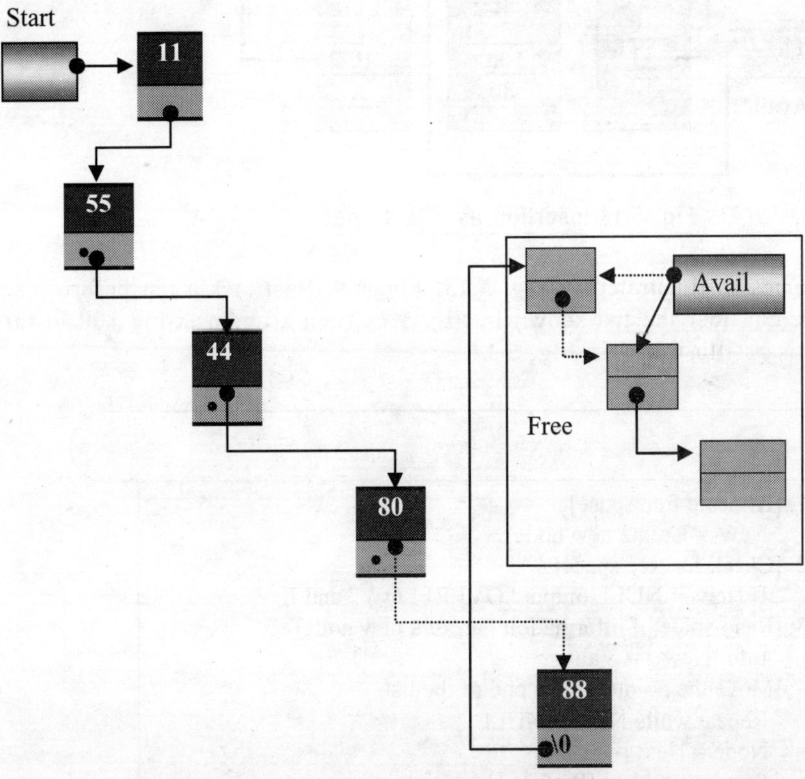

Fig. 5.13 Insertion as a last node

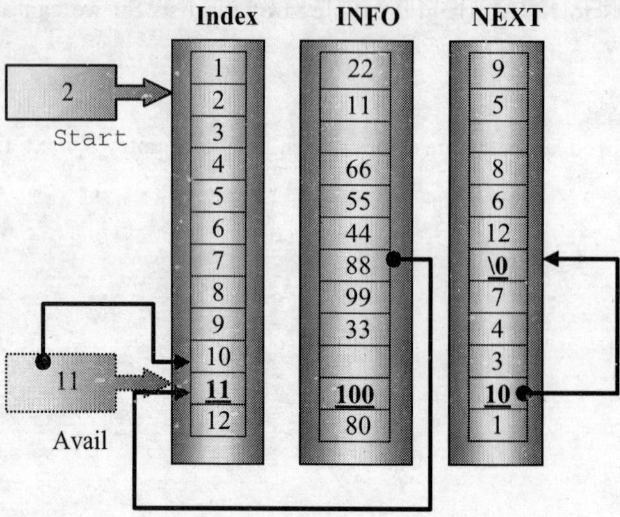

Fig. 5.14 Insertion as a last node

Hence the list becomes as illustrated in **Fig. 5.13. Fig. 5.9** illustrates a list before insertion operation. For example, consider the list shown in **Fig. 5.7**. Then after inserting 100 in this list as a last node, the list is as illustrated in **Fig. 5.14.**

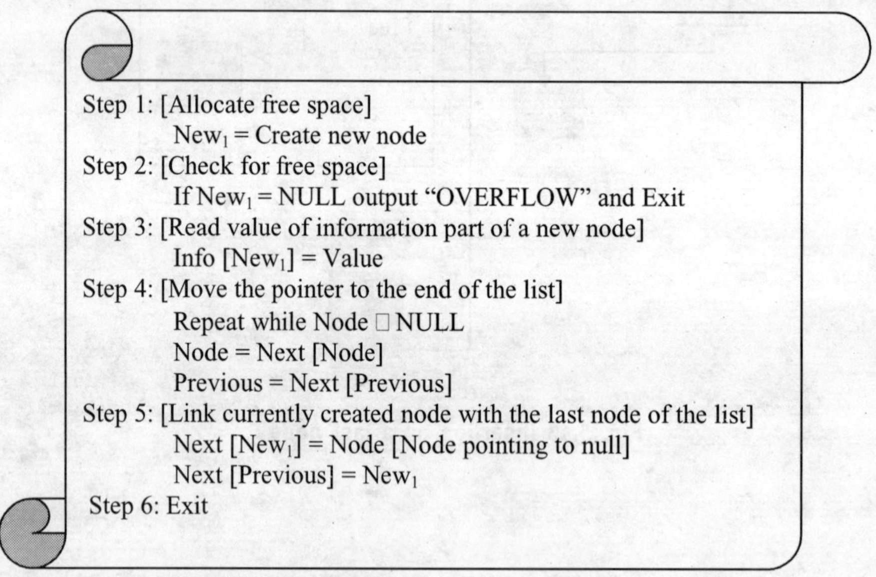

Step 1: [Allocate free space]
New_1 = Create new node
Step 2: [Check for free space]
If New_1 = NULL output "OVERFLOW" and Exit
Step 3: [Read value of information part of a new node]
Info [New_1] = Value
Step 4: [Move the pointer to the end of the list]
Repeat while Node □ NULL
Node = Next [Node]
Previous = Next [Previous]
Step 5: [Link currently created node with the last node of the list]
Next [New_1] = Node [Node pointing to null]
Next [Previous] = New_1
Step 6: Exit

Fig. 5.15 Algorithm to insert a node at the end of a list

The insertion operation is clearer from **Fig. 5.15.** Program segment **LINK_IL.C** implements algorithm shown in **Fig. 5.15.**

```
// INSERT A NODE INTO A SIMPLE LINKED LIST AT THE END OF THE LIST
// LINK_IL.C

# include <iostream.h>
# include <malloc.h>
# include<stdio.h>

struct link
{
	char info[20];
	struct link *next;
};
class insert
{
	private:
		int i;
		int number;
		link start, *previous, *new1;

	public:
		void insertion(link *);
		void create_list(link *);
		void display(link *);
};

// Function create a linked list
void insert :: create_list( link *node)
{
	start.next = NULL; // Empty list

	node = &start; // Point to the start of the list
	i = 0;
	cout<<"\n Input choice n for break: ";
	char ch = getchar();

	while(ch != 'n')
	{
		node->next = (struct link* ) malloc(sizeof(struct link));
		node = node->next;
		cout<<"\n Input the node :"<<(i+1)<<" : ";
		cin>>node->info;
		node->next = NULL;
		cout<<"\n Input choice n for break: ";
		ch = getchar();
		i++;
	}
}
```

```
// Inserting a node

void insert :: insertion(link *node)
{
	node = start.next;
	previous = &start;

	while(node)
	{
		node = node->next;
		previous= previous->next;
	}
	if(node == NULL)
	{
		new1 = (struct link* ) malloc(sizeof(struct link));
		new1->next = node ;
		previous->next = new1;
		cout<<"\n Input the last node value: ";
		cin>>new1->info;
	}
}

// Display the list
void insert :: display(link *node)
{
	node = start.next;
	cout<<"\n After Inserting a node list is as follows:\n";
	while (node)
	{
		cout<<"\n "<<node;
		cout<<" "<< node->info;
		node = node->next;
	}
}

// Function main

void main()
{
	insert i_mode;
	link *node = (link *) malloc(sizeof(link));

	i_mode.create_list(node);
	i_mode.insertion(node);
	i_mode.display(node);
}
```

```
Input choice n for break:
Input the node :1 : TOM
Input choice n for break:
Input the node :2 : RACHITA
Input choice n for break:
Input the node :3 : DOLLY
Input choice n for break:
Input the node :4 : NEOLIN
Input choice n for break:
Input the node :5 : CHAIPPEL
Input choice n for break:
Input the node :6 : LARA
Input choice n for break:
Input the node :7 : LILLY
Input choice n for break:
Input the node :8 : JAISURIA
Input choice n for break:
Input the node :9 : ARVIND
 Input choice n for break:
Input the node :10 : SUNIL
Input choice n for break:n

Input the last node value: DAVID
After inserting a node list is as follows:

Address      Value
0x2ecc116e   TOM
0x2ecc1188   RACHITA
0x2ecc11a2   DOLLY
0x2ecc11bc   NEOLIN
0x2ecc11d6   CHAPPEL
0x2ecc11f0   LARA
0x2ecc120a   LILLY
0x2ecc1224   JAISURIA
0x2ecc123e   ARVIND
0x2ecc1258   SUNIL
0x2ecc1272   DAVID
```

5.4.3 INSERTION OF A NODE AT SPECIFIC LOCATION

In some cases, one might want to place elements at specific locations in a list. For example, if we want to create a linked list that contains the sorted names of files in the current directory, program needs to place each file name into the list at the correct position. To insert an item at a specific place (location) in a list, the program will normally track the starting node, current node and the previous node. To achieve this we scan the list from the beginning and move up to the desired node where we want to insert the new node. Here, we create a new node and insert it into the list and restructure the complete list. **Fig. 5.9** illustrates linked list before insertion at a desired place and **Fig. 5.16** illustrates the linked after insertion.

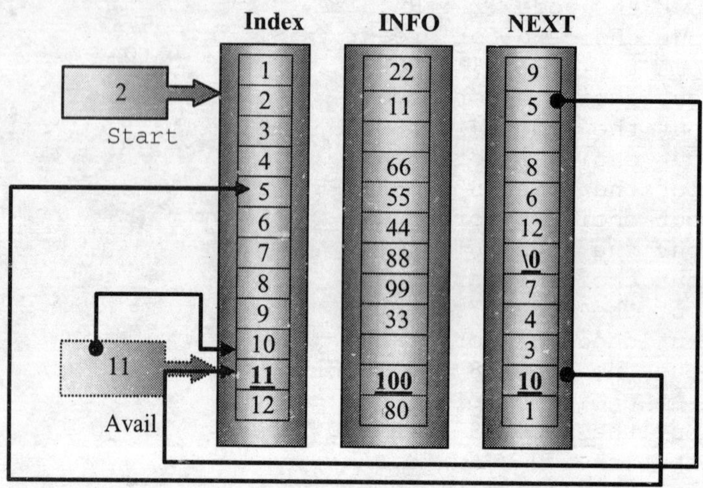

Fig. 5.17 Insertion of a node at a specific place

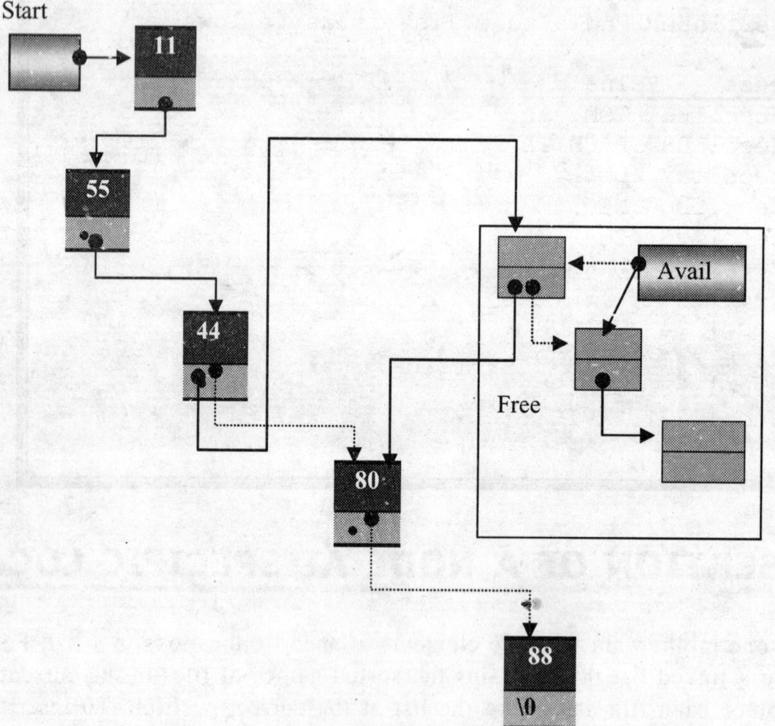

Fig. 5.16 Insertion of a node at a specific place

When a program needs to insert a new element, it will perform the following processing:

```
new1 = malloc(sizeof(struct list_member);
```

Hence, the list becomes as illustrated in **Fig. 5.16. Fig. 5.9** illustrates a list before insertion operation. For example, consider the list shown in **Fig. 5.7**. Then after inserting 100 in this list at a specific place, the list becomes as shown in **Fig. 5.17.**

Fig. 5.17 illustrates the insertion operation. From the result it is clear that insertion operation simply places new node between node 1 and 2. The next field of node 1 is now linked with newly inserted node and next field of newly inserted node is linked with node 2. Thus, new node that was inserted occupies the place of 2nd node. The program segment **LINK_IN.C** illustrates the same operation as discussed in **Fig. 5.17.**

```
// INSERTION OF A NODE INTO A SIMPLE LINKED LIST
// LINK_IN.C

# include <iostream.h>
# include <malloc.h>
# include<stdio.h>

struct link
{
	int info;
	struct link *next;
};

class insert
{
	private:
		int i;
		int number;
		link start, *previous, *new1;

	public:
		void insertion(link *);
		void create_list(link *);
		void display(link *);
};

// Function create a linked list

void insert :: create_list( link *node)
{
	start.next = NULL; // Empty list
```

```
    node = &start; // Point to the start of the list
    i = 0;

    cout<<"\n Input choice n for break: ";
    char ch = getchar();
    while(ch != 'n')
    {
        node->next = (struct link* ) malloc(sizeof(struct link));
        node = node->next;
        cout<<"\n Input the node :"<<(i+1)<<" : ";
        cin>>node->info;
        node->next = NULL;
        cout<<"\n Input choice n for break: ";
        ch = getchar();
        i++;
    }
    cout<<"\n Total nodes = "<< i;
}

// Inserting a node

void insert :: insertion(link *node)
{
    node = start.next;
    previous = &start;

    int node_number = 0;
    int insert_node;

    cout<<"\n Input node number you want to insert:";
    cout<<"\n Value should be less are equal to the";
    cout<<"\n number of nodes in the list: ";
    cin >> insert_node;

    while(node)
    {
        if((node_number+1) == insert_node)
        {
            new1 = (struct link* ) malloc(sizeof(struct link));
            new1->next = node ;
            previous->next = new1;
            cout<<"\n Input the node value: ";
            cin>>new1->info;
            break ;
        }
        else
```

```
        {
            node = node->next;
            previous= previous->next;
        }
        node_number ++;
    }
}

// Display the list

void insert :: display(link *node)
{
    node = start.next;
    cout<<"\n After Inserting a node list is as follows:\n";
    while (node)
    {
        cout<<"\n "<<node;
        cout<<" "<< node->info;
        node = node->next;
    }
}

// Function main

void main()
{
    insert i_mode;
    link *node = (link *) malloc(sizeof(link));

    i_mode.create_list(node);
    i_mode.insertion(node);
    i_mode.display(node);
}
```

```
Input choice n for break:
 Input the node: 1: 22
 Input choice n for break:
 Input the node: 2: 11
 Input choice n for break:
 Input the node: 3: 77
 Input choice n for break:
 Input the node: 4: 66
 Input choice n for break:
 Input the node: 5: 55
 Input choice n for break:
 Input the node: 6: 44
 Input choice n for break:
 Input the node: 7: 88
 Input choice n for break:
 Input the node: 8: 99
 Input choice n for break:
 Input the node: 9: 33
 Input choice n for break:
 Input the node: 10: 100
 Input choice n for break: n
 Total nodes = 10
 Input node number you want to insert:
 Value should be less are equal to the
 Number of nodes in the list: 5
 Input the node value: 9999
 After inserting a node list is as follows:

Address        Value

 0x147911d6   22
 0x147911de   11
 0x147911e6   77
 0x147911ee   66
 0x14791226   9999 <== Newly inserted node
 0x147911f6   55
 0x147911fe   44
 0x14791206   88
 0x1479120e   99
 0x14791216   33
 0x1479121e   100
```

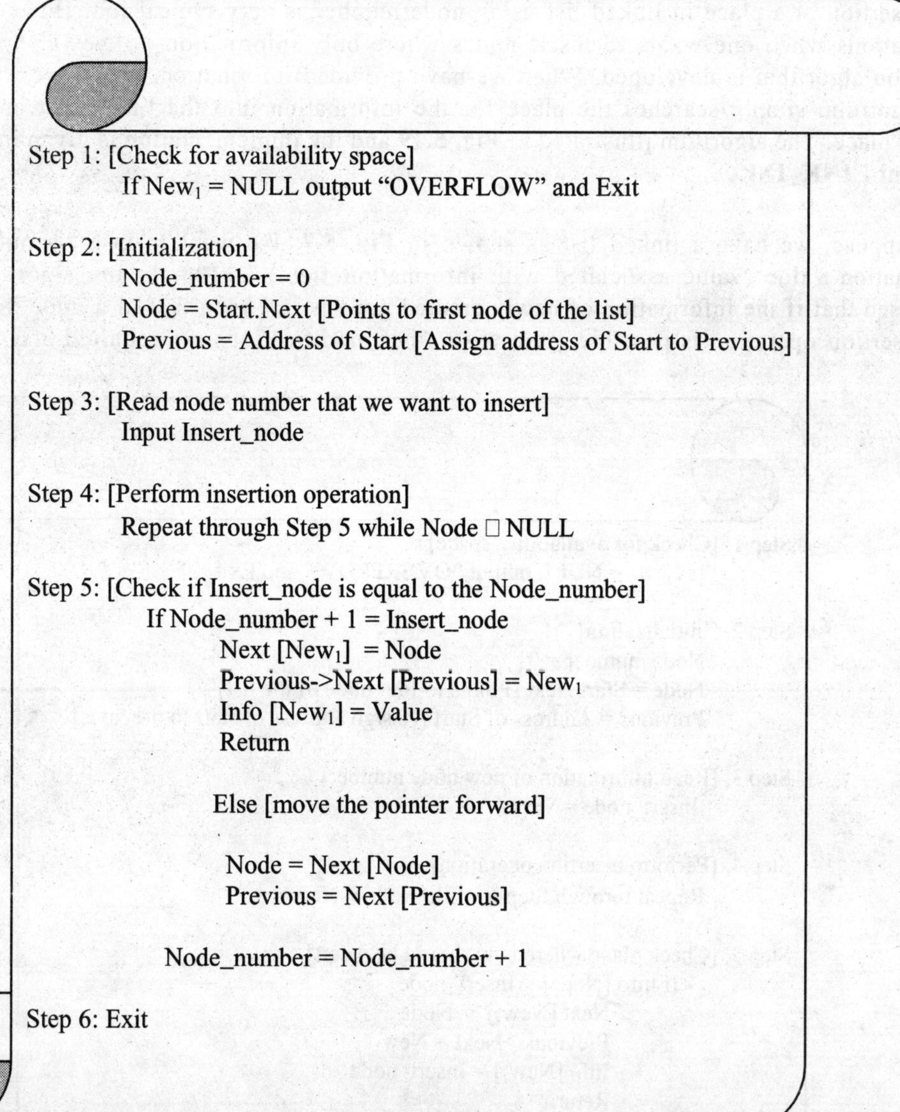

```
Step 1: [Check for availability space]
        If New1 = NULL output "OVERFLOW" and Exit

Step 2: [Initialization]
        Node_number = 0
        Node = Start.Next [Points to first node of the list]
        Previous = Address of Start [Assign address of Start to Previous]

Step 3: [Read node number that we want to insert]
        Input Insert_node

Step 4: [Perform insertion operation]
        Repeat through Step 5 while Node □ NULL

Step 5: [Check if Insert_node is equal to the Node_number]
          If Node_number + 1 = Insert_node
                Next [New1]  = Node
                Previous->Next [Previous] = New1
                Info [New1] = Value
                Return

               Else [move the pointer forward]

                Node = Next [Node]
                Previous = Next [Previous]

           Node_number = Node_number + 1

Step 6: Exit
```

Fig. 5.18 Algorithm to insert a node in a linked list at a desired place, when node number is known.

From the algorithm shown in **Fig. 5.18** it is clear that when one wants to insert a node into a linked list, one should know the node number where he/she wants to insert a new node in the list. If one does not know the node number it is not easy job to insert a new node into the list. If one goes through trial and error method may insert the new node in the list but it requires much more time. In trial and error method if one input a new node number but that particular node does not exists in the list that may create problems. Some times it may crash the list.

Insertion at a place in linked list using node number is very typical job. However, there are applications when one wants to insert nodes where only information is known. For this a new insertion algorithm is developed. When we have provided information, which we want to insert, the algorithm simply searches the place for the information into the linked list and insert into proper place. The algorithm illustrated in **Fig. 5.19** and the implementation is given in the program segment **LINK_INI.C.**

Suppose, we have a linked list as shown in **Fig. 5.7**. We want to insert a node for which information value (value associated with information field) is **100.** In the algorithm we have discussed that if the information of newly created node is less than that of a node in the list then the insertion operation is possible, otherwise other modifications are required accordingly.

```
Step 1: [Check for availability space]
        If New1 = NULL output "OVERFLOW" and Exit

Step 2: [Initialization]
        Node_number = 0
        Node = Start.Next [Points to first node of the list]
        Previous = Address of Start [Assign address of start to previous]

Step 3: [Read information of new node number]
        Insert_node = Value

Step 4: [Perform insertion operation]
        Repeat through Step 6 while Node ≠ NULL

Step 5: [Check place where new should be insert]
          If Info [Node] < Insert_node
                Next [New1]  = Node
                Previous->Next = New1
                Info [New1] = Insert_node
                Return
                Else [move the pointer forward]
                 Node = Next [Node]
                 Previous = Next [Previous]
Step 6:   Node_number = Node_number + 1

Step 7: Exit
```

Fig. 5.19 Algorithm to insert a node in a linked list at a desired place, when information is known

```
// INSERT A NODE INTO A SIMPLE LINKED LIST, INFORMATION IS KNOWN
// AND PUT AFTER SOME SPECIFIED NODE
// LINK_INI.C
# include <iostream.h>
# include <malloc.h>
# include<stdio.h>

struct link
{
    int info;
    struct link *next;
};

class insert
{
    private:
        int i;
        int number;
        link start, *previous, *new1;

    public:
        void insertion(link *);
        void create_list(link *);
        void display(link *);
};
// Function create a linked list
void insert :: create_list( link *node)
{
    start.next = NULL; // Empty list

    node = &start; // Point to the start of the list
    i = 0;
    cout<<"\n Input choice n for break: ";
    char ch = getchar();
    while(ch != 'n')
    {
        node->next = (struct link* ) malloc(sizeof(struct link));
        node = node->next;
        cout<<"\n Input the node :"<<(i+1)<<" : ";
        cin>>node->info;
        node->next = NULL;
        cout<<"\n Input choice n for break: ";
        ch = getchar();
        i++;
    }
    cout<<"\n Total nodes = "<< i;
}
```

```
// Inserting a node

void insert :: insertion(link *node)
{
        node = start.next;
        previous = &start;

        int node_number = 0;
        int insert_node;

        cout<<"\n Input value node the node you want to insert:";
        cin >> insert_node;
        while(node)
        {
                if(node->info < insert_node)
                {
                        new1 = (struct link* ) malloc(sizeof(struct link));
                        new1->next = node;
                        previous->next = new1;
                        new1->info = insert_node;
                        break ;
                }
                else
                {
                        node = node->next;
                        previous= previous->next;
                }
                node_number ++;
        }
}

// Display the list
void insert :: display(link *node)
{
        node = start.next;
        cout<<"\n After Inserting a node list is as follows:\n";
        while (node)
        {
                cout<<"\n "<<node;
                cout<<" "<< node->info;
                node = node->next;
        }
}

// Function main
void main()
```

```
{
        insert i_mode;
        link *node = (link *) malloc(sizeof(link));
        i_mode.create_list(node);
        i_mode.insertion(node);
        i_mode.display(node);
}
```

```
Input choice n for break:
Input the node :1 : 44
Input choice n for break:
Input the node :2 : 55
Input choice n for break:
Input the node :3 : 66
Input choice n for break:
Input the node :4 : 77
Input choice n for break:
Input the node :5 : 88
Input choice n for break:
Input the node :6 : 99
Input choice n for break:
Input the node :7 : 33
Input choice n for break:
Input the node :8 : 22
Input choice n for break:
Input the node :9 : 5
Input choice n for break: n
Total nodes = 9
Input value node the node you want to insert:21
After inserting a node list is as follows:

Address      Value

0x2f04117e  44
0x2f041186  55
0x2f04118e  66
0x2f041196  77
0x2f04119e  88
0x2f0411a6  99
0x2f0411ae  33
0x2f0411b6  22
0x2f0411c6  21
0x2f0411be  5
```

5.5 DELETION IN A LINKED LIST

If one is interested in deletion of a node from a linear linked list, before performing the deletion, one should take into account following points:

1. *If the linked list is empty, the deletion is not possible and the output should display **Underflow** message.*
2. *Consider the Step 3 while end of the list has not been reached and the node has not been found.*
3. *Obtain the next node in the list and record its predecessor.*
4. *If the end of the list has been reached, "**node not found**" message can be displayed.*
5. *Delete the node from the list.*
6. *Return the node to the free area.*

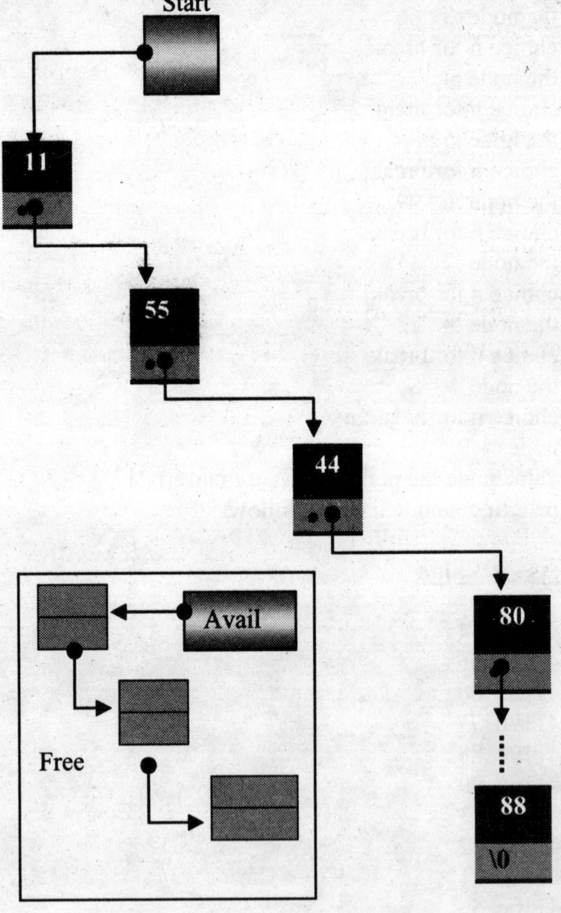

Fig. 5.20 List before deletion

Fig. 5.20 represents the list before deletion and **Fig. 5.21** represents the list after deletion. The deletion operation is classified into following three categories:

- *Deletion of first node*
- *Deletion of last node*
- *Deletion of desired node from any place in the list*

5.5.1 Deletion of First Node

Suppose we have a linked list as shown in **Fig 5.22** and want to delete first node. Then accomplish the following operations:

- *Make link of start pointer to the second node in the list.*
- *Free the space associated with first node.*
- *Operating system then collects the free space and makes link for currently freed node with available free space.*

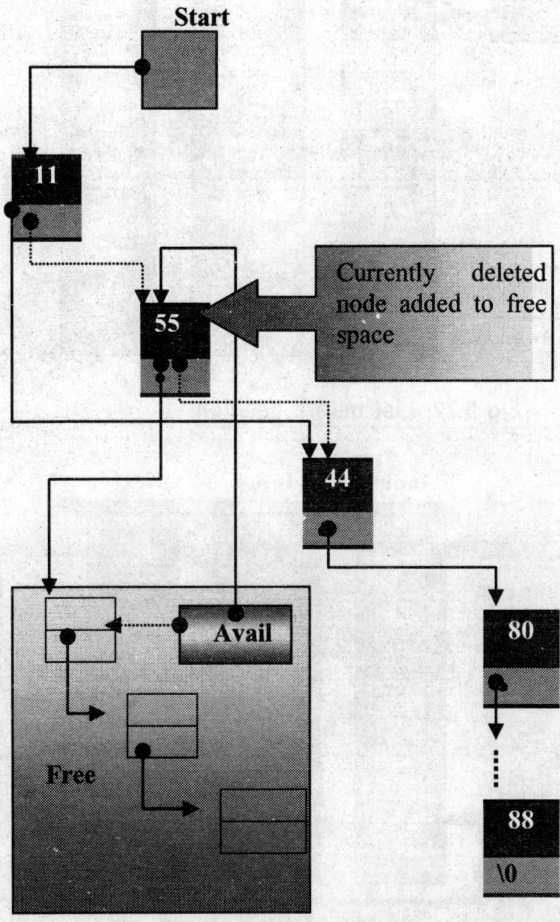

Fig 5.21. List with deletion operation

A variable has been defined to keep the address of **start** and **previous** variable; **start.next** points to first element in the list. The value associated with it is stored into **node** variable. If the value of this node is **NULL,** it means that the list is empty and messages **UNDERFLOW** is displayed and function exits. If the list is not empty, the address of the next node is assigned to **previous->next** variable and the list becomes as shown in **Fig 5.23.** When we free the space associated with a node, it is attached to the free list. The above discussion can be formulated in the following statements:

node = start.next [Points to the first element of the list]
previous = &start
previous->next = node->next [This statement makes link of start to link of the next node that is linked with second node]
free (node)

Fig 5.23 illustrates the deletion of first node from a linked list.

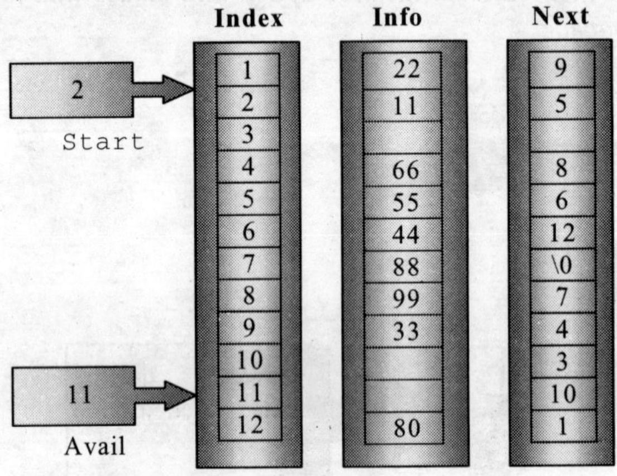

Fig 5.22. List before deletion

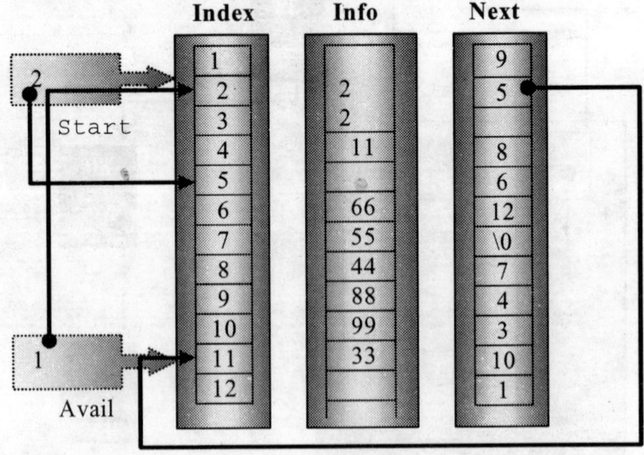

Fig 5.23. List after deletion of first node

The deletion algorithm is discussed in **Fig 5.24.** The program segment **LINK_DF.C** implements the algorithm.

Step 1: [Initialization]
Node = Start.Next [Points to the first node in the list]
Previous = Assign address of start

Step 2: [Perform deletion operation]
If Node = NULL
Output "UNDERFLOW" and Exit
Else [Delete first node]
Next [Previous] = Next [Node] [Move pointer to next node in the list]
Free the space associated with **Node**

Step 3: Exit

Fig. 5.24 Algorithm for deletion of first node from a linked list

```
/* DELETING FIRST NODE FROM A SIMPLE LINKED LIST */
/* LINK_DF.C*/

# include <stdio.h>
# include <malloc.h>

struct link
{
	int data;
	struct link *next;
};

int i;
int number ;
struct link start, *node, *previous;

void Delete_node();
void creat_node();
void creat_node()
{
	char ch;
	i = 0;
	start.next = NULL; /* Empty list */
	node = &start; /* Point to the start of the list */
```

```
    printf("\n Input choice n for break:");
    ch = getchar();
    while(ch != 'n')
    {
        node->next = (struct link* ) malloc(sizeof(struct link));
        node = node->next;
        printf("\n Input the node: %d: ", i+1);
        scanf("%d", &node->data);
        node->next = NULL;
        fflush(stdin);
        printf("\n Input choice n for break:");
        ch = getchar();
        i++;
    }
    node = start.next;
    previous = &start;
    printf("\n Created list is as follows\n");

    while (node)
    {
        printf("\n 0x%x", node);
        printf(" %d", node->data);
        node = node->next;
    }
}

/* Removing a node */
void Delete_node()
{
    node = start.next;
    previous = &start;

    if (node == NULL)
    {
        printf("\n Under flow");
    }
    else
    {
        previous->next = node->next;
        free(node);
    }

    /* Display the list */
    node = start.next;
    printf("\n After deleting first node list is as follows\n");
    while (node)
```

```
    {
        printf("\n 0x%x", node);
        printf(" %d", node->data);
        node = node->next;
    }
}

/* Function main */
void main()
{
    creat_node();
    Delete_node();
}
```

```
Input choice n for break:
Input the node: 1: 2
Input choice n for break:
Input the node: 2: 1
Input choice n for break:
Input the node: 3: 77
Input choice n for break:
Input the node: 4: 66
Input choice n for break:
Input the node: 5: 55
Input choice n for break:
Input the node: 6: 44
Input choice n for break:
Input the node: 7: 88
Input choice n for break:
Input the node: 8: 99
Input choice n for break:
Input the node: 9: 33
Input choice n for break:
Input the node: 10: 100
Input choice n for break: n
 Created list is as follows
Address        Value
0x14751166     2
0x1475116e     1
0x14751176     77
0x1475117e     66
0x14751186     55
0x1475118e     44
0x14751196     88
0x1475119e     99
0x147511a6     33
0x147511ae     100
```

```
After deleting first node list is as follows
Address         Value
0x1475116e      1
0x14751176      77
0x1475117e      66
0x14751186      55
0x1475118e      44
0x14751196      88
0x1475119e      99
0x147511a6      33
0x147511ae      100
```

5.5.2 Deletion of Last Node

The simplest method to delete last node of a linked list is described as follows. First count the number of nodes in the list. Scan the list from beginning to end of the list, it will effectively counts the number of nodes in the list. Let it contain **n** nodes. Now second time once again we scan the list from beginning to **n-1** nodes of the list. At last we free the last node. The deletion mechanism is similar to the previous one. Suppose we have a list as shown in **Fig 5.20.** Then after deletion of last node the list becomes as illustrated in **Fig 5.25.** The code segment, which is used to perform this task, is:

```
node = &start;
    while (node->next)
        node = node->next;
```

Fig 5.22 represents a linked list of which each node has integer number as an information. If we want to traverse the list we can easily traverse the list from starting end to end of the list. **Fig 5.26** illustrates the deletion operation. The program segment **LINK_DL.C** implements the deletion algorithm shown in **Fig 5.27.**

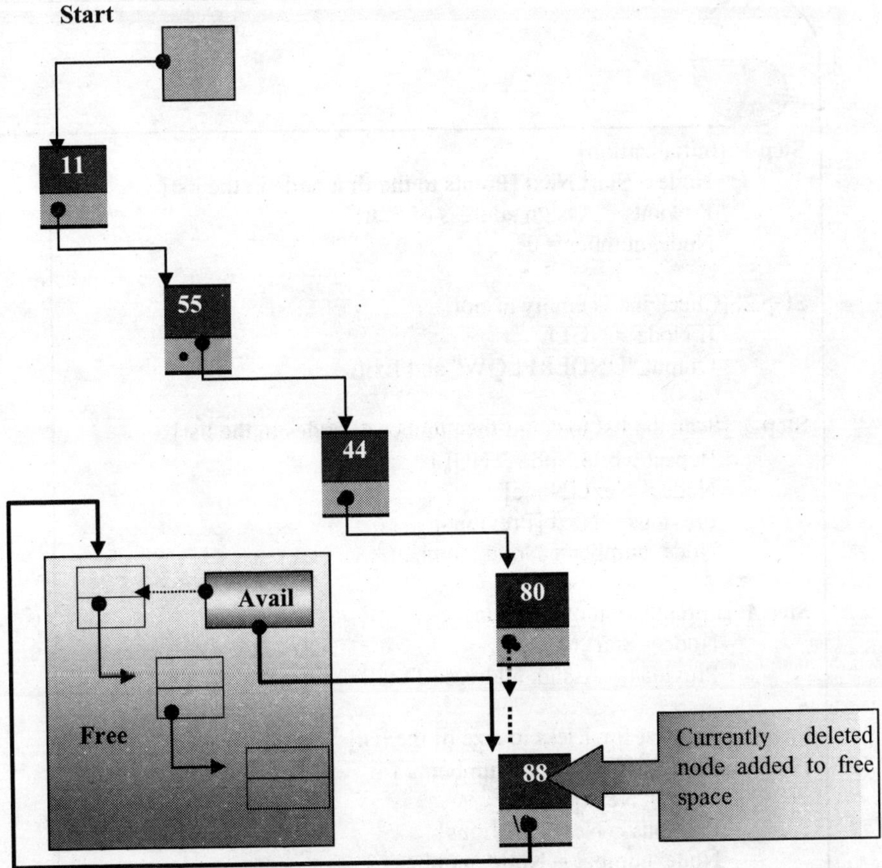

Fig 5.25. List with deletion of last node

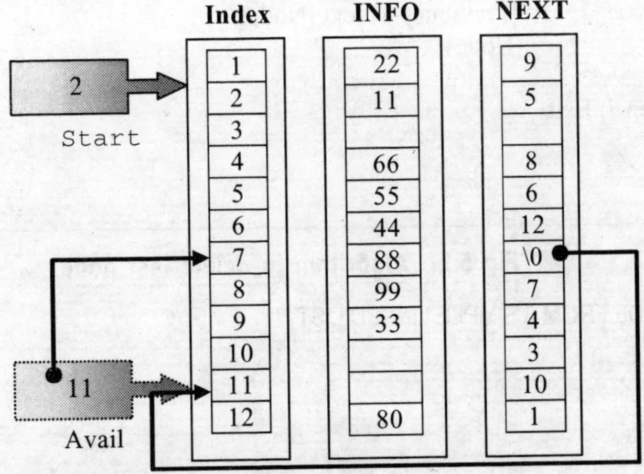

Fig 5.26. List after deletion of last node

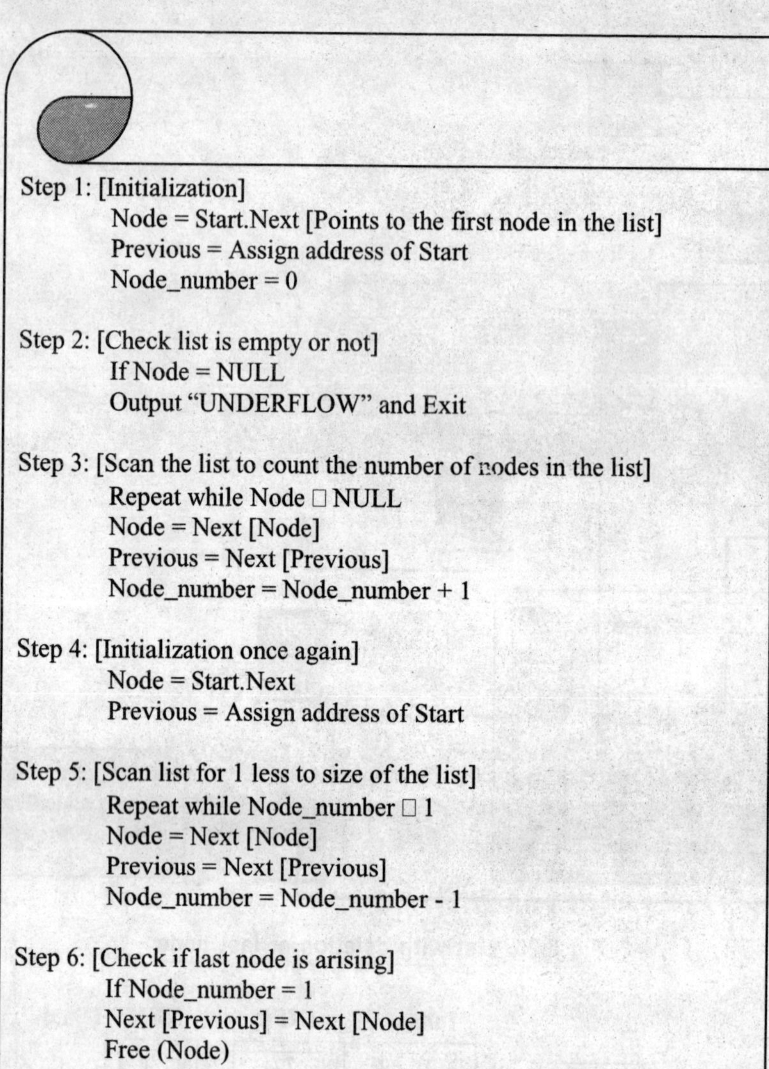

Step 1: [Initialization]
Node = Start.Next [Points to the first node in the list]
Previous = Assign address of Start
Node_number = 0

Step 2: [Check list is empty or not]
If Node = NULL
Output "UNDERFLOW" and Exit

Step 3: [Scan the list to count the number of nodes in the list]
Repeat while Node □ NULL
Node = Next [Node]
Previous = Next [Previous]
Node_number = Node_number + 1

Step 4: [Initialization once again]
Node = Start.Next
Previous = Assign address of Start

Step 5: [Scan list for 1 less to size of the list]
Repeat while Node_number □ 1
Node = Next [Node]
Previous = Next [Previous]
Node_number = Node_number - 1

Step 6: [Check if last node is arising]
If Node_number = 1
Next [Previous] = Next [Node]
Free (Node)

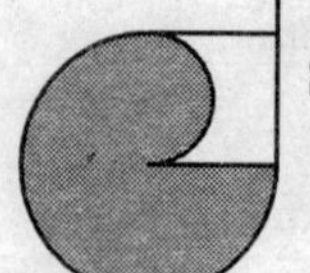

Step 7: Exit

Fig 5.27. Algorithm to delete last node

```
/* DELETING LAST NODE FROM A SIMPLE LINKED LIST */
/* LINK_DL.C */

# include <stdio.h>
# include <malloc.h>
struct link
{
```

```
        char info;
        struct link *next;
};

int i;
int number ;
struct link start, *previous;

void Delete_node(struct link *);
void creat_node(struct link *);
void creat_node(struct link *node)
{
        char ch;
        i = 0;
        start.next = NULL; /* Empty list */
        node = &start; /* Point to the start of the list */
        printf("\n Input choice n for break:");
        ch = getchar();

        while(ch != 'n')
        {
                node->next = (struct link* ) malloc(sizeof(struct link));
                node = node->next;
                printf("\n Input the node: %d: ", (i+1));
                scanf("%c", &node->info);
                node->next = NULL;
                fflush(stdin);
                printf("\n Input choice n for break:");
                ch = getchar();
                i++;
        }
        node = start.next;
        previous = &start;
        printf("\n Created list is as follows\n");

        while (node)
        {
                printf("\n 0x%x", node);
                printf(" %c", node->info);
                node = node->next;
        }
}

/* Removing a node */

void Delete_node(struct link *node)
```

```
{
    int node_number = 0;

    node = start.next;
    previous = &start;

    if (node == NULL)
    {
        printf("\n Underflow");
    }

    else

        while(node)
        {
            node = node->next;
            previous = previous->next;
            node_number ++;
        }
    printf("\n Total Nodes = %d", node_number);

    node = start.next;
    previous = &start;

    while(node_number != 1)
    {
        node = node->next;
        previous = previous->next;
        node_number —;
    }
    if(node_number == 1)
    {
        previous->next = node->next;
        free(node);
    }
    /* Display the list */

    node = start.next;
    printf("\n After deleting last node list is as follows\n");
    while (node)
    {
        printf("\n 0x%x", node);
        printf(" %c", node->info);
        node = node->next;
    }
}
```

```
/* Function main */

void main()
{
    struct link *node = (struct link *) malloc(sizeof(struct link));
    creat_node(node);
    Delete_node(node);
}
```

```
Input choice n for break:
Input the node :1 :A
Input choice n for break:
Input the node :2 :B
Input choice n for break:
Input the node :3 :C
Input choice n for break:
Input the node :4 : D
Input choice n for break:
Input the node :5 : E
Input choice n for break:
Input the node :6 : F
Input choice n for break:
Input the node :7 : G
Input choice n for break:
Input the node :8 : H
Input choice n for break:
Input the node :9 : I
Input choice n for break:
Input the node :10 : J
Input choice n for break:n
Created list is as follows
 Address    Value

0x1448117e  A
0x14481186  B
0x1448118e  C
0x14481196  D
0x1448119e  E
0x144811a6  F
0x144811ae  G
0x144811b6  H
0x144811be  I
0x144811c6  J
Total Nodes = 10
After deleting last node list is as follows

0x1448117e  A
0x14481186  B
0x1448118e  C
0x14481196  D
0x1448119e  E
0x144811a6  F
0x144811ae  G
0x144811b6  H
0x144811be  I
```

5.5.3 Deletion of A Desired Node

Suppose we want to delete a desired node from a linked list. In this section we have assumed that we know the node number, which we want to delete. First of all we provide node number to which we want to delete. We scan the list up to that node. If the node exists in the list, we move the pointer to that particular node, free the node and adjust the pointer to make the list in linked form (The pointer of the previous node of this node will now point to the successor of this node). Before deletion operation we must check whether the list is empty or not. If the list is empty a message **UNDERFLOW** is displayed and the program terminates. The deletion operation is same as discussed in the section {5.5}.

The deletion operation is illustrated in **Fig 5.28. Fig 5.22** represents a linked list of which each node has integer number as an information. If we want to traverse the list we can easily traverse the list from starting end to the desired node in the list after getting the desired node deletion operation can be done as discussed in the section {5.5}. **Fig 5.29** illustrates the deletion operation.

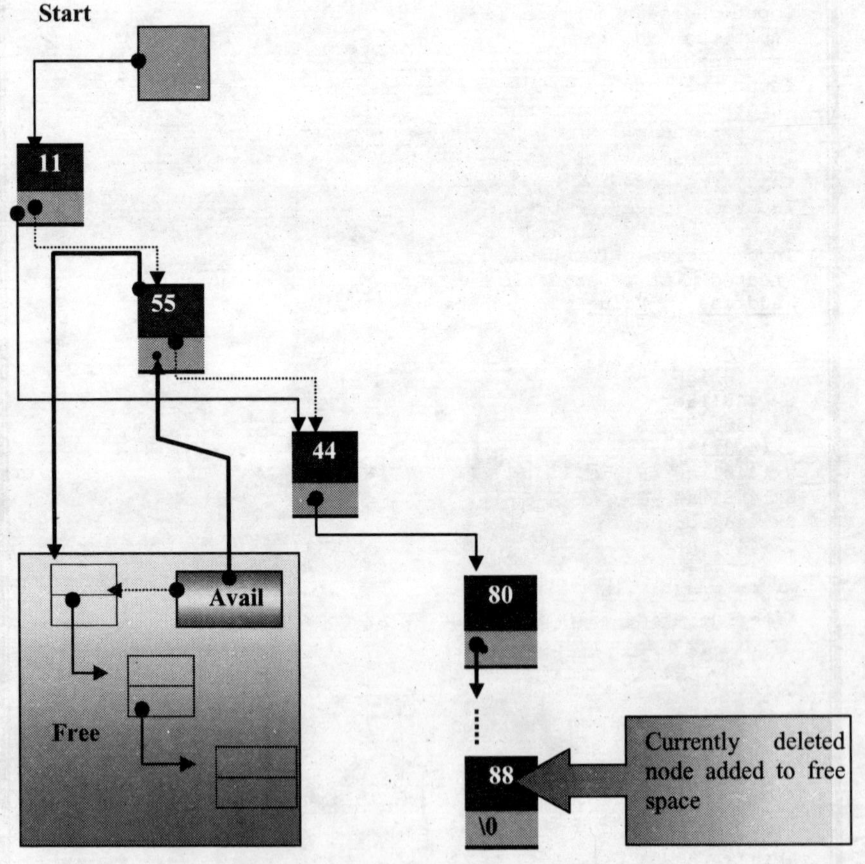

Fig 5.28. List with deletion of a desired node

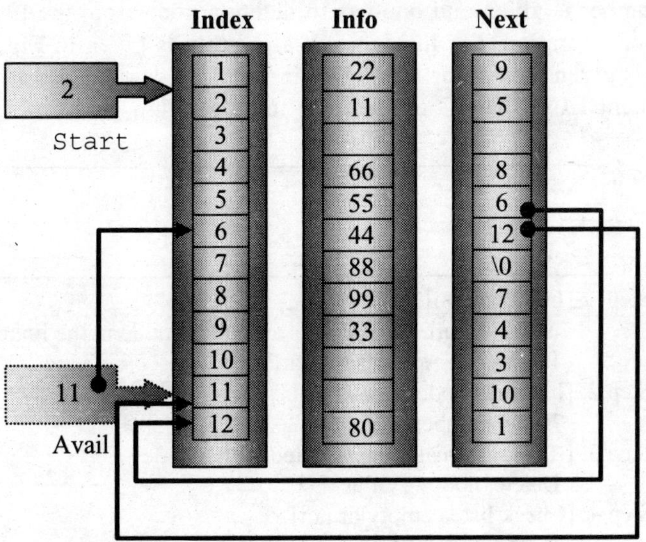

Fig 5.29. List after deletion of a desired node

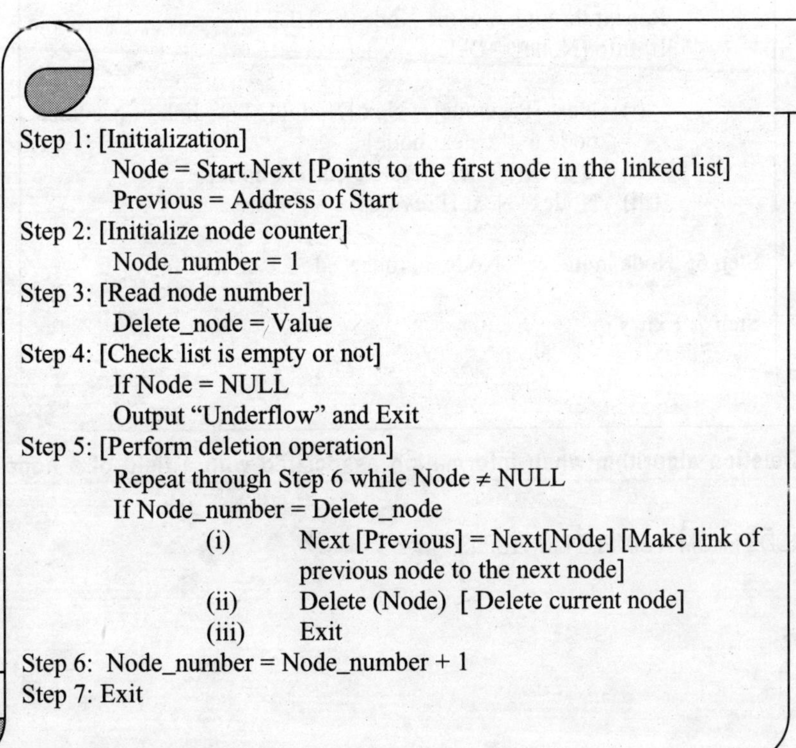

Step 1: [Initialization]
    Node = Start.Next [Points to the first node in the linked list]
    Previous = Address of Start
Step 2: [Initialize node counter]
    Node_number = 1
Step 3: [Read node number]
    Delete_node = Value
Step 4: [Check list is empty or not]
    If Node = NULL
    Output "Underflow" and Exit
Step 5: [Perform deletion operation]
    Repeat through Step 6 while Node ≠ NULL
    If Node_number = Delete_node
        (i) Next [Previous] = Next[Node] [Make link of previous node to the next node]
        (ii) Delete (Node) [Delete current node]
        (iii) Exit
Step 6: Node_number = Node_number + 1
Step 7: Exit

Fig 5.30. Algorithm for deletion on the basis of node number

When node number is given and one has to delete a node from the list. It is very easy task to perform the deletion operation. For the same an algorithm is given in **Fig 5.30.** If the information associated a node is given then algorithm given in **Fig 5.31** can be used for the deletion operation. The program segment **LINK_DN.C** implements the algorithm given in **Fig 5.30.**

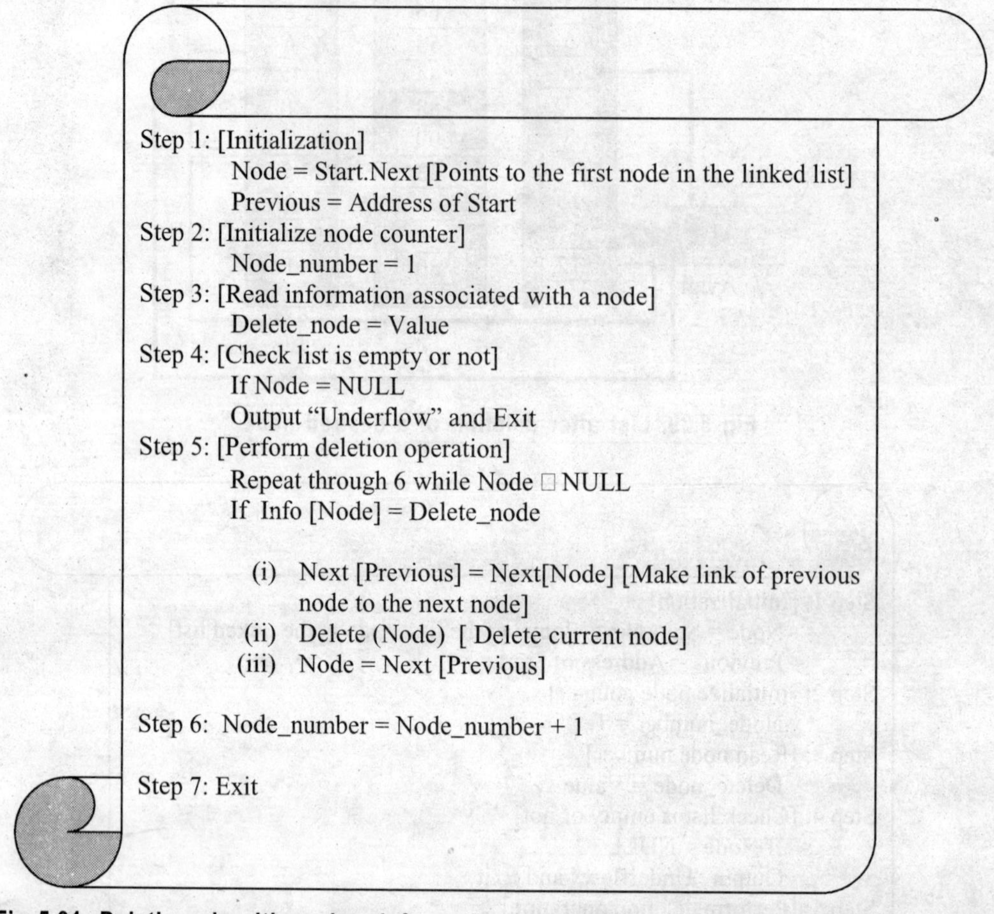

Fig 5.31. Deletion algorithm when information associated with a field of a node is known

```
/* DELETING A NODE FROM A SIMPLE LINKED LIST */
/* LINK_DN.C */

# include <stdio.h>
# include <malloc.h>
struct link
{
	char info[20];
	struct link *next;
};
```

```
int i;
int number ;
struct link start, *previous;
void Delete_node(struct link *);
void creat_node(struct link *);

/* Create linked list */
void creat_node(struct link *node)
{
      char ch;
      i = 0;

      start.next = NULL;
      // Empty list
      node = &start;

      // Point to the start of the list
      printf("\n Input choice n for break: ");
      ch = getchar();

      while(ch != 'n')
      {
            node->next = (struct link* ) malloc(sizeof(struct link));
            node = node->next;
            fflush(stdin);
            printf("\n Input the node: %d: ", i+1);
            gets(node->info);
            node->next = NULL;

            printf("\n Input choice n for break: ");
            ch = getchar();
            i++;
      }
      printf("\n Total nodes = %d", i);
      node = start.next;
      printf("\n Created list is as follows:\n");
      while (node)
      {
            printf("\n 0x%x", node);
            printf(" %s", node->info);
            node = node->next;
      }
}

/* Removing a node */
void Delete_node(struct link *node)
```

```
{
    int node_number = 1;
    int delete_node;
    node = start.next;
    previous = &start;
    printf("\n Input node number you want to delete:");
    scanf(" %d", &delete_node);

    while(node)
    {
        if((node_number) == delete_node)
        {
            previous->next = node->next;
            free(node);
            break ;
        }
        else
        {
            node = node->next;
            previous = previous->next;
        }
        node_number ++;
    }

    /* Display the list */

    node = start.next;
    printf("\n After deleting a node list is as follows:\n");
    while (node)
    {
        printf("\n 0x%x", node);
        printf(" %s", node->info);
        node = node->next;
    }
}

/* Function main */

void main()
{
    struct link *node = (struct link *) malloc(sizeof(struct link));
    creat_node(node);
    Delete_node(node);
}
```

```
Input choice n for break:
Input the node: 1: SACHIN
Input choice n for break:
Input the node: 2: KAMBLE
Input choice n for break:
Input the node: 3: KUMBLE
Input choice n for break:
Input the node: 4: LARA
Input choice n for break:
Input the node: 5: THOMSON
Input choice n for break:
Input the node: 6: LILLY
Input choice n for break:
Input the node: 7: DEEPAK
Input choice n for break:
Input the node: 8: DESMOND
Input choice n for break:
Input the node: 9: HENS
Input choice n for break:
Input the node: 10: BOTHOM
Input choice n for break: n
Total nodes = 10
Created list is as follows:
 Address       Value
0x148511ac   SACHIN
0x148511c6   KAMBLE
0x148511e0   KUMBLE
0x148511fa   LARA
0x14851214   THOMSON
0x1485122e   LILLY
0x14851248   DEEPAK
0x14851262   DESMOND
0x1485127c   HENS
0x14851296   BOTHOM
Input node number you want to delete:6
After deleting a node list is as follows:
Address      Value
0x148511ac   SACHIN
0x148511c6   KAMBLE
0x148511e0   KUMBLE
0x148511fa   LARA
0x14851214   THOMSON
0x1485122e
0x14851248   DEEPAK
0x14851262   DESMOND
0x1485127c   HENS
0x14851296   BOTHOM
```

Implementation of algorithm shown in **Fig 5.31** is given in the program segment **LINK_DIN.C.**

```
/* DELETING A NODE FROM A SIMPLE LINKED LIST */
/* WHEN INFORMATION OF A NODE IS GIVEN */
/* LINK_DIN.C */

# include <stdio.h>
# include <malloc.h>

struct link
{
      int info;
      struct link *next;
};

int i;
int number ;
struct link start, *previous;
void Delete_node(struct link *);
void creat_node(struct link *);

/* Create linked list */

void creat_node(struct link *node)
{
      char ch;

      i = 0;

      start.next = NULL; /* Empty list */
      node = &start; /* Point to the start of the list */

      printf("\n Input choice n for break: ");
      ch = getchar();

      while(ch != 'n')
      {
            node->next = (struct link* ) malloc(sizeof(struct link));
            node = node->next;
            printf("\n Input the node: %d: ", (i+1));
            scanf("%d", &node->info);
            node->next = NULL;
            fflush(stdin);
            printf("\n Input choice n for break: ");
            ch = getchar();

            i++;
```

```
    }
    printf("\n Total nodes = %d", i);

    node = start.next;
    printf("\n Created list is as follows: \n");
    while (node)
    {
        printf("\n 0x%x", node);
        printf(" %d", node->info);
        node = node->next;
    }
}

/* Removing a node */

void Delete_node(struct link *node)
{
    int node_number = 1;
    int delete_node;

    node = start.next;
    previous = &start;


    printf("\n Input information of a node you want to delete: ");
    scanf("%d", &delete_node);

    while(node)
    {
        if(node->info == delete_node)
        {
            printf("\n Position of the information in the list is : %d", node_number);
            previous->next = node->next;

            free(node);
            break ;
        }
        else
        {
            node = node->next;
            previous = previous->next;
        }
        node_number++;
    }
```

```
        /* Display the list */

        node = start.next;
        printf("\n After deleting a node list is as follows:\n");
        while (node)
        {
                printf("\n 0x%x", node);
                printf(" %d", node->info);
                node = node->next;
        }
}

void main()
{
        struct link *node = (struct link *) malloc(sizeof(struct link));
        creat_node(node);
        Delete_node(node);
}
```

```
Input choice n for break:
Input the node :1 : 44
Input choice n for break:
Input the node :2 : 4
Input choice n for break:
Input the node :3 : 88
Input choice n for break:
Input the node :4 : 99
Input choice n for break:
Input the node :5 : 44
Input choice n for break:
Input the node :6 : 33
Input choice n for break:
Input the node :7 : 22
Input choice n for break:
Input the node :8 : 66
Input choice n for break:
Input the node :9 : 77
Input choice n for break: n
Total nodes = 9
Created list is as follows:
Address       Value
0x1dd211d4  44
0x1dd211dc  6
0x1dd211e4  88
```

```
0x1dd211ec 99
0x1dd211f4 44
0x1dd211fc 33
0x1dd21204 22
0x1dd2120c 66
0x1dd21214 77

Input information of a node you want to delete: 66
Position of the information in the lisy is : 8
After deleting a node list is as follows:

Address     Value
0x1dd211d4 44
0x1dd211dc 6
0x1dd211e4 88
0x1dd211ec 99
0x1dd211f4 44
0x1dd211fc 33
0x1dd21204 22
0x1dd21214 77
```

The above program segment can be implemented in another way. The program **REMOVES.C,** creates a linked list containing the numbers 51 to 60. The program then searches the list for the node containing the number 55 and then removes the element.

```
/* REMOVES.C */

#include <stdio.h>
#include <malloc.h>

void main(void)
{
    int i;

    struct ListEntry {
        int number;
        struct ListEntry *next;
    } start, *node, *previous;

    start.next = NULL; /* Empty list */
    node = &start; /* Point to the start of the list */

    for (i = 1; i <= 10; i++)
    {
        node->next = (struct ListEntry *) malloc(sizeof(struct ListEntry));
```

```
        node = node->next;
        node->number = 50+i;
        node->next = NULL;
    }

    /* Remove the number 55 */
    node = start.next;
    printf("\n List before deletion\n");
    while (node)
    {
        printf("%d ", node->number);
        node = node->next;
    }

    node = start.next;
    previous = &start;
    while (node)
        if (node->number == 55)
        {
            previous->next = node->next;
            free(node);
            break; /* End the loop */
        }
        else
        {
            node = node->next;
            previous = previous->next;
        }

    /* Display the list */
    node = start.next;
    printf("\n List after deletion \n");
    while (node)
    {
        printf("%d ", node->number);
        node = node->next;
    }
}
```

```
List before deletion
51 52 53 54 55 56 57 58 59 60
List after deletion
51 52 53 54 56 57 58 59 60
```

5.6 Searching A Linked List

Searching means finding an information in a given linked list. Suppose we have a linked list as illustrated in **Fig 5.32** and we have to search information **33**, whether it is present in the given list or not and if it is present then at which or in how many places. The searching procedure is given below:

Let Search = 33
Node = 1 Info [1] <> Search that is 11 <> 33 Search is unsuccessful
Next [1] = 2 Info [2] <> Search that is 22 <> 33 Search is unsuccessful
Next [2] = 3 Info [3] = Search That is 33 = 33 Search is successful and position = 3
Next [3] = 4 Info [4] <> Search that is 44 <> 33 Search is unsuccessful
Next [4] = 5 Info [5] <> Search that is 55<> 33 Search is unsuccessful
Next [5] = 6 Info [6] = Search that is 33 = 33 Search is successful and position = 6
Next [6] = 7 Info [7] <> Search that is 88 <> 33 Search is unsuccessful
Next [7] = 8 Info [8] = Search that is 33 = 33 Search is successful and position = 8
Next [8] = 9 Info [9] <> Search that is 99 <> 33 Search is unsuccessful
Next [9] = 10 Info [10] = Search that is 33 = 33 Search is successful and position = 10

From the above result it is clear that **33** is found in the linked list at four places. The algorithm for the above operation is shown in **Fig 5.33.** The program segment **LINK_S.C** implements the algorithm given in **Fig 5.33.**

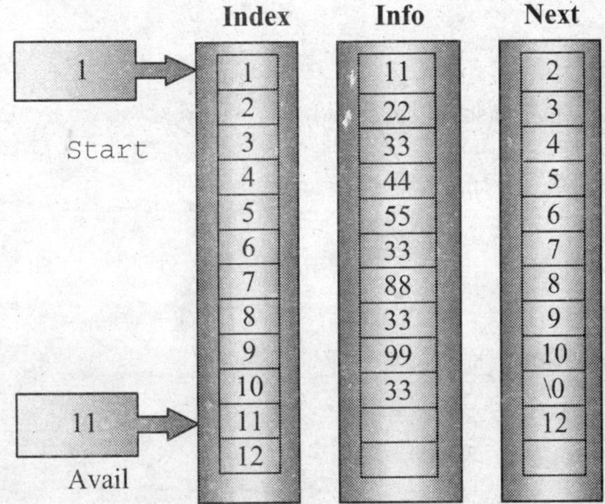

Fig 5.32. List in memory

```
/* Search a node into a simple linked list with information is known */
/* LINK_S.C */

# include <stdio.h>
# include <malloc.h>
struct link
```

```
{
	int info;
	struct link *next;
};

int i;
int number;
struct link start, *new1;

void search(struct link *);
void create_list(struct link *);
void display(struct link *);

/* Function create a linked list */

void create_list(struct link *node)
{
	char ch;
	start.next = NULL; /* Empty list */

	node = &start; /* Point to the start of the list */
	i = 0;
	printf("\n Input choice n for break: ");
	ch = getchar();
	while(ch != 'n')
	{
		node->next = (struct link* ) malloc(sizeof(struct link));

		printf("\n Input the node: %d: ", (i+1));
		scanf("%d", &node->info);
		node = node->next;
		node->next = NULL;
		fflush(stdin);
		printf("\n Input choice n for break: ");
		ch = getchar();
		i++;
	}
	printf("\n Total nodes = %d", i);
}
/* Inserting a node */
void search(struct link *node)
{
	int node_number = 0;
	int search_node;
	int flag = 0;
	node = &start ;
```

```
        printf("\n Input information of a node we want to search:");
        scanf("%d", &search_node);
        if (node == NULL)
        {
            printf("\n List is empty");
        }
        while(node)
        {
            if( search_node == node->info )
            {
                printf("\n Search is successful");
                printf("\n Information to which w want search is: %d",
search_node);
                printf("\n Position from beginning of the list: %d",
node_number+1);
                node = node->next;
                flag = 1;
            }
            else
            {
                node = node->next;
            }
            node_number ++;
        }
        if(!flag)
        {
            printf("\n Search is unsuccessful");
            printf("\n Information does not found in the list: %d", search_node);
        }
}

/* Display the list */
void display(struct link *node)
{
        node = &start;
        while (node->next)
        {
            printf("\n 0x%x", node);
            printf(" %d", node->info);
            node = node->next;
        }
}
/* Function main */

void main()
```

```
{
    struct link *node = (struct link *) malloc(sizeof(struct link));
    create_list(node);
    printf("\n List in which we have to search\n");
    display(node);
    search (node);
}
```

```
Input choice n for break:
Input the node: 1: 11
Input choice n for break:
Input the node: 2: 22
Input choice n for break:
Input the node: 3: 33
Input choice n for break:
Input the node: 4: 44
Input choice n for break:
Input the node: 5: 55
Input choice n for break:
Input the node: 6: 33
Input choice n for break:
Input the node: 7: 88
Input choice n for break:
Input the node: 8: 33
Input choice n for break:
Input the node: 9: 99
Input choice n for break:
Input the node: 10: 33
Input choice n for break: n
Total nodes = 10
List in which we have to search
0x1dd61232  11
0x1dd6123a  22
0x1dd61242  33
0x1dd6124a  44
0x1dd61252  55
0x1dd6125a  33
0x1dd61262  88
0x1dd6126a  33
0x1dd61272  99
0x1dd6127a  33
Input information of a node we want to search:33
Search is successful
Information to which we want search is: 33
Position from beginning of the list: 3
Search is successful
Information to which we want search is: 33
Position from beginning of the list: 6
Search is successful
Information to which we want search is: 33
Position from beginning of the list: 8
Search is successful
Information to which we want search is: 33
Position from beginning of the list: 10
```

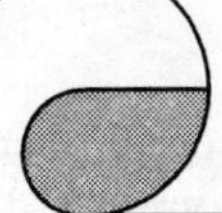

Step 1: [Initialization]
Node = Start.Next [Points to the first node of the list]
Previous = address of first node in the list
Node_number = 1

Step 2: [Set the flag]
Flag = 0

Step 3: [Read the information of a node to which we want to search]
Serach_node = Value

Step 4: [Check the list]
If Node = NULL
Output "List is empty" and Exit

Step 5: [Perform search operation]
Repeat through Step 6 while Node ≠ NULL
If Info [Node] = Search_node
(i) Output "Search is successful" and position is equal to value of Node_number.
(ii) Node = Next [Node]
(iii) Previous = Next [Node]
(iv) Flag = 1
Else
(i) Node = Next [Node]
(ii) Previous = Next [Previous]

Step 6: [Increment the value of Node_number]
Node_number = Node_number+1

Step 7: [Check the flag]
If Flag = 0
Output "Search is unsuccessful"

Step 8: Exit

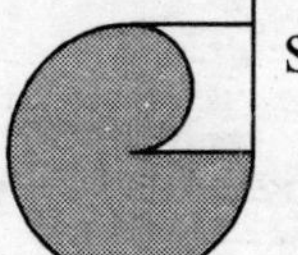

Fig 5.33. Searching algorithm

5.7 Sorting A Linked List

Sometimes it is also required to sort a list in ascending or descending order. The program segment **LINKSORT.C** implements ascending order technique, by some modifications one can change it for descending order technique (details of sorting and searching techniques are given in Chapter 9).

```
/* SORTING A LINKED LIST IN ASCENDING ORDER */
/* LINKSORT.C */

#include <stdio.h>
#include <malloc.h>

struct link
{
    int data;
    struct link *next;
};

int i;
int number ;
struct link *start, *node, *previous, *new1, *counter;

void doubly_link_sort()
{
    printf("\n Input the number of node we need to create: ");
    scanf("%d", &number );

    start->next = NULL; /* Empty list */

    node = start; /* Point to the start of the list */

    /* CREATE A LINKED LIST */

    for (i = 0; i < number ; i++)
    {
        node->next = (struct link* ) malloc(sizeof(struct link));
        node = node->next;
        printf("\n Input the first node: %d: ", i+1);
        scanf("%d", &node->data);
        node->next = NULL;
    }

    /* END OF CREATION */

    /* SORTING THE LINK LIST START FROM HERE */
```

```
    new1 = start;
    for(; new1->next != NULL; new1 = new1->next)
    {
        for(counter = new1->next; counter != NULL; counter = counter->next)
        {
            if(new1->data > counter->data)
            {
                int temp = new1->data;
                new1->data = counter->data;
                counter->data = temp;
            }
        }
    }

    /* END OF SORTING */

    /* Display the list */

    node = start->next;
    printf("\n After sorting the list is as follows:\n");
    while (node)
    {
        printf(" %d", node->data);
        node = node->next;
    }
}

/* Function main */

void main()
{
    doubly_link_sort();
}
```

If we want to create a linked list that contains the sorted names of files in the current directory, program needs to place each file name into the list at the correct position. The program **FILELIST.C** creates a linked list that contains the names of the current directory files. It uses the function **readdir()** to read directory entries. It then allocates the memory to hold an entry and copies to the list entry, the corresponding file name. After all the files have been added to the list the program loops through the list and display list entry.

```
/* FILELIST.C */
#include <stdio.h>
#include <dirent.h>
#include <malloc.h>
#include <string.h>
```

```
#include <stdlib.h>

void main(int argc, char *argv[])
{
    DIR *directory_pointer;
    struct dirent *entry;

    struct FileList {
        char filename[64];
        struct FileList *next;
    } start, *node;

    if ((directory_pointer = opendir(argv[1])) == NULL)
        printf("Error opening %s\n", argv[1]);
    else
    {
        start.next = NULL;
        node = &start;

        while (entry = readdir(directory_pointer))
        {
            node->next = (struct FileList *) malloc(sizeof(struct FileList));
            if (node == NULL)
            {
                printf("Insufficient memory to store list\n");
                exit(1);
            }
            node = node->next;
            strcpy(node->filename, entry->d_name);
            node->next = NULL;
        }

        closedir(directory_pointer);
        node = &start;
        while (node)
        {
            printf("%s\n", node->filename);
            node = node->next;
        }

    }
}
```

```
ARRAYS
LINK
SORT
QUEUE
RECURS
STACK
ARRAYS
STRING
GRAPH
TREE
INTROD
```

How is the sorting performed with the help of linked list structure? We have designed a program segment that sorts the files existing in a directory in alphabetical order. The program segment **SORTLIST.C** illustrates the idea.

```
/* SORTLIST.C */
#include <stdio.h>
#include <dirent.h>
#include <malloc.h>
#include <string.h>
#include <stdlib.h>

void main(int argc, char *argv[])
{
    DIR *directory_pointer;
    struct dirent *entry;

    struct FileList {
        char filename[64];
        struct FileList *next;
    } start, *node, *previous, *new;


    if ((directory_pointer = opendir(argv[1])) == NULL)
        printf("Error opening %s\n", argv[1]);
    else
    {
        start.next = NULL;

        while (entry = readdir(directory_pointer))
        {
            /* Find the correct location */
             previous = &start;
            node = start.next;
```

```
            while ((node) && (strcmp(entry->d_name, node->filename) > 0))
            {
                node = node->next;
                previous = previous->next;
            }

            new = (struct FileList *) malloc(sizeof(struct FileList));
            if (new == NULL)
            {
                printf("Insufficient memory to store list\n");
                exit(1);
            }
            new->next = node;
            previous->next = new;
            strcpy(new->filename, entry->d_name);
        }

        closedir(directory_pointer);


        node = start.next;

        while (node)
        {
            printf("%s\n", node->filename);
            node = node->next;
        }

    }
}
```

```
ARRAYS
GRAPH
INTROD
LINK
QUEUE
RECURS
SORT
STACK
STRING
TREE
```

Sometimes it is also required joining of two lists. This can be done with the help of program segment **LINKCAT.C.**

```
/* CONCATENATE TWO LINKED LIST */
/* LINKCAT.C */

#include <stdio.h>
#include <malloc.h>

struct link
{
	int data;
	struct link *next;
};

struct link *start, *node;
struct link *list_one, *list_two, *list_three;

void display(struct link *);
void create_list(struct link *);
void link_concat_list(struct link *, struct link *, struct link *);

void display(struct link *node)
{
	while (node->next)
	{
		printf(" %d", node->data);
		node = node->next;
	}
}

/* Definition of the function */

void create_list(struct link *node)
{
	int i = 0;
	char ch;

	printf("\n Input choice n for break: ");
	ch = getchar();

	/* CREATE A LINKED LIST */

	while(ch != 'n')
	{
		printf("\n Input the node: %d: ", (i+1));
		scanf("%d", &node->data);
		node->next = (struct link * ) malloc(sizeof(struct link));
		node = node->next;
```

```
            node->next = NULL;
            fflush(stdin);
            printf("\n Input choice n for break: ");
            ch = getchar();
            i ++;
        }
        printf("\n Total nodes = %d", i);
}

void link_concat_list(struct link *list_one, struct link *list_two, struct link *list_three)
{

        /* Copying first list */

        while(list_one->next != NULL)
        {
            list_three->data = list_one->data;
            list_one = list_one->next;
            list_three->next = (struct link* ) malloc(sizeof(struct link));
            list_three = list_three->next;
        }

        /* Copying second list */

        while(list_two->next !=NULL)
        {
            list_three->data = list_two->data;
            list_two = list_two->next;
            list_three->next = (struct link*)malloc(sizeof(struct link));
            list_three = list_three->next;
        }
        list_three->next = NULL;
}

/* Function main */

void main()
{
        struct link *list_one, *list_two, *list_three;

        /* Assign memory to link(struct) type variables */

        list_one = (struct link *)malloc(sizeof(struct link));
        list_two = (struct link *)malloc(sizeof(struct link));
        list_three = (struct link *)malloc(sizeof(struct link));
```

```
    create_list(list_one);
    printf("\n Original list ONE is as follows:\n");
    display(list_one);

    create_list(list_two);
    printf("\n Original list TWO is as follows:\n");
    display(list_two);

    link_concat_list(list_one, list_two, list_three);
    printf("\n Original list ONE + TWO is as follows:\n");
    display(list_three);
}
```

If we want to reverse the contents of a list we use the program segment **LINK_REV.C**. Design of algorithm for this operation is left for the readers.

```
/* REVERSING A LINKED LIST */
/* LINK_REV.C */

#Include <stdio.h>
#include <malloc.h>

struct link
{
    int data;
    struct link *next;
};

int i, number;
struct link *start, *node, *previous, *current1, *counter;

void display(struct link *);
void create_list(struct link *);
struct link * reverse(struct link *);

/* Reversing the list */

struct link * reverse(struct link *start)
{
    current1 = start;
    previous = NULL ;

    while( current1 != NULL )
    {
        counter = (struct link *)malloc(sizeof(struct link));
        counter = current1->next ;
```

```
            current1->next = previous ;
            previous = current1 ;
            current1 = counter;
        }

        start = previous;
        return(start);
}

/* Definition of the function */

void display(struct link *node)
{
        while (node != NULL)
        {
            printf(" %d", node->data);
            node = node->next;
        }
}

/* Definition of the function */

void create_list(struct link *node)
{
        int i;
        int number;

        printf("\n Input the number of nodes you want to create:");
        scanf("%d", &number);

        /* CREATE A LINKED LIST */

        for (i = 0; i < number ; i++)
        {
            printf("\n Input the node: %d: ", i+1);
            scanf("%d", &node->data);
            node->next = (struct link* ) malloc(sizeof(struct link));
            if( i == number - 1)
                node->next = NULL;
            else
                node = node->next;
        }
        node->next = NULL;
}

/* End of function creation */
```

```
/* Function main */
void main()
{
      struct link *node;
      struct link *p;

      node = (struct link *) malloc(sizeof(struct link));
      create_list(node);
      printf("\n Original List is as follows:\n");
      display(node);
      p = ( struct link *)malloc(sizeof(struct link));
      p = reverse(node);
      printf("\n After reverse operation list is as foiiows:\n");
      display(p);
}
```

If we want to examine the operation performed by **DIR** command of **DOS** and **ls** command of **UNIX,** a program segment **LINK_DIR.C** has been developed, design of algorithm is left to the readers as an exercise.

```
/* HOW THE DIR FUNCTION OF DOS WORK SEE IT THROUGH LINKED LIST */
/* LINK_DIR.C */

# include<stdio.h>
# include <dirent.h>
# include <malloc.h>
# include <string.h>
# include <stdlib.h>

struct File_List
{
      char filename[64];
      struct File_List *next;
}
start, *node;
void main(int argc, char *argv[])
{
      DIR *directory_pointer;
      struct dirent *entry;

      if ((directory_pointer = opendir(argv[1])) == NULL)
      {
            perror("Error opening :");
            printf("%s", argv[1]);
      }
      else
      {
```

```
        start.next = NULL;
        node = &start;

        while (entry = readdir(directory_pointer))
        {
            node->next = (struct File_List *) malloc(sizeof(struct File_List));
            if (node == NULL)
            {
                printf("Insufficient memory to store list\n");
                exit(1);
            }
            node = node->next;

            strcpy(node->filename,(char *) entry); /* char * convert dirent to char * constant */

            node->next = NULL;
        }
        closedir(directory_pointer);

        node = start.next;

        while (node)
        {
            printf("\n %s", node->filename);
            node = node->next;
        }
    }
}
```

5.8 Doubly Linked List

A singly linked list is so named because each list element contains a pointer to the next element. We have seen that, to insert elements in a singly linked list, program has to maintain pointers to the current and previous elements.

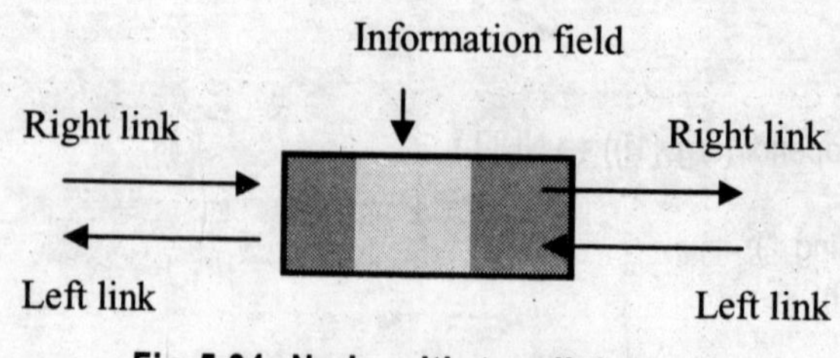

Fig 5.34. Node with two links

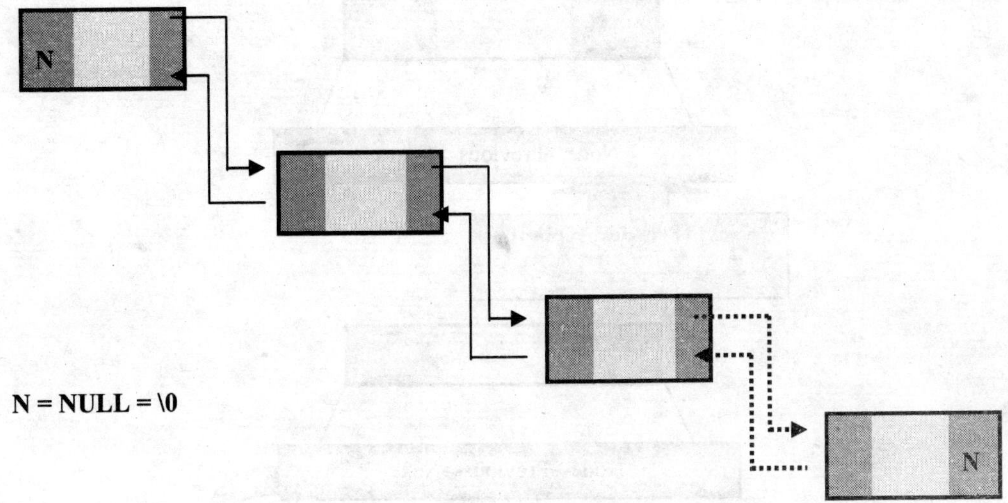

Fig 5.35. Doubly linked list

In linear linked list structure, traversing is possible only in one direction. Sometimes it is required to traverse the list in either direction forward or backward. This increases the performance and efficiency of algorithms. So traversing of linked list in both the directions requires nodes having the links as illustrated in **Fig 5.34.** The links are used to denote the predecessor and successor of a node. The link denoting the predecessor of a node is called the left link and that denoting its successor is right link. A list with this type of arrangement is called doubly linked list as shown in **Fig 5.35.** Now it is possible to define a doubly linked as a collection of nodes, each node having three fields:

- *Pointer to previous node (Pointer to predecessor)*
- *Information field*
- *Pointer to next node (Pointer to successor)*

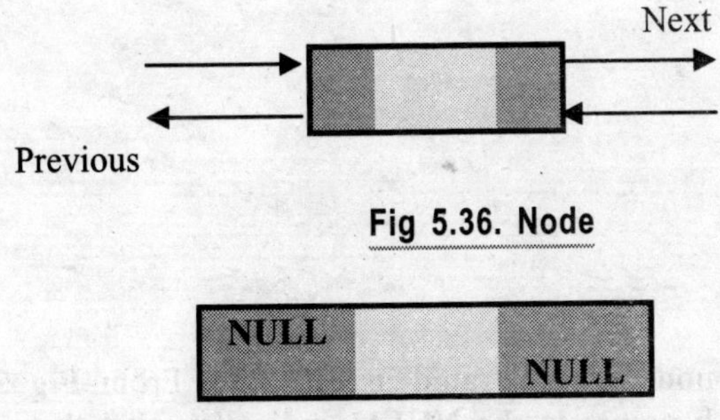

Fig 5.36. Node

Fig 5.37

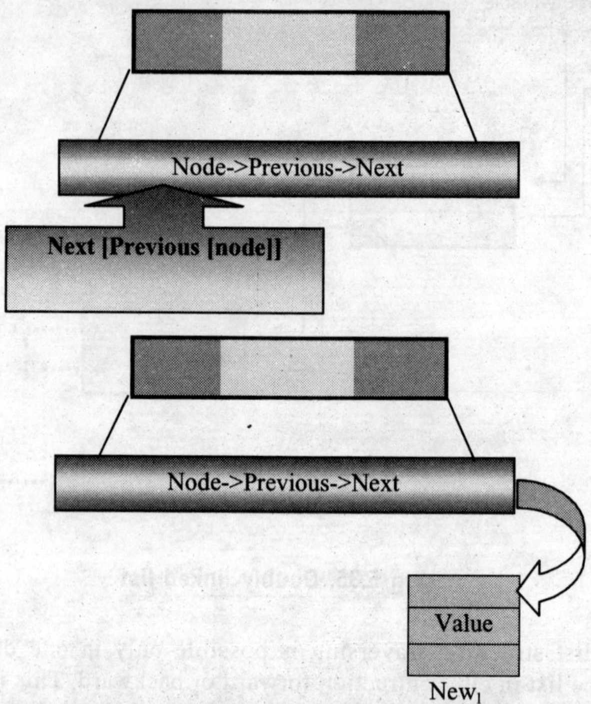

Fig 5.38. Complex pointer resolving

Fig 5.37 illustrates that the left link of the left most node and the right link of the right most node are **NULL**. The **NULL** indicates the end of the list in each direction. How can one create a node of doubly linked? For this consider the following declaration:

```
struct Tag name
{
    Data type information field 1;
    Data type Information field 2;
            ...
            ...
            ...
    Data type information field n;
    struct Tag name *previous;
    struct Tag name *next;
};
```

This definition represents a node as illustrated in **Fig 5.36.** From **Fig 5.37** it is clear that **start.next** and **previous.next** both points to the **NULL,** indicating that there is a single node in the list that is **NULL.** Algorithm to build a doubly linked list is given in **Fig 5.39**. The notations that are used in the algorithm are

Start → structure type variable
Previous → pointer structure type variable

Next → pointer structure type variable
Node → pointer structure type variable

Step 1: Meaning of this step can be clearly illustrated with the help of **Fig 5.40.**

Fig 5.40

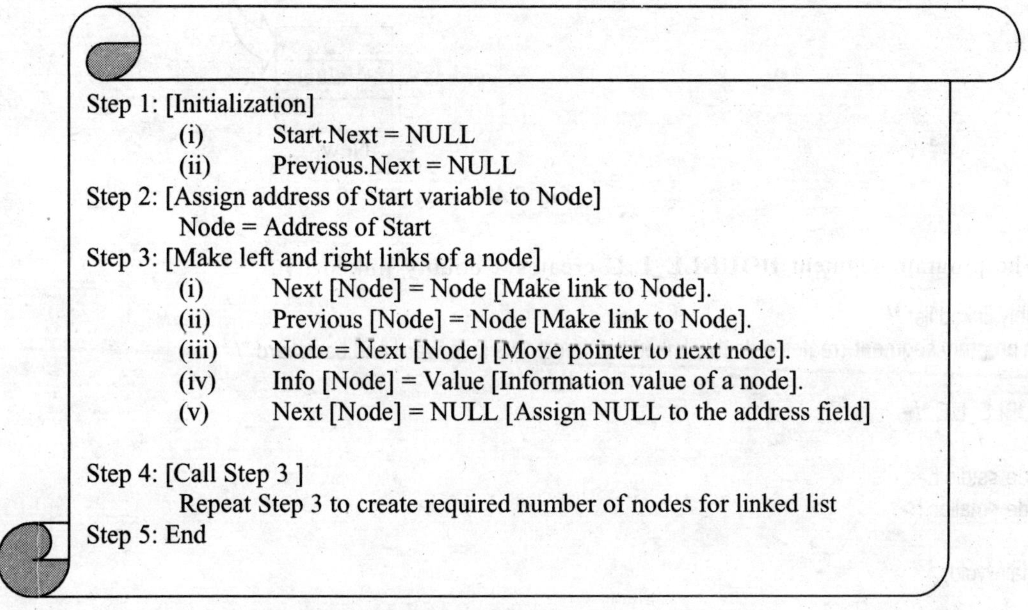

Step 1: [Initialization]
(i) Start.Next = NULL
(ii) Previous.Next = NULL
Step 2: [Assign address of Start variable to Node]
Node = Address of Start
Step 3: [Make left and right links of a node]
(i) Next [Node] = Node [Make link to Node].
(ii) Previous [Node] = Node [Make link to Node].
(iii) Node = Next [Node] [Move pointer to next nodc].
(iv) Info [Node] = Value [Information value of a node].
(v) Next [Node] = NULL [Assign NULL to the address field]

Step 4: [Call Step 3]
Repeat Step 3 to create required number of nodes for linked list
Step 5: End

Fig 5.39. Doubly linked list creation algorithm

From **Fig 5.40** it is clear that **Start.Next** and **Previous.Next** both points to the **NULL,** indicating that there is a single node in the list that is **NULL.**

Step 2: Meaning of first two statements in this step is illustrated in **Fig 5.41.**

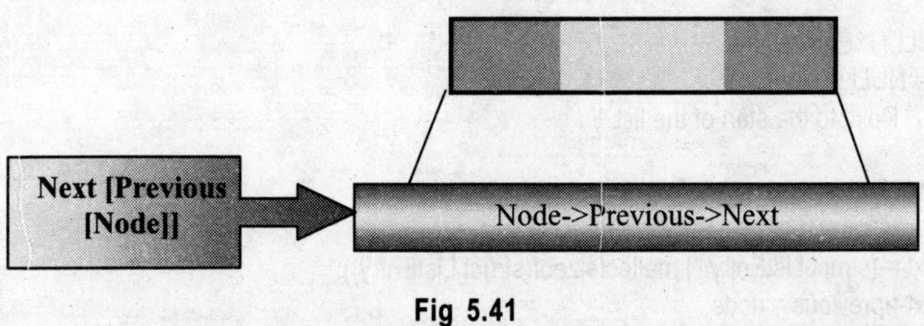

Fig 5.41

If we consider all the statements of this step then **Fig 5.41** becomes like **Fig 5.42.**

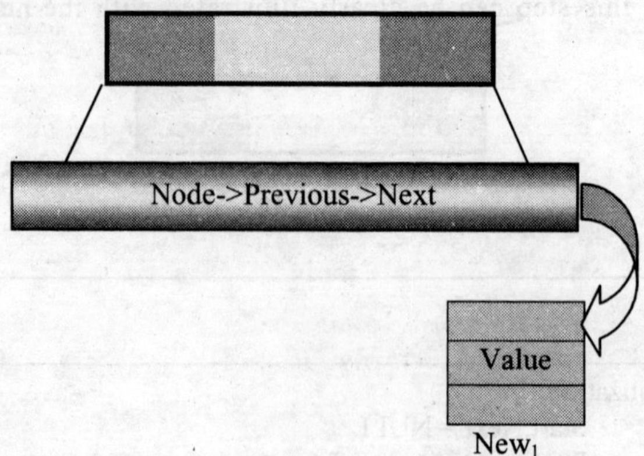

Fig 5.42

The program segment **DOUBLE_L.C** creates a doubly linked list.

```
/* Doubly linked list */
/* This program segment creates a doubly linked list then prints in forward and backward */

/* DOUBLE_L.C */

#include <stdio.h>
#include <malloc.h>

void main(void)
{
    int i;

    struct ListEntry {
        int number;
        struct ListEntry *next;
        struct ListEntry *previous;
    } start, *node;

    start.next = NULL; /* Empty list */
    start.previous = NULL;
    node = &start; /* Point to the start of the list */

    for (i = 1; i <= 10; i++)
    {
        node->next = (struct ListEntry *) malloc(sizeof(struct ListEntry));
        node->next->previous = node;
        node = node->next;
```

```
        node->number = 50+i;
        node->next = NULL;
    }

    /* Display the list */

    node = start.next;

    do {
            printf("%d ", node->number);
            node = node->next;
        } while (node->next); /* Show 60 only one time */


    do {
            printf("%d ", node->number);
            node = node->previous;
        } while (node->previous);
}
```

```
51 52 53 54 55 56 57 58 59 60 59 58 57 56 55 54 53 52 51
```

5.9 Traversing A Doubly Linked List

Traversing a doubly linked list means scanning (processing) each and every node exactly once either in forward or backward direction or in both the directions, *i.e.*, the program can traverse the list from left to right or right to left. Therefore, two **NULL** pointers are maintained. When traversing the list from left to right, it identifies the end of the list when **node->next** is **NULL**. Likewise, when traversing the list from right to left, the end of the list is indicated when **node->previous** is **NULL**. For example, the program **DOUBLE_L.C** creates a doubly linked list and display information associated with each node in forward and backward. **Fig 5.43** illustrates an algorithm for traversing doubly linked in forward and backward directions. According to the requirement of applications one can easily edit this algorithm.

Fig 5.43 clearly indicates that, first of all, it is required to assign address of very first node to the variable **node** with the help of **start.next** variable. Now we move pointer forward and access the information associated with each and every node such as

Start = Node = 1
Info [1] = 11   Next [1] = 2
Info [2] = 22   Next [2] = 3
Info [3] = 33   Next [3] = 4
Info [4] = 44   Next [4] = 5

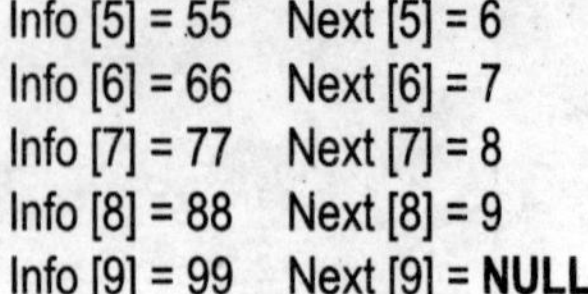

Info [5] = 55 Next [5] = 6
Info [6] = 66 Next [6] = 7
Info [7] = 77 Next [7] = 8
Info [8] = 88 Next [8] = 9
Info [9] = 99 Next [9] = **NULL**

```
Step 1: [Initialization]
        Node = Start.Next [Points to the first node in the list]
Step 2: [Traverse the list in forward direction]
        Repeat while Next [Node] ≠ NULL
        Process  Info [Node]
Step 3: [Traverse the list in backward direction]
        Repeat while Previus[Node] ≠ NULL
        Process  Info [Node]
Step 4: Exit
```

Fig 5.43. Algorithm for traversing a doubly linked list

Index	Info	Next	Previous
1	11	2	NULL
2	22	3	1
3	33	4	2
4	44	5	3
5	55	6	4
6	66	7	5
7	77	8	6
8	88	9	7
9	99	NULL	8

Fig 5.44. Traversing doubly linked list

Similarly in backward direction traversing can be performed as

Node = 9
Info [9] = 99 Previous [9] = 8
Info [8] = 88 Previous [8] = 7
Info [7] = 77 Previous [7] = 6
Info [6] = 66 Previous [6] = 5
Info [5] = 55 Previous [5] = 4
Info [4] = 44 Previous [4] = 3
Info [3] = 33 Previous [3] = 2
Info [2] = 22 Previous [2] = 1
Info [1] = 11 Previous [1] = **NULL**

The program segment **DBLINK.C** illustrates the algorithm shown in **Fig 5.43.** Using the program segment **DBLINK.C** one can easily verify the results shown above.

```
/* CREATING A SIMPLE DOUBLY LINKED LIST */
/* DBLINK.C */

# include <stdio.h>
# include <malloc.h>

struct Double
{
	int info;
	struct Double *next;
	struct Double *previous;
};

int num ;
struct Double start;
void Doubly_link_list (struct Double *);
void display (struct Double *);

/* Function creates a simple doubly linked list */

void Doubly_link_list(struct Double *node)
{
	char ch;
	start.next = NULL; /* Empty list */
	start.previous = NULL;
	node = &start; /* Point to the start of the list */
	num = 0;
	printf("\n Input choice n for break: ");
	ch = getchar();

	while( ch != 'n')
```

```
    {
        node->next = (struct Double *) malloc(sizeof(struct Double));
        node->next->previous = node;
        node = node->next;
        printf("\n Input the values of the node : %d: ", (num+1));
        scanf("%d", &node->info);
        node->next = NULL;
        fflush(stdin);
        printf("\n Input choice n for break: ");
        ch = getchar();
        num ++;
    }
    printf("\n Total nodes = %d", num);
}

/* Display the list */

void display (struct Double *node)
{
    node = start.next;

    do {
        printf("\n 0x%x", node);
        printf(" %d", node->info);
        node = node->next;
    } while (node->next); /* Show value of last node only one time */

    do {
        printf("\n 0x%x", node );
        printf(" %d", node->info);
        node = node->previous;
    } while (node->previous);
}

void main()
{
    struct Double *node = (struct Double *) malloc(sizeof(struct Double));
    Doubly_link_list(node);
    printf("\n Created doubly linked list is as follows\n");
    display(node);
}
```

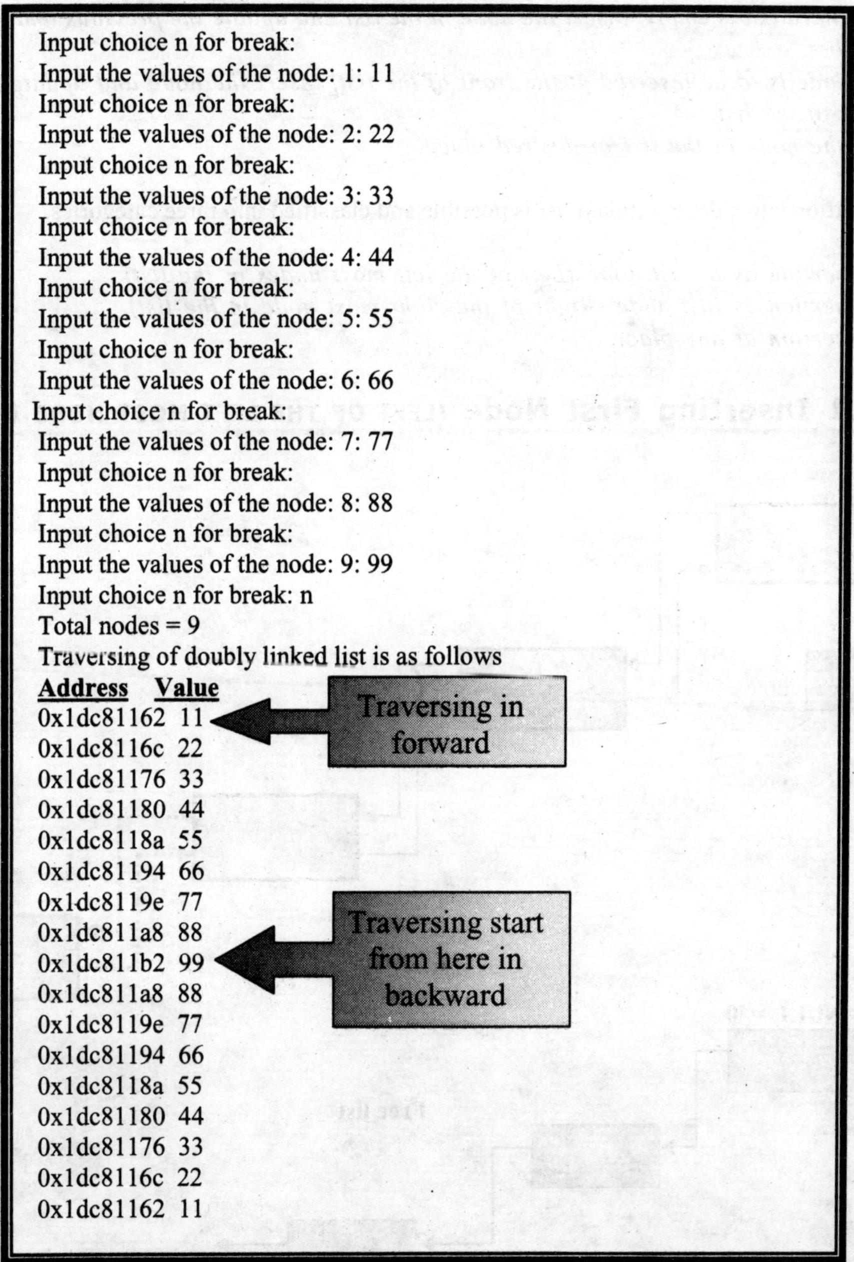

```
Input choice n for break:
Input the values of the node: 1: 11
Input choice n for break:
Input the values of the node: 2: 22
Input choice n for break:
Input the values of the node: 3: 33
Input choice n for break:
Input the values of the node: 4: 44
Input choice n for break:
Input the values of the node: 5: 55
Input choice n for break:
Input the values of the node: 6: 66
Input choice n for break:
Input the values of the node: 7: 77
Input choice n for break:
Input the values of the node: 8: 88
Input choice n for break:
Input the values of the node: 9: 99
Input choice n for break: n
Total nodes = 9
Traversing of doubly linked list is as follows
Address    Value
0x1dc81162  11
0x1dc8116c  22
0x1dc81176  33
0x1dc81180  44
0x1dc8118a  55
0x1dc81194  66
0x1dc8119e  77
0x1dc811a8  88
0x1dc811b2  99
0x1dc811a8  88
0x1dc8119e  77
0x1dc81194  66
0x1dc8118a  55
0x1dc81180  44
0x1dc81176  33
0x1dc8116c  22
0x1dc81162  11
```


5.10 Insertion in A Doubly Linked List

Before making insertion operation, one should go through the following steps to get the idea:

1. *Obtain a new node and set its fields.*

2. *If the linked list is empty, insert the node in the list and update the previous and next pointers of the list.*
3. *If the node is to be inserted at the front of the list, insert the node and update the previous pointer of the list.*
4. *Insert the node in the list at desired place.*

Insertion into a doubly linked list is possible and classified into three categories.

- *Insertion as a first node (Left of the left most nodes in the list)*
- *Insertion as last node (Right of the right most node in the list)*
- *Insertion at any place*

5.10.1 Inserting First Node (LEFT OF THE LEFT MOST NODE IN A LIST)

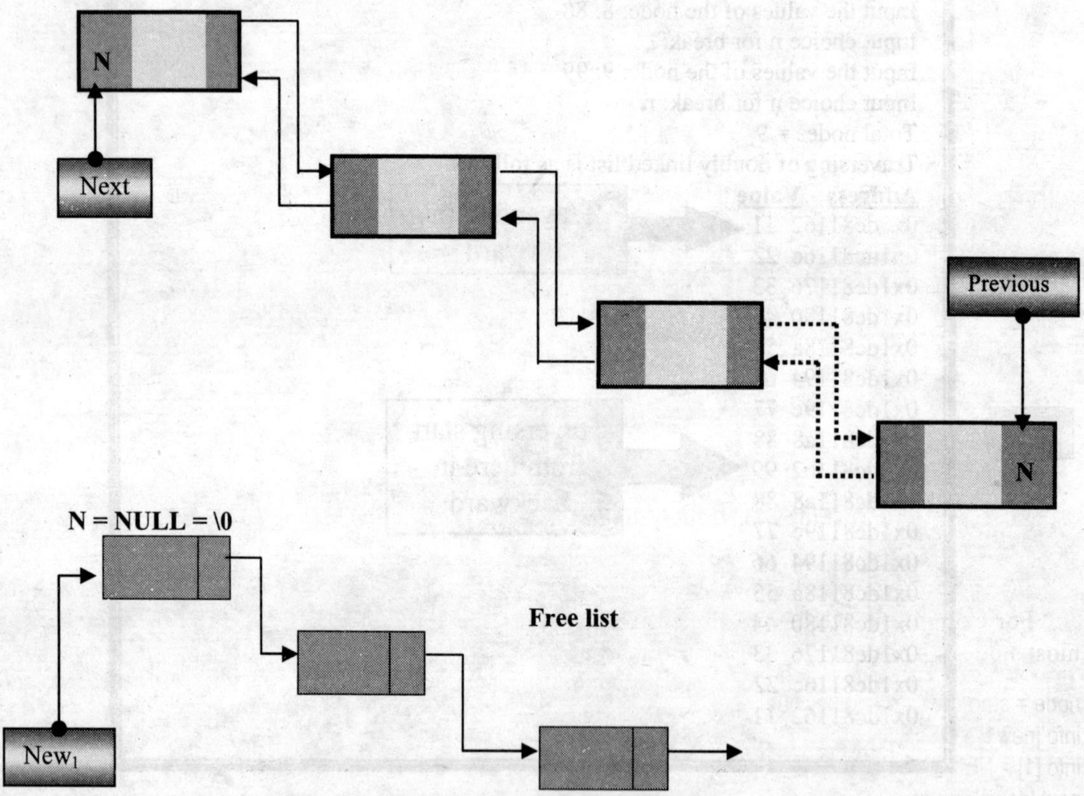

Fig 5.45. Doubly linked list before insertion

Given a doubly linked list whose left most and right most nodes addresses are given by the pointer variables **next** and **previous,** respectively. It is required to insert a node whose address is given by the pointer variable **new**$_1$. The information field of a node is denoted by the variable

info. Suppose we have a doubly linked list as shown in **Fig 5.45,** the insertion operation may be performed as illustrated in **Fig 5.46.**

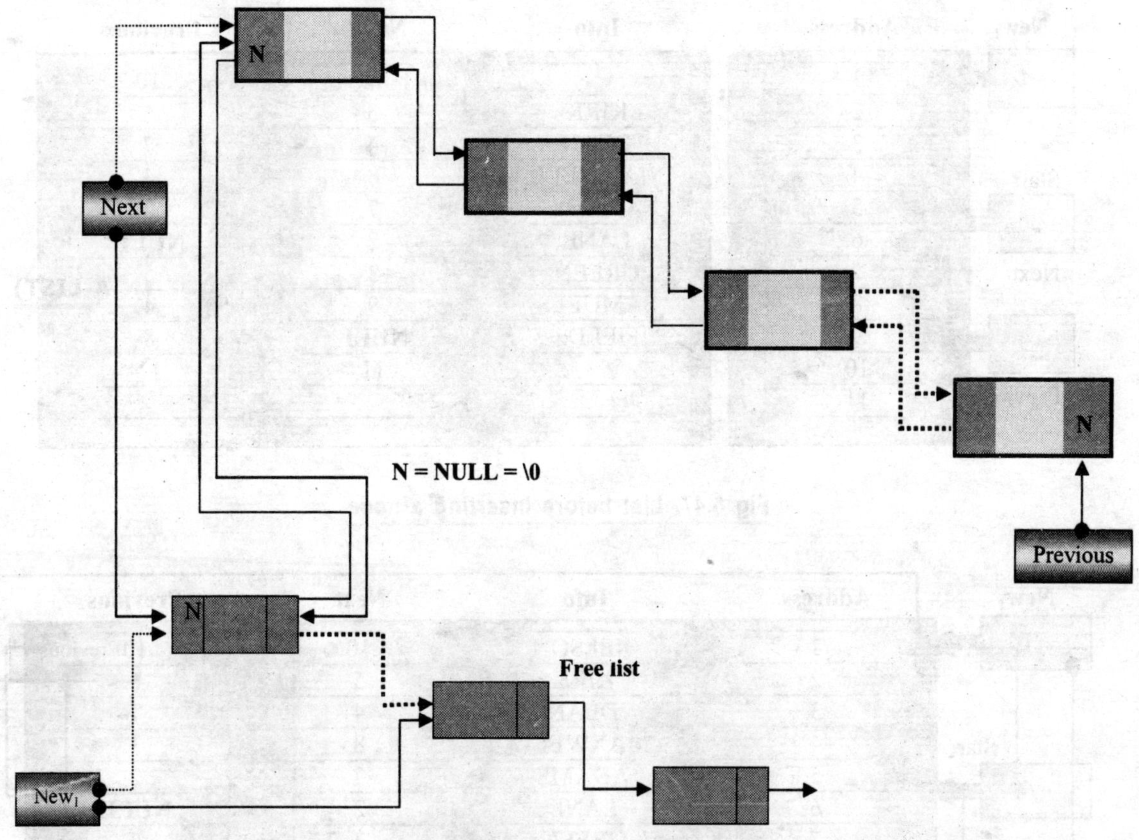

Fig 5.46. Doubly linked list after insertion of first node

For example, if we have a linked list as shown in **Fig 5.47**, the insertion to the left of the left most node in the list may be performed as

node = start.next = 6 [Index value]
info [new1] = NELSON
info [1] = NELSON
next [new1] = node
next [1] = 6
previous [new1] = previous [node] = **NULL**
previous [1] = previous [6] = **NULL**
previous [node] = new1
previous [6] = new1 = 1

Now from the above discussion, it is clear that after insertion of a node to the left of the left most node in the list, the list shown in **Fig 5.47** becomes as shown in **Fig 5.48.** The program segment **DBL_IF.C** implements the algorithm discussed in **Fig 5.49.**

New_1: 1 | Start: 6 | Next: 9 | Previous

Address	Info	Next	Previous
1		10	10
2	KIRK	5	6
3	DEAN	4	7
4	MAXWELL	8	3
5	ADAMS	7	2
6	LANE	2	**NULL**
7	GREEN	3	5
8	SAMUELS	9	4
9	FIELDS	**NULL**	8
10		11	11
11			

Fig 5.47. List before inserting a node

New_1: 1 | Start: 6 | 9 | Previous

Address	Info	Next	Previous
1	NELSON	10	10
2	KIRK	5	6
3	DEAN	4	7
4	MAXWELL	8	3
5	ADAMS	7	2
6	LANE	2	**NULL**
7	GREEN	3	5
8	SAMUELS	9	4
9	FIELDS	**NULL**	8
10		11	11
11			

Fig 5.48. List after inserting a node

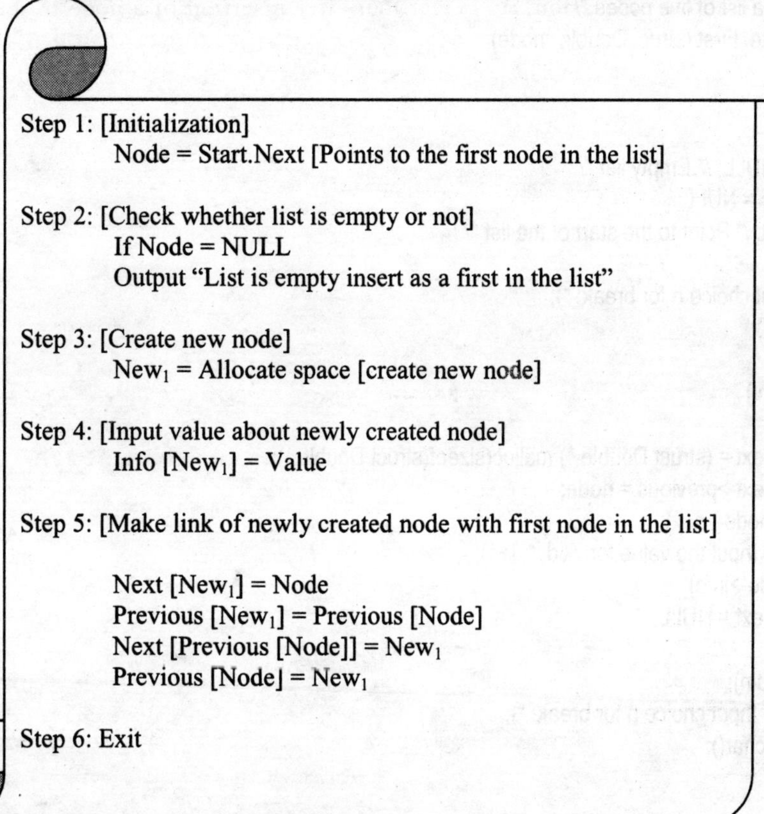

Step 1: [Initialization]
Node = Start.Next [Points to the first node in the list]

Step 2: [Check whether list is empty or not]
If Node = NULL
Output "List is empty insert as a first in the list"

Step 3: [Create new node]
New_1 = Allocate space [create new node]

Step 4: [Input value about newly created node]
Info [New_1] = Value

Step 5: [Make link of newly created node with first node in the list]

Next [New_1] = Node
Previous [New_1] = Previous [Node]
Next [Previous [Node]] = New_1
Previous [Node] = New_1

Step 6: Exit

Fig 5.49. Algorithm to insert left to the left most node in a list

```
/* INSERTING FIRST NODE IN THE DOUBLY LINKED LIST */
/* DBL_IF.C */

# include <stdio.h>
# include <malloc.h>

struct Double
{
	char info[20];
	struct Double *next;
	struct Double *previous;
};
int i;
struct Double start, *new1;
void Doubly_insertion_First (struct Double *);
void Doubly_Create_First (struct Double *);
void Display (struct Double *);
```

```
/* Function create a list of five nodes */
void Doubly_Create_First (struct Double *node)
{
    int i = 0;
    char ch;
    start.next = NULL; /* Empty list */
    start.previous = NULL;
    node = &start; /* Point to the start of the list */
    fflush(stdin);
    printf("\n Input choice n for break: ");
    ch = getchar();

    while (ch != 'n')
    {
        node->next = (struct Double *) malloc(sizeof(struct Double ));
        node->next->previous = node;
        node = node->next;
        printf("\n Input the value for: %d: ", i+1);
        gets(node->info);
        node->next = NULL;
        i++;
        fflush(stdin);
        printf("\n Input choice n for break: ");
        ch = getchar();
    }
}
void Doubly_insertion_First (struct Double *node)
{
    node = start.next;
    new1 = (struct Double *) malloc(sizeof(struct Double ));
    fflush(stdin);
    printf("\n Input the first node value: ");
    gets(new1->info);
    printf("\n new1 address: 0x%x", new1);
    printf("\n Node address: 0x%x", node);
    new1->next = node;
    printf("\n New1 next address: 0x%x", new1->next);
    printf("\n Node previous address: 0x%x", node->previous);
    new1->previous = node->previous;
    node->previous->next = new1;
    printf("\n node->previous.next: 0x%x", node->previous->next);
    printf("\n Node previous address: 0x%x", node->previous);
    printf("\n Node next address: 0x%x", node->next);
    printf("\n new1 address: 0x%x", new1);
    node->previous = new1;
    printf("\n node->previous: 0x%x", node->previous);
}
```

```
/* Display the list */

void Display (struct Double *node)
{
      node = start.next;

      while (node)
      {
            printf("\n 0x%x", node);
            printf(" %s", node->info);
            node = node->next;
      }
}

/* main function */
void main()
{
      struct Double *node = (struct Double *) malloc(sizeof(struct Double));
      Doubly_Create_First (node);
      printf("\n Created list is as follows\n");
      Display(node);
      Doubly_insertion_First (node);
      printf("\n List after insertion of first node \n");
      Display (node);
}
```

```
Input choice n for break:
Input the value for: 1: KIRK
Input choice n for break:
Input the value for: 2: DEAN
Input choice n for break:
Input the value for: 3: MAXWELL
Input choice n for break:
Input the value for: 4: ADAMS
Input choice n for break:
Input the value for: 5: LANE
Input choice n for break:
Input the value for: 6: GREEN
Input choice n for break:
Input the value for: 7: SAMUELS
Input choice n for break:
Input the value for: 8: FIELDS
Input choice n for break:
Input the value for: 9:
Input choice n for break: n
```

```
Created list is as follows
Address      Value
0x1d8f128a
0x1d8f118e  KIRK
0x1d8f11aa  DEAN
0x1d8f11c6  MAXWELL
0x1d8f11e2  ADAMS
0x1d8f1fe   LANE
0x1d8f121a  GREEN
0x1d8f1236  SAMUELS
0x1d8f1252  FIELDS
0x1d8f126e
Input the first node  value: NELSON
List after insertion of first node
Address      Value
0x1d8f128a  NELSON
0x1d8f118e  KIRK
0x1d8f11aa  DEAN
0x1d8f11c6  MAXWELL
0x1d8f11e2  ADAMS
0x1d8f11fe  LANE
0x1d8f121a  GREEN
0x1d8f1236  SAMUELS
0x1d8f1252  FIELDS
0x1d8f126e
```

5.10.2 Inserting A Node At The End

(a node to the right of the right most node in a list)

Suppose we want to insert a node into a doubly linked list at the right of the right most node, it is required to skip all the nodes from beginning, i.e., from the left most node to the right most node where one gets **NULL.** Another way of insertion is add new node after previous pointer (previous pointer contains the address of the right of the right most node). At this point a node is inserted. To insert a newly created node, following arrangement is required:

- *Copy the **NULL** value at the next pointer value of the newly created node.*
- *Copy the **previous** pointer value of the last node to the previous pointer value of a newly created node.*
- *Make arrangements like **Fig 5.50,** i.e., adjust pointers accordingly.*

In **C/C++** language, equivalent of **Fig 5.50** can be implemented as:

```
node->previous->next = new1;
```

- *Copy address of the newly created node to the next pointer value of node.*

INFO
Next [Previous[Node]]
INFO
New1

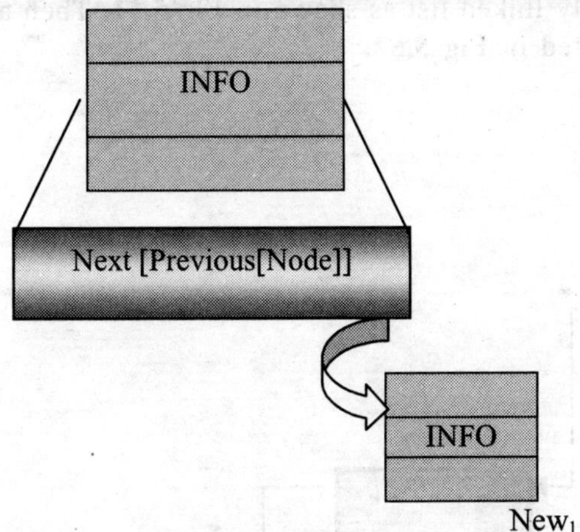

Fig 5.50. Resolving complex pointer

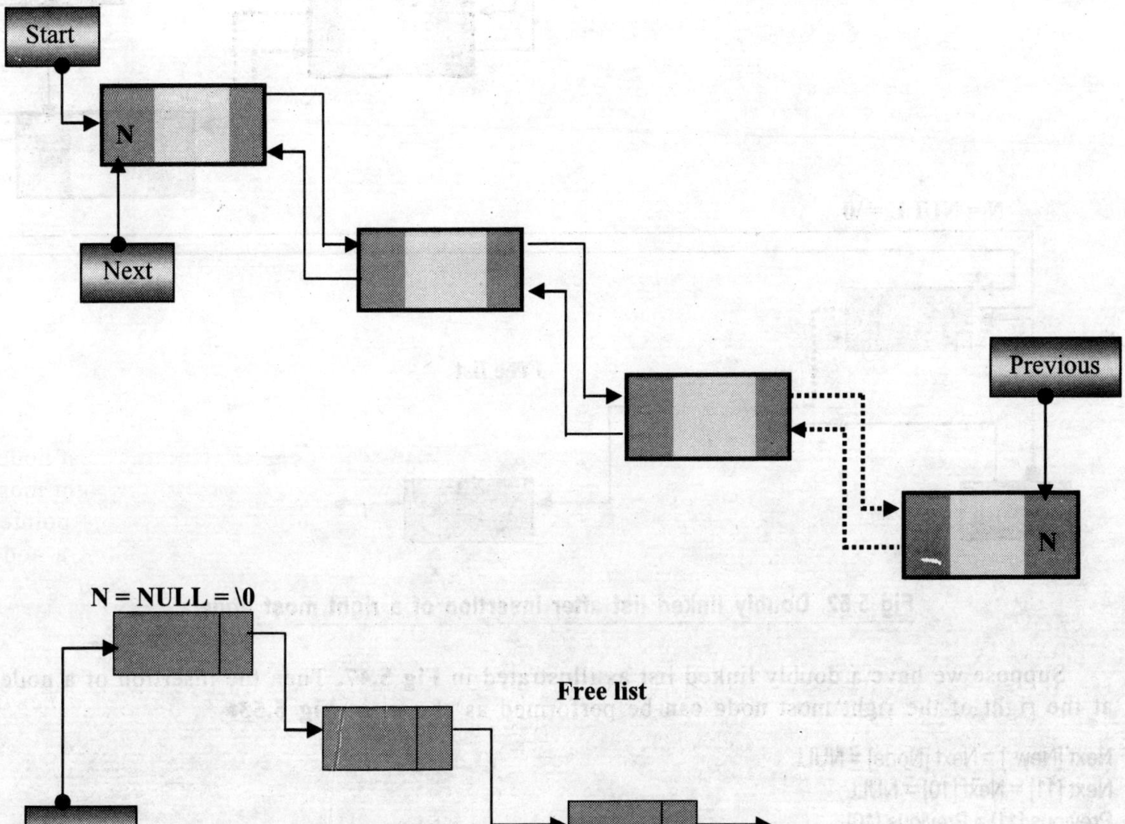

Start
N
Next
Previous
N
N = NULL = \0
Free list
New1

Fig 5.51. Doubly linked list before insertion

Suppose we have a doubly linked list as shown in **Fig 5.51.** Then after insertion of a node at the end of the list is illustrated in **Fig 5.52.**

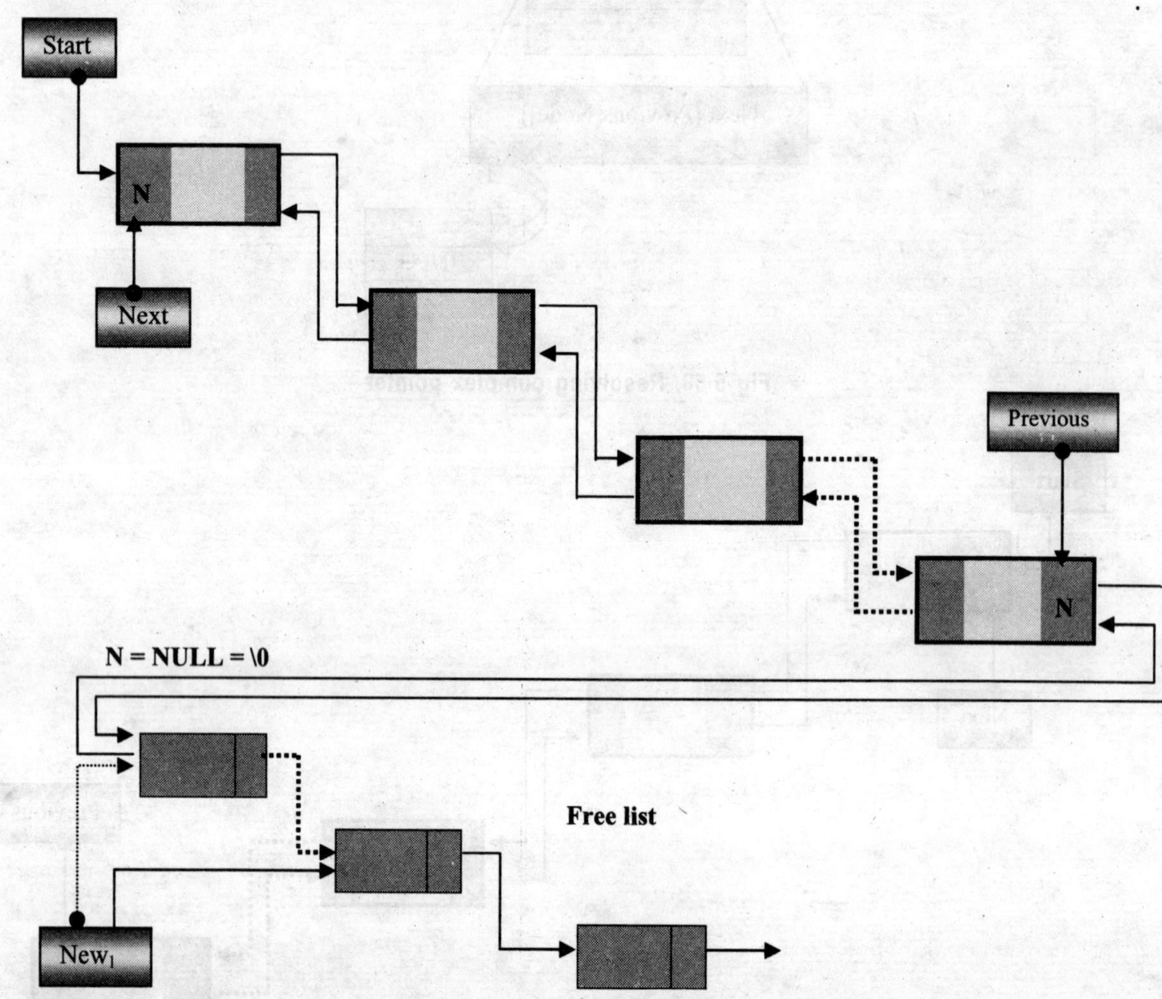

Fig 5.52. Doubly linked list after insertion of a right most node

Suppose we have a doubly linked list as illustrated in **Fig 5.47.** Then the insertion of a node at the right of the right most node can be performed as shown in **Fig 5.53.**

Next [New_1] = Next [Node] = NULL
Next [11] = Next [10] = NULL
Previous [11] = Previous [10]
Next [10] = Next [10] = New_1 = 11

After inserting a node at right of the right most node the list becomes as illustrated in **Fig**

5.53. The algorithm to insert a node at the right of the right most is given in the **Fig 5.54.** For example, the program segment **DBL_IL.C** illustrates the insertion algorithm given in **Fig 5.54.**

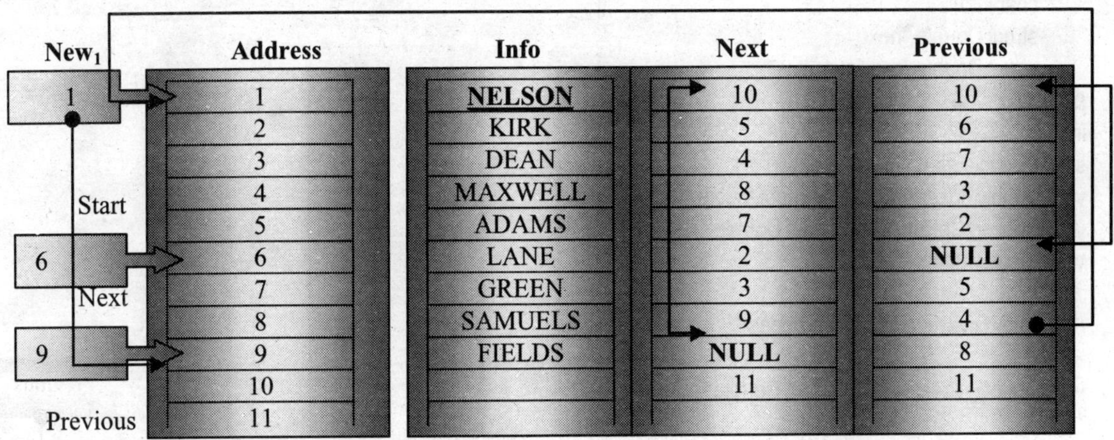

Fig 5.53. List after inserting a node at right of the right most node

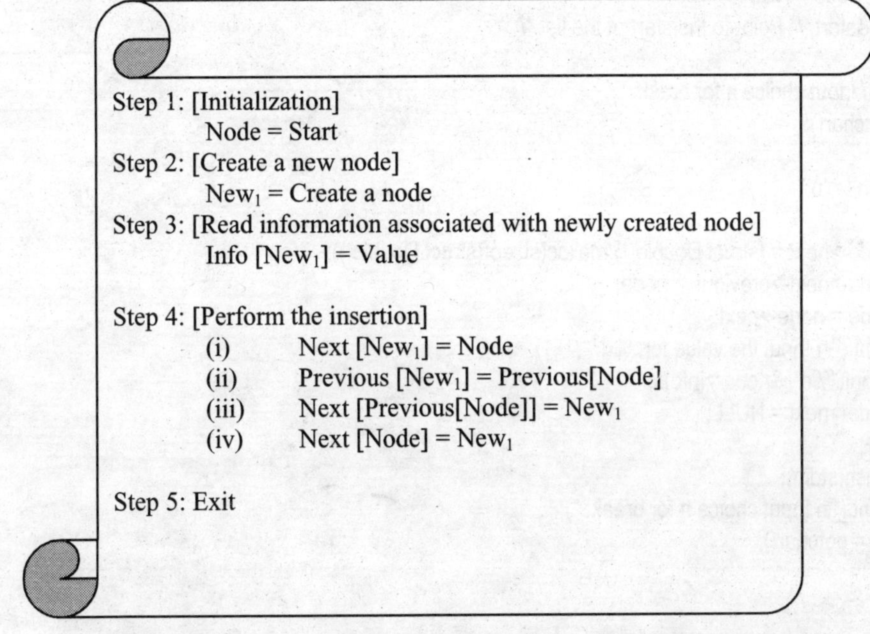

Step 1: [Initialization]
Node = Start
Step 2: [Create a new node]
New_1 = Create a node
Step 3: [Read information associated with newly created node]
Info [New_1] = Value

Step 4: [Perform the insertion]
(i) Next [New_1] = Node
(ii) Previous [New_1] = Previous[Node]
(iii) Next [Previous[Node]] = New_1
(iv) Next [Node] = New_1

Step 5: Exit

Fig 5.54. Algorithm to insert a node at right of the right most node

```
/* INSERTING SOME NODES IN THE DOUBLY LINKED LIST */
/* DBL_IL.C */
```

```
# include <stdio.h>
# include <malloc.h>

struct Double {
      char info;
      struct Double *next;
      struct Double *previous;
};
int i;
struct Double start, *new1;
void Doubly_insertion_Last (struct Double *);
void Doubly_Create_Last (struct Double *);
void Display (struct Double *);

/* Function create a list of five nodes */

void Doubly_Create_Last (struct Double *node)
{
      int i = 0;
      char ch;
      start.next = NULL; /* Empty list */
      start.previous = NULL;
      node = &start; /* Point to the start of the list */

      printf("\n Input choice n for break: ");
      ch = getchar();

      while (ch != 'n')
      {
            node->next = (struct Double *) malloc(sizeof(struct Double ));
            node->next->previous = node;
            node = node->next;
            printf("\n Input the value for: %d: ", i+1);
            scanf("%c", &node->info);
            node->next = NULL;
            i++;
            fflush(stdin);
            printf("\n Input choice n for break: ");
            ch = getchar();
      }
}


void Doubly_insertion_Last (struct Double *node)
{
      node = start.next;
```

```
        new1 = (struct Double *) malloc(sizeof(struct Double ));
        fflush(stdin);
        printf("\n Input the last node value: ");
        scanf("%c", &new1->info);

        if (node == NULL)
        {
            printf("\n List is empty\n");
            printf("\n Insert as last node\n");
        }
        else
            while(node)
            {
                node = node->next;
            }

        new1->next = node;
        new1->previous = node->previous;
        node->previous->next = new1;
        node->next = new1;
}

/* Display the list */

void Display (struct Double *node)
{
        node = start.next;

        while (node)
        {
            printf("\n 0x%x", node);
            printf(" %c", node->info);
            node = node->next;
        }
}

/* Function main */

void main()
{
        struct Double *node = (struct Double *) malloc(sizeof(struct Double));
        Doubly_Create_Last (node);
        printf("\n Created list is as follows\n");
        Display(node);
        Doubly_insertion_Last (node);
```

```
        printf("\n List after insertion of last node \n");
        Display (node);
}
```

```
Input choice n for break:
Input the value for :1 :  A
Input choice n for break:
Input the value for :2 :  B
Input choice n for break:
Input the value for :3 : C
Input choice n for break:
Input the value for :4 : D
Input choice n for break:
Input the value for :5 : E
Input choice n for break:
Input the value for :6 : F
Input choice n for break:
Input the value for :7 : G
Input choice n for break:
Input the value for :8 : H
Input choice n for break:
Input the value for :9 : I
Input choice n for break:
Input the value for :10 :J
Input choice n for break: n

Created list is as follows
ADDRESS   VALUE
 0x1d9b11a2  A
 0x1d9b11ac  B
 0x1d9b11b6  C
 0x1d9b11c0  D
 0x1d9b11ca  E
 0x1d9b11d4  F
 0x1d9b11de  G
 0x1d9b11e8  H
 0x1d9b11f2  I
 0x1d9b11fc  J
 0x1d9b1206
 0x1d9b1210
Input the last node value: Q
 List after insertion of last node
ADDRESS VALUE
 0x1d9b11a2  A
 0x1d9b11ac  B
 0x1d9b11b6  C
 0x1d9b11c0  D
 0x1d9b11ca  E
 0x1d9b11d4  F
 0x1d9b11de  G
 0x1d9b11e8  H
 0x1d9b11f2  I
 0x1d9b11fc  J
 0x1d9b1206  Q
 0x1d9b1210
```

5.10.3 Inserting A Node At Desired Place

The insertion procedure is same as discussed in section {5.10.2}. For the implementation of discussion, consider the program segment **DOUBL_I.C.**

```
/* DOUBLE_I.C */
/* Inserting nodes in a double linked list */

#include <stdio.h>
#include <malloc.h>
void main(void)
{
    int i;
    struct ListEntry     {
                    int number;
                    struct ListEntry *next;
                    struct ListEntry *previous;
               } start, *node, *new;

    start.next = NULL;
    /* Empty list */
     start.previous = NULL;
    node = &start;
    /* Point to the start of the list */

     for (i = 1; i < 10; i += 2)
        {
            node->next = (struct ListEntry *) malloc(sizeof(struct ListEntry));
            node->next->previous = node;
            node = node->next;
            node->number = 50 + i;
            node->next = NULL;
        }

    /* Display the list */
    printf("\n List before inserting nodes\n ");

    node = start.next;
    do {
            printf("%d ", node->number);
            node = node->next;
        } while (node);

    /* inserting some nodes in the list */

    for (i = 2; i <= 10; i += 2)
```

```
    {
        int found = 0;

        new = (struct ListEntry *) malloc(sizeof(struct ListEntry));
        new->number = 50 + i;
        node = start.next;

    do  {
            if (node->number > new->number)
            {
                new->next = node;
                new->previous = node->previous;
                node->previous->next = new;
                node->previous = new;
                found = 1;
            }else
            node = node->next;
        } while ((node->next) && (! found));

    if (! found)
        if (node->number > new->number)
        {
            new->next = node;
            new->previous = node->previous;
            node->previous->next = new;
            node->previous = new;
        }
        else
        {
            new->next = NULL;
            new->previous = node;
            node->next = new;
        }
  }

  /* Display the list */

  printf("\n List after inserting nodes\n ");

  node = start.next;
  do {
      printf("%d ", node->number);
      node = node->next;
  } while (node);
}
```

```
List before inserting nodes
51 53 55 57 59
List after inserting nodes
51 52 53 54 55 56 57 58 59 60
```

5.11 Deletion In A Doubly Linked List

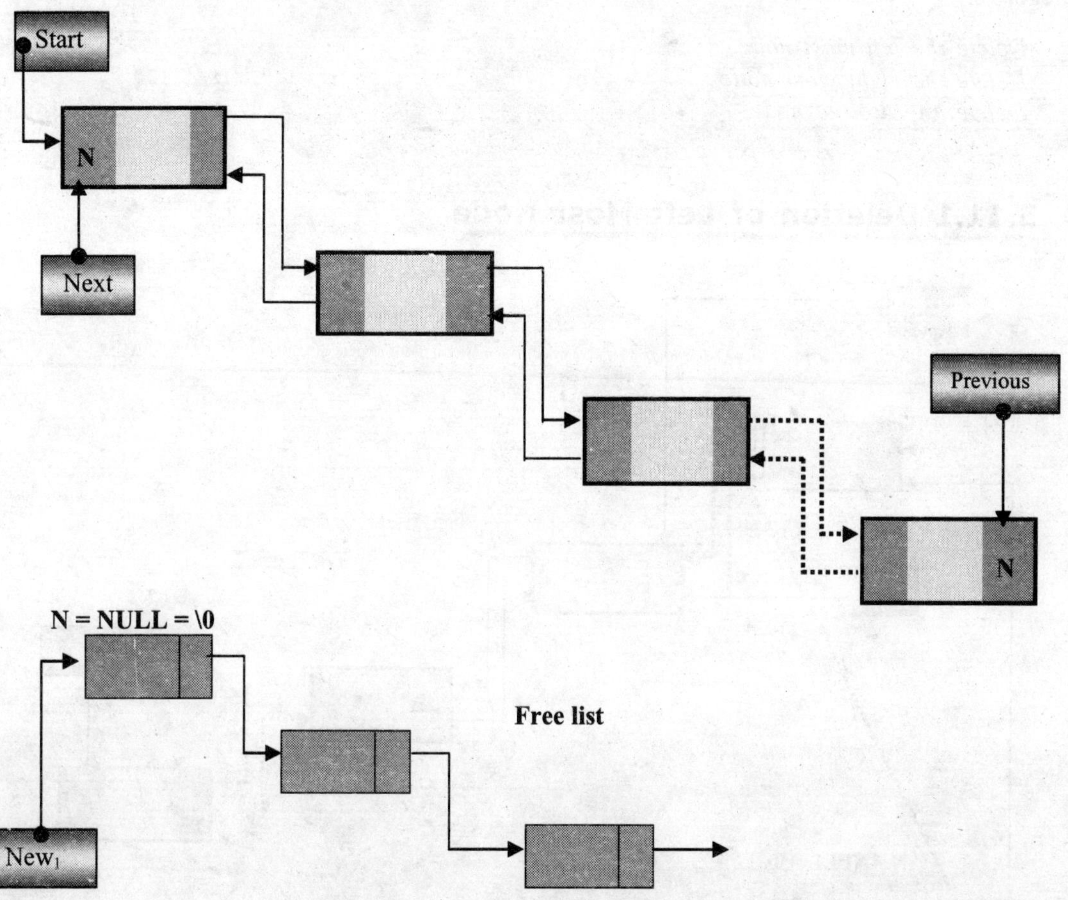

Fig 5.55. List before deleting a node

In the case of deletion, there are several possibilities. If the list contains a single node, a deletion may result in an empty list with the left most and right most pointers set to **NULL**. The node being deleted could be the left most node of the list. In this case, the pointer variable **previous** must be changed. Same situation arises when one is interested in deleting at the right most node of the list. The following points are taken care of at the time of deletion:

- *If the list is empty, flash **UNDERFLOW** message.*
- *If a single node exits in the list, set the left and right pointers of the list as **NULL**. Else if the left most node in the list is to be deleted, delete the node and update the left pointer to the list.*
- *Else if the right most node in the list is to be deleted, delete the node and update the right pointer to the list. Else delete the node from the desired place of the list.*
- *Restore the deleted node to the free area.*

From the above discussion, it is clear that the deletion operation can be classified into three categories:

- *Delete the left most node*
- *Delete the right most node*
- *Delete any desired node*

5.11.1 Deletion of Left Most Node

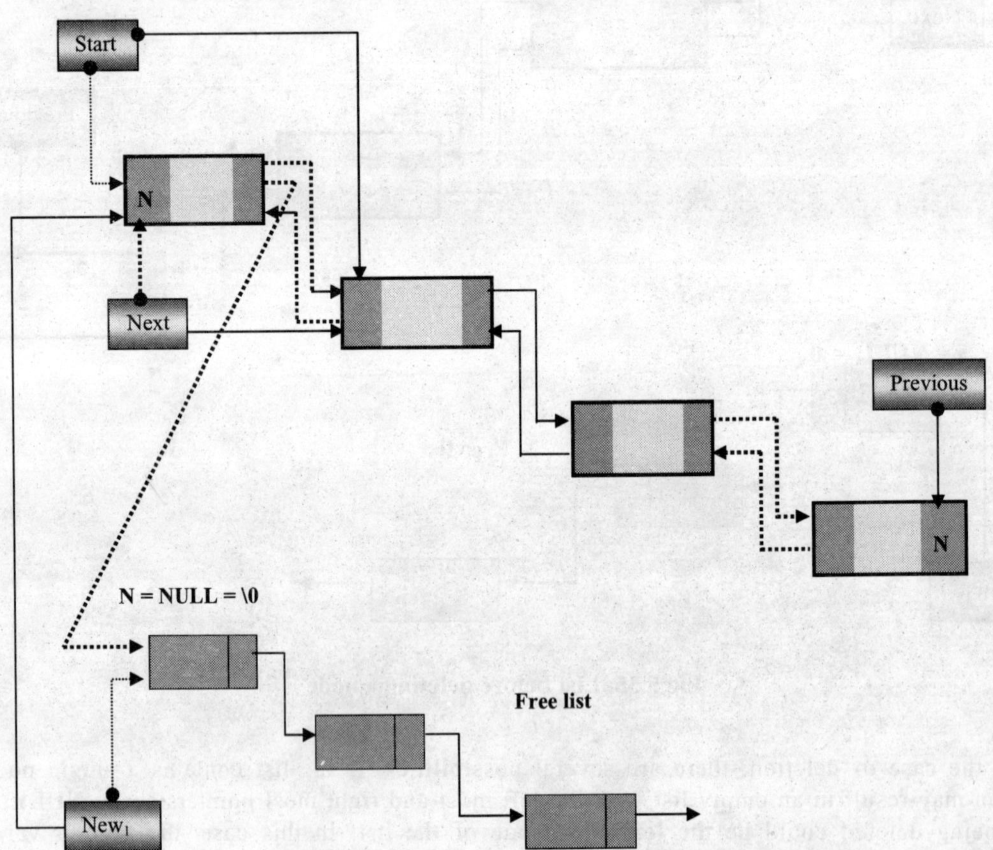

Fig 5.56. List after deleting left most node

Suppose we have a doubly linked list as illustrated in **Fig 5.55.** Then after deleting left most node from the list, it becomes as illustrated in **Fig 5.56.** The algorithm to delete left most node from a doubly linked list is illustrated in **Fig 5.57.** The program segment **DBL_DF.C** implements the discussion. Suppose, we have a doubly linked list as shown in **Fig 5.58** then the deletion operation is done like the illustration shown in **Fig 5.59.**

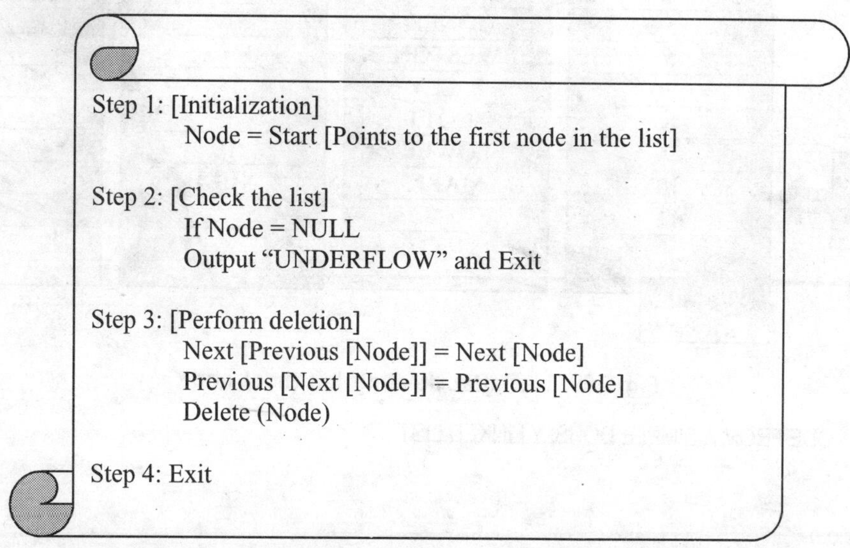

Step 1: [Initialization]
    Node = Start [Points to the first node in the list]

Step 2: [Check the list]
    If Node = NULL
    Output "UNDERFLOW" and Exit

Step 3: [Perform deletion]
    Next [Previous [Node]] = Next [Node]
    Previous [Next [Node]] = Previous [Node]
    Delete (Node)

Step 4: Exit

Fig 5.57. Deletion algorithm for a doubly linked list (left mode node)

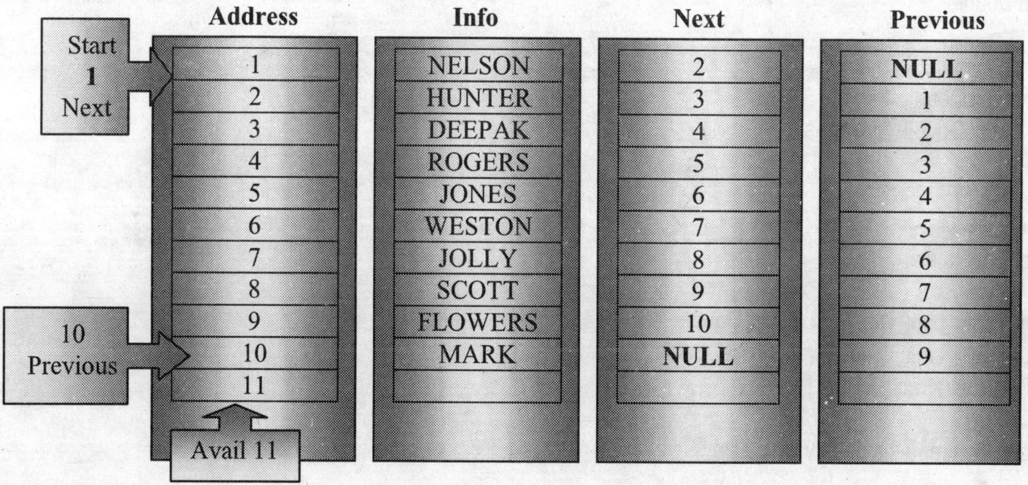

Address	Info	Next	Previous
1	NELSON	2	NULL
2	HUNTER	3	1
3	DEEPAK	4	2
4	ROGERS	5	3
5	JONES	6	4
6	WESTON	7	5
7	JOLLY	8	6
8	SCOTT	9	7
9	FLOWERS	10	8
10	MARK	NULL	9
11			

Fig 5.58. List before deleting a node

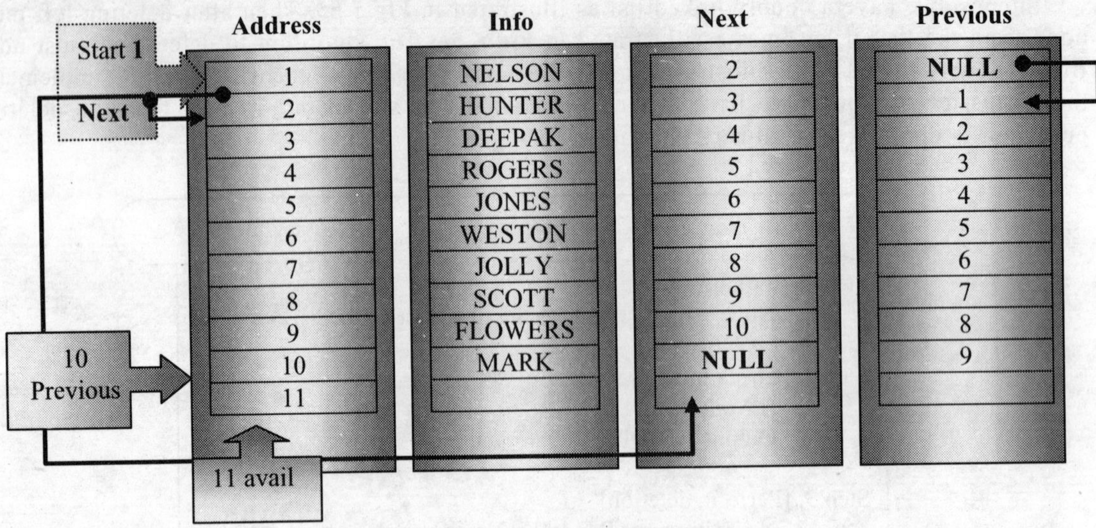

Fig 5.59. List after deleting left most node

```
/* DELETE A NODE FROM A SIMPLE DOUBLY LINKED LIST */
/* DBL_DF.C */

# include <stdio.h>
# include <malloc.h>

struct Double
{
        char info[20];
        struct Double *next;
        struct Double *previous;
};

int num ;
struct Double start;

void Doubly_Link_Del_First (struct Double *);
void Doubly_Link_Creat_First (struct Double *);
void display (struct Double *);

/* Function creates a doubly linked list */

void Doubly_Link_Creat_First (struct Double *node)
{
        char ch;
        start.next = NULL; /* Empty list */
        start.previous = NULL;
        node = &start; /* Point to the start of the list */
```

```
        num = 0;

        printf("\n Input choice n for break:");
        ch = getchar();

        while(ch != 'n')
        {
            node->next = (struct Double *) malloc(sizeof(struct Double));
            node->next->previous = node;
            node = node->next;
            fflush(stdin);
            printf("\n Input the values of the node : %d:", (num+1));
            gets(node->info);
            node->next = NULL;
            fflush(stdin);
            printf("\n Input choice n for break:");
            ch = getchar();
            num ++;
        }
        printf("\n Total nodes = %d", num);
}

/* Function delete */

void Doubly_Link_Del_First (struct Double *node)
{
        node = start.next;
        if( node == NULL)
        {
            printf("\n Underflow");
        }
        else
        {
            node->previous->next = node->next ;
            node->next->previous = node->previous ;
            free(node);
        }
}

/* Display the list */

void display(struct Double *node)
{
        node = start.next;
        if (node == NULL)
```

```
    {
        printf("\n List is empty\n");
    }
    else
        while (node)
        {
            printf("\n 0x%x", node);
            printf(" %s", node->info);
            node = node->next;
        }
}

/* Function main */
void main()
{
    struct Double *node = (struct Double *) malloc(sizeof(struct Double));
    Doubly_Link_Creat_First (node);
    printf("\n Created linked list is as follows\n");
    display (node);
    Doubly_Link_Del_First (node);
    printf("\n After deletion of first node list is as follows\n");
    display(node);
}
```

```
Input choice n for break:
Input the values of the node: 1: NELSON
Input choice n for break:
Input the values of the node: 2: HUNTER
Input choice n for break:
Input the values of the node: 3: DEEPAK
Input choice n for break:
Input the values of the node: 4: ROGERS
Input choice n for break:
Input the values of the node: 5: JONES
Input choice n for break:
Input the values of the node: 6: WESTON
Input choice n for break:
Input the values of the node: 7: JOLLY
Input choice n for break:
Input the values of the node: 8: SCOTT
Input choice n for break:
Input the values of the node: 9: FLOWERS
Input choice n for break:
Input the values of the node: 10: MARK
Input choice n for break: n
Total nodes = 10
```

```
Created linked list is as follows
ADDRESS     VALUE
 0x1d9311b6  NELSON
 0x1d9311d2  HUNTER
 0x1d9311ee  DEEPAK
 0x1d93120a  ROGERS
 0x1d931226  JONES
 0x1d931242  WESTON
 0x1d93125e  JOLLY
 0x1d93127a  SCOTT
 0x1d931296  FLOWERS
 0x1d9312b2  MARK
 After deletion of first node list is as follows
 ADDRESS    VALUE
 0x1d9311d2  HUNTER
 0x1d9311ee  DEEPAK
 0x1d93120a  ROGERS
0x1d931226  JONES
 0x1d931242  WESTON
 0x1d93125e  JOLLY
 0x1d93127a  SCOTT
 0x1d931296  FLOWERS
 0x1d9312b2  MARK
```

5.11.2 Deletion Of Right Most Node

Suppose we have doubly linked list as illustrated in **Fig 5.55** and we have to delete right most from the list. To achieve the purpose, consider **Fig 5.60. Fig 5.61** represents a doubly linked list before deletion of a node and **Fig 5.62** represents necessary arrangement for deletion of right most node from the list. The deletion algorithm is discussed in **Fig 5.63.** The program segment **DBL_DL.C** implements the discussion.

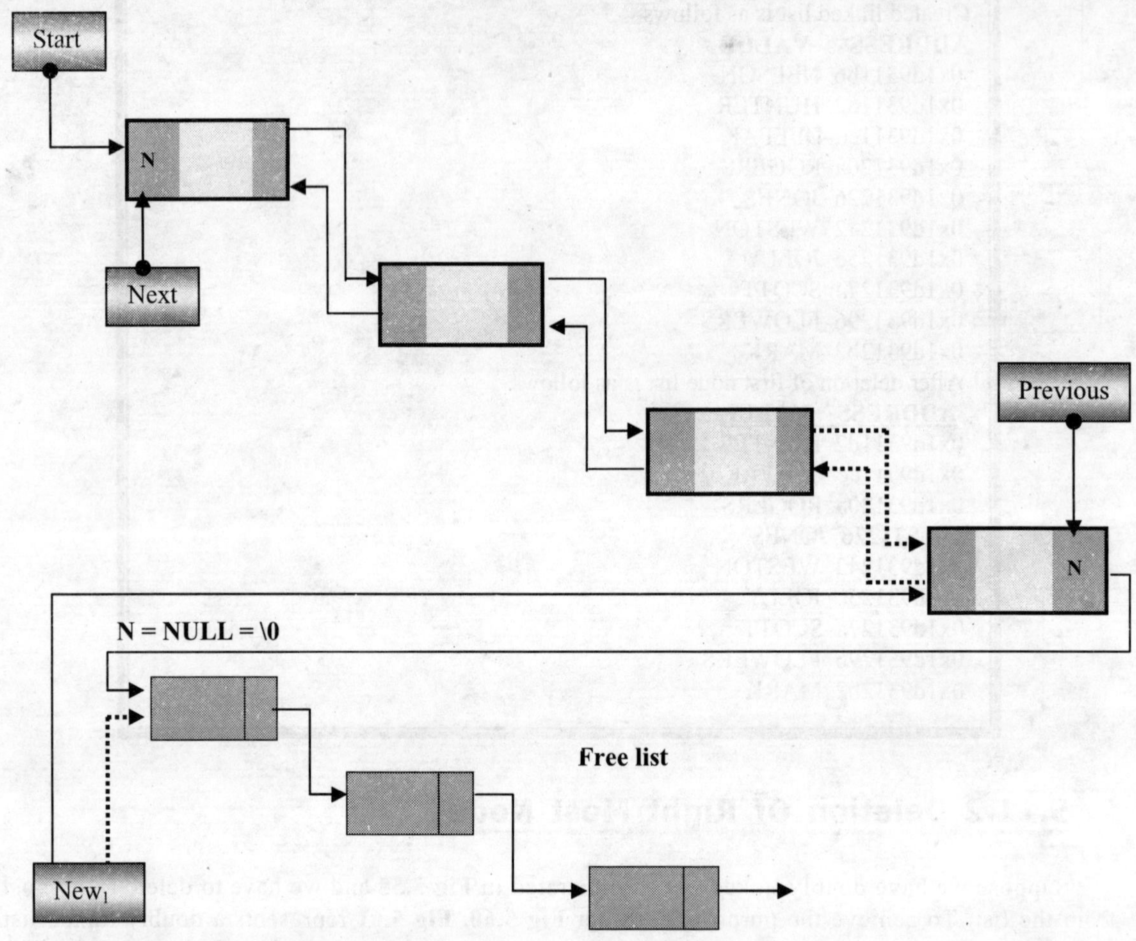

Fig 5. 60. List after deleting right most node

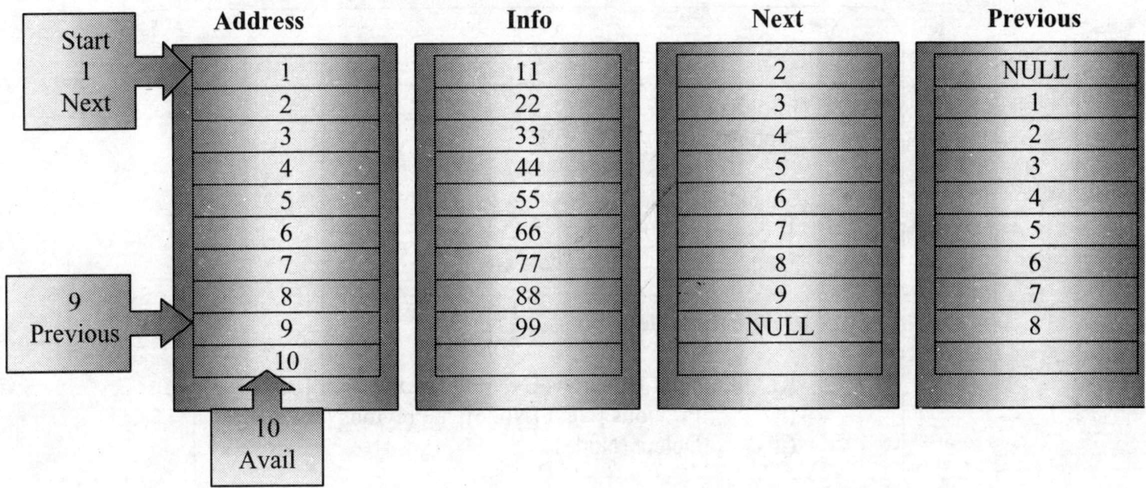

Fig 5.61. List before deleting a node

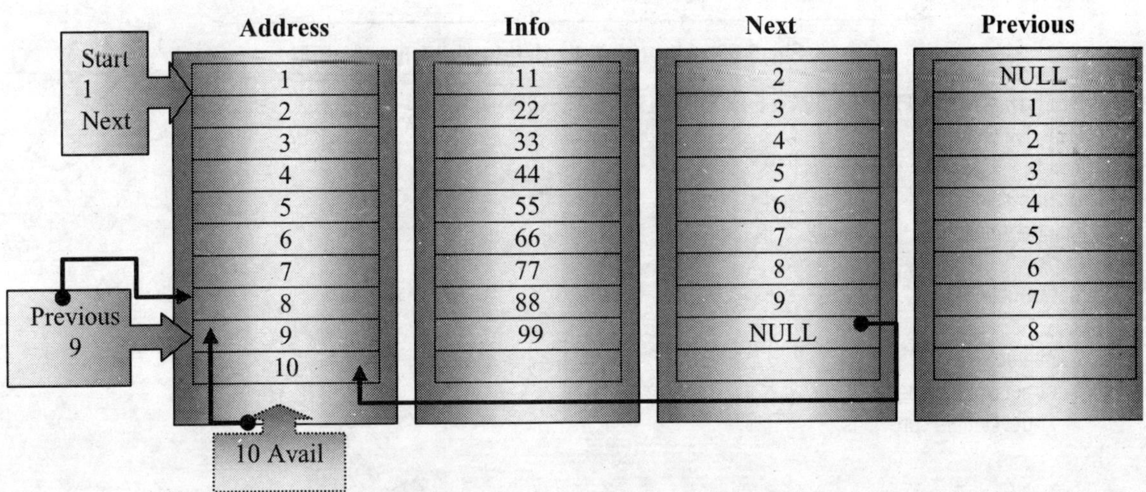

Fig 5.62. List after deleting right most node

Step 1: [Initialization]
Node = Start

Step 2: [Check the list]
If Node = NULL
Output "Underflow" and Exit

Step 3: [Delete the node]

(i) Next [Previous [Node]]= Next [Node]
(ii) Previous [Next [Node]] = Previous [Node]
(iii) Delete (Node)

Step 6: Exit

Fig 5.63. Algorithm to delete right most node

```
/* DELETE A NODE FROM A SIMPLE DOUBLY LINKED LIST*/
/* DBL_DL.C */

# include <stdio.h>
# include <malloc.h>

struct Double
{
	int info;
	struct Double *next;
	struct Double *previous;
};

int num ;
struct Double start;
void Doubly_Link_Del_Last (struct Double *);
void Doubly_Link_Creat_Last (struct Double *);
void display (struct Double *);

/* Function creates a doubly linked list */
void Doubly_Link_Creat_Last (struct Double *node)
{
	char ch;
	start.next = NULL; /* Empty list */
	start.previous = NULL;
```

```
    node = &start; /* Point to the start of the list */

    num = 0;

    printf("\n Input choice n for break: ");
    ch = getchar();

    while(ch != 'n')
    {
        node->next = (struct Double *) malloc(sizeof(struct Double));
        node->next->previous = node;
        node = node->next;
        printf("\n Input the values of the node: %d: ", (num+1));
        scanf("%d", &node->info);
        node->next = NULL;
        fflush(stdin);
        printf("\n Input choice n for break:");
        ch = getchar();
        num ++;
    }
    printf("\n Total nodes = %d", num);
}

/* Function delete */
void Doubly_Link_Del_Last (struct Double *node)
{
    num = 0;
    node = start.next;
    if( node == NULL)
    {
        printf("\n Underflow");
    }
    else
        while(node)
        {
            node = node->next;
            num ++;
        }
    node = start.next;

    while(num != 1)
    {
        node = node->next;
        num —;
    }
```

```
        /* Delete last node */
        node->previous->next = node->next ;
        node->next->previous = node->previous;
        node->next = NULL;
        free(node);
}

/* Display the list */
void display(struct Double *node)
{
        node = start.next;
        if (node == NULL)
        {
                printf("\n List is empty\n");
        }
        else
                while (node)
                {
                        printf("\n 0x%x", node);
                        printf(" %d", node->info);
                        node = node->next;
                }
}

/* Function main */

void main()
{
        struct Double *node = (struct Double *) malloc(sizeof(struct Double));
        Doubly_Link_Creat_Last (node);
        printf("\n Created linked list is as follows\n");
        display(node);
        Doubly_Link_Del_Last(node);
        printf("\n After deletion of last node list is as follows\n");
        display(node);
}
```

```
Input choice n for break:
Input the values of the node :1 :11
Input choice n for break:
Input the values of the node :2 :22
Input choice n for break:
Input the values of the node :3 :33
Input choice n for break:
Input the values of the node :4 :44
Input choice n for break:
Input the values of the node :5 :55
Input choice n for break:
Input the values of the node :6 :66
Input choice n for break:
Input the values of the node :7 :77
Input choice n for break:
Input the values of the node :8 :88
Input choice n for break:
Input the values of the node :9 :99
Input choice n for break: n
Total nodes = 9
Created linked list is as follows
Address    Value
0x1dd011a2  11
0x1dd011ac  22
0x1dd011b6  33
0x1dd011c0  44
0x1dd011ca  55
0x1dd011d4  66
0x1dd011de  77
0x1dd011e8  88
0x1dd011f2  99
After deletion of last node list is as follows
Address    Value
0x1dd011a2  11
0x1dd011ac  22
0x1dd011b6  33
0x1dd011c0  44
0x1dd011ca  55
0x1dd011d4  66
0x1dd011de  77
0x1dd011e8  88
```

5.11.3 Deletion of A Desired Node

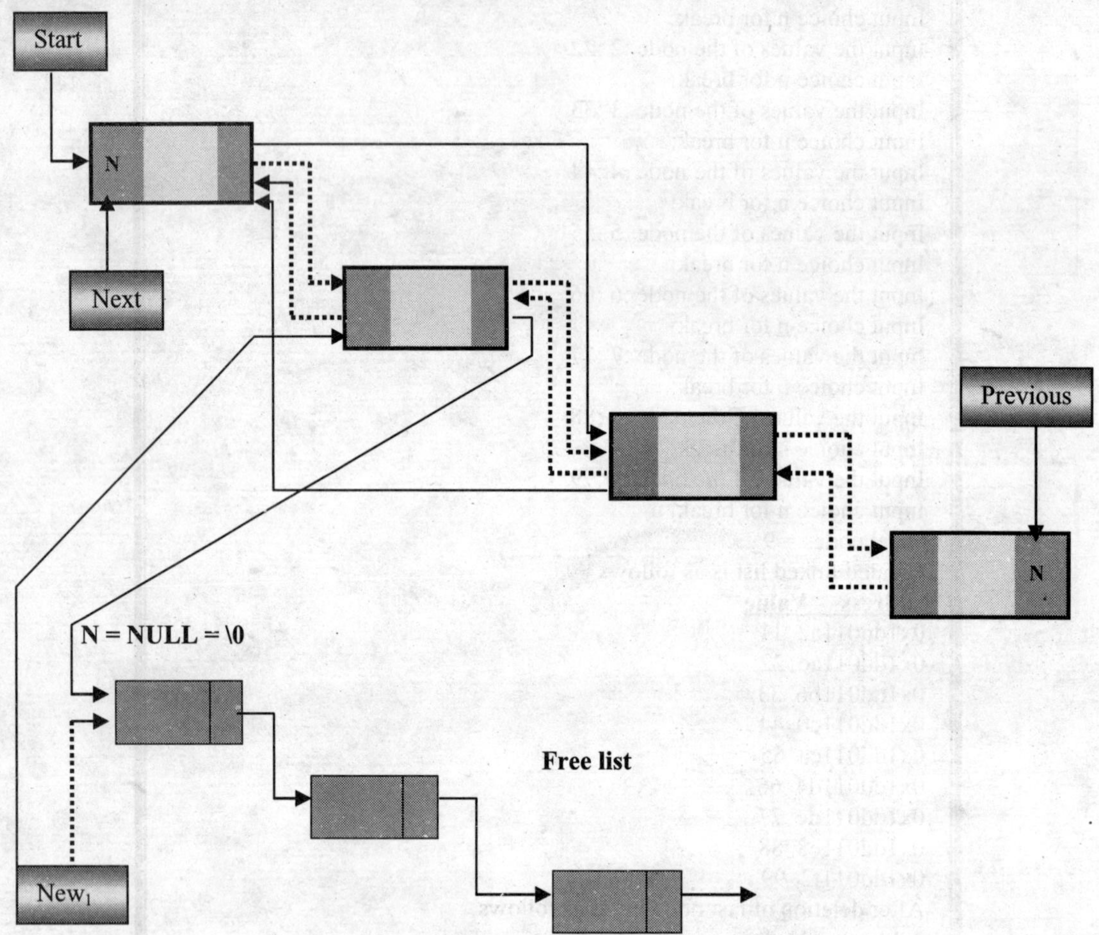

Fig 5.64. List after deleting desired node

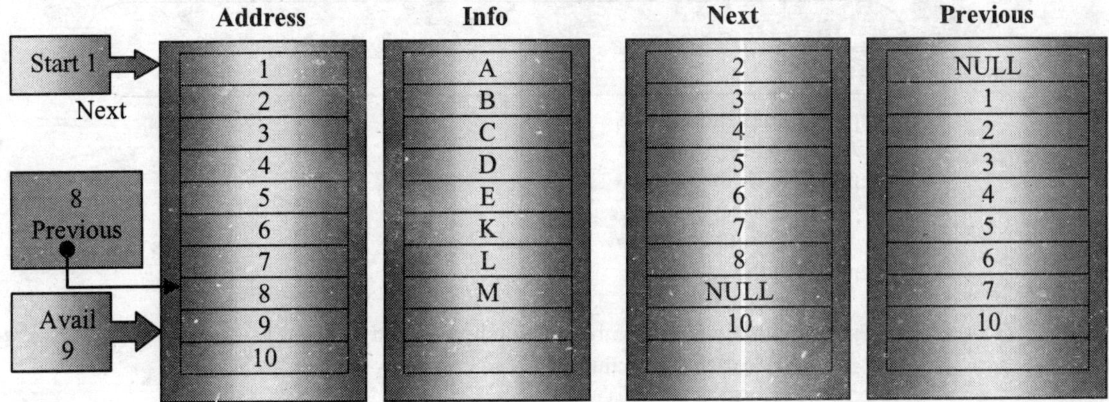

Fig 5.65. List before deleting a node

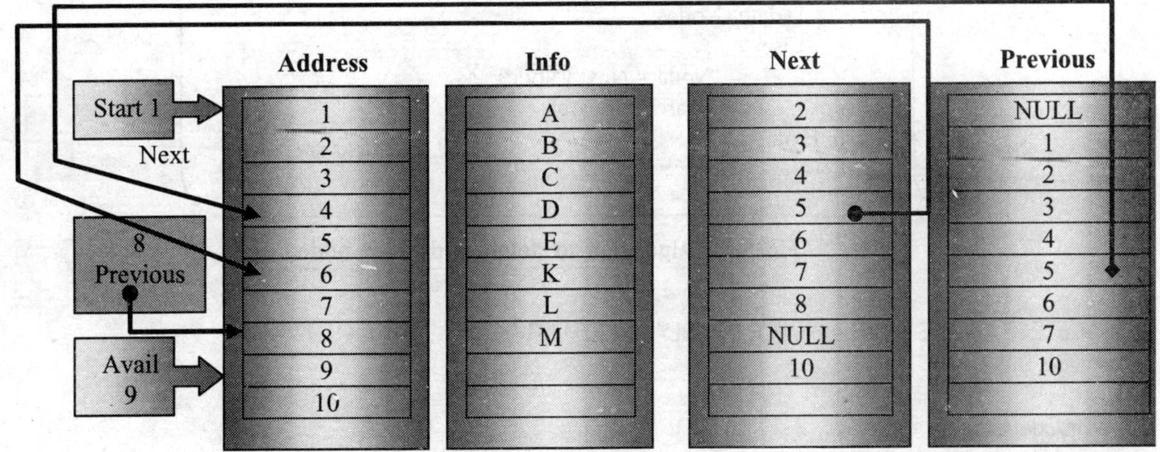

Fig 5.66. List before deleting 5th node

Suppose a doubly linked list is shown in **Fig 5.55,** and we want to delete a desired node from this list. For this, first of all we have to move next pointer to the desired node and then finally delete that node. **Fig 5.64** illustrates the above discussion and the program segment **DBL_D.C** implements the discussion. The deletion algorithm is given in **Fig 5.67. Fig 5.65** represents a list and **Fig 5.66** represents necessary arrangement for deletion of a desired node.

Step 1: [Initialization]
    Node = Start
Step 2: [Check the list]
    If Node = NULL
    Output "Underflow" and exit
Step 3: [Set the counter]
    Search = 0
Step 4: [Input the node number to which you want to delete]
    Node_delete = Value
Step 5: [Perform deletion]
    Repeat while Node □ NULL
    If Search = Delete_node
    Next [Previous [Node]] = Next [Node]
    Previous [Next [Node]] = Previous [Node]
    Delete (Node)
    Else
        Node = Next [Node]
        Search = Search + 1
Step 6: Exit

Fig 5.67. Algorithm to delete a desired node

```
/* DELETE A NODE FROM A SIMPLE DOUBLY LINKED LIST */
/* DBL_D.C */

# include <stdio.h>
# include <malloc.h>

struct Double
{
    char info;
    struct Double *next;
    struct Double *previous;
};

int num ;
struct Double start;
void Doubly_Link_Del (struct Double *);
void Doubly_Link_Creat (struct Double *);
void display (struct Double *);
```

```
/* Function creates a doubly linked list */
void Doubly_Link_Creat (struct Double *node)
{
    char ch;
    start.next = NULL; /* Empty list */
    start.previous = NULL;
    node = &start; /* Point to the start of the list */
    num = 0;
    printf("\n Input choice n for break: ");
    ch = getchar();

    while(ch != 'n')
    {
        node->next = (struct Double *) malloc(sizeof(struct Double));
        node->next->previous = node;
        node = node->next;
        printf("\n Input the values of the node: %d:", (num+1));
        scanf("%d", &node->info);
        node->next = NULL;
        fflush(stdin);
        printf("\n Input choice n for break: ");
        ch = getchar();
        num ++;
    }
    printf("\n Total nodes = %d", num);
}

/* Function delete */

void Doubly_Link_Del (struct Double *node)
{
    int delete_node;
    int search_counter = 0;
    printf("\n Input the node number to which you want delete: ");
    scanf("%d", &delete_node);
    node = start.next;
    if ( node == NULL)
    {
        printf("\n Underflow\n");
        printf("\n List is empty\n");
    }
    else

        while(node)
        {
            if((search_counter + 1) == delete_node)
```

```
                {
                        node->previous->next = node->next ;
                        node->next->previous = node->previous ;
                        free(node);
                }
                else
                {
                        node = node->next;

                }
                search_counter++;
        }
}

/* Display the list */

void display(struct Double *node)
{
        node = start.next;

        while (node)
        {
                printf("\n 0x%x", node);
                printf(" %d", node->info);
                node = node->next;
        }
}

/* Function main */

void main()
{
        struct Double *node = (struct Double *) malloc(sizeof(struct Double));
        Doubly_Link_Creat(node);
        printf("\n Created linked list is as follows\n");
        display(node);
        Doubly_Link_Del(node);
        printf("\n After deletion of a node linked list is as follows\n");
        display(node);
}
```

```
Input choice n for break:
Input the values of the node: 1: A
Input choice n for break:
Input the values of the node: 2: B
Input choice n for break:
Input the values of the node: 3: C
Input choice n for break:
Input the values of the node: 4: D
Input choice n for break:
Input the values of the node: 5: E
Input choice n for break:
Input the values of the node: 6: K
Input choice n for break:
Input the values of the node: 7: L
Input choice n for break:
Input the values of the node: 8: M
Input choice n for break: n
Total nodes = 8
Created linked list is as follows
ADDRESS  VALUE
0x1de811da  A
0x1de811e4  B
0x1de811ee  C
0x1de811f8  D
0x1de81202  E
0x1de8120c  K
0x1de81216  L
0x1de81220  M
Input the node number to which you want delete: 5
After deletion of a node linked list is as follows
ADDRESS  VALUE
0x1de811da  A
0x1de811e4  B
0x1de811ee  C
0x1de811f8  D
0x1de81202
0x1de8120c  K
0x1de81216  L
0x1de81220  M
```

When node number is given and we want to delete a node then the program segment **DBL_D.C** is useful. When information of a node is given and we want to delete the node then the program segment **REMOVES_.C** performs the deletion operation.

```
/* REMOVES_.C */
/* This program segment removes a node from a doubly linked list */

#include <stdio.h>
#include <malloc.h>
```

```
void main(void)
{
    int i, found;

    struct ListEntry {
        int number;
        struct ListEntry *next;
        struct ListEntry *previous;
    } start, *node;

    start.next = NULL;
    /* Empty list */
    start.previous = NULL;
    node = &start;
    /* Point to the start of the list */

    for (i = 1; i <= 10; i++)
    {
        node->next = (struct ListEntry *) malloc(sizeof(struct ListEntry));
        node->next->previous = node;
        node = node->next;
        node->number = 50 + i;
        node->next = NULL;
    }

    /* Display the list */

    printf("\n List before deletion \n");
    node = start.next;
    do {
        printf("%d ", node->number);
        node = node->next;
    } while (node);

    /* Remove the entry */

    node = start.next;
    found = 0;

    do {
        if (node->number == 57)
        {
            found = 1;
            node->previous->next = node->next;
            node->next->previous = node->previous;
```

```
            free(node);
        }
        else
            node = node->next;
    } while ((node) && (! found));

    /* Display the list */

    printf("\n List after deletion \n");
    node = start.next;

    do {
        printf("%d ", node->number);
        node = node->next;
    } while (node);
}
```

```
List before deletion
51 52 53 54 55 56 57 58 59 60
List after deletion
51 52 53 54 55 56 58 59 60
```

5.12 Merging Two Lists

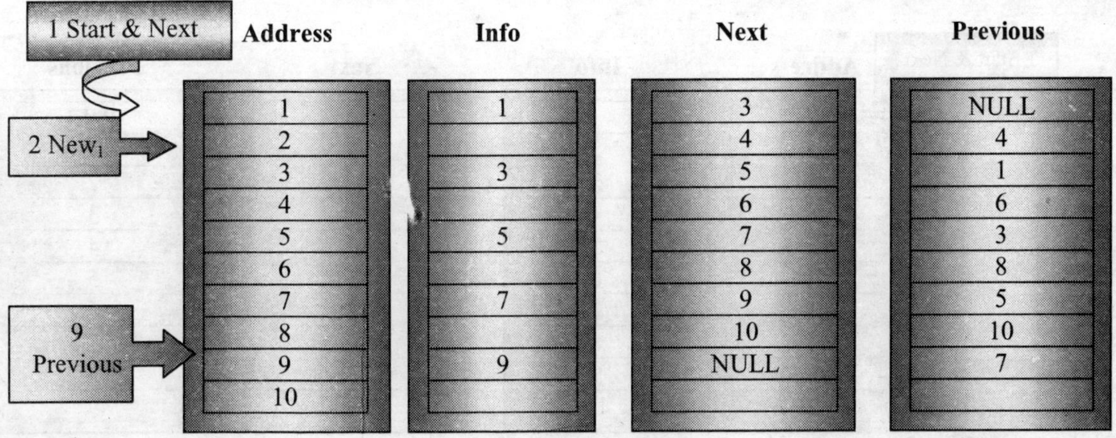

Fig 5.68. List before insertion operation

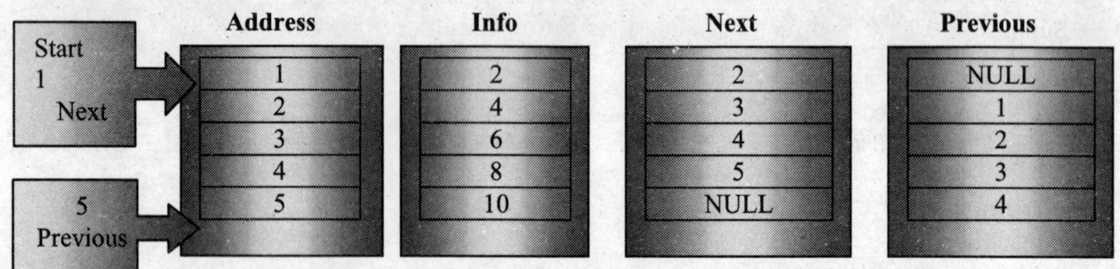

Fig 5.69. List in memory

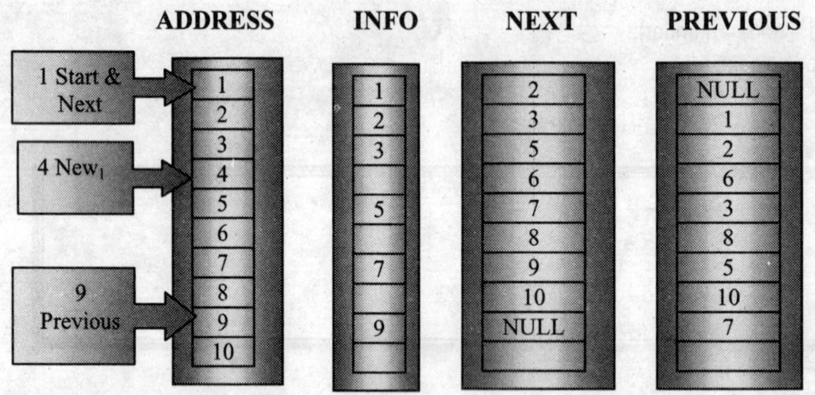

Fig 5.70. List after inserting a node

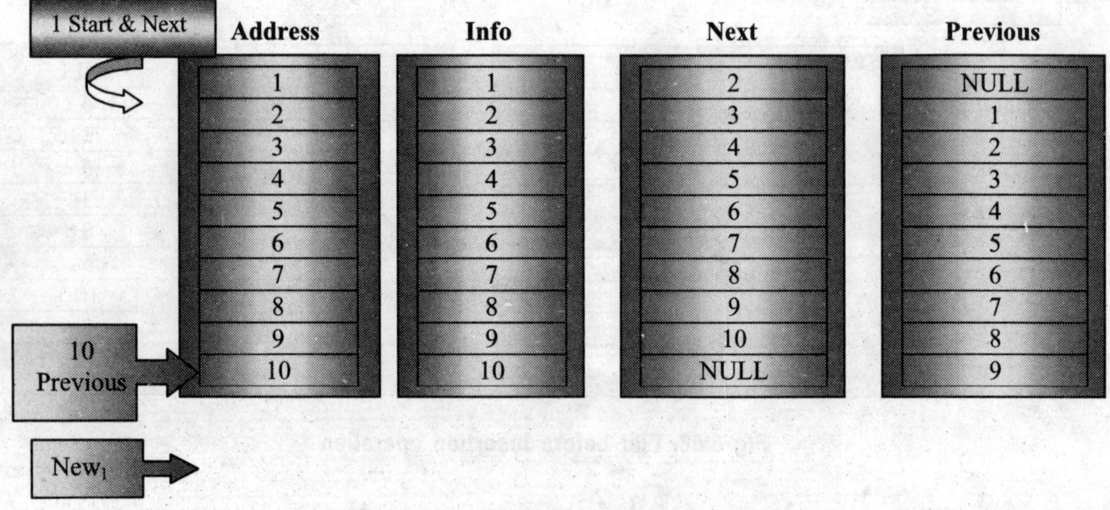

Fig 5.71. List after inserting some nodes

Suppose, we have two doubly linked lists as illustrated in **Fig 5.68** and in **Fig 5.69.** We have to insert each element of the second list into the first so that the resulting list maintains the sorted order.

To accomplish this task first we will remove first node from the second list and find its proper place in the first list. When we find proper place for the first element removed from the second list, we insert it into the first list. Next we remove second element from the second list, and once again we start scanning from the very first node of the first list. When we find the proper place for the removed element from the second list, we insert into the first list. This process continues till the end of second list.

For example, first element of the second list **Fig 5.69** is 2. We remove this element from the list and scan the proper place for it in the first list. We find that the first element takes place in between first and second elements of the list. The resulting list is illustrated in **Fig 5.70.** If one continues this process, he/she gets final list as illustrated in **Fig 5.71.**

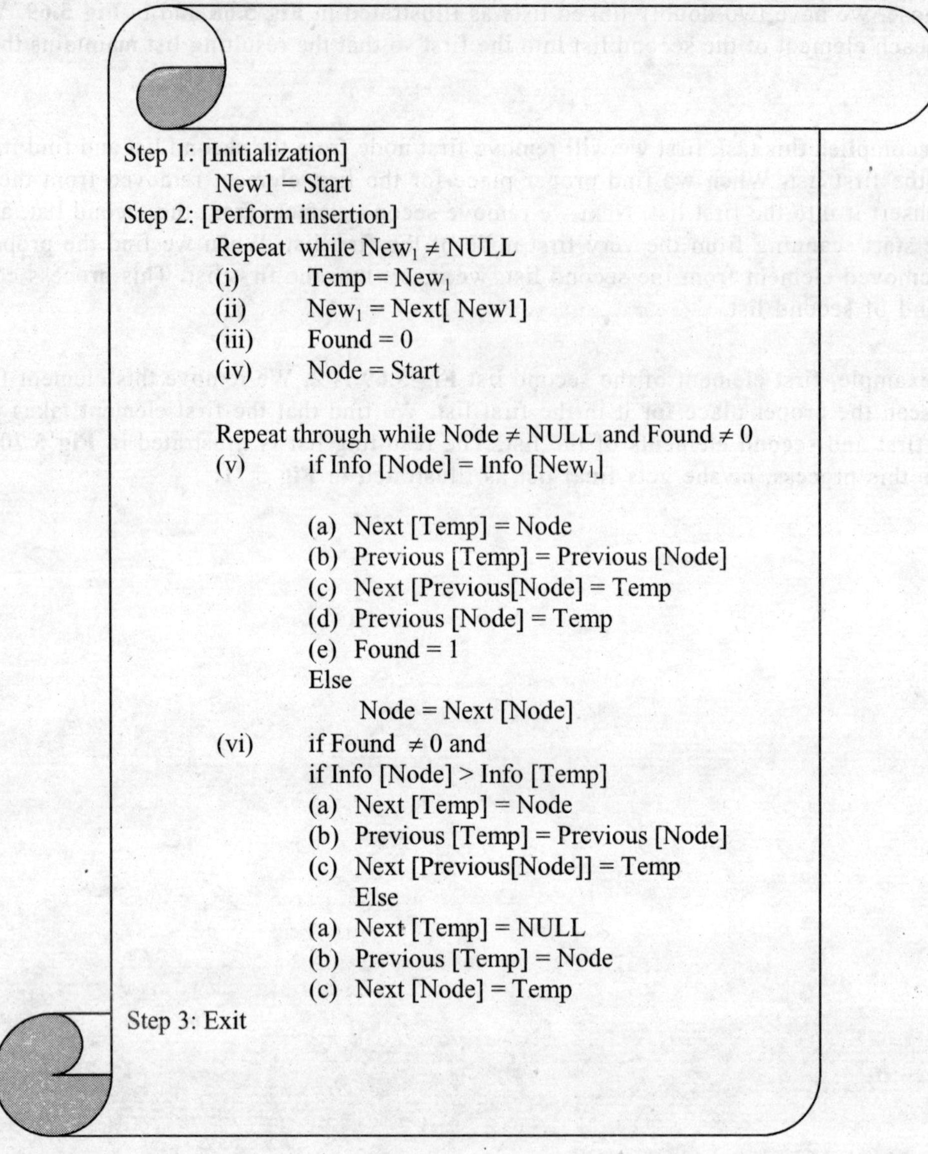

Step 1: [Initialization]
New1 = Start
Step 2: [Perform insertion]
Repeat while $New_1 \neq$ NULL
(i) Temp = New_1
(ii) New_1 = Next[New1]
(iii) Found = 0
(iv) Node = Start

Repeat through while Node $\neq$ NULL and Found $\neq$ 0
(v) if Info [Node] = Info [New_1]

(a) Next [Temp] = Node
(b) Previous [Temp] = Previous [Node]
(c) Next [Previous[Node] = Temp
(d) Previous [Node] = Temp
(e) Found = 1
Else
Node = Next [Node]
(vi) if Found $\neq$ 0 and
if Info [Node] > Info [Temp]
(a) Next [Temp] = Node
(b) Previous [Temp] = Previous [Node]
(c) Next [Previous[Node]] = Temp
Else
(a) Next [Temp] = NULL
(b) Previous [Temp] = Node
(c) Next [Node] = Temp
Step 3: Exit

Fig 5.72. Algorithm to merge a two list

The program segment **DBL_MRG.C** implements the above discussion in better way.

```
/* MERGING TWO DOUBLY LINKED LISTS (ASCENDING ORDER) */
/* DBL_MRG.C */
# include <stdio.h>
# include <malloc.h>
struct Double
{
    int info;
```

```
        struct Double *next;
        struct Double *previous;
};
int i;
struct Double start, start1, *new1, *local;
void Doubly_insertion (struct Double * );
void Doubly_Create (struct Double * );
void Display (struct Double *);
/* Function create a list of five nodes */
void Doubly_Create (struct Double *node)
{
        start.next = NULL; /* Empty list */
        start.previous = NULL;
        node = &start; /* Point to the start of the list */
        for (i = 1; i < 10; i += 2)
        {
                node->next = (struct Double *) malloc(sizeof(struct Double ));
                node->next->previous = node;
                node = node->next;
                node->info = i;
                node->next = NULL;
        }
}
void Doubly_insertion (struct Double *node)
{
        struct Double *new1;
        start1.next = NULL; /* Empty list */
        start1.previous = NULL;
        new1 = &start1; /* Point to the start of the list */
        for (i = 2; i <= 10; i += 2)
        {
                new1->next = (struct Double *) malloc(sizeof(struct Double ));
                new1->next->previous = new1;
                new1= new1->next;
                new1->info = i;
                new1->next = NULL;
        }
        new1 = start1.next;
        printf("\n Second list is as follows");
        while(new1)
        {
                printf("\n 0x%x", new1);
                printf(" %d", new1->info);
                new1 = new1->next;
        }
        new1 = start1.next;
```

```
    while(new1)
    {
        int found = 0;
        local = (struct Double *) malloc(sizeof(struct Double));
        local = new1;
        new1 = new1->next;
        node = start.next;
        do
        {
            if ( node->info > local->info )
            {
                local->next = node;
                local->previous = node->previous;
                node->previous->next = local;
                node->previous = local;
                found = 1;
                break;
            }
            else
                node = node->next;
        } while ((node->next) && (! found));
        if (! found)
            if (node->info> local->info)
            {
                local->next = node;
                local->previous = node->previous;
                node->previous->next = local;
                node->previous = local;
            }
            else
            {
                local->next = NULL;
                local->previous = node;
                node->next = local;

            }
    }
}

/* Display the list */

void Display (struct Double *node)
{
    node = start.next;
    while (node)
```

```
    {
        printf("\n 0x%x", node);
        printf(" %d", node->info);
        node = node->next;
    }
}

/* Function main */
void main()
{
    struct Double *node = (struct Double *) malloc(sizeof(struct Double));
    Doubly_Create (node);
    printf("\n First list is as follows\n");
    Display (node);
    Doubly_insertion (node);
    printf("\n List after merging above two lists (Ascending order)\n");
    Display (node);
}
```

```
Created list is as follows
First list is as follows
Address    Value
0x1c940f48  1
0x1c940f52  3
0x1c940f5c  5
0x1c940f66  7
0x1c940f70  9
Second list is as follows
Address    Value
0x1c940f7a  2
0x1c940f84  4
0x1c940f8e  6
0x1c940f98  8
0x1c940fa2  10
List after merging above two lists (Ascending order)
Address    Value
0x1c940f48  1
0x1c940f7a  2
0x1c940f52  3
0x1c940f84  4
0x1c940f5c  5
0x1c940f8e  6
0x1c940f66  7
0x1c940f98  8
0x1c940f70  9
0x1c940fa2  10
```

5.13 Header Linked List

A header node is a special node that is found at the front of the list. A list, which contains this type of node, is called the header-linked list. This type of list is useful when information other than that found in each node is needed. For example, suppose there is an application in which the number of items in a list is often calculated. Usually a list is always traversed to find the length of the list. However, if the current length is maintained in an additional header node, that information can be easily obtained. The following are two widely used header linked lists:

(i) Grounded header linked list
(ii) Circular header linked list

5.13.1 Grounded Header Linked List

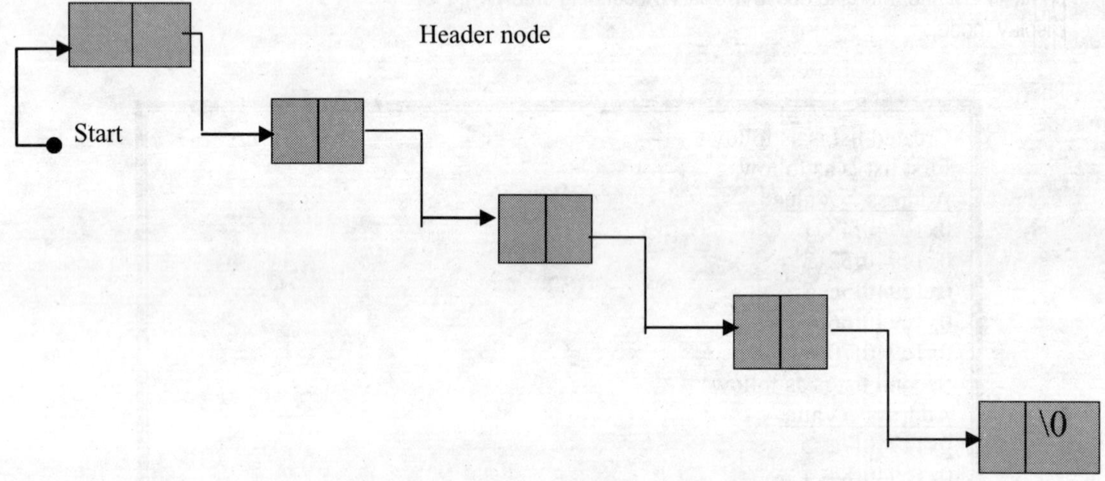

Fig 5.73. Grounded header linked list

A grounded header linked list is the one whose last node contains **NULL** pointer. **Fig 5.73** illustrates header-linked list. In the header linked list the **Start** pointer always points to the header node. **Next [Start] = NULL** indicates that a grounded header linked list is empty. The operations that are possible on this type of linked list are:

- *Insertion*
- *Deletion*
- *Traversing*

Algorithm to build a header-linked list is illustrated in **Fig 5.74.** Algorithm to traverse a header-linked list is illustrated in **Fig 5.75.**

Suppose, we have a header linked as illustrated in **Fig 5.76** and want to traverse this list. The header node contains 10 in **Fig 5.76** and the list contains the 10 elements. Then traversing can be performed as follows:

Node = Start = 1
Count = Info [Node] = Info [1] = 10 Header node value
Now moving pointer from header to very first node of the list
Node = Next [Node]
Next [1] = 2 Info [2] =11
Next [2] = 3 Info [3] = 22
Next [3] = 4 Info [4] = 33
Next [4] = 5 Info [5] = 44
Next [5] = 6 Info [6] = 55
Next [6] = 8 Info [8] = 66
Next [8] = 9 Info [9] = 77
Next [9] = 10 Info [10] = 88
Next [10] = 11 Info [11] = 99
Next [11] = 12 Info [12] = 100
Next [12] = NULL that is end of the list

The program segment **LINK_CH.C** illustrates **creation, insertion** and **traversing** of the header-linked list.

```
Step 1: [Initialization]
        Node = Start [Points to header node]
Step 2: [Create header node]
        Next [Node] = Create a node
Step 3: [Initialize counter]
        I = 0
Step 4: [Create linked list]
        Repeat while choice = n
        (i)     Next [Node] = Create  new node
        (ii)    Node = Next [Node] [Make link of the current node to the
                next node]
        (iii)   Info [Node] = Value [Read information of the node]
        (iv)    Next [Node] = NULL [Assign NULL to the next node
                value]
        (v)     I = I + 1[Increment the counter]

Step 5: [Copy totals number of nodes in the list into the header node]
        (i)     Node = Start
        (ii)    Info [Node] = I

Step 6: Exit
```

Fig 5.74. Algorithm to build a header linked list

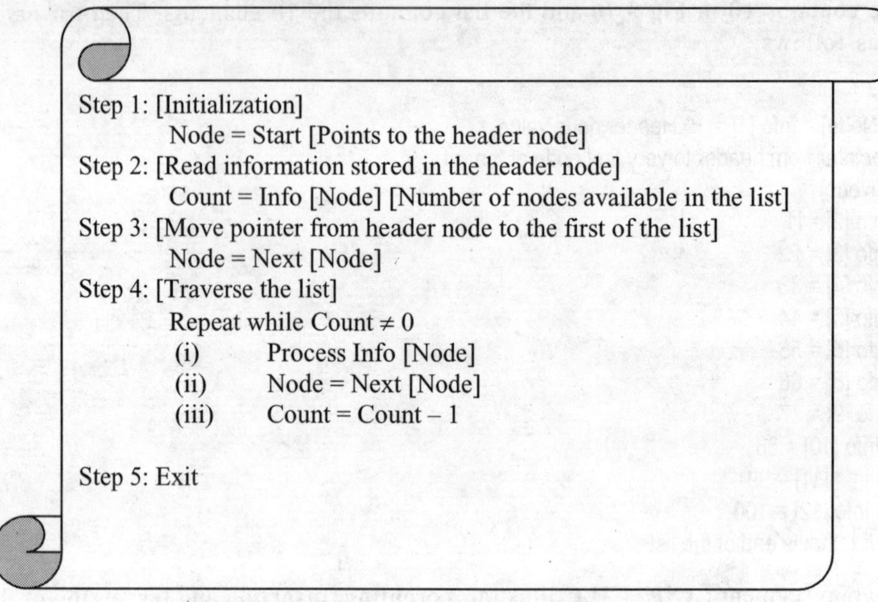

Fig 5.75. Algorithm to traverse a header linked list

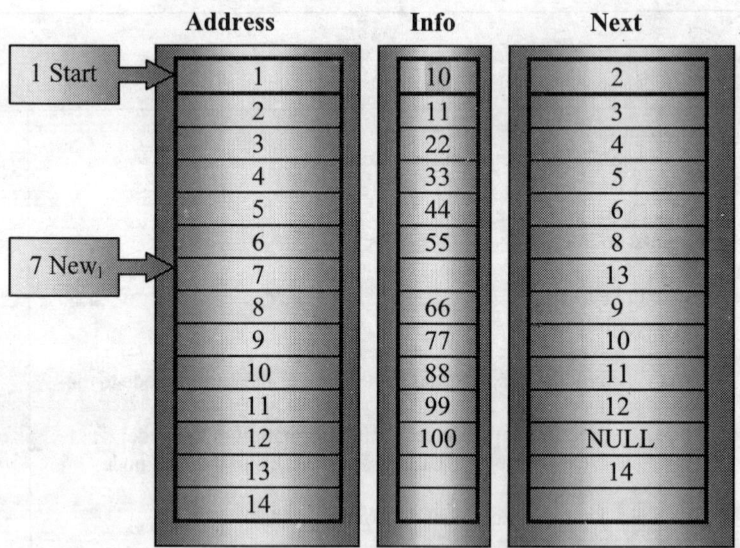

Fig 5.76. Header linked list in memory

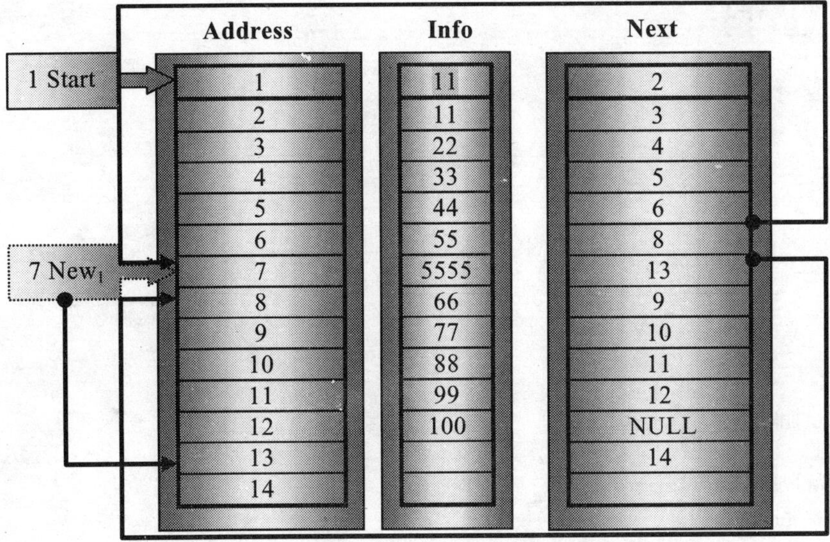

Fig 5.77. Header linked list after inserting a node

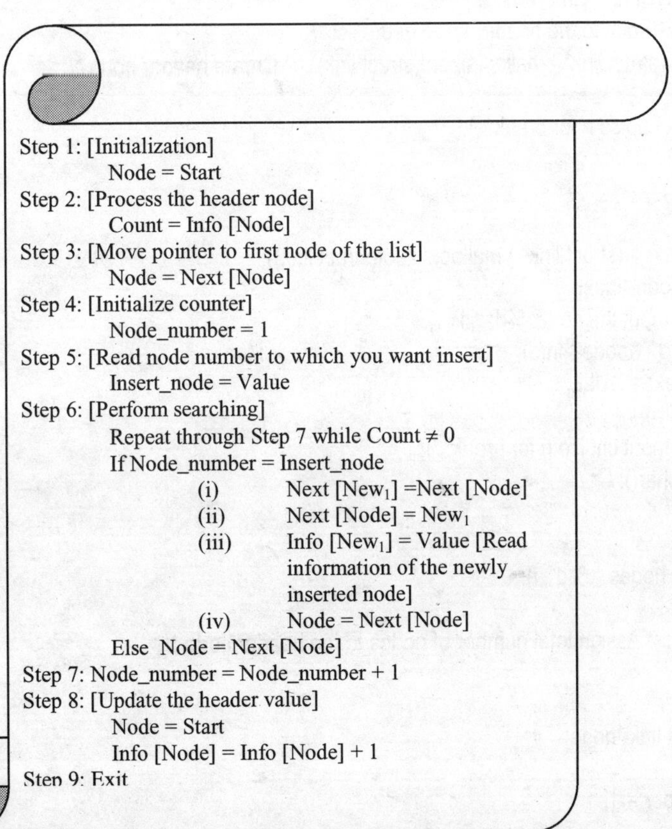

Step 1: [Initialization]
Node = Start
Step 2: [Process the header node]
Count = Info [Node]
Step 3: [Move pointer to first node of the list]
Node = Next [Node]
Step 4: [Initialize counter]
Node_number = 1
Step 5: [Read node number to which you want insert]
Insert_node = Value
Step 6: [Perform searching]
Repeat through Step 7 while Count $\neq$ 0
If Node_number = Insert_node
(i) Next [New$_1$] =Next [Node]
(ii) Next [Node] = New$_1$
(iii) Info [New$_1$] = Value [Read information of the newly inserted node]
(iv) Node = Next [Node]
Else Node = Next [Node]
Step 7: Node_number = Node_number + 1
Step 8: [Update the header value]
Node = Start
Info [Node] = Info [Node] + 1
Step 9: Exit

Fig 5.78. Algorithm to insert a node in a header linked list

```
/* CREATING HEADER LINKED LIST */
/* LINK_CH.C */
# include <stdio.h>
# include <malloc.h>
struct link
{
	int info;
	struct link *next;
};
int i;
int number;
struct link *start, *new1;
void insertion(struct link *);
void create_header_list(struct link *);
void Traverse (struct link *);
/* Function to create a header linked list */
void create_header_list(struct link *node)
{
	char ch;
	start->next = NULL; /* Empty list */
	node = start; /* Point to the header node of the list */
	node->next = (struct link* ) malloc(sizeof(struct link)); /* Create header node */
	i = 0;
	printf("\n Input choice n for break: ");
	ch = getchar();
	while(ch != 'n')
	{
		node->next = (struct link* ) malloc(sizeof(struct link));
		node = node->next;
		printf("\n Input the node: %d: ", i+1);
		scanf("%d", &node->info);
		node->next = NULL;
		fflush(stdin);
		printf("\n Input choice n for break: ");
		ch = getchar();
		i++;
	}
	printf("\n Total nodes = %d", i);
	node = start;
	node->info = i; /* Assign total number of nodes to the header node */
}
/* Inserting a node */
void insertion(struct link *node)
{
	int node_number = 1;
	int insert_node;
	int count = node->info;
```

```
        node = node->next;
        node = start;
        printf("\n Input node number you want to insert: ");
        printf("\n Value should be less are equal to the");
        printf("\n number of nodes in the list: ");
        scanf("%d", &insert_node);
        while(count)
        {
                if((node_number) == insert_node)
                {
                        new1 = (struct link* ) malloc(sizeof(struct link));
                        new1->next = node->next ;
                        node->next = new1;
                        printf("\n Input the node value: ");
                        scanf("%d", &new1->info);
                        node = node->next;
                }
                else
                {
                        node = node->next;
                        count—;
                }
                node_number ++;
        }
        node = start;
        node->info = node->info+1;
}
/* Traversing the header list */
void Traverse(struct link *node)
{
        int count = node->info;
        node = start;
        node = node->next;
        printf("\n After Inserting a node list is as follows:\n");
        while (count)
        {
                printf("\n 0x%x", node);
                printf(" %d", node->info);
                node = node->next;
                count —;
        }
}

/* Function main */
void main()
{
        struct link *node = (struct link *) malloc(sizeof(struct link));
```

```
create_header_list (node);
Traverse (node);
insertion (node);
Traverse (node);
}
```

```
Input choice n for break:
Input the node: 1: 11
Input choice n for break:
Input the node: 2: 22
Input choice n for break:
Input the node: 3: 33
Input choice n for break:
Input the node: 4: 44
Input choice n for break:
Input the node: 5: 55
Input choice n for break:
Input the node: 6: 66
Input choice n for break:
Input the node: 7: 77
Input choice n for break:
Input the node: 8: 88
Input choice n for break:
Input the node: 9: 99
Input choice n for break:
Input the node: 10: 100
Input choice n for break:
Total nodes = 10
Before inserting a node list is as follows:
ADDRESS  VALUE
0x147b120e  11
0x147b1216  22
0x147b121e  33
0x147b1226  44
0x147b122e  55
0x147b1236  66
0x147b123e  77
0x147b1246  88
0x147b124e  99
0x147b1256  100

Input node number you want to insert:
Value should be less are equal to the
number of nodes in the list:5
Input the node value: 5555
```

After inserting a node list is as follows:
ADDRESS VALUE
0x147b120e 11
0x147b1216 22
0x147b121e 33
0x147b1226 44
0x147b122e 55
0x147b125e 5555
0x147b1236 66
0x147b123e 77
0x147b1246 88
0x147b124e 99
0x147b1256 100

5.13.2 Circular Header Linked List

A linked list in which last node points to the header node is called circular linked list. The chains do not indicate first or last nodes. In this case, external pointers provide a frame of reference because last node of a circular linked list does not contain the **NULL** pointer. **Fig 5.79** illustrates this type of linked list and the possible operations on this type of linked list are:

- *Insertion*
- *Deletion*
- *Traversing*

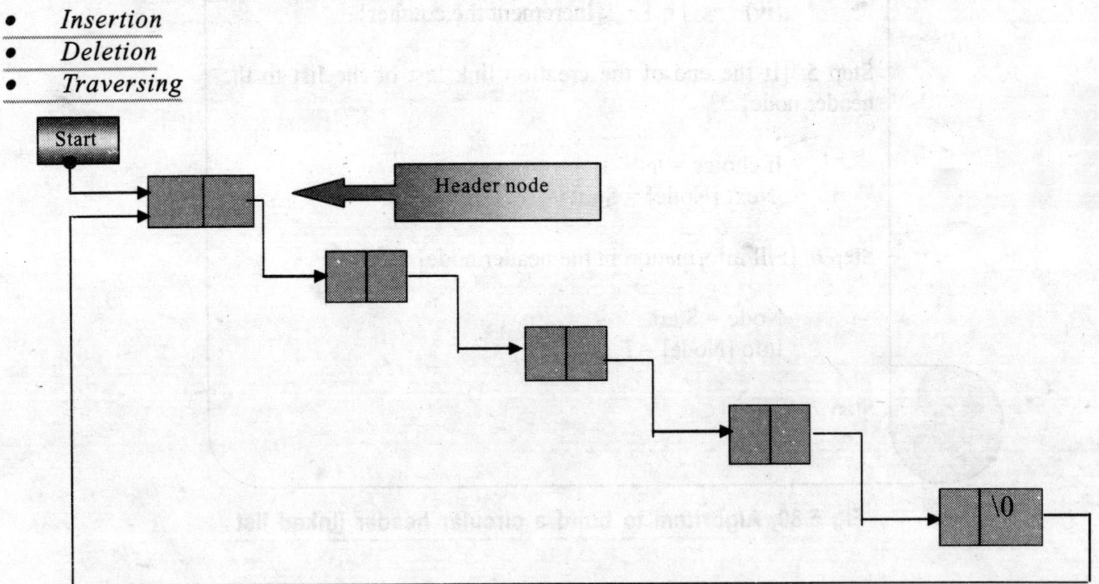

Fig 5.79. Circular header linked list

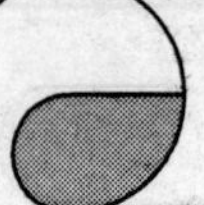

Step 1: [Initialization]

Node = Start [Points to header node]

Step 2: [Create header node]

Next [Node] = Create header node

Step 3: [Initialize counter]

I = 0

Step 4: [Create linked list]

Repeat while choice = n
(i) Next [Node] = Create new node
(ii) Node = Next [Node] [Make link of the current node to the next node]
(iii) Info [Node] = Value [Read information of the node]
(iv) I = I + 1[Increment the counter]

Step 5: [If the end of the creation link last of the list to the header node]

If choice = n
Next [Node] = Start

Step 6: [Fill information in the header node]

Node = Start
Info [Node] = I

Step 7: Exit

Fig 5.80. Algorithm to build a circular header linked list

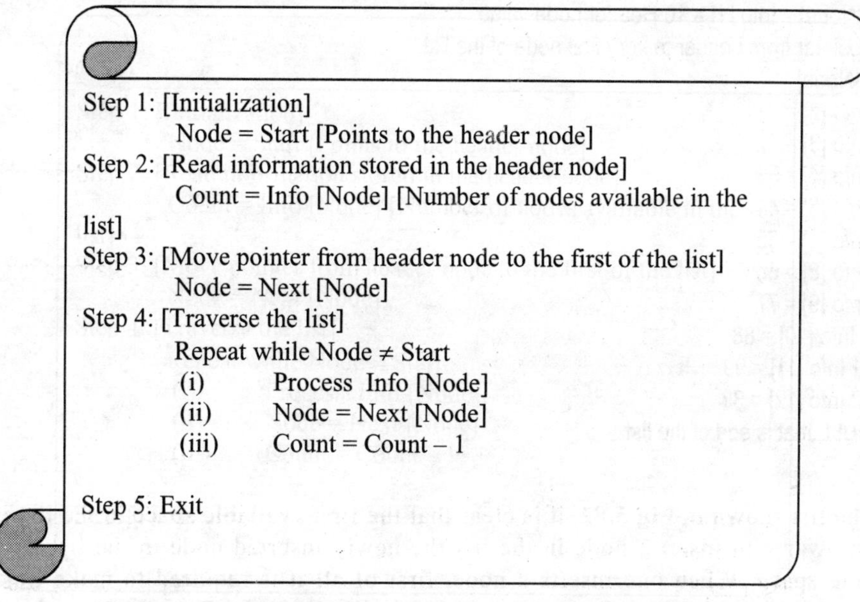

Step 1: [Initialization]
Node = Start [Points to the header node]
Step 2: [Read information stored in the header node]
Count = Info [Node] [Number of nodes available in the list]
Step 3: [Move pointer from header node to the first of the list]
Node = Next [Node]
Step 4: [Traverse the list]
Repeat while Node ≠ Start
(i) Process Info [Node]
(ii) Node = Next [Node]
(iii) Count = Count – 1

Step 5: Exit

Fig 5.81. Algorithm to traverse a circular header linked list

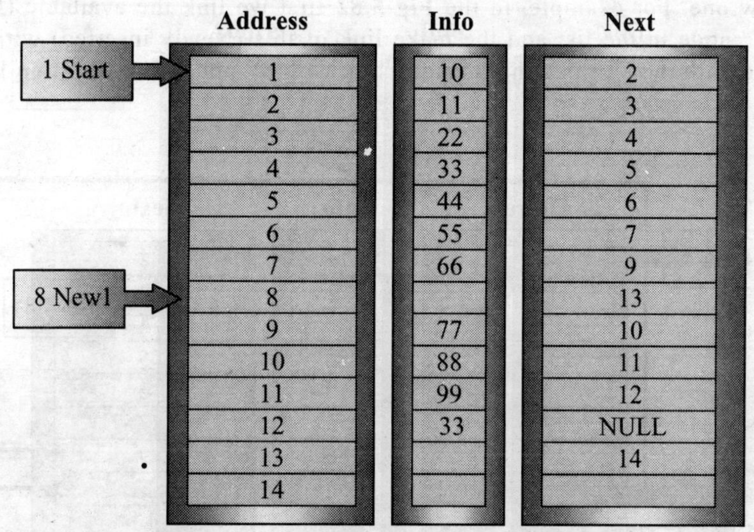

Address	Info	Next
1	10	2
2	11	3
3	22	4
4	33	5
5	44	6
6	55	7
7	66	9
8		13
9	77	10
10	88	11
11	99	12
12	33	NULL
13		14
14		

Fig 5.82. Circular header linked list in memory

Algorithm to traverse a circular header-linked list is illustrated in **Fig 5.81.** If we have a header linked as illustrated in **Fig 5.82** and wants to traverse this list. Here, header node has information 10 meaning that the list contains 10 elements. The traversing is as follows:

Node = Start = 1

Count = Info [Node] = Info [1] = 10 Header node value
Now moving pointer from header to very first node of the list
Node = Next [Node]
Next [1] = 2 Info [2] =11
Next [2] = 3 Info [3] = 22
Next [3] = 4 Info [4] = 33
Next [4] = 5 Info [5] = 44
Next [5] = 6 Info [6] = 55
Next [6] = 8 Info [8] = 66
Next [8] = 9 Info [9] = 77
Next [9] = 10 Info [10] = 88
Next [10] = 11 Info [11] = 99
Next [11] = 12 Info [12] = 33
Next [12] = NULL that is end of the list

From the list shown in **Fig 5.82**, it is clear that the first available space in the list is at position 8. When one wants to insert a node in the list the newly inserted node in the list firstly occupies this available space. When one inserts a node, first of all it is required to make link of the first free space with the node after that one wants to insert the node. Then make link of this newly inserted node with the next node in the list that was previously linked with previous node before inserting the new one. For example, in the **Fig 5.82** first we link the available (Newly inserted) node with the 7th node in the list and the make link of this (Newly inserted) with node that was previously linked with the 7th node that is make link with 8th node. The resulting list is illustrated in **Fig 5.83.**

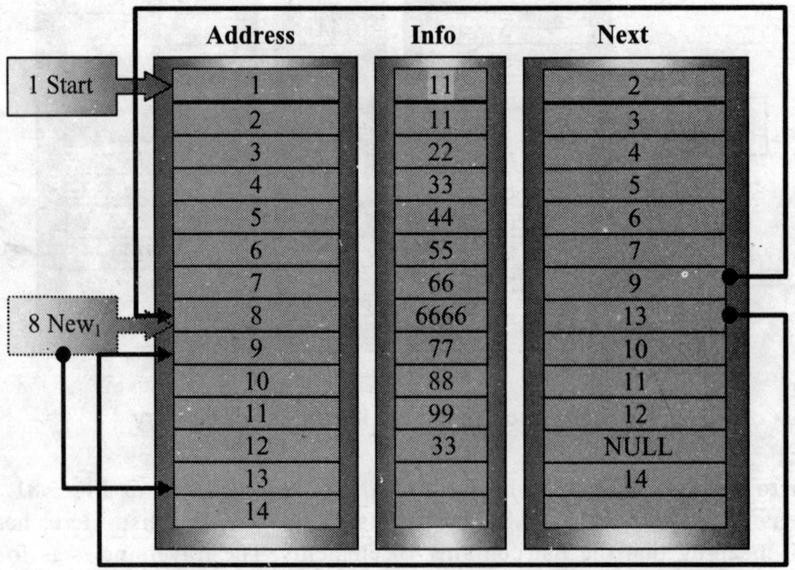

Fig 5.83. Circular header linked list after inserting a node

The program segment **CIRCLIST.C** illustrates the **creation, traversing** and **insertion** operation of a circular linked.

Step 1: [Initialization]
Node = Start
Step 2: [Process the header node]
Count = Info [Node]
Step 3: [Move pointer to first node of the list]
Node = Next [Node]
Step 4: [Initialize counter]
Node_number = 1
Step 5: [Read node number to which you want insert]
Insert_node = Value
Step 6: [Perform searching]
Repeat through Step 7 while Node ≠ Start
If Node_number = Insert_node
(i) Next [New_1] =Next [Node]
(ii) Next [Node] = New_1
(iii) Info [New_1] = Value [Read information of the newly inserted node]
Else
Node = Next [Node]
Step 7: Node_number = Node_number + 1
Step 8: [Update the header node]
Node = Start
Info [Node] = Info [Node] + 1
Step 9 : Exit

Fig 5.84. Algorithm to insert a node in a header linked list

```
/* CREATING CIRCULAR HEADER LINKED LIST */
/* CIRCLIST.C */

# include <stdio.h>
# include <malloc.h>
struct link
{
	int info;
	struct link *next;
};
int i; /* Represents number of nodes in the list */
int number;
struct link *start, *new1;
```

```
void insertion(struct link *);
void create_circular_list(struct link *);
void display(struct link *);


/* Function create a circular header linked list */

void create_circular_list( struct link *node)
{
      char ch;

      node = start; /* Point to the header node in the list */
      node->next = (struct link *) malloc(sizeof(struct link));
      i = 0;
      printf("\n Input choice n for break: ");
      ch = getchar();
      while(ch != 'n')
      {
            node->next = (struct link* ) malloc(sizeof(struct link));
            node = node->next;
            printf("\n Input the node: %d:", (i+1));
            scanf("%d", &node->info);
            fflush(stdin);
            printf("\n Input choice n for break: ");
            ch = getchar();
            i++;
      }
      printf("\n Total nodes = %d", i);
      node = start;
      node->info = i; /* Assign total number of nodes to the header node */
}

/* Inserting a node in circular header linked */
void insertion(struct link *node)
{
      int count = node->info;
      int node_number = 0;
      int insert_node;

      node = start;
      node = node->next;

      printf("\n Input node number you want to insert: ");
      printf("\n Value should be less are equal to the");
      printf("\n number of nodes in the list: ");
      scanf("%d", &insert_node);
```

```
    while(count)
    {
        if((node_number+1) == insert_node)
        {
            new1 = (struct link* ) malloc(sizeof(struct link));
            new1->next = node->next ;
            node->next = new1;
            printf("\n Input the node value: ");
            scanf("%d", &new1->info);
            node = node->next;
            count—;
        }
        else
        {
            node = node->next;
            count—;
        }
        node_number ++;
    }
    if (count == 0)
    {
        node = start; /* Points to header node */
        node->info = node->info+1;
    }
}

/* Display the list */
void display(struct link *node)
{
    int count = node->info;

    node = start;
    node = node->next;

    while (count-1)
    {
        printf("\n 0x%x", node);
        printf(" %d ", node->info);
        node = node->next;
        count —;
    }
}

/* Function main */
void main()
{
```

```
    struct link *node = (struct link *) malloc(sizeof(struct link));
    create_circular_list(node);
    printf("\n Before inserting a node list is as follows:\n");
    display(node);
    insertion(node);
    printf("\n After inserting a node list is as follows:\n");
    display(node);
}
```

```
Input choice n for break:
Input the node: 1: 11
Input choice n for break:
Input the node: 2: 22
Input choice n for break:
Input the node: 3: 33
Input choice n for break:
Input the node: 4: 44
Input choice n for break:
Input the node: 5: 55
Input choice n for break:
Input the node: 6: 66
Input choice n for break:
Input the node: 7: 77
Input choice n for break:
Input the node: 8: 88
Input choice n for break:
Input the node: 9: 99
Input choice n for break:
Input the node: 10: 33
Input choice n for break: n
Total nodes = 10
Before inserting a node list is as follows:
ADDRESS  VALUE
0x147a11e0  11
0x147a11e8  22
0x147a11f0  33
0x147a11f8  44
0x147a1200  55
0x147a1208  66
0x147a1210  77
0x147a1218  88
0x147a1220  99
0x147a1228  33
```

```
Input node number you want to insert:
Value should be less are equal to the
number of nodes in the list: 6
Input the node value: 6666
After inserting a node list is as follows:
ADDRESS  VALUE
 0x147a11e0  11
 0x147a11e8  22
 0x147a11f0  33
 0x147a11f8  44
 0x147a1200  55
 0x147a1208  66
 0x147a1230  6666
 0x147a1210  77
 0x147a1218  88
 0x147a1220  99
 0x147a1228  33
```

5.14 Application of Header Linked List

In this section we will consider polynomial and possible operations on it such as addition.

5.14.1 POLYNOMIALS

The header-linked lists are frequently used to maintain the polynomials in memory. The header node is used to represents the zero polynomial. For example, suppose we have

$F(x) = 5x^5 - 3x^3 + 2x^2 + x^1 + 10x^0$

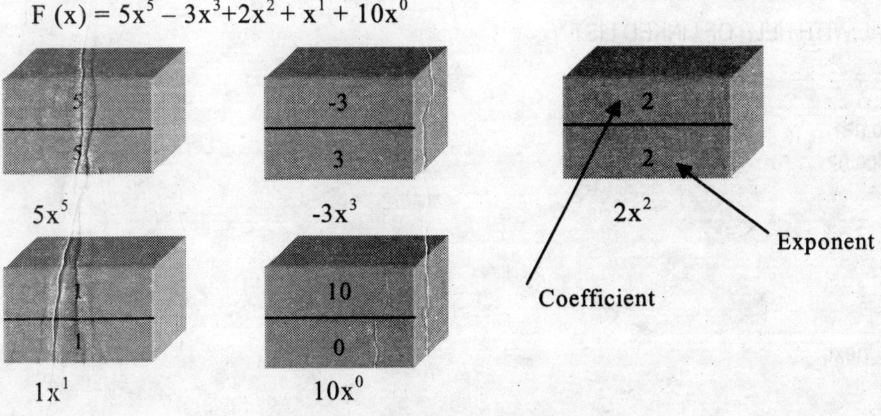

Fig 5.85. Nodes of a polynomial

From the polynomial represented by **F (x)** it is clear that this polynomial contains two things coefficient and exponent, where **x** is a formal parameter. Hence, we can say that a polynomial is sum of terms, each of which consists of a coefficient and an exponent. The computer implementation requires implementing polynomials as a list of pairs of coefficient and exponent. Each of these pairs will constitute a structure, so a polynomial will be represented as a list of structures. If one wants to represent **F (x)** with the help of linked list then the list will contain 5 nodes. The individual nodes are illustrated in **Fig 5.85.** When we link each node represented in **Fig 5.85,** we get a linked list structure that represents polynomial **F (x). Fig 5.86** illustrates the polynomial **F (x)**.

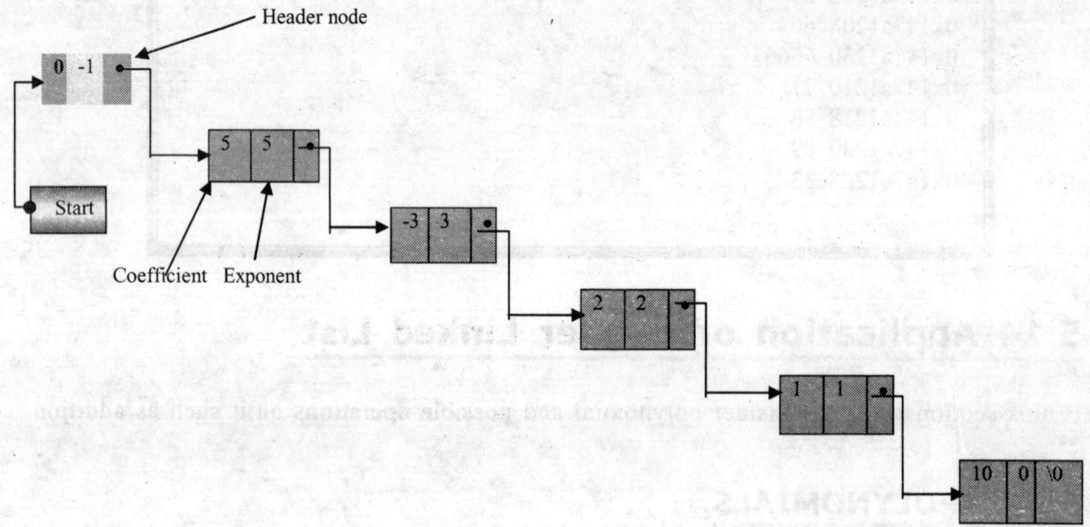

Fig 5.86. Polynomial

The program segment **POLY.C** illustrates the polynomial creation procedures.

```
/* POLY NOMIAL WITH HELP OF LINKED LIST */
/* POLY.C */

# include <stdio.h>
# include <malloc.h>

struct link
{
	float coef;
	int expo;
	struct link *next;
};

int i;
```

```
int number;
struct link start, *previous, *new1;

void insertion(struct link *);
void create_poly(struct link *);
void display(struct link *);

/* Function create a ploynomial list */

void create_poly(struct link *node)
{
    char ch;

    start.next = NULL; /* Empty list */
    node = &start; /* Point to the start of the list */
    i = 0;
    printf("\n Input choice n for break: ");
    ch = getchar();

    while(ch != 'n')
    {
        node->next = (struct link* ) malloc(sizeof(struct link));
        node = node->next;
        printf("\n Input the coeficient value: %d: ", i+1);
        scanf("%f", &node->coef);
        printf("\n Input the exponent value: %d: ", i+1);
        scanf("%d", &node->expo);
        node->next = NULL;
        fflush(stdin);
        printf("\n Input choice n for break: ");
        ch = getchar();
        i++;
    }
    printf("\n Total nodes = %d", i);
}

/* Display the polynomial */

void display(struct link *node)
{
    node = &start;
    node = node->next;

    while (node)
    {
        printf("+ %f", node->coef);
```

```
        printf("X^%d", node->expo);
        node = node->next;
    }
}

/* Function main */

void main()
{
    struct link *node = (struct link *) malloc(sizeof(struct link));
    create_poly(node);
    display(node);
}
```

```
Input choice n for break:
Input the coefficient value:1 :5
Input the exponent value:1 :6
Input choice n for break:
Input the coefficient value:2 :3
Input the exponent value:2 :4
Input choice n for break:
Input the coefficient value:3 :-1
Input the exponent value:3 :-3
Input choice n for break:
Input the coefficient value:4 :1
Input the exponent value:4 :1
Input choice n for break:
Input the coefficient value:5 :10
Input the exponent value:5 :0
Input choice n for break:
Input header node values:
Coefficient value:0
Exponent value:-1

POLYNOMIAL IS

            + 5X^6+ 3X^4+ -1X^-3+ 1X^1+ 10X^0
```

5.14.2 Addition of Polynomials

To add two polynomials we need to scan them once. If we find terms with the same exponent in the two polynomials, then we add the coefficients, otherwise, we copy the term of larger exponent into the sum and go on. When we reach at the end of one of the polynomial, then remaining part of the other is copied into the sum. Suppose we have two polynomials as illustrated in **Fig 5.87** and **Fig 5.88** and we have to perform addition of these polynomials.

When we scan first node of the two polynomials, we find that exponential power of first node in the second polynomial is greater than that of first node of the first polynomial. Here the exponent of the first node of the second polynomial is greater, hence we have to copy first node of the second polynomial into the sum. Then we consider the first node of the first polynomial and once again first node value of first polynomial is compared with the second node value of the second polynomial. Here the first node exponent value of the first polynomial is greater than second node exponent value the second polynomial. We copy the first node of the first polynomial into the sum. Now consider the second node of the first polynomial and it compared with the second node of the second polynomial. Here the exponent value of the second node of the second list greater than the second node of the first polynomial, hence we copy the second node of the second list into sum. Now we consider the third node exponent of the second polynomial and compare it with second node exponent value of the first polynomial. We find that both are equal, hence perform addition of their coefficient and copied into the sum. This process is continuing till all the nodes of both the polynomials are exhausted. For example, after adding the above two polynomial, we get the polynomial illustrated in **Fig 5.89.**

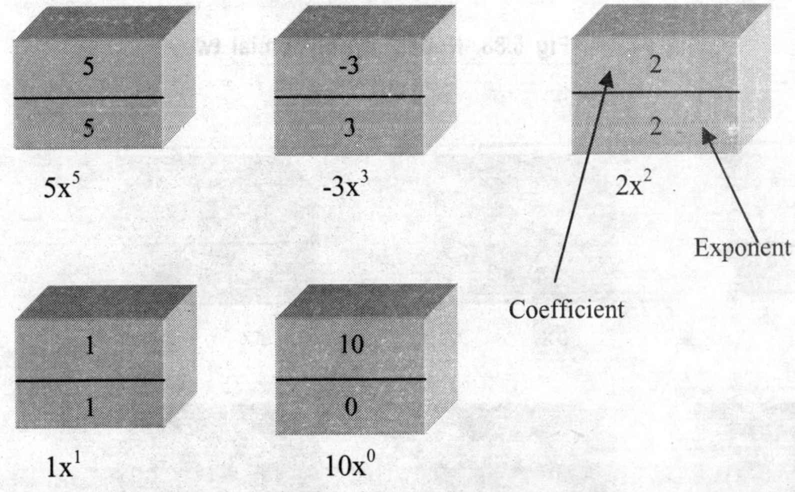

Fig. 5.87 Nodes of polynomial one

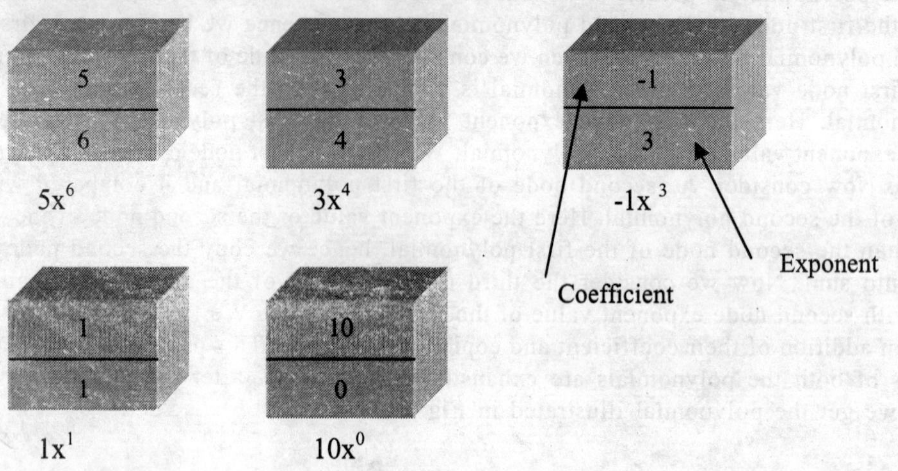

Fig 5.88. Nodes of polynomial two

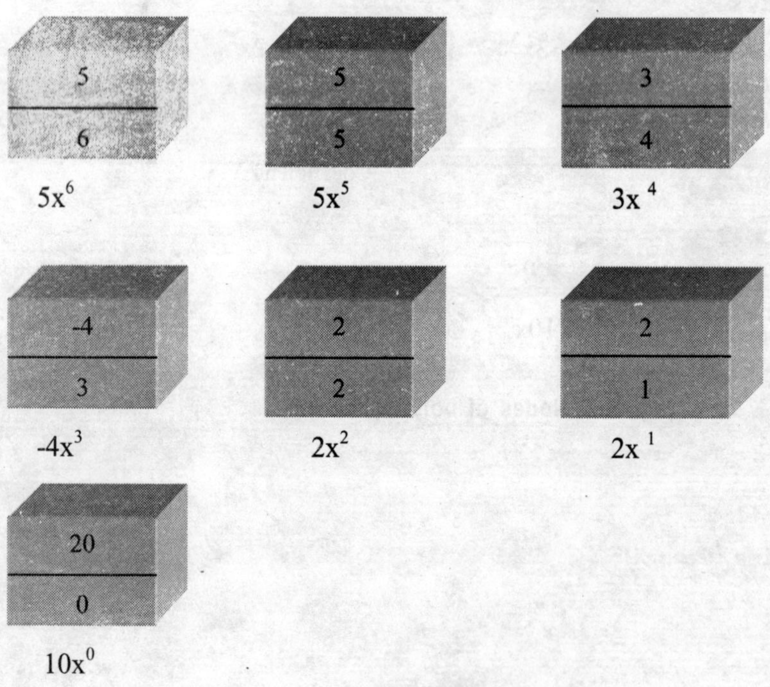

Fig 5.89. Resulting polynomial

EXERCISE

5.1 *Discuss the advantages, if any of a two-way linked list over a one-way linked list for each of the following operations:*

(i) *Traversing the list to process each node*
(ii) *Deleting a node whose location is given*
(iii) *Searching an unsorted list for a given element*
(iv) *Searching a sorted list for a given element*
(v) *Inserting a node before the node with a given location*
(vi) *Inserting a node after the node with a given location*

5.2 *Write an algorithm, which deletes the last node from the **LIST**. Suppose **LIST** is a header list in memory.*

5.3 *Find the polynomials **$POLY_1$** and **$POLY_2$** stored in **Fig 5.90.***

5.4 *Consider **Fig 5.91** and find the following:*

(i) *Sequence of characters in the list.*
(ii) *Suppose **A** then **L** are deleted from the list and then **G** is inserted at the beginning of the list. Find the final structure.*
(iii) *Suppose **L** then **A** are deleted from the list and then **G** is inserted at the beginning of the list. Find the final structure.*
(iv) *Suppose **G** is inserted at the beginning of the list and then **A** and then **L** are deleted from the list. Find the final structure.*

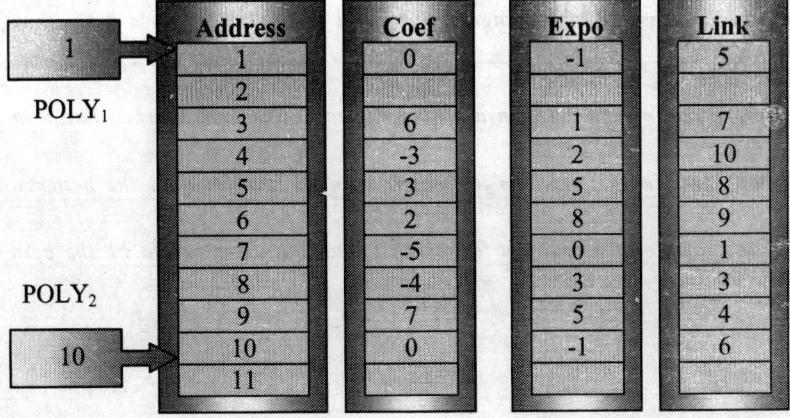

Address	Coef	Expo	Link
1	0	-1	5
2			
3	6	1	7
4	-3	2	10
5	3	5	8
6	2	8	9
7	-5	0	1
8	-4	3	3
9	7	5	4
10	0	-1	6
11			

Fig 5.90. Polynomials in memory

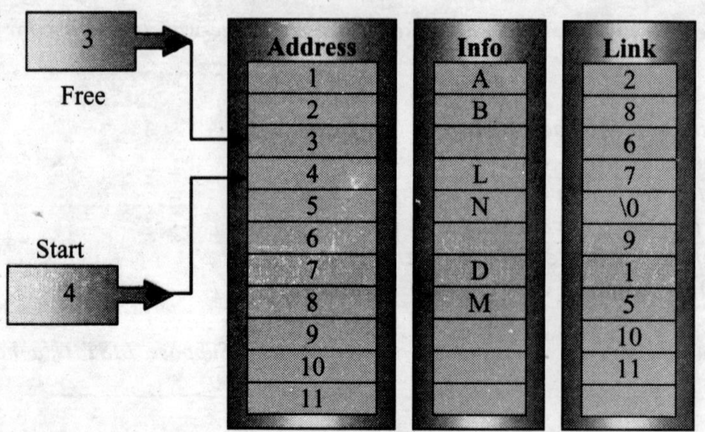

Fig 5.91. List in memory

5.2 *Write a program that takes as input an integer number, split the number in its digits and stores the digits in a linked list structure.*

5.3 *Suppose **LIST** is a linked list in memory consists of numerical values. Write a procedure for each of the following:*

*(i) Finding the minimum **Min** of the values in **LIST**.*
*(ii) Finding the average of the values in **LIST**.*
(iii) Finding the summation of the elements.

5.4 *Write a procedure, which interchanges the **k**th and **k+1**st elements in a list without affecting any other values.*

5.5 *(a) Explain the difference between a sequential and linked list representation of a list.*

(b) Give an example of a problem for which a linked list would be the better solution.

(c) Give an example of a problem for which a sequential list would be the better solution.

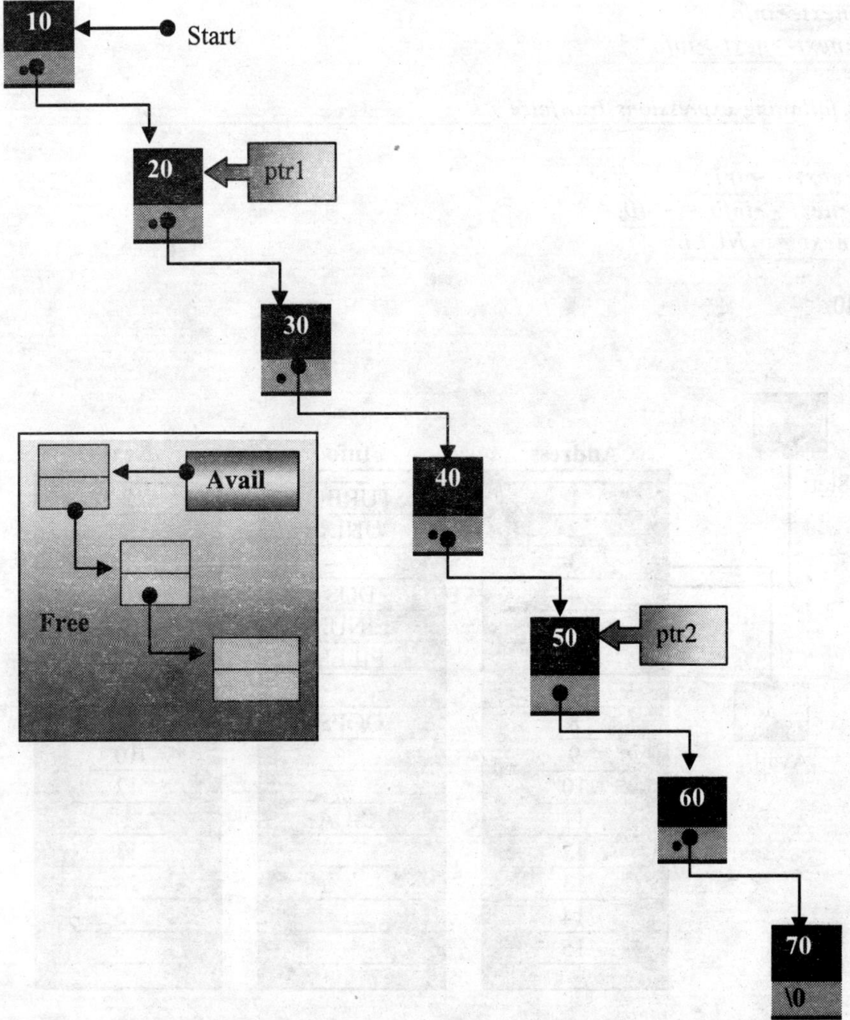

Fig 5.92. List in memory

5.2 True/False? Justify.

(i) An array is a random access structure.
(ii) A linked list is a random access structure.
(iii) A sequential list is a random access structure.
(iv) A sequential list is always stored in a statically allocated structure.

Consider **Fig 5.92** for the questions **5.10 - 5.13.**

5.3 Find the values of the following expressions:

(i) ptr1 -> info
(ii) ptr2->next->info
(iii) start->next->next->info

5.4 *Are the following expressions true/false?*

(i) start->next = ptr1;
(ii) ptr1 ->next ->info == 40;
(iii) ptr2->next == NULL;

start-> info = 10;

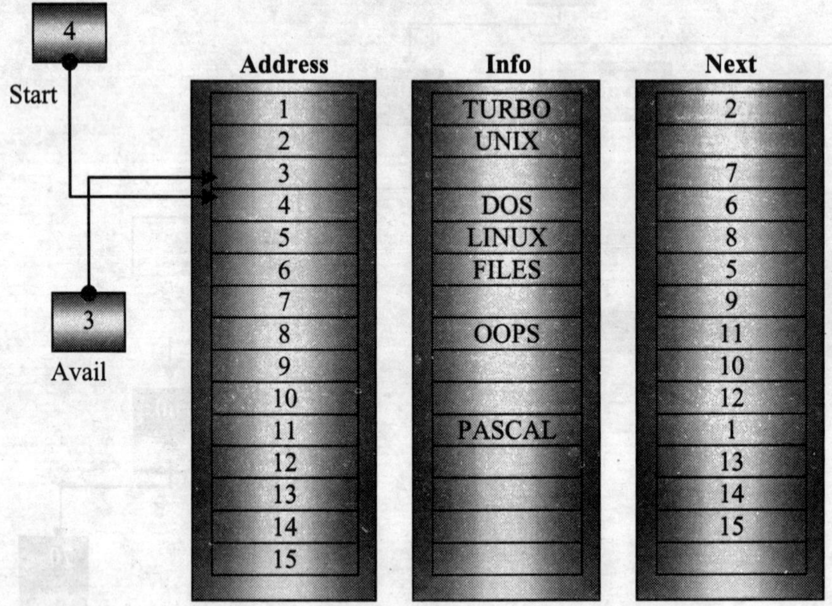

Fig 5.93. List in memory

5.2 *Discuss whether the syntax of the each of the following statements are valid or invalid.*

(i) start->next = ptr1->next;
*(ii) start->next = *(ptr2->next);*
*(iii) *start = ptr2;*
(iv) ptr2=ptr1->next->info;
(v) ptr1->info = ptr2->info;
(vi) ptr2 = ptr2->next->next;

5.3 *Write one statement to do each of the following:*

(i) *Make **start** point to the node containing 30.*
(ii) *Make **ptr2** point to the last node in the list*
(iii) *Make **start** point to an empty list.*
(iv) *Set the **info** member of the node containing 30 to 40.*

5.4 *Consider the linked list shown in **Fig 5.93.***

(a) *Find the alphabetical list of strings.*
(b) *Suppose **LINUX** is deleted and then **C** and **SQL** are inserted into the list. Find the final structure.*

5.5 *Suppose we have following list of months:*

January, February, March, April, May, June, July, August, September, October, November, and December.

Create a linked structure to sort months in their alphabetical order.

5.6 *Suppose **LIST** is in memory and contains duplicate information. Write an algorithm that removes all the duplicates.*

5.7 *Write a function that removes the first element of a linked list and adds it to the end of the list without changing any value in information field. [It is required to change only **Start** and **Next** field values.]*

5.8 *Let **LIST** be a linked list in memory. Write a function that*

(a) *Adds a given information (That is k) to each element in **LIST**.*
(b) *Finds the number **N** of times a given element occurs in **LIST.***

5.9 *Suppose **LIST** is in memory. Write an algorithm, which reverse the list.*

5.10 *Write an algorithm, which sort files of a directory in alphabetical order and implement the same using linear linked list.*

Suppose **ls** is a **UNIX** command. The **ls** command lists all the files in a directory. Write an algorithm, which represents implementation of **ls** command. Implement the designed algorithm using **C++**.

5.11 *Write a function to delete a node from a circular linked list.*

5.12 *Write a function that concatenates two circular linked lists, producing a circular linked list.*

5.13 Write a function that split a circular linked list into three circular linked lists.

5.14 Write a function that creates a two-way header linked list.

5.15 Write a function that creates a two-way circular linked list.

5.16 Write a function that splits a circular two way linked list in two two-way circulars linked list.

5.17 Write a function that multiplies two polynomials.

5.18 Write a function that multiplies a polynomial with a monomial.

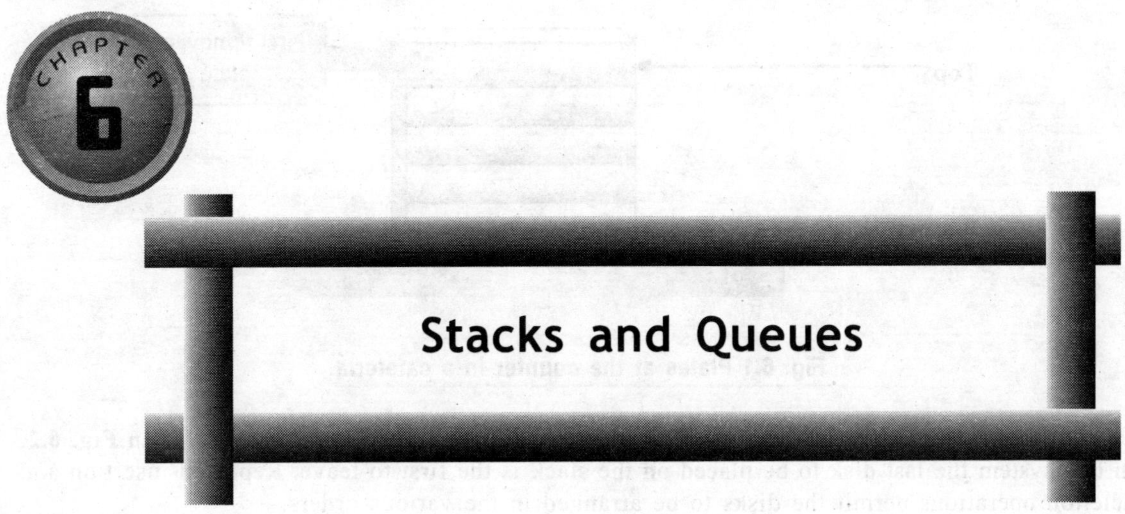

Stacks and Queues

In this chapter we will discuss in detail about stacks and queues. First we will discuss the basic stack operations and their implementation. After that we will explore about queues.

6.1 STACK

A stack is defined formally as a list (a linear data structure) in which all insertions and deletions are made at one end called the top of stack (**TOS**). The fundamental operations, which are possible on a stack, are:

- *Push* ⟶ *Insertion*
- *Pop* ⟶ *Deletion*
- *Peep* ⟶ *Extract information*
- *Update* ⟶ *Update information associated at some location in the stack*

The most recently pushed element can be checked prior to performing a pop operation. A stack is based on the **last-in first-out** algorithm **(LIFO)** in which insertion and deletion operations are performed at one end of a stack. Also, the information can only be removed in the opposite order in which it was added to the stack. The most accessible information in a stack is at the top of the stack and least accessible information is at the bottom of the stack.

For example, consider a stack of plates placed on the counter in a cafeteria. During the dinner time customers take plates from the top of the stack and waiter puts the washed plates on the top of the stack. The plate that is put most recently on the stack is the first one to be taken off. The plate at the bottom is the last one to be used. This discussion can further be understood with the help of **Fig. 6.1.**

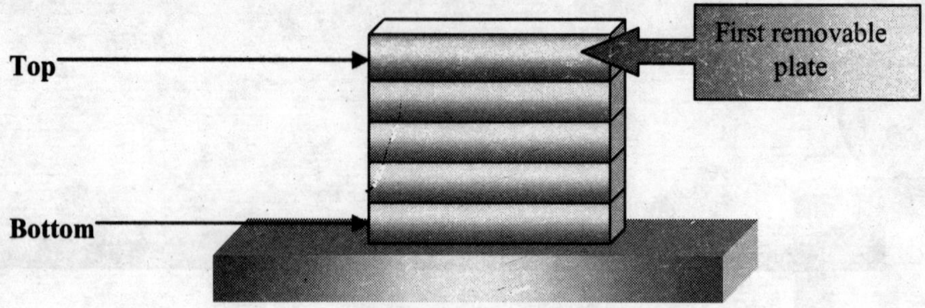

Fig. 6.1 Plates at the counter in a cafeteria

Another example of a stack is a collection of disk system on a peg as illustrated in **Fig. 6.2**. In this system the last disk to be placed on the stack is the first to leave. Repeated insertion and deletion operations permit the disks to be arranged in the various orders.

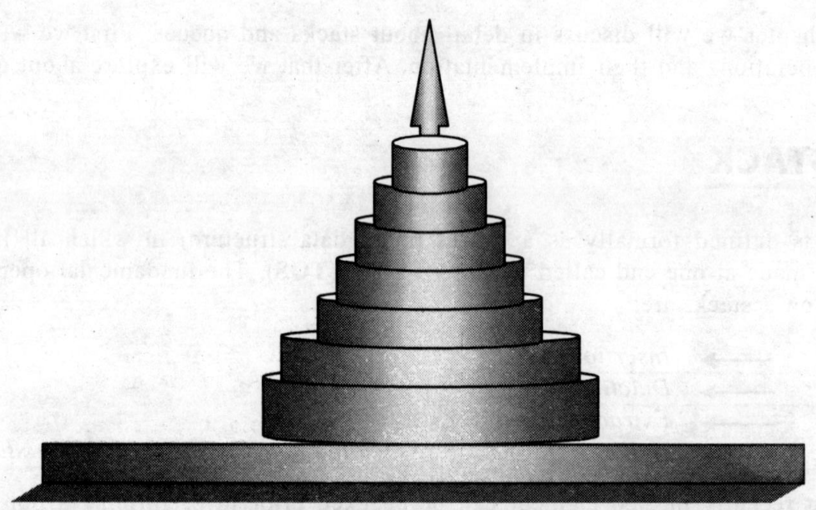

Fig. 6.2 Disks on a peg

6.2 REPRESENTATION OF STACK

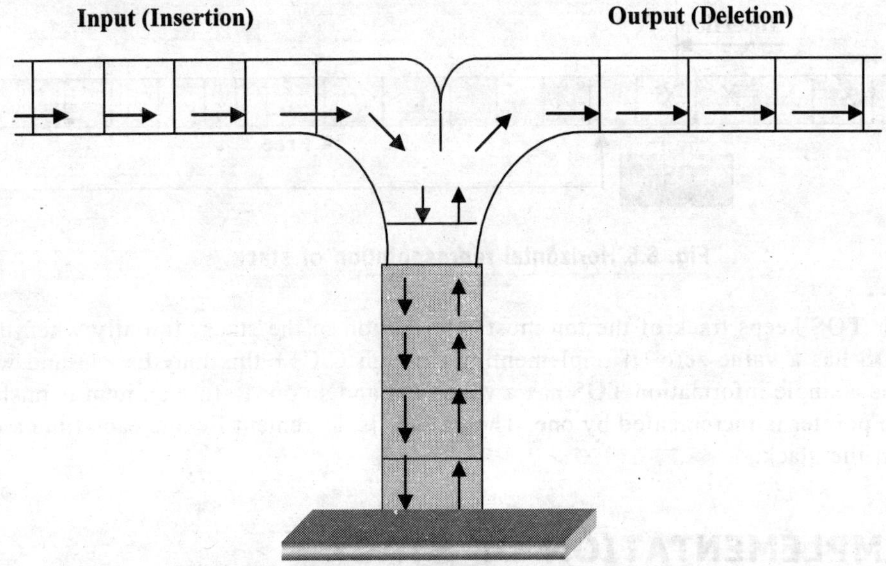

Fig. 6.3 Railway shunting system representation

There are various ways to represent a stack, such as railway shunting method, vertical vector method and horizontal vector method (See **Fig. 6.3, Fig. 6.4** and **Fig. 6.5**).

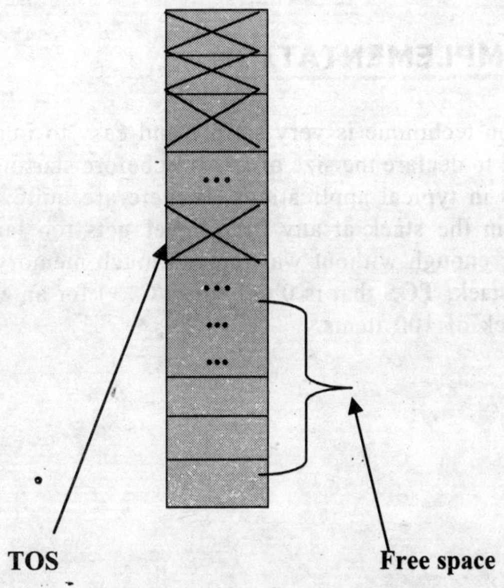

Fig. 6.4 Vertical representation of stack

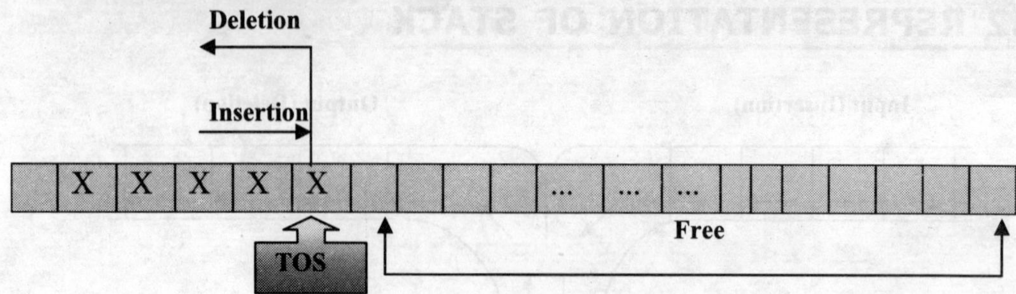

Fig. 6.5 Horizontal representation of stack

A pointer **TOS** keeps track of the top most information in the stack. Initially when the stack is empty, **TOS** has a value zero (if implementing through C/C++ this may be –1) and when the stack contains a single information **TOS** has a value one and so on. Before an item is pushed on to the stack, the pointer is incremented by one. The pointer is decrement by one each time a deletion is made from the stack.

6.3 IMPLEMENTATION OF STACK

We have already discussed that a stack is a list and hence any of the list implementation techniques may be used to implement a stack. Two common implementations are:

- *Pointer (Linked list)*
- *Array*

6.3.1 ARRAY'S IMPLEMENTATION

The array implementation technique is very simple and easy to implement. But there is one potential hazard that we need to declare the size of an array before starting the operation. Generally this is not a big problem as in typical applications, if there are quite few stack operations, the actual number of elements in the stack at any time never gets too large. It is usually easy to declare the array to be large enough without wasting too much memory spaces. Associated with each stack there is a top of stack, **TOS** that is 0 (–1 for C/C++) for an empty stack. For example, let **Fig. 6.6** represents a stack of 100 items.

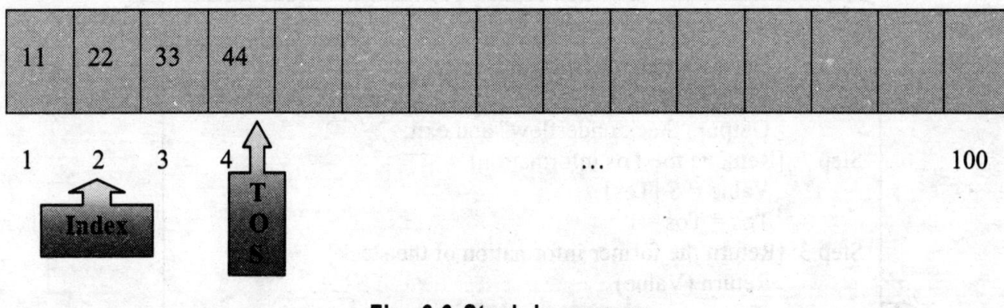

Fig. 6.6 Stack in memory

Now, we will discuss the basic stack operations one by one.

6.3.1.1 PUSH OPERATION

Push means to insert an item onto the stack. The push algorithm is illustrated in **Fig. 6.7**. The algorithm illustrated in **Fig. 6.7** inserts an item to the top of a stack, which is represented by vector **S** and containing **Size** number of items with a pointer **TOS** denoting the position of top most item in the stack.

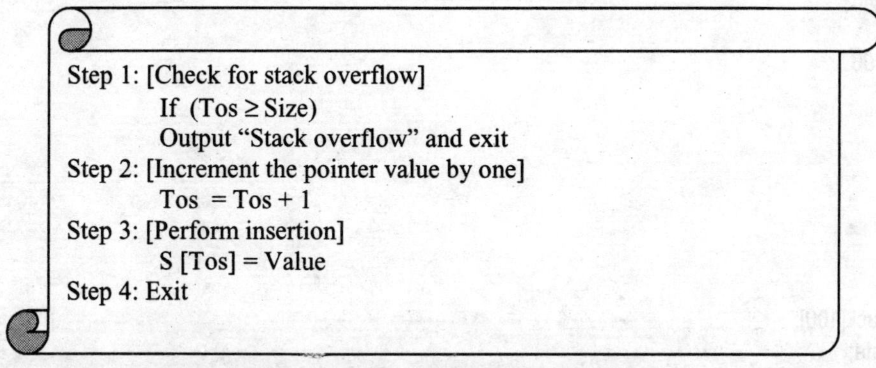

Step 1: [Check for stack overflow]
    If (Tos ≥ Size)
    Output "Stack overflow" and exit
Step 2: [Increment the pointer value by one]
    Tos = Tos + 1
Step 3: [Perform insertion]
    S [Tos] = Value
Step 4: Exit

Fig. 6.7 Algorithm to push information in the stack

6.3.1.2 POP OPERATION

The pop operation deletes or removes the topmost item from the stack. After removal of top most information, new value of the pointer **TOS** becomes the previous value of **TOS** that is **TOS = TOS - 1** and freed position is allocated to free space. The algorithm to remove an item from the stack is illustrated in **Fig. 6.8**.

Step 1 [Check whether the stack is empty]
    If (Tos = 0)
    Output "Stack underflow" and exit
Step 2: [Remove the Tos information]
    Value = S [Tos]
    Tos = Tos – 1
Step 3: [Return the former information of the stack]
    Return (Value)

Fig. 6.8 Pop algorithm

The program segment **STACK_A.C** implements algorithm illustrated in **Fig. 6.7** and **Fig. 6.8**.

```
// IMPLEMENTATION OF THE STACK USING ARRAYS
// STACK_A.C

# include<iostream.h>
# include<stdio.h>
# include<string.h>
# include<ctype.h>

# define size  100

int top = -1;
int flag = 0;

class stacks
{
    private:
        int stack[100];
        int data;

    public:
        void push(int *, int);
        int pop(int *);
        void display(int *);
};
// Definition of the push function

void stacks :: push(int s[], int d)
{
    if(top ==(size-1))
        flag = 0;
```

```
        else
        {
            flag = 1;
            ++top;
            s[top] = d;
        }
}

// Definition of the pop function
int stacks :: pop(int s[])
{
        int popped_element;
        if(top == -1)
        {
            popped_element = 0;
            flag = 0;
        }
        else
        {
            flag = 1;
            popped_element = s[top];
            —top;
        }
        return (popped_element);
}

// Definition of the display function
void stacks :: display(int s[])
{
        if(top == -1)
        {
            cout<<"Stack is empty";
        }
        else
        {
            for(int i = top; i>=0; —i)
                cout<<" "<<s[i];
        }
}

// Function main
void main()
{
        stacks s;
        int stack[size];
        int  data;
```

```
char choice;
int q = 0;
int top = -1;

do
{
      cout<<" \nPush->i Pop->p Quit->q: ";
      cout<<"\nInput the choice: ";

      do
      {
            cin>>choice;
            choice =tolower(choice);
      }while(strchr("ipq", choice)==NULL);

      cout<<"Your choice is ->"<<choice;
      switch(choice)
      {
      case 'i':
            cout<<"\n Input the element to pushed: ";
            cin>>data;
            s.push(stack,data);
            if(flag)
            {
                  cout<<"\n After inserting ";
                  s.display(stack);
                  if(top == (size-1))
                        cout<<"\n Stack is full";
            }
            else
                  cout<<"\n Stack overflow after pushing";
            break;

      case 'p':
            data = s.pop(stack);
            if(flag)
            {
                  cout<<"\n Data is popped: "<<data;
                  cout<<"\n Rest data in stack is as follows:\n";

                  s.display(stack);
            }
            else
                  cout<<"\n Stack underflow";
            break;
      case 'q':
```

```
            q = 1;
        }
    } while(!q);
}
```

```
Push->i Pop->p Quit->q:
Input the choice: i
Your choice is -> i
Input the element to push: 111
After inserting  111
Push->i Pop->p Quit->q:
Input the choice: i
Your choice is -> i
Input the element to push: 999
After inserting   999  111
Push->i Pop->p Quit->q:
Input the choice: i
Your choice is ->i
Input the element to push: 666
After inserting   666  999  111
Push->i Pop->p Quit->q:
Input the choice : i
Your choice is ->i
Input the element to push: 555
After inserting   555  666  999  111
Push->i Pop->p Quit->q:
Input the choice : p
Your choice is ->p
Data is popped: 555
Rest data in stack is as follows:
666  999  111
Push->i Pop->p Quit->q:
Input the choice : i
Your choice is ->i
Input the element to push: 444
After inserting   444  666  999  111
Push->i Pop->p Quit->q:
Input the choice : i
Your choice is ->i
Input the element to push: 333
After inserting   333  444  666  999  111
Push->i Pop->p Quit->q:
Input the choice : p
Your choice is ->p
Data is popped:333
Rest data in stack is as follows:
444  666  999  111
Push->i Pop->p Quit->q:
Input the choice : p
Your choice is ->p
Data is popped:444
Rest data in stack is as follows:
666 999 111
```

```
Push->i Pop->p Quit->q:
Input the choice : p
Your choice is ->p
Data is popped:666
Rest data in stack is as follows:
999  111
Push->i Pop->p Quit->q:
Input the choice : Your choice is ->p
Data is popped:999
Rest data in stack is as follows:
111
Push->i Pop->p Quit->q:
Input the choice : i
Your choice is ->i
Input the element to push:
After inserting  1000  111
Push->i Pop->p Quit->q:
Input the choice : q
Your choice is ->q
```

The program segment **STACK_L.C** implements the algorithm given in **Fig. 6.7** and **Fig. 6.8** with the help of linked list.

```
// STACK IMPLEMENTATION USING LINKED LIST
// STACK_L.C
# include<iostream.h>
# include<malloc.h>

struct link
{
    int info;
    link *next;
};

class stack_link
{
    private:
        link *start;
    public:
        void display(link *);
        link *push(link *);
        link *pop(link *);
        int main_menu();
};
void stack_link :: display(link *rec)
```

```
{
    while(rec != NULL)
    {
        cout<<" "<<rec->info;
        rec = rec->next;
    }
}
link * stack_link :: push(link *rec)
{
    link *new_rec;
    cout<<"\n Input the new value for next location of the stack:";

    new_rec = (link *)malloc(sizeof(link));
    cin>>new_rec->info;
    new_rec->next = rec;
    rec = new_rec;
    return(rec);
}

link * stack_link :: pop(link *rec)
{
    link *temp;

    if(rec == NULL)
    {
        cout<<"\n Stack is empty";
    }
    else
    {
        temp = rec->next;
        free(rec);
        rec = temp;
        cout<<"\n After pop operation the stack is as follows:\n";
        display(rec);
        if(rec  == NULL)
            cout<<"\n Stack is empty";
    }
    return(rec);
}
int stack_link :: main_menu ()
{
    int choice;
    do
    {
        cout<<"\n 1<-Push ";
        cout<<"\n 2<-Pop";
        cout<<"\n 3<-Quit";
```

```
        cout<<"\n Input your choice :";
        cin>>choice;
        if(choice <1 || choice >3)
            cout<<"\n Incorrect choice-> Try once again";
    } while(choice <1 || choice >3);
    return(choice);
}

// main function
void main()
{
    stack_link stack;
    link *start ;
    int choice;
    start = NULL;

    do'
    {
        choice = stack.main_menu();
        switch(choice)
        {
        case 1:
            start = stack.push(start);
            cout<<"\n After push operation stack is as follows:\n";
            stack.display(start);
            break;
        case 2:
            start = stack.pop(start);
            break;
        default:
            cout<<"\n End of session";
        }
    }while(choice != 3);
}
```

```
1<-Push
2<-Pop
3<-Quit
Input your choice: 1
Input the new value for next location of the
stack: 1111
After push operation stack is as follows:
1111
1<-Push
2<-Pop
3<-Quit
```

```
Input your choice: 1
Input the new value for next location of the
stack: 3333
After push operation stack is as follows:
3333  1111
1<-Push
2<-Pop
3<-Quit
Input your choice: 1

Input the new value for next location of the
stack: 8888
After push operation stack is as follows:
8888  3333  1111
1<-Push
2<-Pop
3<-Quit
Input your choice: 2
After pop operation the stack is as follows:
3333  1111
1<-Push
2<-Pop
3<-Quit
Input your choice: 1
Input the new value for next location of the
stack: 9999
After push operation stack is as follows:
9999  3333  1111
1<-Push
2<-Pop
3<-Quit
Input your choice: 1
Input the new value for next location of the
stack: 8888
After push operation stack is as follows:
8888  9999  3333  1111
1<-Push
2<-Pop
3<-Quit
Input your choice: 2
After pop operation the stack is as follows:
9999  3333  1111
1<-Push
2<-Pop
3<-Quit
Input your choice:
End of session
```

6.3.1.3 PEEP OPERATION

If one is interested only about an information stored at some location in a stack then peep operation is required. In this operation we simply move the pointer to the desired location and then fetch the information associated with that location. The algorithm for the peep operation is illustrated in **Fig. 6.9.** The program segment **PEEPCH.C** implements the algorithm given in **Fig. 6.9.**

Step 1: [Check for the stack overflow]
    If (Tos – i = 0)
    Output "Stack overflow" and exit
Step 2: [Return the ith element from the top of stack]
    Return (S [Tos – i])

Fig. 6.9 Peep algorithm

```
// PEEP OPERATION ON THE STACK USING ARRAYS
// PEEPCH.C

# include<iostream.h>
# include<stdio.h>
# include<string.h>
# include<ctype.h>

# define size 100

int top = -1;
int flag = 0;
class stacks
{
    private:
        int stack[100];
        int data;

    public:
        void push(int *, int);
        int peep(int *);
        void display(int *);
};
// Definition of the push function
void stacks :: push(int s[], int d)
{
```

```
        if(top ==(size-1))
                flag = 0;
        else
        {
                flag = 1;
                ++top;
                s[top] = d;
        }
}
// Definition of the peep function
int stacks :: peep(int s[])
{
        int i;
        cout<<"\n Input the information number to which you want access:";
        cin>> i;
        int peepped_element;
        if(top - i + 1 < 0)
        {
                peepped_element = 0;
                flag = 0;
        }
        else
        {
                flag = 1;
                peepped_element = s[top-i +1];
        }
        return (peepped_element);
}
// Definition of the display function
void stacks :: display(int s[])
{
        if(top == -1)
        {
                cout<<"Stack is empty";
        }
        else
        {
                for(int i = top; i>=0; —i)
                        cout<<" "<<s[i];
        }
}
// Function main
void main()
{
        stacks s;
        int stack[size];
        int data;
```

```
char choice;
int q = 0;
int top = -1;

do
{
	cout<<" \nPush->i Peep->p Quit->q:";
	cout<<"\nInput the choice : ";
	do
	{
		cin>>choice;
		choice =tolower(choice);
	}while(strchr("ipq",choice)==NULL);
	cout<<"Your choice is ->"<<choice;

	switch(choice)
	{
	case 'i' :
		cout<<"\n Input the element to pushed:";
		cin>>data;
		s.push(stack,data);
		if(flag)
		{
			cout<<"\n After inserting ";
			s.display(stack);
			if(top == (size-1))
				cout<<"\n Stack is full";
		}
		else
			cout<<"\n Stack overflow after pushing";
		break;

	case 'p' :
		data = s.peep(stack);
		if(flag)
		{
			cout<<"\n Data is peepped:"<<data;
			cout<<"\n Stack is as follows:\n";
			s.display(stack);
		}
		else
			cout<<"\n Stack underflow";
		break;
	case 'q':
		q = 1;
	}
```

```
    } while(!q);
}
```

```
Push->i Peep->p Quit->q:
Input the choice: i
Your choice is -> i
Input the element to push: 11
After inserting   11
Push->i Peep->p Quit->q:
Input the choice: i
Your choice is -> i
Input the element to push: 22
After inserting   22  11

Push->i Peep->p Quit->q:
Input the choice: i
Your choice is -> i
Input the element to push: 33
After inserting   33  22  11
Push->i Peep->p Quit->q:
Input the choice: i
Your choice is -> i
Input the element to push: 55
After inserting   55  33  22  11
Push->i Peep->p Quit->q:
Input the choice: i
Your choice is -> i
Input the element to push: 666
After inserting   666  55  33  22  11
Push->i Peep->p Quit->q:
Input the choice: i
Your choice is -> i
Input the element to push:  99
After inserting   99  666  55  33  22  11
Push->i Peep->p Quit->q:
Input the choice: p
Your choice is -> p
Input the information number to which you want access: 4
Data is peeped: 33
Stack is as follows:
99  666  55  33  22  11
Push->i Peep->p Quit->q:
Input the choice : p
Your choice is ->p
Input the information number to which you want access: 6
Data is peeped: 11
Stack is as follows:
99  666  55  33  22  11
Push->i Peep->p Quit->q:
Input the choice:  p
Your choice is -> p
```

```
Input the information number to which you want access: 1

Data is peeped: 99
Stack is as follows:
99  666  55  33  22  11
Push->i Peep->p Quit->q:
Input the choice : p
Your choice is ->p
Input the information number to which you want access: 3
Data is peeped: 55
Stack is as follows:
99  666  55  33  22  11
Push->i Peep->p Quit->q:
Input the choice : q
Your choice is ->q
```

6.3.1.4 UPDATE OPERATION

Update operation is required when the content of some location in a stack is to be changed. Suppose one wants to update information at the ith location in the stack **S**. We move **TOS** pointer to the ith location from the top of the stack and input the new value of that location. The update algorithm is illustrated in **Fig. 6.10.** The program segment **UPDATE.C** illustrates the algorithm given in **Fig. 6.10.**

```
Step 1: [Check the underflow condition]
        If (Tos – i = 0)
        Output "Stack underflow" and return
Step 2: [Change the element]
        S [Tos – i] = Value

Step 3: Return
```

Fig. 6.10 Update algorithm

```
// UPDATING A STACK IMPLEMENTED WITH THE HELP OF ARRAYS.
// UPDATE.C

# include<iostream.h>
# include<stdio.h>
# include<string.h>
# include<ctype.h>
# define size  100
int top = -1;
int flag = 0;
```

```
class stacks
{
	private:
		int stack[100];
		int data;

	public:
		void push (int *, int);
		int update (int *);
		void display (int *);
};

// Definition of the push function
void stacks :: push(int s[], int d)
{
	if(top ==(size-1))
		flag = 0;
	else
	{
		flag = 1;
		++top;
		s[top] = d;

	}
}

// Definition of the pop function
int stacks :: update(int s[])
{
	int i;
	cout<<"\n Input the information number to which you want to update:";
	cin>> i;
	int update_element;
	if(top - i + 1 < 0)
	{
		update_element = 0;
		flag = 0;
	}
	else
	{
		flag = 1;
		update_element = s[top-i +1];
		cout<<"\n Input the new value:";
		cin>> s[top-i+1];
	}
	return (update_element);
```

```
}

// Definition of the display function
void stacks :: display(int s[])
{
    if(top == -1)
    {
        cout<<"Stack is empty";
    }
    else
    {
        for(int i = top; i>=0; —i)
            cout<<" "<<s[i];
    }
}

// Function main
void main()
{
    stacks s;
    int stack[size];
    int  data;
    char choice;
    int q = 0;
    int top = -1;

    do
    {
        cout<<" \nPush->i Update->u Quit->q:";
        cout<<"\nInput the choice : ";
        do
        {
            cin>>choice;
            choice =tolower(choice);
        }while(strchr("iuq",choice)==NULL);
        cout<<"Your choice is ->"<<choice;

        switch(choice)
        {
        case 'i':
            cout<<"\n Input the element to pushed:";
            cin>>data;
            s.push(stack,data);
            if(flag)
            {
                cout<<"\n After inserting ";
```

```
                s.display(stack);
                if(top == (size-1))
                        cout<<"\n Stack is full";
            }
            else
                cout<<"\n Stack overflow after pushing";
            break;
        case 'u':
            data = s.update(stack);
            if(flag)
            {
                cout<<"\n Data is peepped:"<<data;
                cout<<"\n Stack is as follows:\n";
                s.display(stack);
            }
            else
                cout<<"\n Stack underflow";
            break;
        case 'q':
            q = 1;
        }
    } while(!q);
}
```

```
Push->i Update->u Quit->q:
Input the choice: i
Your choice is ->i
Input the element to push: 99
After inserting 99
Push->i Update->u Quit->q:
Input the choice: i
Your choice is ->i
Input the element to push: 88
After inserting 88 99
Push->i Update->u Quit->q:
Input the choice: i
Your choice is ->i
Input the element to push: 77
After inserting 77 88 99
Push->i Update->u Quit->q:
Input the choice: i
Your choice is ->i
Input the element to push: 6
After inserting 6 77 88 99
Push->i Update->u Quit->q:
Input the choice: i
Your choice is ->i
```

```
Input the element to push: 5
After inserting 5 6 77 88 99
Push->i Update->u Quit->q:
Input the choice: i
Your choice is ->I
Input the element to push: 44
After inserting 44 5 6 77 88 99
Push->i Update->u Quit->q:
Input the choice: i
Your choice is ->i
Input the element to push: 33
After inserting 33 44 5 6 77 88 99
Push->i Update->u Quit->q:
Input the choice: i
Your choice is ->i
Input the element to push: 22
After inserting 22 33 44 5 6 77 88 99
Push->i Update->u Quit->q:
Input the choice: i
Your choice is ->i
Input the element to push: 11
After inserting 11 22 33 44 5 6 77 88 99
Push->i Update->u Quit->q:
Input the choice: u
Your choice is ->u
Input the information number to which you want to
update: 4
Input the new value: 55
Data is updated: 44
Stack is as follows:
11 22 33 55 5 6 77 88 99
Push->i Update->u Quit->q:
Input the choice: u
Your choice is ->u
Input the information number to which you want to
update: 5
Input the new value: 66
Data is updated: 5
Stack is as follows:
11 22 33 55 66 6 77 88 99
Push->i Update->u Quit->q:
Input the choice: q
Your choice is ->q
```

6.4 POLISH NOTATION

The process of writing the operators of an expression either before their operands or after them is called the **Polish** notation in honour of its discoverer, the **Polish** mathematician ***Jan Luksiewicz.*** The fundamental property of **Polish** notation is that the order in which the operations are to be performed is completely determined by the positions of the operators and operands in the expression. Accordingly, one never needs parenthesis when writing expression in **Polish** notation. The **Polish** notations are classified into three categories. These are:

- *Infix*
- *Prefix*
- *Postfix*

When the operators exist between two operands then the expression is called **infix** expression. For example, let **a + b * c** is an expression, by inspection we find that the operator + exists between the operands **a** and **b**, and operator * exists between the operands **b** and **c**, hence we can say that **a + b * c** is an infix expression.

When the operators are written before their operands then the resulting expression is called the prefix Polish notation. Suppose we want to change the infix expression **a + b * c** into it's prefix form. First of all we consider the precedence of the operators present in the infix expression. Here in the given infix expression there are two operands + and *. The precedence of the * is higher than that of the +. The steps which are required to change infix expression **a + b * c** into it's equivalent prefix form are as follows:

*Step 1: a + * b c* *[Putting * before operands **b** and **c**]*

*Step 2: + a * b c* *[Putting + before operands **a** and **b**]*

When the operators come after their operands the resulting expression is called the reverse Polish notation or postfix expression.

For example, suppose **a + b * c** is an infix expression then after changing this expression into post form we get **a b c * +.** Thus, we can say that post expression is not a mirror image of prefix expression but a different one.

For example, the transformation of infix expression **z + (y * x - (w / v ↑ u) * t)*s** into its postfix form is as follows:

z+(y * x – (w / v ↑ u) * t) * s

z+(y * x – (w / vu ↑) * t) * s

z+(y * x – (w vu ↑/)* t) * s

z+(y * x – w vu ↑ / t *) * s

z+(yx* – w vu ↑ / t *) * s

z+(y x * w vu ↑/ t * –) * s

z+y x* w vu ↑ / t * – s *

z+y x* w vu ↑ / t * – s * + [Resulting postfix expression]

The steps shown above to translate infix expression into postfix expression can be implemented with the help of stack. For this we insert '(' at the end of the infix expression then we label each and every elements of the infix expression.

Attached parenthesis ⇩

z	+	(	y	*	x	–	(	w	/	v	^	u	)	*	t	)	*	s	)	
1	2	3	4	5	6	7	8	9	10	11	12	13	14	15	16	17	18	19	20	⇐ Label

The stack implementation of the above infix expression is illustrated in **Table 6.1.**

6.4.1 USES OF STACK

The stack is a region of memory within which programs temporarily store data as they execute. For example, when a program sends parameters to a function, the parameters are placed on the stack. When the function completes, the items from the stack are popped. Similarly, when the function passes local variables the values of these local variables are stored on the stack during the execution of the function. When the subprogram completes the variables are discarded.

What happens in the computer system, when subprograms are called? The system must remember the place where the call was made so that it can return there when the subprograms complete. It must also remember all the local variables, **CPU** registers, jump addresses and intermediate results, so that the information is not lost when the subprogram is working on. We can think of all this information as one large structure a temporary storage area for each subprogram.

Table 6.1 stack implementation of infix expression z + (y * x – (w / v ^ u) * t) *s

Label Number	Symbol Scanned	Stack	Expression
1	z	(	z
2	+	(+	z
3	(	(+(	z
4	y	(+(	zy
5	*	(+(*	zy
6	x	(+(*	zyx
7	-	(+(-	zyx*
8	(	(+(-(	zyx*
9	w	(+(-(	zyx*w
10	/	(+(-(/	zyx*w
11	v	(+(-(/	zyx*wv
12	^	(+(-(/^	zyx*wv
13	u	(+(-(/^	zyx*wvu
14	)	(+(-	zyx*wvu^ /
15	*	(+(- *	zyx*wvu^ /
16	t	(+(-*	zyx*wvu^ /t
17	)	(+	zyx*wvu^ /t*-
18	*	(+ *	zyx*wvu^ /t*-
19	s	(+ *	zyx*wvu^ /t*-s
20	)		zyx*wvu^ /t*-s*+

For example, suppose we have three subprograms **X, Y** and **Z**. Let **X** invokes **Y** and **Y** invokes **Z** then **Y** will not finish it's work until **Z** has finished and returned. Similarly **X** is the first to execute work, but is last to be finished. Thus, the sequence by which subprograms' activity proceed are summed up as the property **LIFO**. Assigning temporary storage areas for subprograms, by the machine is similar to the property of stack. The above discussion is illustrated in **Fig. 6.12.**

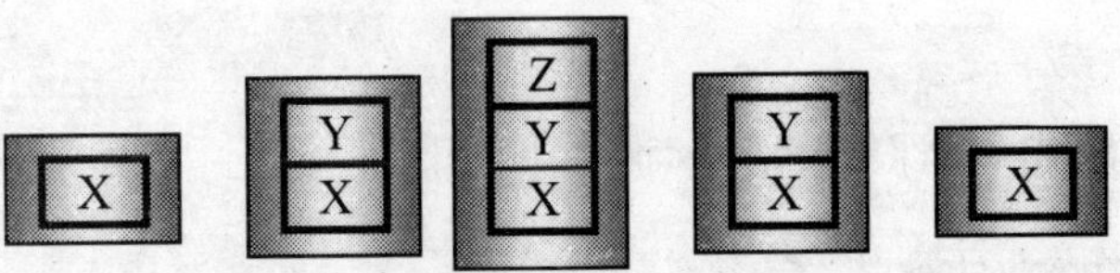

Fig. 6.12 Frames of the stack

Step 1: Initialize the stack.

Step 2: Scan the leftmost symbol in the given infix expression and denote it as the current input symbol.

Step 3: Repeat through **Step 6** while infix expression.

Step 4: Remove and output all stack symbols whose precedence values are greater than or equal to the precedence of the current input symbol.

Step 5: Push the current input symbols onto the stack.

Step 6: Scan the leftmost symbol in the infix expression and let it be the current input symbol.

Fig. 6.11 Algorithm to convert infix expression into Polish postfix form

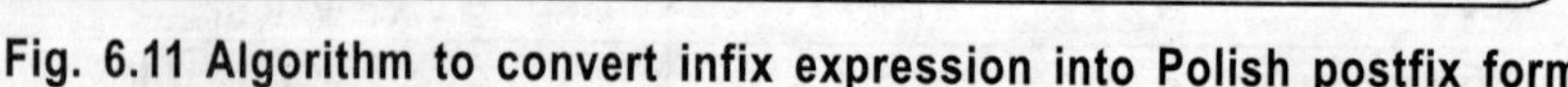

The program segment **POSTFIX.C** implements the algorithm illustrated in **Fig6.11.**

```
// POSTFIX.C
# include<iostream.h>
# include<stdio.h>
# include<string.h>
# include<ctype.h>
# include<stdlib.h>

# define Arnold '\0'
# define Blank ' '
# define Tab '\t'

#define Maxlen 64

static char infix [Maxlen+1], stack[Maxlen], postfix[Maxlen+1];

# define Empty (-1) /* empty stack */
static int top;

/* symbol types */

#define Operator (-10)
# define Operand (-20)
```

```
# define LeftParen (-30)
# define RightParen (-40)

static char *symbols = "()+-%*/";

// Symbol precedence

# define LeftParenPrec 0  /* ( */
# define AddPrec 1 /* + */
# define SubPrec 1 /* - */
# define MultPrec 2 /* * */
# define DivPrec 2 /* / */
# define RemPrec 2 /* % */
# define None 999 /* all else */
class Postfix
{
	public:
		void read_input(void);
		void infix_to_postfix(void);
		void write_output(void);
		void push(char symbol);
		char pop (void);

		int get_type(char );
		int get_prec(char );
		int white_space(char );

		void full_stack();
		void empty_stack();
};

// Function main

void main()
{
	Postfix Postorder;
	char ans[2];
	do
	{
		top = Empty; /* reset stack */
		Postorder.read_input();
		Postorder.infix_to_postfix();
		Postorder.write_output();

		// Selection
```

```
        printf("\n\n Another (y/n)");
        gets(ans);
    } while (toupper(ans[0]) == 'Y');
}

// Function infix to postfix conversion

void Postfix :: infix_to_postfix(void)
{
    int i,p, len, type, precedence;
    char next ;

    // i for infix, p for postfix

    i = p = 0;
    len = strlen(infix);

    // loop through input string
    while(i < len)
    {
        // Ignore whitepsce in infix expression
        if( !white_space(infix[i]))
        {
            type = get_type(infix[i]);
            switch(type)
            {
                // push left paren onto stack
            case LeftParen:
                push(infix[i]);
                break;

                // Pop stack until matching left paren
            case RightParen:
                while((next = pop()) != '(')
                    postfix[p++] = next;
                break;
            case Operand: postfix[p++] = infix[i];
                break;
// Pop stack until first operator of higher precedence and then stack this operator

            case Operator:
                precedence = get_prec(infix[i]);

                // Anything on stack to pop
                while(top > Empty && precedence<= get_prec(stack[top]))
                    postfix[p++] = pop();
```

```
                    push(infix[i]);
                    break;
                }
            }
            i++; // Next symbol in infix expression
        }

        // Pop any remaining operators

        while(top > Empty )
            postfix[p++] = pop();
        postfix[p] = Arnold ; // ensure a string
}

// Function to find operator type

int Postfix :: get_type(char symbol )
{
        switch(symbol)
        {
        case '(' :
            return (LeftParen);
        case ')':
            return (RightParen);
        case '+':
        case '-':
        case '%':
        case '*':
        case '/':
            return (Operator);
        default:
            return (Operand);
        }
}

// Find precedence of the operator

int Postfix :: get_prec(char symbol )
{
        switch(symbol)
        {
        case '+':
            return (AddPrec);
        case '-':
            return (SubPrec);
        case '*':
```

```
            return (MultPrec);
        case '/':
            return (DivPrec);
        case '%':
            return (RemPrec);
        case '(':
            return (LeftParenPrec);
        default:
            return (None);
        }
}

// Function push

void Postfix :: push(char symbol)
{
        // Check for overflow

        if(top > Maxlen)
            full_stack();
        else
            stack[++top] = symbol;
}

// Function pop

char Postfix :: pop(void)
{
        // check for underflow

        if (top <= Empty )
            empty_stack();
        else
            return (stack[top—]);
}

// Exit in case of overflow

void Postfix :: full_stack(void )
{
        cout<<"\n Full Stsck ... exiting. \n";
        exit(1);
}

// Exit in case of underflow
```

```
void Postfix :: empty_stack(void)
{
      cout<<"\n Empty Stack ... exiting \n";
      exit(2);
}

// Input function

void Postfix :: read_input(void)
{
      printf("\n Infix (up to %d chars): ", Maxlen);
      gets(infix);
}

// Output function

void Postfix :: write_output(void)
{
      cout<<"\n Infix: "<< infix;
      cout<<"\n Postfix: "<<postfix;
}

// Function white space checking

int Postfix :: white_space(char symbol)
{
      return( symbol == Blank || symbol == Tab || symbol == Arnold);
}
```

```
Infix (up to 64 chars): a+b*c/d
Infix: a+b*c/d
Postfix: abc*d/+


Another (y/n) y
Infix (up to 64 chars): x+y*q-w/t
Infix: x+y*q-w/t
Postfix: xyq*+wt/-

Another (y/n) n
```

6.4.1.1 EVALUATION OF THE POSTFIX EXPRESSION

Let **E** is an arithmetic expression written in Polish postfix notation. We add a right parenthesis ')' at the end of **E**. Now we scan **E** from left to right. If an operand is encountered it is put on the stack. If an operator **op** is encountered then we remove the two top elements of stack, let **x** is the top element and **y** is the next top element, we evaluate **x op y** and place the result back on the stack. We repeat this process until we get last element of the stack that is right parenthesis ')'. Suppose the expression **E** is as follows:

E: 2 3 10 + * 8 2 / -

The equivalent infix expression is

I: 2 * (3 + 10) – 8 / 2

E :	2	3	10	+	*	8	2	/	-	)
Label:	1	2	3	4	5	6	7	8	9	10

The evaluation procedure is given **Table 6.2.**

Table 6.2

Label Number	Symbol Scanned	Stack Contents
1	2	2
2	3	2 3
3	10	2 3 10
4	+	2 13
5	*	26
6	8	26 8
7	2	26 8 2
8	/	26 4
9	-	22
10	)	

6.5 QUEUES

This is a linear data structure used to represent a linear list and permits deletion to be performed at one end of the list and the insertion at the other. The information in such a list is processed in the same order as it was received, that is on **first-come-first-serve** basis **(FCFS)**.

An example of queue is time sharing computer system where many users share the system simultaneously. The procedure, which is used to design such type of system, is **Round Robin Technique.** The railway reservation counter is also an example of queue where the people collect their tickets on the **first-come-first-serve** basis.

6.5.1 IMPLEMENTATION OF QUEUES

Two common ways in which queues may be implemented are as follows:

- *Arrays*
- *Pointers (One way linear linked list)*

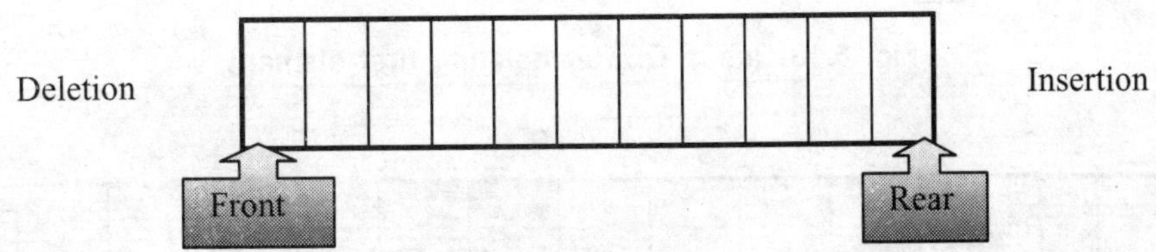

Fig. 6.13 Queue

A queue has two pointers **Front** and **Rear**, pointing to the front and rear elements of the queue, respectively. Consider a queue **Q** consisting of **n** elements and an element **Value,** which we have to insert into the **Q**. The value NULL (0) of front pointer implies an empty queue. **Fig. 6.13** illustrates a queue and **Fig. 6.14** illustrates a queue with the help of vector.

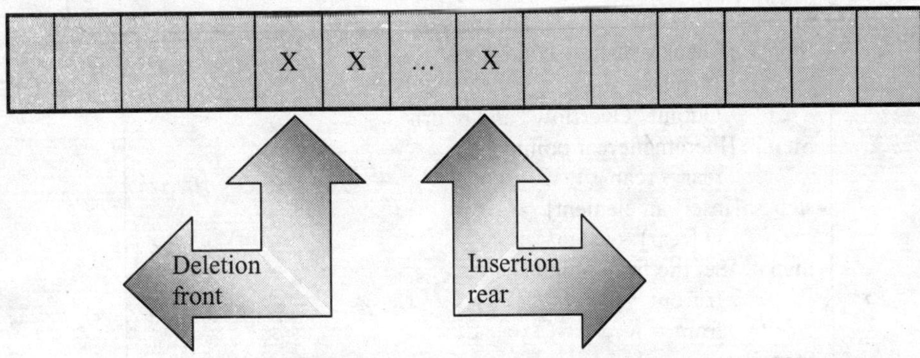

Fig. 6.14 vector representation of a queue

For example, suppose **Q** has 40 elements. But at present there are only 4 elements in the queue. **Fig. 6.15** illustrates the **Q.**

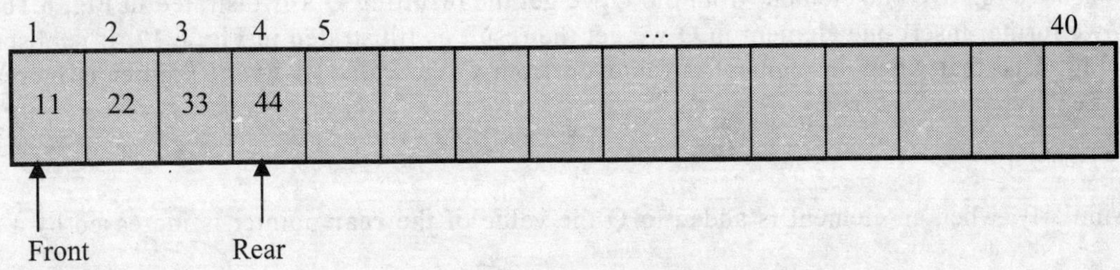

Fig. 6.15 Queue Q in memory

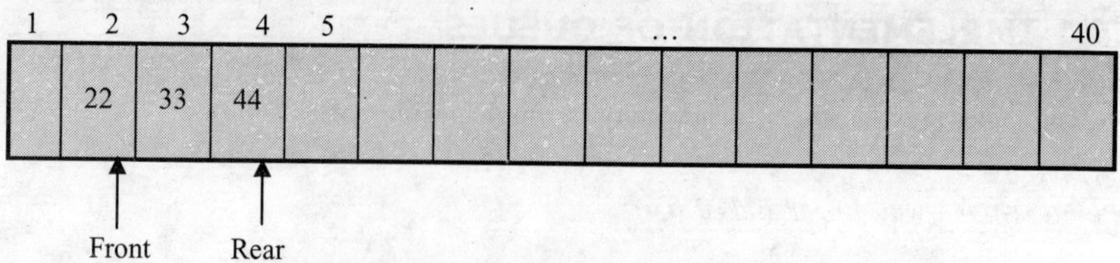

Fig. 6.16 Queue Q after deleting first element

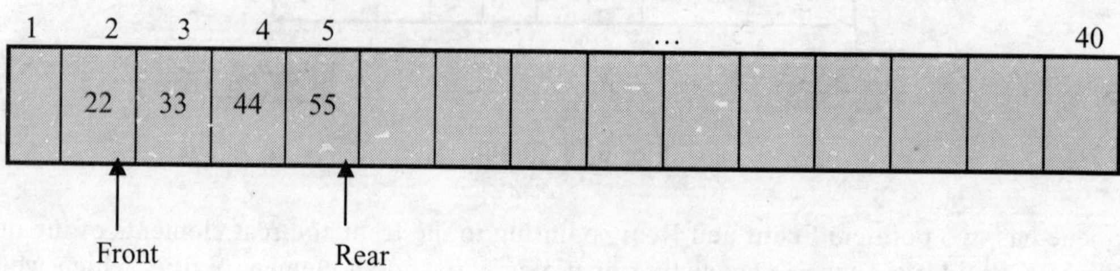

Fig. 6.17 Queue Q after inserting one element

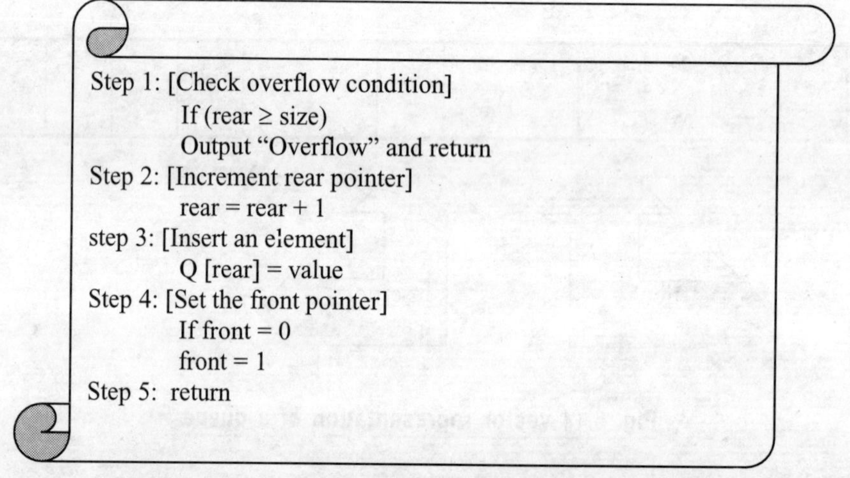

Fig. 6.18 algorithm to insert an element in a queue

When we remove one element from the **Q** we get the resulting **Q** as illustrated in **Fig. 6.16** and when we further insert one element in **Q** we get the result as illustrated in **Fig. 6.17.** It is observed from **Fig. 6.16** that when an element is removed from **Q** the value of **Front** pointer is increased by 1, i.e.,

Front = Front + 1.

Similarly, when an element is added to **Q** the value of the **rear** pointer is increased by 1 that is:

Rear = Rear + 1

The deletion algorithm is illustrated in **Fig. 6.19.**

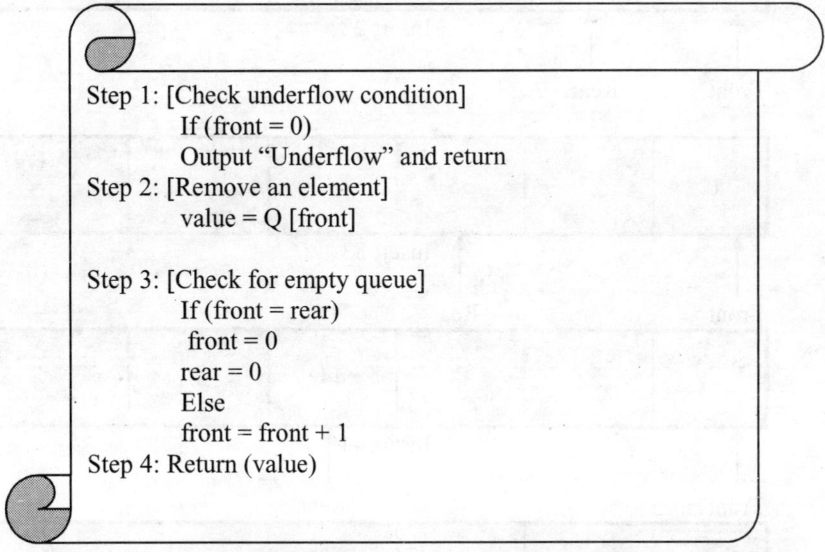

Fig. 6.19 Deletion algorithm for queue

When we continue insertion of elements in **Q** then after a stage we have **Rear = 40**, i.e., the **Rear** pointer points to end of the array. Now suppose we still want to insert an element into the queue then this can be done by moving entire queue to the beginning of the array, changing **Front** and **Rear** pointers value accordingly and then inserting an element into the queue. But for an array, such operation is time consuming and expensive. Here, circular queue comes as a solution, which we shall discuss in {6.6}. **Fig. 6.18** illustrates the insertion algorithm. For example, consider a queue, which has 6 rooms. Initially the queue is empty. It is required to insert integers 11, 22, 33, 44, remove 11 and 22 and then insert 55, 66 and 77. **Fig. 6.20** illustrates the trace of above problem.

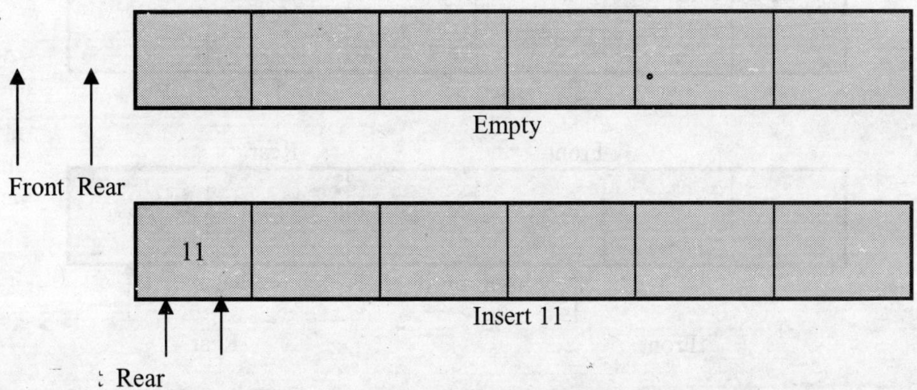

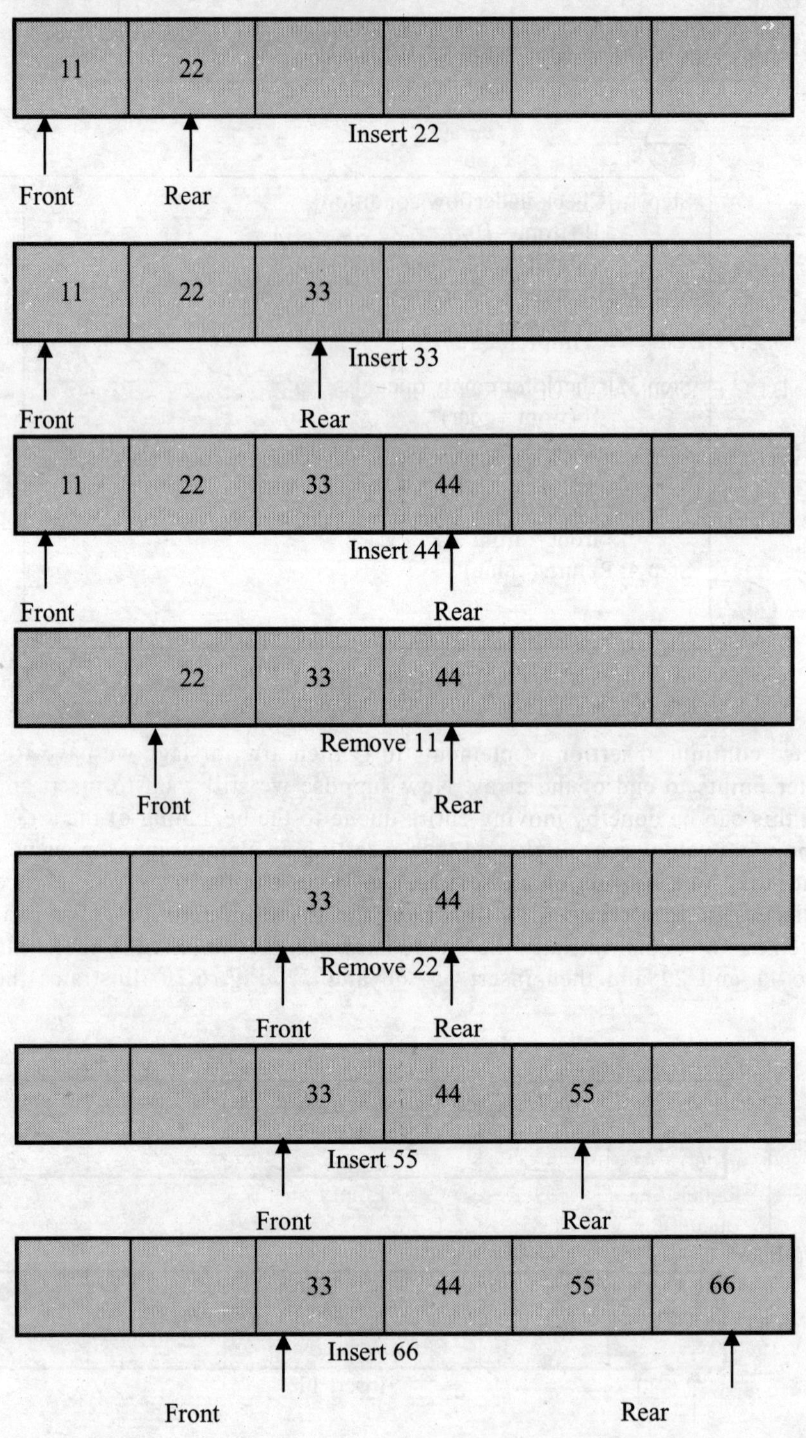
11
22
Insert 22
Front
Rear
11
22
33
Insert 33
Front
Rear
11
22
33
44
Insert 44
Front
Rear
22
33
44
Remove 11
Front
Rear
33
44
Remove 22
Front
Rear
33
44
55
Insert 55
Front
Rear
33
44
55
66
Insert 66
Front
Rear

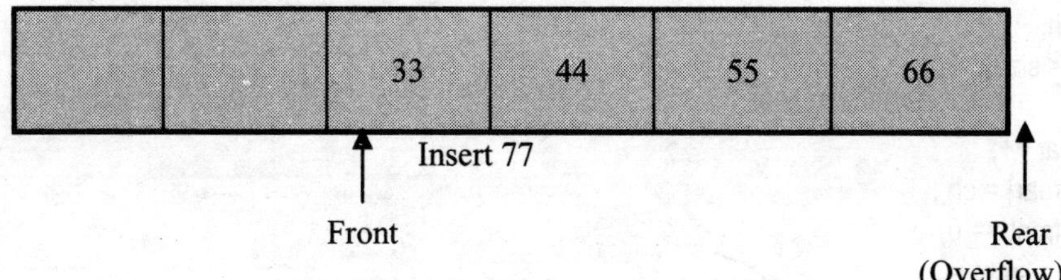

Fig. 6.20 Trace of a queue

When we try to insert integer 77 overflow occur even though the first two rooms are free. The program segment **QUEUE_A.C** implements the algorithm given in **Fig. 6.18** and **Fig. 6.19.**

```
// INSERTION AND DELETION IN A QUEUE ARRAY IMPLEMENTATION
// QUEUE_A.C

# include<iostream.h>
# include<stdio.h>
# include<string.h>
# include<ctype.h>
# include<stdlib.h>

# define size 10

class Queue
{
    public:
        int rear, front;
        int ch;
        int q[size];

    public:
        Queue()
        {
            rear = front = 0;
        }

        void Insert_queue();
        void Delete_queue();
        void Display_queue();
};

// Function to create queue

void Queue :: Insert_queue()
{
    cout<<"\n Input the element:";
```

```
        cin>>ch;
        if(rear < size)
        {
            rear ++;
            q[rear] = ch ;
            if(front == 0)
                front = 1;
        }
        else
            cout<<"\nQueue is overflow";
}
```

```
// Function to perform delete operation

void Queue :: Delete_queue() //char q[], char ch)
{
        if (front == 0)
        {
            cout<<"\nUnderflow";
            return ;
        }
        else
        {
            ch = q[front];

            cout<<"\nElement deleted :"<<ch;
        }
        if(front == rear)
        {
            front = 0;
            rear = 0;
        }
        else
            front = front + 1;
}

// Output function

void Queue :: Display_queue()  //char q[])
{
        if (front == 0)
            return;
        for( int i = front ; i <= rear; i++)
            cout<<" "<<q[i];
}
```

```
//Function main

void main()
{
    Queue Q;
    int k = 0;
    char choice;

    do
    {
        cout<<"\nInsert->i Delete->d Quit->q:";
        cout<<"\nInput the choice : ";
        do
        {
            cin>>choice;
            choice = tolower(choice);
        }while(strchr("idq",choice)==NULL);
        cout<<"Your choice is ->"<<choice;

        switch(choice)
        {
        case 'i':
            Q.Insert_queue();
            cout<<"\nQueue after inserting ";
            Q.Display_queue();
            break;

        case 'd':
            Q.Delete_queue();
            cout<<"\nQueue content after deleteion is as follows:\n";
            Q.Display_queue();
            break;

        case 'q':
            k = 1;
        }
    } while(!k);
}
```

```
Insert->i Delete->d Quit->q:
Input the choice: i
Your choice is -> i
Input the element: 11
Queue after inserting  11
Insert->i Delete->d Quit->q:
Input the choice: i
Your choice is -> i
Input the element: 22
Queue after inserting  11 22
Insert->i Delete->d Quit->q:
Input the choice: i
Your choice is -> i
Input the element: 33
Queue after inserting  11 22 33
Insert->i Delete->d Quit->q:
Input the choice: i
Your choice is -> i
Input the element: 44
Queue after inserting  11 22 33 44
Insert->i Delete->d Quit->q:
Input the choice: d
Your choice is -> d
Element deleted: 11
Queue content after deletion is as follows:
22 33 44
```

```
Insert->i Delete->d Quit->q:
Input the choice: d
Your choice is -> d
Element deleted: 22
Queue content after deletion is as follows:
33 44
Insert->i Delete->d Quit->q:
Input the choice: i
Your choice is -> i

Input the element: 66
Queue after inserting  33 44 66
Insert->i Delete->d Quit->q:
Input the choice: i
Your choice is -> i
Input the element: 77
Queue after inserting  33 44 66 77
Insert->i Delete->d Quit->q:
Input the choice: d
Your choice is -> d
Element deleted: 33
Queue content after deletion is as follows:
44 66 77
Insert->i Delete->d Quit->q:
Input the choice: d
Your choice is -> d
Element deleted: 44
Queue content after deletion is as follows:
66 77
Insert->i Delete->d Quit->q:
Input the choice: i
Your choice is -> i
Input the element: 88
Queue after inserting  66 77 88
Insert->i Delete->d Quit->q:
Input the choice: q
Your choice is ->q
```

6.6 CIRCULAR QUEUES

Let we have an array **Q** that contains **n** elements in which **Q[1]** comes after **Q[n]** in the array. When this technique is used to construct a queue then the queue is called circular queue. In other word we can say that a queue is called circular when the last room comes just before the first room. **Fig. 6.21** illustrates a circular queue.

In a circular queue when **Rear = n,** if we insert an element then this element is assigned to **Q [1].** That is instead of increasing rear to **n + 1,** we reset **rear** to 1. Similarly, if **Front** = **n** and an element of the queue is removed, we reset **Front** to 1 instead of **n + 1**. Suppose queue contains only one element that is **Front** = **Rear** = **1** and suppose that the element is removed then the **Front** and **Rear** pointers are now assigned NULL to indicate that the queue is empty.

Suppose we have a circular queue with 6 rooms that is **n** = **6**. Insert 99, 88, 66, 55 and 44 remove 99 and 88 then insert 33, 22 and 11. The trace of this operation is illustrated in **Fig. 6.22.**

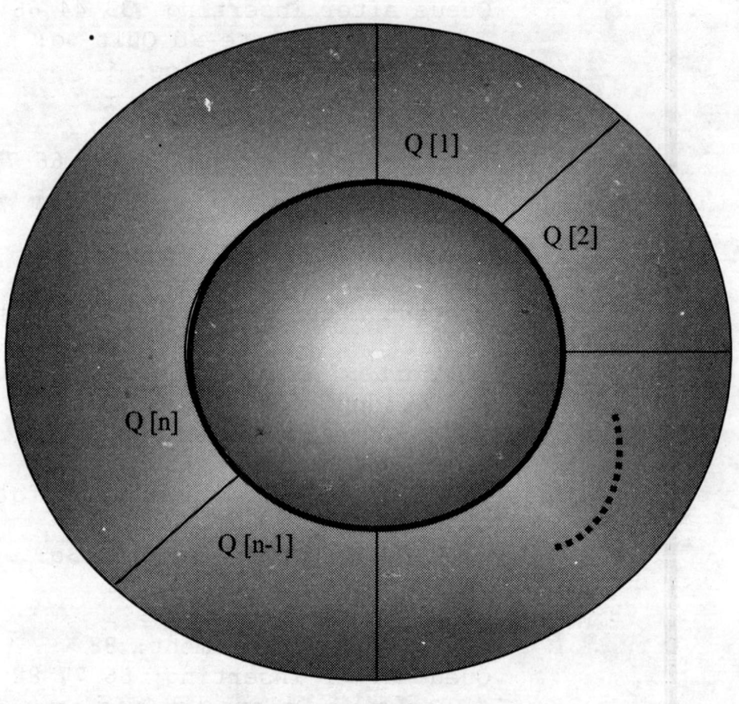

Fig. 6.21 Circular queue

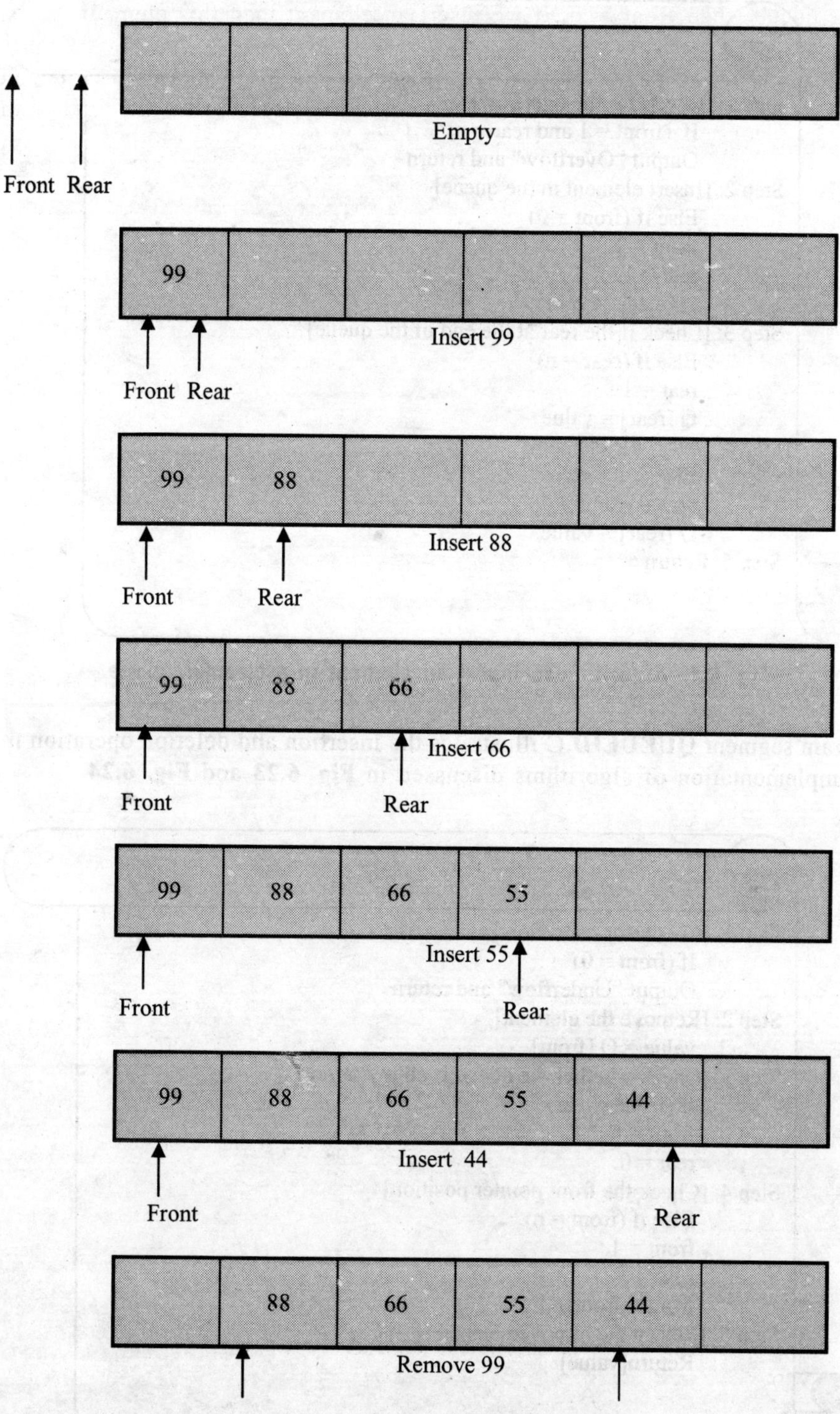

Fig. 6.22 Trace of a circular queue

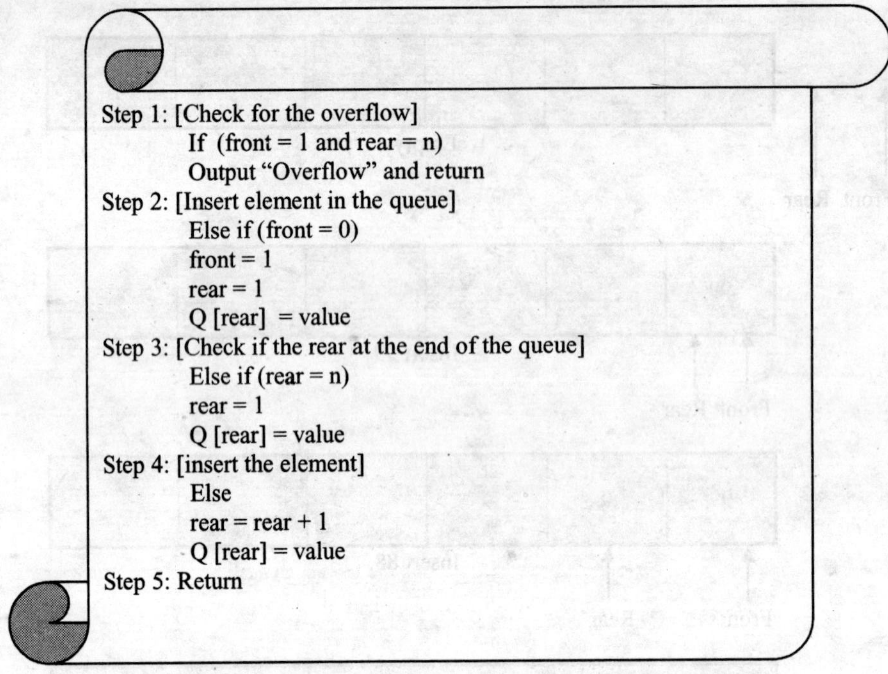

Step 1: [Check for the overflow]
If (front = 1 and rear = n)
Output "Overflow" and return
Step 2: [Insert element in the queue]
Else if (front = 0)
front = 1
rear = 1
Q [rear] = value
Step 3: [Check if the rear at the end of the queue]
Else if (rear = n)
rear = 1
Q [rear] = value
Step 4: [insert the element]
Else
rear = rear + 1
Q [rear] = value
Step 5: Return

Fig. 6.23 Algorithm to insert an element in a circular queue

The program segment **QUEUEID.C** illustrates the insertion and deletion operation in a circular queue. It is implementation of algorithms discussed in **Fig. 6.23** and **Fig. 6.24.**

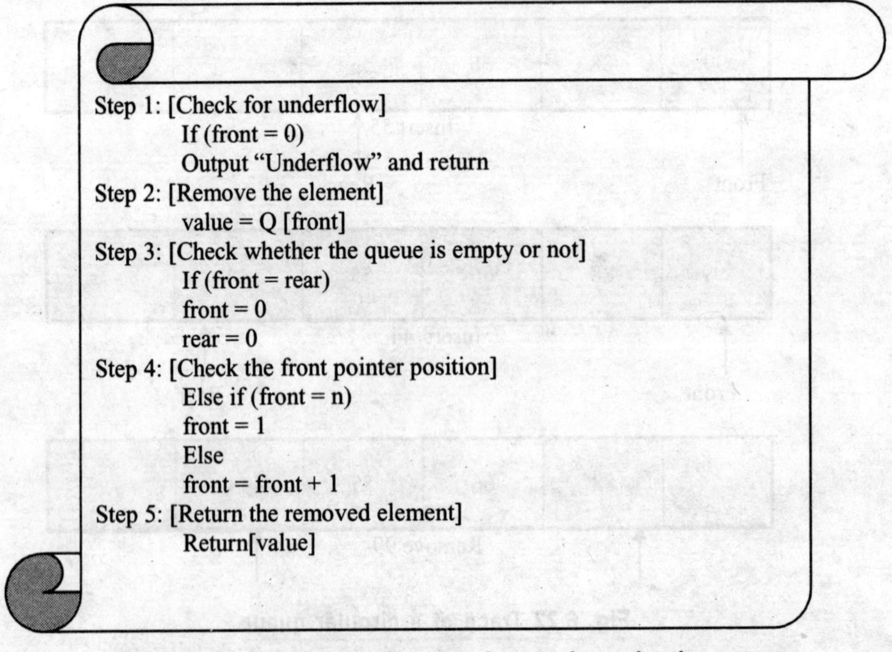

Step 1: [Check for underflow]
If (front = 0)
Output "Underflow" and return
Step 2: [Remove the element]
value = Q [front]
Step 3: [Check whether the queue is empty or not]
If (front = rear)
front = 0
rear = 0
Step 4: [Check the front pointer position]
Else if (front = n)
front = 1
Else
front = front + 1
Step 5: [Return the removed element]
Return[value]

Fig. 6.24 Algorithm to delete an element in a circular queue

```
// INSERTION AND DELETION IN A CIRCULAR QUEUE ARRAY MPLEMENTATION
// QUEUEID.C

# include<iostream.h>
# include<stdio.h>
# include<string.h>
# include<ctype.h>
# include<stdlib.h>
# define size 6

int L, U; // L means lower bound U means upper bound

class Queue
{
	public:
		int rear, front;
		int ch;
		int q[size];

	public:

		Queue()
		{
			rear = front = -1;
		}

		void Insert_queue();
		void Delete_queue();
		void Display_queue();
};

// Function to create queue
void Queue :: Insert_queue()
{
	if ((front == 0) && (rear == size-1))
	{
		cout<<"\n Overflow";
		rear = 1;
		return;
	}
	else
		if (front < 0) // Insert first element
		{
			front = 0;
			rear = 0;
			cout<<"\nInput the element :";
```

```
            cin>>ch;
            q[rear] = ch ;
        }
        else
            if (rear == size-1)
            {
                rear = 0;
                cout<<"\n Input the element :";
                cin>>ch;
                q[rear] = ch ;
            }
            else
            {
                rear ++;
                cout<<"\n Input the element :";
                cin>>ch;
                q[rear] = ch ;
            }
}

// Function to perform deletion operation
void Queue :: Delete_queue()
{
    if (front < 0)
    {
        cout<<"\nUnderflow";
        return ;
    }
    ch = q[front];
    q[front] = NULL;
    cout<<"\nElement deleted :"<<ch;
    if(front == rear)
    {
        front = -1;
        rear = -1;
    }
    else
        if ( front == size-1)
        {
            front = 0;
        }
        else
        {
            front++ ;
        }
```

```
// Output function
void Queue :: Display_queue()
{
	if (front < 0)
		return;
	if ( rear >= front)
	{
		for( int i = front; i <= rear; i++)
		{
			cout <<"\n i="<<i;
			cout<<" "<<q[i];
		}
	}
	else
	{
		for( int i = front; i < size; i++)
		{
			cout <<"\n i="<<i;
			cout<<" "<<q[i];
		}
		for( i = 0; i <= rear; i++)
		{
			cout <<"\n i="<<i;
			cout<<" "<<q[i];
		}
	}
}

//Function main
void main()
{
	Queue Q;
	int k = 0;
	char choice;

	do
	{
		cout<<"\nInsert->i Delete->d Quit->q:";
		cout<<"\nInput the choice : ";
		do
		{
			cin>>choice;
			choice = tolower(choice);
		}while(strchr("idq",choice)==NULL);
		cout<<"Your choice is ->"<<choice;
```

```
        switch(choice)
        {
        case 'i' :
            Q.Insert_queue();
            cout<<"\nQueue after inserting ";
            Q.Display_queue();
            break;

        case 'd' :
            Q.Delete_queue();
            cout<<"\nQueue content after deleteion is as follows:\n";
            Q.Display_queue();
            break;

        case 'q':
            k = 1;
        }
    } while(!k);
}
```

```
Insert->i Delete->d Quit->q:
Input the choice: i
Your choice is -> i
Input the element: 11
Queue after inserting
i=0 11
Insert->i Delete->d Quit->q:
Input the choice: i
Your choice is -> i
Input the element: 22
Queue after inserting
i=0 11
i=1 22
```

```
Insert->i Delete->d Quit->q:
Input the choice: i
Your choice is -> i
Input the element: 55
Queue after inserting
i=0 11
i=1 22
i=2 55
Insert->i Delete->d Quit->q:
Input the choice: i
Your choice is -> i
Input the element: 66
Queue after inserting
i=0 11
i=1 22
i=2 55
i=3 66
Insert->i Delete->d Quit->q:
Input the choice: d
Your choice is -> d
Element deleted: 11
Queue content after deletion is as follows:
i=1 22
i=2 55
i=3 66
Insert->i Delete->d Quit->q:
Input the choice: d
Your choice is -> d
Element deleted: 22
Queue content after deletion is as follows:
i=2 55
i=3 66
Insert->i Delete->d Quit->q:
Input the choice: i
Your choice is -> i
Input the element: 77
Queue after inserting
i=2 55
i=3 66
i=4 77
Insert->i Delete->d Quit->q:
Input the choice: i
Your choice is -> i
Input the element: 88
Queue after inserting
i=2 55
i=3 66
i=4 77
i=5 88
```

```
Insert->i Delete->d Quit->q:
Input the choice: i
Your choice is -> i
Input the element: 99
Queue after inserting
i=2 55
i=3 66
i=4 77
i=5 88
i=0 99
Insert->i Delete->d Quit->q:
Input the choice: q
Your choice is -> q
```

6.7 DOUBLE ENDED QUEUE

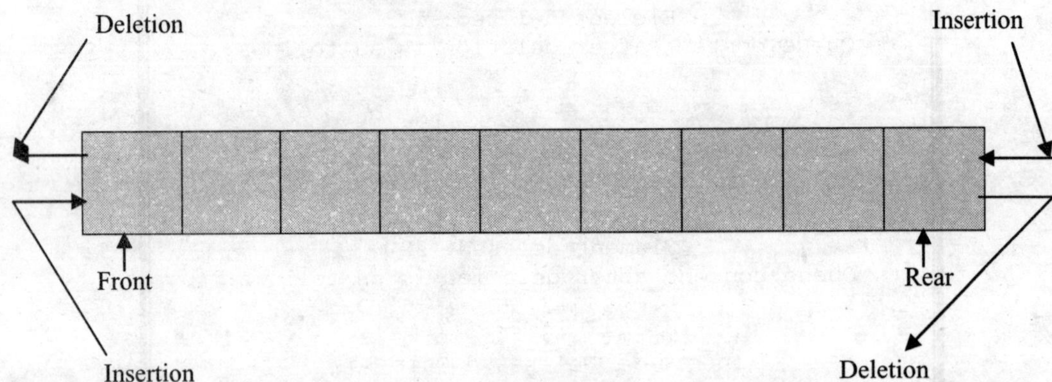

Fig. 6.25 Deque

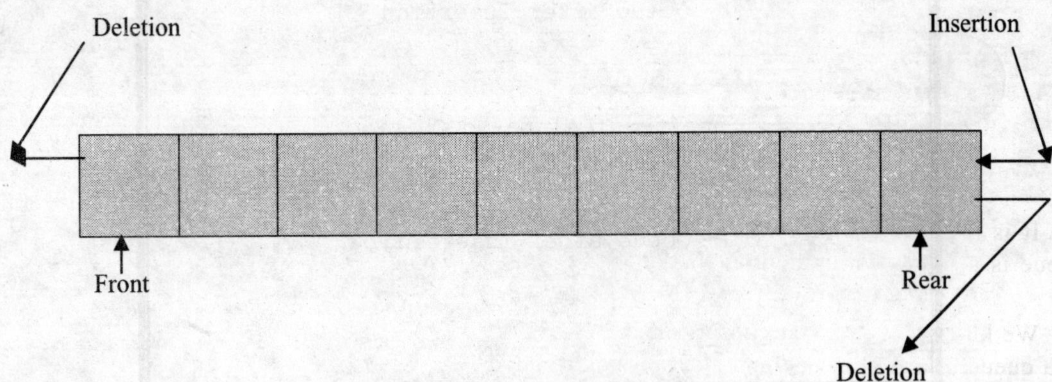

Fig. 6.26 Input restricted deque

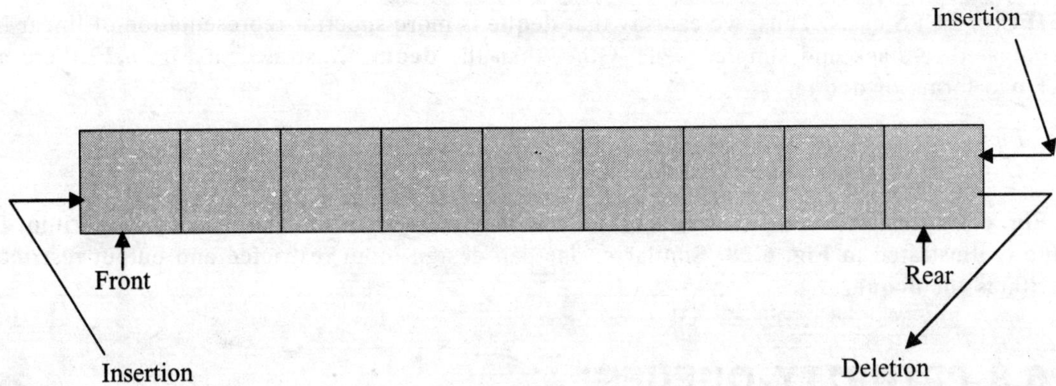

Fig. 6.27 Output restricted deque

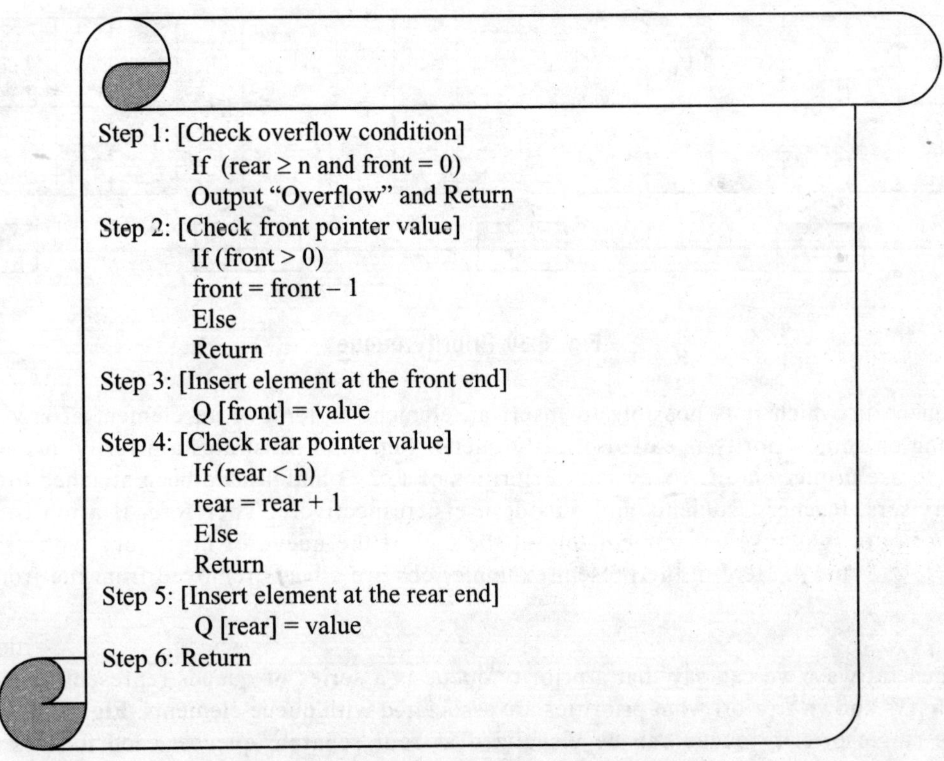

```
Step 1: [Check overflow condition]
        If (rear ≥ n and front = 0)
        Output "Overflow" and Return
Step 2: [Check front pointer value]
        If (front > 0)
        front = front – 1
        Else
        Return
Step 3: [Insert element at the front end]
        Q [front] = value
Step 4: [Check rear pointer value]
        If (rear < n)
        rear = rear + 1
        Else
        Return
Step 5: [Insert element at the rear end]
        Q [rear] = value
Step 6: Return
```

Fig. 6.28 Algorithm for insertion in deque

It is a linear list in which insertion and deletions are possible at either end. Double-ended queue is also known as **deque**. **Fig. 6.25** represents a **deque**.

We know that in a stack insertions and deletions are possible only at one end (**LIFO).** While in a queue insertion at one end and deletion at other end. That is operation in queue is performed in **FIFO** or **FCFS** basis. Thus, we can say that **deque** is more superior representation of linear list as compared to stack and simple queue. Other than the **deque** illustrated in **Fig. 6.25** there are other two forms of **deque**.

- *Input restricted* ***deque*** *[Insertion at one end]*
- *Output restricted* ***deque*** *[Deletion at one end]*

Fig. 6.26 illustrates a **deque** and **Fig. 6.27** with input restricted. The insertion algorithm for **deque** is illustrated in **Fig. 6.28.** Similarly, one can design input restricted and output restricted algorithms for **deque**.

6.8 PRIORITY QUEUES

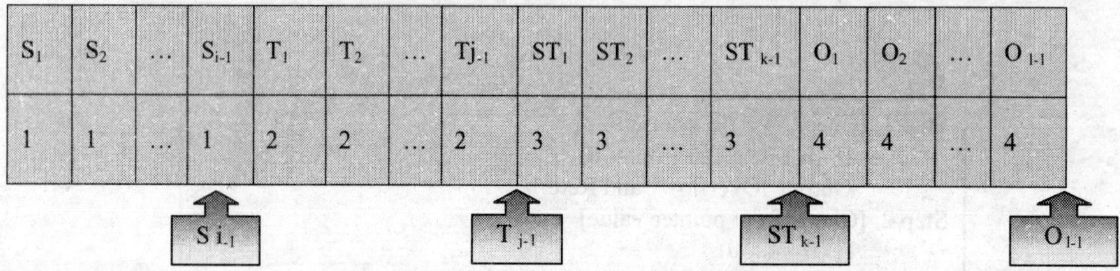

Fig. 6.30 Priority queue

A queue in which it is possible to insert an element or remove an element at any position depending on some priority is called priority queue. **Fig. 6.30** illustrates a priority queue of jobs waiting to use printer on a **LAN** system. Priorities of 1, 2, 3 and 4 have been attached to the jobs of supervisors, teachers, students and outside users, respectively. Therefore, if a job is initiated with priority **p**, it is inserted immediately at the end of the queue of other jobs with priority **p,** for **p** = 1, 2, 3 and 4. Here in the present example jobs are always removed from the front of the queue.

In general way, we can say that a priority queue is a series of queues representing situations in which it is known a priori what priorities are associated with queue elements. **Fig. 6.31** illustrates how the single priority queue can be visualized as four separate queues; each follows a **FIFO** behaviour. The elements in the second queue are removed only when the first queue is empty, elements from the third queue are removed only when the first and second queues are empty and so on. This separation of a single priority queue into a series of queues also suggests an efficient storage representation of a priority queue. When the elements are added, they are always added at the end of one of the queues as determined by priority. If one uses a single sequential storage structure for the priority queue then insertion may mean that the new element must be placed in the middle of the queue. This can require the movement of several elements. Thus, we can say that it is better to split a priority queue in several queues, each having its own storage structure.

Let telephone department contains the list of telephone holders in their alphabetical order. Suppose some new users we have to add into the list at their proper place. It means we have to insert new users some where in middle, it will require more and more processing time if the list is very large. The remedies for it to divide the list into 26 sub-lists then the processing automatically will be reduced. If it is required to sort the list use radix technique for efficient processing. **Fig. 6.32** illustrates such type of representation.

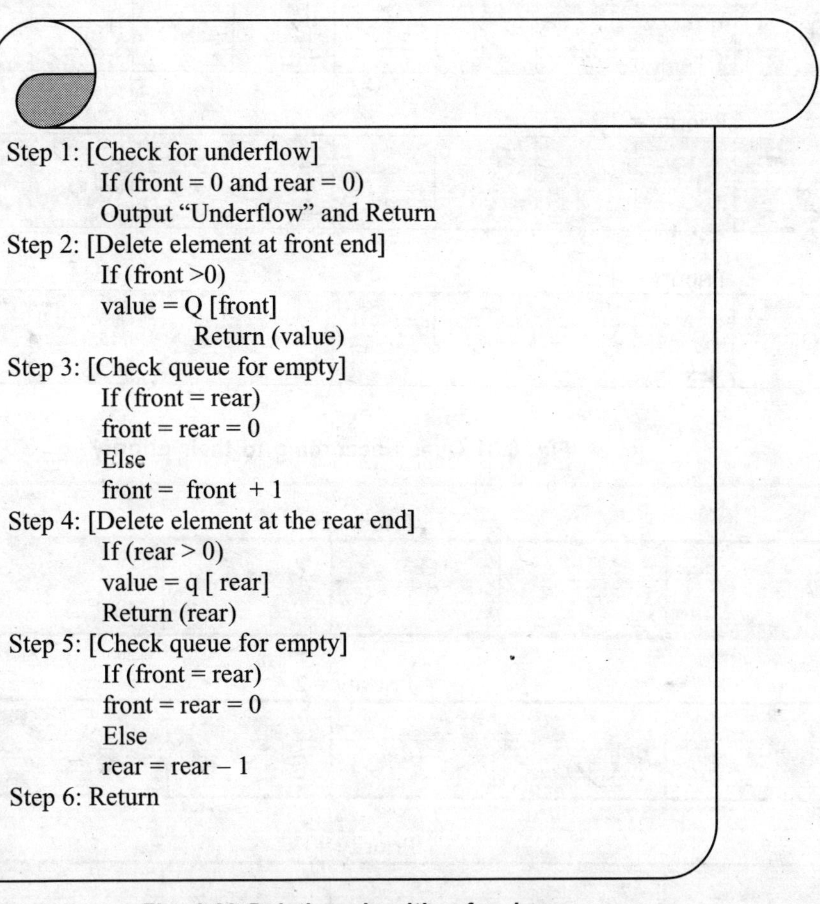

```
Step 1: [Check for underflow]
        If (front = 0 and rear = 0)
        Output "Underflow" and Return
Step 2: [Delete element at front end]
        If (front >0)
        value = Q [front]
              Return (value)
Step 3: [Check queue for empty]
        If (front = rear)
        front = rear = 0
        Else
        front =  front  + 1
Step 4: [Delete element at the rear end]
        If (rear > 0)
        value = q [ rear]
        Return (rear)
Step 5: [Check queue for empty]
        If (front = rear)
        front = rear = 0
        Else
        rear = rear – 1
Step 6: Return
```

Fig. 6.29 Deletion algorithm for deque

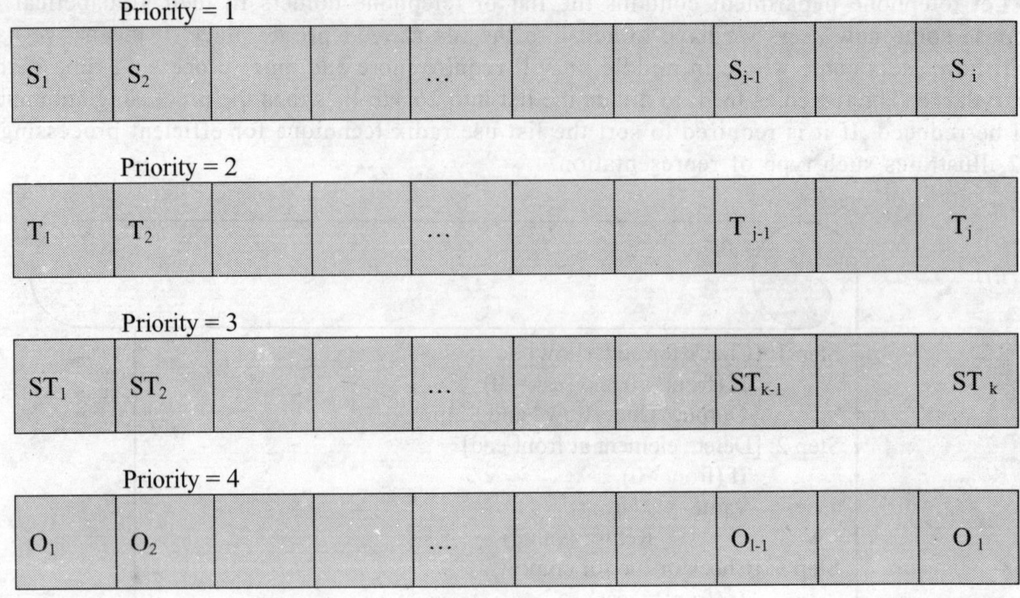

Fig. 6.31 Queue according to their priority

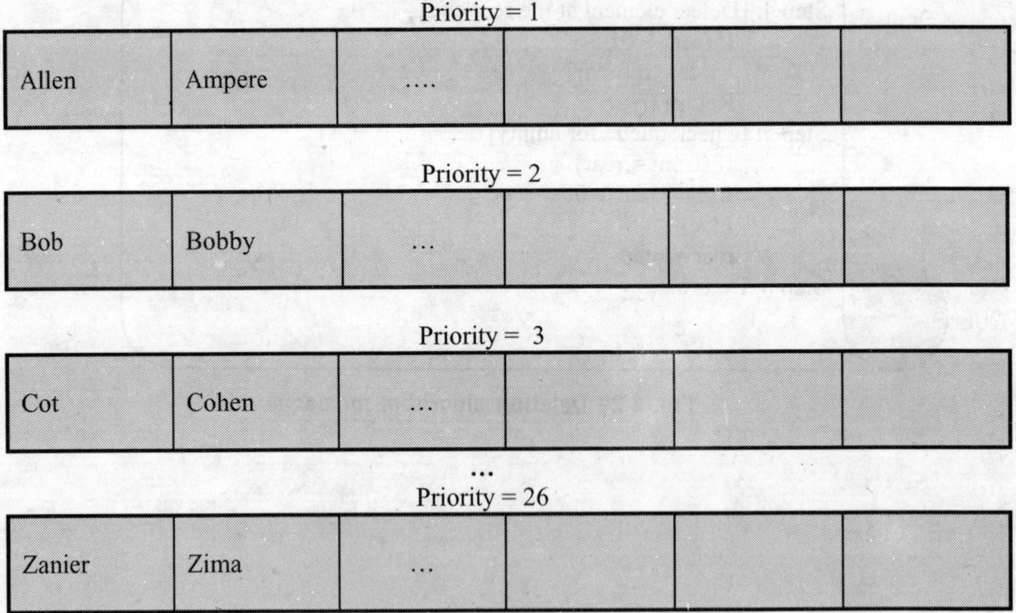

Fig. 6.32 Alphabetized list of telephone holders

EXERCISE

6.1 *Translate the following infix expression into its equivalent postfix expression:*

(i) (x-y) * ((z+v) / f)
(ii) ((a+b)/d↑ ((e-f) + g)
(iii) 12/3*6+6-6+8/2

6.2 *Evaluate the following expressions:*

(i) 10+3 ↑ 2 – 8/2 * 6 – 7
(ii) 12-2 ↑ 3+10/2+4*2
(iii) 3+4/2+5-3*4+3

6.3 *Translate the following infix expression into its equivalent prefix expression:*

(i) (a+b) ↑ c – d / e * f – g
(ii) a – b ↑ c + d / e + f *g
(iii) c+d/e+a-b*c

6.4 *Consider the following postfix expression:*

(i) 5, 3, +, 2, *, 6, 9, 7, -, /, -
(ii) 6, 10, +, 12, 8, -, *, 8, 2,-, 4, ↑, +

Translate each expression into infix notation and then evaluate.

6.5 *Consider the following queue where **QUEUE** is allocated 10 rooms:*

Front = 2, Rear = 6
QUEUE: ________, Pauri, Bombay, Delhi, Chennai, Lucknow, _________, ________, _________, ________.

*Describe the **QUEUE**, including **Front** and **Rear**, as the following operations take place:*

(i) Ahmedabad is added
(ii) Two cities are deleted
(iii) Varanasi is added
(iv) Bangalore is added
(v) Goa is added
(vi) Four cities are deleted
(vii) Hyderabad is added

6.6 *Consider the following deque where **DEQUE** is allocated 10 rooms:*

Left = 3, Right = 6
DEQUE: ______, ______, Tokyo, Now York, London, Masco, ______, ______,
______, ______.

*Describe the **DEQUE** including **Left** and **Right** as following operations take place:*

(i) *Athens is added on the left*
(ii) *India is added on the right*
(iii) *Bombay is added on the right*
(iv) *Two cities are deleted from the left*
(v) *California is added on the right*
(vi) *UAE is added on the left*
(vii) *Two cities are deleted from the right*

6.7 *Suppose a queue is maintained by a circular array **QUEUE** with **n = 20** rooms. Find the number of elements in the **QUEUE**, if*

(i) *Front = 6 and Rear = 14*
(ii) *Front = 20 and Rear = 6*
(iii) *Front = 5, Rear = 15 and then two elements are deleted.*

6.8 *Consider the following **Stack** of fibonacci numbers:*

Stack: 0, 1, 1, 2, 3, 5, _____, _____, _____, _____.

(a) *Describe the **Stack** when the following operation take place:*

(i) *pop(Stack, 5)*
(ii) *push(Stack, Num)*
(iii) *push(Stack, Num)*
(iv) *pop(Stack, Num)*

(b) *Describe the stack if the operation **pop(Stack, Num)** deletes 3.*

6.9 *Suppose the following **Stack** of names is in memory where **Stack** is allocated **n = 10** rooms:*

TOP = 7
Stack: DON, RACHITA, MISTHI, TOM ALTER, NAFIZ, JEF, DONO MANN, _____, ______, ______.

Find the output of the following code slices:

(a)
```
pop(Stack, Name1)
pop(Stack, Name2)
push(Stack, Name3)
```

(c)

Do while (TOP ≠ 0)
pop (Stack, Name)
[End of loop]

6.10 *Write a program segment that uses a stack to read an integer and print all its prime divisors in ascending order. For example, with integer 2100 the output should be*

2, 2, 3, 5, 5, 7

6.11 *Write an algorithm that translates an infix expression into Polish prefix notation. Implement the designed algorithm with the help of stack.*

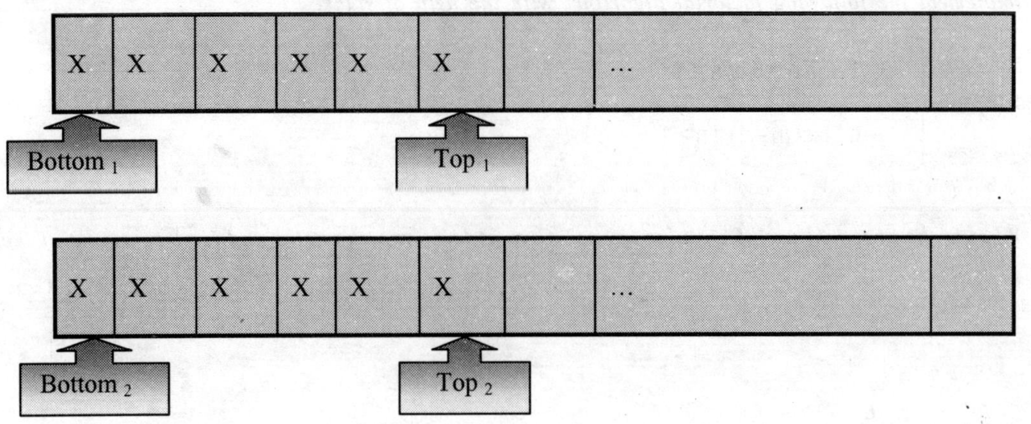

Fig. 6.33 stacks in memory

6.12 *Is it possible to implement a queue with the help of two stacks?*

6.13 *Implement a queue with the help of doubly linked list.*

6.14 *Implement a* ***deque*** *with the help of an array.*

6.15 *Implement a* ***deque*** *with the help of linear linked list.*

6.16 *Design an algorithm for a input restricted* ***deque****. Implement the designed algorithm.*

6.17 *Design an algorithm for a output restricted* ***deque.*** *Implement the designed algorithm.*

6.18 *Consider the grammar*

G = (V_N, V_T, S, P)

where

V_N = {<S>}
V_T = {a, b, c}
P = {<S> ::= a<S>a
<S> ::= b <S> b
<S> ::= c }

Implement it with the help of stack.

6.19 *Two stacks are given as illustrated in **Fig. 6.33,** join these stacks in such a way that the efficiency of stacks should not be affected.*

6.20 *Implement the following factorial algorithm with the help of stack:*

$$\text{fact}(n) = \begin{cases} 1 & \text{if } n = 0 \text{ or } n = 1 \\ n * \text{fact}(n-1) & \text{if } n > 1 \end{cases}$$

6.21 *What is the practical use of circular queue? Give at least two examples and implement one of them.*

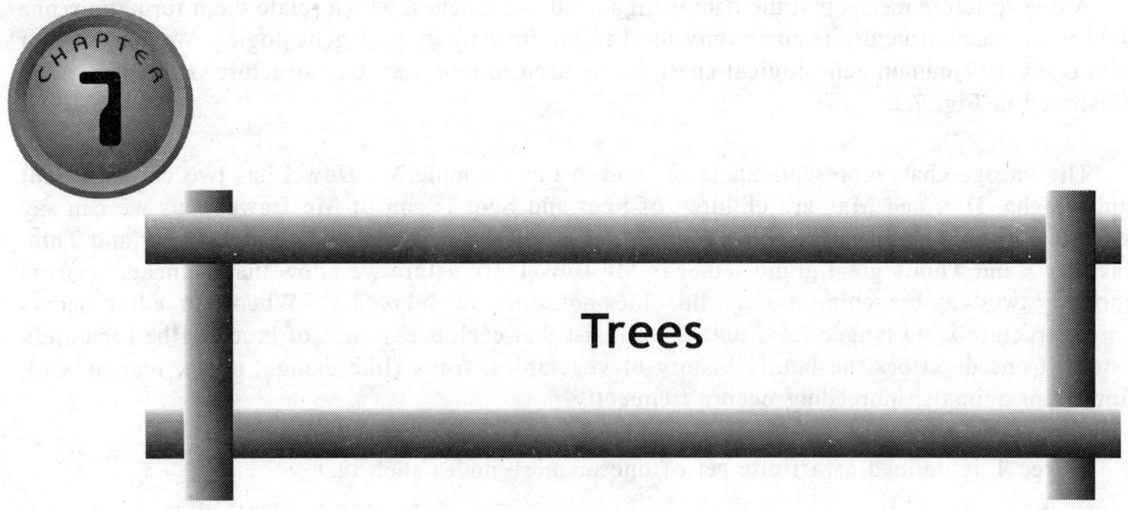

In this chapter we will explore one of the non-linear data-structure trees: Binary tree, Complete Binary tree, Expression tree, Search tree, B-tree, AVL tree. Operations possible on tree such as insertion, deletion and searching.

7.1 INTRODUCTION

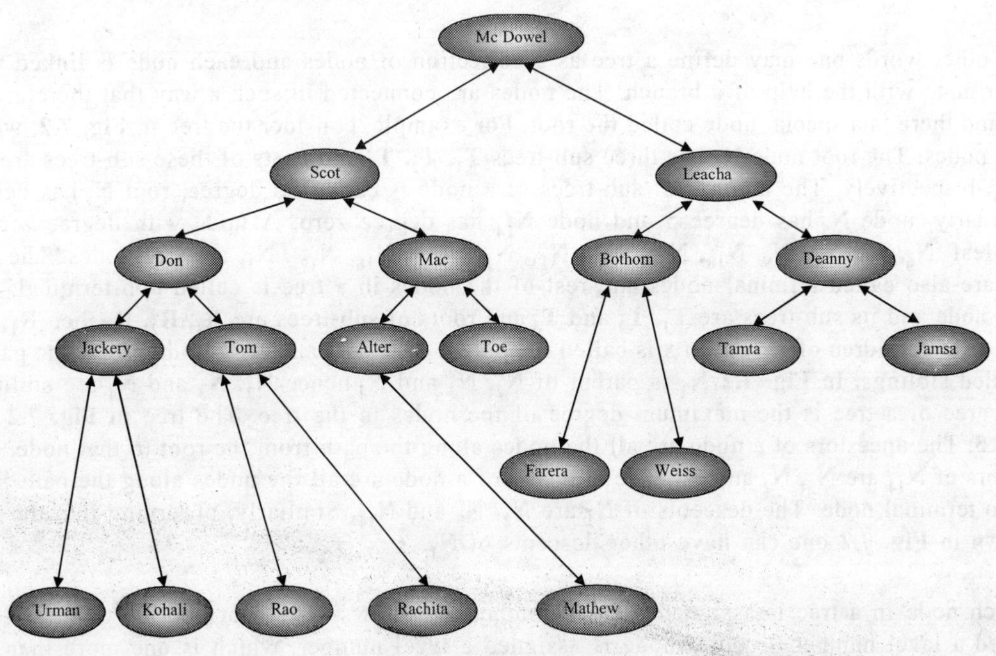

Fig. 7.1 Lineage Chart

A tree structure means that the data is organized as branches, which relate the information, one field where such structure is commonly used in the investigation of genealogies. We are familiar with one very common genealogical chart that is used to represent tree structure is lineage and is illustrated in **Fig. 7.1**.

The lineage chart represents ancestors and in this example **Mc Dowel** has two children **Scot** and **Leacha**. **Don** and **Mac** are children of **Scot** and **Scot** is son of **Mc Dowel** thus we can say that **Mc Dowel** is grand father of **Don** and **Mac**. Similarly, **Don** has two child **Jackery** and **Tom**. **Jackery**'s and **Tom**'s great grand father is **Mc Dowel**. By nature we know that a lineage chart is normally two-way branching, though this does not allow for inbreeding. When inbreeding occurs a tree structure is no longer valid unless we insist that each occurrence of breeding be separately listed. If one describes the family history of vegetables, fruits (like mango, apple, orange, etc), flowers or animals, inbreeding occurs frequently.

A tree **T** is defined as a finite set of one or more nodes such that

- *there is a special node called the root **R**.*
- *the remaining nodes are divided into **n** ³ 0 disjoint sets* $T_1, T_2, T_3 \ldots T_n$, *where each of these sets is a tree.* $T_1, T_2, T_3 \ldots T_n$ *is called the sub-trees of the root.*

For example, if we consider **Fig. 7.1** then we can say that **Mc Dowel** is father and **Scot** and **Leacha** are two sons of **Mc Dowel**. In other words we can say that **Mc Dowel** is root and the tree has two sub-trees whose roots are **Scot** and **Leacha.** The condition that $\mathbf{T_1, T_2, T_3 \ldots T_n}$ be disjoint sets prevents sub-trees from connecting with each other (No cross breeding) thus it follows that every element in a tree is the root of some sub-tree of the whole.

In other words one may define a tree as a collection of nodes and each node is linked with another node with the help of a branch. The nodes are connected in such a way that there are no loops and there is a special node called the root. For example, consider the tree in **Fig. 7.2**, which has 18 nodes. The root node N_1 has three sub-trees $\mathbf{T_1, T_2, T_3}$ and roots of these sub-trees are $\mathbf{N_2}$, $\mathbf{N_3}$, $\mathbf{N_4}$, respectively. The number of sub-trees of a node is called its degree, root $\mathbf{N_1}$ has degree 3. Similarly, node $\mathbf{N_5}$ has degree 5 and node $\mathbf{N_{14}}$ has degree zero. A node with degree zero is called leaf. $\mathbf{N_6, N_7, N_8, N_9, N_{10}, N_{11}, N_{12}, N_{13}, N_{14}, N_{15}, N_{16}, N_{17}, N_{18}}$ are leaf nodes. The leaf nodes are also called terminal nodes and rest of the nodes in a tree is called non-terminal. If **x** is root node and its sub-trees are $\mathbf{T_1}$, $\mathbf{T_2}$ and $\mathbf{T_3}$ and roots of sub-trees are $\mathbf{R_1, R_2, R_3}$ then $\mathbf{R_1, R_2, R_3}$ are called children of **x**. In turn **x** is called the parent of $\mathbf{R_1}$, $\mathbf{R_2}$ and $\mathbf{R_3}$. Children of same parent are called siblings. In **Fig. 7.2** $\mathbf{N_1}$ is parent of $\mathbf{N_2}$, $\mathbf{N_3}$ and $\mathbf{N_4}$ hence $\mathbf{N_2}$, $\mathbf{N_3}$ and $\mathbf{N_4}$ are siblings. The degree of a tree is the maximum degree of the nodes in the tree. The tree in **Fig. 7.2** has degree 5. The ancestors of a node are all the nodes along the path from the root to that node. The ancestors of $\mathbf{N_{14}}$ are $\mathbf{N_5}$, $\mathbf{N_2}$ and $\mathbf{N_1}$. The descents of a node are all the nodes along the path from node to terminal node. The descents of $\mathbf{N_1}$ are $\mathbf{N_2}$, $\mathbf{N_5}$ and $\mathbf{N_{14}}$. Similarly, observing into the tree **T** shown in **Fig. 7.2** one can have other descents of $\mathbf{N_1}$.

Each node in a tree is assigned a level number as follows- The root node **R** of the tree is assigned a level number 0, and a node is assigned a level number, which is one more than the level number of its parent (Root) of the sub-tree to which it belongs. The nodes, which are at the same level, are said to be of the same generation. The height or depth of a tree is the maximum number of nodes in a branch. This turns out to be one more than the largest level number of the tree.

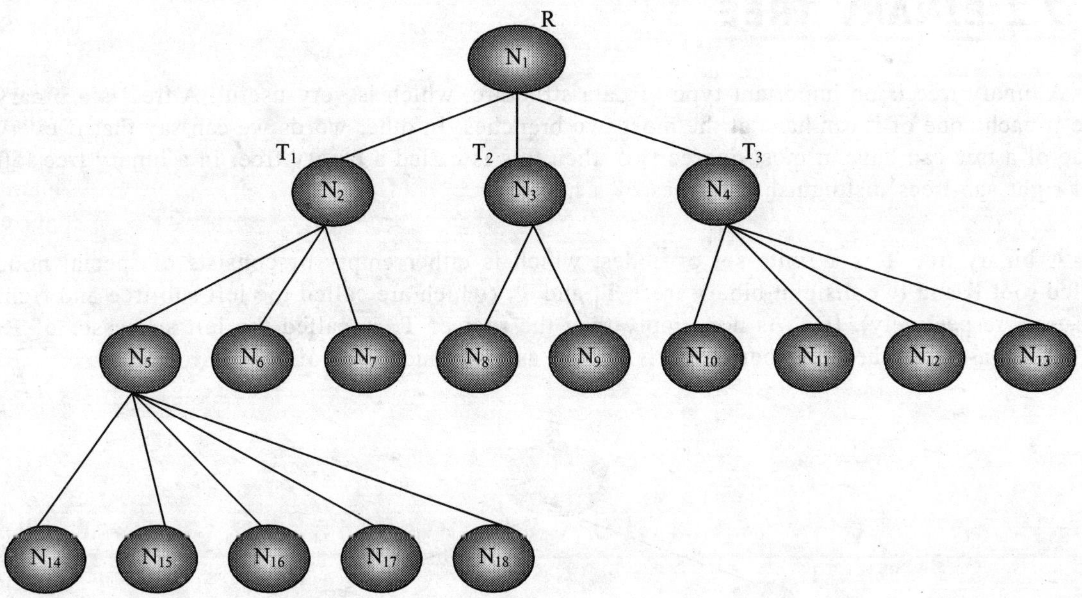

Fig. 7.2 Tree T with 18 nodes

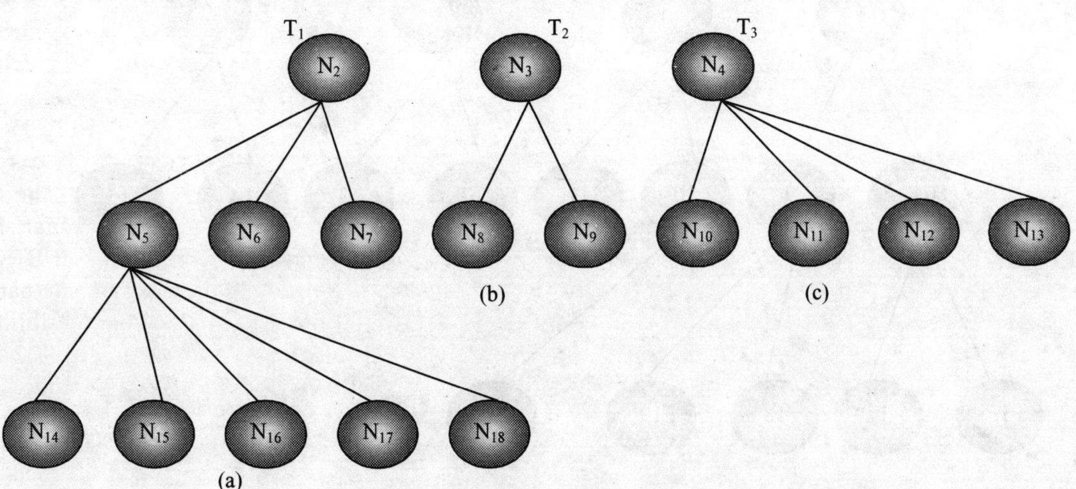

Fig. 7.3 Forest of Trees

A forest is a set of **n ≥ 0** disjoint trees, where **n** represents number of nodes in the tree. The meaning of a forest is very close to a tree, because if we remove the root of a tree, we get a forest. For example, in **Fig. 7.2** if we remove N_1, we get a forest of three trees. It is illustrated in **Fig. 7.3.**

7.2 BINARY TREE

A binary tree is an important type of data structure, which is very useful. A tree is a binary tree if each node of it can have at the most two branches. In other words we can say that if every node of a tree can have at most degree two, then this is called a binary tree. In a binary tree left and right sub-trees distinguish sub-trees of a node.

A binary tree **T** is a finite set of nodes, which is either empty or consists of special node called root **R** and two disjoint binary trees T_1 and T_2 (which are called the left sub-tree and right sub-tree, respectively). If T_1 is non-empty then the root of T_1 is called the left successor of **R**. If T_2 is non-empty then the root of T_2 is known as right successor of **R**.

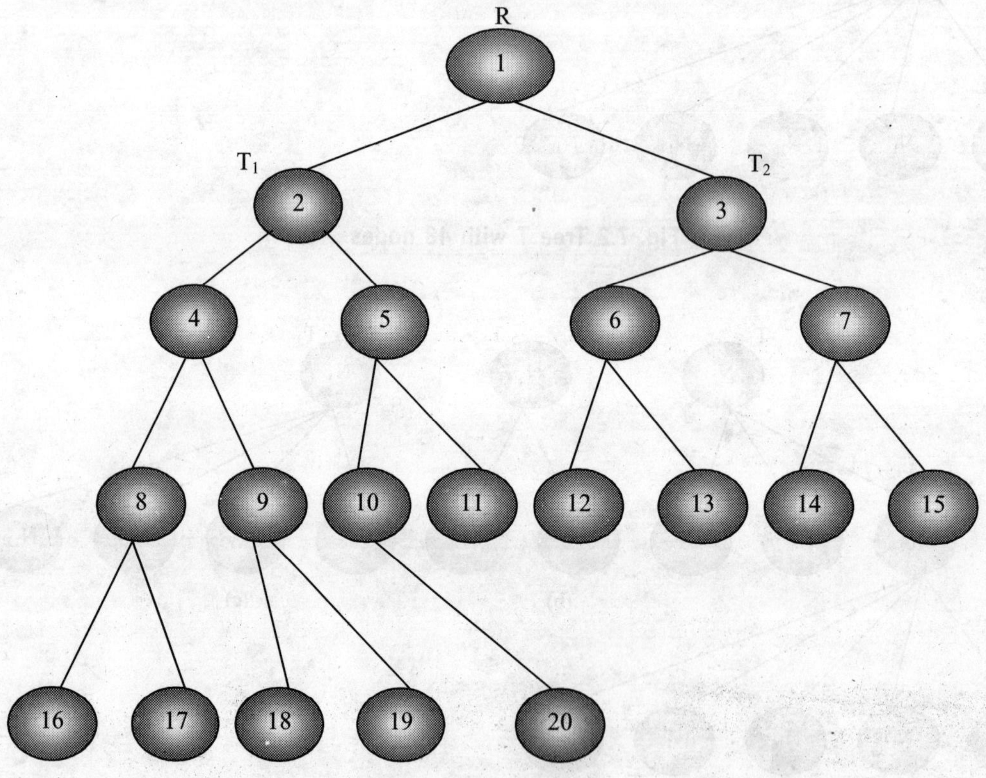

Fig. 7.4 Binary tree

For example, **Fig. 7.4** illustrates a binary tree **T** that consists of 20 nodes and the value of each node is equivalent to its node number. Root is 1, its left successor is 2 and right successor is 3.

Similarly, left successor of 2 is 4 and right successor is 5. Thus, we can say that the left sub-tree of root node 1 is equivalent to **Fig. 7.5 (a)** and the right sub-tree is equivalent to **Fig. 7.5 (b).**

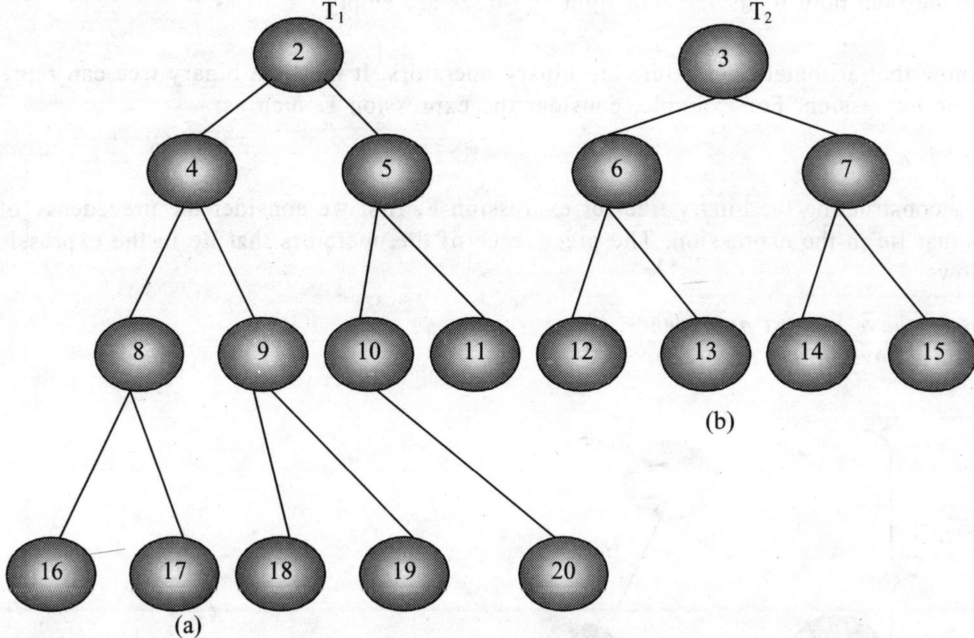

Fig. 7.5 Left sub-tree and right sub-tree of Binary tree T (Fig. 7.4))

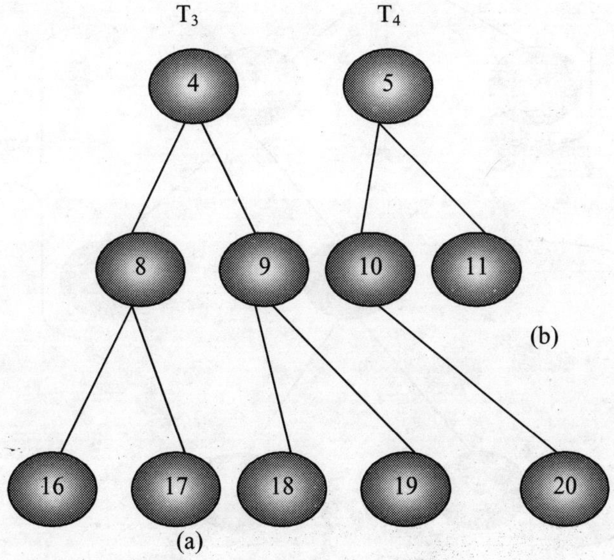

Fig. 7.6 Left sub-tree and right sub-tree of Binary tree T_1 (Fig. 7.5a))

The above definition of binary tree **T** is recursive since **T** is defined in terms of the binary sub-trees $\mathbf{T_1}$ and $\mathbf{T_2}$. Similarly, we can define $\mathbf{T_1}$ in terms of its sub-trees $\mathbf{T_3}$ and $\mathbf{T_4}$ as illustrated in **Fig. 7.6.** This means, in particular every node **N** of **T** contains a left and right sub-trees. If **N** is terminal node then both of its left and right sub-trees are empty.

We know that arithmetic operators are binary operators. It means a binary tree can represent an algebraic expression. For example, consider the expression **E** such as:

E = v + u / x * y - z

Before constructing the binary tree for expression **E,** first we consider the precedence of the operators that lie in the expression. The precedence of the operators that lie in the expression **E** is as follows:

(i) */ and * have highest precedence.*
(ii) *+ and - have lowest precedence.*

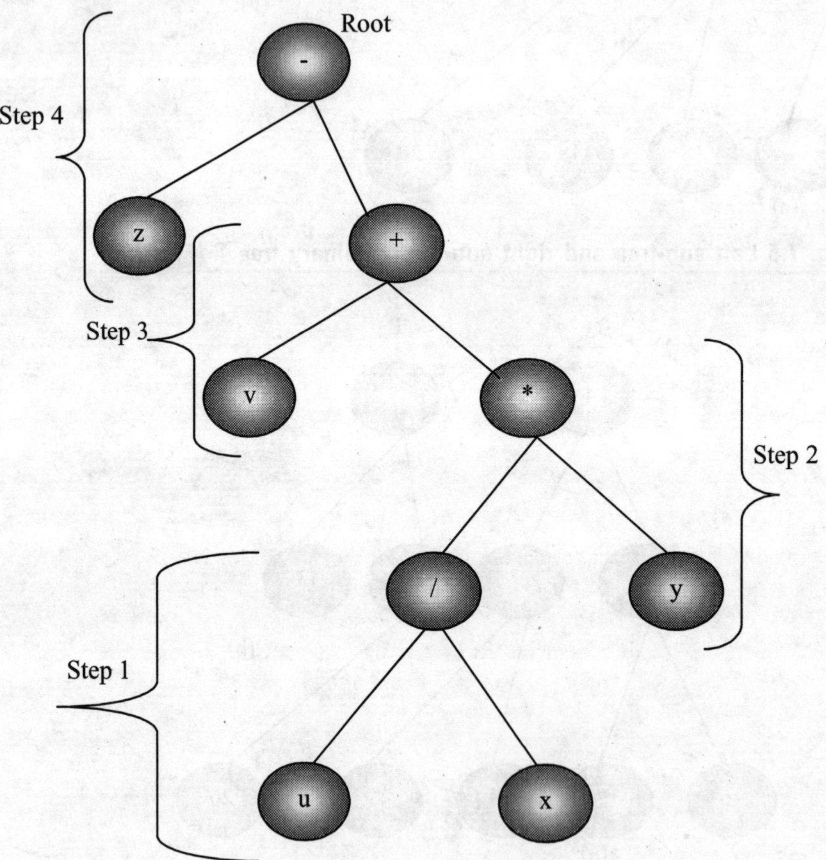

Fig. 7.7 Binary tree for the expression E

Now the construction of the binary tree may be done in the following steps.

(i) *In the expression* **E**, *the operands of / are* ***u*** *and* ***x***.
(ii) *The operands of * are* ***u/x*** *and* ***y***.
(iii) *The operands of + are* ***v*** *and* ***u/x*y***.
(iv) *The operands of - are* ***v+u/x*y*** *and* ***z***.

If we consider the above steps for the expression **E**, we will get binary tree as illustrated in **Fig. 7.7,** where all the steps of derivations are clearly mentioned.

```
Create_Tree (Info, Node)

Where Info → Information for which we have to create a node.
Node  → structure type variable to points both left and right child.

Step 1: [Check whether the tree is empty]
        If (Node = NULL)
        Node = Create a Node
        Left_Child [Node] = NULL
        Right_Child [Node] = NULL

Step 2: [Test for the left child]
        If (Info[Node] ≥ Info)
        Left_child [Node] = Call Create_Tree (Info, Left_Child [Node])

        Else
        Right_child [Node] = Call Create_Tree (Info, Right_Child [Node])

Step 3: Return (Node)
```

Fig. 7.8 Recursive algorithm for binary tree creation

The binary tree creation algorithm is illustrated in **Fig. 7.8.** This is a recursive algorithm that creates a binary tree by inserting the desired information. After insertion of the information at proper place in the tree, next information is inserted into the binary tree in the second step. This process is continued till last information is inserted. The recursive algorithm of **Fig. 7.8** is implemented in the program segment **CREAT_T.C.** Program segment **CREAT_BT.C** illustrates the algorithm discussed in **Fig. 7.9.**

```
// Create TREE
// CREAT_T.C
# include<iostream.h>
```

```
# include<stdio.h>
struct NODE
{
    int Info;
    NODE *Left_Child;
    NODE *Right_Child;
};
class Create_T
{
    public:
        NODE *Create_Tree (int , NODE *);
        void Output(NODE *, int );
};

// Function to create a tree
NODE *  Create_T :: Create_Tree (int Info, NODE *Node)
{
    if (Node == NULL)
    {
        Node = new (NODE);
        Node->Info = Info;
        Node->Left_Child = NULL;
        Node->Right_Child = NULL;
        return (Node);
    }

    // Test for the left child

      if (Node->Info >= Info )
        Node->Left_Child = Create_Tree (Info, Node->Left_Child);
    else

        // Set all the rest of the elements as right child

          Node->Right_Child = Create_Tree (Info, Node->Right_Child);

    return(Node);
}
// Output function
void Create_T :: Output(NODE *T, int Level)
{
    if (T)
    {
        Output(T->Right_Child, Level+1);
        cout<<"\n ";
        for (int i = 0; i < Level; i++)
```

```
            cout<<"  ";
        cout<< T->Info;
        cout<<"\n";
        Output(T->Left_Child, Level+1);
    }
}

// Function main
void main()
{
    Create_T C_Tree;
    int Info ;
    char choice;
    NODE *T = new (NODE);
    T = NULL;
    cout<<"\n Input choice 'b' to break:";
    choice = getchar();
    while(choice != 'b')
    {
        cout<<"\n Input information of the node: ";
        cin>>Info;
        T = C_Tree.Create_Tree (Info, T);
        cout<<"\n Tree is ";
        C_Tree.Output(T, 1);
        cout<<"\n Input choice 'b' to break:";
        choice = getchar();
    }
}
```

```
Input information of the node: 11
 Tree is
    11

 Input choice 'b' to break:
 Input information of the node: 22
 Tree is
       22

    11

 Input choice 'b' to break:
 Input information of the node: 33
 Tree is
        33

       22

  11

 Input choice 'b' to break:
 Input information of the node: 99
 Tree is
           99

        33

       22

  11
```

```
Input choice 'b' to break:
 Input information of the node: 66
 Tree is
           99

            88

               77

                  66

        33

       22

    11

 Input choice 'b' to break:
 Input information of the node: 88
 Tree is
           99

            88

        33

       22

    11

 Input choice 'b' to break:
 Input information of the node: 77
 Tree is
           99

            88

               77

        33

       22

    11
```

```
Input choice 'b' to break:
Input information of the node: 23
Tree is
          99

           88

              77

                 66

       33

          23

      22

   11
Input choice 'b' to break:
Input information of the node: 44
Tree is
            99

               88

                  77

                     66

                        44

        33

           23

      22

   11
Input choice 'b' to break: b
```

```
// Deleting in Binary Tree
// DELET_BT.C

# include<iostream.h>
# include<stdio.h>
```

```
struct NODE
{
    int Info;
    NODE *Left_Child;
    NODE *Right_Child;
};

class Operation_BT
{
    public:
        int depth;
    public:
        void Output (NODE *, int );
        NODE *Delet_Node (NODE *, int );
        NODE *Create_Tree (int , NODE *);
        NODE * DELE(NODE *, NODE *);
};

// Output function

void Operation_BT :: Output(NODE *T, int Level)
{
    if (T)
    {
        Output(T->Right_Child, Level+1);
        cout<<"\n";
        for (int i = 0; i < Level; i++)
            cout<<"  ";
        cout<< T->Info;
        Output(T->Left_Child, Level+1);
    }
}

// Delete a node in the binary tree

NODE * Operation_BT :: DELE(NODE *Node1, NODE *Node)
{
    NODE *DNode;
    if (Node1->Right_Child != NULL)
        Node1->Right_Child = DELE(Node1->Right_Child, Node);
    else
    {
        DNode = Node1;
        Node->Info = Node1->Info;
        Node1 = Node1->Left_Child;
        delete(DNode);
    }
```

```
    return (Node1);
}

// Deletion in binary tree

NODE * Operation_BT :: Delet_Node (NODE *Node, int Info)
{
    NODE *Temp;

    if (Node == NULL)
    {
        cout<<"\n Information does not exist in the above tree";
        return (Node);
    }
    else
    {
        if (Info < Node->Info )
            Node->Left_Child = Delet_Node (Node->Left_Child, Info);
        else
            if (Info > Node->Info )

                Node->Left_Child = Delet_Node (Node->Right_Child, Info);
            else
            {
                Temp = Node;
                if (Temp->Right_Child == NULL)
                {
                    Node = Temp->Left_Child;
                    delete(Temp);
                }
                else
                    if (Temp->Left_Child == NULL)
                    {
                        Node = Temp->Right_Child;
                        delete(Temp);
                    }
                    else
                        Temp->Left_Child = DELE(Temp->Left_Child, Temp);
            }
    }
    return(Node);
}

// Create binary tree

NODE *  Operation_BT :: Create_Tree (int Info, NODE *Node)
{
```

```
    if (Node == NULL)
    {
        Node = new (NODE);
        Node->Info = Info;
        Node->Left_Child = NULL;
        Node->Right_Child = NULL;
        return (Node);
    }

    // Test for the left child

      if (Info < Node->Info)

        Node->Left_Child = Create_Tree (Info, Node->Left_Child);

    else

        // Test for the right child

          if (Info > Node->Info)

              Node->Right_Child = Create_Tree (Info, Node->Right_Child);
    return(Node);
}

// Function main

void main()
{
    Operation_BT Delet_BT;
    int Number = 0;
    int Info ;
    char choice;
    int depth;
    NODE *T = new (NODE);
    T = NULL;
    cout<<"\n Input choice 'b' to break:";
    choice = getchar();

    while(choice != 'b')
    {
        cout<<"\n Input information of the node: ";
        cin>>Info;
        T = Delet_BT.Create_Tree(Info, T);
        Number++;
        cout<<"\n Input choice 'b' to break:";
```

```
        choice = getchar();
    }
    cout<<"\n Number of elements in the list is "<<Number;
    cout<<"\n Tree is \n";
    Delet_BT.Output(T,1);

    cout<<"\n Input the information to which want remove from the above tree: ";
    cin>>Info;

    T = Delet_BT.Delet_Node(T, Info);
    cout<<"\n Tree after deletion of a node: ";
    Delet_BT.Output(T,1);
}
```

```
Input choice 'b' to break:
Input information of the node: A
Input choice 'b' to break:
Input information of the node: B
Input choice 'b' to break:
Input information of the node: C
Input choice 'b' to break:
Input information of the node: D
Input choice 'b' to break:
Input information of the node: E
Input choice 'b' to break:
Input information of the node: F
Input choice 'b' to break:
Input information of the node: G
Input choice 'b' to break:
Input information of the node: H
Input choice 'b' to break:
Input information of the node: I
Input choice 'b' to break:

Input information of the node: J
Input choice 'b' to break:
Input information of the node: K
Input choice 'b' to break:
Input information of the node: L
Input choice 'b' to break:
Input information of the node: M
Input choice 'b' to break:
Input information of the node: N
Input choice 'b' to break:
Input information of the node: O
Input choice 'b' to break:
Input information of the node: P
Input choice 'b' to break:
Input information of the node: Q
Input choice 'b' to break:
Input information of the node: P
Input choice 'b' to break:
Input information of the node: R
Input choice 'b' to break: b
```

```
Number of elements in the list is 19
              R
            P
         Q
            P
      O
               N
            M
   L
K
  J
               I
            H
         G
            F
      E
               D
            C
         B
           A
```

7.3 COMPLETE BINARY TREE

A binary tree **T** is called complete if each node of **T** can have at the most two children. A binary tree **T** at level **L** can have at the most 2^L nodes. For example:

- *If L = 0, then 2^0 = 1 implies that there is only one node in the tree that is a root.*
- *If L = 1, then 2^1 = 2 implies that there are only three nodes in the tree root and a left and right successor.*
- *If L = 2, then 2^2 = 4 implies that there are only four nodes in the tree at level 2 and other three nodes.*

Similarly If L = 3, then 2^3 = 8 implies that there are eight nodes in the tree at level 8 and other seven nodes. Thus, there are seven nodes.

Thus, we can say that a tree **T** is said to be complete if all its levels except the last have the maximum number of possible nodes; and if all the nodes at last level appear to be left as far as possible. For example, **Fig. 7.10** illustrates a complete binary tree.

If we look into **Fig. 7.10,** we find that at level 0 there is only one node; at level 1 there are two nodes and at level 2 there are four nodes, etc.

If we assume that $v_1 = 1$ is a root and its left sub-tree's root is $v_2 = 2*v_1 = 2*1 = 2$ and right sub-tree's root is $v_3 = 2*v_1 + 1 = 2*1 + 1 = 3$ and we consider the 4th nodes' its value is 4 then its left sub-tree value is = 4*2 = 8, and right sub-tree's value is 4*2 + 1 = 9 and so on. If we consider node **v** then its left child will be at position **2*v** and right child will be at position **2*v+1**. Thus the depth of the binary tree with **n** nodes is given by

$$D_n = \lfloor \log_2 n+1 \rfloor$$

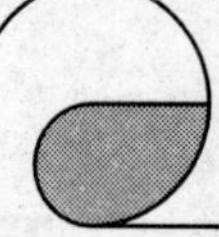

Binary_Tree (List, Lower, Upper)

Where List → Represents list of elements that forms a binary tree.

Lower → Represents lower limit of the list that is lower index value of the list.

Upper → Represents upper limit of the list that is upper index value.

Step 1: [Find middle of the list]

(i) Mid = (Lower + Upper) / 2 [Integer division]
(ii) Info [Node] = List [Mid]

Step 2: If (Lower ≥ Upper)

(i) Left_Child [Node] = NULL
(ii) Right_Child [Node] = NULL
(iii) Return (Node)

Step 3: If (Lower ≤ Mid – 1)
Left_Child = Call Binary_Tree (List, Lower, Mid – 1)
Else
Left_Child [Node] = NULL

Step 4: If (Upper ≥ Mid + 1)
Right_Child = Call Binary_Tree (List, Mid+1, Upper)
Else
Right_Child [Node] = NULL

Step 5: Return (Node)

Fig. 7.9 Algorithm to create binary tree

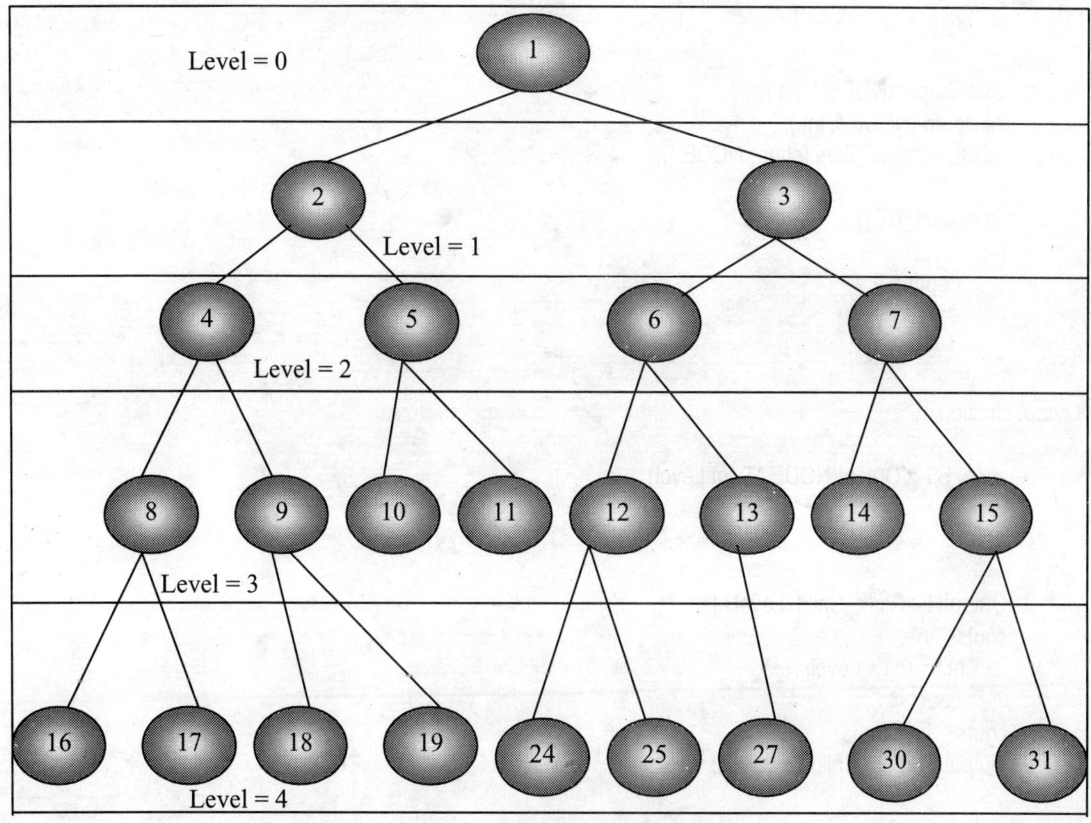

Fig. 7.10 Complete Binary Tree

For example, consider the following program segment that implements the above discussion.

```
// Finding Depth of Binary Tree
// DEPTH_BT.C

# include<iostream.h>
# include<stdio.h>

struct NODE
{
      char Info;
      NODE *Left_Child;
      NODE *Right_Child;
};

class Operation_BT
{
```

```
    public:
        int depth;
    public:
        void Output (NODE *, int );
        int Depth (NODE *, int );
        NODE *Create_Tree (char , NODE *);

        Operation_BT ()
        {
            depth = 0;
        }
};

// Output function

void Operation_BT :: Output(NODE *T, int Level)
{
    if (T)
    {
        Output(T->Right_Child, Level+1);
        cout<<"\n";
        for (int i = 0; i < Level; i++)
            cout<<"  ";
        cout<< T->Info;
        Output(T->Left_Child, Level+1);
    }
}

// Find depth of the tree

int Operation_BT :: Depth (NODE *Node, int Level)
{
    if (Node != NULL)
    {
        if (Level > depth)
            depth = Level;
        Depth (Node->Left_Child, Level + 1);
        Depth (Node->Right_Child, Level + 1);
    }
    return (depth);
}

// Create binary tree

NODE *  Operation_BT :: Create_Tree (char Info, NODE *Node)
{
```

```
    if (Node == NULL)
    {
        Node = new (NODE);
        Node->Info = Info;
        Node->Left_Child = NULL;
        Node->Right_Child = NULL;
        return (Node);
    }

    // Test for the left child

     if (Info < Node->Info)

        Node->Left_Child = Create_Tree (Info, Node->Left_Child);

    else

        // Test for the right child

          if (Info > Node->Info)

            Node->Right_Child = Create_Tree (Info, Node->Right_Child);
    return(Node);
}

// Function main

void main()
{
    Operation_BT Depth_BT;
    int Number = 0;
    char Info;
    char choice;
    int depth;
    NODE *T = new (NODE);
    T = NULL;
    cout<<"\n Input choice 'b' to break:";
    choice = getchar();

    while(choice != 'b')
    {
        cout<<"\n Input information of the node: ";
        cin>>Info;
        T = Depth_BT.Create_Tree(Info, T);
        Number++;
        cout<<"\n Input choice 'b' to break:";
```

```
        choice = getchar();
    }
    cout<<"\n Number of elements in the list is "<<Number;
    cout<<"\n Tree is \n";
    Depth_BT.Output(T,1);

    depth = Depth_BT.Depth(T, 0);
    cout<<"\n Depth of the above tree is: "<<depth;
}
```

```
Input choice 'b' to break:
Input information of the node: A
Input choice 'b' to break:
Input information of the node: P
Input choice 'b' to break:
Input information of the node: T
Input choice 'b' to break:
Input information of the node: F
Input choice 'b' to break:
Input information of the node: B
Input choice 'b' to break: b
Number of elements in the list is 5
Tree is

     B
    T
  P
    F
 A

Depth of the above tree is: 3
```

7.4 EXTENDED BINARY TREE OR 2-TREE

A binary tree is called extended or 2-tree if each node **N** has either 0 or 2 degree. In this case, the nodes with degree 2 are called internal and nodes with degree 0 are called terminal (or external or leaf) nodes. The 2-trees are used to represent algebraic expression and shown in **Fig. 7.7**.

7.5 REPRESENTATION OF BINARY TREE

It is often required to maintain binary trees in the computer memory. There are two traditional popular techniques that are used to maintain binary trees in the memory. These are:

- *Sequential representation*
- *Linked list representation*

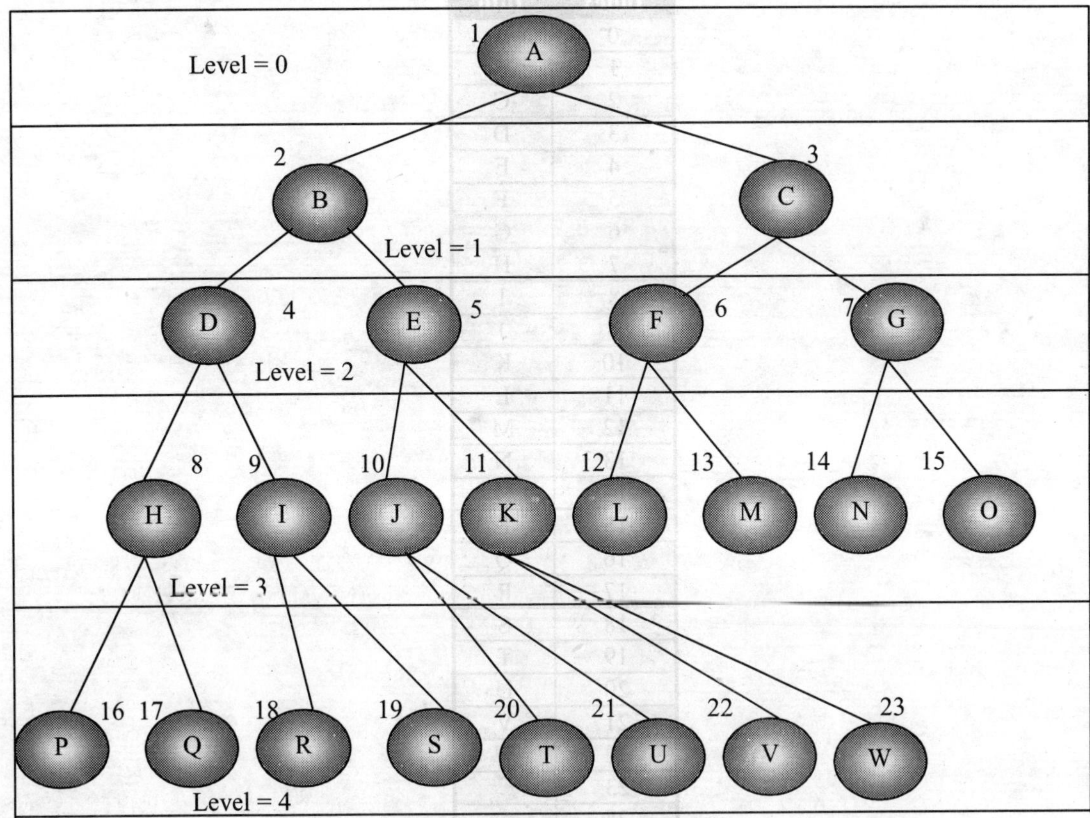

Fig. 7.11 Binary Tree T

7.5.1 SEQUENTIAL REPRESENTATION

A sequential representation of a binary tree requires numbering of nodes; starting with nodes on level 0, then on level 1 and so on. The nodes are numbered from left to right. As we have already discussed that numbering of nodes gives a complete binary tree. The nodes of the binary tree are maintained in a one-dimensional array. For example, consider the binary tree **T** illustrated in **Fig. 7.11**.

Linear_T

Index	Info
0	A
1	B
2	C
3	D
4	E
5	F
6	G
7	H
8	I
9	J
10	K
11	L
12	M
13	N
14	O
15	P
16	Q
17	R
18	S
19	T
20	U
21	V
22	W
23	
24	
25	
26	
27	
28	

Fig. 7.12 Sequential representation of tree T illustrated in Fig. 7.11

In **Fig. 7.11** the root node is numbered as 1, then its left child as 2 and the right child as 3. Now node 2 is the parent and its left child is numbered 4 and right child is numbered 5. The node 3 is right child of node 1 (Root) and is parent of nodes 6 and 7. The nodes at level 2 are 4, 5, 6 and 7 will be treated as children of nodes at level 1, and parent of the nodes at level 3 and so on. If we consider **Fig. 7.12,** we find that the root node occupies rooms at index 0 (Node numbered 1). The left child of node 1 will occupy rooms at index 1, and right child at index 2. Similarly, left child of node 2 at index 3 and right child at index 4, left child of node 3 at index 5 and right child at index 6 occupy rooms, and so on. Till now from above discussion it is clear that if we have any node numbered **k** then its left child will occupy room at index **2k** and right child at **2k+1**.

The above representation of binary tree can also be applied to the complete binary tree. It is an ideal representation for complete binary tree and in this case no space is wasted. However, for other binary trees most of the memory space remains unutilized. For example, if we have a skewed binary tree then more than 50% of the space is unutilized, if it is implemented through the arrays. The sequential representation of the tree shown in **Fig. 7.13** is illustrated in **Fig. 7.14**. From this figure we find that out of 30 spaces only 9 are occupied by the tree thereby wasting about 70% memory.

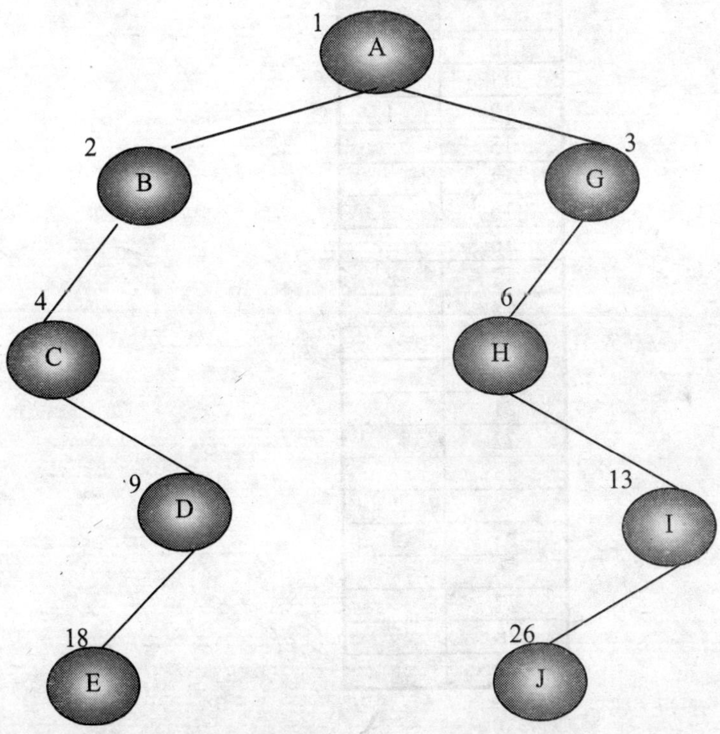

Fig. 7.13 Skewed tree

Other problems arise during the insertion and deletion of new node when information is to be inserted/deleted in the middle of the tree, because it requires much more movement of nodes, requires renumbering of nodes.

Linear_Skewed_Tree

Index	Info
0	A
1	B
2	G
3	C
4	
5	H
6	
7	
8	D
9	
10	
11	
12	I
13	
14	
15	
16	
17	E
18	
19	
20	
21	
22	
23	
24	
25	J
26	
27	
28	
29	

Fig. 7.14 Sequential representation of tree illustrated in Fig. 7.13

7.5.2 LINKED LIST REPRESENTATION

The problem associated with the sequential representation of binary tree can be overcome through the use of the linked list representation. In this representation each node requires three fields, one for the link of the left child, second field for representing the information associated with the node and the third field is used to represent the link of the right child. For example, **Fig. 7.15** illustrates a binary tree, each node having three fields and is represented in computer memory as shown in **Fig. 7.16.**

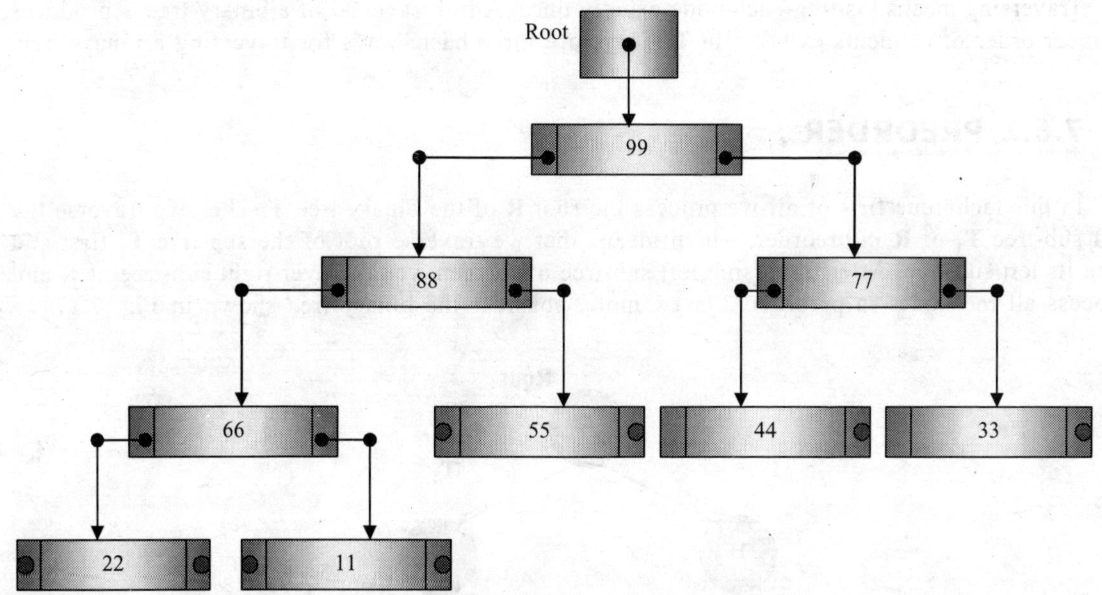

Fig. 7.15 Binary tree T

Root 3

Free 11

Address	Info	Left	Right
1	33	\0	\0
2			
3	99	7	5
4	22	\0	\0
5	77	14	1
6		17	
7	88	9	12
8			
9	66	4	18
10		10	
11		2	
12	55	\0	\0
13		13	
14	44	\0	\0
15		15	\0
16		16	\0
17		8	
18	11	\0	\0

Fig. 7.16 Linked list representation of Binary tree T

7.6 TRAVERSING BINARY TREE

Traversing means visiting each node exactly once. A full traversal of a binary tree **T** produces a linear order of elements existing in **T**. There are three basic ways for traversing a binary tree.

7.6.1 PREORDER

In this technique first of all we process the root **R** of the binary tree **T**. Then we traverse the left sub-tree T_1 of **R** in preorder, which means that we traverse root of the sub-tree T_1 first and then its left sub-tree. After traversing left sub-tree of **R**, then we take over right sub-tree of **R** and process all the nodes in preorder. For example, consider the binary tree shown in **Fig. 7.17.**

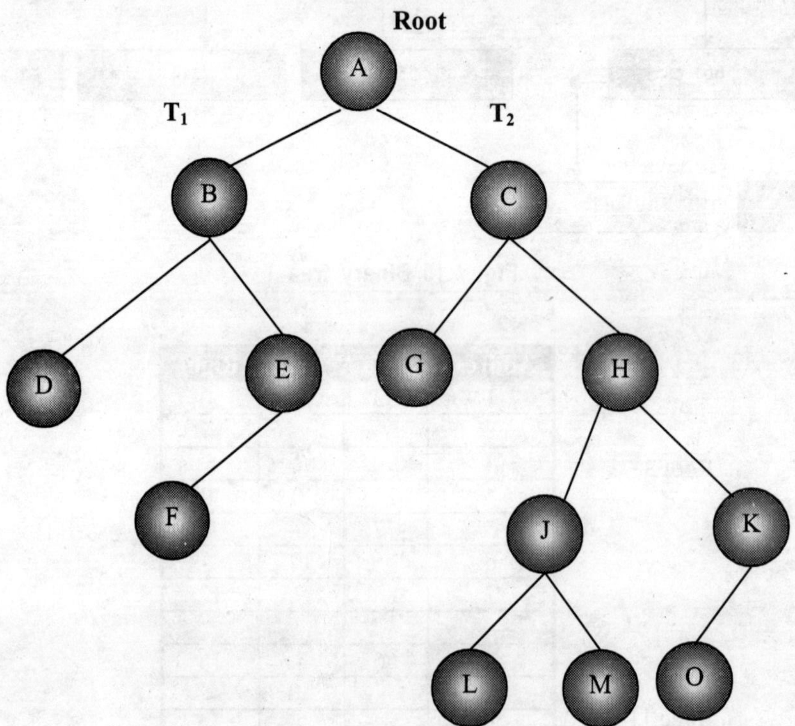

Fig. 7.17 Binary tree T with 13 nodes

According to the above discussion first of all we consider the root node **A**; then consider its left sub-tree as illustrated in **Fig. 7.18**. Now we process root of sub-tree T_1 (node B) then its left sub-tree T_3 that is a terminal node **D.** Now consider the right sub-tree of T_1 (T_4). The root of T_4 is **E** and left sub-tree of T_4 is T_5 that is a terminal node **F**. Thus the processing of all the nodes of the left sub-tree T_1 is finished. Now we will take over right sub-tree T_2 of **R** as illustrated in **Fig. 7.19.** We will process all the nodes of the T_2 in same way as we have processed the nodes of sub-tree T_1. After completion of the preorder traversing of the binary tree we get the linear list of the nodes as A, B, D, E, F, C, G, H, J, L, M, K, O.

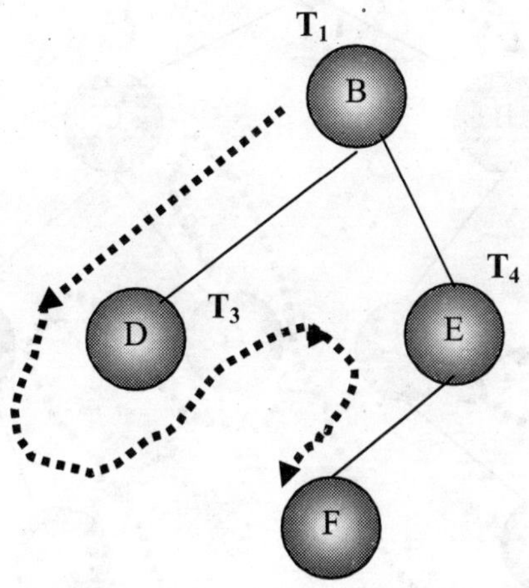

Fig. 7.18 Traversing left Sub-tree T_1 in preorder

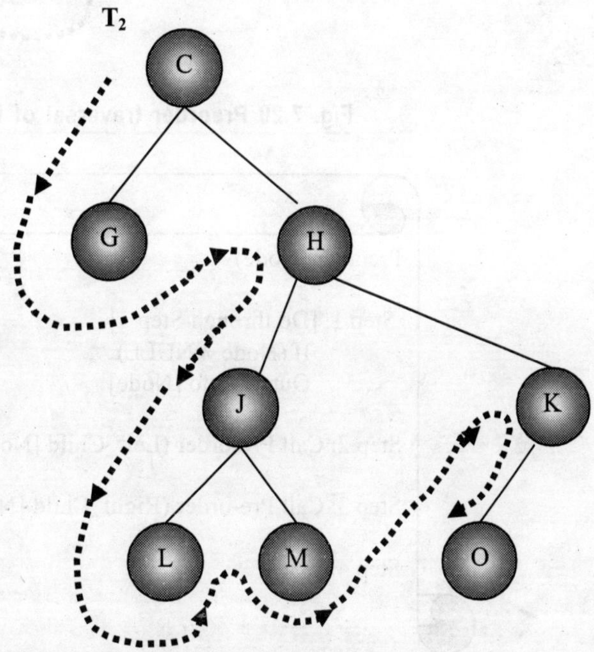

Fig. 7.19 Right sub-tree T_2 traversing in preorder

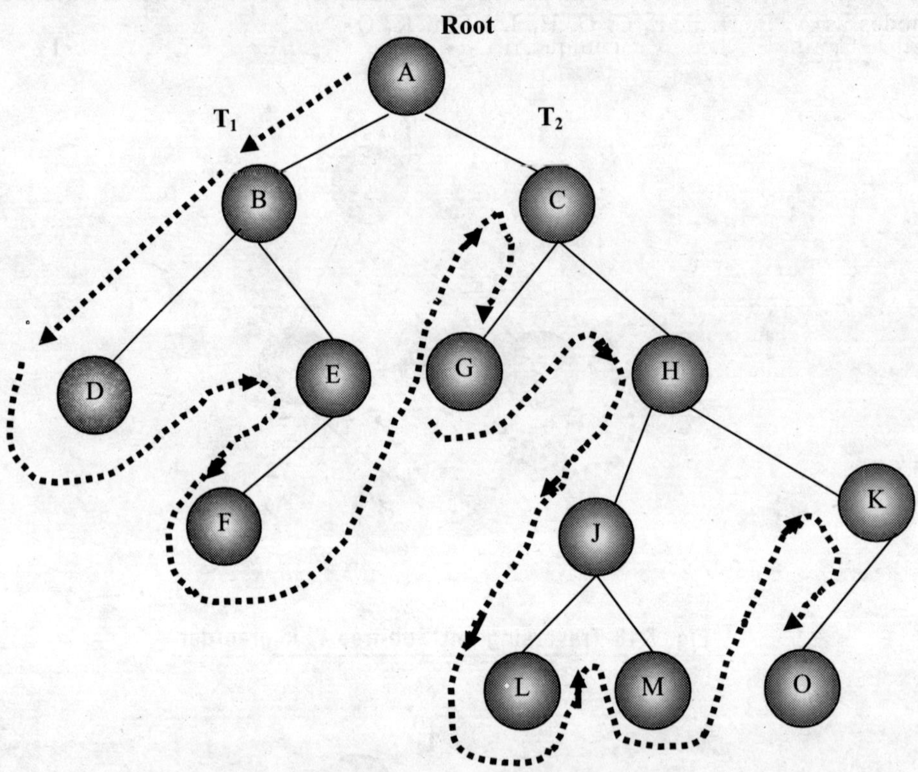

Fig. 7.20 Preorder traversal of Binary tree T

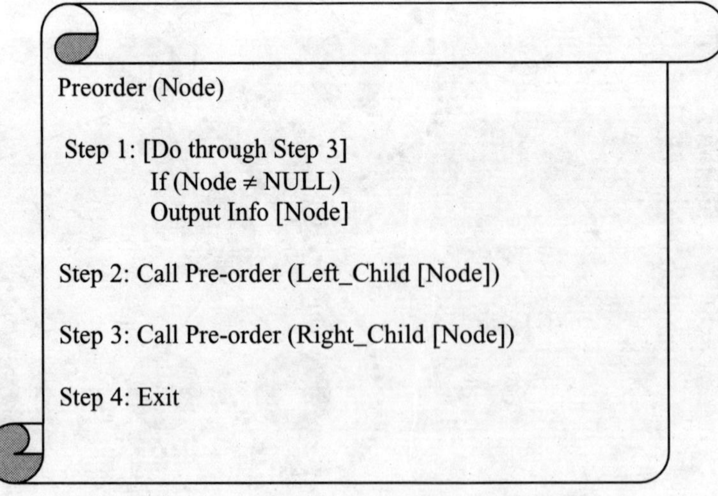

Preorder (Node)

Step 1: [Do through Step 3]
If (Node ≠ NULL)
Output Info [Node]

Step 2: Call Pre-order (Left_Child [Node])

Step 3: Call Pre-order (Right_Child [Node])

Step 4: Exit

Fig. 7.21 Recursive algorithm of preorder traversing

7.6.2 INORDER

In the in-order traversing technique first of all we process the left sub-tree T_1 of the root **R** in the in-order. Then process the root **R** and at the last we process the right sub-tree T_2 of **R.** In **Fig. 7.17, A** is root and its left sub-tree T_1 can be illustrated as in **Fig. 7.18**. The root of T_1 is **B** and its left sub-tree **D** is a terminal node. We first process node **D** then root of **D** (B) and the last the right sub-tree of **B** (E). The left sub-tree of **E** is **F** that is terminal node. We first process **F** and then right sub-tree of **E**. There is no right sub-tree, hence we process **E**. Thus all the nodes of left sub-tree is processed and resulting list is as follows:

DBFE

Secondly we process root **R** and then process right sub-tree T_2 in the similar fashion as T_1. List of processed nodes is as follows:

GCLJMHOK

When we combine list of elements of left sub-tree T_1, root **R** and elements of right sub-tree T_2 we get the list of all the elements in the binary tree **T**:

DBFE**A**GCLJMHOK

The above discussion is straightforward if one consider the tree shown in **Fig. 7.23.** The algorithm to traverse a tree in in-order is illustrated in **Fig. 7.22.**

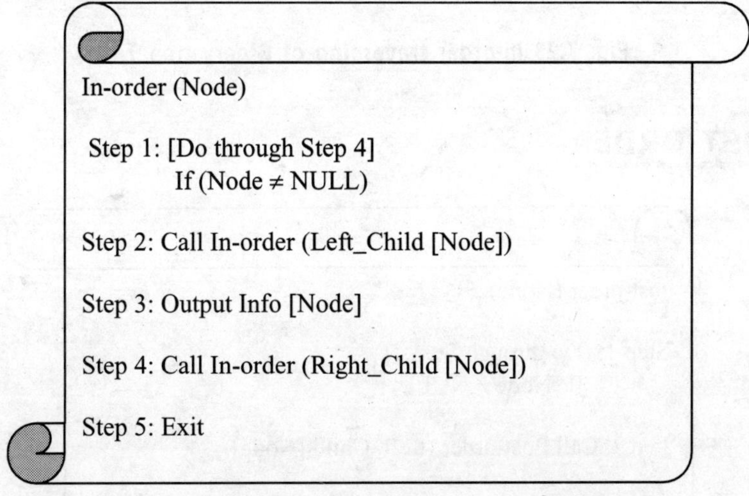

In-order (Node)

Step 1: [Do through Step 4]
If (Node ≠ NULL)

Step 2: Call In-order (Left_Child [Node])

Step 3: Output Info [Node]

Step 4: Call In-order (Right_Child [Node])

Step 5: Exit

Fig. 7.22 Recursive algorithm of in-order traversing

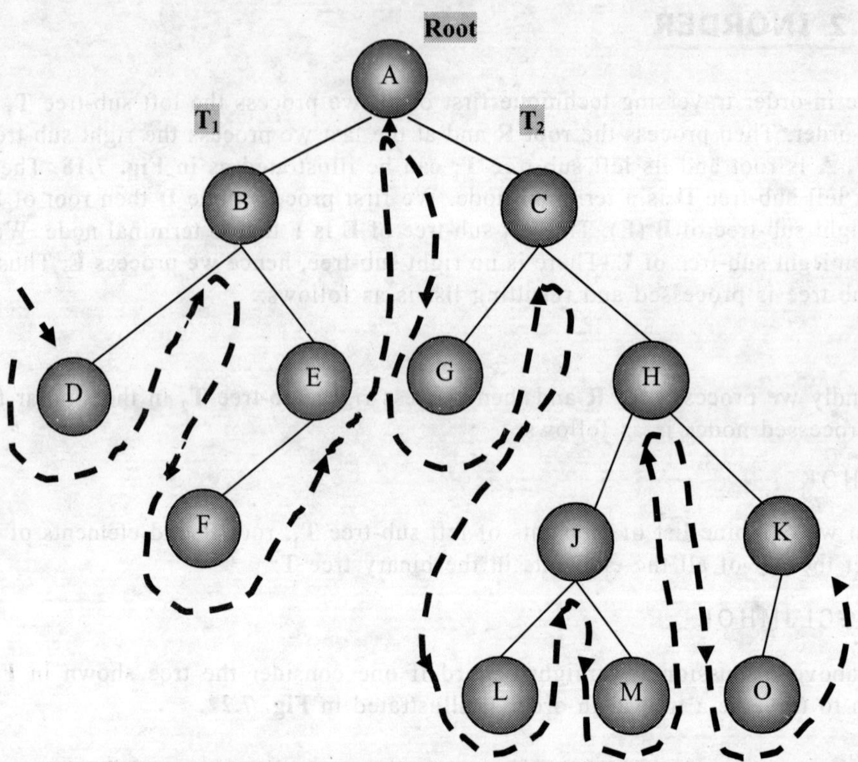

Fig. 7.23 In-order traversing of Binary tree T

7.6.3 POST ORDER

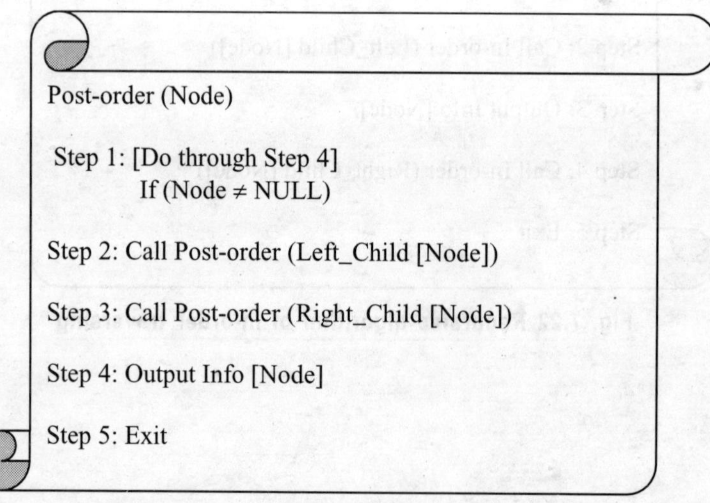
Post-order (Node)

Step 1: [Do through Step 4]
If (Node ≠ NULL)

Step 2: Call Post-order (Left_Child [Node])

Step 3: Call Post-order (Right_Child [Node])

Step 4: Output Info [Node]

Step 5: Exit

Fig. 7.24 Recursive algorithm of postorder traversing

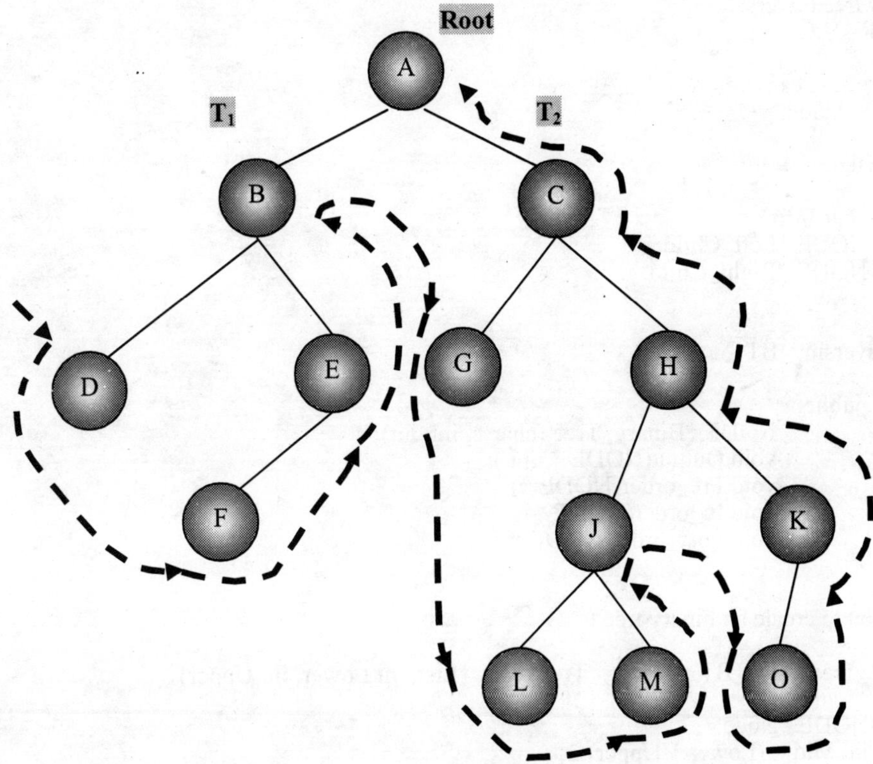

Fig. 7.25 Postorder traversing of Binary tree T

In this technique first of all, we process the left sub-tree T_1 of **R** in post order, then the right sub-tree T_2 in postorder and at the last the root **R**.

Once again we consider the tree illustrated in **Fig. 7.17**. The left sub-tree of **R** is $\mathbf{T_1}$, root of $\mathbf{T_1}$ is **B** and its left sub-tree is **D** that is terminal node. We process **D** first. Now we consider right sub-tree of **B** that is **E**, the left sub-tree of **E** is **F**, so process **F** at the second priority. As there is no right sub-tree of **E** we process **E** and at the last root of the sub-tree $\mathbf{T_1}$, that is **B**. The resulting list of elements after traversing the left sub-tree in postorder is as follows:

DFEB

In the same fashion we process all the nodes of the right sub-tree $\mathbf{T_2}$. The list of elements after processing right sub-tree in postorder is as follows:

GLMJOKHC

The final list of elements after traversing binary tree illustrated in **Fig. 7.17** is as follows:

DFEBGLMJOKHCA

The postorder traversing algorithm is illustrated in **Fig. 7.24**. The program segment **BT_TRAV.C** implements the above discussed traversing algorithms.

```
// Binary tree traversal
// BT_TRAV.C

# include<iostream.h>
# include<stdio.h>

struct NODE
{
        char Info;
        NODE *Left_Child;
        NODE *Right_Child;
};

class Traversing_BT
{
        public:
                NODE *Binary_Tree (char *, int, int);
                void Output(NODE *, int );
                void Pre_order(NODE *);
                void In_order(NODE *);
                void Post_order(NODE *);
};

// Function to create an binary tree

NODE *  Traversing_BT :: Binary_Tree (char *List, int Lower, int Upper)
{
        NODE *Node;
        int Mid = (Lower + Upper)/2;
        Node = new (NODE);

        Node->Info = List [Mid];
        if ( Lower>= Upper)
        {
                Node->Left_Child = NULL;
                Node->Right_Child = NULL;
                return (Node);
        }
        if (Lower <= Mid - 1)
                Node->Left_Child = Binary_Tree (List, Lower, Mid - 1);
        else
                Node->Left_Child = NULL;
        if (Mid + 1 <= Upper)
                Node->Right_Child = Binary_Tree (List, Mid + 1, Upper);
        else
                Node->Right_Child = NULL;
        return(Node);
}

// Output function

void Traversing_BT :: Output(NODE *T, int Level)
{
        if (T)
```

```
        {
                Output(T->Right_Child, Level+1);
                cout<<"\n";
                for (int i = 0; i < Level; i++)
                        cout<<"  ";
                cout<< T->Info;
                Output(T->Left_Child, Level+1);
        }
}

// Preorder traversal

void Traversing_BT :: Pre_order (NODE *Node)
{
        if (Node)
        {
                cout<<"  "<<Node->Info;
                Pre_order(Node->Left_Child);
                Pre_order(Node->Right_Child);
        }
}

// In-order traversal

void Traversing_BT :: In_order (NODE *Node)
{
        if (Node)
        {
                In_order(Node->Left_Child);
                cout<<"  "<<Node->Info;
                In_order(Node->Right_Child);
        }
}

// Postorder traversal

void Traversing_BT :: Post_order (NODE *Node)
{
        if (Node)
        {
                Post_order(Node->Left_Child);
                Post_order(Node->Right_Child);
                cout<<"  "<<Node->Info;

        }
}

// Function main

void main()
{
        Traversing_BT Binary_C_Tree;
        char List[100];
        int Number = 0;
        char Info ;
```

```
        char choice;
        NODE *T = new (NODE);
        T = NULL;
        cout<<"\n Input choice 'b' to break:";
        choice = getchar();
        while(choice != 'b')
        {
                cout<<"\n Input information of the node: ";
                cin>>Info;
                List[Number++] = Info;
                cout<<"\n Input choice 'b' to break:";
                choice = getchar();
        }
        Number --;
        cout<<"\n Number of elements in the list is "<<Number;
        T = Binary_C_Tree.Binary_Tree(List, 0, Number);
        Binary_C_Tree.Output(T,1);
        cout<<"\n Preorder traversal\n";
        Binary_C_Tree.Pre_order (T);
        cout<<"\n In-order traversal\n";
        Binary_C_Tree.In_order (T);
        cout<<"\n Postorder traversal\n";
        Binary_C_Tree.Post_order (T);
}
```

7.7 MINIMUM WEIGHTED PATH LENGTH ALGORITHMS

Suppose we have **n** values $w_1, w_2, w_3 \ldots w_n$ and want to find out the extended binary trees with **n** external (terminal) nodes, and to associate the values $w_1, w_2, w_3 \ldots w_n$ with these nodes in such a way that the sum $\Sigma w_i l_i$ is minimized, where l_i is the length of path from the root and the sum is taken over all external nodes. For example, if we have following list of elements then the complete binary trees for the list are shown in **Fig. 7.26,** where rectangles are used to represent external nodes.

List: 11, 13, 14, 15, 16

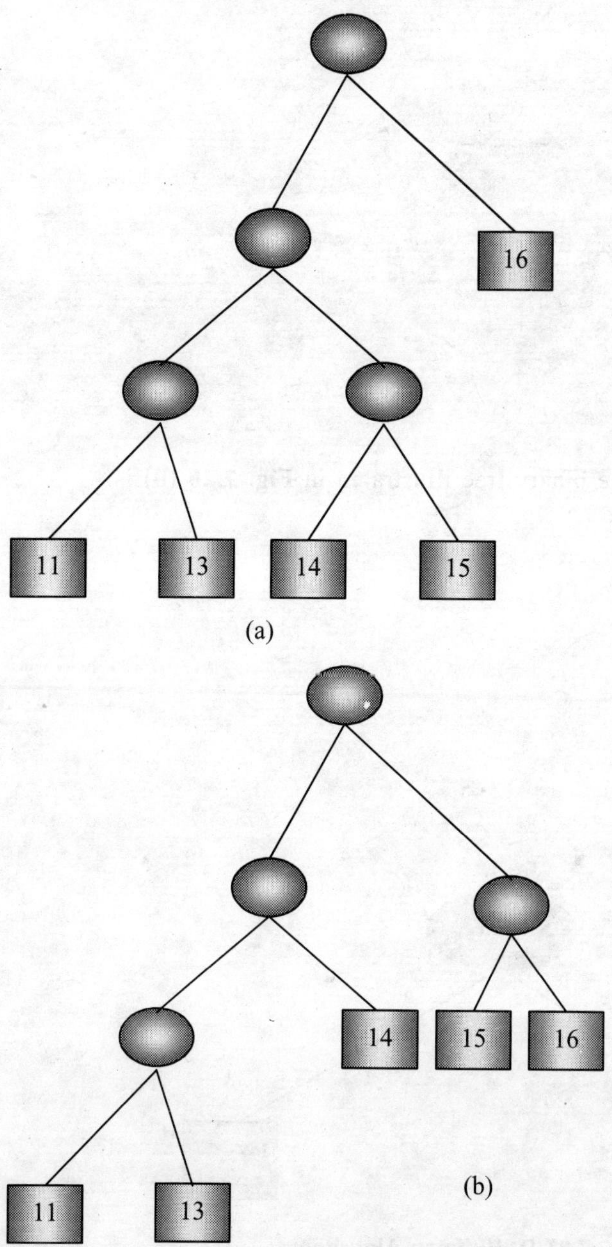

Fig. 7.26 Complete binary tree

The weighted path length for the binary tree illustrated in **Fig. 7.26 (a)** is:

$$\sum_{i=1}^{n} w_i l_i$$

$$\sum_{i=1}^{5} w_i l_i$$

= 11*3+13*3+14*3+15*3+16*1

= 33+39+42+45+16

= 175

The weighted path length for the binary tree illustrated in **Fig. 7.26 (b)** is:

$$\sum_{i=1}^{n} w_i l_i$$

= 11*3+13*3+14*2+15*2+16*2

= 33+39+28+30+32

= 162

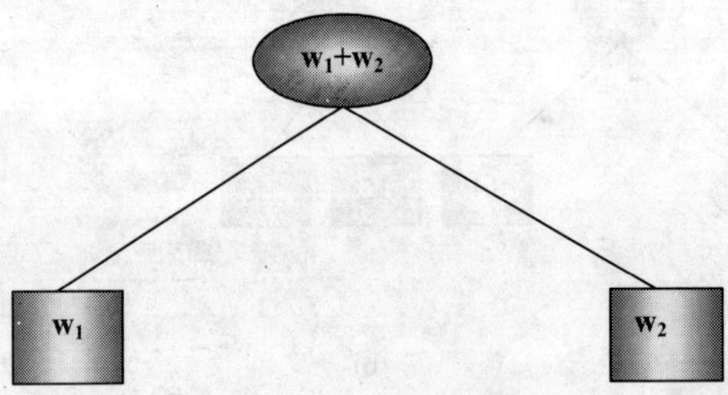

Fig. 7.27 D. Huffman Algorithm

1	**2**	4	6	10	12	16	18	22	28	30	36	40
	3	**4**	6	10	12	16	18	22	28	30	36	40
		7	**6**	10	12	16	18	22	28	30	36	40
			13	**10**	**12**	16	18	22	28	30	36	40
			13		22	**16**	18	22	28	30	36	40
					22	29	**18**	22	28	30	36	40
						29	40	**22**	**28**	30	36	40
						29	40		50	**30**	36	40
							40		50	59	**36**	40
									50	59	76	**40**
										59	**76**	90
											135	**90**
												225

Fig. 7.28 Discussion of D. Huffman algorithm

From the above two results it is clear that a perfectly balanced tree does not give the minimum weighted path length. But a complete binary tree gives a minimum weighted path length only when all the weights of terminal nodes are 1. That is:

$w_1 = w_2 = w_3 = ... = w_n = 1$

To find a tree with minimum weighted path length, an algorithm was developed by ***D. Huffman***. In this algorithm first of all we find two weight's $\mathbf{w_1}$ and $\mathbf{w_2}$ of lowest value and then solve the problem for **n-1** weights $\mathbf{w_1+w_2, w_3, w_4 ... w_n}$, and replace the nodes as illustrated in **Fig. 7.27.**

For example, find the optimal tree for the weight list given below:

List: 1, 2, 4, 6, 10, 12, 16, 18, 22, 28, 30, 36, 40

If we look into the above list we find that 1 and 2 are least values. First of all we combine 1 and 2 and look for the solution weights 1 + 2, 4, 6, 10, 12, 16, 18, 22, 28, 30, 36, 40, then we combine (1+2) = 3 and 4 that is 3+4 = 7 and look for the solution. 7, 6, 10, 12, 16, 18, 22, 28, 30, 36, 40 then combine 7 and 6 and so on. The detail solution for the given list is illustrated in **Fig. 7.28.**

Now the problem is how **Fig. 7.28** can be used to construct **Huffman** tree? **Fig. 7.29** helps to illustrate this.

1	**2**	4	6	10	12	16	18	22	28	30	36	40

Fig. 7.29 (a) Step 1

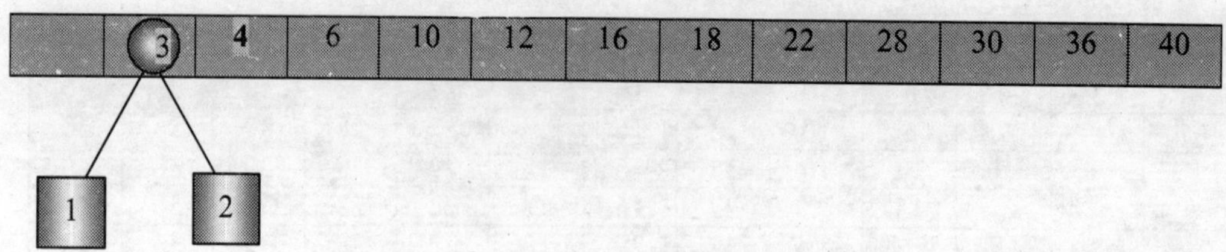

Fig. 7.29 (b) Step 2

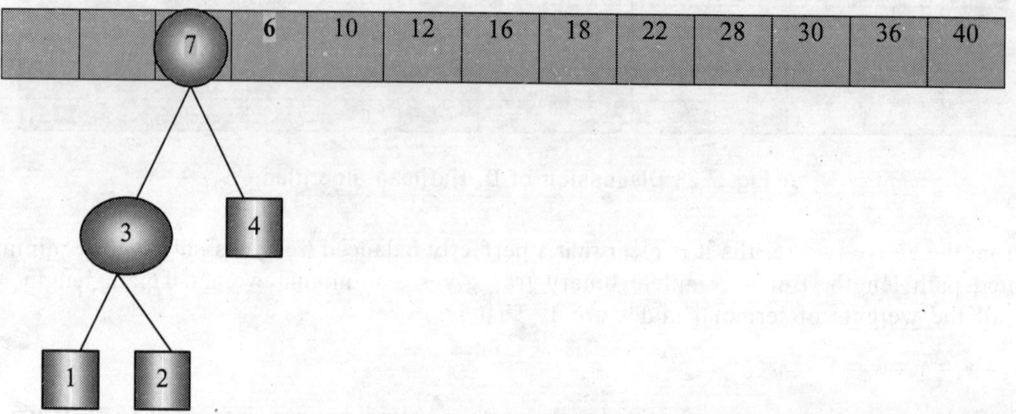

Fig. 7.29 (c) Step 3

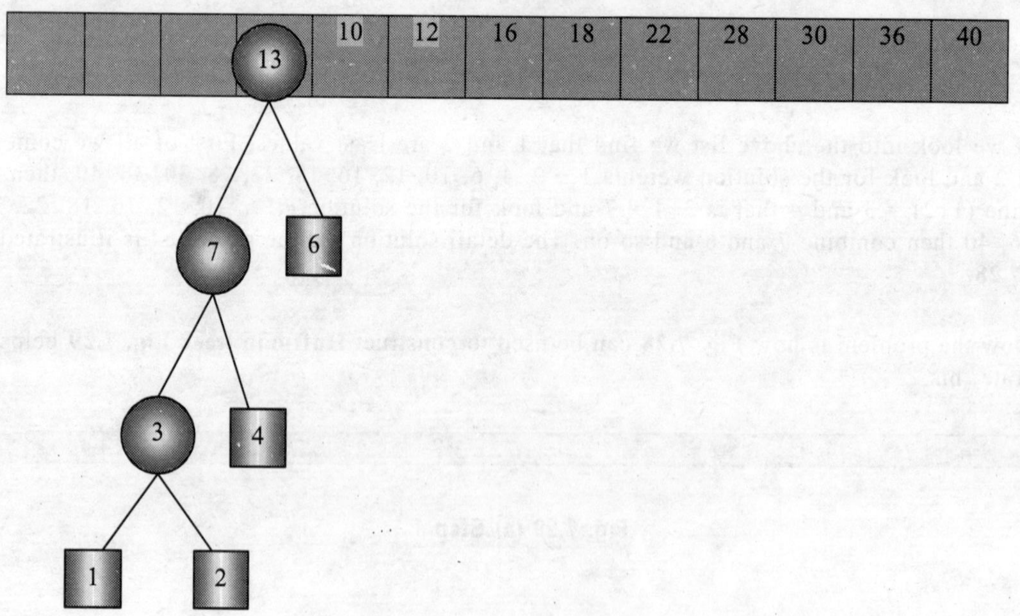

Fig. 7.29 (d) Step 4

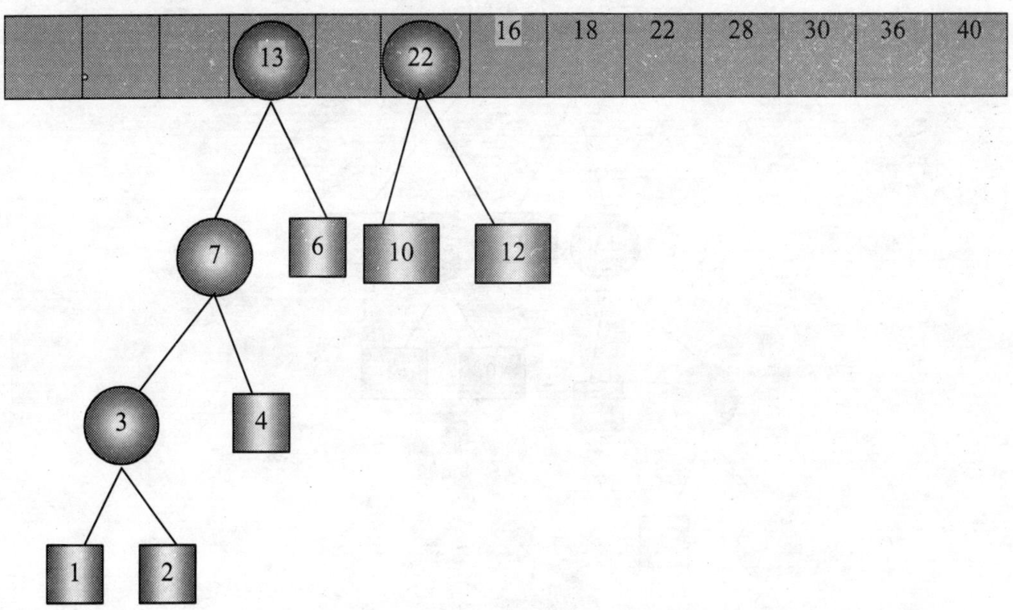

Fig. 7.29 (e) Step 5

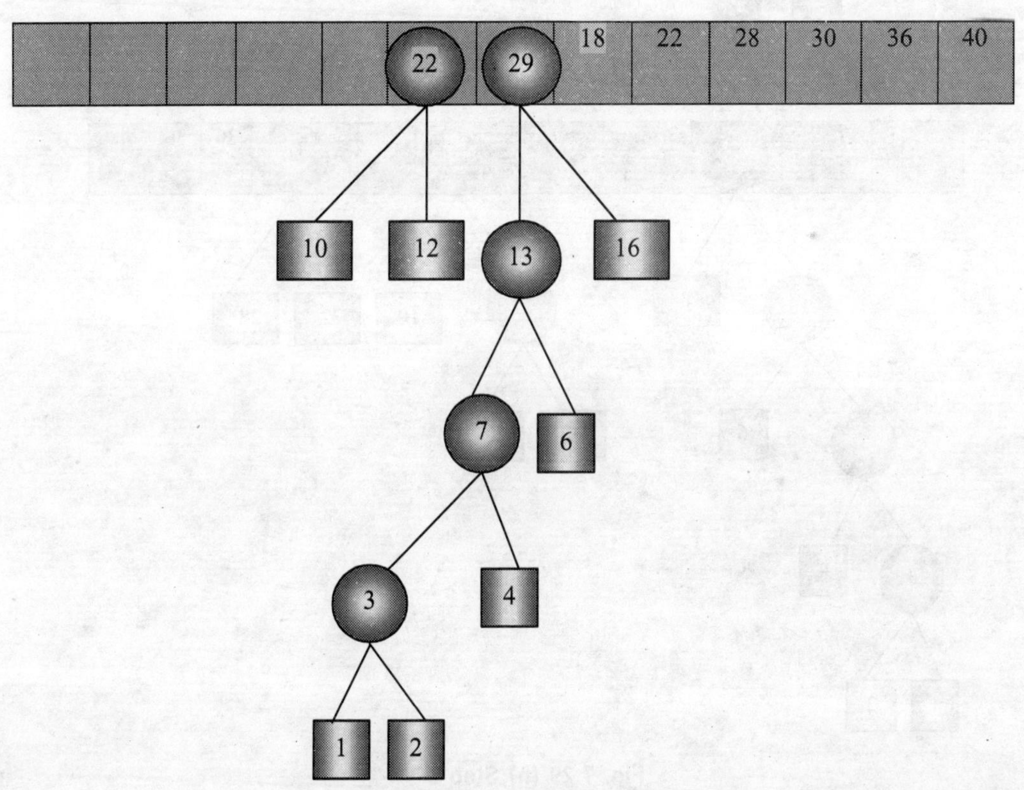

Fig. 7.29 (f) Step 6

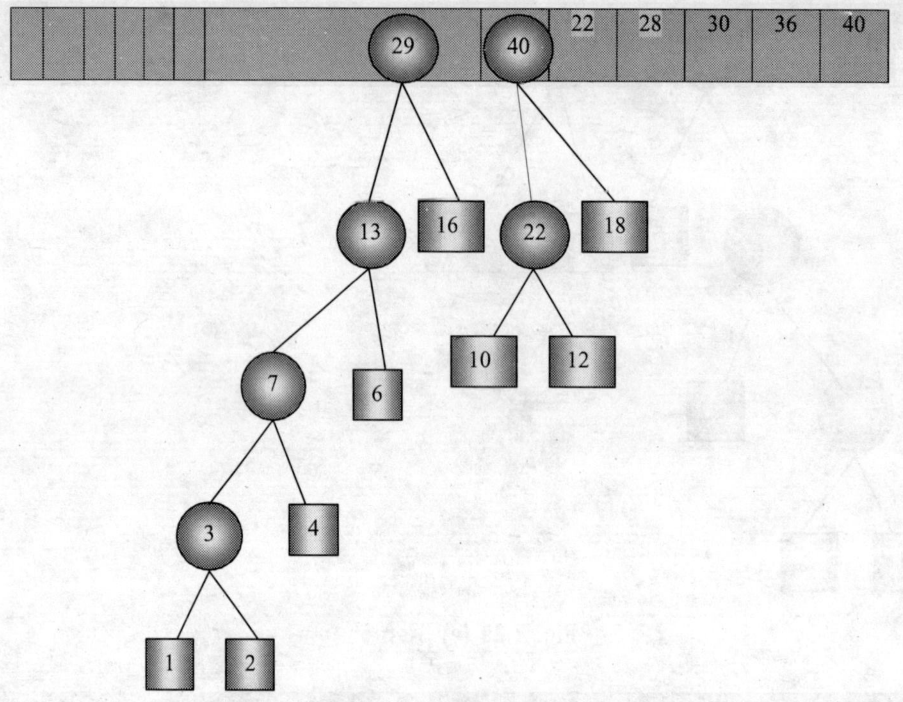

Fig. 7.29 (g) Step 7

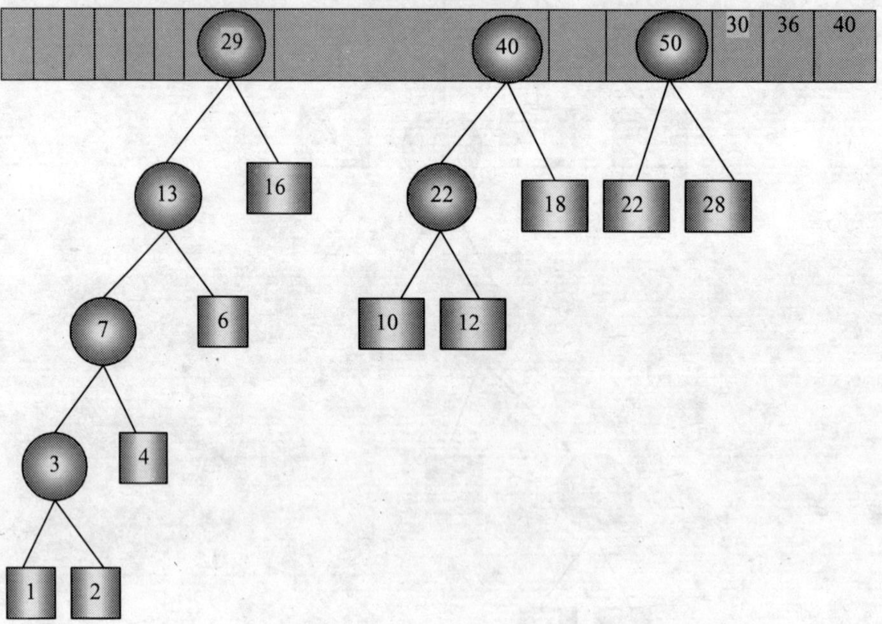

Fig. 7.29 (h) Step 8

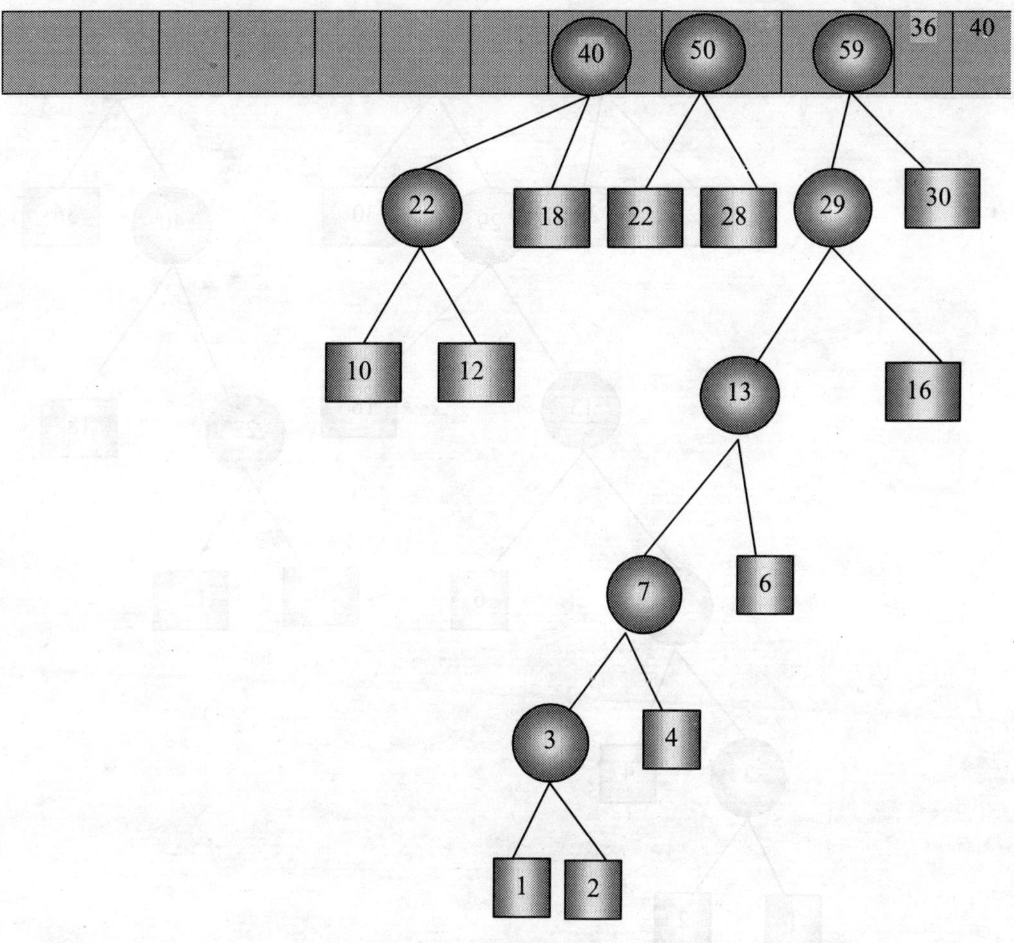

Fig. 7.29 (i) Step 9

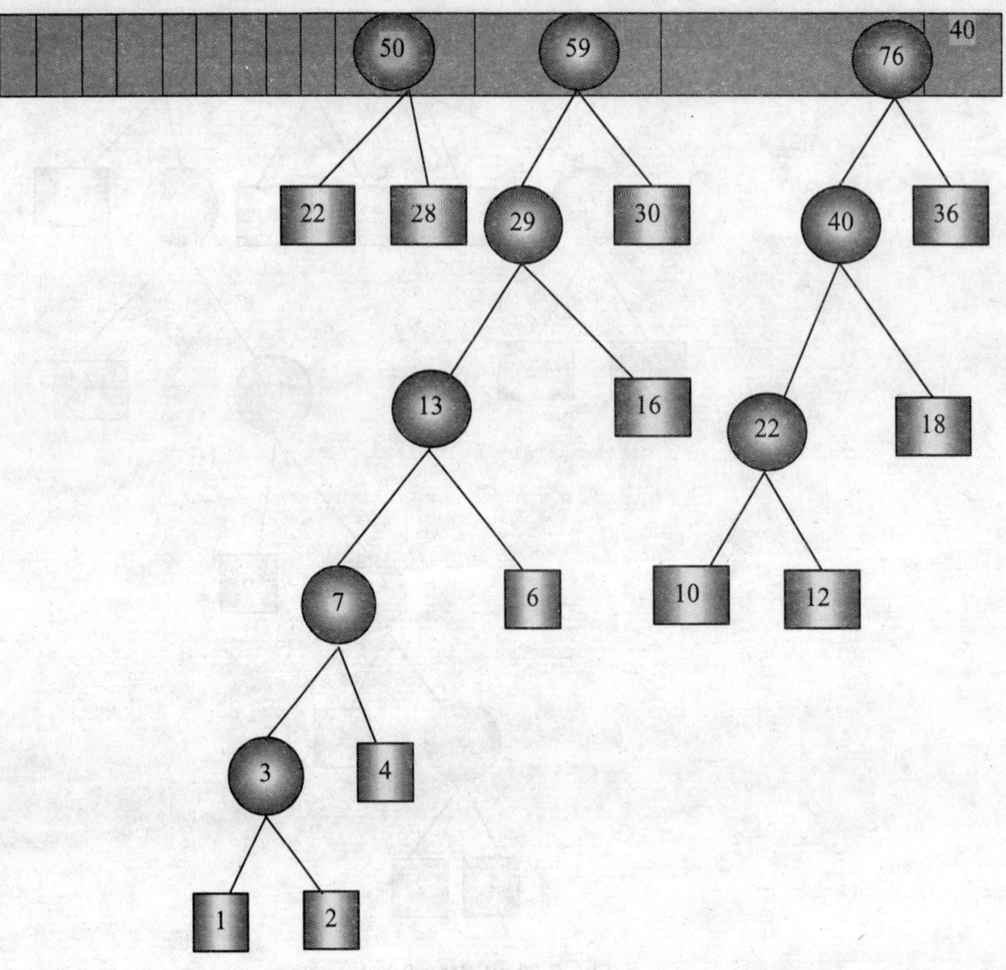

Fig. 7.29 (j) Step 10

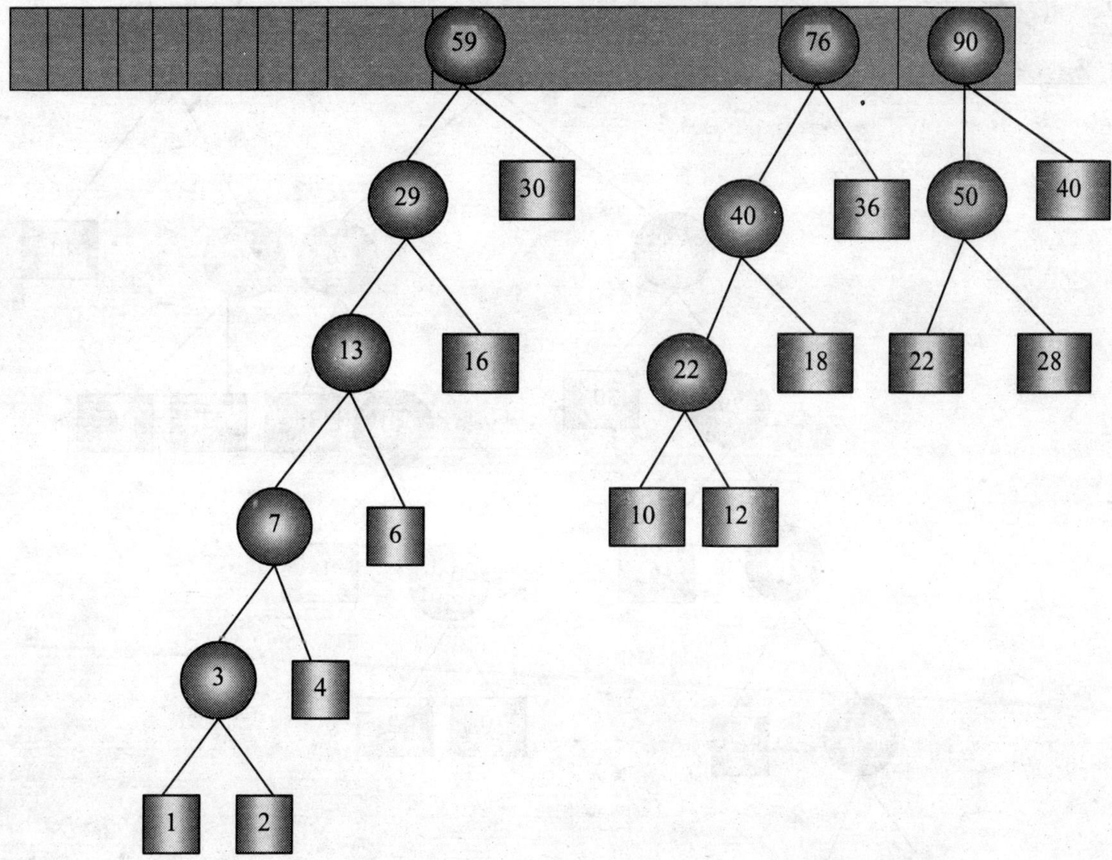

Fig. 7.29 (k) Step 11

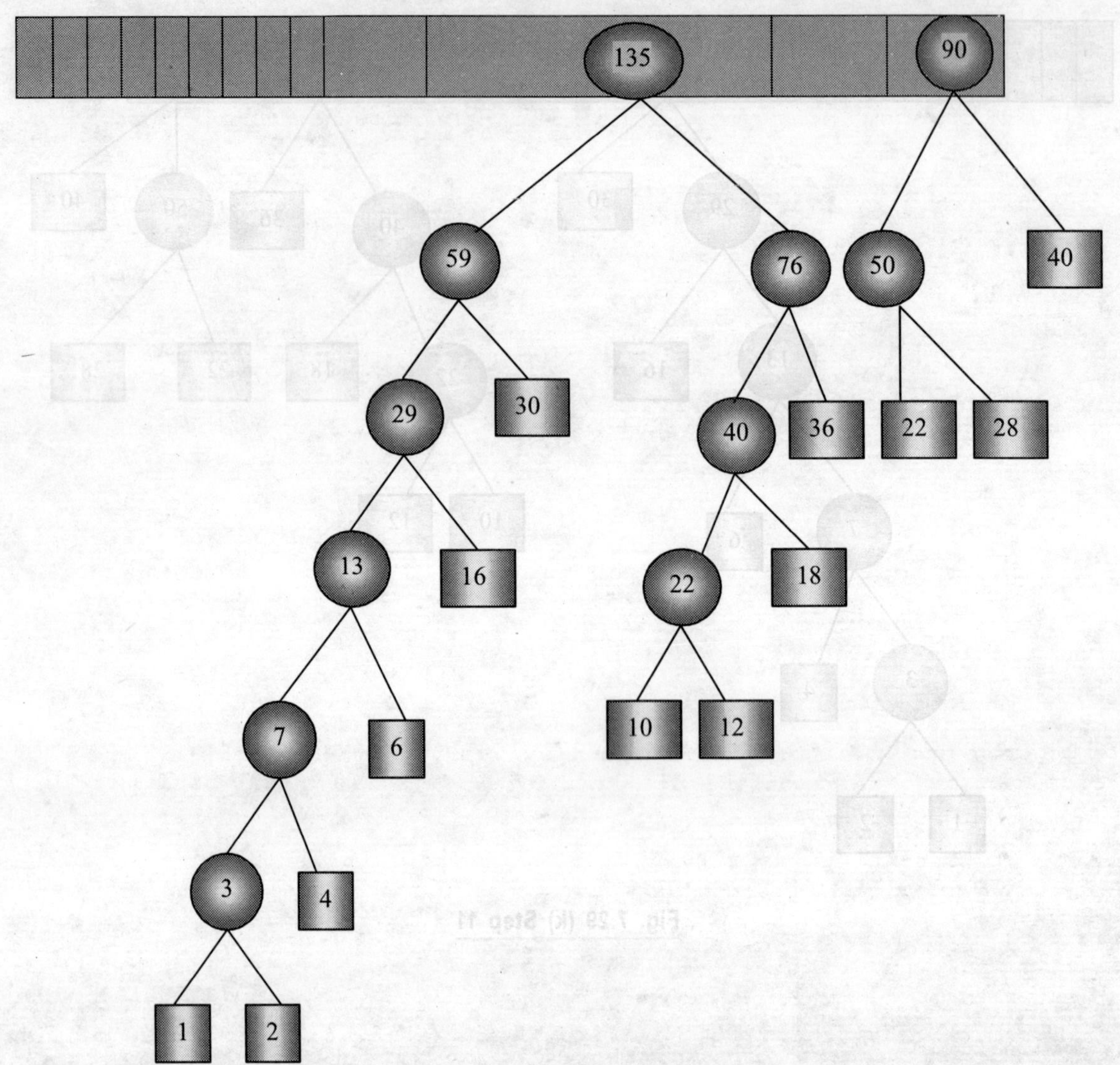

Fig. 7.29 (l) Step 12

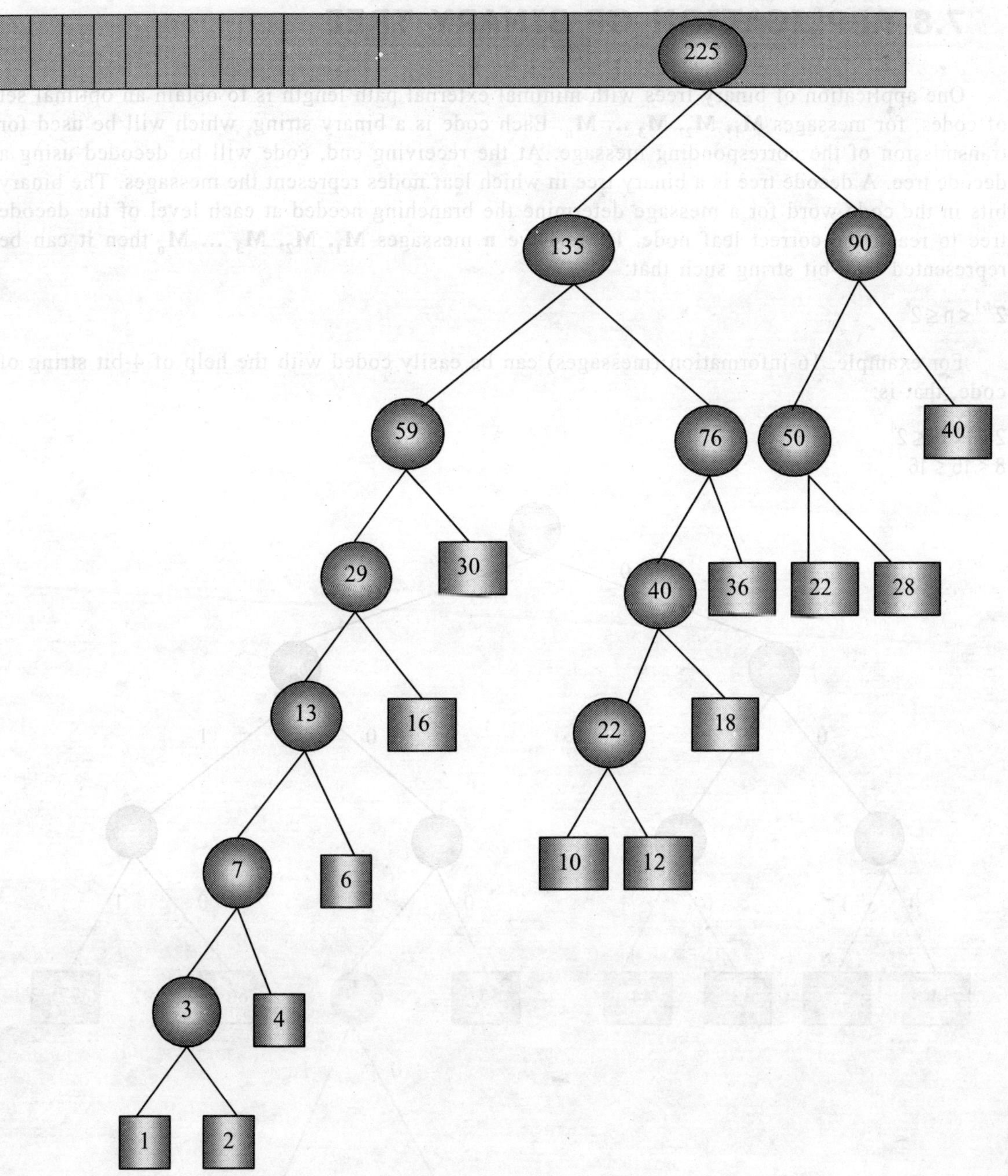

Fig. 7.29 Resulting Huffman tree

7.8 APPLICATION OF BINARY TREE

One application of binary trees with minimal external path length is to obtain an optimal set of codes, for messages $\mathbf{M_1}$, $\mathbf{M_2}$, $\mathbf{M_3}$ ... $\mathbf{M_n}$. Each code is a binary string, which will be used for transmission of the corresponding message. At the receiving end, code will be decoded using a decode tree. A decode tree is a binary tree in which leaf nodes represent the messages. The binary bits in the code word for a message determine the branching needed at each level of the decode tree to reach the correct leaf node. If we have **n** messages $\mathbf{M_1}$, $\mathbf{M_2}$, $\mathbf{M_3}$ ... $\mathbf{M_n}$ then it can be represented by **r**-bit string such that:

$$2^{r-1} < n \leq 2^r$$

For example, 16-information (messages) can be easily coded with the help of 4-bit string of code, that is:

$$2^{4-1} < 16 \leq 2^4$$
$$8 < 16 \leq 16$$

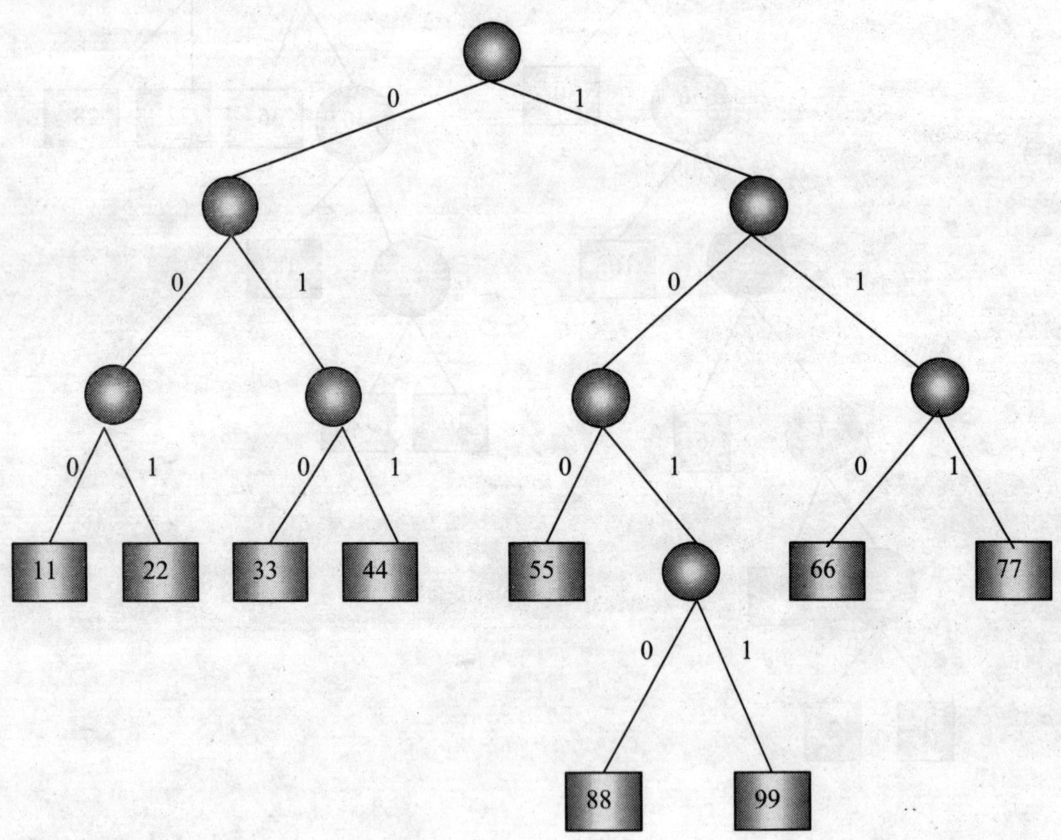

Fig. 7.30 Huffman code tree

When information do not occur with the same probability, then memory space may be conserved using variable length strings where the information which occur frequently are assigned shorter strings and are assigned longer strings, otherwise. For example, consider the 2-tree shown in **Fig. 7.30,** where external nodes have the information 11, 22, 33, 44, 55, 66, 77, 88, 99. In this, the bit 0 labeled each edge from an internal node to the left child and the bit 1 labels each edge to the right child. According to Huffman algorithm, code for each external node is evaluated from root to that node as a sequence of bits. Thus in **Fig. 7.30** codes for the external nodes are illustrated in **Table. 7.1.**

Table. 7.1 Huffman Code for tree shown in Fig. 7.30

Information At Leaf Node	Corresponding Code
11	00
22	001
33	010
44	011
55	100
66	110
77	111
88	1010
99	1011

From **Table. 7.1** it is clear that the code of any information does not contain initial sub-string of the code of any other information. Thus, we can say that there can not be any ambiguity in decoding any message using a Huffman coding scheme.

7.9 SEARCH TREE

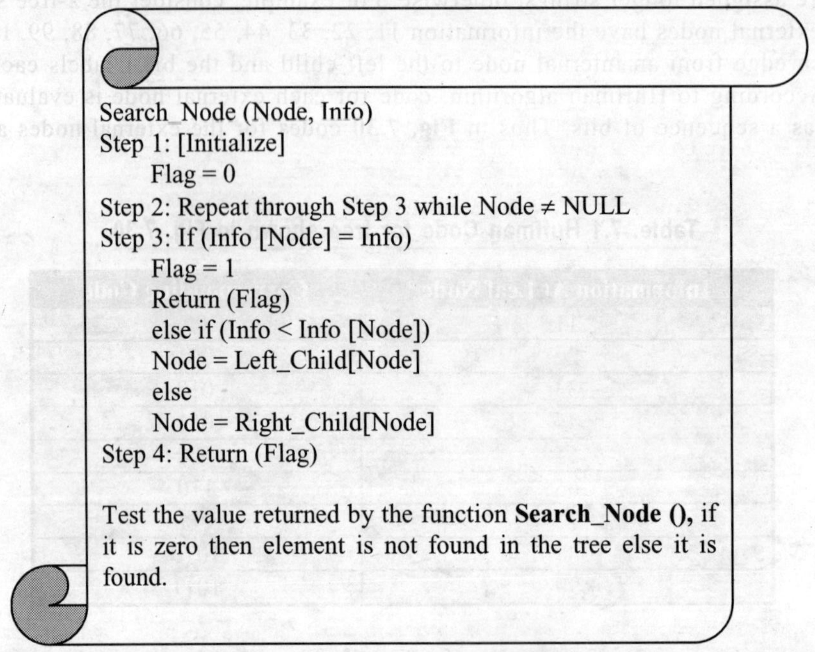

Fig. 7.31 Binary search algorithm

A binary search tree is a binary tree that is either empty or in which each node possesses a key that satisfies the following conditions:

(i) *All keys (if any) in the left sub-tree of the root precede the key in the root.*
(ii) *The key in the root precedes all keys (if any) in its right sub-tree.*
(iii) *The left and right sub-trees of the root are again search trees.*

To search for the target, we first compare it with the key at the root of the tree. If it is not same, we go to either the left sub-tree or right sub-tree as appropriate and repeat the search in that sub-tree. What condition will terminate the execution? Clearly if we find the key, the function succeeds. If not, then we continue searching until we find an empty sub-tree. The details of the search algorithm are given in **Fig. 7.31.** For example, consider the tree shown in **Fig. 7.32,** if we apply binary search to the list of names then the list that arises after processing (in sorted order left and right sub-trees) is:

Amy, Ann, Dot, Eva, Guy, Jan, Jim, Jon, Kay, Kim, Ron, Roy, Tim, Tom

If this list is maintained by linked list then the search requires **O (n)** time, while for binary search tree the time required is **O ($\log_2$ n)**. The program segment **SEARCH_B.C** implements the algorithm discussed in **Fig. 7.31.**

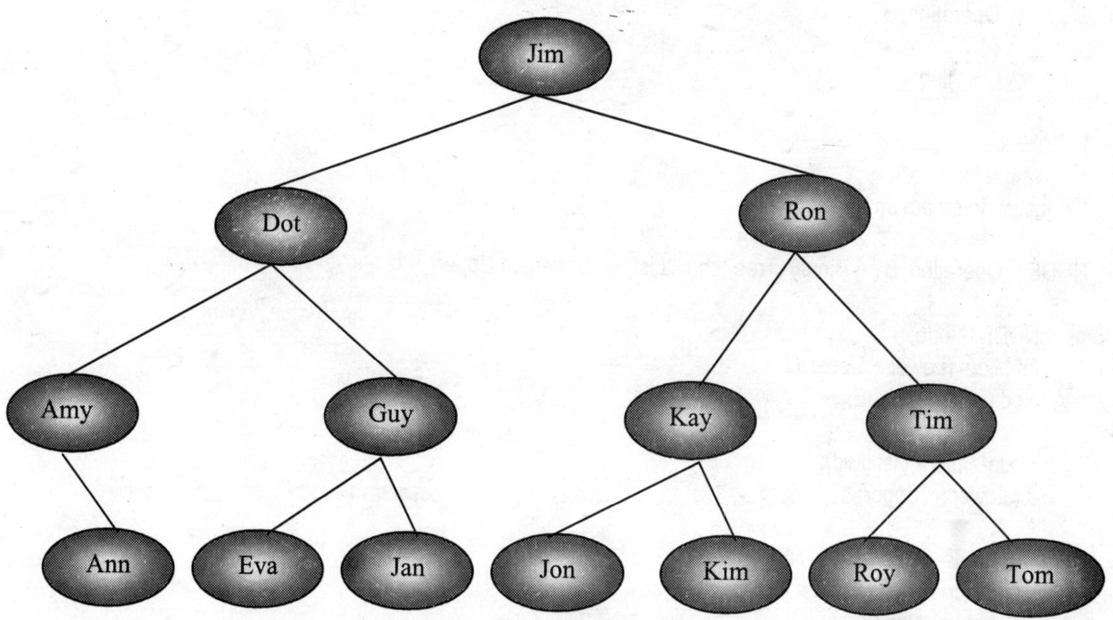

Fig. 7.32 Binary tree

```
// Searching Binary Tree
// SEARCH_B.C

# include<iostream.h>
# include<stdio.h>

struct NODE
{
	char Info;
	NODE *Left_Child;
	NODE *Right_Child;
};

class Operation_BT
{
	public:
		int flag;
	public:
		NODE *Binary_Tree (char *, int, int);
		void Output(NODE *, int );
		int Search_Node(NODE *, char);
```

```
        Operation_BT()
        {
            flag = 0;
        }
};

// Function to create an binary tree

NODE *  Operation_BT :: Binary_Tree (char *List, int Lower, int Upper)
{
    NODE *Node;
    int Mid = (Lower + Upper)/2;
    Node = new (NODE);

    Node->Info = List [Mid];
    if ( Lower>= Upper)
    {
        Node->Left_Child = NULL;
        Node->Right_Child = NULL;
        return (Node);
    }

    if (Lower <= Mid - 1)
        Node->Left_Child = Binary_Tree (List, Lower, Mid - 1);
    else
        Node->Left_Child = NULL;
    if (Mid + 1 <= Upper)
        Node->Right_Child = Binary_Tree (List, Mid + 1, Upper);
    else
        Node->Right_Child = NULL;
    return(Node);
}

// Output function

void Operation_BT :: Output(NODE *T, int Level)
{
    if (T)
    {
        Output(T->Right_Child, Level+1);
        cout<<"\n";
        for (int i = 0; i < Level; i++)
            cout<<"  ";
        cout<< T->Info;
        Output(T->Left_Child, Level+1);
```

```
    }
}

// Insert a node in the tree

int Operation_BT :: Search_Node(NODE *Node, char Info)
{
    while (Node != NULL)
    {
        if (Node->Info == Info)
        {
            flag = 1;
            return(flag);
        }
        else
            if( Info < Node->Info)
            {
                Node = Node->Left_Child;
            }
            else
            {
                Node = Node->Right_Child;
            }
    }
    return(flag);
}

// Function main

void main()
{
    Operation_BT Search_BT;
    char List[100];
    int Number = 0;
    char Info ;
    char choice;
    NODE *T = new (NODE);
    T = NULL;
    cout<<"\n Input choice 'b' to break:";
    choice = getchar();
    while(choice != 'b')
    {
        cout<<"\n Input information of the node: ";
        cin>>Info;
        List[Number++] = Info;
        cout<<"\n Input choice 'b' to break:";
```

```
        choice = getchar();
    }
    Number —;
    cout<<"\n Number of elements in the list is "<<Number+1;
    T = Search_BT.Binary_Tree(List, 0, Number);
    cout<<"\n Tree is \n";
    Search_BT.Output(T,1);
    cout<<"\n Input the information of the node to which want to search: ";
    cin>>Info;
    int flag = Search_BT.Search_Node(T, Info);
    if (flag)
    {
        cout<<"\n Search is successful \n";
    }
}
```

```
Input choice 'b' to break:
Input information of the node: A
Input choice 'b' to break:
Input information of the node: B
Input choice 'b' to break:
Input information of the node: D
Input choice 'b' to break:
Input information of the node: G
Input choice 'b' to break:
Input information of the node: H
Input choice 'b' to break: b
Number of elements in the list is 5
Tree is

          H
      G
  D
          B
      A
Input the information of the node to which wants
to search: G
 Search is successful
```

7.9.1 DELETION IN A BINARY SEARCH TREE

The deletion is an easy task if the deleted node has only one sub-tree. In this case we simply link the parent of the deleted node to its sub-tree. When the element to be deleted has both left and right sub-trees nonempty, the problem becomes more complicated. In this case two questions arise which of the sub-trees should point the parent of the deleted node and what is to be done with the other sub-tree? This is illustrated in **Fig. 7.33.**

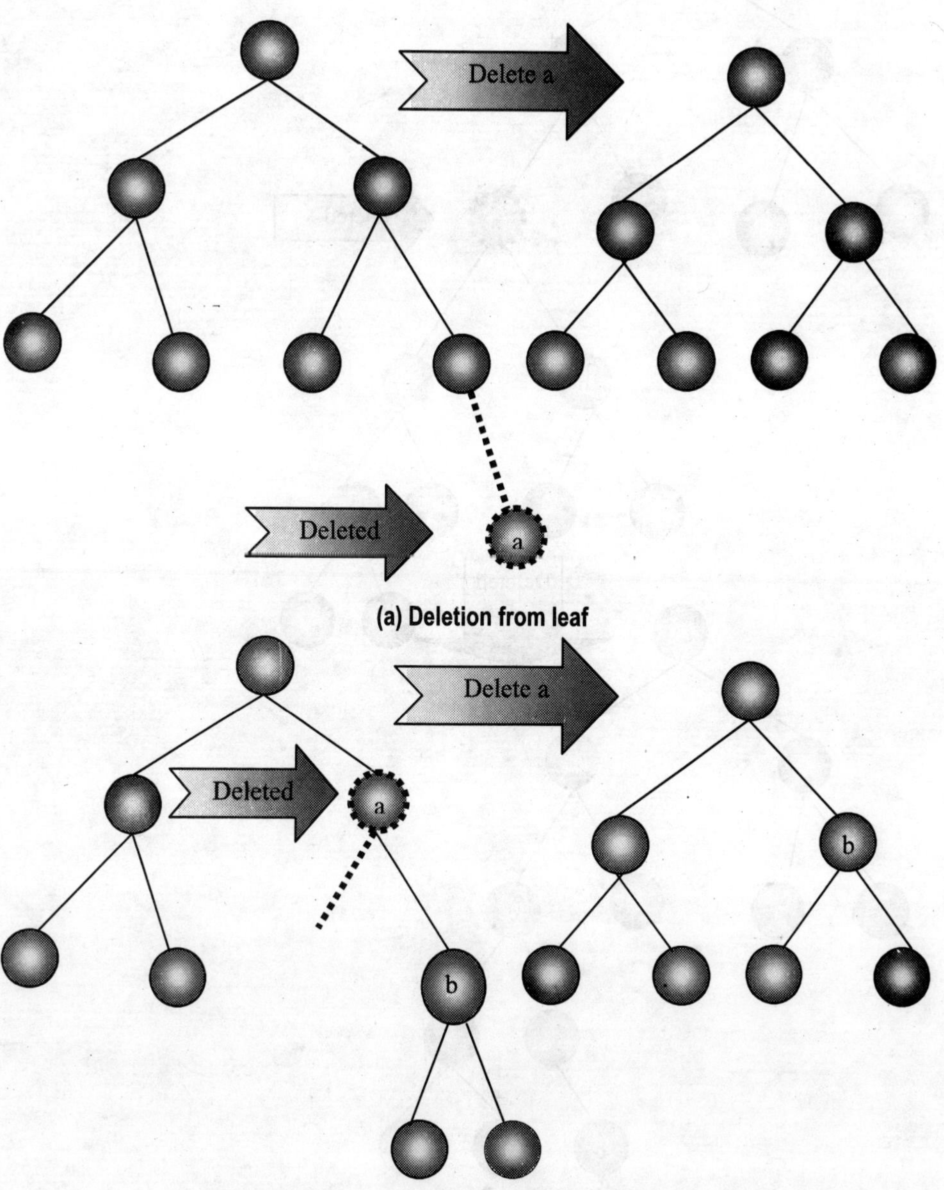

(a) Deletion from leaf

(b) Deletion of non-terminal (Empty left sub-tree)

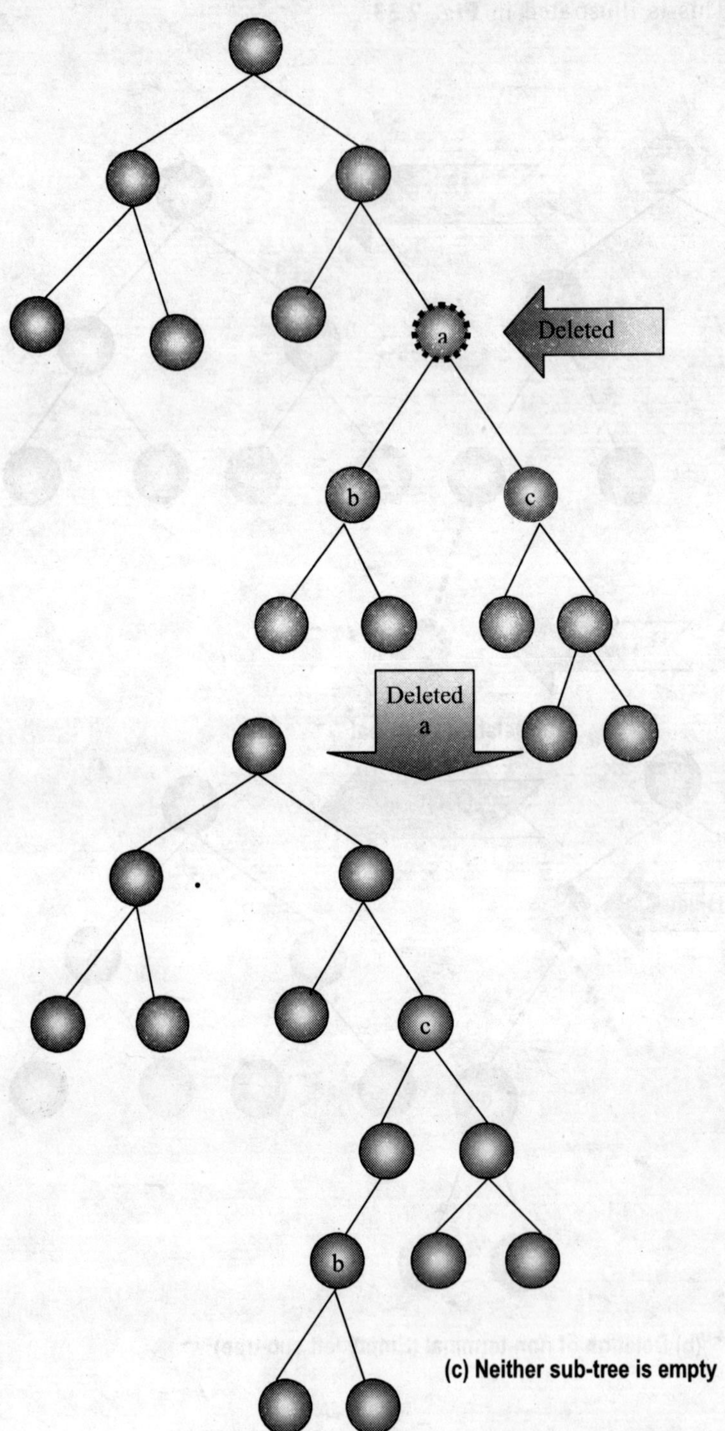

(c) Neither sub-tree is empty

Fig. 7.33 Deletion of node in a search tree

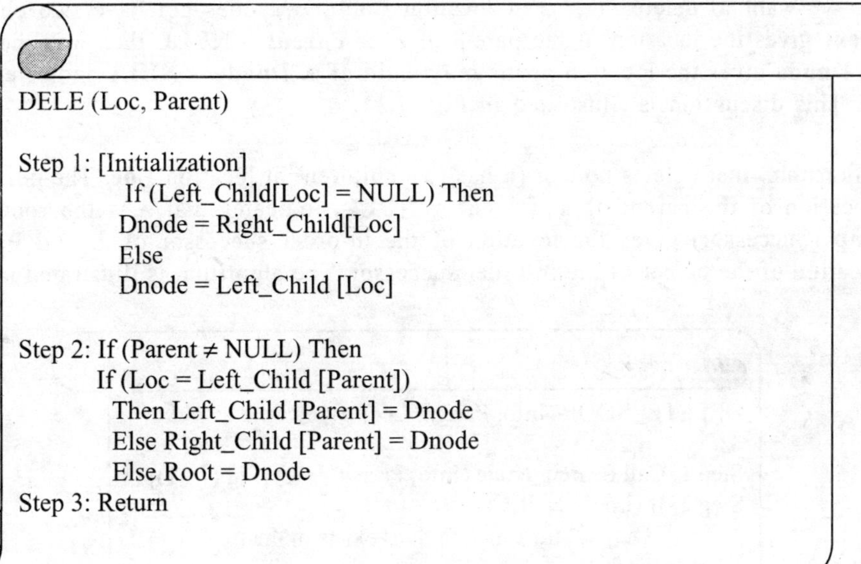

```
DELE (Loc, Parent)

Step 1: [Initialization]
        If (Left_Child[Loc] = NULL) Then
        Dnode = Right_Child[Loc]
        Else
        Dnode = Left_Child [Loc]

Step 2: If (Parent ≠ NULL) Then
        If (Loc = Left_Child [Parent])
          Then Left_Child [Parent] = Dnode
          Else Right_Child [Parent] = Dnode
          Else Root = Dnode
Step 3: Return
```

Fig. 7.34 Deletion in binary search tree phase 1

```
Delete_Node (Parent, Loc)

Step 1:  (i)     Temp = Right_Child [Loc]
         (ii)    Parent_Succ = Loc
Step 2: Repeat while (Left_Child [Temp] ≠ NULL)
         (i)     Parent_Succ = Temp
         (ii)    Temp = Left_Child [Temp]
         (iii)   Successor = Parent
         (iv)    Parent_Successor = Save

Step 3: Call DELE (Temp, Parent_Succ)

Step 4: (i) If (Parent ≠ NULL) Then
            If Loc = Left_Child[Parent] Then
             Left_Child[Parent] = Temp
              Else
                Left_Child[Temp] = Left_Child[Loc]
                Right_Child[Successor] = Right_Child[Loc]
Step 4: Return
```

Fig. 7.35 Deletion in Binary search tree phase 2

Suppose we want to delete node **a** at location **Loc** and **a** does not have two children. The pointer **Parent** gives the location of the parent of **a**. If **Parent** = **NULL** then **a** is the root node. The pointer **Dnode** gives the location of the only child of **a. Dnode** = **NULL** indicates that **a** has no children. This discussion is illustrated in **Fig. 7.34.**

Other algorithm, that deletes node **a** (**a** has two children) at location **Loc.** The pointer **Parent** gives the location of the parent of **a**. **Parent** = **NULL,** indicates that **a** is the root node. The pointer **Temp** (Successor) gives the location of the in-order successor of **a**, and **Parent_Succ** gives the location of the parent of the in-order successor. The algorithm is illustrated in **Fig. 7.35.**

```
DELETE_NODE (Info, Parent, Loc)

Step 1: Call Search_Node (Info, Parent, Loc) [Fig (7.31)]
Step 2: If (Loc = NULL)
            Output" Information does exists in the tree"
            Exit
            Else
            If (Left_Child[Loc] ≠ NULL and
             Right_Child[Loc] ≠ NULL)
Call Delete_Node (Parent, Loc)
Call DELE(Parent, Loc)
```

Fig. 7.36 Deletion in binary search tree

The program segment **DELET_BT.C** implements the above discussion.

```
// Deleting in Binary Tree
// DELET_BT.C

# include<iostream.h>
# include<stdio.h>

struct NODE
{
    int Info;
    NODE *Left_Child;
    NODE *Right_Child;
};

class Operation_BT
{
```

```
    public:
        int depth;
    public:
        void Output (NODE *, int );
        NODE *Delet_Node (NODE *, int );
        NODE *Create_Tree (int , NODE *);
        NODE * DELE(NODE *, NODE *);
};

// Output function

void Operation_BT :: Output(NODE *T, int Level)
{
    if (T)
    {
        Output(T->Right_Child, Level+1);
        cout<<"\n";
        for (int i = 0; i < Level; i++)
            cout<<"  ";
        cout<< T->Info;
        Output(T->Left_Child, Level+1);
    }
}

// Delete a node in the binary tree

NODE * Operation_BT :: DELE(NODE *Node1, NODE *Node)
{
    NODE *DNode;
    if (Node1->Right_Child != NULL)
        Node1->Right_Child = DELE(Node1->Right_Child, Node);
    else
    {
        DNode = Node1;
        Node->Info = Node1->Info;
        Node1 = Node1->Left_Child;
        delete(DNode);
    }
    return (Node1);
}

// Deletion in binary tree

NODE * Operation_BT :: Delet_Node (NODE *Node, int Info)
{
    NODE *Temp;
```

```
	if (Node == NULL)
	{
		cout<<"\n Information does not exist in the above tree";
		return (Node);
	}
	else
	{
		if (Info < Node->Info )
			Node->Left_Child = Delet_Node (Node->Left_Child, Info);
		else
			if (Info > Node->Info )

				Node->Left_Child = Delet_Node (Node->Right_Child, Info);
			else
			{
				Temp = Node;
				if (Temp->Right_Child == NULL)
				{
					Node = Temp->Left_Child;
					delete(Temp);
				}
				else
					if (Temp->Left_Child == NULL)
					{
						Node = Temp->Right_Child;
						delete(Temp);
					}
					else
						Temp->Left_Child = DELE(Temp->Left_Child, Temp);
			}
	}
	return(Node);
}

// Create binary tree

NODE *  Operation_BT :: Create_Tree (int Info, NODE *Node)
{

	if (Node == NULL)
	{
		Node = new (NODE);
		Node->Info = Info;
		Node->Left_Child = NULL;
		Node->Right_Child = NULL;
```

```
        return (Node);
    }

    // Test for the left child

        if (Info < Node->Info)

            Node->Left_Child = Create_Tree (Info, Node->Left_Child);

    else

            // Test for the right child

                if (Info > Node->Info)

                    Node->Right_Child = Create_Tree (Info, Node->Right_Child);
    return(Node);
}

// Function main
void main()
{
    Operation_BT Delet_BT;
    int Number = 0;
    int Info ;
    char choice;
    int depth;
    NODE *T = new (NODE);
    T = NULL;
    cout<<"\n Input choice 'b' to break:";
    choice = getchar();
    while(choice != 'b')
    {
        cout<<"\n Input information of the node: ";
        cin>>Info;
        T = Delet_BT.Create_Tree(Info, T);
        Number++;
        cout<<"\n Input choice 'b' to break:";
        choice = getchar();
    }
    cout<<"\n Number of elements in the list is "<<Number;
    cout<<"\n Tree is \n";
    Delet_BT.Output(T,1);
```

```
        cout<<"\n Input the information to which want remove from the above tree: ";
        cin>>Info;

        T = Delet_BT.Delet_Node(T, Info);
        cout<<"\n Tree after deletion of a node: ";
        Delet_BT.Output(T,1);
}
```

7.10 BALANCED BINARY TREE

Balanced binary trees are classified into two categories:

- *Height Balanced*
- *Weight Balanced*

7.10.1 HEIGHT BALANCED

Two Russian mathematicians, ***G.M. ADEL' SON-VEL'SKII*** and ***E.M. LANDIS***, gave a technique in 1962. It is feasible to balance the height of binary trees using this technique and the resulting tree is called **AVL** trees in their honour. With the help of **AVL** trees searching, insertions and deletions in a tree with **n** nodes achieved in time of order **O (n),** even in the worst case. The height of an **AVL** tree with **n** nodes can never exceed by **1.44** $\mathbf{\log_2 n}$ and thus the behaviour of an **AVL** tree could not be much below that of a random binary search tree. The actual length of a search is near to $\mathbf{\log_2 n}$ and thus the behaviour of **AVL** trees are closed to ideal balanced binary tree.

A tree is called **AVL** tree (Balanced binary tree), if each node possesses one of the following properties:

- *A node is called left heavy, if the longest path in its left sub-tree is one longer than the longest path of its right sub-tree.*
- *A node is called right heavy, if the longest path in the right sub-tree is one longer than the longest path in its left sub-tree.*
- *A node is called balanced, if the longest paths in both the right and left sub-trees are equal. For example, **Fig. 7.37** illustrates a balanced binary tree.*

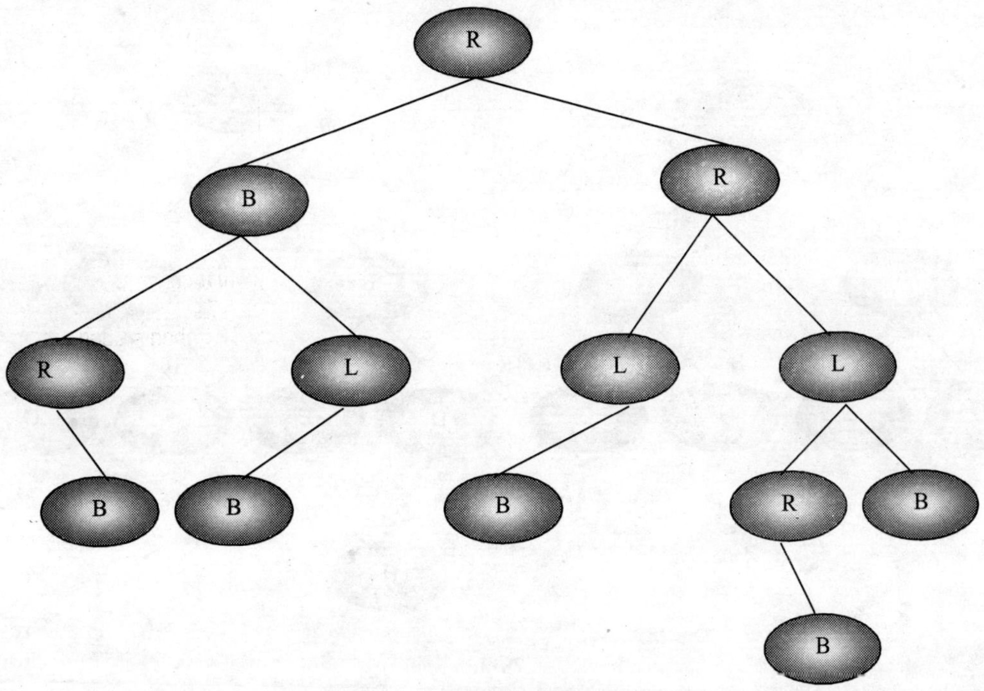

Fig. 7.37 Balanced Binary Tree

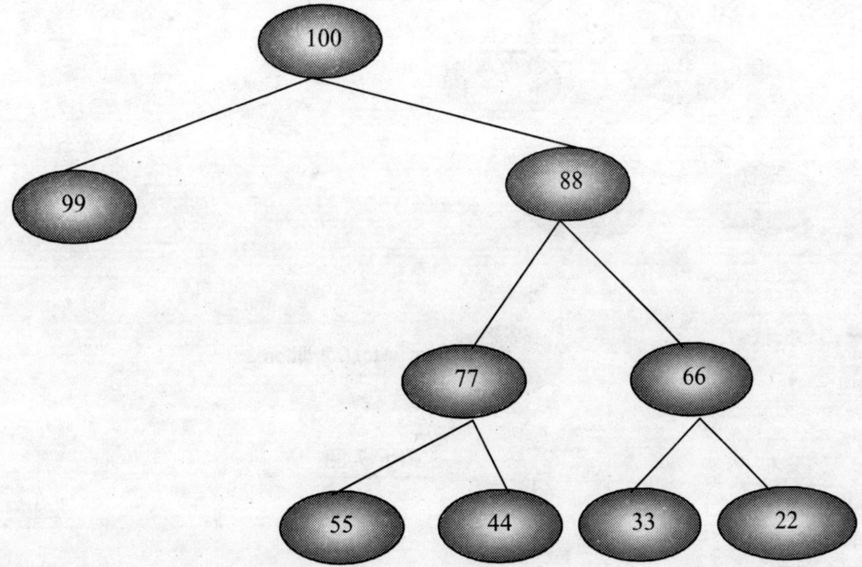

Fig. 7.38 Unbalanced Binary Tree

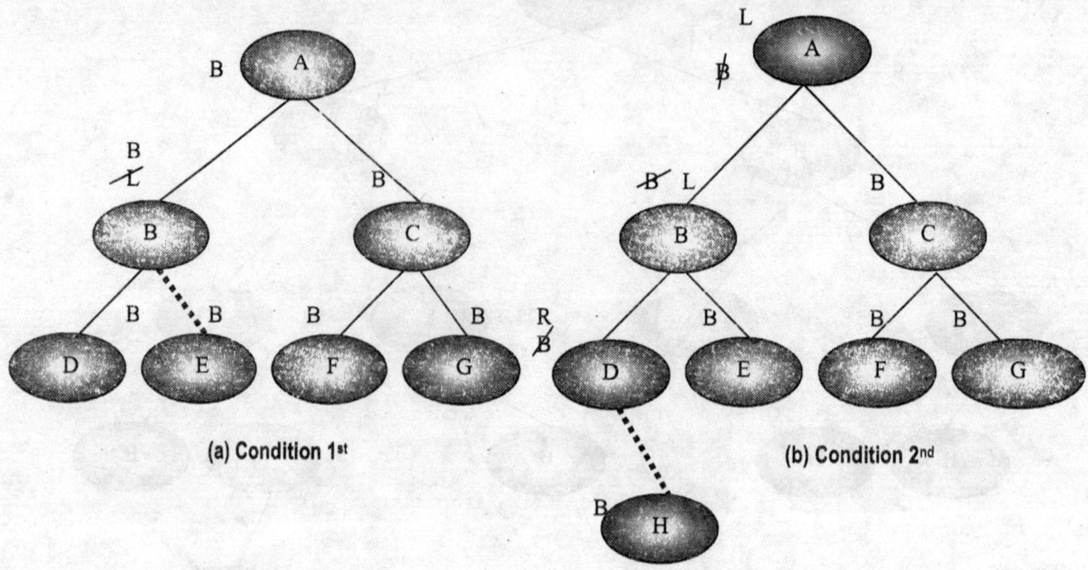

(a) Condition 1st

(b) Condition 2nd

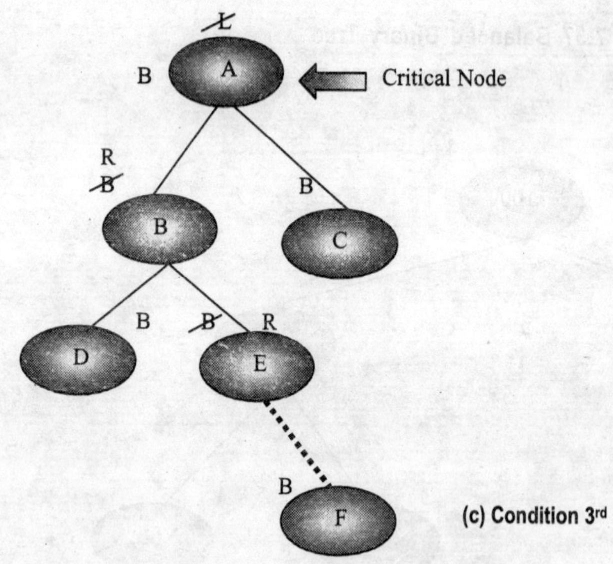

(c) Condition 3rd

Fig. 7.39

B →Balanced

L →Left Heavy

R →Right Heavy

→Newly Inserted Node (Linked with this type of line)

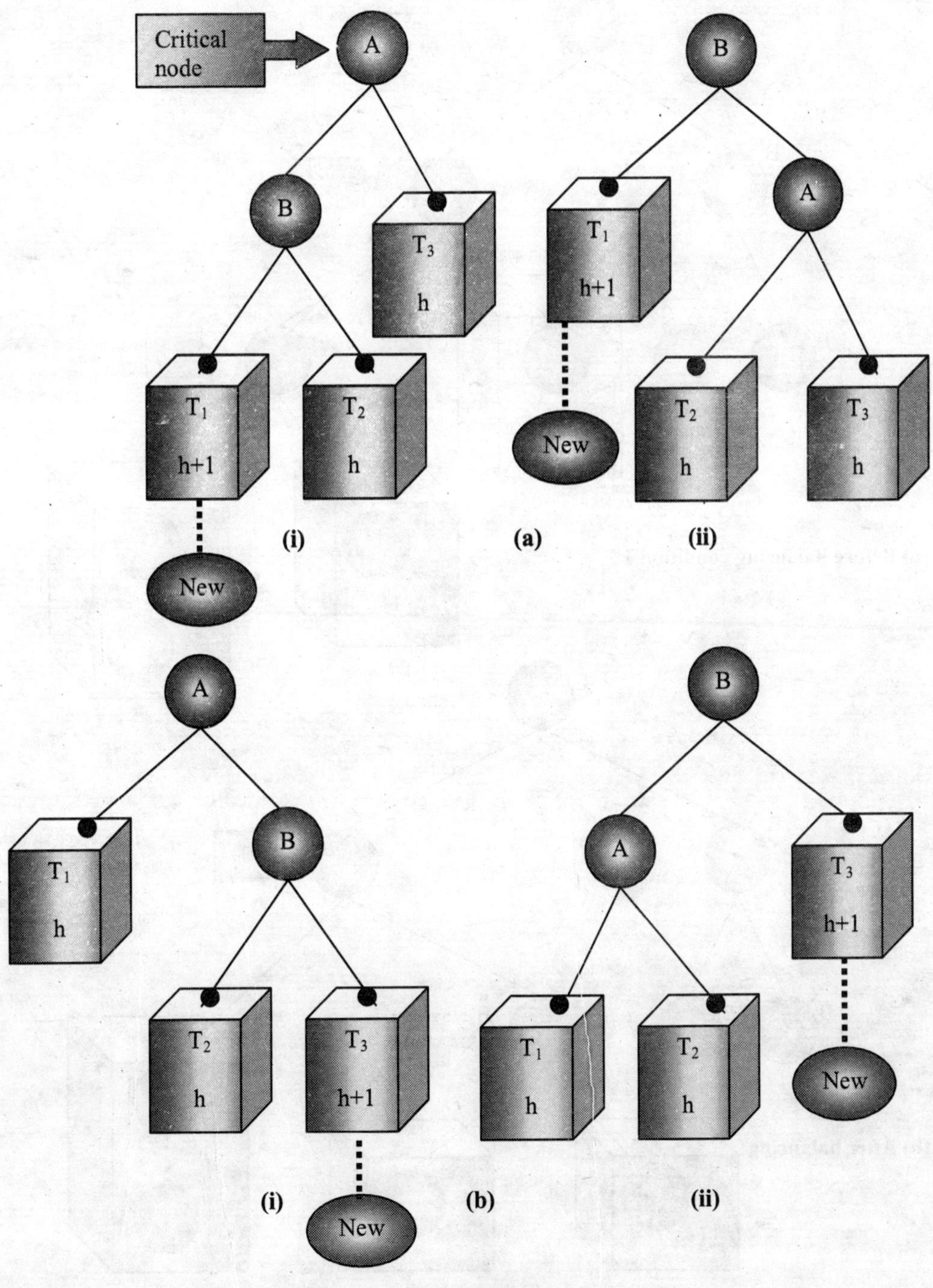
Critical node
A
B
T₃
h
T₁
h+1
T₂
h
New
(i)
B
A
T₁
h+1
New
T₂
h
T₃
h
(a)
(ii)
A
T₁
h
B
T₂
h
T₃
h+1
New
(i)
(b)
B
A
T₃
h+1
New
T₁
h
T₂
h
(ii)

Fig. 7.40

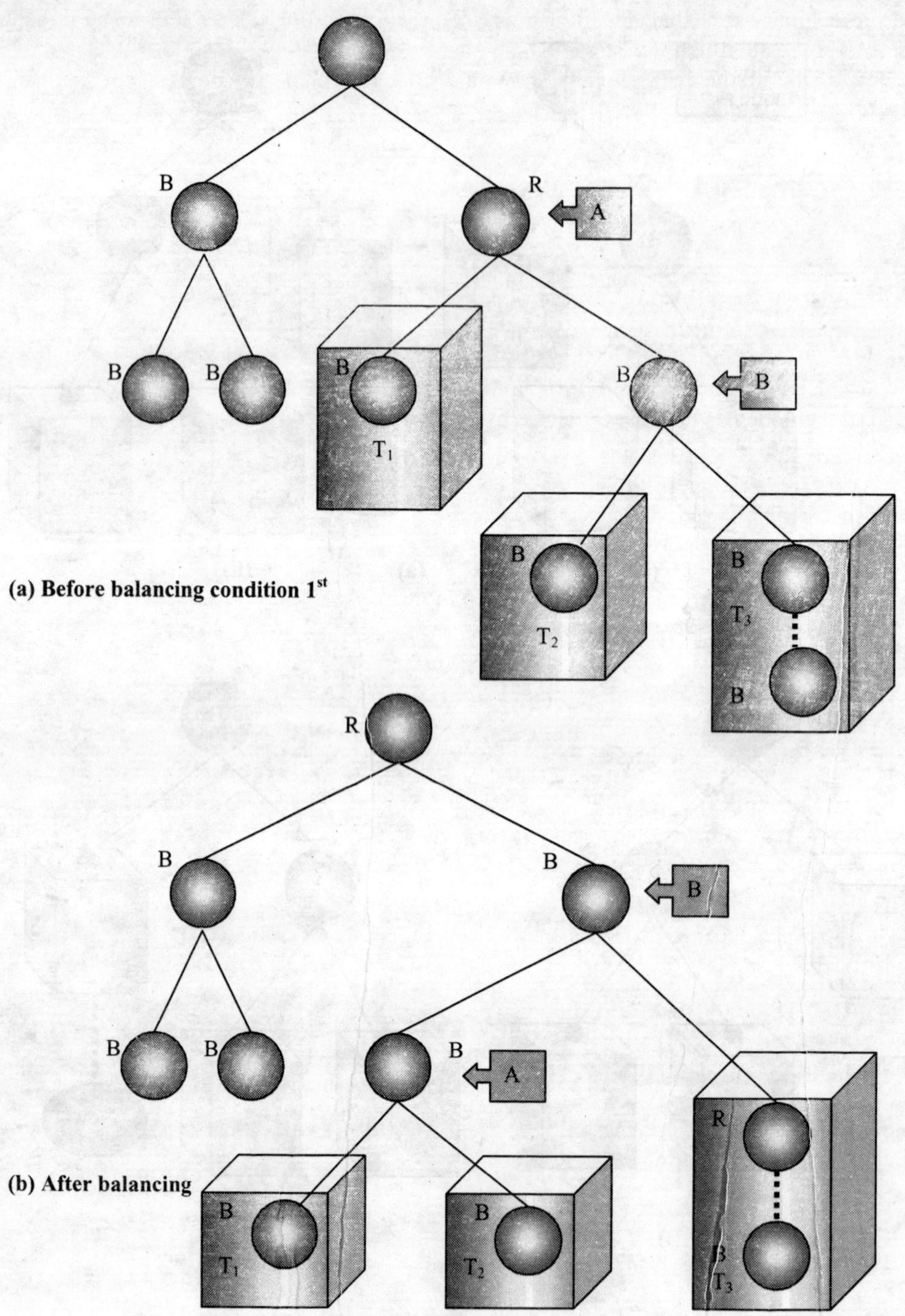

Fig. 7.41 Example

A node in a binary tree that does not contain the above properties is said to be unbalanced. For example, **Fig. 7.38** illustrates an unbalanced binary tree. If one inserts a new node into a balanced binary tree at the leaf, then the possible changes in the status of a node on the path (balanced indicator), which can occur are as follows:

- *The node was either left or right heavy and has now become balanced.*
- *The node was balanced and has now become left or right heavy.*
- *The node was heavy and the new node has been inserted in the heavy sub-tree, thus creating an unbalanced sub-tree, such a node is called a critical node.*

If we apply first condition to current node, then the balance indicators of all the ancestor nodes of this node remain unchanged, since the length of the longest path in the sub-tree remains unchanged. When second condition is applied to a current node, then the balance indicators of the ancestors will change. If the third condition applies to a current node, then the binary tree becomes unbalanced and the node has become critical. For example, **Fig. 7.39** illustrates the above discussion.

Now we discuss re-balancing of a tree when a critical node has been encountered. There are two broad cases, which can arise, each of which can be further sub-divided into two similar sub-cases. A general representation of case 1st is illustrated in **Fig. 7.40,** where the 3-D boxes labeled $\mathbf{T_1}$, $\mathbf{T_2}$, $\mathbf{T_3}$, $\mathbf{T_4}$, etc represent sub-trees and the node attached with dotted line is the node being inserted. The expression shown in the rectangles shows the height of that sub-tree. In **Fig. 7.40.(a),** since node **A** is critical, node **B** must be balanced before inserting a node. It is also possible that **B** becomes heavy in the same direction that **A** was heavy. This discussion is illustrated in **Fig. 7.41.** The 2nd case, which is illustrated in **Fig. 7.42** is much like the first one, except that node **B** becomes heavy in the opposite direction to that in which **A** was heavy. It is clear that node **C** must have been balanced prior to insertion.

7.10.2 INSERTION IN AVL TREE

We can insert a new node into an AVL tree by first using the usual binary tree insertion technique, comparing the key of the new node with that in the root and inserting the new node into the left or right sub-trees accurately. It often turns out that the new node can be inserted without changing the height of the sub-tree, in that case neither the height nor the balance factor of the root is changed. Even when the height of a sub-tree increases, it may be the shorter sub-tree that has grown up, so that only the balance factor of the root will be changed. The only case that can cause difficulty occurs when the new node is added to a sub-tree of the root that is strictly taller than the other sub-tree and the height is increased. This would cause one sub-tree to have height 2 more than other, where as the AVL condition restricts one height difference to be never more than one.

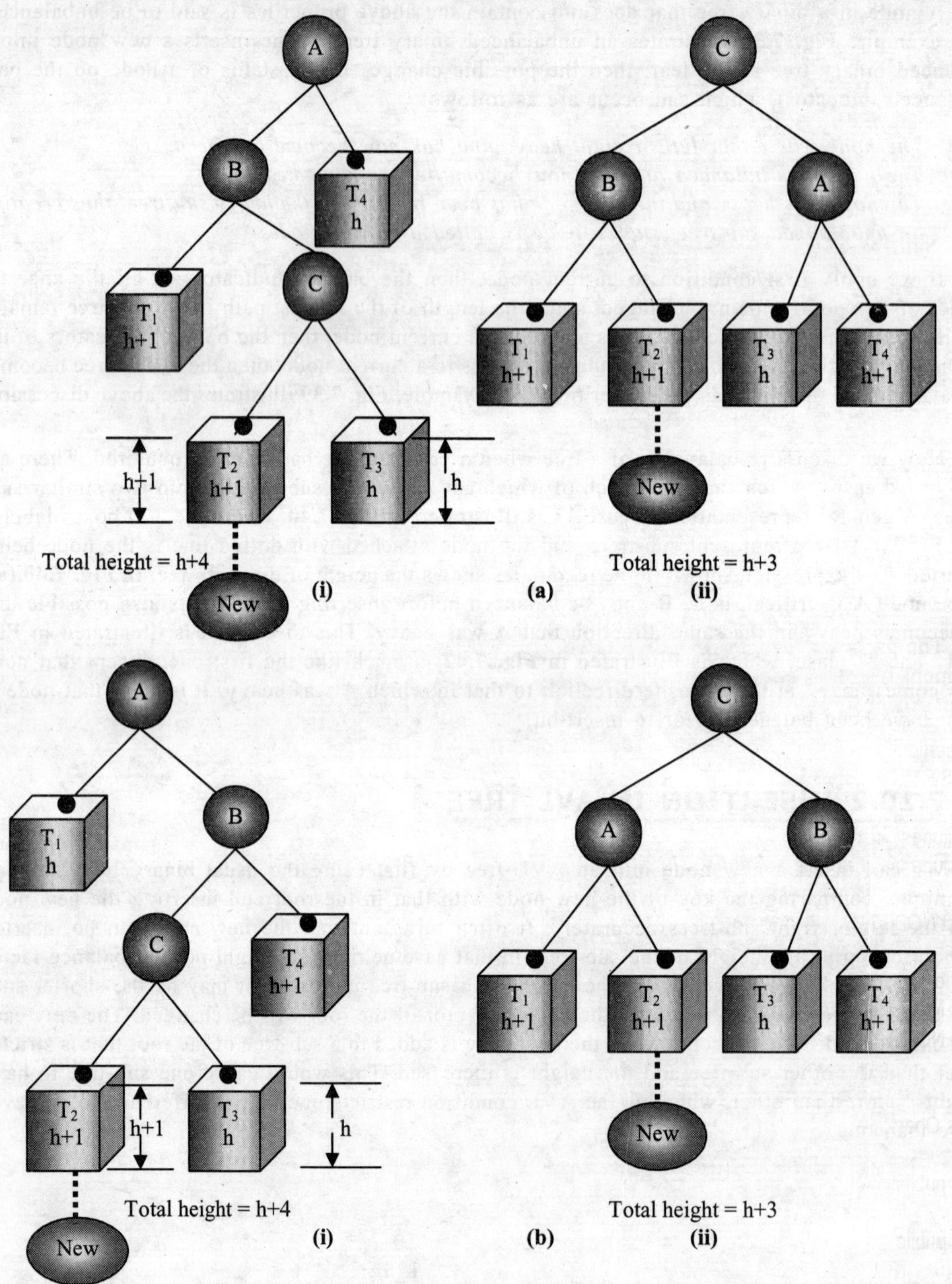

Fig. 7.42 2nd case

Step 1: If this is the first insertion then allocate a node, set its fields and return.

Step 2: If the information we want to insert is not already present in the tree then link the new node to the existing tree else discard the new information and return.

Step 3: Search for an unbalanced node.

Step 4: Adjust the balance factors if there is no critical node return.

Step 5: If the node was balanced and then becomes heavy or the node was heavy and now becomes balanced then adjust the balanced factors and return.

Step 6: Rebalance the tree and return.

Fig. 7.43 Insertion algorithm for AVL tree

The program segment **INSERT.C** implements the algorithm given in **Fig. 7.43.** This program segment insert a node in a binary tree and it does not completely follow the algorithm discussed here. According to need it is required to update this program segment.

```
// Insertion in a Binary Tree
// INSERT.C

# include<iostream.h>
# include<stdio.h>

struct NODE
{
	char Info;
	NODE *Left_Child;
	NODE *Right_Child;
};

class Operation_BT
{
	public:
		int flag;
	public:
		NODE *Binary_Tree (char *, int, int);
		void Output(NODE *, int );
```

```
        NODE *Insert_Node(NODE *, char);

        Operation_BT()
        {
            flag = 0;
        }
};

// Function to create an binary tree

NODE *  Operation_BT :: Binary_Tree (char *List, int Lower, int Upper)
{
    NODE *Node;
    int Mid = (Lower + Upper)/2;
    Node = new (NODE);

    Node->Info = List [Mid];
    if ( Lower>= Upper)
    {
        Node->Left_Child = NULL;
        Node->Right_Child = NULL;
        return (Node);
    }

    if (Lower <= Mid - 1)
        Node->Left_Child = Binary_Tree (List, Lower, Mid - 1);
    else
        Node->Left_Child = NULL;
    if (Mid + 1 <= Upper)
        Node->Right_Child = Binary_Tree (List, Mid + 1, Upper);
    else
        Node->Right_Child = NULL;
    return(Node);
}

// Output function

void Operation_BT :: Output(NODE *T, int Level)
{
    if (T)
    {
        Output(T->Right_Child, Level+1);
        cout<<"\n";
        for (int i = 0; i < Level; i++)
            cout<<"  ";
        cout<< T->Info;
```

```
        Output(T->Left_Child, Level+1);
    }
}

// Insert a node in the tree

NODE * Operation_BT :: Insert_Node(NODE *Node, char Info)
{
    if (Node == NULL)
    {
        Node = new (NODE);
        Node->Info = Info;
        Node->Left_Child = NULL;
        Node->Right_Child = NULL;
        return (Node);
    }

    // Test for the left child

      if (Node->Info >= Info )
        Nodc->Left_Child = Insert_Node (Node->Left_Child, Info);
    else

        // Set all the rest of the elements as right child

          Node->Right_Child = Insert_Node (Node->Right_Child, Info);

    return(Node);
}

// Function main

void main()
{
    Operation_BT Insertion_BT;
    char List[100];
    int Number = 0;
    char Info;
    char choice;
    NODE *T = new (NODE);
    T = NULL;
    cout<<"\n Input choice 'b' to break:";
    choice = getchar();
    while(choice != 'b')
    {
        cout<<"\n Input information of the node: ";
```

```
		cin>>Info;
		List[Number++] = Info;
		cout<<"\n Input choice 'b' to break:";
		choice = getchar();
	}
	Number —;
	cout<<"\n Number of elements in the list is "<<Number+1;
	T = Insertion_BT.Binary_Tree(List, 0, Number);
	cout<<"\n Tree is \n";
	Insertion_BT.Output(T,1);
	cout<<"\n Input the information of the node to which wants to insert: ";
	cin>>Info;
	T = Insertion_BT.Insert_Node(T, Info);
	cout<<"\n Tree is \n";
	Insertion_BT.Output(T,1);
}
```

```
Input choice 'b' to break:
Input information of the node: U
Input choice 'b' to break:
Input information of the node: W
Input choice 'b' to break:
Input information of the node: Y
Input choice 'b' to break:
Input information of the node: P
Input choice 'b' to break:
Input information of the node: T
Input choice 'b' to break:
Input information of the node: Q
Input choice 'b' to break: b
```

```
Number of elements in the list is 6
 Tree is

          Q
       T
          P
    Y
          W
       U

Input the information of the node to which wants to
insert: X
 Tree is

          Q
       T
          P
    Y
             X
          W
       U
```

When a tree does not satisfy the AVL requirements, it is required to rebuild the part of the tree to restore its balance. For example, assume that if we insert a new node into the right sub-tree, its height will increase and the original tree right high. Let **A** is the root of the tree and **B** is the root of its right sub-tree then there are three cases two of them are discussed here.

- *Right high*
- *Left high*
- *Equal high*

The general insertion algorithm illustrated in **Fig. 7.43.**

7.10.2.1 RIGHT HIGH (height of the right sub-tree is greater than left sub-tree)

If **B** is right high as illustrated in **Fig. 7.44** then the action needed in this case is called a left rotation. We rotate the node **B** upward to the root, dropping **A** down into the left sub-tree **B**; the sub-tree $\mathbf{T_2}$ of nodes with keys between **A** and **B** now becomes the right sub-tree of **A** rather than the left sub-tree of **B**.

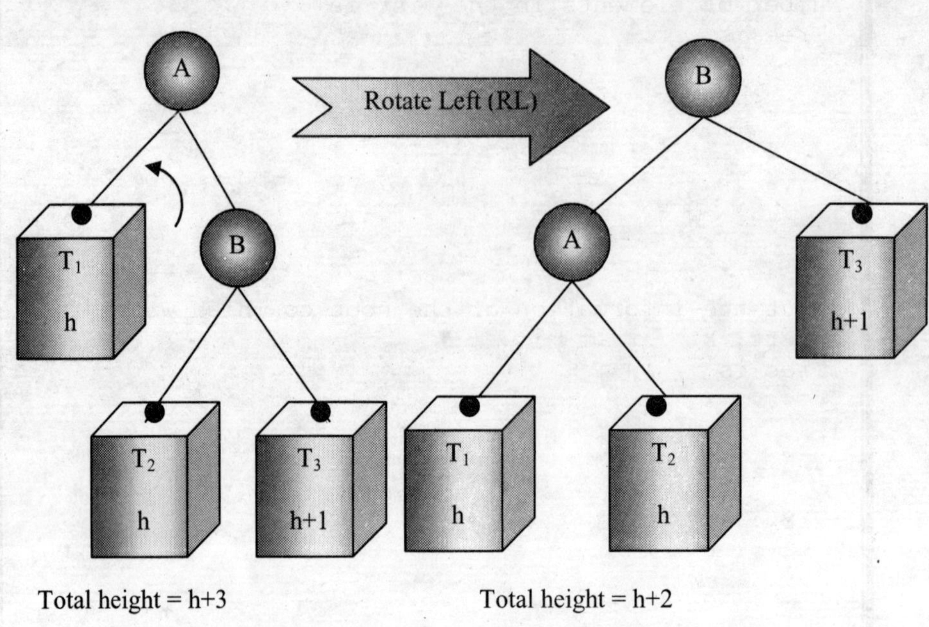

Fig. 7.44 Restoring balance by left rotation

7.10.2.2 LEFT HIGH (height of left sub-tree is greater than right sub-tree)

When the balance factor of **B** is left high then it is required to move two levels to the node **C** that roots the left sub-tree of **B**, to find the new root. This process is called the double rotation, because the transformation can be obtained in two steps, first rotating the sub-tree with root **B** to the right so that **C** becomes its root and then rotating the tree with root **A** to the left (moving **C** up to become the new root). In this case, new balance factors for **A** and **B** depend on the previous balance factor of **C** as illustrated in **Fig. 7.45.** The insertion procedure is illustrated in **Fig. 7.46.**

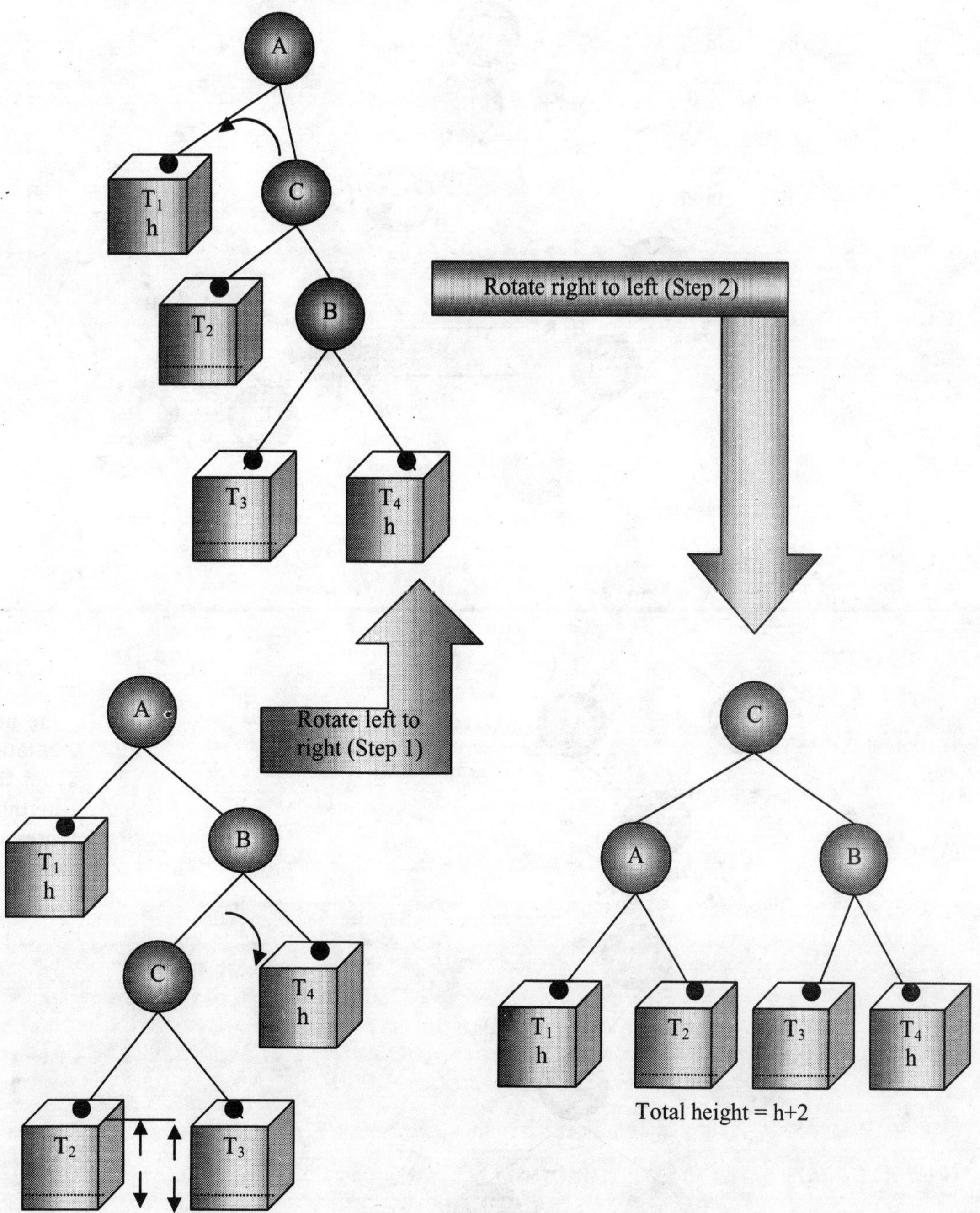

One of T_2 and T_3 has height h and other has h-1
Total height = h+3

Fig. 7.45

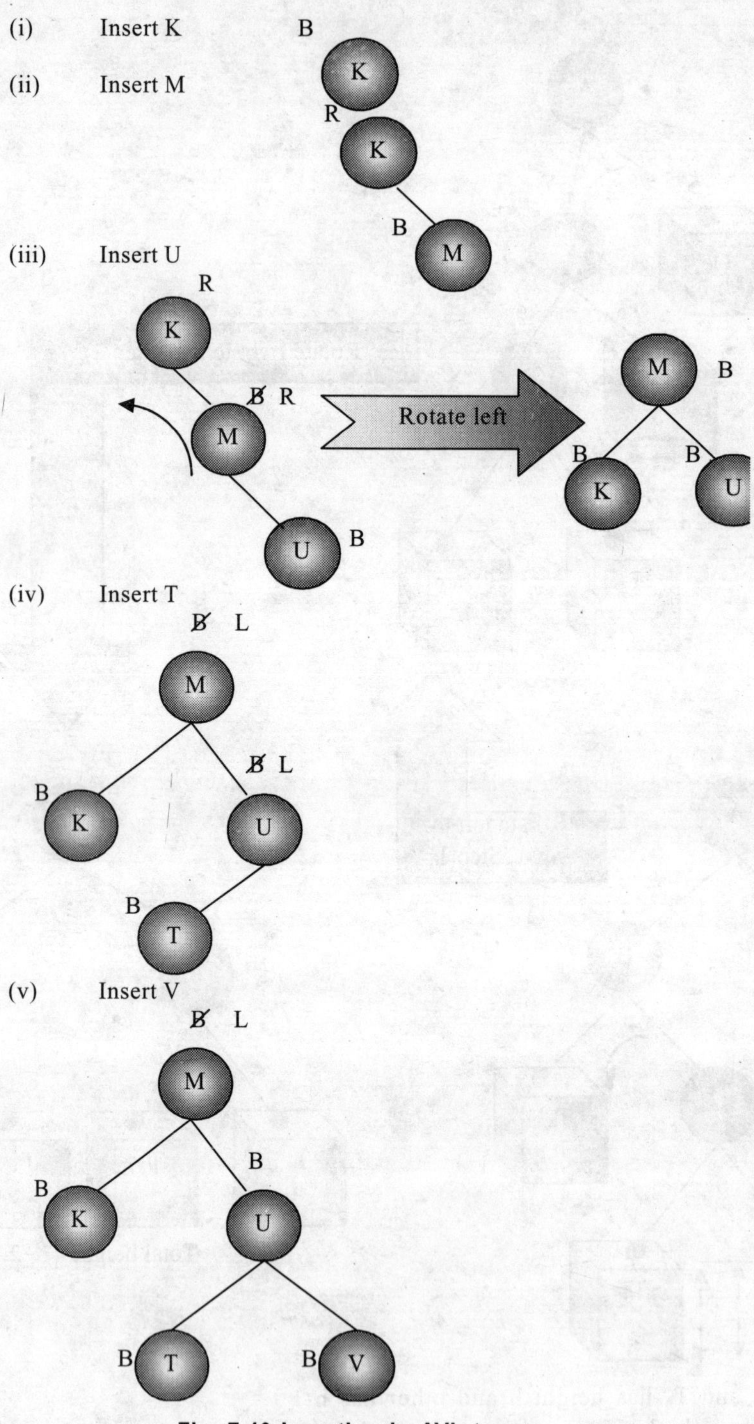

Fig. 7.46 Insertion in AVL tree

7.10.3 THE HEIGHT OF AN AVL TREE

What is the maximum height that an AVL tree with **n** nodes can have? Instead of this we can ask what is the minimum number of nodes that an AVL tree of height **h** can have. If F_h is such a tree, and the left and right sub-trees of its root are F_l and F_r, then one of F_l or F_r must have height **h-1**, say, F_l, and the other has height either **h-1** or **h-2**. Since, F_h has the minimum number of nodes among AVL trees of height **h,** it follows that F_l must have the minimum number of nodes among AVL trees of height **h-1.** F_l is of the form F_{h-1}, and F_r must have height **h-2** with minimum number of nodes simply that F_r is of the form F_{h-2}.

Trees that are built upon the above rules, are therefore as sparse as possible for AVL trees and are called **Fibonacci** trees. The first few trees of this category are illustrated in **Fig. 7.47.** If | **T** | is the number of nodes in a tree **T**, then by recurrence relation

$$|F_h| = |F_{h-1}| + |F_{h-2}| + 1$$

Where $|F_0| = 1$ and $|F_1| = 2$, by adding 1 to both sides, we find that $|F_h| + 1$ satisfy the **Fibonacci** number generator function that is:

$$|F_n| + 1 \approx \frac{1}{\sqrt{5}}\left[\frac{1+\sqrt{5}}{2}\right]^{h+2}$$

Taking logarithms of both sides and discarding small terms we get the approximate result.

$$h \approx 1.44 \log_2 |F_h|$$

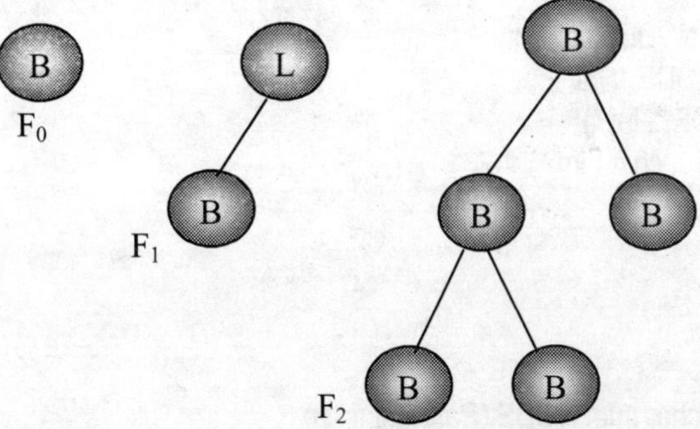

Fig. 7.47 Fibonacci Trees

From the above result it is clear that the sparsest possible AVL tree with **n** nodes has approximate height $\mathbf{1.44 \log_2 n}$. A perfectly balanced binary tree with **n** nodes has height $\mathbf{\log_2 n}$ and a degenerate tree has height as large as **n**. Hence the algorithms for manipulating AVL trees require more than 44% time than the optimum. But in practice, AVL trees do much well than this. It can be shown that for **Fibonacci** trees, which are the worst case for AVL trees, the average search time is only

4% more than the optimum. Most AVL trees are not nearly as sparse as **Fibonacci** trees and therefore it is reasonable to accept that average search times for average AVL trees are very close to the optimum. The average comparisons are:

$\log_2 n + 0.25$ where **n** is large.

```
// Create AVL Binary TREE
// AVL_TREE.C

# include<iostream.h>
# include<stdio.h>

# define F 0
# define T 1

struct NODE
{
	char Info;
	int Flag;
	NODE *Left_Child;
	NODE *Right_Child;
};

class Create_AVL_BT
{
	public: NODE *Binary_Tree (char , NODE *, int *);
		void Output(NODE *, int );
		NODE *Balance_Right_Heavy(NODE *, int *);
		NODE *Balance_Left_Heavy(NODE *, int *);
		NODE *DELETE(NODE *, NODE *, int *);
		NODE *Delete_Element(NODE *, char , int *);

};

// Function to insert an element into tree

NODE * Create_AVL_BT :: Binary_Tree (char Info, NODE *Parent, int *H)
{
	NODE *Node1;
	NODE *Node2;
	if(!Parent)
	{
		Parent = new (NODE);
		Parent->Info = Info;
		Parent->Left_Child = NULL;
```

```
        Parent->Right_Child = NULL;
        Parent->Flag = 0;
        *H = T;
        return (Parent);
    }

    if(Info < Parent->Info)
    {
        Parent->Left_Child = Binary_Tree(Info, Parent->Left_Child, H);
    if(*H) //Left branch has grown higher
    {
    switch(Parent->Flag)
        {
        case 1: //Right heavy
            Parent->Flag = 0;
            *H = F;
            break;
        case 0: //Balanced tree
            Parent->Flag = -1;
            break;
        case -1: //Left heavy
            Node1 = Parent->Left_Child;
            if(Node1->Flag == -1)
            {
                cout<<"\n Left to Left Rotation\n";
                Parent->Left_Child= Node1->Right_Child;
                Node1->Right_Child = Parent;
                Parent->Flag = 0;
                Parent = Node1;
            }
            else
            {
                cout<<"\n Left to right rotation\n";
                Node2 = Node1->Right_Child;
                Node1->Right_Child = Node2->Left_Child;
                Node2->Left_Child = Node1;
                Parent->Left_Child = Node2->Right_Child;
                Node2->Right_Child = Parent;
                if(Node2->Flag == -1)
                    Parent->Flag = 1;
            else
                    Parent->Flag = 0;
                if(Node2->Flag == 1)
                Node1->Flag = -1;
            else
                Node1->Flag = 0;
```

```
                Parent = Node2;
                }

                Parent->Flag = 0;
                *H = F;
            }
        }
}


if(Info > Parent->Info)
{
    Parent->Right_Child = Binary_Tree(Info, Parent->Right_Child, H);
    if(*H) //Right branch has grown higher
    {
        switch(Parent->Flag)
    {
        case -1: //Left heavy
            Parent->Flag = 0;
            *H = F;
            break;
        case 0: //Balanced tree
            Parent->Flag = 1;
            break;

        case 1: //Right heavy
            Node1 = Parent->Right_Child;
            if(Node1->Flag == 1)
            {
                cout<<"\n Right to Right Rotation\n";
                Parent->Right_Child= Node1->Left_Child;
                Node1->Left_Child = Parent;
                Parent->Flag = 0;
                Parent = Node1;
            }
            else
            {
                cout<<"\n Right to Left Rotation\n";
                Node2 = Node1->Left_Child;
                Node1->Left_Child = Node2->Right_Child;
                Node2->Right_Child = Node1;
                Parent->Right_Child = Node2->Left_Child;
                Node2->Left_Child = Parent;

                if(Node2->Flag == 1)
                Parent->Flag = -1;
```

```
                else
                        Parent->Flag = 0;
                        if(Node2->Flag == -1)
                                Node1->Flag = 1;
                else
                        Node1->Flag = 0;
                        Parent = Node2;
                }

                Parent->Flag = 0;
                *H = F;
            }
        }
}
return(Parent);
}

// Output function

void Create_AVL_BT :: Output(NODE *Tree,int Level)
{
        if (Tree)
        {
                Output(Tree->Right_Child, Level+1);
                cout<<"\n";
                for (int i = 0; i < Level; i++)
                        cout<<" ";
                        cout<< Tree->Info;
                        Output(Tree->Left_Child, Level+1);
        }
}

// Balancing Right Heavy

NODE * Create_AVL_BT :: Balance_Right_Heavy(NODE *Parent, int *H)
{
        NODE *Node1, *Node2;

        switch(Parent->Flag)
        {
        case -1: Parent->Flag = 0;
                break;

        case 0: Parent->Flag = 1;
                *H= F;
                break;
```

```
case 1: // Rebalance
        Node1 = Parent->Right_Child;
        if(Node1->Flag >= 0)
        {
        cout<<"\n Right to Right Rotation\n";
        Parent->Right_Child= Node1->Left_Child;
        Node1->Left_Child = Parent;
        if(Node1->Flag == 0)
        {
        Parent->Flag = 1;
        Node1->Flag = -1;
        *H = F;
        }
        else
        {
            Parent->Flag = Node1->Flag = 0;
        }
        Parent = Node1;
    }
        else
        {
            cout<<"\n Right to Left Rotation\n";
            Node2 = Node1->Left_Child;
            Node1->Left_Child = Node2->Right_Child;
            Node2->Right_Child = Node1;
            Parent->Right_Child = Node2->Left_Child;
            Node2->Left_Child = Parent;

        if(Node2->Flag == 1)
            Parent->Flag = -1;
        else
            Parent->Flag = 0;
        if(Node2->Flag == -1)
            Node1->Flag = 1;
        else
            Node1->Flag = 0;
            Parent = Node2;
            Node2->Flag = 0;
        }
    }
    return(Parent);
}

// Balancing Left Heavy
NODE * Create_AVL_BT :: Balance_Left_Heavy(NODE *Parent, int *H)
```

```
{
    NODE *Node1, *Node2;

    switch(Parent->Flag)
    {
     case 1: Parent->Flag = 0;
            break;

     case 0: Parent->Flag = -1;
            *H= F;
            break;

     case -1: // Rebalance
            Node1 = Parent->Left_Child;
            if(Node1->Flag <= 0)
            {
                cout<<"\n Left to Left Rotation\n";
                Parent->Left_Child= Node1->Right_Child;
                Node1->Right_Child = Parent;
                if(Node1->Flag == 0)
                {
                    Parent->Flag = -1;
                    Node1->Flag = 1;
                    *H = F;
                }
                else
                {
                    Parent->Flag = Node1->Flag = 0;
                }
                Parent = Node1;
            }
            else
            {
                cout<<"\n Left to Right Rotation\n";
                Node2 = Node1->Right_Child;
                Node1->Right_Child = Node2->Left_Child;
                Node2->Left_Child = Node1;
                Parent->Left_Child = Node2->Right_Child;
                Node2->Right_Child = Parent;

                if(Node2->Flag == -1)
                    Parent->Flag = 1;
                else
                    Parent->Flag = 0;

                if(Node2->Flag == 1)
```

```
                    Node1->Flag = -1;
                else
                    Node1->Flag = 0;
            Parent = Node2;
            Node2->Flag = 0;
        }
    }
    return(Parent);
}
```

// Replace the node at which key is found with last right key of a left child

```
NODE * Create_AVL_BT :: DELETE(NODE *R, NODE *Temp, int *H)
{
    NODE *Dnode = R;
    if( R->Right_Child != NULL)
    {
        R->Right_Child = DELETE(R->Right_Child, Temp, H);
        if(*H)
        R = Balance_Left_Heavy(R, H);
    }
    else
    {
        Dnode = R;
        Temp->Info = R->Info;
        R = R->Left_Child;
        delete(Dnode);
        *H = T;
    }
    return(R);
}
```

// Delete the key element from the tree

```
NODE *Create_AVL_BT :: Delete_Element(NODE *Parent, char Info, int *H)
{
    NODE *Temp;
    if(!Parent)
    {
        cout<<"\n Information does not exist";
        return(Parent);
    }
    else
    {
        if (Info < Parent->Info )
        {
```

```
                Parent->Left_Child = Delete_Element(Parent->Left_Child, Info, H);
                if(*H)
                    Parent = Balance_Right_Heavy(Parent, H);
            }
            else
            if(Info > Parent->Info)
            {
                Parent->Right_Child = Delete_Element(Parent->Right_Child, Info, H);
                if(*H)
                Parent = Balance_Left_Heavy(Parent, H);
            }
            else
            {
                Temp= Parent;
                if(Temp->Right_Child == NULL)
                {
                    Parent = Temp->Left_Child;
                    *H = T;
                    delete(Temp);
                }
                else
                if(Temp->Left_Child == NULL)
                {
                    Parent = Temp->Right_Child;
                    *H = T;
                     delete(Temp);
                }
                else
                {
                    Temp->Left_Child = DELETE(Temp->Left_Child, Temp, H);
                    if(*H)
                    Parent = Balance_Right_Heavy(Parent, H);
                }
            }
        }
return(Parent);
}

// Function main

void main()
{
    Create_AVL_BT Binary_C_Tree;
    int H;
    char Info ;
    char choice;
```

```
NODE *Tree = new (NODE);
Tree = NULL;
cout<<"\n Input choice 'b' to break:";
choice = getchar();

while(choice != 'b')
{
    cout<<"\n Input information of the node: ";
    cin>>Info;
    Tree = Binary_C_Tree.Binary_Tree(Info, Tree, &H);
    cout<<"\n Tree is:\n";
    Binary_C_Tree.Output(Tree,1);
    cout<<"\n Input choice 'b' to break:";
    choice = getchar();
}
while(1)
{
    cout<<"\n Input choice 'b' to break:";
    cout<<"\n Input the key value want to delete:";
    cin>>Info;
    if (Info == 'b')
        break;
    Tree = Binary_C_Tree.Delete_Element(Tree, Info, &H);
    cout<<"\n Tree is:\n";
    Binary_C_Tree.Output(Tree,1);
}
}
```

```
Input choice 'b' to break:
 Input information of the node: A
 Tree is:

   A
 Input choice 'b' to break:
 Input information of the node: B
 Tree is:

      B
   A

 Input choice 'b' to break:
 Input information of the node: C
 Right to Right Rotation
```

```
Tree is:

      C
   B
      A
 Input choice 'b' to break:
 Input information of the node: D
 Tree is:

       D
      C
   B
      A
 Input choice 'b' to break:
 Input information of the node: F
 Right to Right Rotation

 Tree is:

       F
      D
       C
   B
      A
 Input choice 'b' to break:
 Input information of the node: G
 Right to Right Rotation
 Tree is:

       G
      F
   D
       C
      B
       A
 Input choice 'b' to break:
 Input information of the node: E
 Tree is:

       G
      F
       E
   D
       C
      B
       A
```

```
Input choice 'b' to break:
 Input information of the node: H
 Tree is:

          H
       G
      F
       E
   D
       C
      B
       A
 Input choice 'b' to break:
 Input information of the node: I
 Right to Right Rotation

 Tree is:

          I
       H
          G
      F
       E
   D
       C
      B
       A

 Input choice 'b' to break:
 Input information of the node: K
 Right to Right Rotation

 Tree is:

          K
       I
      H
          G
       F
          E
   D
       C
      B
       A
```

```
Input choice 'b' to break:
Input information of the node: L
Right to Right Rotation

Tree is:

           L
       K
           I
     H
           G
       F
           E
 D
       C
     B
       A

Input choice 'b' to break:
Input information of the node: Q
Right to Right Rotation

Tree is:

           Q
       L
     K
       I
 H
           G
       F
           E
     D
           C
       B
           A
Input choice 'b' to break:
Input choice 'b' to break:
Input the key value want to delete: I
Right to Right Rotation

Tree is:

       Q
     L
       K
 H
           G
       F
           E
     D
           C
       B
           A
```

```
Input choice 'b' to break:
 Input the key value want to delete: F
 Tree is:

      Q
     L
      K
  H
         G
      E
     D
         C
      B
         A

 Input choice 'b' to break:
 Input the key value want to delete: L
 Tree is:

      Q
     K
  H
         G
      E
     D
         C
      B
         A
 Input choice 'b' to break:
Input the key value want to delete: b
```

7.11 B-TREE (Balanced Multi-Way Tree)

Binary search tree can be generalized directly to multi-way search trees in which for some integer **m** called the order of the tree; each node has at most **m** children. If **k ≤ m** is the number of children, and then the node contains exactly **k - 1** keys, which partition all the keys into **k** sub-sets. If some of these sub-sets are empty, then corresponding children in the tree are empty. **Fig. 7.48** illustrates a 5-way search tree in which some of the children of some nodes are empty.

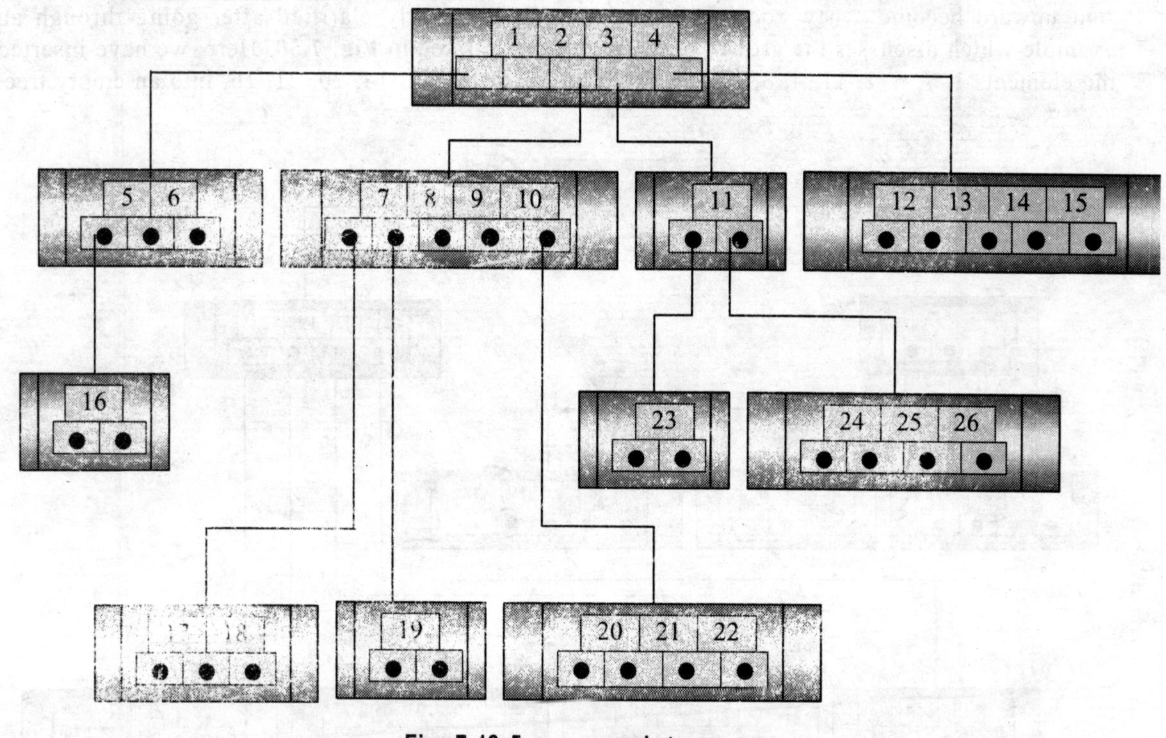

Fig. 7.48 5-way search tree

A B-tree of order **m** is an m-way tree in which

- *All leaves are on the same level.*
- *All the internal nodes except the root have at the most **m** (nonempty) children, and at least* $\lceil m/2 \rceil$ *(nonempty) children.*
- *The number of keys in each internal node is one less than the number of its children, and these keys partition the keys in the children as a search tree.*
- *The root has at the most **m** children and may have at least 2 if it is not a leaf or none if the tree consists of the root only.*

From the above points it is clear that in **Fig. 7.48** some of the nodes have empty children, and also the leaves are not on the same level. **Fig. 7.49** illustrates a B-tree of order 5 whose keys are the 26 integer numbers.

The insertion procedure for B-tree is as follows: First, a search is made to see whether the new element is in the tree or not. This search will terminate where it will return false. The new element is then added to the leaf node. If the node is empty then the insertion is finished. When an element is added to non-empty node, then the node splits into two nodes on the same level, except that the median element is not put either of the two new nodes, but is instead sent up the tree to be inserted into the parent node. When a search is later made through the tree, therefore, a comparison with the median element will serve to direct the search into the proper sub-tree.

When an element is added to non-empty root, then the root splits into two and the median element sent upward become a new root. This process will be greatly clarified after going through an example which discusses the growth of a B-tree as illustrated in **Fig. 7.50**. Here, we have inserted the elements 1, 7, 6, 2, 11, 4, 8, 13, 10, 5, 19, 9, 18, 24, 3, 12, 14, 20, 21, 16, into an empty tree.

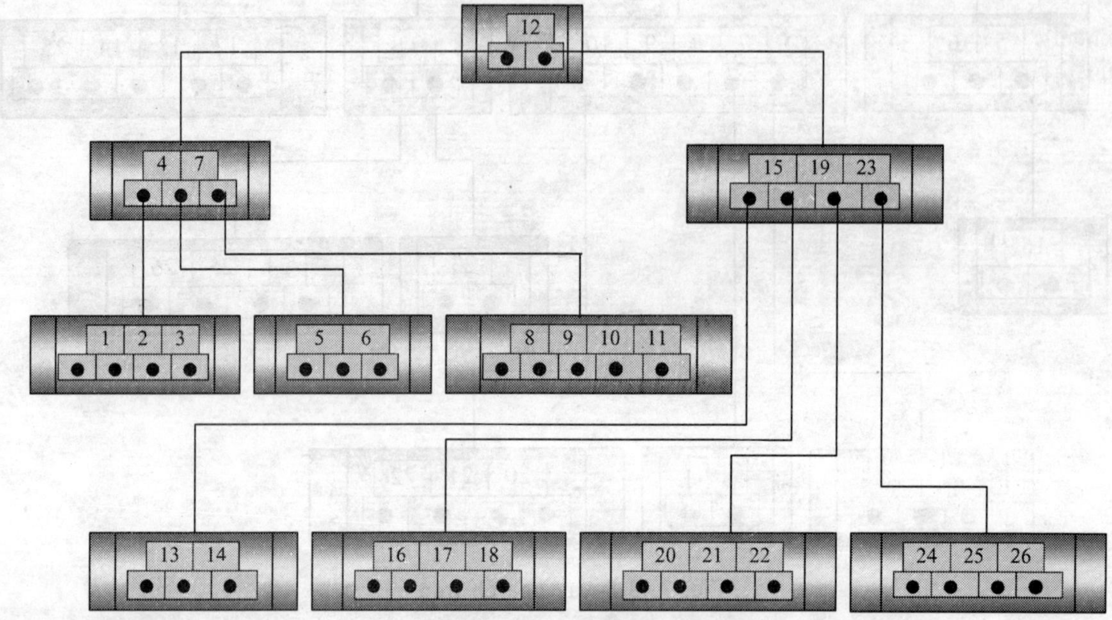

Fig. 7.49 B-tree of order 5

The first four elements will be inserted into one node, as illustrated in the **Fig. 7.50 (i).** They are sorted and put in the proper order as they are inserted. However, as there is no room for the 5th element 11, so its insertion causes the node to split into two and the median element 6, moves up to enter a new node, which now becomes new root. Since the split nodes are now only half full, the next three elements can be inserted without any difficulty. The next insertion, 10, again splits a node, and therefore moves up to join 6 in the root. The next insertions proceed in the same way. But the final insertion, that of 16, is more interesting. This insertion first splits the node originally containing 11,12,13,14, sending the median element 13, upward into the node containing 3, 6, 10, 18, which is, however, already full. Hence this node in turn splits and a new root containing 10 is created.

During the insertion, the new element always attached to a leaf. For deletion we wish to remove an element from a leaf. If an element is to be deleted is not in the leaf, then it's immediate predecessor (or successor) under the natural order of the elements will be definitely in a leaf. Hence, we can promote the immediate predecessor (or successor) into the position previously occupied by the deleted element and delete the element from the leaf. If the leaf contains more than minimum number of elements, then one element can be deleted without further action. If the leaf contains the minimum number of elements then we first look at the two leaves of the same node (or in the case of a node outside, one leaf) immediately adjacent and child. If one of these have more than the minimum number of elements then one of them can be moved into the parent node and the element from the parent can be moved into the leaf where the deletion is occurring. Finally, if the adjacent leaf has only minimum number of elements, then the two leaves and the median element from the parent can all be combined as one leaf, which will contain no more than the maximum number of elements allowed. If this step leaves the parent node with too few elements, then the process propagate upward. In the limiting case, the last element is removed from the root and the height of the tree decreases.

Step 1: Insert 1, 7, 6, 2

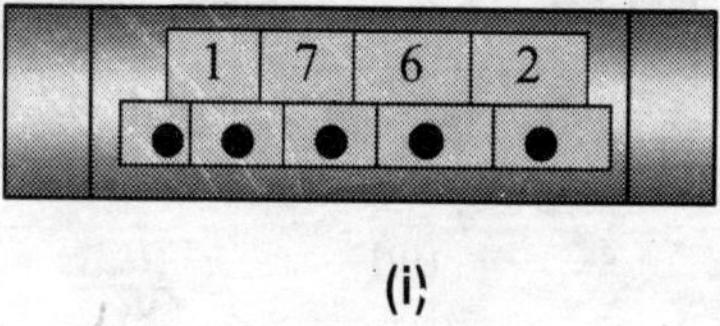

(i)

Step 2: Insert 11

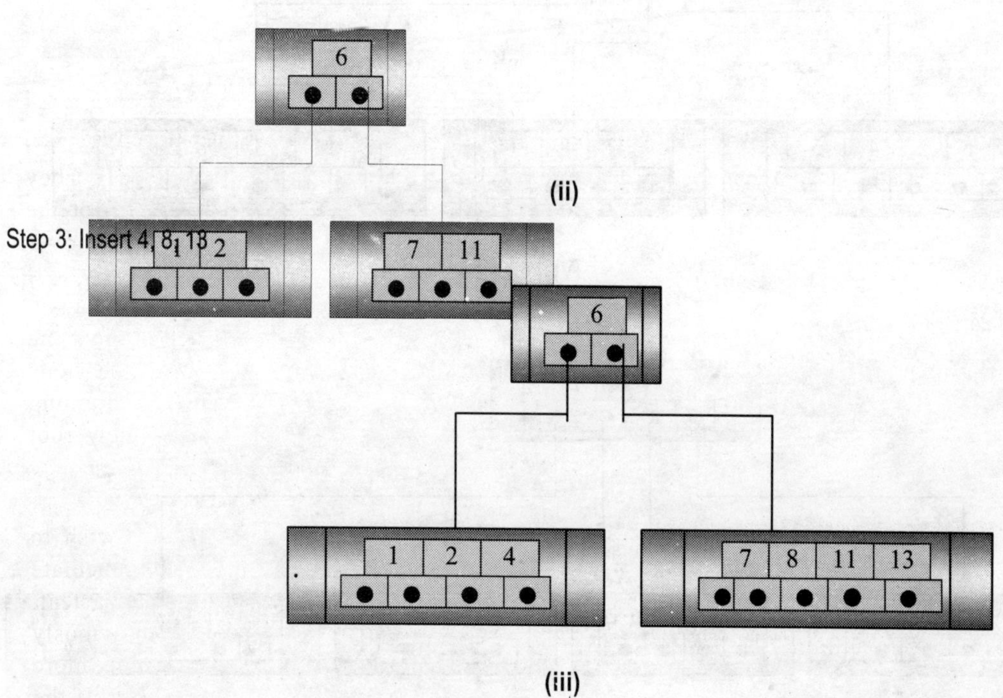

(ii)

Step 3: Insert 4, 8, 13

(iii)

Step 4: Insert 10

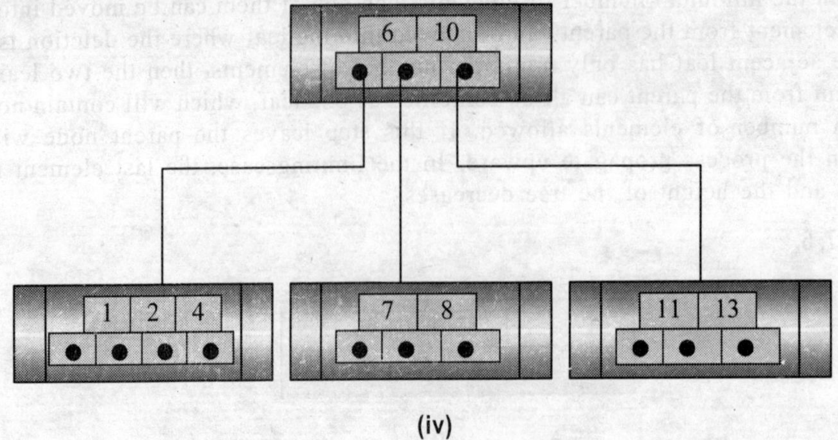

(iv)

Step 5: Insert 5, 19, 9, 18

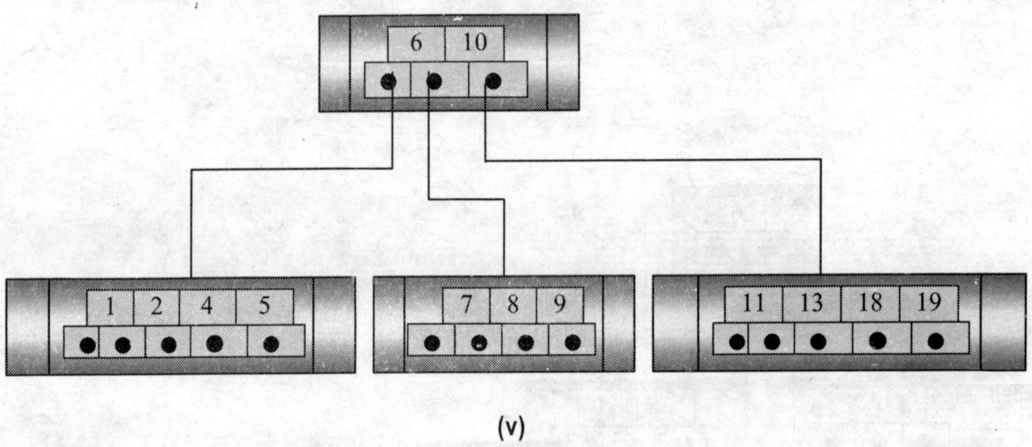

(v)

Step 6: Insert 24

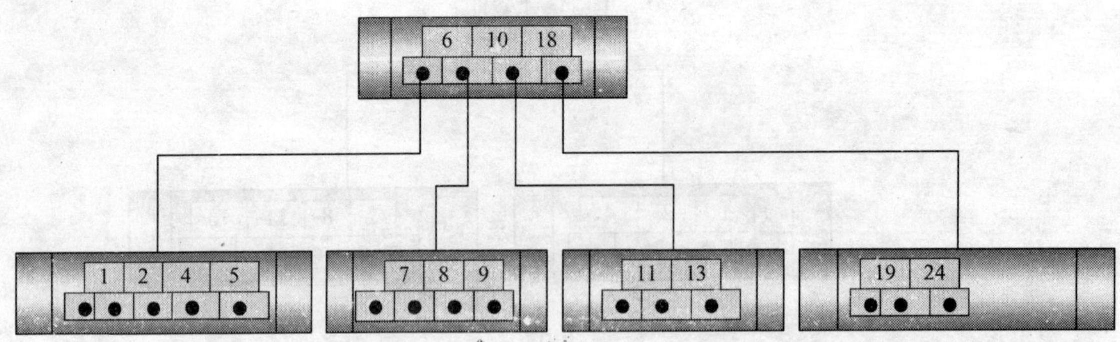

(vi)

Step 7: Insert 3, 12, 14, 20, 21

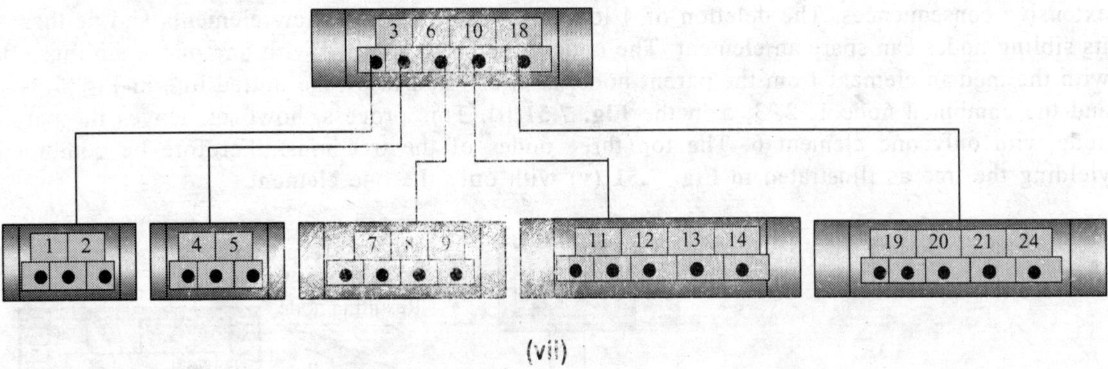

(vii)

Step 8: Insert 16

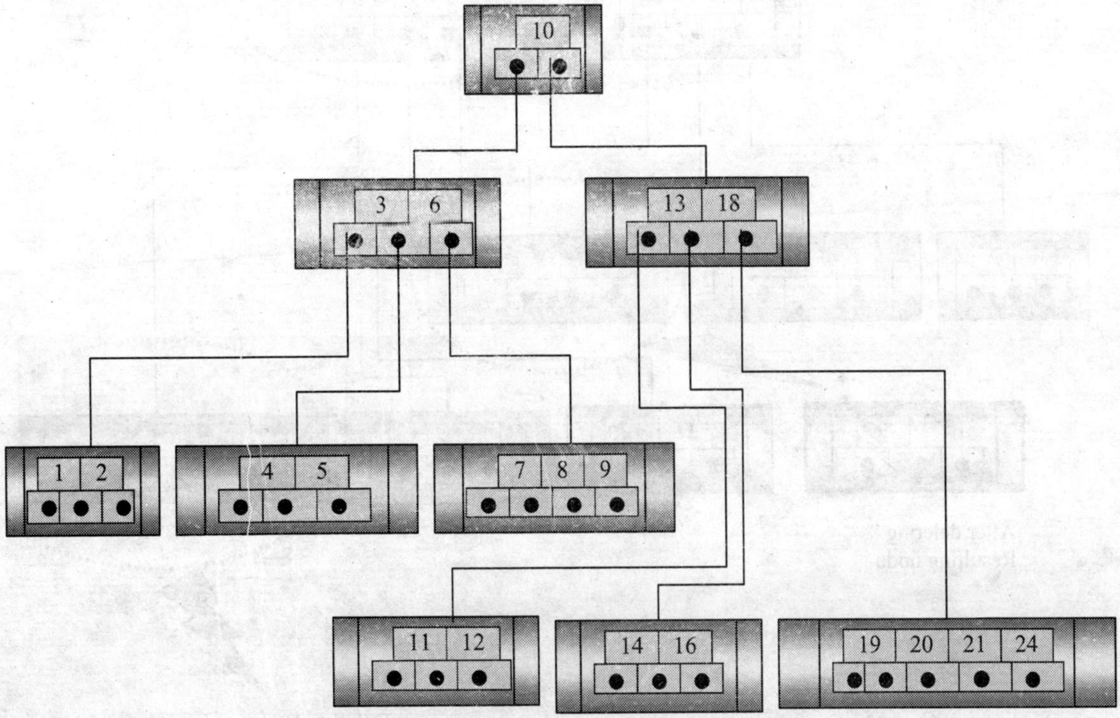

(viii)

Fig. 7.50 Insertion in B-tree

The process of deletion in the previous B-tree of order 5 is illustrated in **Fig. 7.51.** The first deletion of 8, is from a leaf with more than the minimum number of the elements and hence causes no problem. The 2nd deletion of 19 is not from the leaf and therefore the immediate successor of 18; (which is 19) is promoted into the position of 18, and then 19 is deleted from its leaf. The 3rd deletion of 16 leaves its nodes with too few elements. The element 19 from the parent node is therefore brought down and replaced by the element 20. The deletion of 4 has more extensive consequences. The deletion of 4 leaves the node with too few elements and neither of its sibling nodes can spare an element. The node therefore combined with one of the siblings and with the median element from the parent node, as illustrated in by the dotted line in **Fig. 7.51(i)** and the combined node 1, 2, 3, 5 in the **Fig. 7.51(ii).** This process, however, leaves the parent node with only one element 6. The top three nodes of the tree must therefore be combined, yielding the tree as illustrated in **Fig. 7.51 (v)** with only the one element.

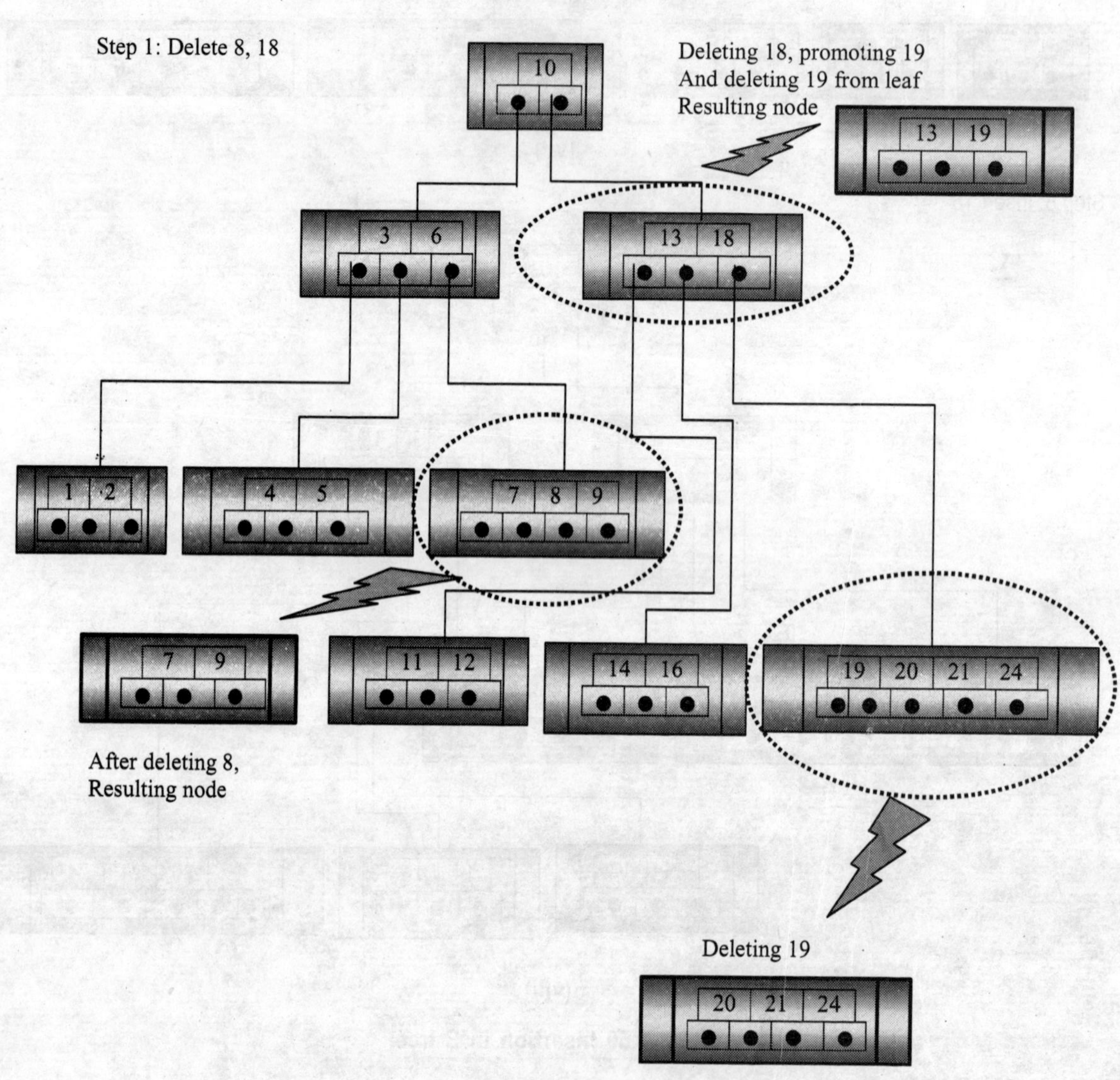

(i)

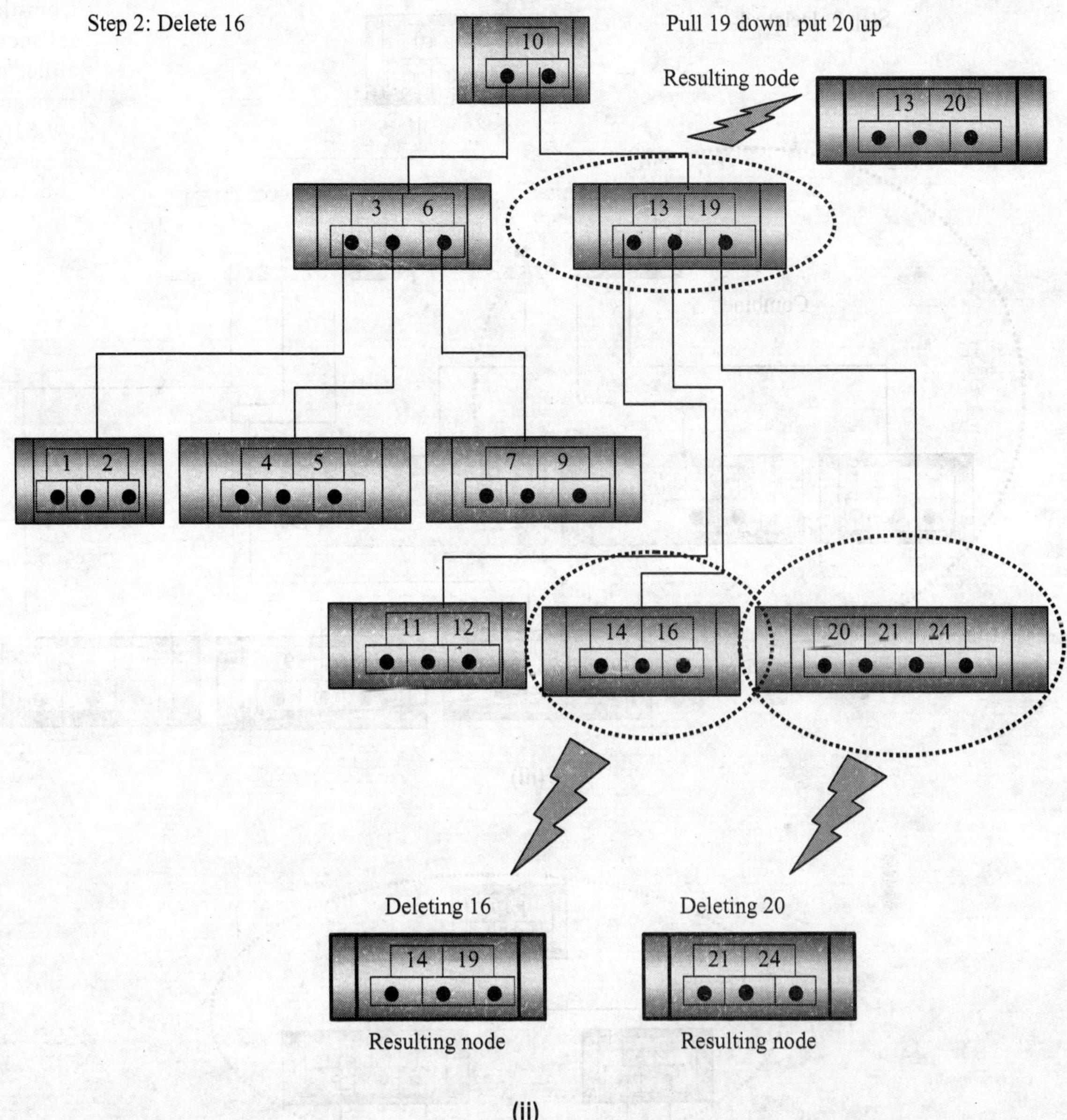

Step 2: Delete 16
Pull 19 down put 20 up
Resulting node
13 20
10
3 6
13 19
1 2
4 5
7 9
11 12
14 16
20 21 24
Deleting 16
Deleting 20
14 19
21 24
Resulting node
Resulting node

(ii)

Step 3: Delete 4

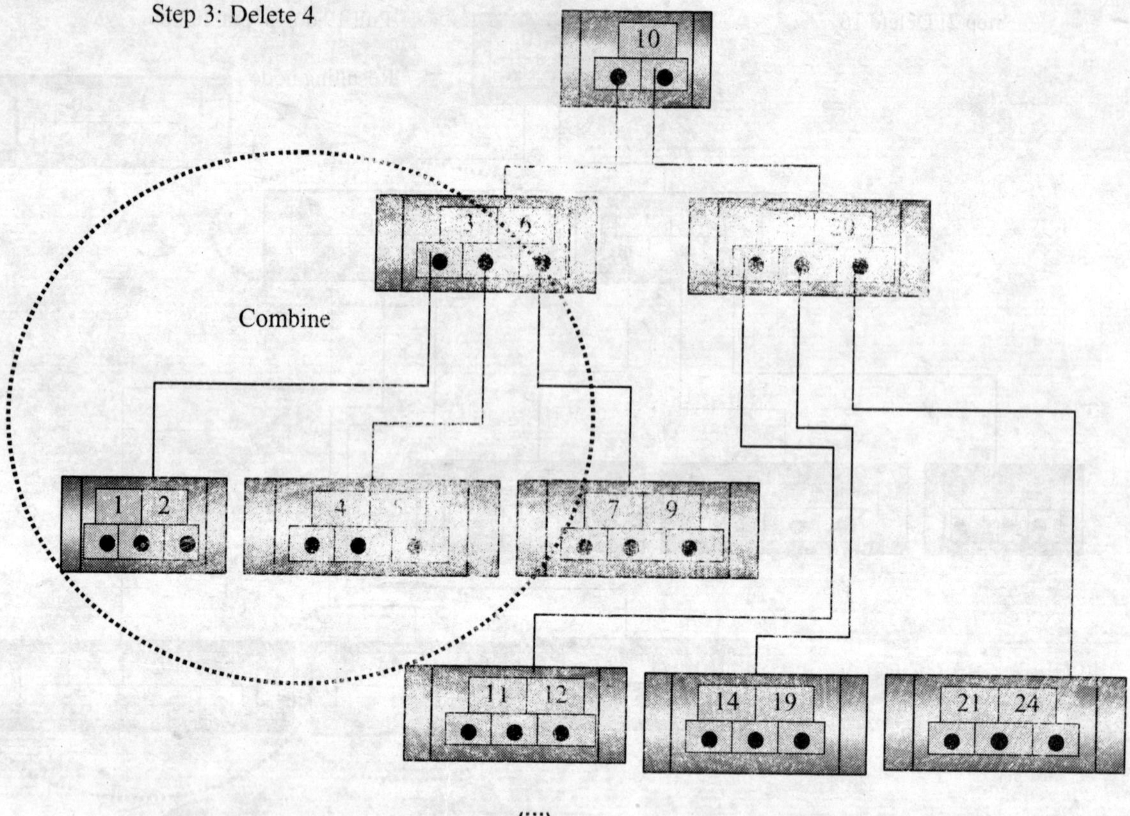

Combine

(iii)

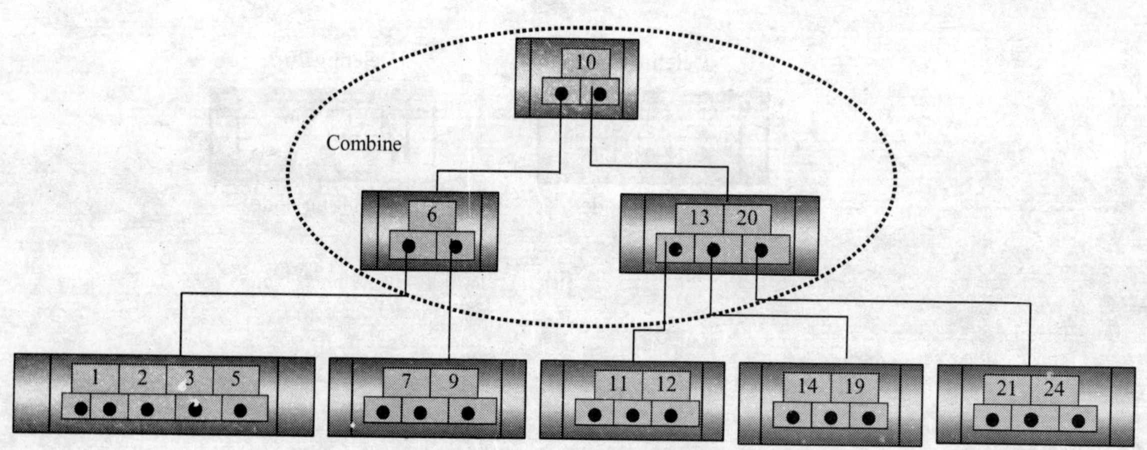

(iv)

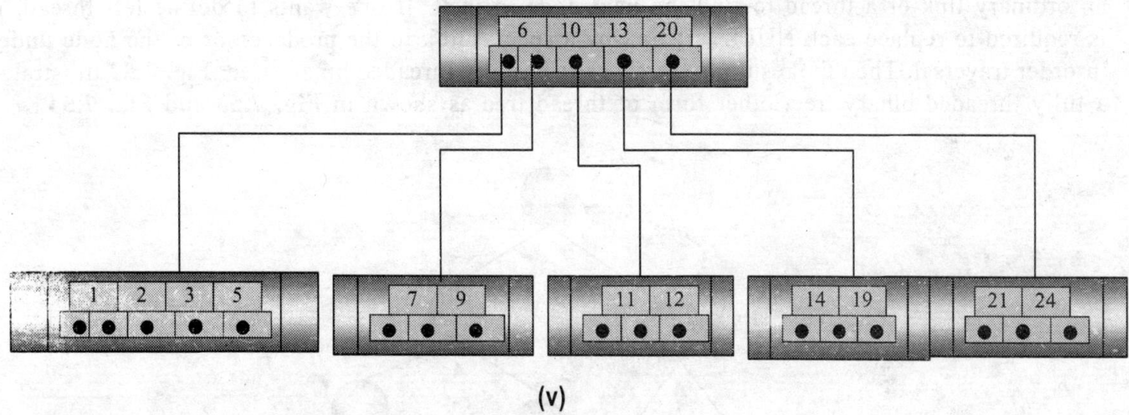

(v)

Fig. 7.51 Deletion in B-tree

7.12 THREADED BINARY TREES

Because of the importance of linked binary trees, it is worth while to develop non-recursive algorithms to manipulate them, and to study the time and space requirement of these algorithms. We shall find that, by changing the NULL links in a binary tree to special links called threads, it is possible to perform traversals, insertions and deletions without using either a stack or recursion. A binary tree with **n** nodes, when **n ≥ 0** has exactly **n+1** NULL links.

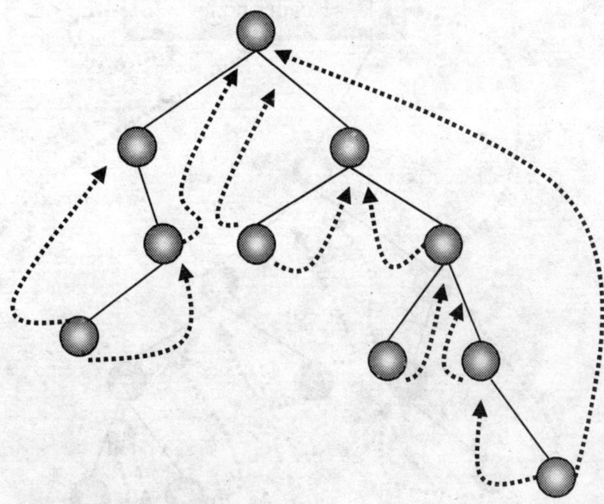

Fig. 7.52 Fully threaded tree binary tree (Two-way)

In a right-threaded binary tree each NULL right link is replaced by a special link to the successor of that node under in-order traversal, called a right thread. Using right threads we shall find that it easy to perform an in-order traversal of the binary tree, since we need to follow either an ordinary link or a thread to find the next node to visit. If one wants to define left thread, it is required to replace each NULL left link by a special link to the predecessor of the node under in-order traversal. Then the resulting tree is called a fully threaded binary tree. **Fig. 7.52** illustrates a fully threaded binary tree, other form of thread tree as shown in **Fig. 7.53** and **Fig. 7.54**.

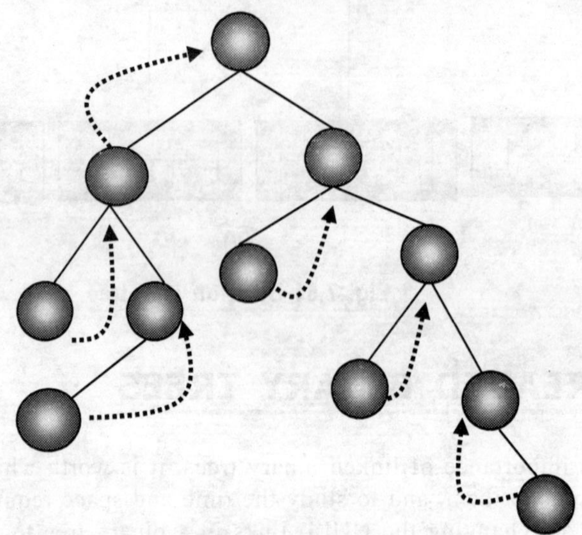

Fig. 7.53 One way threaded tree binary tree

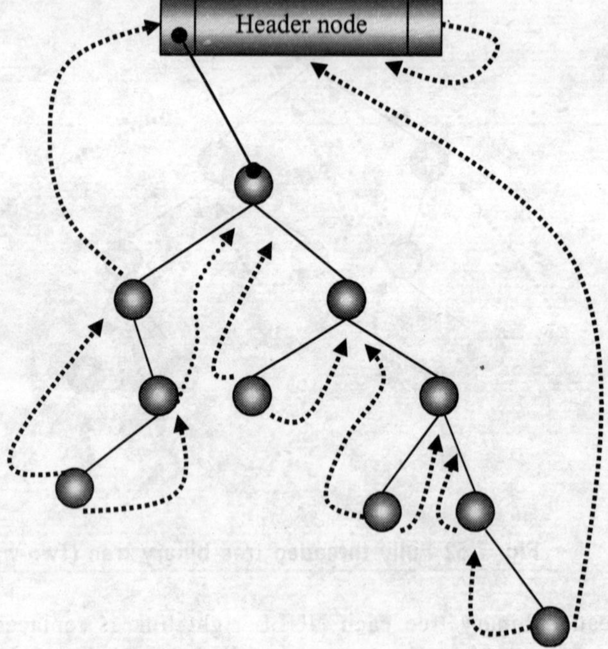

Fig. 7.54 Two-way threading with header node

EXERCISE

7.1 *How many binary trees are possible with four nodes?*

7.2 *Determine the order in which the vertices of the following binary trees will be visited under:*

(i) Preorder
(ii) In-order
(iii) Postorder

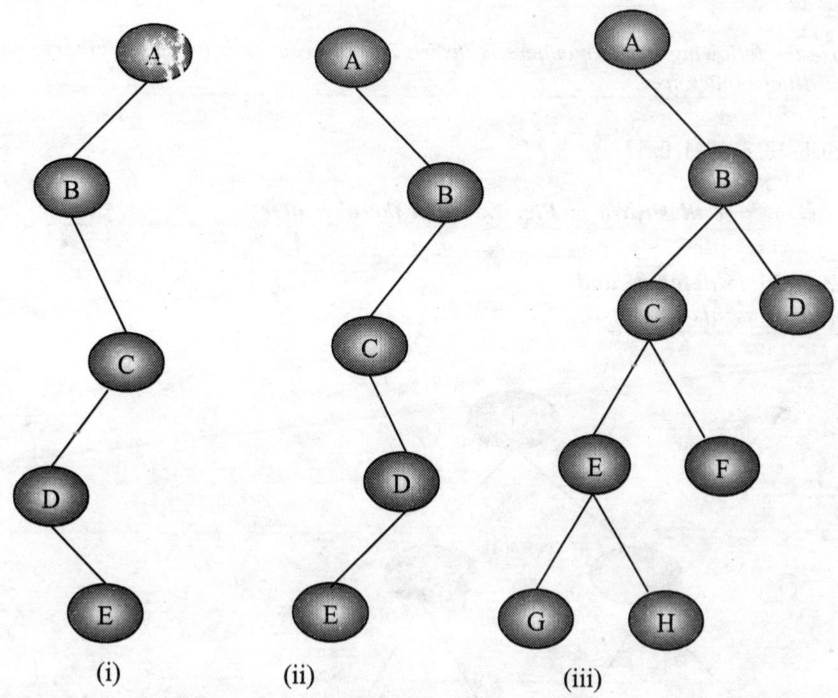

Fig. 7.55

7.3 *Write a function that finds height of a binary tree.*

7.4 *In each of the following, insert the elements, in the order shown, to build them into an AVL tree.*

(i) 1, 26, 2, 25, 3, 24
(ii) 1, 2, 3, 4, 5, 6
(iii) 1, 26, 2, 25, 3, 24, 4, 23, 5, 22, 6

7.5 *A binary tree **T** has 9 nodes. The in-order and Preorder traversals of **T** yield the following sequences of the nodes:*

In-order: 5, 1, 3, 11, 6, 8, 4, 2, 7
Preorder: 6, 1, 5, 11, 3, 4, 8, 7, 2

7.6 *Find the binary tree **T** for the following expression*

$E = (3x - y)(5a + b)^4$

7.7 *Find all the possible non-similar trees **T** where*

(i) ***T** is a binary tree with 3 nodes*
(ii) ***T** is a 2-tree with 4 external nodes*

7.8 *Suppose the following list of numbers is inserted in in-order into an empty binary search tree. Draw the resulting binary tree.*

10, 18, 4, 7, 20, 5, 13, 8, 16, 1, 6, 17

7.9 *Consider the tree illustrated in **Fig. 7.56** find the tree after*

(i) *the node 13 is deleted, and*
(ii) *The node 4 is also deleted.*

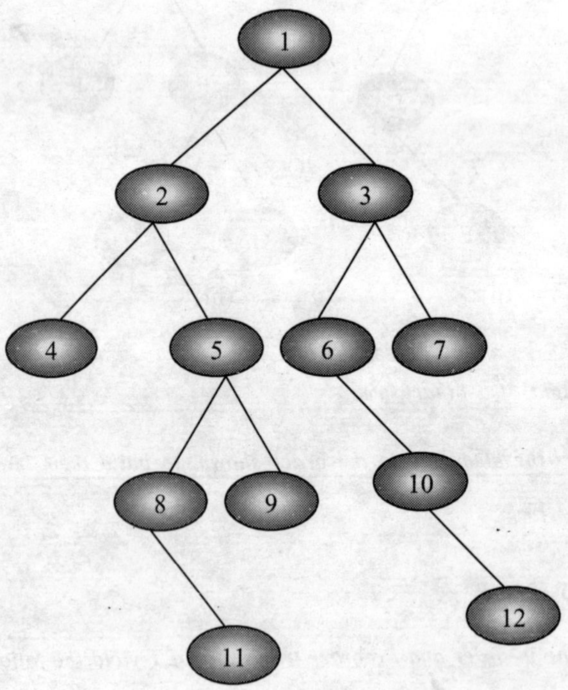

Fig. 7.56 Binary tree

7.10 *Suppose **T** is a complete tree with **n** nodes and depth **D**. Prove that*

(i) $2^{D-1} - 1 < n \le 2^{D} - 1$
(ii) $D \approx \log_2 n$

Use the relation $1 + x + x^2 + x^3 + \ldots + x^n = \frac{x^{n+1}}{x+1} - 1 \text{ for } x = 2$

7.11 *Write a program that implements the list of employees of GBPEC Company. Write a recursive function that searches an employee record using binary search. Sort the list of employees' record in alphabetical order.*

7.12 *Suppose a binary tree **T** is in memory. Write a function that deletes all the terminal nodes from **T**.*

7.13 *Suppose a binary tree **T** is in memory. Write a function that finds number of terminal nodes in **T**.*

7.14 *Suppose a binary tree **T** is in memory. Write a function that finds duplicate elements.*

7.15 *Suppose a binary **T** is memory. Write a function that deletes duplicate elements from **T**.*

7.16 *Write a function that counts number of nodes in a binary tree.*

7.17 *Suppose 8 weights 16, 32, 6, 18, 19, 20, 3, 8 are given. Find a 2-tree **T** with the given weights and a minimum weighted path length.*

7.18 *Write a function that finds minimum weighted path length (use Huffman technique) for a binary tree.*

7.19 *Draw the binary expression tree that represents the following postfix expression:*

x y + c / d *

7.20 *Write a recursive function to print the postfix representation of binary tree.*

7.21 *Find the **prefix, infix** and **postfix** notation of the following binary trees. (supply parenthesis for infix notation)*

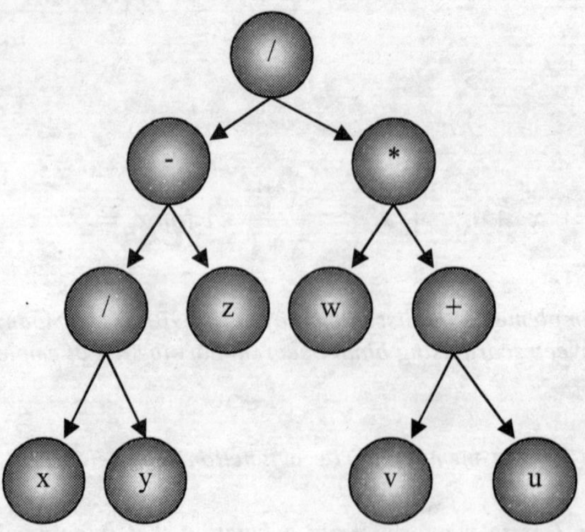

Fig. 7.57 binary tree

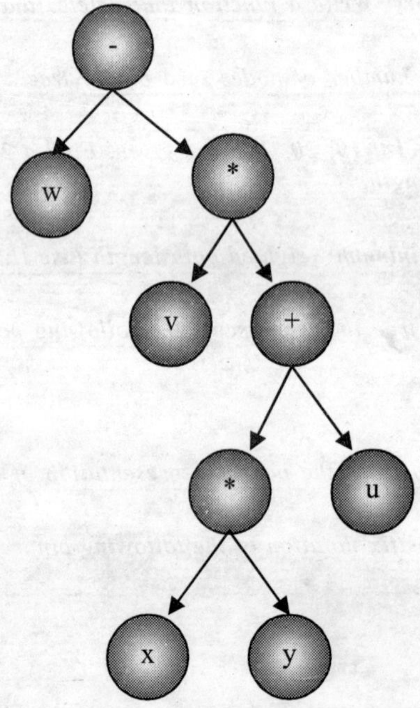

Fig. 7.58 Binary tree

*7.22 Evaluate expression tree in **Fig. 7.57** where*

x = 3u = 10
y = 2v = 30
z = 10 w = 2

*7.23 Evaluate the binary expression tree in **Fig. 7.58***

x = 6u = 10
y = 4v = 30
w = 2

7.23 Draw the binary tree that represents the following prefix expression:

+*x y/- z v w

7.24 Draw the binary tree that represents the following infix expression:

(((x-y) +z) / ((u-v) * w)) +t

7.25 State whether the following trees are [Fig. 7.59, Fig. 7.60 and Fig. 7.61]

(i) Complete
(ii) Full
(iii) Heap

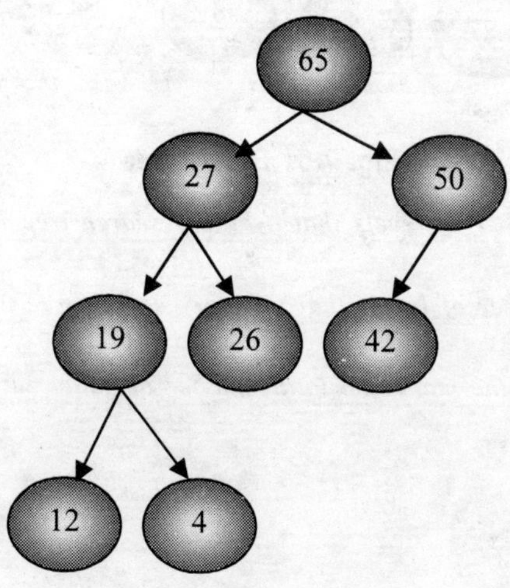

Fig. 7.59 Binary tree

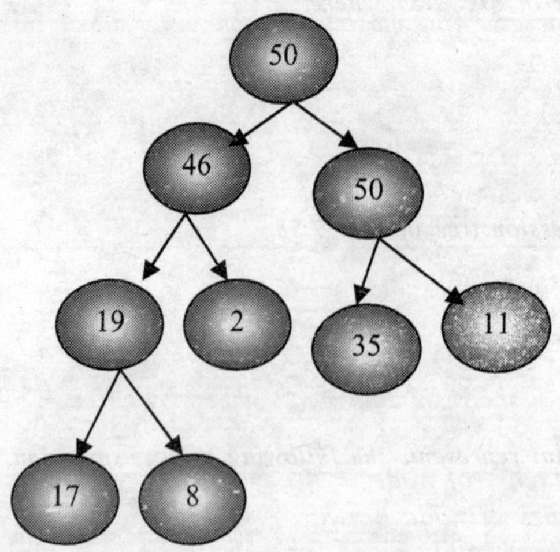

Fig. 7.60 Binary tree

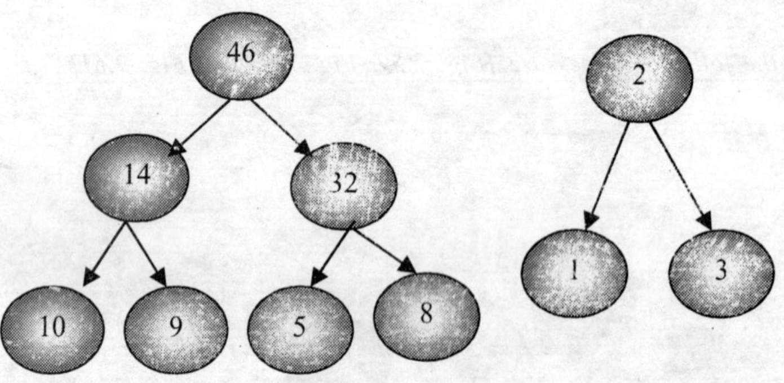

Fig. 7.61 Binary tree

7.26 *What is the maximum number of levels that a binary search tree with 100 nodes can have?*

7.27 *What is the minimum number of levels that a binary search tree with 100 nodes can have?*

7.28 *Which of these form gives the maximum total number of nodes in a tree that has* **n** *levels?*

(i) n^2-1
(ii) 2^n
(iii) 2^n-1
(iv) 2^{n+1}

7.29 *Which of these formulae gives the maximum number of nodes in nth level of a binary tree?*

(i) n^2
(ii) 2^n
(iii) 2^{n+1}
(iv) 2^n-1

7.30 *Draw all the possible binary trees that have four terminal nodes and all the non-terminal nodes have two children.*

7.31 *Consider the binary tree shown in* ***Fig. 7.62*** *and find*

(i) *What are the descendents of node* ***p****?*
(ii) *What are the ancestors of node* ***k****?*
(iii) *What is the maximum possible number of nodes in the tree at the level of node* ***w****?*

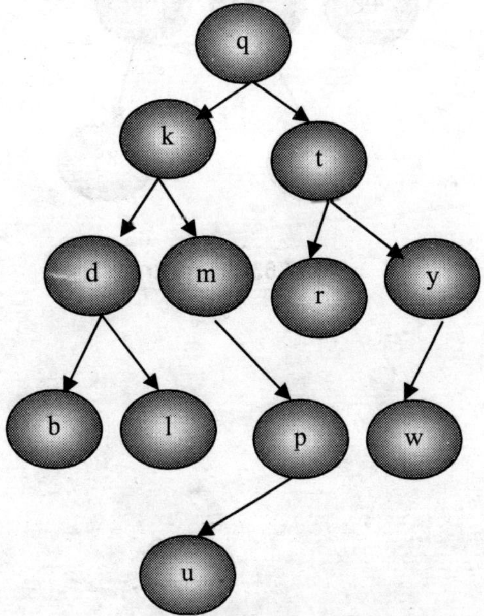

Fig. 7.62 Binary tree

7.32 *Draw binary search tree whose elements are inserted in the following order:*

50, 72, 96, 94, 107, 26, 12, 11, 9, 2, 10, 25, 51, 16, 17, 95

7.33 *Construct the* ***min*** *and* ***max*** *heap for the following data:*

50, 72, 96, 94, 107, 26, 12, 11, 9, 2, 10, 25, 51, 16, 17, 95

7.34 *Examine the binary search tree given in* **Fig. 7.63** *and discuss the following:*

(i) *If an item is to be inserted whose key value is less than the key value in node 1 but greater than the key value in node 5, where would it be inserted?*
(ii) *If node 1 is to be deleted, the value in which node could be used to replace it?*
(iii) *44, 22, 77, 55, 11, 66, 88, 33 is a traversal of the tree in which order?*
(iv) *11, 22, 44, 55, 77, 33, 66, 88 is a traversal of the tree in which order?*

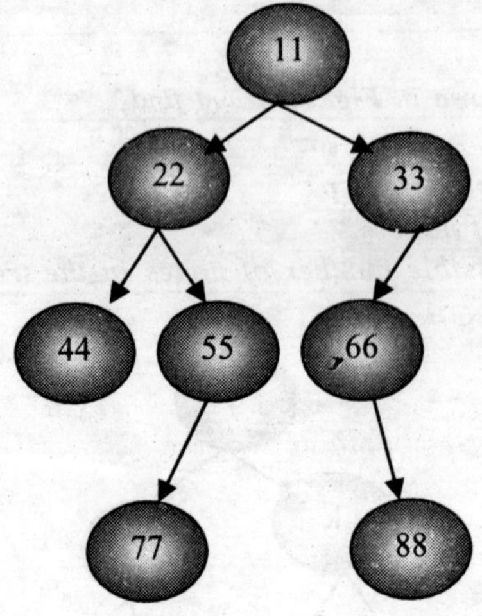

Fig. 7.63 binary tree

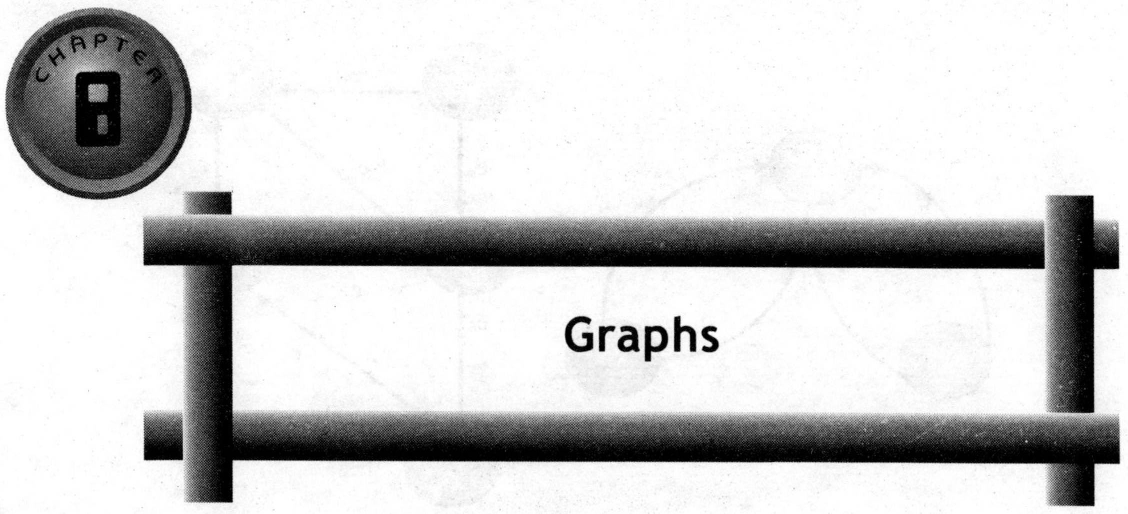

This chapter investigates another nonlinear data structures **Graph.** In this chapter we will discuss the representation of graphs, operations on them and algorithms such as Breadth first search and Depth first search, Dijkstra, Floyd, Warshall's algorithms, etc, certain applications of graphs, including topological sorting is also covered.

8.1 BASIC CONCEPTS AND DEFINITIONS

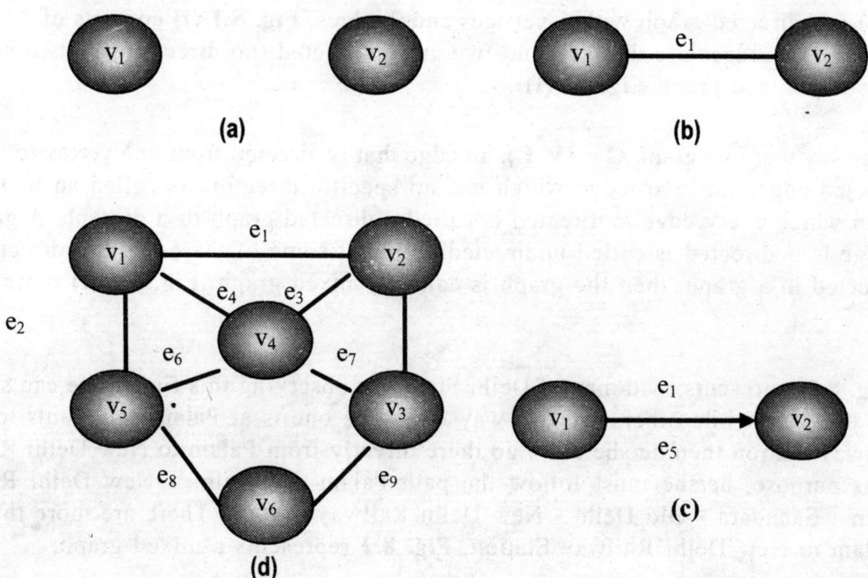

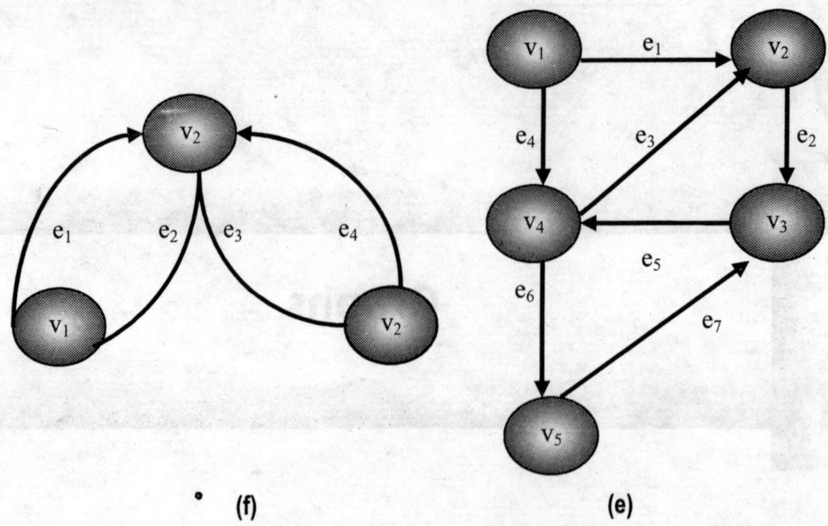

Fig: 8.1 Different types of graph

A graph **G** is defined as a set of two tuples that is **G = (V, E),** where **V** represents set of vertices of **G** and **E** represents the set of edges of **G**. There exists a mapping from the set of edges to a set of pairs of elements of **V**. For example, **Fig. 8.1** illustrates the different type of graphs.

From **Fig. 8.1** it is clear that part (a) consists of 2 vertices each one is stand-alone; (b) contains an undirected graph having one edge and two vertices. Similarly (c) consists of two vertices and one edge and it is directed graph; (d) illustrates an undirected graph with 6 vertices and 9 edges; (e) is a directed graph with 5 vertices and 7 edges. **Fig. 8.1 (f)** consists of 3 vertices and 4 edges in which 2 edges are directed and two are undirected (no direction for two edges is to be shown as it is mixed graph **Fig. 8.1(f)**).

Thus, we can say that in a graph **G = (V, E),** an edge that is directed from one vertex to another is called a directed edge, while an edge which has no specific direction is called an undirected edge. A graph in which every edge is directed is called a directed graph or a digraph. A graph in which every edge is undirected is called undirected graph. If some of the edges are directed and some are undirected in a graph, then the graph is called a mixed graph. **Fig. 8.1 (f)** represents a mixed graph.

Suppose **Fig. 8.2** represents road map of Delhi State. By observing this figure one can say that some roads are one way while others are two-ways. If some one is at Palam and wants to go to New Delhi Railway Station then he/she can't go there directly from Palam to New Delhi Railway Station. For this purpose, he/she must follow the path Palam-Old Delhi – New Delhi Railway Station or Palam – Sahadara - Old Delhi - New Delhi Railway Station. There are more than two routes from Palam to New Delhi Railway Station. **Fig. 8.2** represents a mixed graph.

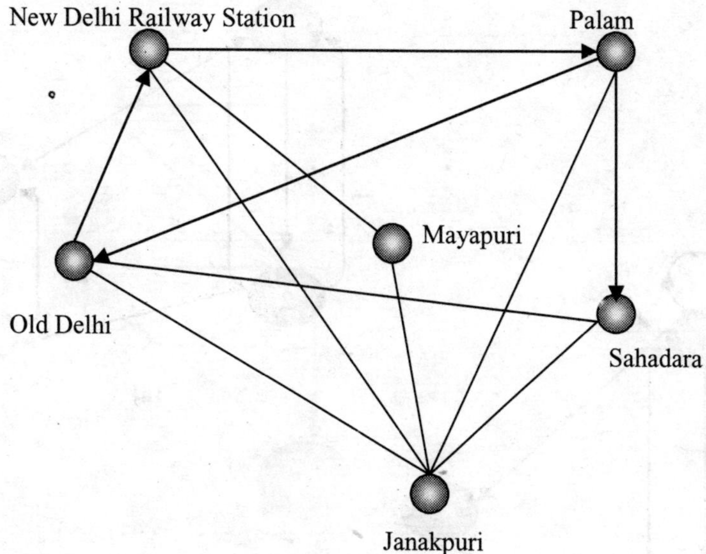

Fig. 8.2 Road map of Delhi

Let **G = (V, E)** be a graph and **e ε E** be a directed edge associated with ordered pair of vertices **(v_1, v_2).** Then the edge **e** is said to be initiating from the vertex **v_1** and terminating at the vertex **v_2**. Thus, vertex **v_1** and **v_2** are also called the initial and terminal vertices of the edge **e**, e **ε E,** which joins the vertices **v_1** and **v_2** in graph **G**. It is an incident to the vertices **v_1** and **v_2.** An edge of a graph that joins a vertex to it is called **sling.** The direction of the loop is of no significance; hence it can be considered either a directed or undirected edge.

When in a graph, two or more than two edges are used to join two vertices, such edges are called parallel edges and the graph is called multi-graph. In **Fig. 8.3** there are three parallel edge between the vertices 1 and 4, and two parallel edge between vertices 6 and 5. If there is only one edge between a pair of vertices then such a graph is called a simple graph **Fig. 8.1 (a) to (e)** are examples of simple graphs.

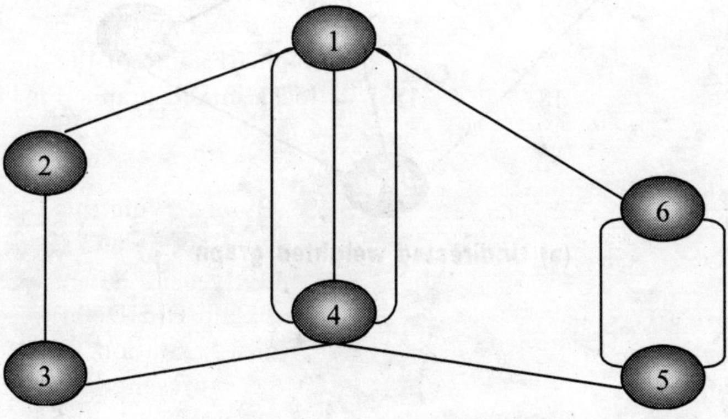

Fig. 8.3 Undirected graph

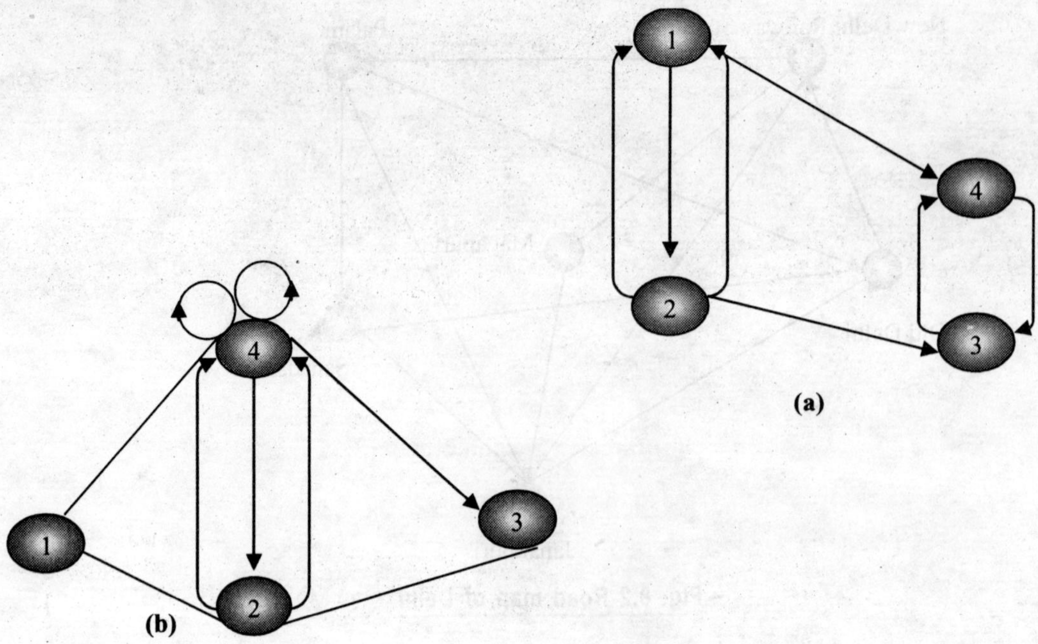

Fig. 8.4 Directed graph

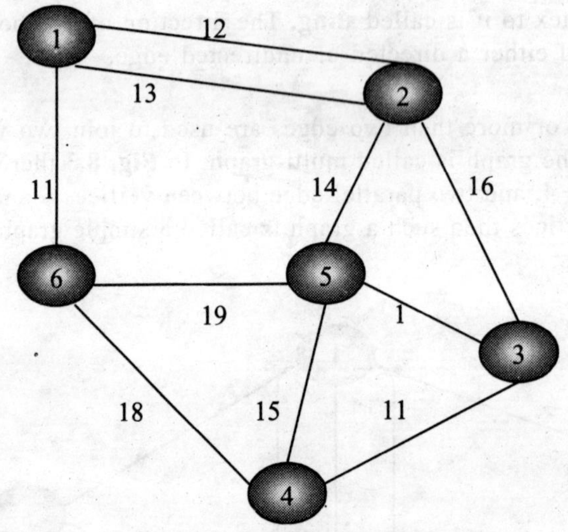

(a) Undirected weighted graph

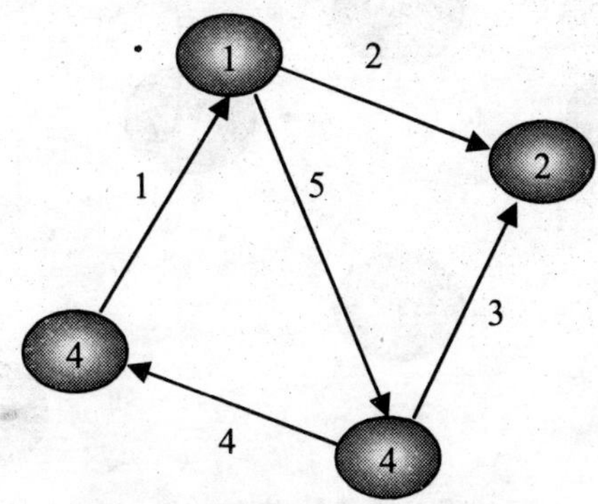

(b) Directed weighted graph

Fig. 8.5 Weighted graphs

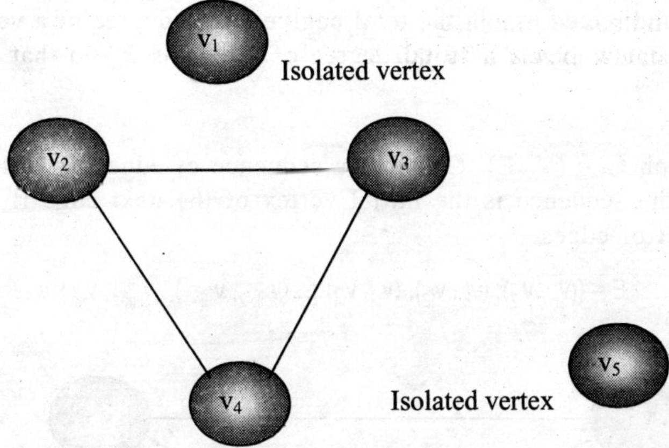

Fig. 8.6 Graph with isolated vertices

In a graph there may exist two or more directed edges between two vertices. Parallel loops are also possible in a graph as illustrated in **Fig. 8.4 (b).** A graph with edge value is called weighted graph as shown in **Fig. 8.5**.

In a graph a vertex which is not adjacent to any other vertices in the graph is called an isolated vertex. A graph containing only isolated vertices is called **null** graph or in other words a graph without an edge is called a null graph (see **Fig. 8.7**). **Fig. 8.6** illustrates a graph with isolated vertices $\mathbf{v_1}$ and $\mathbf{v_5}$.

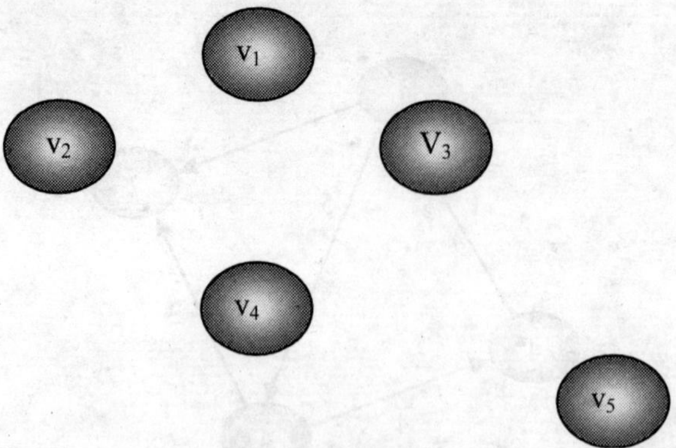

Fig. 8.7 Null graph

In a directed graph for any vertex **v** the number of edges which have **v** as their initial vertex is called the **out-degree** of **v.** The number of edges, which have **v** as their terminal vertex, is called the **in-degree** of **v**. The sum of the out-degree and in-degree of a vertex is called its total degree. In case of an undirected graph, the total degree or the degree of a vertex **v** is equal to the number of edges incident with **v**. The total degree of a loop is 2 and that of an isolated vertex is 0.

Take a simple graph **G = (V, E).** Consider a sequence of edges of **G** such that the terminal vertex of an edge in the sequence is the initial vertex of the next edge if any in the sequence. Suppose we have a set of edges

$$E = \{(v_{i1}, v_{i2}), (v_{i2}, v_{i3}), (v_{i3}, v_{i4}) \ldots (v_{ik-2}, v_{ik-1}), (v_{ik-1}, v_{ik})\}$$

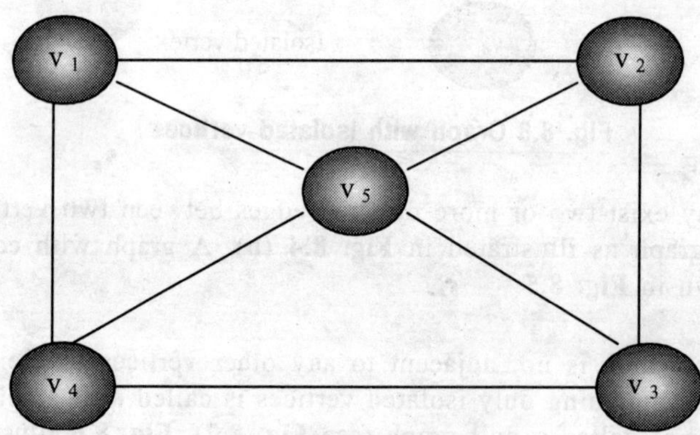

Fig. 8.8 Undirected graph

Then the set of vertices **V** will contain all the vertices existing in the set **E**, that is

$$V = \{v_{i1}, v_{i2}, v_{i3}, v_{i4} \ldots v_{ik-2}, v_{ik-1}, v_{ik}\}$$

Let we have a graph as illustrated in **Fig. 8.8,** then from the above description, we have

E = {(v_1, v_2), (v_1, v_4), (v_1, v_5), (v_2, v_1), (v_2, v_3), (v_2, v_5), (v_3, v_2), (v_3, v_4), (v_3, v_5), (v_4, v_1), (v_4, v_3), (v_4, v_5), (v_5, v_1), (v_5, v_2), (v_5, v_3), (v_5, v_4)}
V = {v_1, v_2, v_3, v_4, v_5}

If we consider **Fig. 8.9** then we have

E = {(v_1, v_2), (v_1, v_4), (v_2, v_3), (v_3, v_5), (v_3, v_4), (v_3, v_5), (v_4, v_5), (v_5, v_1), (v_5, v_2)}
V = {v_1, v_2, v_3, v_4, v_5}

8.2 PATH

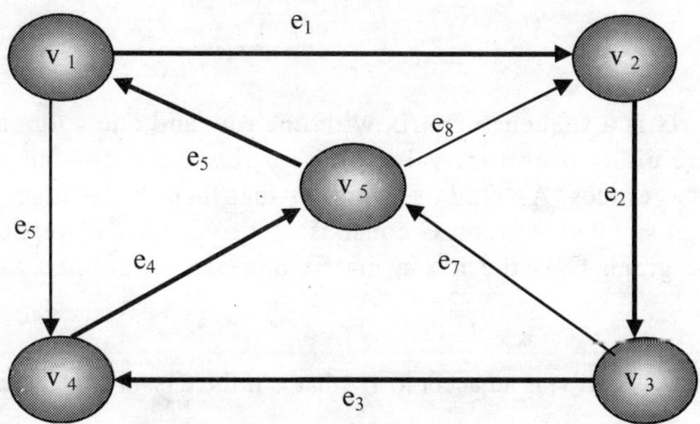

Fig. 8.9 Directed graph

A sequence of edges of a digraph such that the terminal vertex of an edge sequences in the initial vertex of the next edge if exists is called the path. For example, let we have

E = {(v_1, v_2), (v_2, v_3), (v_3, v_4), (v_4, v_5), (v_5, v_1)}

If we consider the elements of **E**, we find that **E** is a set of 5 tuples, that is

e_1 = (v_1, v_2)
e_2 = (v_2, v_3)
e_3 = (v_3, v_4)
e_4 = (v_4, v_5)
e_5= (v_5, v_1)

From $\mathbf{e_1}$ and $\mathbf{e_2}$ we find that $\mathbf{v_2}$ is common in both. In the $\mathbf{e_1}$, $\mathbf{v_2}$ is the terminal vertex and it is initial vertex of $\mathbf{e_2}$. Similarly, in $\mathbf{e_2}$ and $\mathbf{e_3}$, $\mathbf{v_3}$ is common and so on. Thus, we can say that there is a cycle, i.e., there exists a circular path. The circular path is illustrated in **Fig. 8.9** with the help of dark line.

8.3 REPRESENTATION OF GRAPH

There is two popular ways that are used to maintain a graph in a computer memory. These are:

- *Sequential*
- *Linked list*

8.3.1 SEQUENTIAL REPRESENTATION

The graphs can be represented as matrices in sequential representation. There are two most common matrices. These are:

- *Adjacency*
- *Incidence*

The adjacency matrix is a sequence matrix with one row and one column for each vertex. The values of the matrix are either 0 or 1. A value of 1 for row **i** and column **j** implies that edge $\mathbf{e_{ij}}$ exists between $\mathbf{v_i}$ and $\mathbf{v_j}$ vertices. A value of 0 implies that there is no edge between vertex $\mathbf{v_i}$ and $\mathbf{v_j}$. In other words we can say that if graph **G** consists of $\mathbf{v_1, v_2, v_3 \ldots v_n}$ vertices then the adjacency matrix $\mathbf{A} = [\mathbf{a_{ij}}]$ of the graph **G** is the **n x n** matrix and can be defined as:

$$\mathbf{a_{ij}} = \begin{cases} 1 & \text{If } \mathbf{v_i} \text{ is adjacent to } \mathbf{v_j} \text{ (that is if there is an edge between } \mathbf{v_i} \text{ and } \mathbf{v_j}\text{)} \\ 0 & \text{If there is no edge between } \mathbf{v_i} \text{ and } \mathbf{v_j} \end{cases}$$

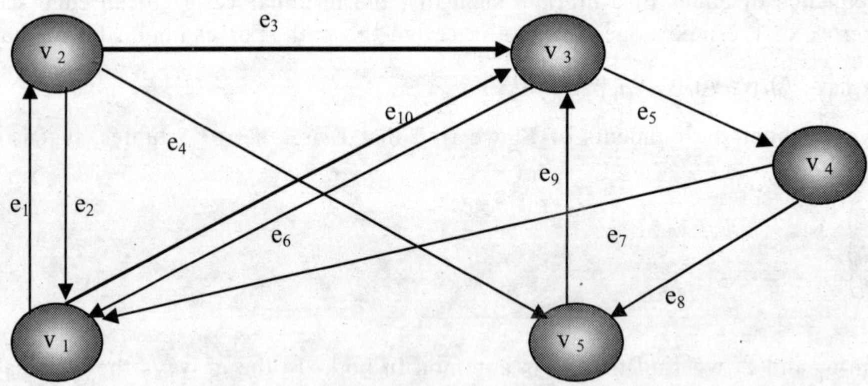

Fig. 8.10 5 Vertices and 10 edges of a directed graph

Such a matrix **A**, which contains entries of only 0 or 1, is called a bit matrix or a Boolean. For example, consider the graph **G** illustrated in **Fig. 8.10,** which consists of 5 vertices and 10 edges. The set of vertices is as follows:

$V = \{v_1, v_2, v_3, v_4, v_5\}$

and the set of edges is:

$E = \{(v_1, v_2), (v_1, v_3), (v_2, v_1), (v_2, v_3), (v_2, v_5), (v_3, v_1), (v_3, v_4), (v_4, v_1), (v_4, v_5), (v_5, v_3)\}$

The adjacency matrix **A** for **G** is as follows:

$$A = \begin{array}{c} \\ v_1 \\ v_2 \\ v_3 \\ v_4 \\ v_5 \end{array} \begin{array}{c} \begin{array}{ccccc} v_1 & v_2 & v_3 & v_4 & v_5 \end{array} \\ \begin{pmatrix} 0 & 1 & 1 & 0 & 0 \\ 1 & 0 & 1 & 0 & 1 \\ 1 & 0 & 0 & 1 & 0 \\ 1 & 0 & 0 & 0 & 1 \\ 0 & 0 & 1 & 0 & 0 \end{pmatrix} \end{array}$$

From the matrix **A**, it is clear that number of 1's in an adjacency matrix is equal to the number of edges in the graph. When one is constructing an adjacency matrix for a graph, one must follows the following points:

- *Adjacency matrix **A** does not depend on the ordering of the vertex of a graph **G**, that is different ordering of the vertices may result in a different adjacency matrix. One can obtain the same matrix by interchanging rows and columns.*
- *If graph **G** is undirected then the adjacency matrix of **G** will be symmetric. That is:*

$[a_{ij}] = [a_{ji}]$ for every **i** and **j**

The incidence matrix consists of a row for every vertex and a column for every edge. The values of the matrix are –1, 0 or 1. If the kth edge is (v_i, v_j), the kth column has a value 1 in the ith row, -1 in the jth row and 0 else where. For example, the incidence matrix **I** for the graph illustrated in **Fig. 8.10** is as follows:

$$I = \begin{pmatrix} 1 & 1 & -1 & 0 & 0 & -1 & 0 & -1 & 0 & 0 \\ -1 & 0 & 1 & 1 & 1 & 0 & 0 & 0 & 0 & 0 \\ 0 & -1 & 0 & -1 & 0 & 1 & 1 & 0 & 0 & -1 \\ 0 & 0 & 0 & 0 & 0 & 0 & -1 & 1 & 1 & 0 \\ 0 & 0 & 0 & 0 & -1 & 0 & 0 & 0 & -1 & 1 \end{pmatrix}$$

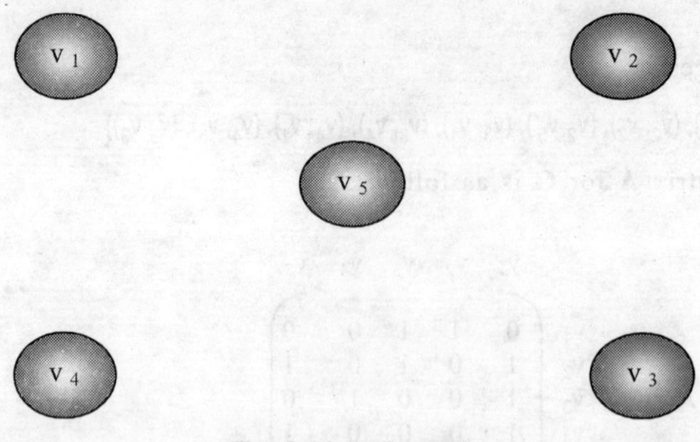

Fig. 8.11 Null graph

For a null graph, which consists of **V** vertices but no edges, the adjacency matrix has all of its entire elements zero. For example, consider the graph illustrated in **Fig. 8.11,** there are 5 vertices in the graph but no edges. Hence the resulting adjacency matrix will be

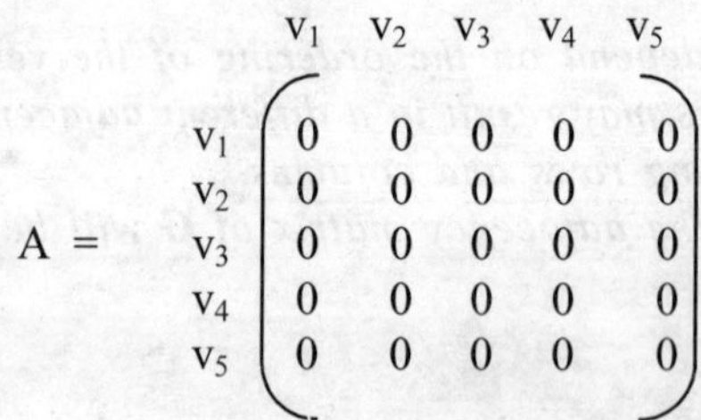

$$A = \begin{array}{c} \\ v_1 \\ v_2 \\ v_3 \\ v_4 \\ v_5 \end{array} \begin{array}{c} \begin{array}{ccccc} v_1 & v_2 & v_3 & v_4 & v_5 \end{array} \\ \begin{pmatrix} 0 & 0 & 0 & 0 & 0 \\ 0 & 0 & 0 & 0 & 0 \\ 0 & 0 & 0 & 0 & 0 \\ 0 & 0 & 0 & 0 & 0 \\ 0 & 0 & 0 & 0 & 0 \end{pmatrix} \end{array}$$

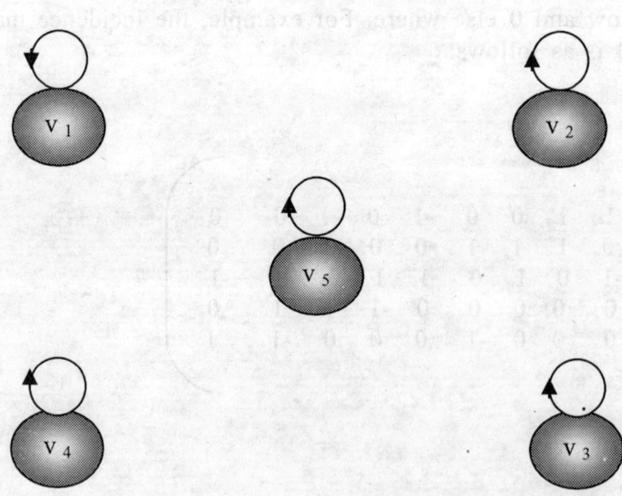

Fig. 8.12 Graph in which loop at each vertex

If there are loops at each vertex but no edges in the graph, then the adjacency matrix is the unit matrix. For example, consider the graph illustrated in **Fig. 8.12.** The adjacency matrix for this graph will be:

$$U = \begin{array}{c} \\ v_1 \\ v_2 \\ v_3 \\ v_4 \\ v_5 \end{array} \begin{array}{c} \begin{array}{ccccc} v_1 & v_2 & v_3 & v_4 & v_5 \end{array} \\ \begin{pmatrix} 1 & 0 & 0 & 0 & 0 \\ 0 & 1 & 0 & 0 & 0 \\ 0 & 0 & 1 & 0 & 0 \\ 0 & 0 & 0 & 1 & 0 \\ 0 & 0 & 0 & 0 & 1 \end{pmatrix} \end{array}$$

Let us now consider the powers of an adjacency matrix. As we know that an entry of 1 in the ith row and j^{th} column of adjacency **A** shows existence of an edge of (v_i, v_j), that is, a path of length 1 from v_i to v_j. Let us denote the elements of A^2 by $a_{ij}^{\ 2}$, then

$$a_{ij}^{\ 2} = \Sigma\, a_{ik}\, a_{kj}$$

For any fixed value of **k**; $a_{ik}\, a_{kj} = 1$ if and only if both a_{ik} and a_{kj} are equal to **1**; that is (v_i, v_k) and (v_k, v_j) are the edges of the graph. For each such **k** we get a contribution of 1 in the sum. Which implies that there is a path from v_i to v_j of length 2. Therefore, $a_{ij}^{\ 2}$ is equal to the number of different paths of length 2 from v_i to v_j. Similarly, the diagonal element $a_{ij}^{\ 2}$ shows the number of cycles of length 2 at the vertex v_i for **i = 1, 2, 3 ... n.**

In the similar way, we can show that the element in the ith row and j^{th} column of A^3 gives the number of paths of length 3 from v_i to v_j. Hence in general we can say that the element in the ith row and j^{th} column A^n $(n > 1)$ is equal to the number of paths of length **n** from v_i to v_j. For example, consider the graph **G** illustrated in **Fig. 8.10.** The adjacency matrix **A** for **G** is as follows:

$$A = \begin{array}{c} \\ v_1 \\ v_2 \\ v_3 \\ v_4 \\ v_5 \end{array} \begin{array}{c} \begin{array}{ccccc} v_1 & v_2 & v_3 & v_4 & v_5 \end{array} \\ \begin{pmatrix} 0 & 1 & 1 & 0 & 0 \\ 1 & 0 & 1 & 0 & 1 \\ 1 & 0 & 0 & 1 & 0 \\ 1 & 0 & 0 & 0 & 1 \\ 0 & 0 & 1 & 0 & 0 \end{pmatrix} \end{array}$$

Now consider A^1, A^2, A^3, A^4 and A^5 if **A** is the adjacency matrix of the graph **G** illustrated in **Fig. 8.10.** The A^1 is same as adjacency matrix **A** and other powers are as follows:

$$A^1 = \begin{pmatrix} 0 & 1 & 1 & 0 & 0 \\ 1 & 0 & 1 & 0 & 1 \\ 1 & 0 & 0 & 1 & 0 \\ 1 & 0 & 0 & 0 & 1 \\ 0 & 0 & 1 & 0 & 0 \end{pmatrix}$$

$$A^2 = \begin{pmatrix} 2 & 0 & 1 & 1 & 1 \\ 1 & 1 & 2 & 1 & 0 \\ 1 & 1 & 1 & 0 & 1 \\ 0 & 1 & 2 & 0 & 0 \\ 1 & 0 & 0 & 1 & 0 \end{pmatrix}$$

$$A^3 = \begin{pmatrix} 2 & 2 & 3 & 1 & 1 \\ 4 & 1 & 2 & 2 & 2 \\ 2 & 1 & 3 & 1 & 1 \\ 3 & 0 & 1 & 2 & 1 \\ 1 & 1 & 1 & 0 & 1 \end{pmatrix}$$

$$A^4 = \begin{pmatrix} 6 & 2 & 5 & 3 & 3 \\ 5 & 4 & 7 & 2 & 3 \\ 5 & 2 & 4 & 3 & 2 \\ 3 & 3 & 4 & 1 & 2 \\ 2 & 1 & 3 & 1 & 1 \end{pmatrix}$$

$$A^5 = \begin{pmatrix} 10 & 6 & 11 & 5 & 5 \\ 13 & 5 & 12 & 7 & 6 \\ 9 & 5 & 9 & 4 & 5 \\ 8 & 3 & 8 & 4 & 4 \\ 5 & 2 & 4 & 3 & 2 \end{pmatrix}$$

Now we define the matrix $\mathbf{B_r}$ as follows:

$$B_r = A^1 + A^2 + A^3 + A^4 + A^5 + \ldots + A^r$$

Then the ith row and j^{th} column entry of the matrix $\mathbf{B_r}$ gives the number of the paths of length **r** or less than **r** from vertex $\mathbf{v_i}$ to $\mathbf{v_j}$.

Let **G = (V, E)** be a simple directed graph with **n** vertices $\mathbf{v_1, v_2, v_3 \ldots v_n}$. Then path matrix or the reachability matrix of **G** is the **n x n** matrix $\mathbf{P = p_{ij}}$ defined as:

$$p_{ij} = \begin{cases} 1 & \text{If there is a path from } v_i \text{ to } v_j \\ 0 & \text{Otherwise} \end{cases}$$

If there is path from $\mathbf{v_i}$ to $\mathbf{v_j}$ then there must be a simple path, path without loop, etc, from $\mathbf{v_i}$ to $\mathbf{v_j}$ when $\mathbf{v_i} \neq \mathbf{v_j}$ or there must be a cycle from $\mathbf{v_i}$ to $\mathbf{v_j}$ when $\mathbf{v_i} = \mathbf{v_j}$. Since **G** has **n** vertices, such a simple path must have length **n – 1** or less or such a cycle must have length **n** or less. The path matrix can be calculated from the matrix $\mathbf{B_n}$ by choosing $\mathbf{p_{ij}} = \mathbf{1}$ if the elements in the ith row and j^{th} column of $\mathbf{B_n}$ is nonzero and $\mathbf{p_{ij}} = \mathbf{0}$, otherwise. From this method one can easily calculate path matrix. For example, once again consider the graph illustrated in **Fig. 8.10**, the adjacency matrix and powers of adjacency matrix of this graph, i.e., calculated $\mathbf{A^2}$, $\mathbf{A^3}$, $\mathbf{A^4}$ and $\mathbf{A^5}$. We have

$$B_5 = A^1 + A^2 + A^3 + A^4 + A^5$$

$$B_5 = \begin{pmatrix} 20 & 11 & 21 & 10 & 10 \\ 24 & 11 & 24 & 12 & 12 \\ 19 & 9 & 17 & 9 & 9 \\ 15 & 7 & 15 & 7 & 8 \\ 9 & 4 & 9 & 5 & 4 \end{pmatrix}$$

The path matrix for **G** will be:

$$\mathbf{P} = \begin{pmatrix} 1 & 1 & 1 & 1 & 1 \\ 1 & 1 & 1 & 1 & 1 \\ 1 & 1 & 1 & 1 & 1 \\ 1 & 1 & 1 & 1 & 1 \\ 1 & 1 & 1 & 1 & 1 \end{pmatrix}$$

8.4 SHORTEST PATH ALGORITHMS

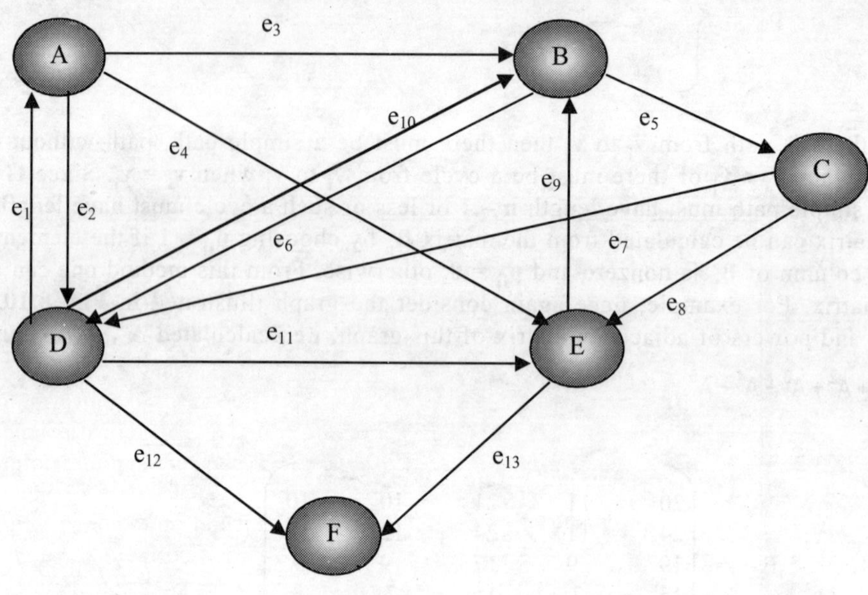

Fig. 8.13

Graphs may be used to represent the highway structure, communication lines, heavy structures in Civil Engineering, etc of a city, state or country. The vertices representing highway cities or Telecommunication towers (Transmitters) or heavy structures load centered (column) edges representing for high sections or Telecommunication link lines and or heavy structure supporting walls. The edges may be assigned weights, which might be either distance between the two cities and average time to spend along that section of highway. A pilot wishing to drive from city **A** to city **B** would be interested in getting the answers of the following questions:

- *Is there a path from **A** to **B**?*
- *If there is more than one path from **A** to **B**, which is the shortest one?*

Similarly, in the case of the Telecommunication the edges can be assigned weights, which might be either distance between the two transmitters area or pulse rate to transmit messages along the line of communication. A customer wishing to send a message from city **A** to city **B** may ask about pulse rate and distance.

8.4.1 WARSHALL'S ALGORITHM

Let **G = (V, E)** is a multi-graph with **n** vertices $v_1, v_2 \ldots v_n$. Suppose we want to find the path matrix **P** of the graph, **G**. ***Warshall*** gave an algorithm for this purpose that is much more efficient to find the shortest path between two vertices in a graph. ***Warshall*** had defined **n+1, n x n** matrices $P_0, P_1, P_2 \ldots P_n$. Such as:

$$P_k[i][j] = \begin{cases} 1 & \text{If there is simple path from } \mathbf{v_i} \text{ to } \mathbf{v_j}\text{, which does not use any other vertices except possibly } \mathbf{v_1, v_2 \ldots v_k}. \\ 0 & \text{Otherwise} \end{cases}$$

For example:

P_0 [i][j] = 1 if there is an edge from $\mathbf{v_i}$ to $\mathbf{v_j}$.
P_1 [i][j] = 1 If there is a path from $\mathbf{v_i}$ to $\mathbf{v_j}$ which does not use any other vertex except possibly $\mathbf{v_1}$.
P_2 [i][j] = 1 If there is a path from $\mathbf{v_i}$ to $\mathbf{v_j}$ which does not use any other vertices except possibly $\mathbf{v_1}$ and $\mathbf{v_2}$.

From the above discussion it is clear that matrix $\mathbf{P_0}$ is equivalent to adjacency matrix **A** of the graph **G**. Since **G** consists of **n** vertices, the last matrix $\mathbf{P_n}$ = **P** becomes the path matrix of **G**.

Warshall said that $\mathbf{P_k}$ **[i][j] = 1** can occur only when one of the following two cases occurs:

- *There exists an edge between v_i and v_j which does not use any other vertex except possibly $v_1, v_2 \ldots v_{k-1}$; hence*

P_{k-1} [i][j] = 1

- *There exists an edge between v_i and v_k and an edge between v_k and v_l where each edge does not use any other vertex except possibly $v_1, v_2 \ldots v_{k-1}$; hence*

P_{k-1} [i][k] = 1 and P_{k-1} [k][j] = 1

One can obtain the elements of matrix $\mathbf{P_k}$ with the help of the following formula:

P_k [i][j] = P_{k-1} [i][j] V (P_{k-1} [i][k] Λ P_{k-1} [k][j])

where

Λ → Means logical AND operations (For example: 1 Λ 1 = 1 and 1 Λ 0 = 0)

V → Means logical OR operations (For example: 1 V 1 = 1, 1 V 0 = 1 and 0 V 0 = 0)

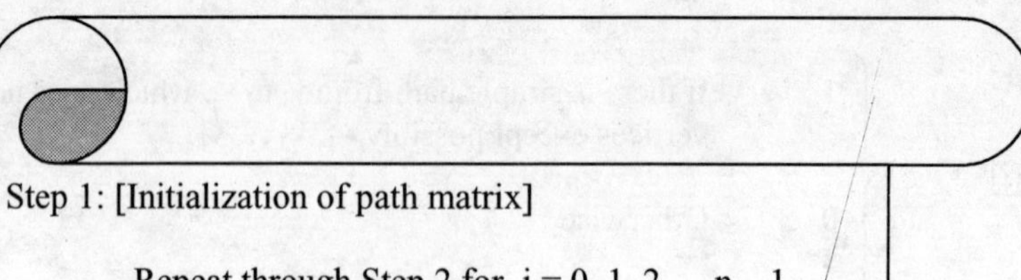

Step 1: [Initialization of path matrix]

Repeat through Step 2 for i = 0, 1, 2 … n – 1
Repeat through Step 2 for j = 0, 1, 2 … n – 1

Step 2: [Test the condition and assign value to path matrix accordingly]

If (a [i][j] = 0)
p [i][j] = 0
Else
p [i][j] = 1

Step 3: [Evaluate path matrix]

Repeat through Step 4 for k = 0, 1, 2, … n – 1
Repeat through Step 4 for i = 0, 1, 2 … n – 1
Repeat through Step 4 for j = 0, 1, 2 … n – 1

Step 4: p[i][j] = p[i][j] V (p[i][k] □ p[k][j])

Step 5: Exit

Fig. 8.14 Warshall's algorithm of path matrix

Warshall's algorithm is illustrated in **Fig. 8.14.** Consider the graph illustrated in **Fig. 8.15** and the adjacency matrix of this graph is

$$A = \begin{pmatrix} 0 & 1 & 0 & 1 \\ 1 & 0 & 0 & 0 \\ 1 & 1 & 0 & 1 \\ 0 & 1 & 0 & 0 \end{pmatrix}$$

If we apply the above ***Warshall***'s technique we find the path matrix **P** that is as follows:

$$P = \begin{pmatrix} 1 & 1 & 0 & 1 \\ 1 & 1 & 0 & 1 \\ 1 & 1 & 0 & 1 \\ 1 & 1 & 0 & 1 \end{pmatrix}$$

If we apply general procedure to find path matrix, we get the same result. For example, for the graph illustrated in **Fig. 8.15.** Consider the following steps:

$$A = \begin{pmatrix} 0 & 1 & 0 & 1 \\ 1 & 0 & 0 & 0 \\ 1 & 1 & 0 & 1 \\ 0 & 1 & 0 & 0 \end{pmatrix}$$

$$A^2 = A \times A = \begin{pmatrix} 1 & 1 & 0 & 0 \\ 0 & 1 & 0 & 1 \\ 1 & 2 & 0 & 1 \\ 1 & 0 & 0 & 0 \end{pmatrix}$$

$$A^3 = A \times A \times A = \begin{pmatrix} 1 & 1 & 0 & 1 \\ 1 & 1 & 0 & 0 \\ 2 & 2 & 0 & 1 \\ 0 & 1 & 0 & 1 \end{pmatrix}$$

$$A^4 = A \times A \times A \times A = \begin{pmatrix} 1 & 2 & 0 & 1 \\ 1 & 1 & 0 & 1 \\ 2 & 3 & 0 & 2 \\ 1 & 1 & 0 & 0 \end{pmatrix}$$

Path matrix can be evaluated with the help of general formula:

$P = A \vee A^2 \vee A^3 \vee A^4$

If we apply the above formula to find path matrix, we get the following resultant matrix. Thus, we can say that the general technique to find path matrix requires much more theoretical work and it is slow in comparison to ***Warshall***'s algorithm even if we implement it on computer.

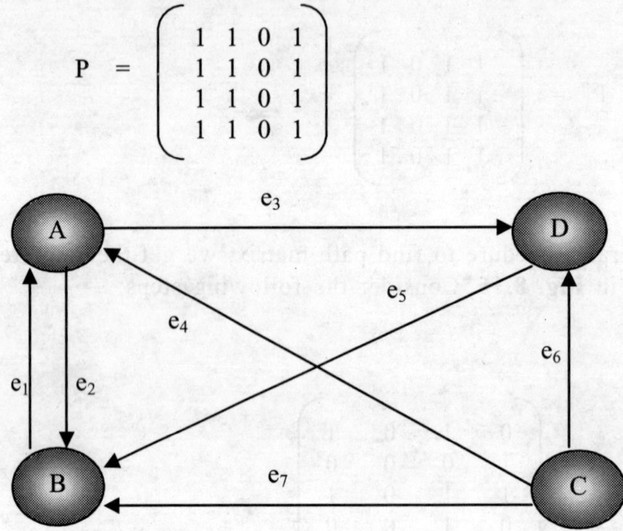

Fig. 8.15

The program segment **WARSHALL.C** illustrates the algorithm given in **Fig. 8.14.** The result of this program segment can be tested with the help of **Fig. 8.15.**

```
// SHORTEST PATH
// WARSHALL.C
# include<iostream.h>

# define size 10

class Shortest_path
{
    public:
        int a [size][size];
        int p [size][size];
        int i,k,j;
        int n;

    public:
        void Input ();
        void Warshall ();
        void Output ();
};

// Input function
void Shortest_path :: Input()
{
    cout<<"\n Input the number of vertices:";
```

```
    cin>>n;
    cout<<"\n Input adjency matrix\n";
    for ( i = 0; i < n; i++)
    {
        for ( j = 0; j < n; j++)
        {
            cin>>a[i][j];
        }
        cout<<"\n";
    }
    cout<<"\n Adjency matrix \n";
    for ( i = 0; i < n; i++)
    {
        for ( j = 0; j < n; j++)
        {
            cout<<" "<<a[i][j];
        }
        cout<<"\n";
    }
}

// Output function

void Shortest_path :: Output()
{
    for ( i = 0; i < n; i++)
    {
        for ( j = 0; j < n; j++)
        {
            cout<<" "<<p [i][j];
        }
        cout<<"\n";
    }
}

// Shortest path function
void Shortest_path :: Warshall ()
{
    // Initialization of matrix m

    for ( i = 0; i < n; i++)
    {
        for ( j = 0; j < n; j++)
        {
            if (a[i][j] == 0)
                p [i][j] = 0;
            else
```

```
                p[i][j] = 1;
            }
        }

        // Shortest Path evaluation start from here
        for ( k = 0; k < n; k++)
        {
            for ( i = 0; i < n; i++)
            {
                for ( j = 0; j < n; j++)
                {
                    p[i][j] = p[i][j] | ( p[i][k] & p[k][j]);
                }
            }
        }
}

// Function main
void main()
{
        Shortest_path S;
        S.Input ();
        S.Warshall ();
        cout<<"\n Path matrix:\n";
        S.Output ();
}
```

```
Input the number of vertices: 4
Input adjacency matrix

0 1 0 1
1 0 0 0
1 1 0 1
0 1 0 0

Adjacency matrix
0 1 0 1
1 0 0 0
1 1 0 1
0 1 0 0

Path matrix:

1 1 0 1
1 1 0 1
1 1 0 1
1 1 0 1
```

8.4.2 WARSHALL'S MODIFIED ALGORITHM

Warshall's algorithm can be modified to obtain a matrix, which gives the length of the shortest paths between the vertices of a graph **G**. For example, suppose **A** is adjacency matrix of **G**, replace all those elements of **A** which are zero by infinity (∞ or by a very-very large number), which now indicates that there is no edge between the vertices. In this technique we obtain a set of matrices $\mathbf{M_0}$, $\mathbf{M_1}$, $\mathbf{M_2}$ ... $\mathbf{M_n}$, with the help of following formula:

$M_k [i][j] = Min (M_{k-1} [i][j], M_{k-1} [i][k] + M_{k-1} [k][j])$

The input matrix is same as adjacency matrix **A** except that each 0 is replaced by infinity (∞ or by a very-very large number). The final resulting matrix $\mathbf{M_n}$ will be the desired shortest path matrix. For example, consider the graph illustrated in **Fig. 8.16.** The adjacency matrix for this graph is:

$$A = \begin{pmatrix} 0 & 1 & 0 & 1 \\ 1 & 0 & 0 & 0 \\ 1 & 1 & 0 & 1 \\ 0 & 1 & 0 & 0 \end{pmatrix}$$

$$M_0 = \begin{pmatrix} 9999 & 1 & 9999 & 1 \\ 1 & 9999 & 9999 & 9999 \\ 1 & 1 & 9999 & 1 \\ 9999 & 1 & 9999 & 9999 \end{pmatrix}$$

Step0

$$M_1 = \begin{pmatrix} 9999 & 1 & 9999 & 1 \\ 1 & 2 & 9999 & 2 \\ 1 & 1 & 9999 & 1 \\ 9999 & 1 & 9999 & 9999 \end{pmatrix}$$

Step1

$$M_2 = \begin{pmatrix} 2 & 1 & 9999 & 1 \\ 1 & 2 & 9999 & 2 \\ 1 & 1 & 9999 & 1 \\ 2 & 1 & 9999 & 3 \end{pmatrix}$$

Step2

$$M_3 = \begin{pmatrix} 2 & 1 & 9999 & 1 \\ 1 & 2 & 9999 & 2 \\ 1 & 1 & 9999 & 1 \\ 2 & 1 & 9999 & 3 \end{pmatrix}$$

Step3

$$M_4 = \begin{pmatrix} 2 & 1 & 9999 & 1 \\ 1 & 2 & 9999 & 2 \\ 1 & 1 & 9999 & 1 \\ 2 & 1 & 9999 & 3 \end{pmatrix}$$

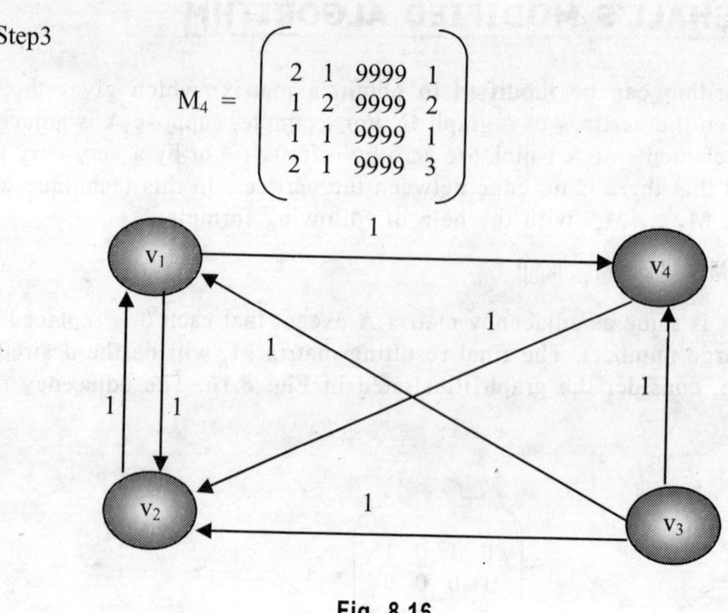

Fig. 8.16

M_4 is the shortest path matrix for the graph illustrated in **Fig. 8.16.**

If graph **G** is a weight graph, we can find its weight matrix and apply the above procedure to find the shortest path matrix if the length of the edges is the weights. If the weight of each edge is the cost then the shortest path matrix gives the minimal cost matrix. For example, let the graph **G** illustrated in **Fig. 8.17.**

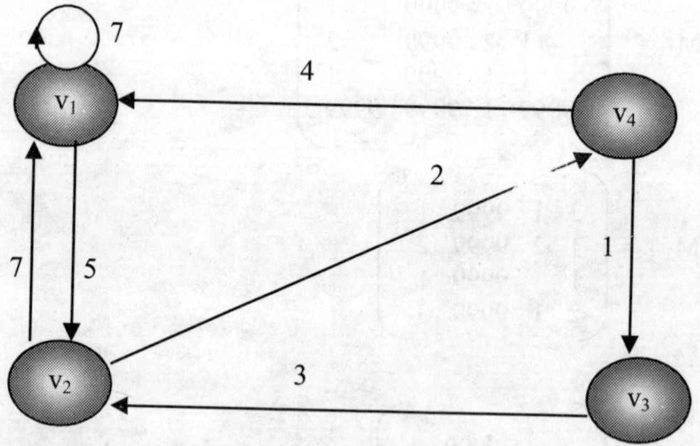

Fig. 8.17

The adjacency matrix **A** for **G** is as follows.

$$A = \begin{pmatrix} 7 & 5 & 0 & 0 \\ 7 & 0 & 0 & 2 \\ 0 & 3 & 0 & 0 \\ 4 & 0 & 1 & 0 \end{pmatrix}$$

Matrix after replacing all 0's elements by a large value

$$M_0 = \begin{pmatrix} 7 & 5 & 9999 & 9999 \\ 7 & 9999 & 9999 & 2 \\ 9999 & 3 & 9999 & 9999 \\ 4 & 9999 & 1 & 9999 \end{pmatrix}$$

Step0

$$M_1 = \begin{pmatrix} 7 & 5 & 9999 & 9999 \\ 7 & 12 & 9999 & 2 \\ 9999 & 3 & 9999 & 9999 \\ 4 & 9 & 1 & 9999 \end{pmatrix}$$

Step1

$$M_2 = \begin{pmatrix} 7 & 5 & 9999 & 7 \\ 7 & 12 & 9999 & 2 \\ 10 & 3 & 9999 & 5 \\ 4 & 9 & 1 & 11 \end{pmatrix}$$

Step 1: [Initialize matrix m]
Repeat through Step 2 for i = 0, 1, 2, 3 … n - 1
Repeat through Step 2 for j = 0, 1, 2, 3 … n – 1

Step 2: [Test the condition and assign the required value to matrix m]
If a[i][j] = 0
m [i][j] = Infinity
Else
m[i][j] = a [i][j]

Step 3: [Shortest Path evaluation]
Repeat through Step 4 for k = 0, 1, 2, 3 … n – 1
Repeat through Step 4 for i = 0, 1, 2, 3 … n - 1
Repeat through Step 4 for j = 0, 1, 2, 3 … n – 1

Step 4: If m [i][j] < m [i][k] + m [k][j]
m [i][j] = m [i][j]
Else
m [i][j] = m [i][k] + m [k][j]

Step 5: Exit

Fig. 8.18 Modified Warshall's algorithm

Step2

$$M_3 = \begin{pmatrix} 7 & 5 & 9999 & 7 \\ 7 & 12 & 9999 & 2 \\ 10 & 3 & 9999 & 5 \\ 4 & 4 & 1 & 6 \end{pmatrix}$$

Step3

$$M_4 = \begin{pmatrix} 7 & 5 & 8 & 7 \\ 6 & 6 & 3 & 2 \\ 9 & 3 & 6 & 5 \\ 4 & 4 & 1 & 6 \end{pmatrix}$$

$\mathbf{M_4}$ represents shortest path matrix for the graph illustrated in **Fig. 8.17.**

The program segment **SPATH.C** illustrates the algorithm given in **Fig. 8.18** and result is tested for graph illustrated in **Fig. 8.16** and **Fig. 8.17.**

```
// SHORTEST PATH
// SPATH.C

# include<iostream.h>

# define size 10
# define infinity 9999

class Shortest_path
{
    public:
        int a[size][size];
        int m[size][size];
        int i,k,j;
        int n;

    public:
        void Input ();
        void Short ();
        void Output ();
};

// Input function

void Shortest_path :: Input()
{
    cout<<"\n Input the number of vetices: ";
    cin>>n;
```

```
    cout<<"\n Input adjacency matrix\n";
    for ( i = 0; i < n; i++)
    {
        for ( j = 0; j < n; j++)
        {
            cin>>a[i][j];
        }
        cout<<"\n";
    }
    cout<<"\n Adjacency matrix \n";
    for ( i = 0; i < n; i++)
    {
        for ( j = 0; j < n; j++)
        {
            cout<< " "<<a[i][j];
        }
        cout<<"\n";
    }
}

// Output function

void Shortest_path :: Output()
{
    for ( i = 0; i < n; i++)
    {
        for ( j = 0; j < n; j++)
        {
            cout<< " "<<m[i][j];
        }
        cout<<"\n";
    }
}

// Shortest path function

void Shortest_path :: Short ()
{
    // Initialization of matrix m

    for ( i = 0; i < n; i++)
    {
        for ( j = 0; j < n; j++)
        {
            if (a[i][j] == 0)
                m[i][j] = infinity;
```

```
            else
                m[i][j] = a[i][j];
        }
    }
    cout<<"\n Adjacency matrix after replacing zeros by very large value";
    Output();

    // Shortest path evaluation start from here

    for ( k = 0; k < n; k++)
    {
        for ( i = 0; i < n; i++)
        {
            for ( j = 0; j < n; j++)
            {
                if ( m [i][j] <= m [i][k] + m [k][j] )
                    m [i][j] = m [i][j];
                else
                    m [i][j] = m[i][k] + m [k][j];
            }
        }
        cout<<"\n STEP"<<k<<"\n";
        Output();
    }
}

// Function main

void main()
{
    Shortest_path S;
    S.Input();
    S.Short();
    cout<<"\n Shortest path matrix is as follows \n";
    S.Output();
}
```

```
Input the number of vertices: 4
Input adjacency matrix
  0   1   0   1
  1   0   0   0
  1   1   0   1
  0   1   0   0

Adjacency matrix
  0   1   0   1
  1   0   0   0
  1   1   0   1
  0   1   0   0
Matrix after replacing zeros by large value

  9999       1   9999      1
     1    9999   9999   9999
     1       1   9999      1
  9999       1   9999   9999

STEP0
  9999   1   9999      1
     1   2   9999      2
     1   1   9999      1
  9999   1   9999   9999

STEP1
  2   1   9999   1
  1   2   9999   2
  1   1   9999   1
  2   1   9999   3

STEP2
  2   1   9999   1
  1   2   9999   2
  1   1   9999   1
  2   1   9999   3

STEP3
  2   1   9999   1
  1   2   9999   2
  1   1   9999   1
  2   1   9999   3

Shortest path matrix is as follows
  2   1   9999   1
  1   2   9999   2
  1   1   9999   1
  2   1   9999   3
```

```
Input the number of vertices: 4
 Input adjacency matrix
  7  5  0  0
  7  0  0  2
  0  3  0  0
  4  0  1  0

 Adjacency matrix
  7  5  0  0
  7  0  0  2
  0  3  0  0
  4  0  1  0
 Matrix after replacing zeros by large value

      7      5  9999  9999
      7   9999  9999     2
   9999      3  9999  9999
      4   9999     1  9999

 STEP0
      7     5  9999  9999
      7    12  9999     2
   9999     3  9999  9999
      4     9     1  9999

 STEP1
    7    5  9999  7
    7   12  9999  2
   10    3  9999  5
    4    9     1 11

 STEP2
    7    5  9999  7
    7   12  9999  2
   10    3  9999  5
    4    4     1  6

 STEP3
  7  5  8  7
  6  6  3  2
  9  3  6  5
  4  4  1  6

 Shortest path matrix is as follows
  7  5  8  7
  6  6  3  2
  9  3  6  5
  4  4  1  6
```

8.4.3 DIJKSTRA' S TECHNIQUE

This technique is used to determine the shortest path between two arbitrary vertices in a graph. Let, weight **w** $(\mathbf{v_i}, \mathbf{v_j})$ is associated with every edge $(\mathbf{v_i}, \mathbf{v_j})$ in a given graph **G**. Furthermore, the weights are such that the total weight from vertex $\mathbf{v_i}$ to the vertex $\mathbf{v_k}$ via vertex $\mathbf{v_j}$ is **w** $(\mathbf{v_i}, \mathbf{v_j})$ + **w** $(\mathbf{v_j}, \mathbf{v_k})$. Using this technique, the weight from a vertex $\mathbf{v_s}$ (starting of the path) to vertex $\mathbf{v_t}$ (the end of the path) in the graph **G** for a given path $(\mathbf{v_s}, \mathbf{v_1}), (\mathbf{v_1}, \mathbf{v_2}), (\mathbf{v_2}, \mathbf{v_3}) \ldots (\mathbf{v_i}, \mathbf{v_t})$ is given by **w** $(\mathbf{v_s}, \mathbf{v_1})$ + **w** $(\mathbf{v_1}, \mathbf{v_2})$ + **w** $(\mathbf{v_2}, \mathbf{v_3})$+ ... + **w** $(\mathbf{v_i}, \mathbf{v_t})$. In a graph there are many possible paths between $\mathbf{v_s}$ and $\mathbf{v_t}$.

Dijkstra's method is a very popular and efficient one to find each and every path from starting to terminal vertices. If there is an edge between two vertices, then the weight of this edge is its length. If several edges exist however, use the shortest length edge. If no edge actually exists set the length to infinity. Edge $(\mathbf{v_i}, \mathbf{v_j})$ does not necessarily have the same length as edge $(\mathbf{v_j}, \mathbf{v_i})$. This allows different routes between two vertices that take different paths depending on the direction of travel.

Dijkstra's technique is based on assigning labels to each vertex. The label is equal to the distance (weight) from the starting vertex to that vertex. Obviously, the starting vertex $\mathbf{v_s}$ has a label 0. A label can be in one of two states-temporary or permanent. A permanent label that lies along the shortest path while a temporary label is one that has uncertainty as to whether the label is along the shortest path.

Step 1: Assign a temporary label $l(v_i) = \infty$ to all vertices except $\mathbf{v_s}$.

Step 2: [Mark v_s as permanent by assigning 0 label to it]

$l(v_s) = 0$

Step 3: [Assign value of v_s to v_r where v_r is last vertex to be made permanent]

$v_r = v_s$

Step 4:

if $l(v_i) > l(v_k) + w(v_k, v_i)$

$l(v_i) = l(v_k) + w(v_k, v_i)$

Step 5: $v_r = v_i$

Step 6: If $\mathbf{v_t}$ has temporary label, repeat Step 4 to Step 5 otherwise the value of $\mathbf{v_t}$ is permanent label and is equal to the shortest path $\mathbf{v_s}$ to $\mathbf{v_t}$.

Step 7: Exit

Fig. 8.19 Dijkstra's algorithm

This technique gradually changes the temporary labels to permanent labels until the end vertex has a permanent label. At each step, the aim is to make the temporary labels shorter by finding paths to the associated vertices using the shortest paths to the permanent labeled vertices. After this the temporary label with the smallest value is made permanent. This process eliminates one temporary vertex at each step, ensuring that the shortest path from $\mathbf{v_s}$ to $\mathbf{v_t}$ will eventually be found.

For example, consider the graph **G** illustrated in **Fig. 8.20** and the weight matrix of **G** is as follows:

$$W = \begin{array}{c} \\ v_1 \\ v_2 \\ v_3 \\ v_4 \end{array} \begin{array}{c} \begin{array}{cccc} v_1 & v_2 & v_3 & v_4 \end{array} \\ \begin{pmatrix} 0 & 5 & 0 & 4 \\ 7 & 0 & 0 & 2 \\ 0 & 3 & 0 & 0 \\ 0 & 0 & 1 & 0 \end{pmatrix} \end{array}$$

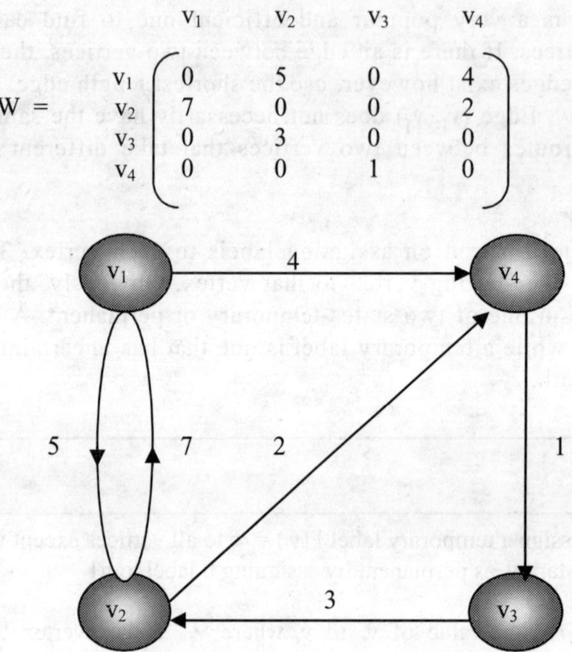

Fig. 8.20 Weighted graph

If we replace the elements, which have 0 with 9999 (very large value) except diagonal elements, we get a distance matrix **D**.

$$D = \begin{array}{c} \\ v_1 \\ v_2 \\ v_3 \\ v_4 \end{array} \begin{array}{c} \begin{array}{cccc} v_1 & v_2 & v_3 & v_4 \end{array} \\ \begin{pmatrix} 0 & 5 & 9999 & 4 \\ 7 & 0 & 9999 & 2 \\ 9999 & 3 & 0 & 9999 \\ 9999 & 9999 & 1 & 0 \end{pmatrix} \end{array}$$

Now, we have to travel from $\mathbf{v_1}$ to $\mathbf{v_4}$ in the graph **G** illustrated in **Fig. 8.20.** There are two possible route (a) from vertex $\mathbf{v_1}$ to $\mathbf{v_4}$ (direct) and (b) vertex $\mathbf{v_1}$ to $\mathbf{v_2}$ and then from $\mathbf{v_2}$ to $\mathbf{v_4}$. The distances for the two possible routes are 4 and 7 represented.

Step 1, Step 2 and Step 3: Assign labels as follows and set $\mathbf{v_r} = \mathbf{v_s} = \mathbf{v_1}$.

	v_s	v_2	v_3	v_t
Label:	*0*	*9999*	*9999*	*9999*
Permanent:	*Y*	*N*	*N*	*N*

Step 4 and Step 5: Redefine temporary labels as follows:

Label (v_2) = min (9999, 0 + 5) = 5
Label (v_3) = min (9999, 0 + 9999) = 9999
Label (v_t) = min (9999, 0 + 4) = 4
Make Label (v_2) permanent, $v_r = v_2$

	v_s	v_2	v_3	v_t
Label:	*0*	*5*	*9999*	*9999*
Permanent:	*Y*	*Y*	*N*	*N*

Step 6: Repeat Step 4 and Step 5, redefine the temporary labels as follows:

Label (v_3) = min (9999, 7 + 0) = 7
Label (v_t) = min (4, 7+2) = 4
Make Label (v_3) permanent set $v_r = v_3$

	v_s	v_2	v_3	v_t
Label:	*0*	*5*	*7*	*9999*
Permanent:	*Y*	*Y*	*Y*	*N*

Step 6: Repeat Step 4 and Step 5, redefine

Label (v_t) = min (4, 0+9999) 4
Make Label (v_t) permanent set $v_r = v_t$

	v_s	v_2	v_3	v_t
Label:	*0*	*5*	*7*	*4*
Permanent:	*Y*	*Y*	*Y*	*Y*

Step 6: Label (v_t) is permanent. The shortest path length is 4.

The program segment **DIJKSTRA.C** implements ***DIJKSTRA***'s algorithm.

```
// DIJKSTRA METHOD
// DIJKSTRA.C
# include<iostream.h>
# include<stdio.h>
```

```
# define size 20
# define P 1
# define T 0
# define infinity 9999

struct Label
{
    int predecessor;
    int length;
    int flag;
};

class Dijkstra
{
    public:
        int k, min, count;
        Label state[size];
        int visit_path[size];

    public:
        int Short_Path(int a[size][size], int , int , int ,
        int path [size], int *);
        void Input(int , int a[size][size]);
        void Output(int , int a[size][size]);
};

// Shortest path computing function
int Dijkstra :: Short_Path(int a[size][size], int n, int s, int t,
int path[size], int *dist)
{
    *dist = 0;

    for( int i = 1; i <= n; i ++)
    {
        state[i].predecessor = 0;
        state[i].length = infinity ;
        state[i].flag = T;
    }

    // Make source vertex permanent

    state[s].predecessor = 0;
    state[s].length = 0;
    state[s].flag = P;

    // Start from source vertex
```

```
k = s;

do
{
    // Check all the paths from kth vertex and find their distance from k vertex

    for ( i = 1; i <= n; i++)
    {
        if ((a[k][i] > 0) && (state[i].flag == T))
        {
            if ((state[k].length + a[k][i]) < state[i].length)
            {
                state[i].predecessor = k;
                state[i].length = state[k].length + a[k][i];
            }
        }
    }
    min = infinity;
    k = 0;
    for ( i =1; i <= n; i++)
    {
        if ((state[i].flag == T) && (state[i].length < min))
        {
            min = state[i].length;
            k = i;
        }
    }
    if ( k==0)
        return (0);
    state[k].flag = P;
} while(k != t);

// Store optimal path
k = t;
count = 1;

do
{

    visit_path[count] = k;
    count ++;
    k = state[k].predecessor;
} while(k!= 0);

// Reverse the vertices since algorithm stores path in reverse direction

count —;
```

```
        for ( i = 1; i <= count ; i++)
            path[i] = visit_path[count-i+1];

        int t1, t2;

        for ( i = 1; i < count ; i ++)
        {
            t1 = path[i];
            t2 = path [i+1];
            *dist += a[t1][t2];
        }
        return (count);
}

// Input function
void Dijkstra :: Input(int n, int a[size][size])
{
        cout<<"\n Input adjacency matrix \n";
        for(int i =0; i < n; i++)
        {
            for(int j =0; j < n; j++)
            {
                cin >> a[i][j];
            }
            cout<<"\n";
        }
}

// Output function
void Dijkstra :: Output(int n, int a[size][size])
{
        cout<<"\n Adjacency matrix \n";
        for(int i =0; i < n; i++)
        {
            for(int j =0; j < n; j++)
            {
                cout<<" "<< a[i][j];
            }
            cout<<"\n";
        }
}

// Function main
void main()
{
        Dijkstra Dijk;
```

```
    int a[size][size];
    int path [size];
    int org , dest, dist;
    int count, n;

    cout<<"\n Input the number of vertices in the graph: ";
    cin >> n;

    Dijk.Input(n,a);
    Dijk.Output(n,a);

    cout<<"\n Input starting vertex: ";
    cin >> org;
    cout<<"\n Input destination: ";
    cin >> dest;
    count = Dijk.Short_Path(a,n,org,dest, path, &dist);
    cout<<"\n "<<dist;

    if (dist)
    {
        cout<<"\n Shortest path: "<<path[1];
        for (int i=2; i<=count; i++);
        cout<<" => "<<path[i];
        cout<<"\n Minimum distance = "<<dist;
    }
    else
        cout<<"\n Path does not exist \n";
}
```

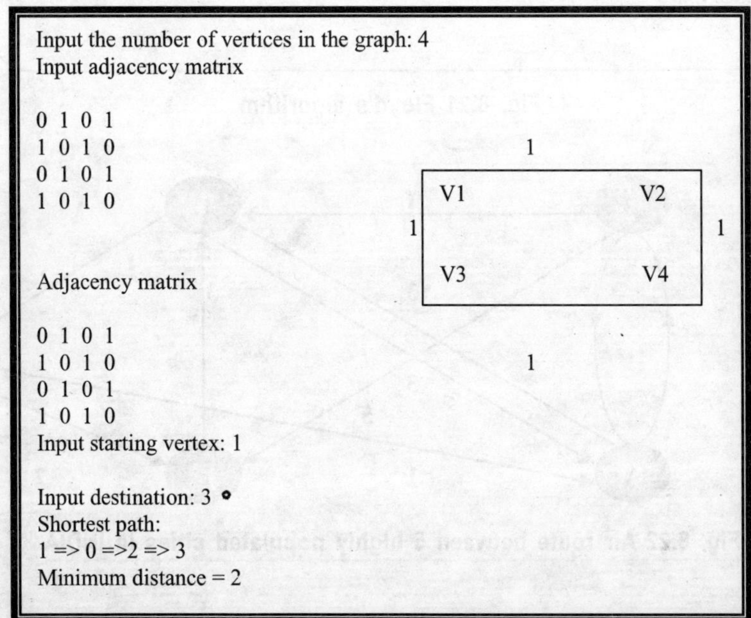

```
Input the number of vertices in the graph: 4
Input adjacency matrix

0 1 0 1
1 0 1 0
0 1 0 1
1 0 1 0

Adjacency matrix

0 1 0 1
1 0 1 0
0 1 0 1
1 0 1 0
Input starting vertex: 1

Input destination: 3
Shortest path:
1 => 0 =>2 => 3
Minimum distance = 2
```

8.4.4 FLOYD'S TECHNIQUE

Floyd's technique starts by numbering each vertex from $\mathbf{v_1}$ to $\mathbf{v_n}$ and uses the weight matrix (Distance matrix or adjacency matrix) first to find the shortest paths that are either direct or use vertex $\mathbf{v_1}$ as an intermediate vertex. Then it finds the shortest path that uses vertex $\mathbf{v_1}$ or vertex $\mathbf{v_2}$ as intermediate vertices. This process continues until the shortest paths are found that are either direct or use some or all of the vertex $\mathbf{v_1}$ to $\mathbf{v_n}$ as intermediate vertices.

```
Step 1: [Initialize matrix m]
        Repeat through Step 2 for i = 0, 1, 2, 3 … n - 1
        Repeat through Step 2 for j = 0, 1, 2, 3 … n – 1

Step 2: [Test the condition and assign the required value to matrix m]
        If a[i][j] = 0
            m [i][j] = Infinity
        Else
            m[i][j] = a [i][j]

Step 3: [Shortest Path evaluation]
        Repeat through Step 4 for k = 0, 1, 2, 3 … n – 1
        Repeat through Step 4 for i = 0, 1, 2, 3 … n - 1
        Repeat through Step 4 for j = 0, 1, 2, 3 … n – 1

Step 4: If m [i][j] < m [i][k] + m [k][j]
                m [i][j] = m [i][j]
        Else
                m [i][j] = m [i][k] + m [k][j]

Step 5: Exit
```

Fig. 8.21 Floyd's algorithm

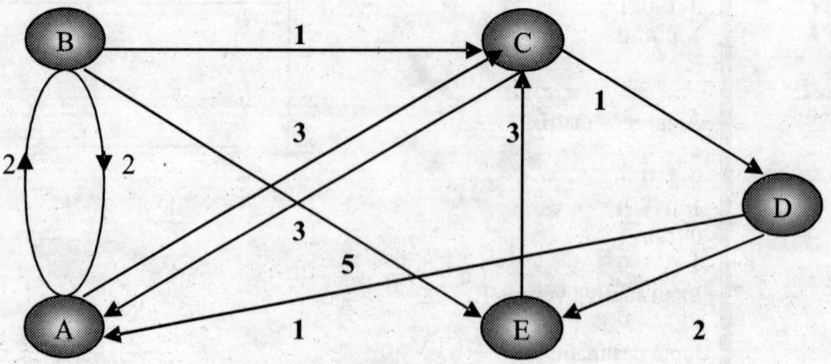

Fig. 8.22 Air route between 5 highly populated cities in INDIA

The intermediate results are stored in an **n x n** matrix **r**, where element $\mathbf{r_k}$ **[i][j]** represents the shortest path between vertices $\mathbf{v_i}$ and $\mathbf{v_j}$, **when** the vertices $\mathbf{v_1}$ to $\mathbf{v_k}$ are used as intermediate vertices. The element $\mathbf{r_{k+1}}$ **[i][j]** is either $\mathbf{r_k}$ **[i][j]** or $\mathbf{r_k}$ **[i][k]** + $\mathbf{r_k}$ **[k][j]**. **Fig. 8.21**illustrates the algorithm for **Floyd's** technique.

For example, consider the graph **G** illustrated in **Fig. 8.22.** The adjacency (weight) matrix for **G** is as follows:

$$W = \begin{pmatrix} 0 & 2 & 3 & 0 & 0 \\ 2 & 0 & 1 & 0 & 5 \\ 3 & 0 & 0 & 1 & 0 \\ 1 & 0 & 0 & 0 & 2 \\ 0 & 0 & 3 & 0 & 0 \end{pmatrix}$$

Step 2 and Step 3:

Replacing zero elements by very large value (9999) except diagonal elements, we get distance matrix D.

$$D = \begin{pmatrix} 0 & 2 & 3 & 9999 & 9999 \\ 2 & 0 & 1 & 9999 & 5 \\ 3 & 9999 & 0 & 1 & 9999 \\ 1 & 9999 & 9999 & 0 & 2 \\ 9999 & 9999 & 3 & 9999 & 0 \end{pmatrix}$$

Step 4 and Step 5:

r_0 (0, 0) = min (0, 0+0) = 0
r_0 (0, 1) = min (2, 0+2) = 2
r_0 (0, 2) = min (3, 0+3) = 3
r_0 (0, 3) = min (9999, 0+9999) = 9999
r_0 (0, 4) = min (9999, 0+9999) = 9999

r_0 (1, 0) = min (2, 2+0) = 2
r_0 (1, 1) = min (0, 2+2) = 0
r_0 (1, 2) = min (1, 2+3) = 1
r_0 (1, 3) = min (9999, 2+9999) = 9999
r_0 (1, 4) = min (5, 2+9999) = 9999

r_0 (2, 0) = min (3, 3+0) = 3
r_0 (2, 1) = min (9999, 3+2) = 5
r_0 (2, 2) = min (0, 3+3) = 0
r_0 (2, 3) = min (1, 3+9999) = 1
r_0 (2, 4) = min (9999, 3+9999) = 9999

If we continue the above process we get the final shortest distance matrix $\mathbf{r_n}$. The program segment **FLOYD.C** is the implementation of the algorithm given in **Fig. 8.21**.

$$\mathbf{r_n} = \begin{pmatrix} 0 & 2 & 3 & 4 & 6 \\ 2 & 0 & 1 & 2 & 4 \\ 2 & 4 & 0 & 1 & 3 \\ 1 & 3 & 4 & 0 & 2 \\ 5 & 7 & 3 & 4 & 0 \end{pmatrix}$$

```
// FLYOD'S METHOD
// FLOYD.CPP
# include<iostream.h>

# define Infinity 9999
# define size 20

class Fly
{
      public: int i, k, j;
      public: void Input(int , int a[size][size]);
            void Output(int , int a[size][size]);
            void Flyod(int , int a[size][size], int r[size][size]);
};

// Input function

void Fly :: Input(int n, int a[size][size])
{
 cout<<"\n Input adjacency matrix\n";
 for ( int i =0; i < n; i++)
 {
      for ( int j =0; j < n; j++)
      {
       cin >>a[i][j];
      }
      cout<<"\n";
 }
}

// Output function

void Fly :: Output (int n, int a[size][size])
{
 for ( int i =0; i < n; i++)
      {
            for ( int j =0; j < n; j++)
```

```
        {
            cout<< " "<<a[i][j];
        }
        cout<<"\n";
    }
}

// Shortest path evaluation function

void Fly :: Flyod(int n, int a[size][size], int r[size][size])
{
    for ( i = 0; i < n; i ++)
    a[i][i] = 0;        // Set diagonal elements zero
    cout<<"\n After setting diagonal elements to zero \n";
    Output(n, a);
    for (i=0; i < n; i++)
    {
        for ( j=0; j < n; j++)
        {
            if (( a[i][j] == 0) && (i != j))
                r[i][j] = Infinity;
            else
                r[i][j] = a[i][j];
        }
    }
    cout<<"\n Replacing zeros by very large value \n";
    Output(n,r);
    for (k = 0; k < n; k++)
    {
    for (i=0; i < n; i++)
    {
        for ( j=0; j < n; j++)
        {
            if (r[i][k] + r[k][j]< r[i][j])
            {
                cout<<"\n r["<<i<<"]["<<k<<"]="<<r[i][k];
                cout<<"\n r["<<k<<"]["<<j<<"]= "<<r[k][j];
                cout<<"\n r["<<i<<"]["<<j<<"]=" <<r[i][j];
                r[i][j] = r[i][k] + r[k][j];
                cout<<"\n r["<<i<<"]["<<j<<"]="<<"r["<<i<<"]["<<k<<"]+"<<"r["<<k<<"]["<<j<<"] = "<<r[i][j];
            }
            else
            {
            r[i][j] = r[i][j];
            cout<<"\n r["<<i<<"]["<<j<<"]="<<"r["<<i<<"]["<<j<<"]= "<<r[i][j];
            }
```

```
            }
            cout<<"\n";
        }
        cout<<"\n Step "<<k<<"\n";
        Output (n, r);
        }
}

// Function main

void main()
{
        Fly FLY;
        int a[size][size];
        int r[size][size];
        int n;
        cout<<"\n Input number of vertices in the graph: ";
        cin >> n;
        FLY.Input(n, a);
        cout<<"\n Adjacency matrix\n";
        FLY.Output(n,a);
        FLY.Flyod(n, a, r);
        cout<<"\n Shortest path matrix \n";
        FLY.Output(n, r);
}
```

```
Input number of vertices in the graph: 4
Input adjacency matrix
0 1 0 1
1 0 1 0
0 1 0 1
1 0 1 0

Adjacency matrix

0 1 0 1
1 0 1 0
0 1 0 1
1 0 1 0
After setting diagonal elements to zero
0 1 0 1
1 0 1 0
0 1 0 1
1 0 1 0

Replacing zeros by very large value
0 1 9999 1
1 0 1 9999
9999 1 0 1
1 9999 1 0
```

```
Step 1
0 1 2 1
1 0 1 2
2 1 0 1
1 2 1 0

Step 2
0 1 2 1
1 0 1 2
2 1 0 1
1 2 1 0

Step 3
0 1 2 1
1 0 1 2
2 1 0 1
1 2 1 0

Shortest path matrix
0 1 2 1
1 0 1 2
2 1 0 1
1 2 1 0
```

```
Input number of vertices in the graph: 5
Input adjacency matrix
0 2 3 0 0
2 0 1 0 5
3 0 0 1 0
1 0 0 0 2
0 0 3 0 0

Adjacency matrix
0 2 3 0 0
2 0 1 0 5
3 0 0 1 0
1 0 0 0 2
0 0 3 0 0

After setting diagonal elements to zero
0 2 3 0 0
2 0 1 0 5
3 0 0 1 0
1 0 0 0 2
0 0 3 0 0
```

```
Replacing zeros by very large value [by 9999 except diagonal elements]
     0      2      3   9999   9999
     2      0      1   9999      5
     3   9999      0      1   9999
     1   9999   9999      0      2
  9999   9999      3   9999      0

Step 0 [Resulting matrix after first iteration]
     0      2  3   9999   9999
     2      0  1   9999      5
     3      5  0      1   9999
     1      3  4      0      2
  9999   9999  3   9999      0

Step 1[Resulting matrix after second iteration]
     0      2  3   9999   7
     2      0  1   9999   5
     3      5  0      1  10
     1      3  4      0   2
  9999   9999  3   9999   0

Step 2 [Resulting matrix after 3rd iteration]
 0  2  3  4   7
 2  0  1  2   5
 3  5  0  1  10
 1  3  4  0   2
 6  8  3  4   0

Step 3 [Resulting matrix after 4th iteration]
 0  2  3  4  6
 2  0  1  2  4
 2  4  0  1  3
 1  3  4  0  2
 5  7  3  4  0

Step 4 [Resulting matrix after 5th  and last iteration]
 0  2  3  4  6
 2  0  1  2  4
 2  4  0  1  3
 1  3  4  0  2
 5  7  3  4  0
Shortest path matrix [RESULT]
 0  2  3  4  6
 2  0  1  2  4
 2  4  0  1  3
 1  3  4  0  2
 5  7  3  4  0
```

8.5 ADJACENCY LIST

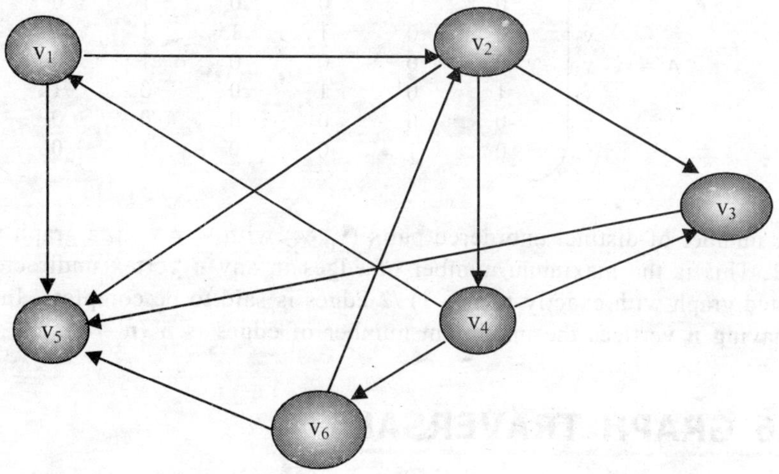

Fig. 8.23 Directed graph

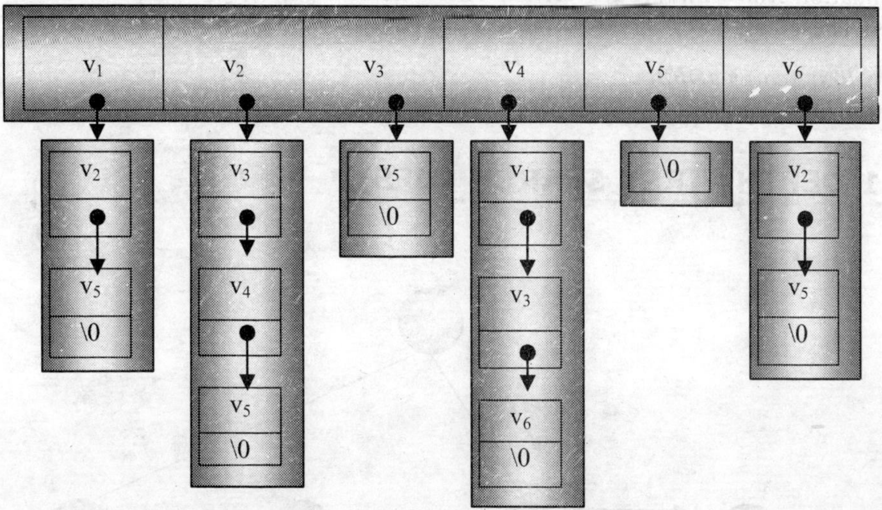

Fig. 8.24 Adjacency lists for the graph G

Let **G = (V, E)** is a graph with **n** vertices. This graph can be represented by **n x n** adjacency matrix. The **n** linked lists represent the **n** rows of the adjacency matrix **A** and there is one linked list for each vertex in **G**. The vertices in the list **L** represent the vertices that are adjacent to the vertex **L,** each vertex represented by two fields: **Vertex** and **Link.** The **Vertex** fields contain the indices of the vertices adjacent to vertex **L**. The adjacency list for the graph illustrated in **Fig. 8.23** is given in **Fig. 8.24.** The adjacency matrix for **G** is as follows:

$$A = \begin{pmatrix} & v_1 & v_2 & v_3 & v_4 & v_5 & v_6 \\ v_1 & 0 & 1 & 0 & 0 & 1 & 0 \\ v_2 & 0 & 0 & 1 & 1 & 1 & 0 \\ v_3 & 0 & 0 & 0 & 0 & 1 & 0 \\ v_4 & 1 & 0 & 1 & 0 & 0 & 1 \\ v_5 & 0 & 0 & 0 & 0 & 0 & 0 \\ v_6 & 0 & 1 & 0 & 0 & 1 & 0 \end{pmatrix}$$

The number of distinct unordered pairs **(v_i, v_j)** with $v_i \neq v_j$ in a graph with **n** vertices is **n (n – 1) / 2**. This is the maximum number of edges in any **n** vertex undirected graph. An **n** vertex undirected graph with exactly **n (n – 1) /2** edges is said to be complete. In the case of a directed graph having **n** vertices the maximum number of edges is **n (n – 1).**

8.6 GRAPH TRAVERSAL

Some times it is required to examine all the vertices in a graph in some systemic orders, as we have seen in the case of binary trees where we use pre-order, post-order or in-order to examine the vertices. For examining all the vertices we start from the root for trees while in the graph we start examination from an arbitrary vertex. There are two popular techniques for examination of the graphs. These are:

- *Depth first search (DFS)*
- *Breadth first search (BFS)*

8.6.1 DEPTH FIRST SEARCH (DFS)

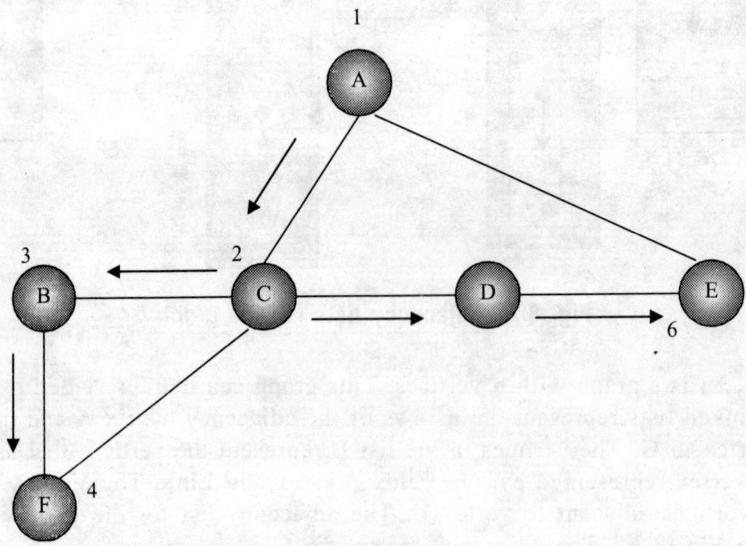

Fig. 8.25

This is similar to pre-order examination of an order tree. Suppose the examination has just examined a vertex v_i and let $w_1, w_2, w_3 \ldots w_k$, be the vertices adjacent to v_i. We next examine w_1 and keep $w_2, w_3 \ldots w_k$ waiting. After examining w_1 we examine all the vertices to which it is adjacent to before returning to examine $w_2, w_3 \ldots w_k$.

For example, consider the graph **G** illustrated in **Fig. 8.25**. The **DFS** strategy results the examination indicated by the arrows, assuming that each edge has been assigned a value of 1. Starting at vertex **A** the examination numbers all the vertices down until vertex **F** is reached, where all the adjacent vertices have already been marked (examined). The **DFS** algorithm returns to **C**, which still has an unlabeled adjacent vertex **D**. After vertex **D** and **E** are labeled, all vertices are numbered and the examination is complete.

In graph traversal two problems arise if we design a recursive algorithm.

- *Graph may contain cycles, so examination algorithm may reach to the same vertex second time and repeat itself.*
- *Graph may not be connected so the examination algorithm may fail to reach all the vertices from a single starting point.*

To prevent infinite recursion, we can use a Boolean valued array **B**, assigning **B [v] = True,** before the recursion begins and check the value of **B [w]** before processing **w**.

A graph is called a bi-connected if there is no single vertex whose removal causes the graph break into two or more pieces refer **Fig. 8.26**. A vertex whose removal causes the graph to become disconnected is called a cut-vertex.

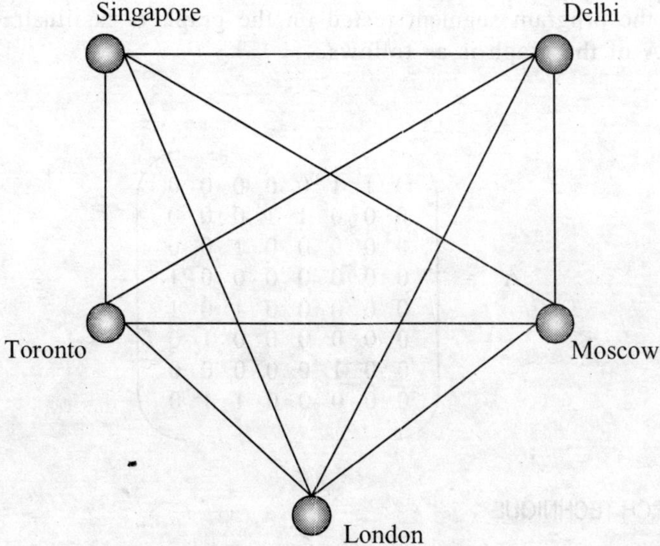

Fig. 8.26 Bi-connected graph

A vital communications network may be described by a graph, allowing each vertex to representing a communication line and each edge indicating the presence of an interconnection between the lines. For a cut-vertex destruction of the line would result in a break down of communications. If the graph is bi-connected the removal of one line (vertex) would not affect the communication, since there will still be other links.

The **DFS** algorithm is illustrated in **Fig. 8.27** and the program segment **DFS.C** implements the algorithm.

Step 1: Define an array **B** that store Boolean values, its size should be greater or equal to the number of vertices in the graph **G**.

Step 2: Initialize the array **B** to False.

Step 3: For all vertices v in **G**

If B[v] = False
Process (v)

Step 4: Exit

Fig. 8.27 Depth first search algorithm

The result of the program segment tested on the graph **G** is illustrated in **Fig. 8.30.** The adjacency matrix **A** of the graph is as follows:

$$A = \begin{pmatrix} 0 & 1 & 1 & 0 & 0 & 0 & 0 & 0 \\ 0 & 0 & 0 & 1 & 1 & 0 & 0 & 0 \\ 0 & 0 & 0 & 0 & 0 & 1 & 0 & 0 \\ 0 & 0 & 0 & 0 & 0 & 0 & 0 & 1 \\ 0 & 0 & 0 & 0 & 0 & 1 & 0 & 1 \\ 0 & 0 & 0 & 0 & 0 & 0 & 1 & 0 \\ 0 & 0 & 1 & 0 & 0 & 0 & 0 & 0 \\ 0 & 0 & 0 & 0 & 0 & 1 & 1 & 0 \end{pmatrix}$$

```
// DEPTH FIRST SEARCH TECHNIQUE
// DFS.C

# include<iostream.h>
# include<stdio.h>
```

```
# define size 20
# define T 1
# define F 0

struct Edge
{
      int terminal;
      Edge *next;
};

struct Vertex
{
      int visit;
      int vertex_no;
      char info;
      int path_length;
      Edge *Edge_Ptr;
};

class Depth_First_Search
{
      public:
            void Table(int , int matrix [size][size], Vertex vert[size]);
            Edge *Insert_Vertex (int , Edge *);
            void DFS ( int , int *dist, Vertex vert [size]);
            void Input(int, int a [size][size]);
            void Output(int, int a [size][size]);
};

Edge * Depth_First_Search :: Insert_Vertex (int vertex_no, Edge *first)
{
      Edge *new1, *current;
      new1 = new (Edge);
      new1->terminal = vertex_no;
      new1->next = NULL;
      if (!first)
            return (new1);
      for (current = first; current->next; current = current->next);
      current->next = new1;
      return (first);
}

// Initializing entries

void Depth_First_Search :: Table(int vertex_num, int matrix [size][size],
```

```
Vertex vert[size])
{
      for ( int i = 0; i < vertex_num; i++)
      {
            vert [i].visit = F;
            vert [i].vertex_no = i+1;
            vert [i].info = 'A'+ i;
            vert [i].path_length = 0;
            vert [i].Edge_Ptr = NULL;
      }

      for (i =0; i < vertex_num ; i++)
            for (int j =0; j < vertex_num ; j++)
                  if (matrix [i][j] > 0)
                        vert [i].Edge_Ptr = Insert_Vertex (j, vert [i].Edge_Ptr);
}

// Computing path length
void Depth_First_Search :: DFS ( int index, int *dist,
Vertex vert [size])
{
      Edge *Link;
      vert [index].visit = T;
      vert [index].path_length = *dist;
      *dist += 1;
      for ( Link = vert [index].Edge_Ptr; Link; Link = Link->next)
            if (vert [Link->terminal].visit == F)
                  DFS (Link->terminal, dist, vert);
}

// Input function to read adjacency matrix
void Depth_First_Search :: Input(int number, int a [size][size])
{
      cout<<"\n Input the adjacency matrix \n";

      for (int i =0; i < number; i++)
      {
            for ( int j=0; j < number; j ++)
            {
                  cin >> a [i][j];
            }
            cout<<"\n";
      }
}

// Output function
```

```
void Depth_First_Search :: Output(int number, int a [size][size])
{
    cout<<"\n Adjacency matrix \n";
    for (int i =0; i < number; i++)
    {
        for ( int j=0; j < number; j ++)
        {
            cout<<" "<< a [i][j];
        }
        cout<<"\n";
    }
}

// Function main
void main()
{
    Depth_First_Search D_F_S;
    int number, index, dist;
    int a [size][size];
    Vertex vert [size];
    Edge *List;
    cout<<"\n Input the number of vertices in the graph: ";
    cin>>number;
    D_F_S.Input(number, a);
    D_F_S.Output(number, a);

    D_F_S.Table(number, a, vert);
    cout <<"\n Input the starting vertex 0-"<<number-1<<": ";
    cin>>index;
    dist = 0;
    D_F_S.DFS (index, &dist, vert);
    cout<<"\n Path length of the vertex from " <<vert[index].info;
    cout<<"\n Vertex Length Vertex Connectivity \n ";
    for (int i = 0; i < number; i++)
    {
        cout <<"\n "<< vert[i].info<<" "<<vert[i].path_length<<" ";
        for (List= vert[i].Edge_Ptr; List; List = List->next)
        {
            cout<<" ";
            putchar(List->terminal+'A');
        }
    }
}
```

```
Input the number of vertices in the graph: 8
 Input the adjacency matrix

 0 1 1 0 0 0 0 0
 0 0 0 1 1 0 0 0
 0 0 0 0 0 1 0 0
 0 0 0 0 0 0 0 1
 0 0 0 0 0 1 0 1
 0 0 0 0 0 0 1 0
 0 0 1 0 0 0 0 0
 0 0 0 0 0 1 1 0

Adjacency matrix

 0 1 1 0 0 0 0 0
 0 0 0 1 1 0 0 0
 0 0 0 0 0 1 0 0
 0 0 0 0 0 0 0 1
 0 0 0 0 0 1 0 1
 0 0 0 0 0 0 1 0
 0 0 1 0 0 0 0 0
 0 0 0 0 0 1 1 0

Input the starting vertex 0-7: 0
Path length of the vertex from A
Vertex Length Vertex Connectivity

 A      0      B C
 B      1      D E
 C      6      F
 D      2      H
 E      7      F H
 F      4      G
 G      5      C
 H      3      F G
```

8.6.2 BREADTH FIRST SEARCH (BFS)

Breadth first examination (search) of a graph is similar to level by level examination of an ordered tree. If the examination has just visited a vertex **v**, then it visits all the vertices adjacent to **v** by putting the vertices adjacent to those in a waiting queue to be examined, after all vertices adjacent to **v** have been visited.

For example, consider the undirected graph **G** illustrated in **Fig. 8.28.** A breadth first examination beginning at vertex **A** of the graph **G** would first visit **A** and then **B** and **C**. Next visits **D, E, F** and **G** will be visited and finally **H**. The adjacency lists of **G** are shown in **Fig. 8.29.** The directed graph **G** and the adjacency lists corresponding to this are illustrated in **Fig. 8.30** and **Fig. 8.31,** respectively.

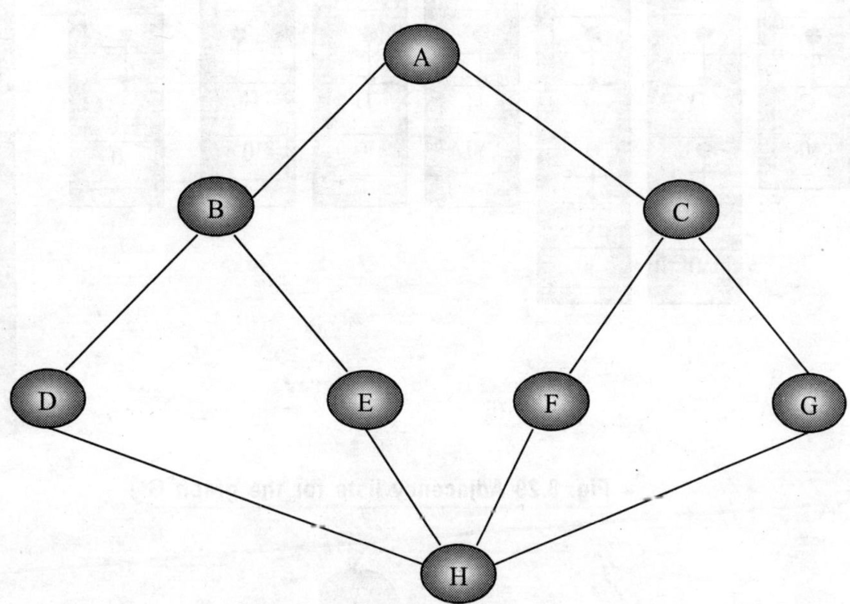

Fig. 8.28 Undirected graph

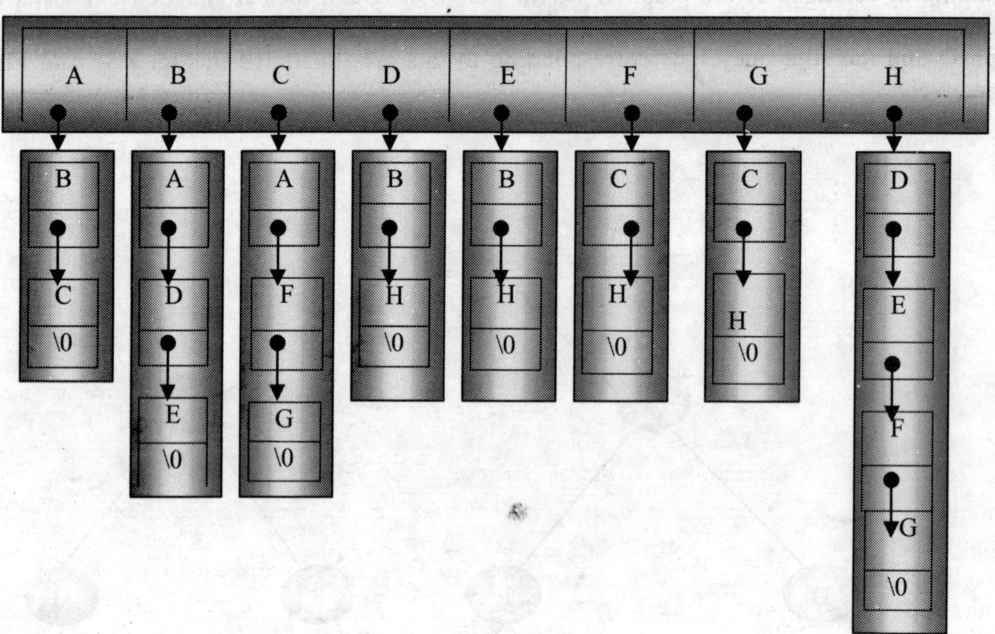

Fig. 8.29 Adjacency lists for the graph G

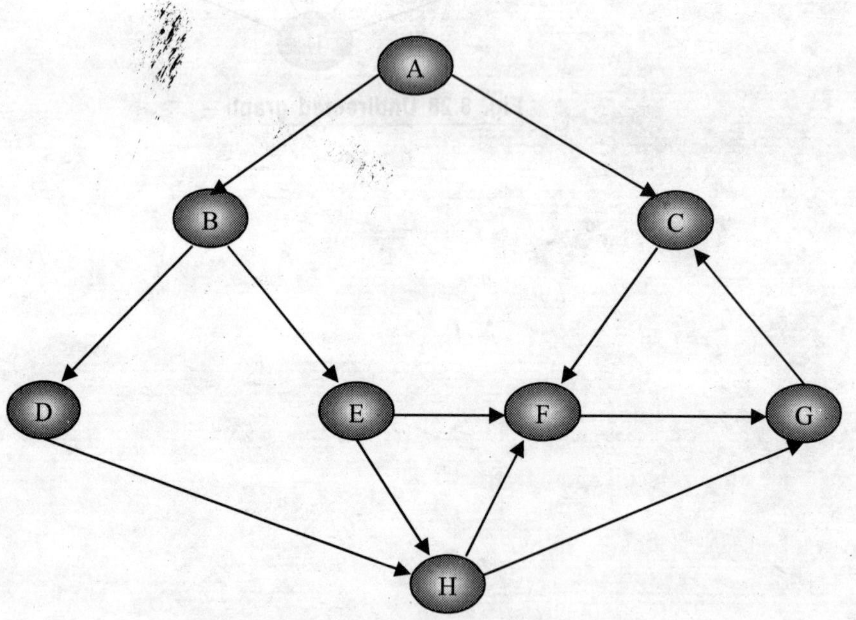

Fig. 8.30 Directed graph

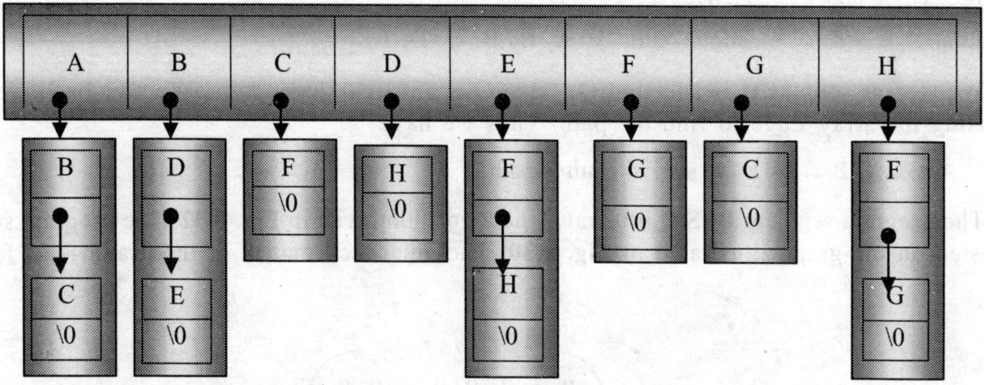

Fig. 8.31 Adjacency lists for the graph G

Suppose **Fig. 8.30** represents bus stops and we want to go from stop **A** to stop **G** with minimum number of stops in between. That means we want the minimum path length **P** from **A** to **G.** With the help of breadth first search algorithm we have to find out minimum path **P** beginning at **A** and ending at **G.** During the execution one thing which should be kept in mind is the origin of each edge. Let we have two arrays **Edge** and **Q**. The discussion of algorithm with reference to **Fig. 8.30** is as follows:

(i) Add **A** to **Q** and add **NULL** to **Edge**
Front = 0 Q: A
Rear = 0 Edge: Null

(ii) Remove the front element **A** from **Q** and add to **Q** the neighbors of **A**
Front = 1 Q: B, C
Rear = 2 Edge: Null, A, A
Here origin of each of the two edges is added to **Edge**.

(iii) Remove the front element **B** from **Q** and add to **Q** the neighbors of **B**.
Front = 2 Q: C, D, E
Rear = 4 Edge: Null, A, A, B, B

(iv) Remove the front element **C** from **Q** and add to **Q** the neighbors of **C.**
Front = 3 Q: D, E, F
Rear = 6 Edge: Null, A, A, B, B, C

(v) Remove the front element **D** from **Q** and add to **Q** the neighbors of **D**.
Front = 4 Q: E, F, H
Rear = 7 Edge: Null, A, A, B, B, C, D

(vi) Remove the front element **E** from **Q** and add to **Q** neighbors of **E**.
Front = 5 Q: F, H
Rear = 7 Edge: Null, A, A, B, B, C, D, E

(vii) Remove the front element **F** from **Q** and add to **Q** neighbors of **F**.
Front = 6 Q: H, G
Rear = 8 Edge: Null, A, A, B, B, C, D, E, F

We stop as soon as **G** is added to **Q**; since **G** is our final destination, We now backtrack from **G**, using the array Edge to find the path. Thus we have

A ⟶ **B** ⟶ **E** ⟶ **F** is required path.

The program segment **BFS.C** illustrates the algorithm given in **Fig. 8.32**. The program segment is tested on the graph illustrated in **Fig. 8.30.** The adjacency matrix of the graph is as follows:

$$A = \begin{pmatrix} 0 & 1 & 1 & 0 & 0 & 0 & 0 & 0 \\ 0 & 0 & 0 & 1 & 1 & 0 & 0 & 0 \\ 0 & 0 & 0 & 0 & 0 & 1 & 0 & 0 \\ 0 & 0 & 0 & 0 & 0 & 0 & 0 & 1 \\ 0 & 0 & 0 & 0 & 0 & 1 & 0 & 1 \\ 0 & 0 & 0 & 0 & 0 & 0 & 1 & 0 \\ 0 & 0 & 1 & 0 & 0 & 0 & 0 & 0 \\ 0 & 0 & 0 & 0 & 0 & 1 & 1 & 0 \end{pmatrix}$$

Step 1: Initialize all the vertices by setting **Flag = 1**

Step 2: Put the starting vertex **A** in **Q** and change its status to the waiting state by setting **Flag = 0**

Step 3: Repeat through Step 5 while **Q** is not **NULL.**

Step 4: Remove the front vertex **v** of **Q**. Process **v** and set the status of **v** to the processed status by setting **Flag = -1**

Step 5: Add to the rear of **Q** all the neighbors of **v** that are in the ready state by setting **Flag = 1**, and change their status to the waiting state by setting **Flag = 0**

Step 6: Exit

Fig. 8.32 Breadth first search algorithm

```
// BREADTH FIRST SEARCH TECHNIQUE
// BFS.C

# include<iostream.h>
# include<stdio.h>

# define size 20
# define T 1
# define F 0

struct Edge
{
	int terminal;
	Edge *next;
};

struct Vertex
{
	int visit;
	int vertex_no;
	char info;
	int path_length;
	Edge *Edge_Ptr;
};

struct Q
{
	int info;
	Q *next;
};

class Breadth_First_Search
{
	public:
		void Table(int , int matrix [size][size], Vertex vert[size]);
		Edge *Insert_Vertex (int , Edge *);
		void BFS ( int , Vertex vert [size]);
		void Input(int, int mat [size][size]);
		void Output(int number, int mat [size][size]);
		Q *Insert_Queue(int vertex_no, Q *first);
		Q *Delete_Queue(int *vertex_no, Q *first);
};

// Insert vertex into connectivity list
```

```
Edge * Breadth_First_Search :: Insert_Vertex (int vertex_no, Edge *first)
{
    Edge *new1, *current;
    new1 = new (Edge);
    new1->terminal = vertex_no;
    new1->next = NULL;
    if (!first)
        return (new1);
    for (current = first; current->next; current = current->next);
    current->next = new1;
    return (first);
}

// Insert vertices into queue

Q * Breadth_First_Search :: Insert_Queue(int vertex_no, Q *first)
{
    Q *new1, *current;
    new1 = new (Q);
    new1->info = vertex_no;
    new1->next = NULL;
    if (!first)
        return (new1);
    for (current = first; current->next; current = current->next);
    current->next = new1;
    return (first);
}

// This function deletes
Q * Breadth_First_Search :: Delete_Queue(int *vertex_no, Q *first)
{
    Q *previous;
    if (!first)
        return (NULL);
    *vertex_no = first->info;
    previous = first;
    first = first->next;
    delete(previous);
    return (first);
}

// Initializing entries
void Breadth_First_Search :: Table(int vertex_num, int matrix [size][size],
Vertex vert[size])
{
    for ( int i = 0; i < vertex_num; i++)
```

```
    {
        vert [i].visit = F;
        vert [i].vertex_no = i+1;
        vert [i].info = 'A'+ i;
        vert [i].path_length = 0;
        vert [i].Edge_Ptr = NULL;
    }

    for (i =0; i < vertex_num ; i++)
        for (int j =0; j < vertex_num ; j++)
            if (matrix [i][j] > 0 )
                vert [i].Edge_Ptr = Insert_Vertex (j, vert [i].Edge_Ptr);
}

// Computing path length
void Breadth_First_Search :: BFS ( int index, Vertex vert [size])
{
    Q *queue = NULL;
    Edge *Link;
    vert [index].visit = T;
    queue = Insert_Queue(index, queue);
    while(queue)
    {
        queue = Delete_Queue(&index, queue);
        for ( Link = vert [index].Edge_Ptr; Link; Link = Link->next)
        {
            if (vert [Link->terminal].visit == F)
            {
                vert[Link->terminal].visit = T;
                vert[Link->terminal].path_length=vert[index].path_length+1;
                queue = Insert_Queue(Link->terminal, queue);
            }
        }
    }
}

// Input function to read adjacency matrix
void Breadth_First_Search :: Input(int number, int mat [size][size])
{

    cout<<"\n Input the adjacency matrix \n";
    for (int i =0; i < number; i++)
    {
        for ( int j=0; j < number; j ++)
        {
            cin >> mat [i][j];
```

```
            }
            cout<<"\n";
        }
}

// Output function to display adjacency matrix

void Breadth_First_Search :: Output(int number, int mat [size][size])
{

        cout<<"\n Adjacency matrix \n";
        for (int i =0; i < number; i++)
        {
            for ( int j=0; j < number; j ++)
            {
                cout<<" "<< mat [i][j];
            }
            cout<<"\n";
        }
}

// Function main
void main()
{
        Breadth_First_Search B_F_S;
        int number, index;
        int mat [size][size];
        Vertex vert [size];
        Edge *List;
        cout<<"\n Input the number of vertices in the graph: ";
        cin>>number;
        B_F_S.Input(number, mat);
        B_F_S.Output(number, mat);
        B_F_S.Table(number, mat, vert);
        cout <<"\n Input the starting vertex 0-"<<number-1<<": ";
        cin>>index;
        B_F_S.BFS (index, vert);
        cout<<"\n Path length of the vertex from " <<vert[index].info ;
        cout<<"\n Vertex Length Vertex Connectivity \n ";
        for (int i = 0; i < number; i++)
        {
            cout <<"\n "<< vert[i].info<<" "<<vert[i].path_length<<" ";
            for (List= vert[i].Edge_Ptr; List; List = List->next)
            {
                cout<<" ";
                putchar(List->terminal+'A');
```

```
        }
    }
}
```

```
Input the number of vertices in the graph: 8
Input the adjacency matrix
 0  1  1  0  0  0  0  0
 0  0  0  1  1  0  0  0
 0  0  0  0  0  1  0  0
 0  0  0  0  0  0  0  1
 0  0  0  0  0  1  0  1
 0  0  0  0  0  0  1  0
 0  0  1  0  0  0  0  0
 0  0  0  0  0  1  1  0

Adjacency matrix
 0  1  1  0  0  0  0  0
 0  0  0  1  1  0  0  0
 0  0  0  0  0  1  0  0
 0  0  0  0  0  0  0  1
 0  0  0  0  0  1  0  1
 0  0  0  0  0  0  1  0
 0  0  1  0  0  0  0  0
 0  0  0  0  0  1  1  0

Input the starting vertex 0-7: 4
Path length of the vertex from E
Vertex Length Vertex Connectivity

A        0        B C
B        0        D E
C        3        F
D        0        H
E        0        F H
F        1        G
G        2        C
H        1        F G
```

8.7 TOPOLOGICAL SORTING

If **G** is a directed graph with no directed cycles then a topological order **T** is a sequential listing of all the vertices in **G,** such that for all vertices **v**, **w ε G,** if there is an edge from **v** to **w**, then **v** precedes **w** in the sequential listing. Consider the graph illustrated in **Fig. 8.33.** The topological order is equivalent to this as illustrated in **Fig. 8.34** and **Fig. 8.35.**

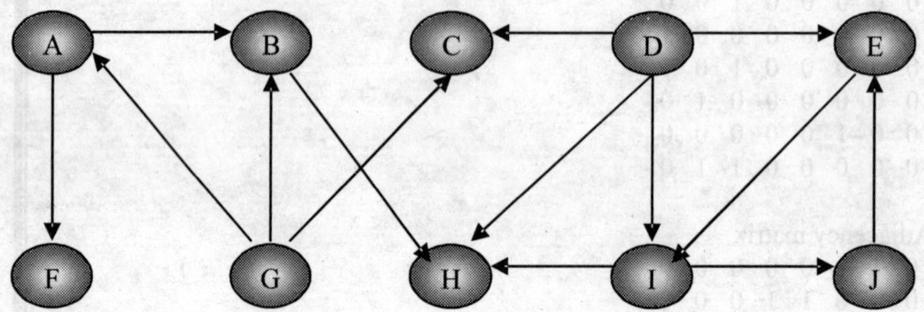

Fig. 8.33 Directed graph

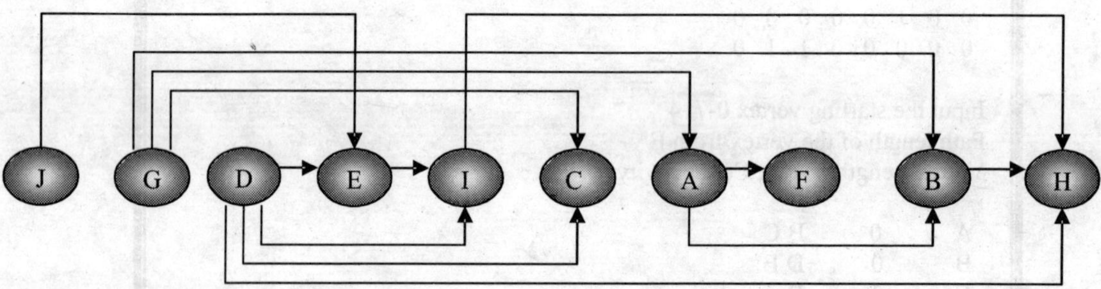

Fig. 8.34 Topological ordering

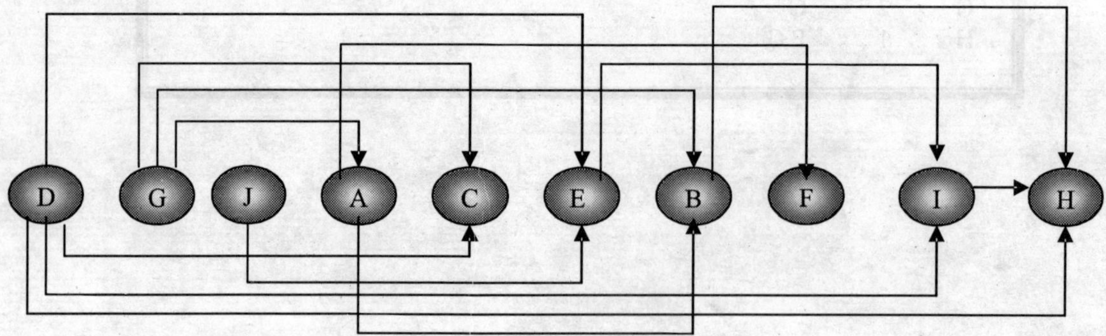

Fig. 8.35 Topological ordering

The main idea behind our algorithm to find a topological order **T** of a graph without cycles is that any vertex **v** with zero in-degree (i.e., without any predecessors) may be selected as the first element in the order **T**. We repeat the following steps until the graph **G** is empty:

- *Find a vertex **v** with zero in-degree.*
- *Remove vertex **v** and its edges from the graph **G**.*

The detail of the algorithm is illustrated in **Fig. 8.36** and the development of the program is left as an exercise to the readers.

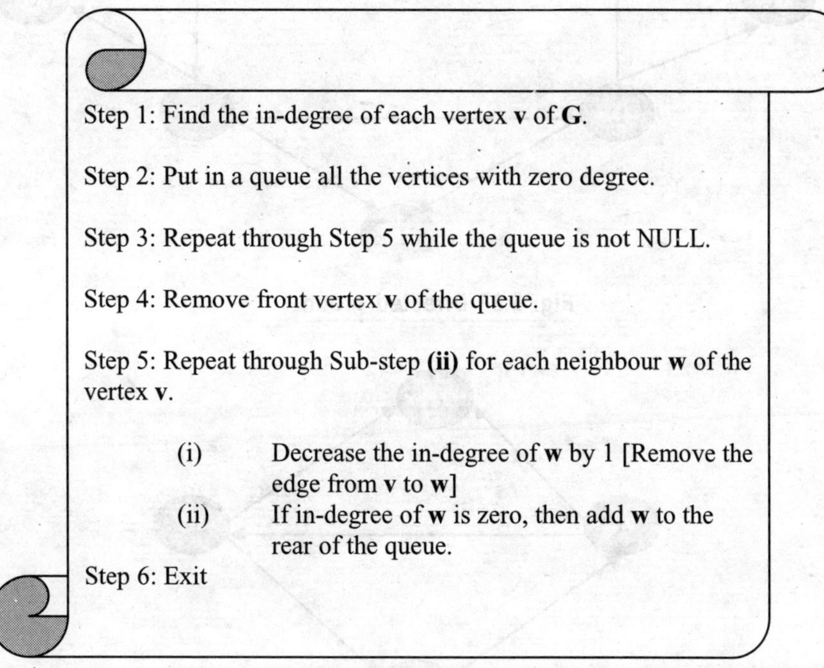

Fig. 8.36 Topological algorithm

EXERCISE

*8.1 Consider the graph **G** illustrated in **Fig. 8.37**.*

*(i) Find adjacency matrix **A** of the graph **G**.*
*(ii) Find the path matrix **P** of **G** using powers of the adjacency matrix **A**.*
(iii) Is this graph bi-connected?

*8.2 Consider the graph **G** illustrated in **Fig. 8.37**. Find path matrix of **G** using* **Warshall**'*s algorithm.*

*8.3 Find the depth of the graph **G** illustrated in **Fig. 8.37**.*

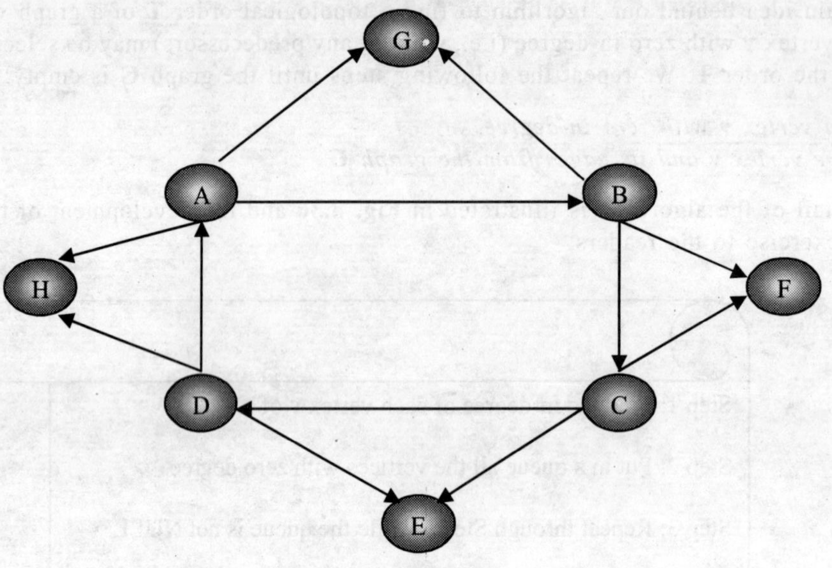

Fig. 8.37 Directed graph

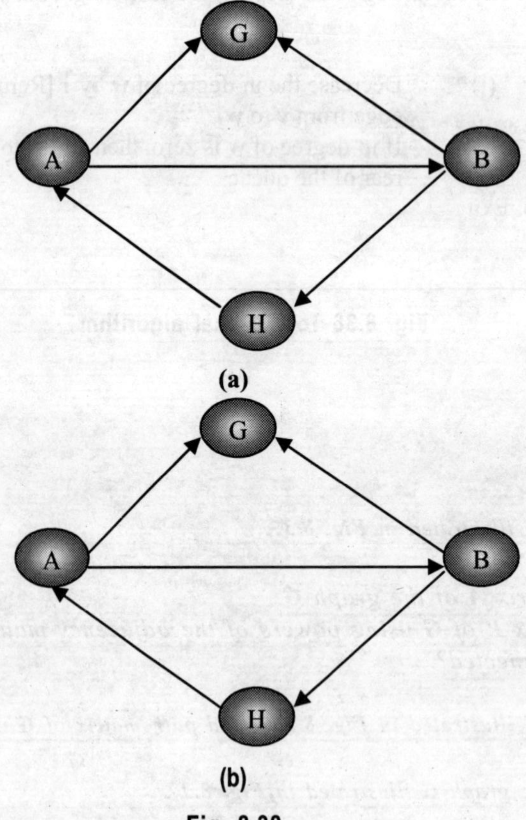

Fig. 8.38

*8.5 Is the graph illustrated in **Fig. 8.38** complete? Comment.*

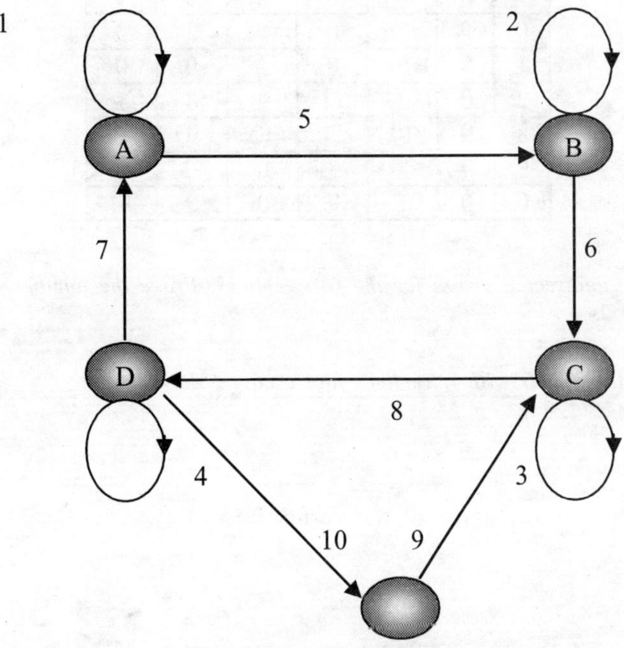

Fig. 8.39

8.6 *Consider the graph **G** illustrated in **Fig. 8.39.** Find the shortest path matrix using* **Warshall**'*s modified algorithm.*

8.7 *Suppose a weighted graph **G** is stored in computer memory by a vertex array **V** and a weighted matrix **W** such as:*

V => vertex array

A	B	C	D	E	F	G

W => Weight matrix

7	0	0	0	3	0	4
0	9	7	0	0	3	3
1	0	10	0	2	0	0
2	0	3	11	4	0	7
8	9	10	11	12	0	1
0	9	8	3	0	13	0
0	0	1	7	0	0	14

8.7 *Draw the complete undirected graph for the five vertices. Prove the number of edges in an* ***n*** *vertex graph is* ***n (n – 1)/2.***

8.8 *For an undirected graph* **G** *with* ***n*** *vertices and* ***e*** *edges show that*

$$\sum_{i=1}^{n} d_i = 2.e$$ where d_i is in-degree of the vertex **i**.

8.9 *For the directed graph* **G** *shown in* ***Fig. 8.40,*** *find its distance matrix (weight) and shortest distance matrix using* **Floyd**'*s technique.*

8.10 *Using* **Dijkstra** *technique find the shortest distance between* ***A*** *and* ***F*** *in the graph* **G** *illustrated in* ***Fig. 8.40.***

8.11 *Apply Depth-first and Breadth-first search technique to visit all the vertices in the graph* **G** *illustrated in* ***Fig. 8.40****. Show each and every step clearly.*

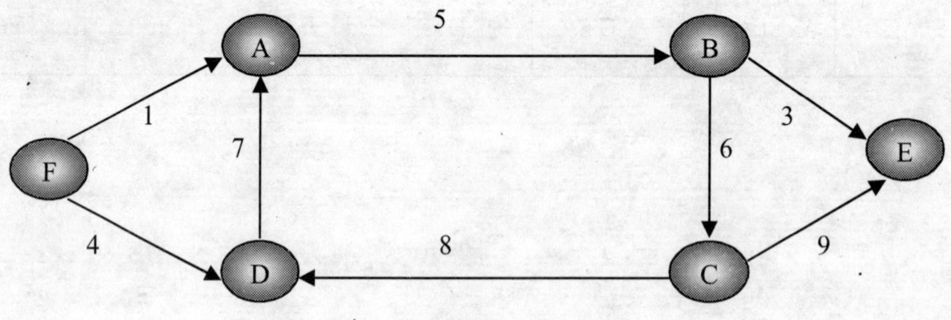

Fig. 8.40

*8.12 For any **n x n** Boolean matrix **A**, prove that*

$(U+A)^2 = (U+A) L (U+A) = U + A + A^2$

*where **U** is the **n x n** identity matrix and $A^2 = A\ L\ A$. Also prove that for any positive integer **r***

$(U+A)^r = U + A + A^2 + ... + A^r$

8.13 For what kind of graph is the topological sorting defined?

8.14 Explain the difference between Depth-first and Breadth-first traversing techniques of a graph.

SEARCHING AND SORTING

In this chapter we will discuss some sorting and searching techniques. First we will take searching techniques, then sorting and in the end hashing.

9.1 LINEAR SEARCH

This is the simplest technique to find out an element in an unsorted list. Suppose we have an unsorted list **l** which consists of **n** elements and want to search the value of a particular element in the list, as illustrated in **Fig. 9.1.**

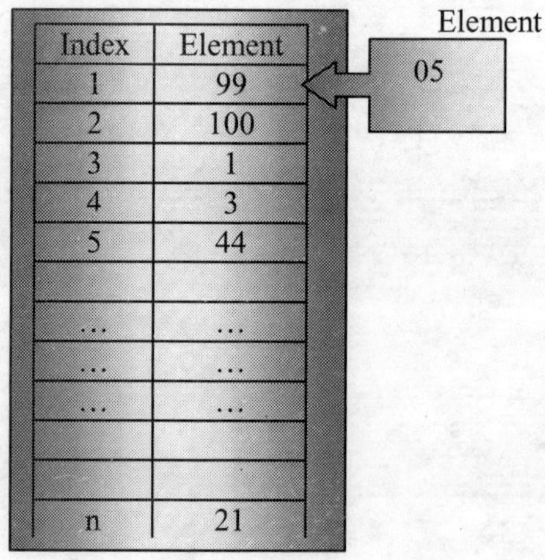

Fig. 9.1 Linear list l in memory

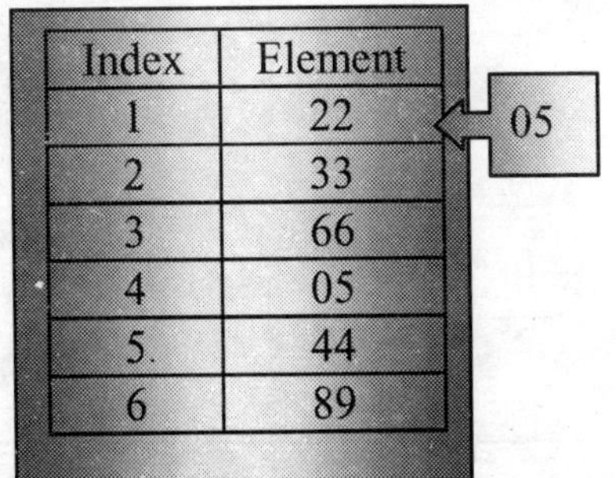

Index	Element
1	22
2	33
3	66
4	05
5.	44
6	89

Fig. 9.2

Index	Element
1	22
2	33
3	66
4	05
5	44
6	89

05

Fig. 9.2 (a)

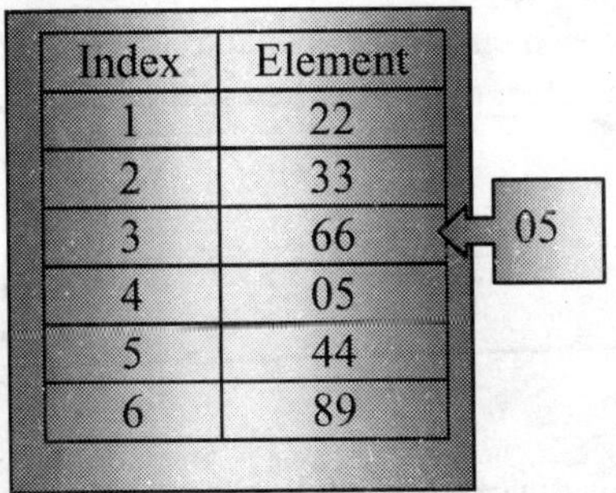

Index	Element
1	22
2	33
3	66
4	05
5	44
6	89

Fig. 9.2 (b)

Index	Element
1	22
2	33
3	66
4	05
5	44
6	89

05

Fig. 9.2 (c) *Result*

In this technique the value of the **key** is compared with the first element of the list, if match is found then the search is terminated. Otherwise next element from the list is fetched and compared with the **key** and this process is continued till the **key** is found or list is completely exhausted. For example, **Fig. 9.2** represents the list of elements in the memory, having 6 elements 22, 33, 66, 05, 44, 89 and we want to search for **key** = 05. **Fig. 9.2, Fig. 9.2 (a), Fig. 9.2 (b)** and **Fig. 9.2 (c)** illustrate the idea.

The performance of linear search algorithm can be measured by counting the key comparisons performed to find out an element in the list. There are two cases:

- *Average case*
- *Worst case*

In the above algorithm there are **n** key comparisons in worst case and **n/2** in average case. The time taken in the average and the worst case is proportional to **n,** i.e., **O (n).** These results are based on the assumption that the probability of finding an element or record in the list is same as for any other element or record. Let $\mathbf{P_i}$ is the probability of finding an element or record $\mathbf{E_i}$ $(0 \le i < n)$ in the list. The average length of search for **n** elements or records is given by:

$E(n) = 1^* P_1 + 2^*P_2 + 3^*P_3 + 4^*P_4 \ldots +n^*P_n$
$(1 + 2 + 3 + 4 + \ldots + n)\ P_a$
where $P = 1 = P_1 + P_2 + P_3 + \ldots + P_n$

If P_a = P/n average probability then

$(1 + 2 + 3 + 4 + \ldots + n)\ P_a$
- $P_a * (n(n+1))/2$
- $1/n * n(n+1)/2$
- $(n+1)/2$, *i.e.*, $O(n)$

Linear_search(L, n, Element)

Where L → Represents the list of elements,
n → Represents number of elements in the list, and
Element → Represents the value to be searched in the list

Step 1: [initialize]
K =1
Flag = 1
Step 2: Repeat through Step 3 for K = 1, 2, 3 … n
Step 3: If L[K] = Element
(i) Flag = 0
(ii) Output " search is successful" and element is found at location K

Step 4: If Flag output " Search in unsuccessful" and Exit
Step 5: Exit

Fig. 9.3 Algorithm for Linear Search

The algorithm for linear search is given in **Fig. 9.3.** Following program segment implements the above discussion **(LENEAR.C).**

```
// LINEAR SEARCH
// LINEAR.C
# include<iostream.h>
# include<stdio.h>

int search;
class linear_s
{
    public:
```

```
        int flag;
        input( int *, int , int);
        int n, key;
        int list[200];

    public:
        void linear_search(int * , int , int ); // prototypes
        void display(int *, int);
};

// Definition of function

void  linear_s :: linear_search(int l[], int n, int element)
{
    flag = 1;
    for( int k = 0; k< n; k++)
    {
        if(l[k] == element)
        {
            cout <<"\n Search is successful \n";
            cout <<"\n Element:  " <<element
                << "  " <<"Found at Location : "<< (k+1);
            flag = 0 ;
        }
    }
    if (flag)
        cout<< "\n Search is unsuccessful";
}

void linear_s :: display(int list[], int n)
{
    for( int i = 0 ; i < n ; i++)
    {
        cout<<"  "<< list[i];
    }
}

linear_s :: input(int list[], int number, int key)
{
    cout <<"Input the number of elements in the list:";
    cin >> number;
    cout <<"\n Number  of elements in the list is :"<<number<<"\n";

    for( int i = 0 ; i < number ; i++)
    {
        cout<<" Input the elements of the list : "<<i+1<<" : ";
```

```
        cin >> list[i];
    }
    cout<<"\n Element to be searched :";
    cin>>key;
    search = key;
    return number;
}

// Function main

void main()
{
    linear_s sort;

    int number, key, list[200];

    number = sort.input( list, number, key);

    key = search ;
    cout<<"\n Entered list as follows: \n";
    sort.display(list, number);
    sort.linear_search(list, number, key);
    cout<<"\n In the following list \n";
    sort.display(list, number);
}
```

```
Input the number of elements in the list:6

Number  of elements in the list is :6

Input the elements of the list : 1 : 22
Input the elements of the list : 2 : 33
Input the elements of the list : 3 : 66
Input the elements of the list : 4 : 5
Input the elements of the list : 5 : 44
Input the elements of the list : 6 : 89

Element to be searched : 05
Entered list as follows:
22  33  66  5  44  89
Search is successful

Element:  5  Found at Location : 4
In the following list
22  33  66  5  44  89
```

9.2 BINARY SEARCH

Binary search works for sorted lists and is a very efficient searching technique. It is used to find the location of a given element or record in a list. Other information associated with the element can also be fetched if required. To find the location of a file in the computer directory one can use this searching technique. If we are on the **Internet** then it is not a easy task using linear search to find out the information about some records or files. For this one prefers Binary searching technique. Let **low** represents lower limit of the list **l**, **high** upper and **mid** is average of **low** and **high** that is middle of the lower and upper limits, it is

mid = (low + high)/2

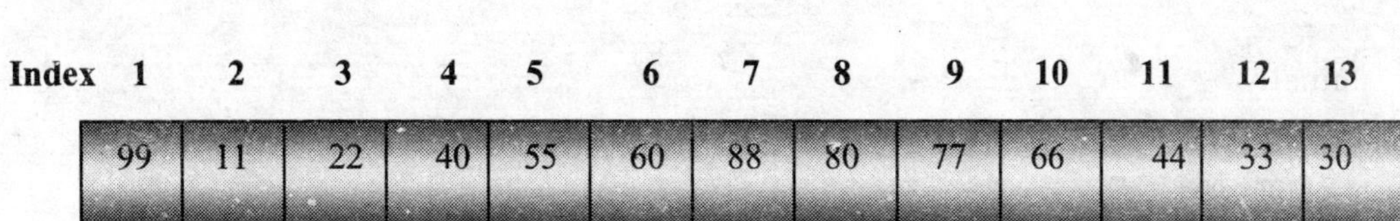

Fig. 9.4 List in the memory

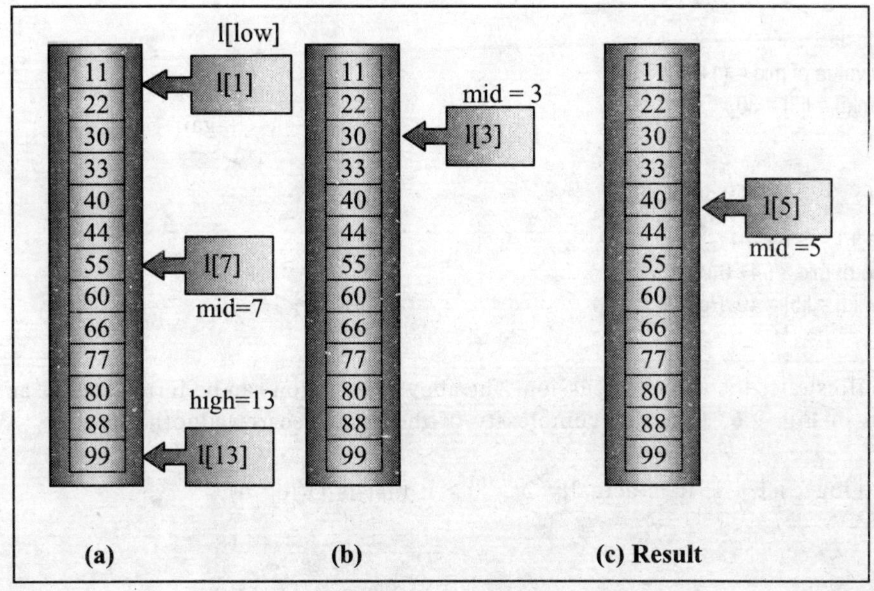

Fig. 9.5 Binary search operation

We compare the middle element with **key** to be searched. If the value of middle element is greater than **key**, then **key** will exist in lower half of the list, take **high = mid - 1** and find new value of **mid**, i.e., mid = (low + high)/2

Otherwise, **key** will exist in upper half and take

low = mid + 1
and mid = (low + high)/2

This process continues until the entire list is exhausted or **key** is searched. For example, consider the list given in **Fig. 9.4.** This list contains 13 elements, i.e., from 1- 13, suppose we want to search for **key = 40**.

The list is unsorted so that it is required to sort the list before starting the searching. The sorted list is given in **Fig. 9.5 (a).** How does the binary search technique work?

1. Initially

(i) l[low] = l[1] = 11
(ii) l[high] = l[13] = 99
(iii) mid = (low + high)/2 = (1+13)/2 = 7
(iv) l[mid] = l[7] = 55

1. Since 40 < 55 means element < l[mid] so that

(i) high = mid-1
(ii) now new value of mid = (1+6)/2 = 3
(iii) so that l[mid] = l[3] = 30

1. Since 40> 30 so that

(i) low = mid +1 = 3 + 1 = 4
(ii) new value of mid = (4+ 6)/2 = 5
(iii) and so l[mid] = l[5] = 40 ***Result***

Fig. 9.5 illustrates the above discussion. The above discussion can be formulated as an algorithm and is given in **Fig. 9.6.** The time complexity of the binary search algorithm is:

$E(n) = \lfloor \log_2 n \rfloor + 1$, it is actually $2^{E(n)} > n$ that is $O(\log_2 n)$

Binary_search(element, n, l)
Where
element → To which we have to search in the list
n → Represents number of elements in the list
l → Represents list of the elements
Step 1: [Initialize]
low = 1
high = n
flag = 1
Step 2: Repeat through Step 4 while (low ≤ high)
Step 3: mid = (low high)/2
Step 4: if(element < l[mid])
then
high = mid –1
else if (element > l[mid])
then
low = mid + 1
else if (element == l[mid])
Output " Search is successful" and location of the element is mid
flag = 0
return
Step 5: if(flag) output "Search is unsuccessful"
return
Step 6: Exit

Fig. 9.6 Algorithm for Binary Search

The following program segment implements the above discussion **(BINARY.C)**.

```
// BINARY SEARCH
// BINARY.C

# include<iostream.h>
# include<stdio.h>

class binary_s
{
    public:
        void binary_search(int , int , int *); // prototypes
        void sorting(int *, int );
```

```
        void display(int *, int);
};

void binary_s :: binary_search(int element, int n, int l[])
{
    int flag = 1;
    int low, mid, high;
    low = 0 ;
    high = n - 1 ;

    while(low <= high)
    {
        mid = (low + high)/2;
        if( element < l[mid]) // element in lower half
        high =  mid - 1 ;
        else
            if(element > l[mid]) // element in upper half
            low = mid + 1 ;
            else
                if(element == l[mid])
                {
                    cout <<"\n Search is successful \n";
                    cout <<"\n Element:" <<element << " :Found at Location : "<< (mid+1);
                    flag = 0 ;
                    break ;
                }
    }
    if (flag)
        cout<< "\n Search is unsuccessful";
}

// Ascending the list

void binary_s :: sorting(int list[], int number)
{
    for(int j = 0 ; j<number; j++)
        for(int k = 0 ; k<number-1; k++)
        {
            if(list[k] > list[k+1])
            {
                int  temp = list[k];
                list[k] = list[k+1];
                list[k+1] = temp ;
            }
        }
}
```

```
void binary_s :: display(int list[], int number)
{
      cout<<"\n Entered  list as  follows in\n";
      cout<<"\n Ascending order: ";
      for(int i = 0 ; i < number ; i++)
            cout<<"  "<< list[i];
}

// Function main

void main()
{
      binary_s search;
      int number, key, list[200];

      cout <<"Input the number of elements in the list:";
      cin >> number;
      cout <<"\n Number  of elements in the list is :"<<number<<"\n";

      for( int i = 0 ; i < number ; i++)
      {
            cout<<" Input the elements of the list :"<<(I + 1) <<" : ";
            cin >> list[i];
      }
      cout<<"\n Entered list is as  follows:\n";
      for( i = 0 ; i < number ; i++)
            cout<<"  "<< list[i];
      cout<<"\n Element to be searched :";
      cin>>key;

      search.sorting(list,number);
      search.display(list,number);
      search.binary_search(key, number, list);
}
```

```
Input the number of elements in the list: 13
Number of elements in the list is: 13

Input the elements of the list: 1: 99
Input the elements of the list: 2: 11
Input the elements of the list: 3: 22
Input the elements of the list: 4: 40
Input the elements of the list: 5: 55
Input the elements of the list: 6: 60
Input the elements of the list: 7: 88
Input the elements of the list: 8: 80
Input the elements of the list: 9: 77
Input the elements of the list: 10: 66
Input the elements of the list: 11: 44
Input the elements of the list: 12: 33
Input the elements of the list: 13: 30

Entered list is as follows:
99 11 22 40 55 60 88 80 77 66 44 33 30

Element to be searched: 40

Entered list as follows in ascending order:
11 22 30 33 40 44 55 60 66 77 80 88 99

Search is successful

Element: 40: Found at Location: 5
```

9.3 BUBBLE SORT

It is very simple sorting technique. However, this sorting technique is not efficient in comparison to other sorting techniques. But for smaller lists this sorting technique works fine. Suppose we sort the elements in descending order, the bubble sort loops through the elements in the list comparing the adjacent element and moves the largest element to the top of the list.

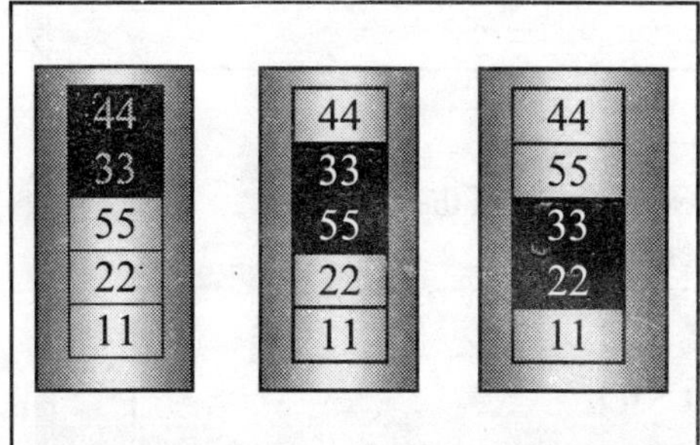

Fig. 9.7 Operation of Bubble sort

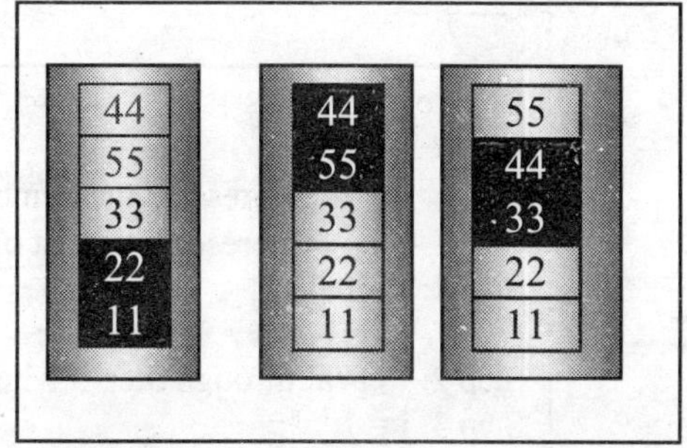

Fig. 9.7 (a) Operation of Bubble sort

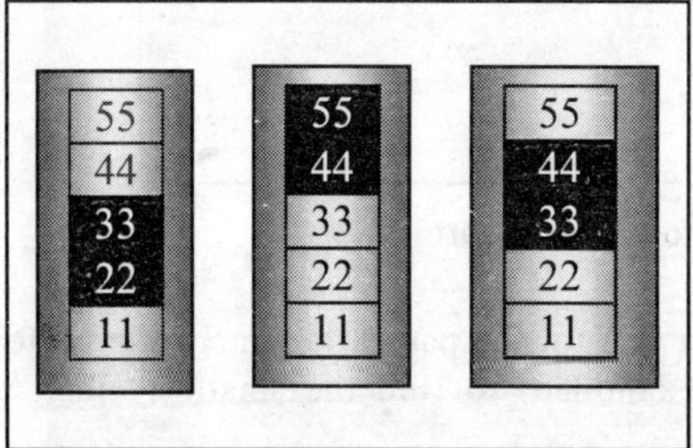

Fig. 9.7 (b) Operation of Bubble sort

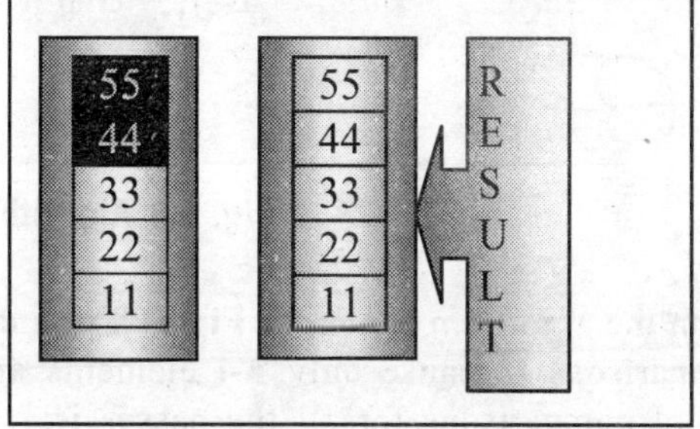

Fig. 9.7 (c) Operation of Bubble sort

The bubble sort algorithm is given in **Fig. 9.8.** From this algorithm it is clear that the bubble sort places the smallest element in the proper position and selects the second element and searches for the second smallest element. **Fig. 9.7, Fig. 9.7 (a), Fig. 9.7 (b)** and **Fig. 9.7 (c)** illustrate the complete operation performed on 5-element list.

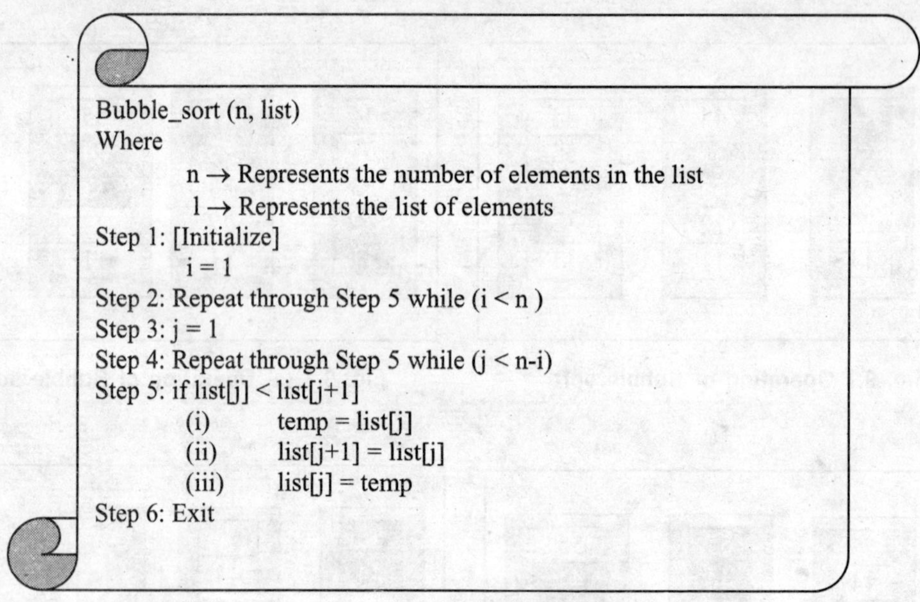

Bubble_sort (n, list)
Where
n → Represents the number of elements in the list
l → Represents the list of elements
Step 1: [Initialize]
i = 1
Step 2: Repeat through Step 5 while (i < n)
Step 3: j = 1
Step 4: Repeat through Step 5 while (j < n-i)
Step 5: if list[j] < list[j+1]
(i) temp = list[j]
(ii) list[j+1] = list[j]
(iii) list[j] = temp
Step 6: Exit

Fig. 9.8 Algorithm for Bubble sort

From the algorithm shown in **Fig. 9.8** it is clear that for the pass **i** the inner loop performs the **n-i** comparisons (because only **n-i** elements are examined) to find the smallest element. Total number of comparisons for all the passes is:

$$E(n) = \sum_{i=1}^{n} n-1$$

⇨ $(n - 1) + (n - 2) + (n-3) + \ldots + 2 + 1$

⇨ $n(n - 1)/2$

⇨ $n^2/2 + O(n)$, i.e., $O(n^2)$

Following program segment illustrates the algorithm given in **Fig. 9.8 (BUBBLES.C)**:

```
// BUBBLE SORT
// BUBBLES.C

# include<iostream.h>
# include<stdio.h>

class bubble
{
    public:

        void bubble_sort(int , int *); // prototype
```

```
        void display(int *, int);
};

// Definition of function

void bubble :: bubble_sort(int n, int l[])
{
    int limit = n - 1 ;
    int flag = 1 ;

    for(int j = 0 ; j< n - 1; j++)
    {
        for(int k = 0 ; k<  limit - j ; k++)
        {
            if(l[k] > l[k+1])
            {
                int  temp = l[k];
                l[k] = l[k+1];
                l[k+1] = temp ;
                flag = 0;

            }
        }
        if(flag)
            break ;
        else
            flag = 1;
    }
}

void bubble :: display(int list[], int number)
{
    for( int i = 0 ; i < number ; i++)
        cout<<"  "<< list[i];
}

// Function main

void main()
{
    bubble sort;
    int number, key, list[200];

    cout <<"Input the number of elements in the list:";
    cin >> number;
    cout <<"\n Number  of elements in the list is :"<<number;
```

```
    for(int i = 0 ; i < number; i++)
    {
        cout<<"\nInput the elements of the list : "<< i+1<<" : ";
        cin >> list[i];
    }
    cout<<"\n Entered list is as follows:\n";
    sort.display(list,number);
    sort.bubble_sort(number, list);
    cout<<"\n After sorting list is as  follows:\n";
    sort.display(list, number);
}
```

```
Input the number of elements in the list:5

Number of elements in the list is :5

Input the elements of the list : 1 :44
Input the elements of the list : 2 :33
Input the elements of the list : 3 :55
Input the elements of the list : 4 :22
Input the elements of the list : 5 :11

Entered list is as follows:
44 33 55 22 11

After sorting list is as  follows:
11 22 33 44 55
```

If one is interested in sorting of strings can choose the following program segment.

```
// BUBBLE SORT FOR SORTING STRINGS
// BUB_STR.C

# include <iostream.h>
# include <stdlib.h>
# include <string.h>
# include <malloc.h>
# include <stdio.h>

class bubble_string
{
    private:
        char *temp;
        int i, j;
    public:
```

```
        void bubble_sort(char *array[], int );
        void display(char *list[], int);
};

void bubble_string :: bubble_sort(char *array[], int size)
{
    for (i = 0; i < size; i++)
        for (j = 0; j < size; j++)
            if (strcmp(array[i], array[j]) < 0)
            {
                temp =(char *) malloc(sizeof(array[i]));
                temp = array[i];
                array[i] = array[j];
                array[j] = temp;
            }
}

// Output function

void bubble_string :: display(char *list[], int n)
{
    for(int i = 0 ; i < n; i++)
    {
        cout<<"\n "<<list[i];
    }
}

// Function main

void main(void)
{
    bubble_string b_sort;
    char *list[100] = {
        "MONDAY", "TUESDAY", "WEDNESDAY", "FRIDAY", "SATURDAY"};
    cout<<"\n Input list is as follows:";
    b_sort.display(list, 5);
    b_sort.bubble_sort(list, 5);
    cout<<"\n Sorted list is as follows:\n";
    b_sort.display(list, 5);
}
```

```
Input list is as follows:
MONDAY
TUESDAY
WEDNESDAY
FRIDAY
SATURDAY
Sorted list is as follows:

WEDNESDAY
TUESDAY
SATURDAY
MONDAY
FRIDAY
```

9.4 INSERTION SORT

Suppose **l** is the list of **n** elements. The insertion sort technique scans the list **l** from **l[1]** to **l[n]**, inserting each element into its proper position in the previously sorted sub-list **l[1]**, **l[2]** ... **l[i-1]**.

step = 1	**-0**	**7**	**3**	**4**	**1**	**8**	**2**	**6**	**5**
step = 2	**-0**	**3**	**7**	**4**	**1**	**8**	**2**	**6**	**5**
step = 3	**-0**	**3**	**4**	**7**	**1**	**8**	**2**	**6**	**5**
step = 4	**-0**	**1**	**3**	**4**	**7**	**8**	**2**	**6**	**5**
step = 5	**-0**	**1**	**3**	**4**	**7**	**8**	**2**	**6**	**5**
step = 6	**-0**	**1**	**2**	**3**	**4**	**7**	**8**	**6**	**5**
step = 7	**-0**	**1**	**2**	**3**	**4**	**6**	**7**	**8**	**5**
step = 8	**-0**	**1**	**2**	**3**	**4**	**5**	**6**	**7**	**8**

Fig. 9.9 insertion sort

The discussion of the algorithm given in **Fig. 9.10** can be explained with the help of following steps:

Step 1: l [1] by itself is trivially sorted.
Step 2: l [2] is inserted before or after l [1] so that l [1], l [2] is sorted.

Step 3: l [3] is inserted into its proper place in l [1], l [2], i.e., l [3] is inserted in between l [1] and l [2] or after l [2] so that l [1], l [2], l [3] is sorted.

...

...

...

Step n: l [n] is inserted into its proper place in l [1], l [2] ... l [n-1] so that, l [1], l [2], l [3] ... l [n] is sorted.

For smaller values of **n** this algorithm is useful. The inner loop of the algorithm performs **i-1** comparisons. Hence:

$$E(n) = \sum_{i=1}^{n} i - 1$$

⇨ $1 + 2 + 3 + 4 + \ldots + n - 1$
⇨ $n(n-1)/2$
⇨ $O(n^2)$

Insertion_sort (l, n)

Where l → Represents the list of elements.
N → Represents number of elements in the list.

Step 1: [Initialize]
l[0] = -0

Step 2: Repeat through Step 5 for i = 1, 2, 3, 4 … n

Step 3: (i) temp = l[i]
(ii) pointer = i – 1

Step 4: while(temp < l[pointer])

(i) l[pointer + 1] = l[pointer]
(ii) pointer = pointer – 1

Step 5: l[pointer] = temp

Step 6: Exit

Fig. 9.10 Algorithm for Insertion sort

For average case the inner loop performs **(i-1) / 2** comparisons.

$$E(n) = \sum_{i=1}^{n} (i-1)/2$$

⇨ $(1 + 2 + 3 + 4 + ... + n - 1) / 2$

⇨ $n(n-1) / 4$

⇨ $O(n^2)$

Fig. 9.9 illustrates the algorithm given in **Fig. 9.10.** The program segment **INSERT.C** implements the above discussion.

```
// Insertion sort algorithm implementation
// INSERT.C

# include<iostream.h>

class insertion
{
    private:
        int i, k;
    public:
        void insertion_sort(int *, int);
        void display(int*, int);
};

void insertion :: insertion_sort(int l[], int n)
{
    l[0] = -0;
    for( int i=1 ; i<=n; i++)
    {
        int pointer = i -1;
        int temp = l[i];
        while(temp<l[pointer])
        {
            l[pointer+1] = l[pointer];
            pointer --;
        }
        l[pointer+1] = temp;
        cout<<"step = "<<i;
        for( k =1; k<=n; k++)
            cout<< "  "<<l[k];
        cout<<"\n";
    }
}
void insertion :: display(int l[], int n)
{
    cout<<"\n Sorted list is as follows\n";
```

```
    for(i =1; i<=n; i++)
        cout<<" "<<l[i];
}

// Function main

void main()
{
    insertion ins_sort;
    int number;
    int list[100];
    cout<<"\n Input the number of elements in the list:";
    cin>>number;
    for( int i = 1; i<= number; i++)
        cin>>list[i];

    ins_sort.insertion_sort(list, number);
    ins_sort.display(list, number);
}
```

```
Input the number of elements in the list: 8

Elements of the list: 7 3 4 1 8 2 6 5

step = 1  7 3 4 1 8 2 6 5  Initially list was
step = 2  3 7 4 1 8 2 6 5
step = 3  3 4 7 1 8 2 6 5
step = 4  1 3 4 7 8 2 6 5
step = 5  1 3 4 7 8 2 6 5
step = 6  1 2 3 4 7 8 6 5
step = 7  1 2 3 4 6 7 8 5
step = 8  1 2 3 4 5 6 7 8

Sorted list is as follows
1 2 3 4 5 6 7 8
```

Another way of implementation of above technique is given below:

```
// INSERTION SORT
// INSERS.C
# include<iostream.h>
class insertion_s
{
    private:
        int key;
```

```
    public:
        int  insertion_sort(int *); // prototypes
        void display(int *, int);
};

// Definition of the insertion sort function

int insertion_s :: insertion_sort(int list[])
{
    cout<<"\nElement to be inserted Break condition is -0 : ";
    cin>>key;
    cout<<"\nSelected Element is :"<<key;
    int i = 0;
    int k ;

    while( key != -0 ) // -0 is break condition
    {
        k = i - 1;
        while((key < list[k]) && (k >= 0))
        {
            list[k+1] = list[k];
            --k;
        }

        list[k+1] = key ;
        cout<<"\n List after inserting an element ";
        for(int j = 0 ; j<=i; j++)
            cout<<"  "<<list[j];

        cout<<"\nElement to be inserted Break condition is -0: " ;
        cin>>key;
        cout<<"\nSelected Element is :"<<key;
        i ++;
    }
    return i;
}

// End of the insertion sort function

// Definition of the function

void insertion_s :: display(int list[], int n)
{
    cout<<"\n Final sorted list is as follows:\n";
    for(int j = 0 ; j < n ; j++)
        cout<<"  "<<list[j];
```

```
}

// End of the display function

// Function main

void main()
{
      insertion_s sort;
      int list[200];
      int n ;

      n = sort.insertion_sort(list);
      sort.display(list,n);
}
```

9.5 QUICK SORT

Quick sort treats an array as a list of elements. When sort begins it selects the list's middle element as the list pivot. The sort then divides the list into two sub-lists, one with elements that are less than the list pivot and a second list with elements greater than or equal to the list pivot. The sort then recursively invoke itself with both lists. Each time when the sort is invoked, it further divides the elements into smaller sub-lists. The list in **Fig. 9.11** contains the elements: 8, 9, 11, 13, 99, 44, 77, 66, 12 and the leaves of the tree in **Fig. 9.11** represents the sorted list. The quick sort algorithm is given in **Fig. 9.12.** For example, for the discussion of this algorithm consider the list having 9 elements and are 6, 2, 1, 3, 4, 5, 8, 7, 0.

List contains 9 elements

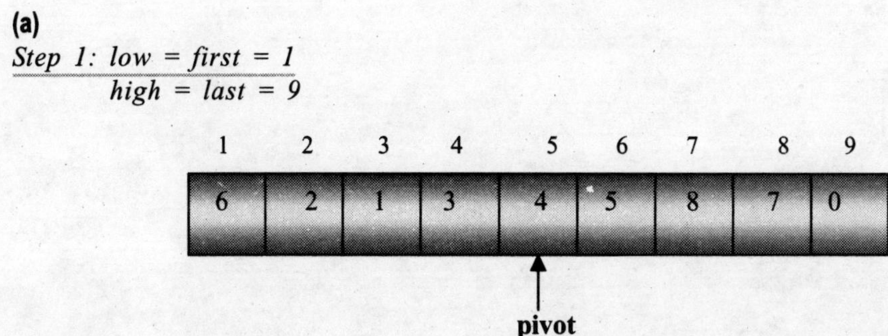

Step 2: low ≤ high, i.e., 1 < 9

Step 3: array [low] < pivot is false because array[1] > pivot, i.e., 6 > 4

Step 4: low = 1 [remains previous value]

Step 5: array[high] > pivot is false because array[9] < pivot, i.e., 0 < 4

Step 6: high = 9 [remains previous value]

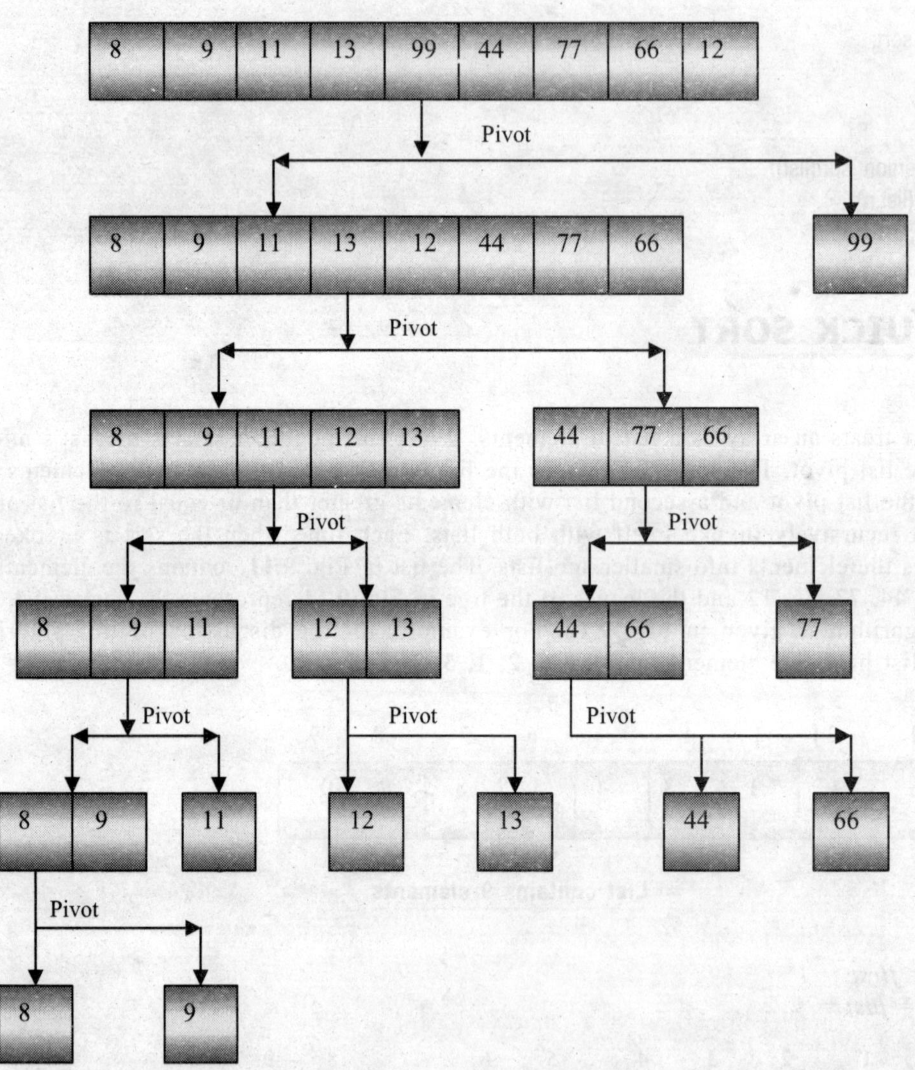

Fig. 9.11 Quick Sort Operation

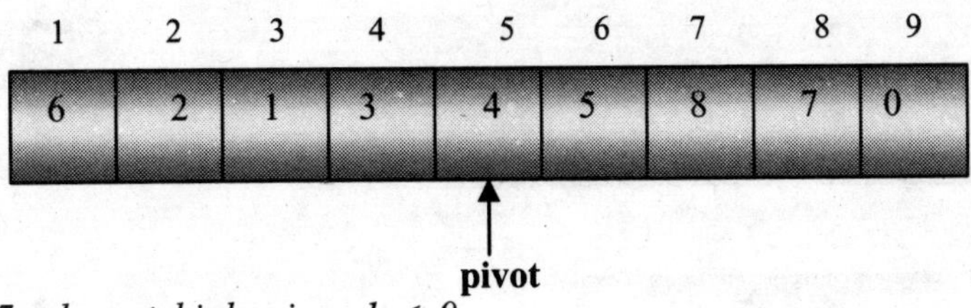

Step 7: low < high, i.e., 1 < 9

temp = array[low] = array[1] = 6
array[1] = array[high] = array[9] = 0
array[9] = temp = 6
low = low +1 = 1 + 1 = 2
high = high - 1 = 9 - 1 = 8

Now the list becomes

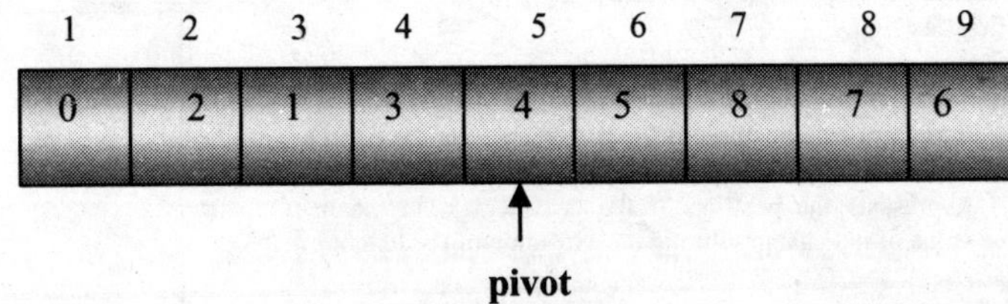

(b)

Step 2 : low ≤ high, i.e., 2 < 8

Step 3: } *array[low] < pivot, i.e., array[2] < pivot, i.e., 2 < 4*
Step 4: } *(i) low = low + 1 = 2 + 1 = 3*

Step 3: } *array[3] < pivot, i.e., 1 < 4*
Step 4: } *(ii) low = low + 1 = 3 + 1 = 4*

Step 3: } *array[4] < pivot, i.e., 3 < 4*
Step 4: } *(iii) low = low + 1 = 4 + 1 = 5*

Step 5: } *array[high] > pivot, i.e., array[8] > pivot, i.e., 4 < 7*
Step 6: } *(i) high = high -1 = 8 - 1 = 7*

Step 5: } *array[high] > pivot, i.e., array[7] > pivot, i.e., 4 < 8*
Step 6: } *(ii) high = high -1 = 7 - 1 = 6*

Step 5: } *array[high] > pivot, i.e., array[6] > pivot, i.e., 4 < 5*
Step 6: } *(iii) high = high -1 = 6 - 1 = 5*

Now the list is broken into two sub-list

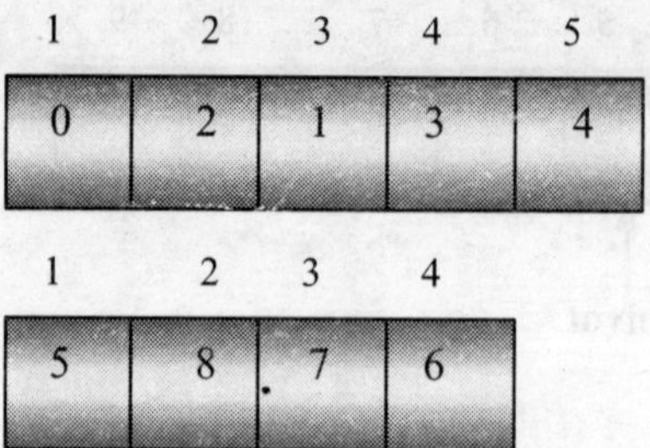

If we continue above process, finally we will get a sorted list.

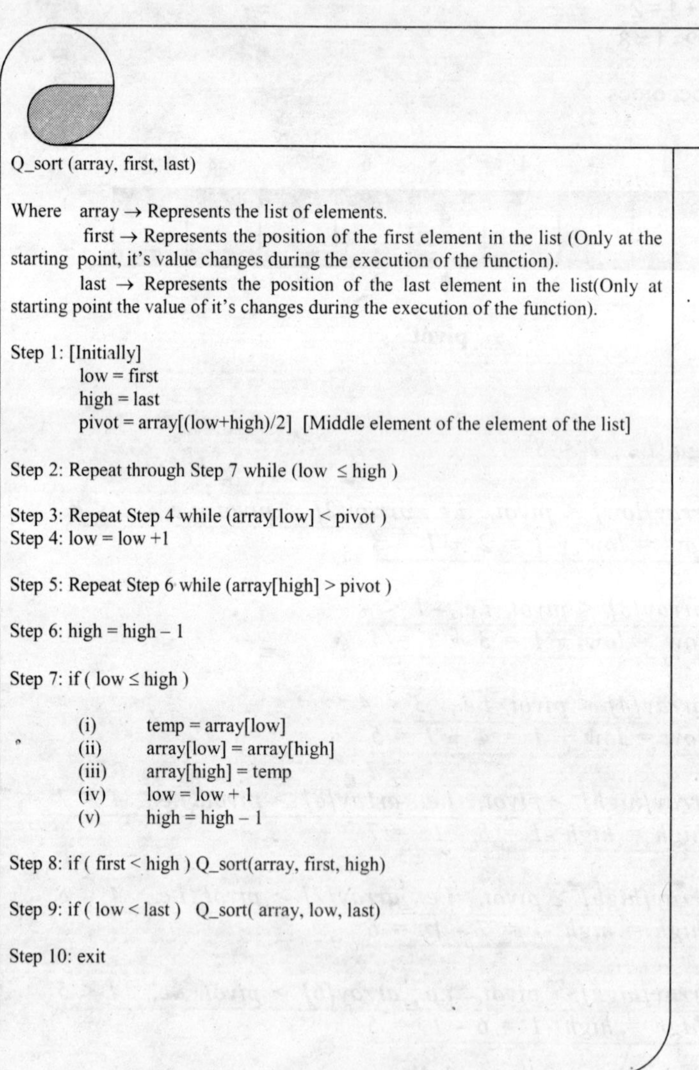

Q_sort (array, first, last)

Where array → Represents the list of elements.
first → Represents the position of the first element in the list (Only at the starting point, it's value changes during the execution of the function).
last → Represents the position of the last element in the list(Only at starting point the value of it's changes during the execution of the function).

Step 1: [Initially]
low = first
high = last
pivot = array[(low+high)/2] [Middle element of the element of the list]

Step 2: Repeat through Step 7 while (low ≤ high)

Step 3: Repeat Step 4 while (array[low] < pivot)
Step 4: low = low +1

Step 5: Repeat Step 6 while (array[high] > pivot)

Step 6: high = high – 1

Step 7: if (low ≤ high)

(i) temp = array[low]
(ii) array[low] = array[high]
(iii) array[high] = temp
(iv) low = low + 1
(v) high = high – 1

Step 8: if (first < high) Q_sort(array, first, high)

Step 9: if (low < last) Q_sort(array, low, last)

Step 10: exit

Fig. 9.12 Algorithm of Quick Sort

The partition process involves **n** comparisons with the pivot, with at most **n/2** swaps and, hence, is **O (n).** The question, then is how many partitions are performed? If the pivot is such that, then array is divided into two sub-arrays of the same size, then the situation is similar to merge sort. In this case, the algorithm is **O (n log n).** However, in the worst case, each partitioning will divide the array into parts of size **1** and **n-1**. Partition would then be called **n** times, with array sizes ranging from **1** to **n**. The average case performance for quick sort algorithm is **O(n log n).**

The following program segment implements the quick sort technique **(QUICK.C)**.

```
// QUICK SORT
// QUICK.C

# include<iostream.h>
# include <stdlib.h>
class quick
{
    private:
        int temp, low, high, pivot;
    public:
        void Q_sort(int *, int , int );
        void display(int *, int );
};

// sorting function
void quick :: Q_sort(int array[], int first, int last)
{
    low = first;
    high = last;
    pivot = array[(first + last) / 2];

    do {
        while (array[low] < pivot )
            low++;

        while (array[high] > pivot)
            high--;
        if (low <= high)
        {
            temp = array[low];
            array[low++] = array[high];
            array[high--] = temp;
        }
    } while (low <= high);
    if (first < high)
        Q_sort(array, first, high);
```

```
    if (low < last)
        Q_sort(array, low, last);
}

// Display function
void quick :: display(int list[], int n)
{
    cout<<"\n List after sorting the elements:\n";
    for( int i = 1 ; i <= n ; i++)
    {
        cout<<"  "<<list[i];
    }
}

// Function main
void main(void)
{
    quick sort;
    int list[100];
    int number ;

    cout<< "\n Input the number of elements in the list:";
    cin>> number;

    for ( int i = 1; i <= number; i++)
    {
        cout<<" Input the value for : "<< i <<" : ";
        cin>>list[i];
    }
    sort.Q_sort(list, 1, number);
    sort.display(list, number);
}
```

```
Input the number of elements in the list:9

Input the value for : 1 :6
Input the value for : 2 :2
Input the value for : 3 :1
Input the value for : 4 :3
Input the value for : 5 :4
Input the value for : 6 :5
Input the value for : 7 :8
Input the value for : 8 :7
Input the value for : 9 :0

List after sorting the elements:
0 1 2 3 4 5 6 7 8
```

Implementation of Hoare's quick sort algorithm is as follows:

```
// QUICK SORT
// QUICK1.C

# include<iostream.h>

// Sorting an array by using Hoare's quicksort

        quick_sort(int *, int, int, int (*p_cmp_f)(int *,int *));
        int *select_pivot(int data[], int n, int size,  int (*p_cmp_f)(int *,int *));
        void memswap(int *s, int *t, int count);

void main()
{
        int n ;
        int list[100];
        int (*p_cmp_f)(int *, int *);
        int size ;
        cout<<"\n Number of elements in the list: ";
        cin>> n;

        cout<<"\n Input the elements :\n";
        for( int i = 0 ; i < n ; i++)
    cin>>list[i];
        cout<<"\n Sorted list\n";

        quick_sort(list, n, size, p_cmp_f);
        for( i = 0 ; i < n ; i++)
                cout<<"  "<<list[i];
}

quick_sort(int data[], int n, int size, int (*p_cmp_f)(int *,int *))
{
        int *p_left, *p_right, *p_pivot;
        int lsize;

        if(n <= 1)
                return 0;
          p_left = data;
          p_right = data + ( n - 1 ) * size;

          // find pivot and move it to the right end
          p_pivot = select_pivot(data, n, size, p_cmp_f);
          memswap(p_pivot, p_right, size);
```

```
        p_pivot = p_right;

        // partition

        while(p_left < p_right)
        {
          while((*p_cmp_f)(p_left, p_pivot) >= 0 && (p_left < p_right))
          p_left += size ;
          while((*p_cmp_f)(p_right, p_pivot) >= 0 && (p_left < p_right))
          p_right -= size ;

          if(p_left < p_right)
          {
              memswap(p_left, p_right, size);
              p_left += size ;
          }
        }

          if(p_right == data )
          {
              memswap(p_right, p_pivot, size);
              p_right += size ;
          }

          lsize = (p_right -data) / size ;
          quick_sort(data, lsize, size, p_cmp_f);
          quick_sort(p_right, n- lsize, size, p_cmp_f);
}

int *select_pivot(int data[], int n, int size,  int (*p_cmp_f)(int *, int *))
{
        return data;
}

void memswap(int *s, int *t, int count)
{
        int temp ;
        while(count --> 0)
        {
          temp = *s ;
          *s ++ = *t ;
          *t++ = temp ;
        }
}
```

9.6 SELECTION SORT

The selection sort starts from first element and searches the entire list until it finds the minimum value. The sort places the minimum value in the first place, selects the second element and searches for the second smallest element. The process continues until the complete list is sorted.

For example, suppose we have a list, which contains the elements: 44, 33, 55, 22 and 11. If we want to sort this list using the selection sort technique, the details of this technique are illustrated in **Fig. 9.13** to **Fig. 9.13 (b).**

In **Fig. 9.13, Fig. 9.13 (a)** and **Fig. 9.13 (b),** the parts **(i), (ii), (iii)** and **(iv)** are generated during the first iteration, similarly **(v), (vi)** and **(vii)** in the second iteration and in the third iteration **(viii), (ix)** and **(x)** are produced.

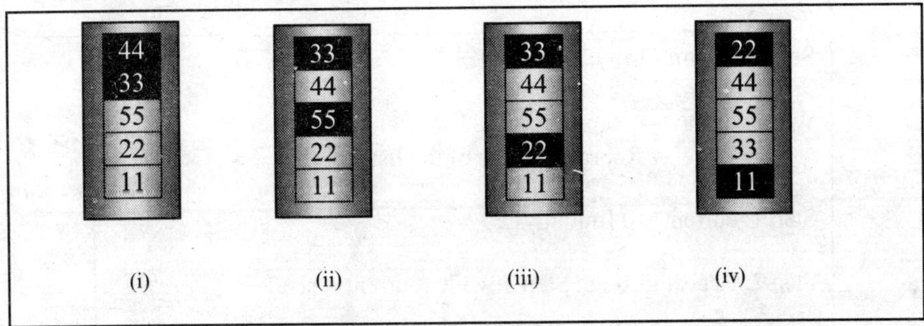

Fig. 9.13 Selection Sort

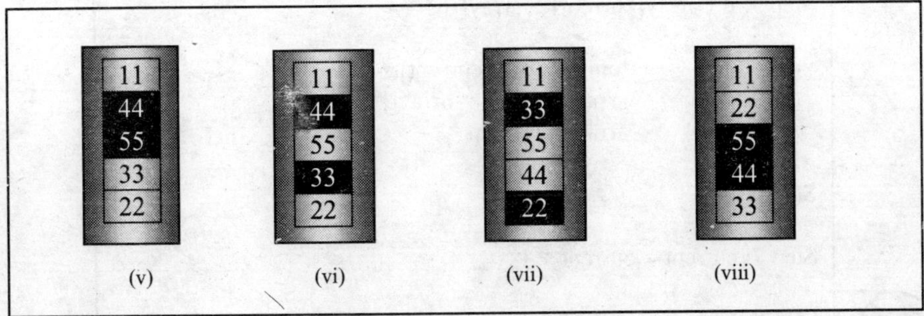

Fig. 9.13 (a) Selection Sort

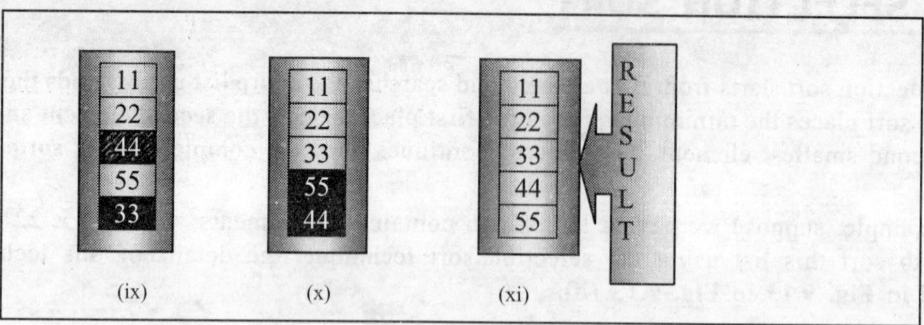

Fig. 9.13 (b) Selection Sort

Selection_sort (array, size)

Where array → Represents the list of elements
size → Represents size of the list

Step 1: current = 0 [initially]

Step 2: Repeat through Step 7 while (current < size)

Step 3: j = current + 1

Step 4: Repeat through Step 6 while (j < size)

Step 5: if (array[current] > array[j])

(i) temp = array[current]
(ii) array[current] = array[j]
(iii) array[j] = temp

Step 6: j = j + 1

Step 7: current = current + 1

Step 8: Exit

Fig. 9.14 Algorithm of Selection Sort

From the algorithm given in **Fig. 9.14**, it is clear that the algorithm consumes most of its time in the inner loop. During the pass **current** of the outer loop **size - current** elements are examined to find the smallest remaining elements. This requires **size - current - 1** comparisons. The number of comparisons for all passes is:

$$E(n) = \sum_{current=0}^{size-1} (size - current - 1)$$

Let k = size - current - 1
k = size - 1 at current = 0
k = 0 at current = size - 1

$$E(n) = \sum_{k=0}^{size-1} k$$

size(size - 1)/2
n(n - 1)/2 Let size = n
$O(n^2)$

Following program segment implements the discussion (**SELECT.C**):

```
// SELECTION SORT

// SELECT.C

# include<iostream.h>
#include <stdio.h>
#include <stdlib.h>

class selection
{
    private:
        int temp, current, j;

    public:
        void selection_sort(int *, int);
        void display(int *, int );
};

void selection :: selection_sort(int array[], int size)
{
    for (current = 0; current < size; current++)
        for (j = current + 1; j < size; j++)
            if (array[current] > array[j])
            {
                temp = array[current];
                array[current] = array[j];
```

```
                array[j] = temp;
            }
}

void selection :: display( int list[], int n)
{
    cout<<"\n Sorted list is as follows :\n";
    for(int i = 0 ; i < n ; i++)
    {
        cout<<"  "<<list[i];
    }
}

// Function main

void main(void)
{
    selection sort;

    int list[30];
    int number;

    cout<<"\n Input the number of the elements:";
    cin>>number;
    for (int i = 0; i < number; i++)
    {
        cout<<"\n Input the values for | "<<i+1<<" | ";
        cin>>list[i];
    }
    sort.selection_sort(list, number);
    sort.display(list, number);
}
```

```
Input the number of the elements: 5
    Input the values for | 1 |44
    Input the values for | 2 |33
    Input the values for | 3 |55
    Input the values for | 4 |22
    Input the values for | 5 |11

    Sorted list is as follows:
        11  22  33  44  55
```

The **SELECTS.C** program segment illustrates the algorithm shown in **Fig. 9.14** in some another way.

```
// SELECTION SORT
// SELECTS.C

# include<iostream.h>

selection_sort(int , int *); // prototype

void main()
{
      int number, list[200];
      cout <<"Input the number of elements in the list:";
      cin >> number;
      cout <<"\n Number  of elements in the list is :"<<number;

      cout<<"\n Input the elements of the list \n";
      for( int i = 0 ; i < number ; i++)
            cin >> list[i];

      selection_sort( number, list);
}

// Definition of function
selection_sort(int n, int l[])
{
      int min ;

      for( int index = 0; index< n - 1 ; index++)
      {
            min = index ;
            for( int k = index + 1; k < n ; k ++)
            {
                  if(l[min] > l[k])
                        min = k ;
            }
            if( min != index)
            {
                  int temp = l [index];
                  l[index] = l[min];
                  l[min] = temp ;
            }
      }

      cout<<"\n Entered list is as  follows:\n";
      for( index = 0 ; index < n; index++)
            cout<<"  "<< l[index];
      return 0;
}
```

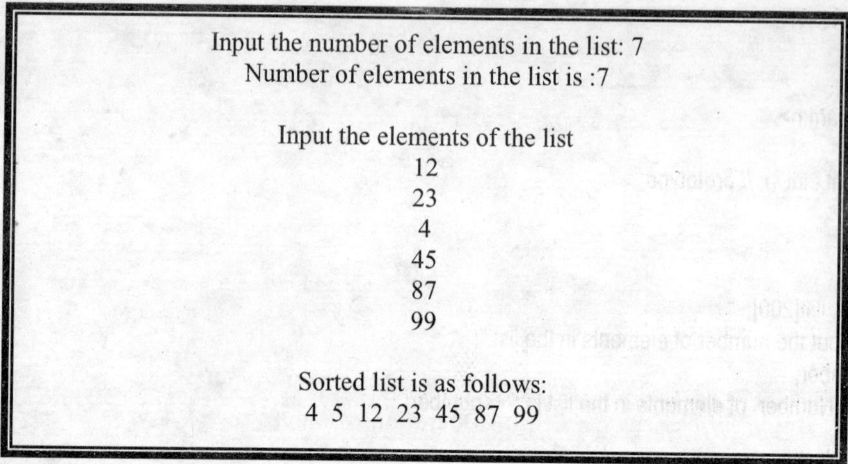

```
Input the number of elements in the list: 7
Number of elements in the list is :7

Input the elements of the list
12
23
4
45
87
99

Sorted list is as follows:
4 5 12 23 45 87 99
```

9.7 SHELL SORT

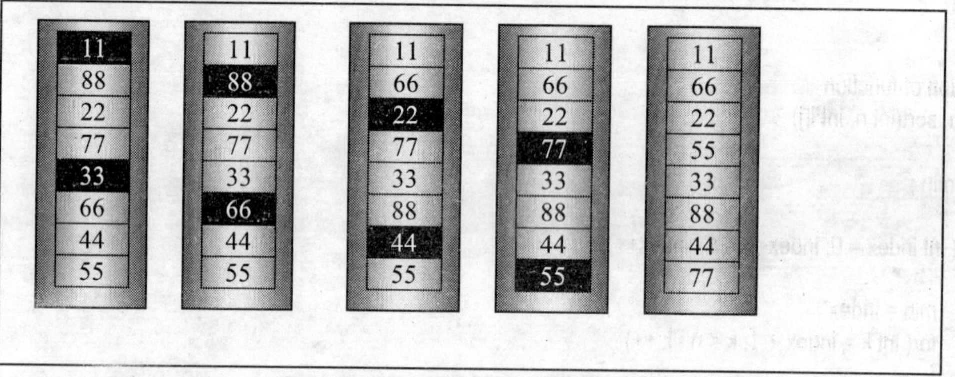

Fig. 9.15 (a) Operation of Shell Sort

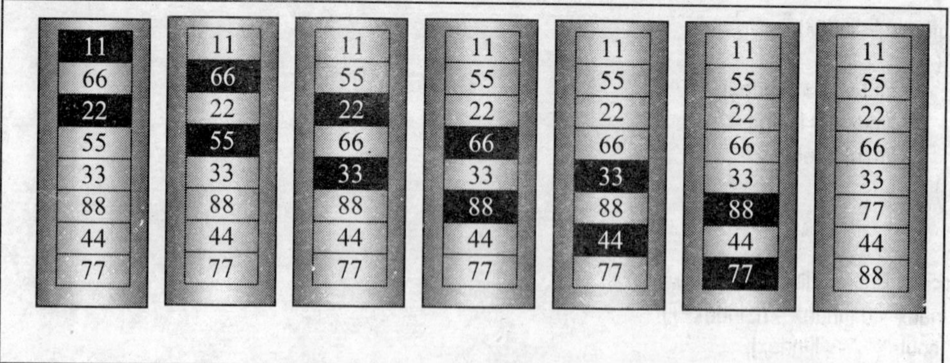

Fig. 9.15 (b) Operation of Shell Sort

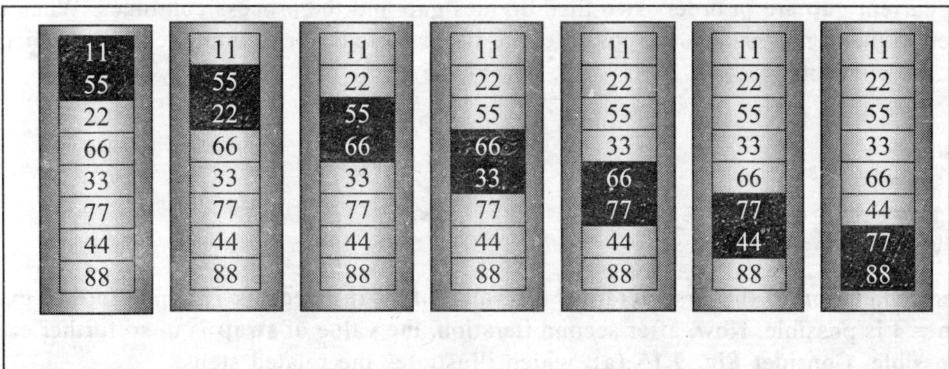

Fig. 9.15 (c) Operation of Shell Sort

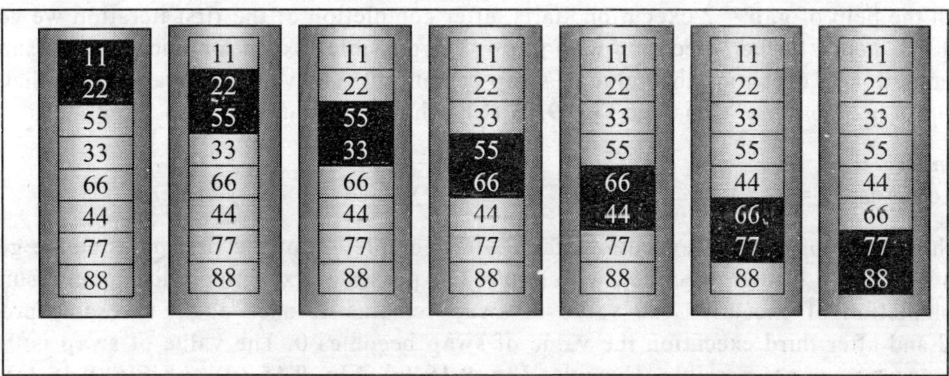

Fig. 9.15 (d) Operation of Shell Sort

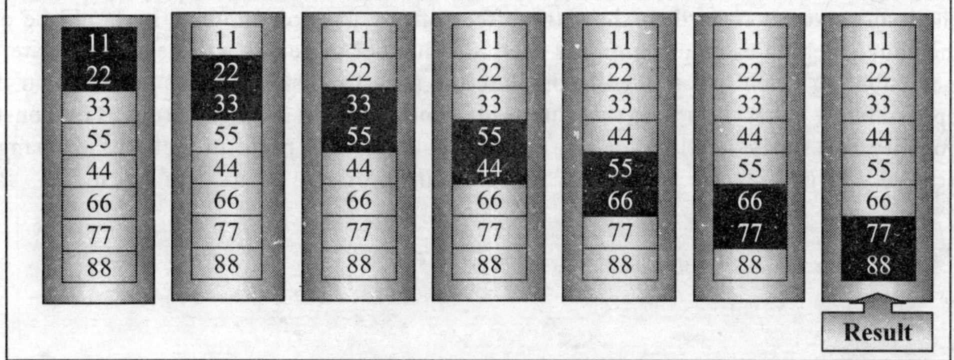

Fig. 9.15 (e) Operation of Shell Sort

The shell sort is named after its developer ***Donald Shell.*** The sort technique works by comparing the list elements that are separated by a specific distance, i.e., a **gap** until the elements compared with the current **gap** are in order. Two then divides **gap** and the process continues. When the **gap** is reached to 0 and no changes are possible, the list is sorted. For example, consider a list, which contains the elements: 11, 88, 22, 77, 33, 66, 44, 55.

Iteration 1:

size = 8

gap = size/2 = 8/2 = 4

and initial value of swap = 0

After completion of the first iteration the value of **swap** becomes 1, hence further execution with **gap = 4** is possible. Now, after second iteration, the value of **swap** is 0, so further execution is not possible. Consider **Fig. 9.15 (a)**, which illustrates the related steps.

Iteration 2:

gap = gap /2 = 4/2 = 2

With the help of **gap = 2** execution starts, after completion of the first iteration we get value of **swap = 1**, hence further execution with **gap = 2** is possible. Execution once again resumes and after completion of execution the value of **swap** becomes 0. The value of **swap** is 0 so that further execution is not possible. Consider **Fig. 9.15 (b)**, which illustrate the associated steps.

Iteration 3:

gap = gap / 2 = 2/2 = 1

With the help of **gap = 1** execution starts, after completion of the first iteration we get value of **swap = 1**, hence further execution with **gap = 1** is possible. Execution once again resumes and after completion of execution the value of **swap** remains 1, once again the same process is repeated and after third execution the value of **swap** becomes 0. The value of **swap** is 0 so that further execution is not possible. Consider **Fig. 9.15 (c)**, **Fig. 9.15 (d)** and **Fig. 9.15 (e)**, which illustrate each step clearly.

The algorithm for shell sort is given in **Fig. 9.16.** It is difficult to predict the time requirements of the shell sort since it is hard to show the effect of one pass on another. It should be obvious that is the above method calculating **gap** is used, the number of passes will be approximately **($\log_2$ gap)** since bubbling when **gap = 1** will complete the sort. Empirical studies have shown that the shell approximately takes **$B*n*(\log_2 n)^2$** units of time for an **n** element array. The constant of proportionality **B** is fairly small so for small **n** the shell sort will perform the radix exchange sort. When **n** is very large then the number of moves is in the range of **$n^{1.5}$** to **$1.6\ n^{1.5}$**.

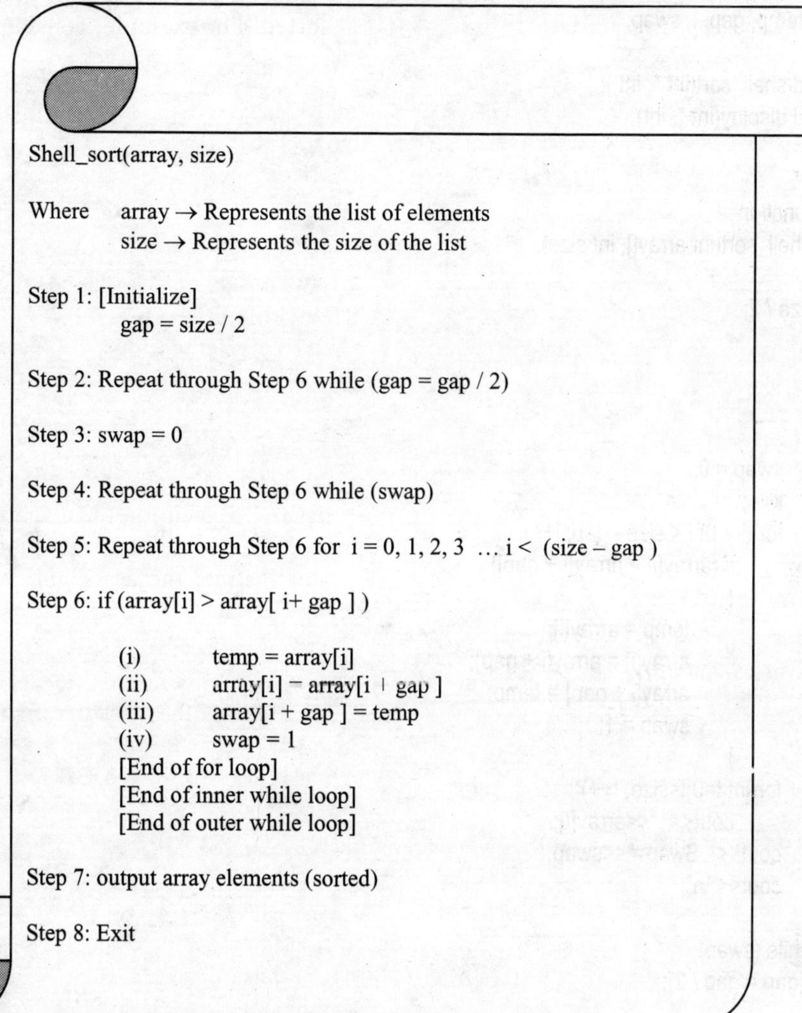

Shell_sort(array, size)

Where array → Represents the list of elements
size → Represents the size of the list

Step 1: [Initialize]
gap = size / 2

Step 2: Repeat through Step 6 while (gap = gap / 2)

Step 3: swap = 0

Step 4: Repeat through Step 6 while (swap)

Step 5: Repeat through Step 6 for i = 0, 1, 2, 3 … i < (size – gap)

Step 6: if (array[i] > array[i+ gap])

(i) temp = array[i]
(ii) array[i] = array[i + gap]
(iii) array[i + gap] = temp
(iv) swap = 1
[End of for loop]
[End of inner while loop]
[End of outer while loop]

Step 7: output array elements (sorted)

Step 8: Exit

Fig. 9.16 Shell sort algorithm

The following program segment implements the above discussion (**SHELL.C**):

```
// SHELL SORTING
// SHELL.C
# include<iostream.h>
#include <stdio.h>
#include <stdlib.h>

class shell
{
    private:
```

```
        int temp, gap, i, swap;
    public:
        void shell_sort(int *, int );
        void display(int *, int);
};

// Shell sort function
void shell :: shell_sort(int array[], int size)
{
    gap = size / 2;
    int k =0;

    do {
        do {
            swap = 0;
            k++;
            for (i = 0; i < size - gap; i++)
                if (array[i] > array[i + gap])
                {
                    temp = array[i];
                    array[i] = array[i + gap];
                    array[i + gap] = temp;
                    swap = 1;
                }
            for(int t=0;t<size; t++)
                cout<<" "<<array[t];
            cout<<"  Swap="<<swap;
            cout<<"\n";

        } while (swap);
    } while (gap = gap / 2);
}

// Output function
void shell :: display(int list[], int n)
{
    cout<<"\n Sorted list is as follows:\n";
    for( int i = 0; i < n; i++)
        cout<<" " << list[i];
}

// Function main
void main(void)
{
    shell sort;
    int list[50];
```

```
    int number;
    cout<<"\n Input the number of elements in the list:";
    cin>>number;
    for (int i = 0; i < number; i++)
    {
        cout<<"\n Input the value for the "<< i+1<<" : ";
        cin>>list[i];
    }
    sort.shell_sort(list, number);
    sort.display(list, number);
}
```

```
Input the number of elements in the list:8
Input the value for the 1 :11
Input the value for the 2 :88
Input the value for the 3 :22
Input the value for the 4 :77
Input the value for the 5 :33
Input the value for the 6 :66
Input the value for the 7 :44
Input the value for the 8 :55
Steps of execution
11 66 22 55 33 88 44 77  Swap=1
11 66 22 55 33 88 44 77  Swap=0
11 55 22 66 33 77 44 88  Swap=1
11 55 22 66 33 77 44 88  Swap=0
11 22 55 33 66 44 77 88  Swap=1
11 22 33 55 44 66 77 88  Swap=1
11 22 33 44 55 66 77 88  Swap=1
11 22 33 44 55 66 77 88  Swap=0
Sorted list is as follows:

11 22 33 44 55 66 77 88
```

9.8 MERGE SORT

Suppose **list_a** is a list with **n** elements and **list_b** with **m** elements. The operation that combines the elements of **list_a** and **list_b** into a single **result_list** list with **r = n+m** elements is called *merging*. If the elements of **list_a** and **list_b** are in sorted order then we may get a **result_list** in sorted order. If the **list_a** and **list_b** are not in sorted order we can make them in sorted order and then both the lists can be merged. It is also possible that first merging of **list_a** and **list_b** is done and then sort the merged **result_list.** In the later case execution time will be less.

For example, suppose we have two rows of police men sorted by increasing heights and we want to merge them into a single sorted row. Choosing at the head of their respective rows forms the new row. When one of these rows has no more policemen, the remaining policemen line up at the end of the combined row. Suppose we have two lists as shown in **Fig. 9.17.** The top row of **Fig. 9.17** to **Fig. 9.19** represents index of the lists.

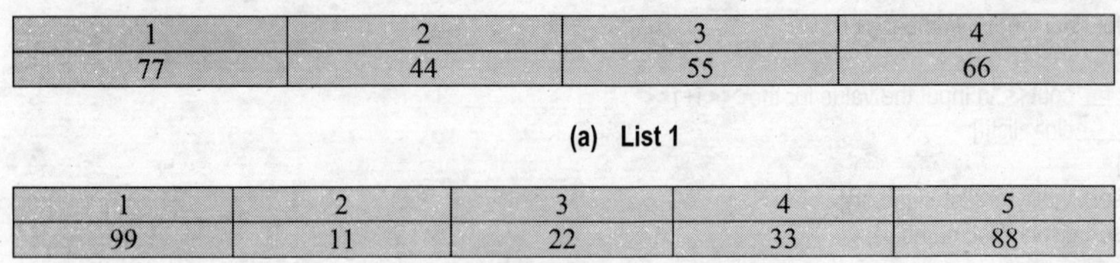

1	2	3	4
77	44	55	66

(a) List 1

1	2	3	4	5
99	11	22	33	88

(b) List 2

Fig. 9.17 Two list of elements

From the **Fig. 9.17** it is clear that the two lists are unsorted. Before merging, it is required to sort the list individually. The sorted lists are given in **Fig. 9.18.**

1	2	3	4
44	55	66	77

(a) List 1

1	2	3	4	5
11	22	33	88	99

(a) List 2

Fig. 9.18 List after sorting their elements

1								
11								

Step 1

1	2							
11	22							

Step 2

1	2	3						
11	22	33						

Step 3

1	2	3	4					
11	22	33	44					

Step 4

1	2	3	4	5				
11	22	33	44	55				

Step 5

1	2	3	4	5	6			
11	22	33	44	55	66			

Step 6

1	2	3	4	5	6	7		
11	22	33	44	55	66	77		

Step 7

1	2	3	4	5	6	7	8	
11	22	33	44	55	66	77	88	

Step 8

1	2	3	4	5	6	7	8	9
11	22	33	44	55	66	77	88	99

Step 9

Fig. 9.19 Illustration of Merging and Sorting

The algorithm for the merge sort is given in **Fig. 9.20.** From the algorithm given in **Fig. 9.20** it is clear that the total number of comparisons performed is **r = n + m** at the most so:

$E(r) = r = n + m$, i.e., $O(r)$

```
Merge_sort(n, list_a, m, list_b, result)

Where   n → Represents number of elements in first list(list_a)
        list_a → Represents the list of elements(first list)
        m → Represents number of elements in the second list(list_b)
        list_b → Represents the list of elements(second list)
Step 1: [initialize]
        i = 0
        j = 0
        k = 0
Step 2: Repeat step 3 while(( i < n ) and ( j < m))
Step3: if(list_a[i] < list_b[j])
        (i)      result_list[k] = list_a[i]
        (ii)     i = i + 1
        (iii)    k = k + 1
        else if(list_a[i] > list_b[j])
        (iv)     result_list[k] = list_b[j]
        (v)      j = j + 1
        (vi)     k = k + 1

        else  [ Means elements of both the list are equal and insert only
        one of them into the result_list]
        (vii)    result_list[k] = list_a[i]
        (viii)   i = i + 1
        (ix)     j = j + 1
        (x)      k = k + 1
Step4: if( i < n)  [ size of list_a  is larger than the list_b]
Step 5: Repeat through Step 5 for l =i, i+1, i+2  … n-1
        (i)      result_list[k] = list_a[i]
        (ii)     i = i + 1
        (iii)    k = k + 1

Step 6: [Size of lits_b is larger than list_a]
       else if( j < m )
Step 7: Repeat through Step 7 for l = j, j+1, j + 2 … m –1
        (i)      result_list[k] = list[j]
        (ii)     j = j + 1
        (iii)    k = k + 1
Step 8: return
```

Fig. 9.20 Algorithm of Merge sort

The program segment **MERGES.C** implements the above discussion.

```
// SIMPLE MERGE SORT
// MERGES.C

# include<iostream.h>
# include<stdio.h>

class merge_s
{
	public:
		int i, j, k;
	public:
		merge_sort( int , int *, int  , int *, int * );
		bubble_sort(int , int *);
};

// Definition of function
merge_s :: bubble_sort(int n, int l[])
{
	int flag = 1 ;
	for(int j = 0 ; j< n - 1; j++)
	{
		for(int k = 0 ; k<  n - j - 1 ; k++)
		{
			if(l[k] > l[k+1])
			{
				int  temp = l[k];
				l[k] = l[k+1];
				l[k+1] = temp ;
				flag = 0;
			}
		}
		if(flag)
			break ;
		else
			flag = 1;
	}
	cout<<"\n Entered  list as  follows in";
	cout<<"\n Ascending order: ";
	for(int i = 0 ; i < n ; i++)
		cout<<"  "<< l[i];
	return 0 ;
}

// Definition of function
merge_s :: merge_sort( int n, int list_a[], int m, int list_b[], int result_list[] )
```

```
{
    int i = 0;
    int j = 0;
    int k = 0;

// Repeat the process until the elements of list_a and list_b are exhausted
    while((i < n) &&(j<m))
    {
        if(list_a[i] < list_b[j])
        {
            result_list[k] = list_a[i];
            i++;
            k++;
        } //  End of if statement
    else
    if(list_a[i] > list_b[j])
    {
        result_list[k] = list_b[j];
        j++;
        k++;
    } // end of if statement
    else
    {
        result_list[k] = list_a[i];
        i++;
        j++;
        k++;
    } // end of else statement
    cout<<"\n";
    for( int ch = 0; ch < k; ch++)
        cout<<" "<<result_list[ch];

    } // end of while statement

    // checks if size of list_a larger than list_b
    // copy rest of the elements of list_a into result_list

    if(i <n )
    {
        for(int l = i ; l <n ; l++)
        {
            result_list[k] = list_a[i];
            i++;
            k++;
            cout<<"\n";
            for( int ch = 0; ch < k; ch++)
                cout<<" "<<result_list[ch];
```

```
            }
        }
        else
            // checks if size of list_b larger than list_a
            // copy rest of the elements of list_b into result_list
            if(j < m)
            {
                for(int l = j; l<m; l++)
                {
                    result_list[k] = list_b[j];
                    j++;
                    k++;
                    cout<<"\n";
                    for( int ch = 0; ch < k; ch++)
                    cout<<" "<<result_list[ch];
                }
            }

        return (k);
}

// Function main
void main()
{
        merge_s sort;
        int list_a[100],list_b[100];
        int result[200];
        int n,m,k;

        cout<<"\n Input the number of elements of list_a : ";
        cin>>n;
        for(int i = 0; i<n ; i++)
        {
            cout<<" Input the element : " << i+1;
            cout<<" : ";
            cin>>list_a[i];
        }
        // Sort the elements of list_a
           sort.bubble_sort(n, list_a);
        // End of sorting
        cout<<"\n Input the number of elements of list_b :";
        cin>>m;
        for( i = 0 ; i< m ; i++)
        {
            cout<<" Input the element : " << i+1;
            cout<<" : ";
            cin>>list_b[i];
```

```
    }

    // Sort the elements of list_b
        sort.bubble_sort(m, list_b);
    // End of sorting
    k= sort.merge_sort( n, list_a, m , list_b, result);
    cout<<"\n Duplicates are :"<<(m+n-k);
    cout<<"\n";
    cout<<"\n Sorted list is as follows:\n";
    for(i = 0 ; i< k ; i++)
    {
        cout<<" "<<result[i];
    }
}
```

```
Input the number of elements of list_a :5
Input the element : 1 :99
Input the element : 2 :11
Input the element : 3 :22
Input the element : 4 :33
Input the element : 5 :88
Entered  list as  follows in
Ascending order:   11  22  33  88  99

Input the number of elements of list_b :4
Input the element : 1 :77
Input the element : 2 :44
Input the element : 3 :55
Input the element : 4 :66
Entered  list as  follows in
Ascending order:   44  55  66  77

11
11 22
11 22 33
11 22 33 44
11 22 33 44 55
11 22 33 44 55 66
11 22 33 44 55 66 77
11 22 33 44 55 66 77 88
11 22 33 44 55 66 77 88 99

Duplicates are: 0

 Sorted list is as follows:
 11 22 33 44 55 66 77 88 99
```

Now we will simplify the algorithm discussed in **Fig. 9.20.** The simplified algorithm discussed in **Fig. 9.21.** Assumptions, which are taken into account: Given two ordered sub-tables stored in an array **A** with **First, Second** and **Third (First** through **Second -1** elements and **Second** through the **Third** elements represents the first and second tables, respectively), this algorithm performs a simple merge. **Temp** is a temporary array variable used in the merging process. The variables **I** and **J** denote the cursor associated with the first and second sub-tables, respectively. The **L** is the index variable associated with the array **Temp.** Performance of this algorithm is also **O (n)** and is equivalent to the algorithm given in **Fig. 9.20.**

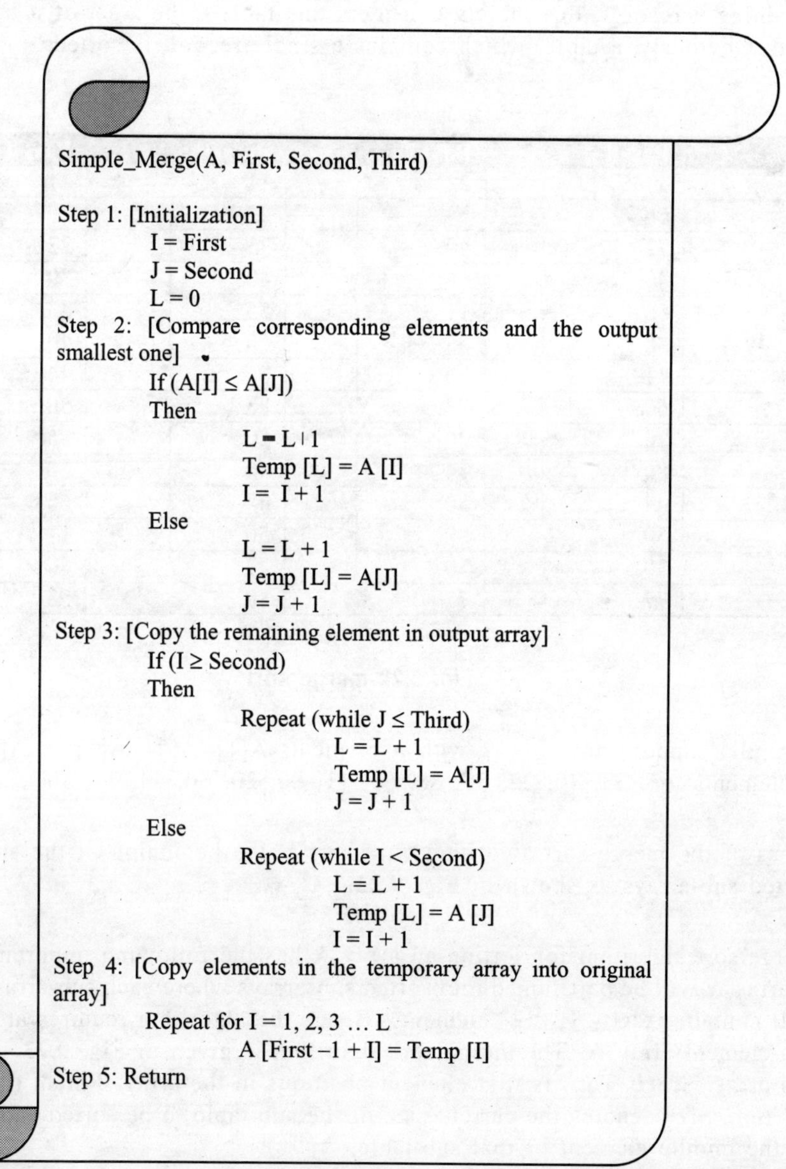

```
Simple_Merge(A, First, Second, Third)

Step 1: [Initialization]
        I = First
        J = Second
        L = 0
Step 2: [Compare corresponding elements and the output
smallest one]
        If (A[I] ≤ A[J])
        Then
                L = L + 1
                Temp [L] = A [I]
                I = I + 1
        Else
                L = L + 1
                Temp [L] = A[J]
                J = J + 1
Step 3: [Copy the remaining element in output array]
        If (I ≥ Second)
        Then
                Repeat (while J ≤ Third)
                        L = L + 1
                        Temp [L] = A[J]
                        J = J + 1
        Else
                Repeat (while I < Second)
                        L = L + 1
                        Temp [L] = A [J]
                        I = I + 1
Step 4: [Copy elements in the temporary array into original
array]
        Repeat for I = 1, 2, 3 … L
                A [First –1 + I] = Temp [I]
Step 5: Return
```

Fig. 9.21 Simple merge algorithm (Simplified from of the algorithm given in Fig. 9.20

The algorithm given **Fig. 9.21** can also be generalized to merge **k** sorted tables into a single sorted table. Such merging operation is called multiple merging or **k-way** merging. Multiple merging can also be accomplished by performing a single merge repeatedly. For example, if we have 16 tables to merge, we can first merge them in pairs using algorithm simple merge (Fig. 9.21). The result of this first step yields eight tables, which again merged in pairs to give four tables. This process is repeated until a single table is obtained. Result of this example, four separate passes is required to yield a single table. In general, **k** separate passes are required to merge $\mathbf{2^k}$ separate tables into a single table. This technique can also be applied for sorting. Given a table containing **n** records, one merely considers this table to be a set of **n** tables, each with a single record. Obviously, a table, which contains a single record, is sorted.

Values	Pass 1	Pass 2	Pass 3	Pass 4
66	33	22	11	11
33	66	33	22	20
40	22	40	33	22
22	40	66	40	30
55	55	11	55	33
88	88	55	60	40
60	11	60	66	44
11	60	88	88	50
80	20	20	20	55
20	80	44	30	60
50	44	50	44	66
44	50	80	50	77
77	30	30	77	80
30	77	77	80	88

Fig. 9.22 merge sort

For example, suppose an array **A** with **n** elements A[1], A[2], A[3] ... A[n] is in memory, having 14 elements: 66, 33, 40, 22, 55, 88, 60, 11, 80, 20, 50, 44, 77, 30.

Each pass of the merge sort algorithm will start at the beginning of the array **A** and merge pairs of sorted sub-arrays as shown in **Fig. 9.22.**

The merge sort algorithm for sorting an array **A** has the following important property. After pass **k**, the array **A** will be partitioned into sorted sub-arrays where each sub-array, except possibly the last, will contain exactly $\mathbf{L = 2^k}$ elements. Hence the algorithm requires at most $\mathbf{\log_2 n}$ pass to sort an n-element array **A**. The merge sort algorithm is given in **Fig. 9.23.** The assumptions are: **A** is an array, **Start** (Top) is first element positions in the array, **Finish** (bottom) is the last element position, **Size** denotes the current size of the sub-table to be sorted and **Mid** denotes the position of the middle element of that sub-table.

The above informal description of merge sort will now be translated into a formal algorithm, which will be divided into two parts. The first part will be a merge pass algorithm, which is given in **Fig. 9.24** to execute a single pass of the algorithm and the second part will repeatedly apply merge pass until **A** is sorted. The merge pass algorithm applies to an n-element array **A** consists of a sequence of sorted sub-arrays. Moreover, each sub-array consists of **L** elements except that the last sub-array may have fewer than **L** elements. Dividing **N** by **2*L**, we obtain the quotient **Q**, which tells the number of pairs of **L** element sorted sub-arrays, i.e.,

Q = N/(2*L)

Setting **S = 2*L*Q,** we get the total number **S** of elements in the **Q** pairs of sub-arrays. Hence **R = N - S** denotes the number of remaining elements. The procedure first merges the initial **Q** pairs of L-element sub-arrays then the procedure takes care of the case where there is an odd number of sub-arrays (when R ≤ L) or where the last sub-array has fewer than **L** elements. The merge sort algorithm is given in **Fig. 9.25.**

```
Two_Way_Merge_Sort (A, Start, Finish)

Staep 1: [Compute the size of the current sub-table]
         Size = Finish – Start + 1

Step 2: [Test base condition for sub-tables of size one]
         If Size ≤ 1
         Then
                  Return

Step 3: [Calculate midpoint position of current sub-table]
         Mid =  Start + Size/2 – 1

Step 4: [Recursively sort the first sub-table]
         Call Two_Way_Merge_Sort(A, Start, Mid)

Step 6: [Recursively sort the second sub-table]
         Call Two_Way_Merge_Sort (A, Mid +1, Finish)

Step 7: Call Simple  Merge (A, Start, Mid+1, Finish)
```

Fig. 9.23 Merge sort algorithm

Let **f (n)** denote the number of comparisons needed to sort an n-element array **A** using the merge sort algorithm. Recall that the algorithm requires at most $\mathbf{log_2 n}$ pass. Moreover each pass merges a total of **n** elements and by the discussion on the complexity of merging each pass will require at most **n** comparisons. Accordingly, for both the worst case and average case:

f (n) £ n $\log_2$ n

Observe that this algorithm has the same order as heap sort and the same average as quick sort. The main drawback of merge sort is that it requires an auxiliary array with **n** elements. Each of the other sorting algorithms we have studied requires only a finite number of extra locations, which is independent of **n**. The summarized result is as follows:

Algorithm	Worst case	Average case	Extra memory
Merge sort	$n \log_2 n = O(n \log_2 n)$	$n \log_2 n = O(n \log_2 n)$	O(n)

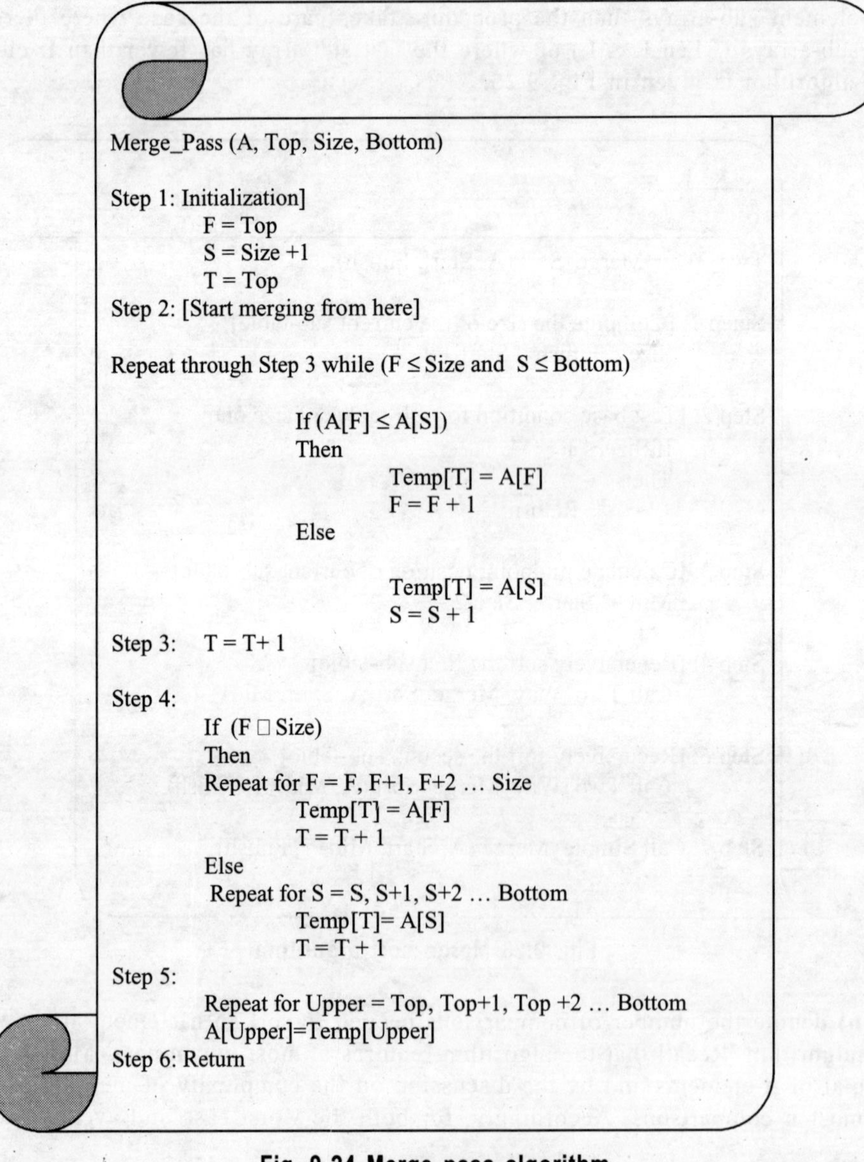

```
Merge_Pass (A, Top, Size, Bottom)

Step 1: Initialization]
        F = Top
        S = Size +1
        T = Top
Step 2: [Start merging from here]

Repeat through Step 3 while (F ≤ Size and  S ≤ Bottom)

                If (A[F] ≤ A[S])
                Then
                        Temp[T] = A[F]
                        F = F + 1
                Else

                        Temp[T] = A[S]
                        S = S + 1
Step 3:  T = T+ 1

Step 4:
        If  (F □ Size)
        Then
        Repeat for F = F, F+1, F+2 … Size
                Temp[T] = A[F]
                T = T + 1
        Else
         Repeat for S = S, S+1, S+2 … Bottom
                Temp[T]= A[S]
                T = T + 1
Step 5:
        Repeat for Upper = Top, Top+1, Top +2 … Bottom
        A[Upper]=Temp[Upper]
Step 6: Return
```

Fig. 9.24 Merge pass algorithm

```
Merge_Sort(A, M, N )

Step 1: [Compute Middle index value]
        Mid = M + N/2

Step 2: [Test Non equality of M and N]
        If  M ≠ N)
        Call Merge_Pass(A, M, Mid )
        Call Merge_Pass(A, Mid+1, N)
        Call  Merge_Sort(A, M, Mid, N)

Step 3: Return
```

Fig. 9.25 Merge sort algorithm

The algorithm in **Fig. 9.23** and **Fig. 9.25** are almost same. Program segment **MERGE.C** implements the above discussion of the merge sort technique.

```
// MERGE SORT
// MERGE.C
# include <iostream.h>
# include<stdio.h>
# include<stdlib.h>

void Merge_Pass(float *, int , int , int );
void Merge_Sort(float *, int , int );

// Definition of the function

void Merge_Pass(float l[], int top, int size, int bottom)
{
    float temp[1000];
    int f = top;
    int s = size +1 ;
    int t = top ;
    int upper;
    while(( f <= size)&&(s <=bottom))
    {
        if(l[f] <= l[s])
        {
            temp[t] = l[f] ;
```

```
            f ++;
        }

        else
        {
            temp[t] = l[s] ;
            s ++;
        }

        t ++;
    }

    if(f <=size)
    {
        for(f = f ; f<=size; f++)
        {
            temp[t] = l[f];
            t++;
        }
    }

    else
    {
        for(s = s ; s<= bottom ; s++)
        {
            temp[t]=l[s];
            t++;
        }
    }

    for(upper = top; upper <= bottom ; upper++)
    {
        l[upper]=temp[upper];
    }
}

// Definition of the function

void Merge_Sort( float append[], int m, int n )
{
    if( m!= n)
    {
        int mid = (m+n)/2;
        Merge_Sort(append, m, mid );
        Merge_Sort(append, mid+1, n );
        Merge_Pass(append, m, mid, n );
```

```
    }
}

// main function

void main()
{
    float list[1000];
    int i, n = 30;
    cout<<"\n Size of the list:" << n;

    for(i = 0 ; i < n ; i++)
    {
        list[i] = (float) (rand() %100);
    }

    cout<<"\n Entered list as follows: \n";
    for( i = 0 ; i<n ; i++)
        cout<< (int) list[i];

    i = 0 ;

    Merge_Sort (list, i, n-1);

    cout<<"\n Merge sorted list is as follows: \n";
    for( i = 0 ; i<n ; i++)
        cout<< (int) list[i];
}
```

```
Size of the list: 30
Entered list as follows:
10 11 12 25 27 31 36 37 38 43 67 78 82 83 84 86 89 95 45 49 51 54 58 60
66 66 67 13 15 19

Merge sorted list is as follows:
10 11 12 13 15 19 25 27 31 36 37 38 43 45 49 51 54 58 60 66 66 67 67 78
82 83 84 86 89 95
```

9.9 HEAP SORT

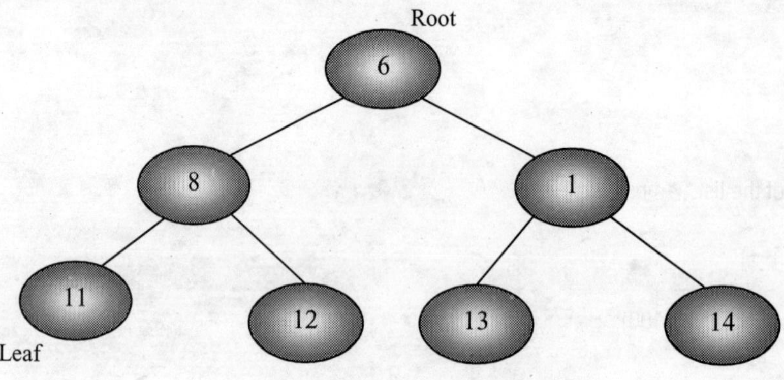

Fig. 9.26 Heap (Min-heap)

A heap is an ordered balanced binary tree in which the value of the node at the root of any sub-tree is less than or equal to the value of either of its children. This inherent ordering implies that only valued items may be placed in the heap. In general a heap represents a table of **n** elements or records satisfying the following property:

$N_j \geq N_i$ for $2 \leq j \leq n$ and $i = \lfloor j/2 \rfloor$

A heap satisfying the above definition is called a min-heap. For example, **Fig. 9.26** illustrate a min-heap.

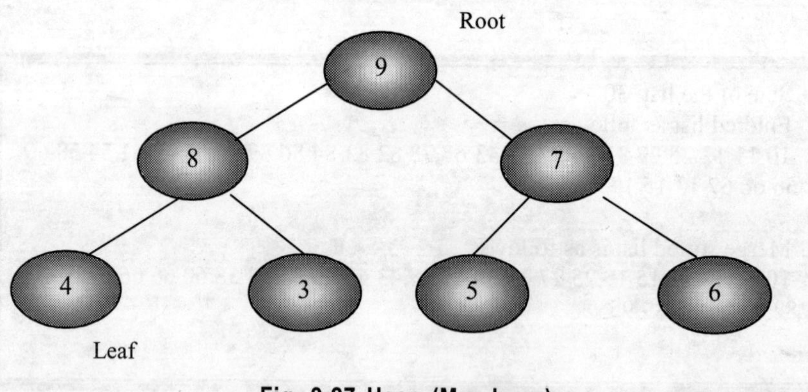

Fig. 9.27 Heap (Max-heap)

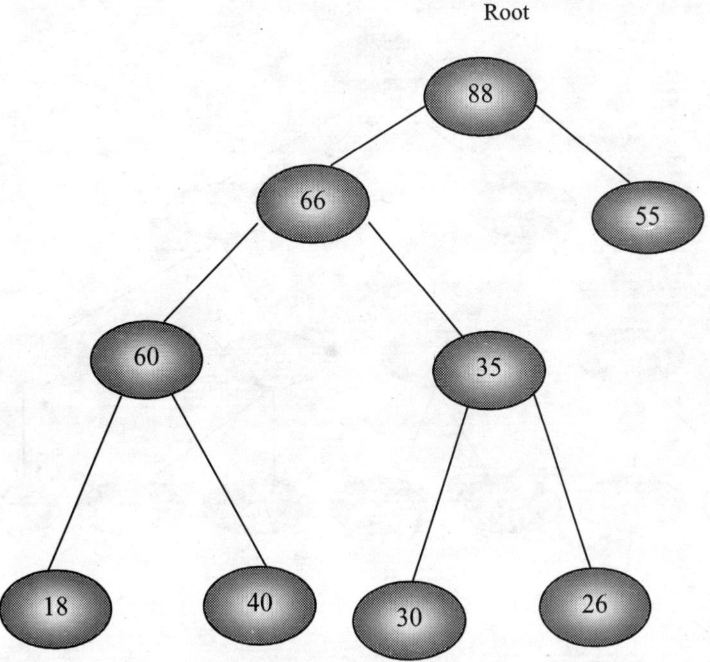

Fig. 9.28 Tree but not a heap

If the value at the node **N** is greater than or equal to the value at each of the children of **N** then heap is called a max-heap **Fig. 9.27.** In general a heap represents a table of **n** elements or records satisfying the following property:

$N_j \leq N_i$ for $2 \leq j \leq n$ and $i = \lfloor j/2 \rfloor$

In a balanced tree the number of links traversed between the root of the tree and any leaf node will differ by only one. Due to this restriction the tree shown in **Fig. 9.28** is not a heap.

The binary tree is allocated sequentially such that the indices of the left and right children (if exist) of elements **i** are **2i** and **2i + 1,** respectively. Similarly, the index of the parent of element **j** (if exists) is **j / 2**. In other words, let the root of any sub-tree be at position **i** in the list then left child will be at position **2i** and the right child will be at position **2i + 1**.

For example, if we have the list shown in **Fig. 9.29** then **Fig. 9.30** represents a heap equivalent to this list.

1	2	3	4	5	6	7	8	9	10	11	12	13	14	15	16	17	18
97	88	95	66	55	95	48	60	45	48	55	62	77	25	38	18	40	38

Fig. 9.29 List in the memory

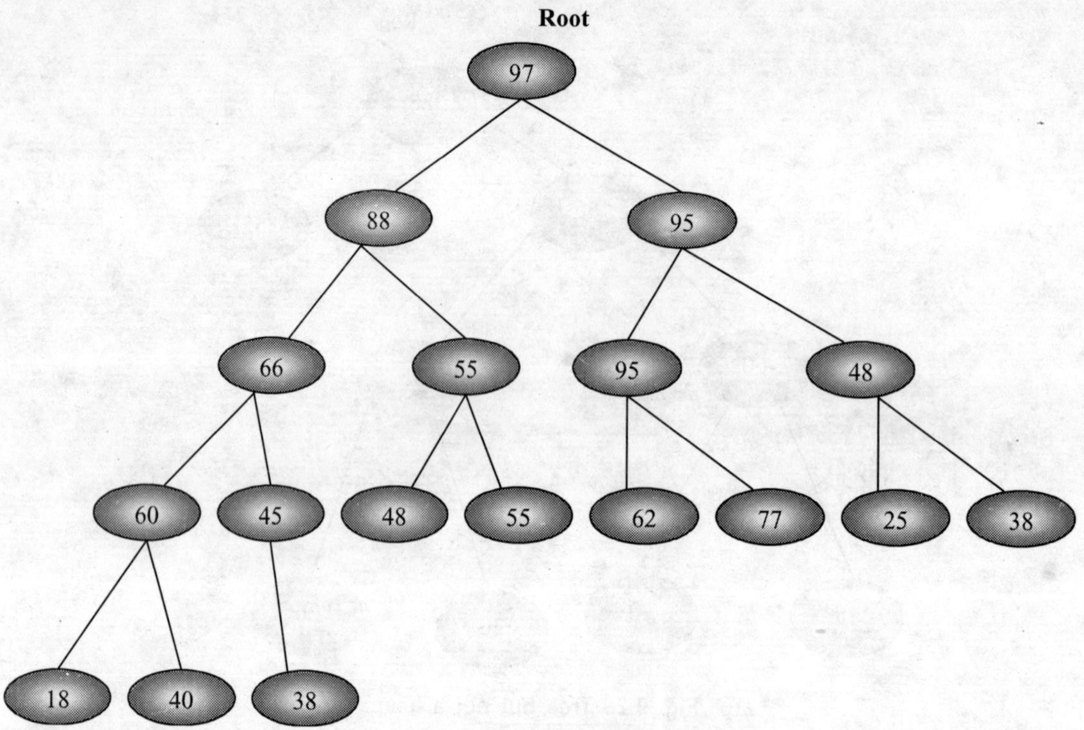

Fig. 9.30 Binary tree (Heap)

From the list shown in **Fig. 9.29** it is clear that **n = 18**. Following steps show the construction of a binary tree:

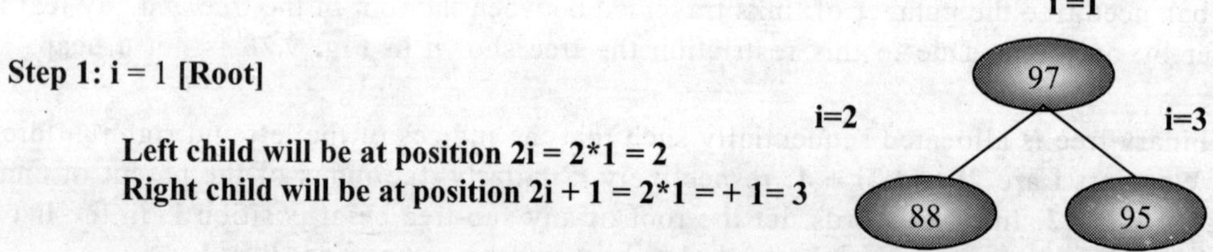

Fig. 9.31 Heap

Step 2: i = 2(New root)
Left child 2i = 2*2=4
Right child 2i+1 = 2*2+1=5

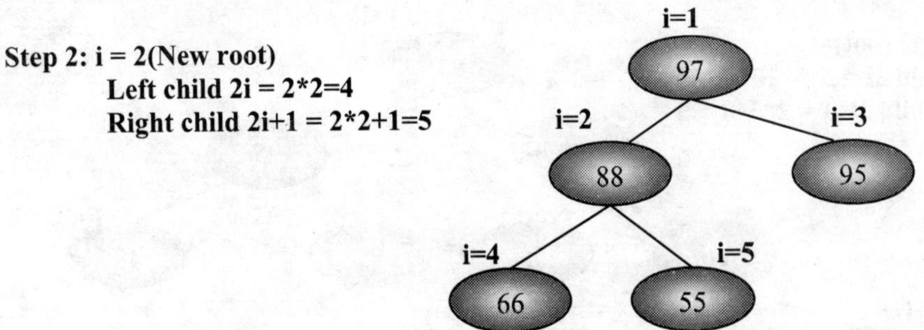

Fig. 9.32 Heap

Step 3: i = 3 (New root)
Left child 2i = 2*3=6
Right child 2i+1 = 2*3+1=7

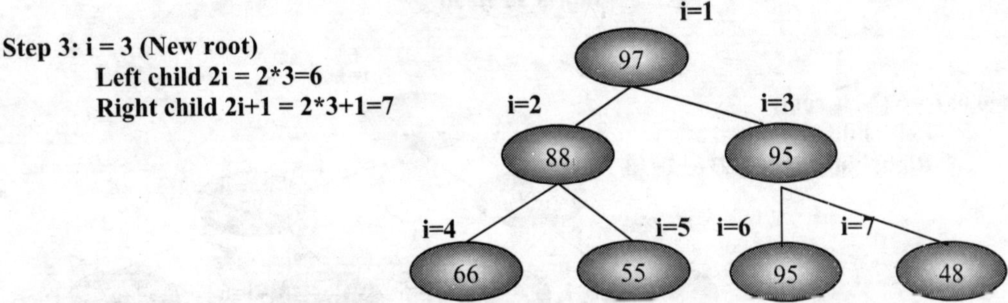

Fig. 9.33 Heap

Step 4: i = 4 (New root)
Left child 2i = 2*3=8
Right child 2i+1 = 2*4+1=9

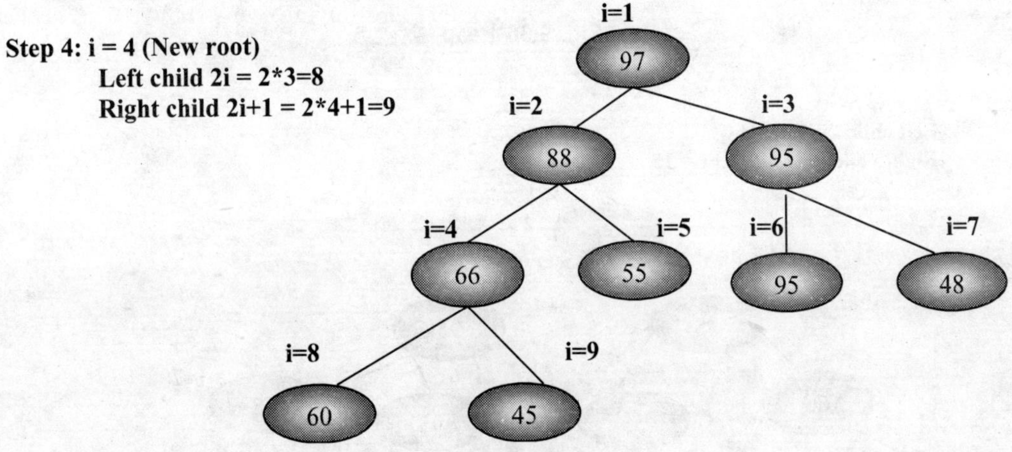

Fig. 9.34 Heap

Step 5: i = 5 (New root)
Left child 2i = 2*5=10
Right child 2i+1 = 2*5+1=11

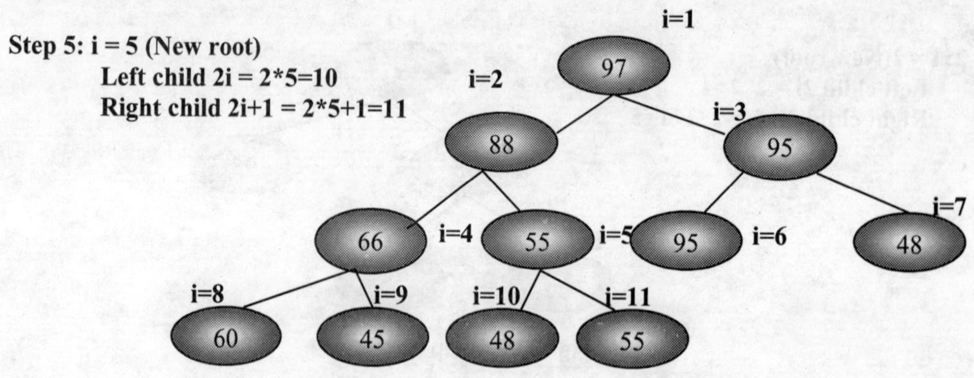

Fig. 9.35 Heap

Step 6: i = 6 (New root)
Left child 2i = 2*6=12
Right child 2i+1 = 2*6+1=13

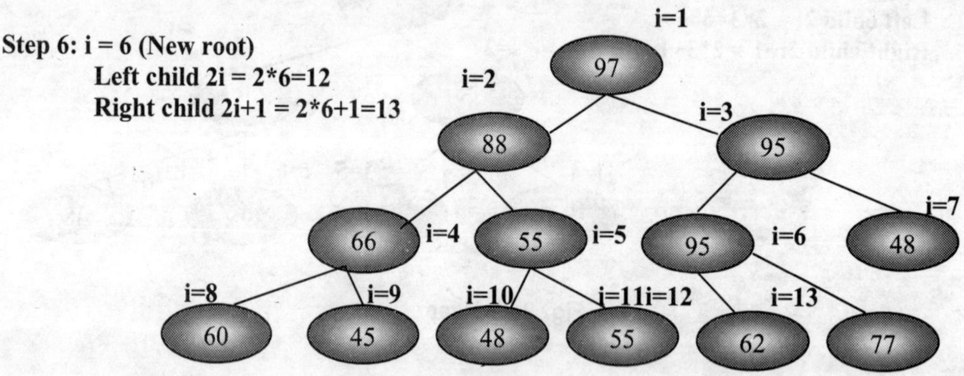

Fig. 9.36 Heap

Step 7: i=7 (New root)
Left child 2i=2*7 = 14
Right child 2i+1 = 2*7+1 = 15

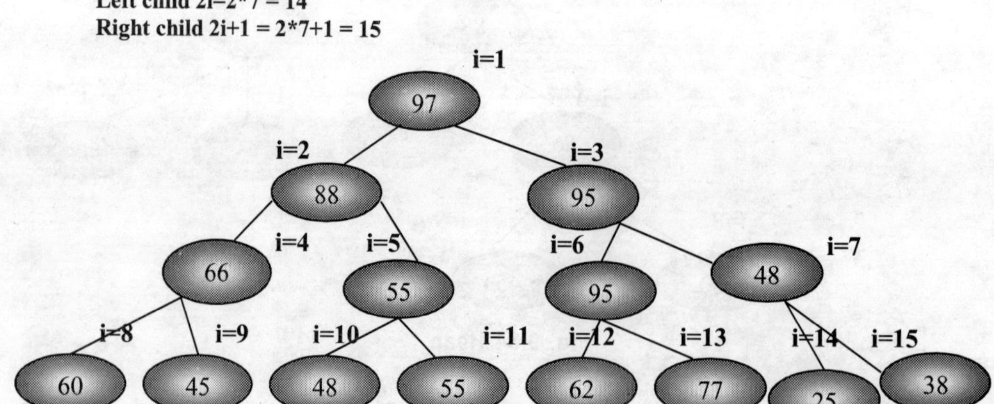

Fig. 9.37 Heap

Step 8: i=8 (New root)
Left child 2i=2*8 = 16
Right child 2i+1 = 2*8+1 = 17

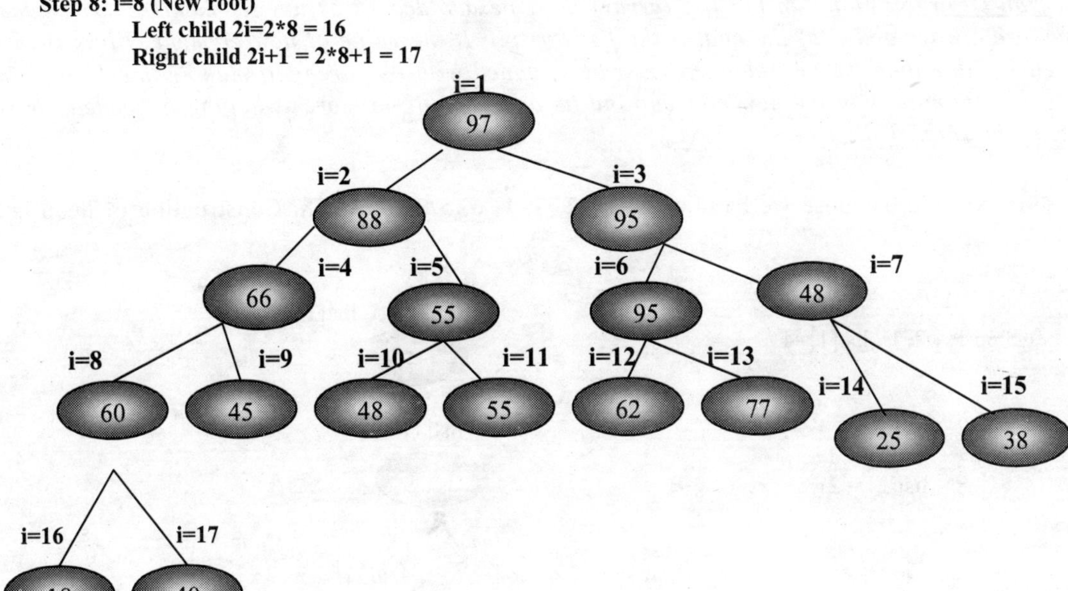

Fig. 9.38 Heap

Step 9: i=9 (New root)
Left child 2i=2*9 = 18
Right child 2i+1 = 2*9+1 = 19(*value not available*)

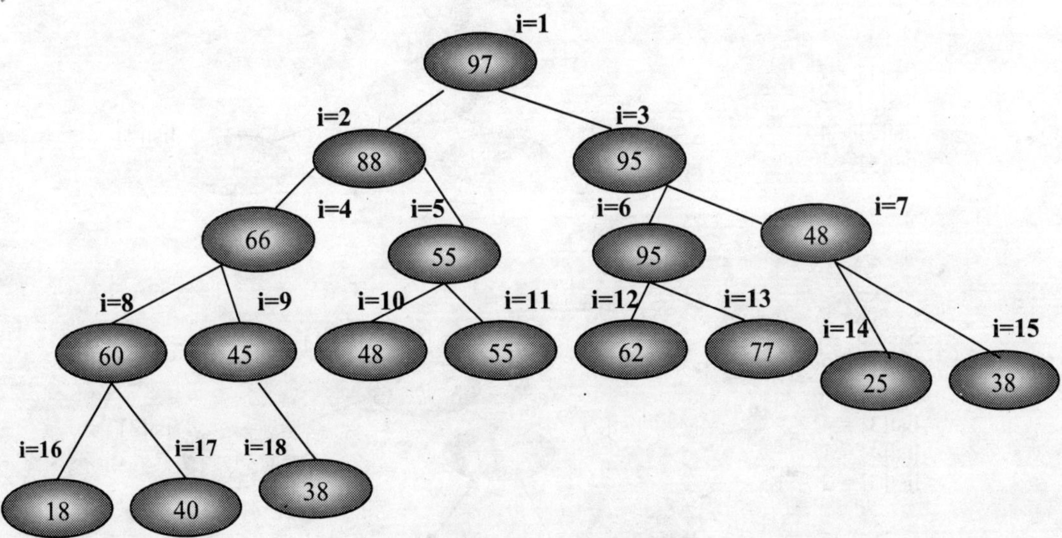

Fig. 9.39 Binary Tree Created

Don't Forget: *Holes in the list (array) must be avoided so as new elements can be added. They are always added at the end of the list (array). If the value of new element is less than its parent's value then the new element must be swapped with its parent (if making min-heap). This process continues with the new element and its parent until no more swapping is needed, or you are at the root of the tree.*

For example, suppose we have a list: 4, 2, 7, 1, 6, 5, 9, 3, 99, 8. Construction of heap is as follows:

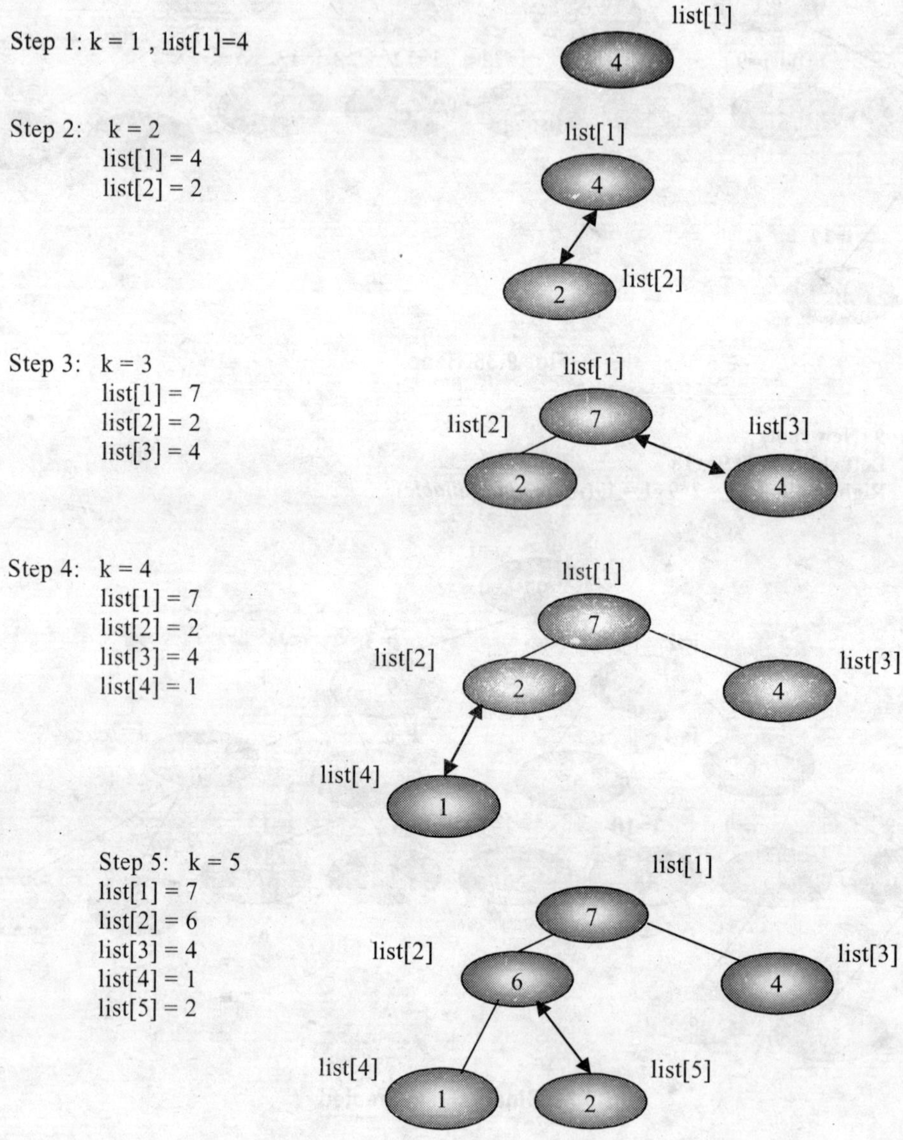

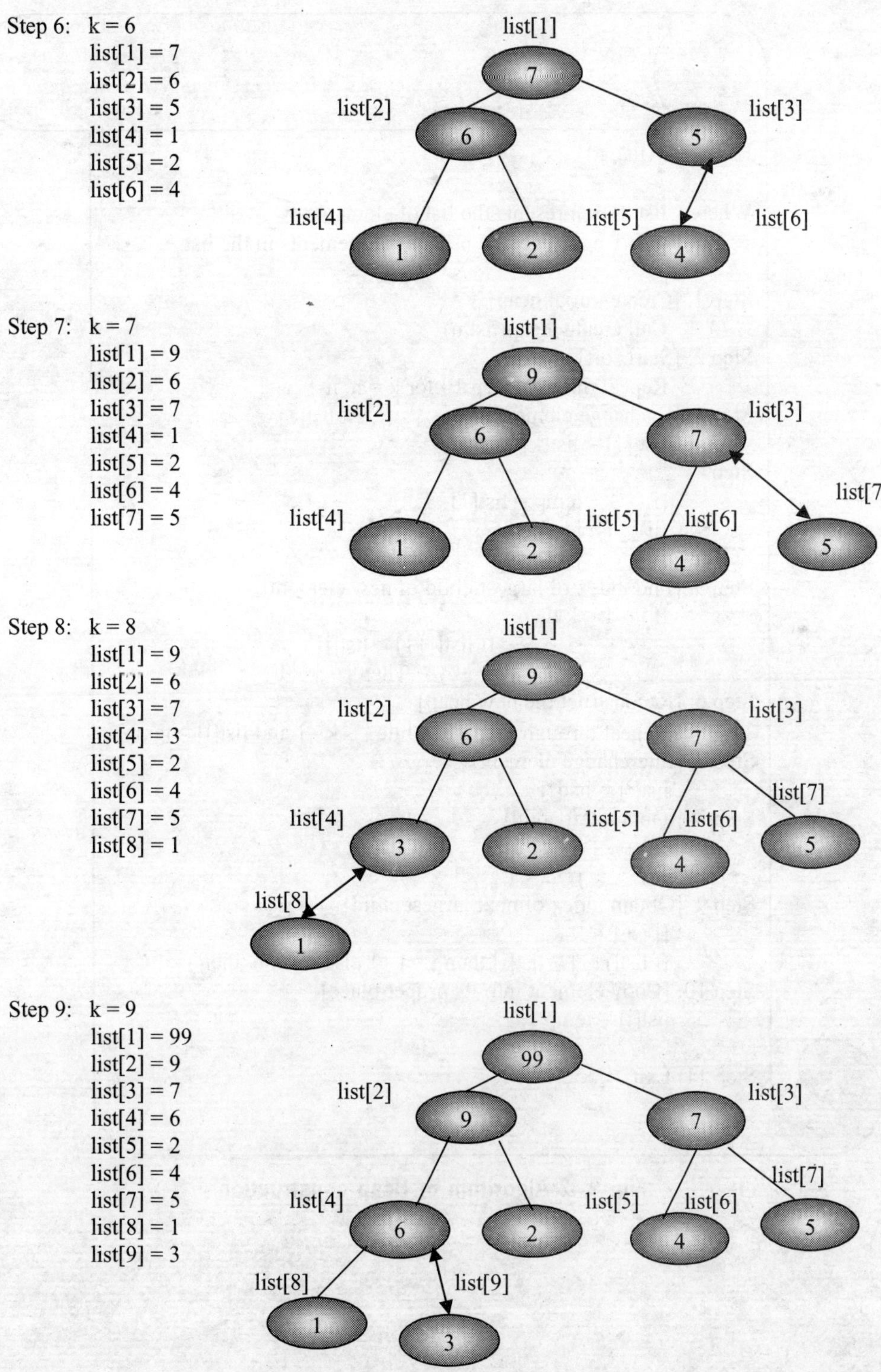

Fig. 9.40 Result (Heap)

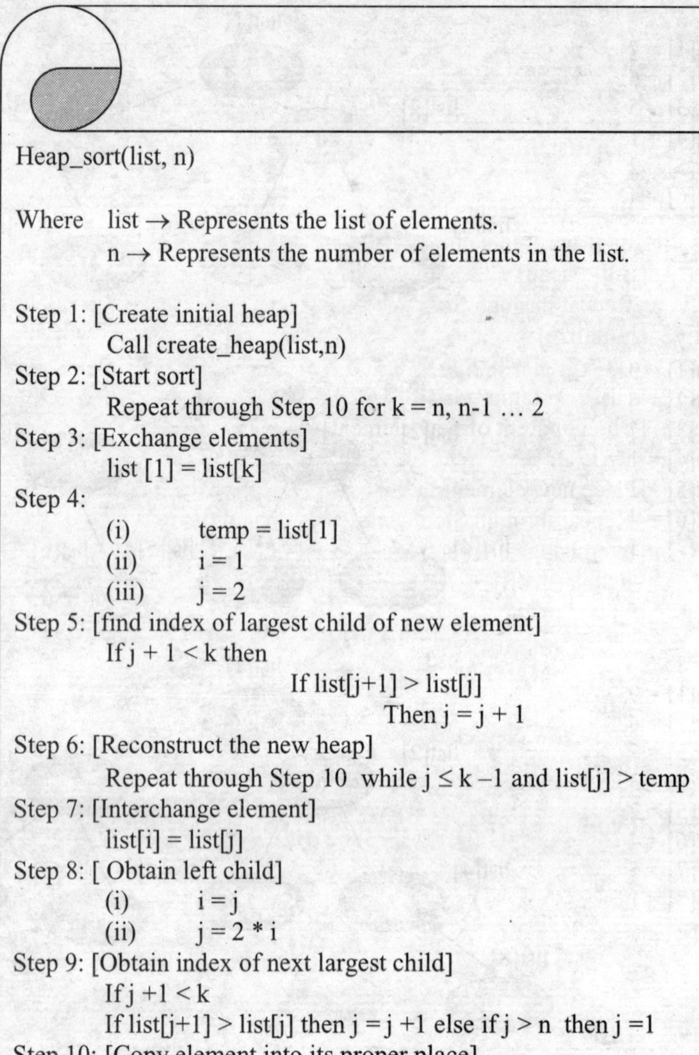

Heap_sort(list, n)

Where list → Represents the list of elements.
n → Represents the number of elements in the list.

Step 1: [Create initial heap]
Call create_heap(list,n)
Step 2: [Start sort]
Repeat through Step 10 for k = n, n-1 … 2
Step 3: [Exchange elements]
list [1] = list[k]
Step 4:
(i) temp = list[1]
(ii) i = 1
(iii) j = 2
Step 5: [find index of largest child of new element]
If j + 1 < k then
If list[j+1] > list[j]
Then j = j + 1
Step 6: [Reconstruct the new heap]
Repeat through Step 10 while j ≤ k –1 and list[j] > temp
Step 7: [Interchange element]
list[i] = list[j]
Step 8: [Obtain left child]
(i) i = j
(ii) j = 2 * i
Step 9: [Obtain index of next largest child]
If j +1 < k
If list[j+1] > list[j] then j = j +1 else if j > n then j =1
Step 10: [Copy element into its proper place]
list[j] = temp

Step 11: Exit

Fig. 9.42 Algorithm of Heap construction

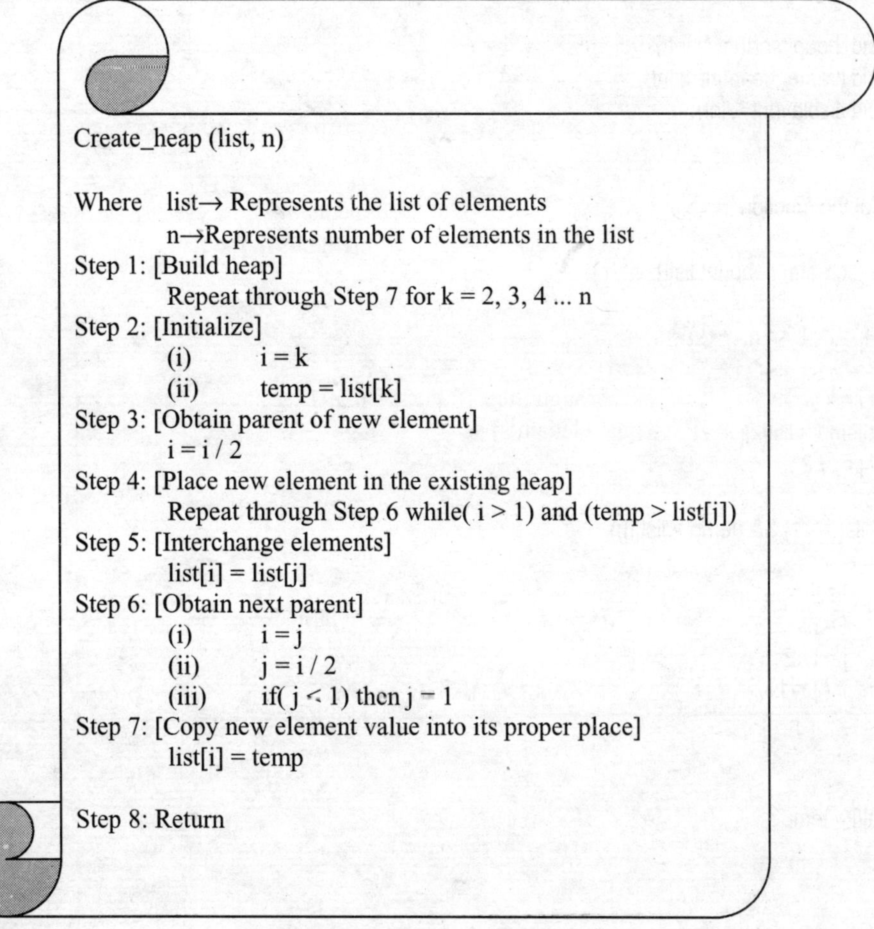

```
Create_heap (list, n)

Where   list→ Represents the list of elements
        n→Represents number of elements in the list
Step 1: [Build heap]
        Repeat through Step 7 for k = 2, 3, 4 ... n
Step 2: [Initialize]
        (i)     i = k
        (ii)    temp = list[k]
Step 3: [Obtain parent of new element]
        i = i / 2
Step 4: [Place new element in the existing heap]
        Repeat through Step 6 while( i > 1) and (temp > list[j])
Step 5: [Interchange elements]
        list[i] = list[j]
Step 6: [Obtain next parent]
        (i)     i = j
        (ii)    j = i / 2
        (iii)   if( j < 1) then j = 1
Step 7: [Copy new element value into its proper place]
        list[i] = temp

Step 8: Return
```

Fig. 9.41 Heap sort algorithm

***Note** : Here in **Fig. 9.40** double arrow (⟷) represents node from where the next entry of new item will take place.*

The algorithm of heap creation is given in **Fig. 9.41.** We have completed construction of the heap, now it is time to discuss heap sort algorithm. The heap sort algorithm is given in **Fig. 9.42.** The program segment **HEAP.C** discusses the implementation of this algorithm.

```
// HEAP SORT
// HEAP.C

# include<iostream.h>

class heap_s
{
```

```
    public:
        void  heap_sort(int *, int );
        void create_heap(int *, int);
        void display(int *, int);
};

// Definition of the function

void heap_s :: create_heap(int list[], int n )
{
    for( int k = 2 ; k <= n;  ++k)
    {
        int i = k ;
        int temp = list[k];
        int j = i / 2 ;

        while((i > 1) && (temp > list[j]))
        {
            list[i] = list[j];
            i = j ;
            j = i / 2 ;
            if ( j < 1 )
                j = 1 ;
        }

        list[i] = temp ;
    }
}

// End of heap creation function

// Definition of the function

void  heap_s :: heap_sort(int list[], int n)
{
    for( int k = n ; k >= 2; --k)
    {
        int temp = list[1] ;
        list[1] = list[k];
        list[k] = temp ;

        int i = 1 ;
        int value = list[1];
        int j = 2 ;

        if((j+1) < k)
```

```
                if(list[j+1] > list[j])
                        j ++;
            while((j <= ( k-1)) && (list[j] > value))
            {
                list[i] = list[j];
                i = j ;
                j = 2*i ;
                if((j+1) < k)
                        if(list[j+1] > list[j])
                                j++;
                        else
                                if( j > n)
                                        j = n ;
                list[i] = value;
            } // End of while statement
            cout<<"\n";
            for(int p=1; p<=n; p++)
                cout<<"  "<<list[p];
        } //End for loop
}

void heap_s :: display(int list[], int n)
{
        for( int i = 1 ; i <= n; ++ i)
        {
            cout<<"  "<<list[i];
        }
}

// Function main

void main()
{
        heap_s sort;

        int list[100];
        int size ;

        cout<<"\n Input the size of the list :";
        cin>>size;

        for(int i = 1 ; i <= size ; ++i)
        {
            cout<<"\n Input values for :" <<i<< " : ";
            cin>>list[i];
        }
```

```
    cout<<"\n Entered list is as follows: \n";
    sort.display(list, size);
    sort.create_heap(list, size);
    cout<<"\n Heap\n";
    sort.display(list, size);
    sort.heap_sort(list, size);

    cout<<"\n Sorted list is as follows :\n";
    sort.display(list, size);
}
```

```
Input the size of the list :10

Input values for :1 :4
Input values for :2 :2
Input values for :3 :7
Input values for :4 :1
Input values for :5 :6
Input values for :6 :5
Input values for :7 :9
Input values for :8 :3
Input values for :9 :99
Input values for :10 :8

Entered list is as follows:
4 2 7 1 6 5 9 3 99 8
Heap
99 9 7 6 8 4 5 1 3 2
9 8 7 6 2 4 5 1 3 99
8 6 7 3 2 4 5 1 9 99
7 6 5 3 2 4 1 8 9 99
6 3 5 1 2 4 7 8 9 99
5 3 4 1 2 6 7 8 9 99
4 3 2 1 5 6 7 8 9 99
3 1 2 4 5 6 7 8 9 99
2 1 3 4 5 6 7 8 9 99
1 2 3 4 5 6 7 8 9 99

Sorted list is as follows :
1 2 3 4 5 6 7 8 9 99
```

9.10 RADIX SORT

Radix sort is a technique, which is usually used when large lists of names are to be sorted alphabetically. Using this sorting technique one can classify the list of names into 26 groups. The list is first sorted on the first letter of each name, i.e., the names are arranged in 26 classes where the first class consists of those names that begin with alphabet '**A**', the second class consists of those names that begin with alphabet '**B**' and so on. During the second pass each class is alphabetized according to the second letter of the name and so on. For example, if no name contains more than 20 characters then the sort requires 20 passes.

The radix sort is a technique, which is used by a card sorter. A card sorter contains 13 receiving pockets labeled as

9, 8, 7, 6, 5, 4, 3, 2, 1, 0, 11, 12, R

Here **R** represents reject, if any card comes in this pocket.

Each pocket other than **R** corresponds to a row on a card in which a hole can be punched. Decimal numbers where the radix is 10 are punched in the obvious way and hence use only the first 10 pockets on the sorter. The sorter uses a radix reverse digit sort on numbers. For example, suppose a card sorter is given a collection of cards where each card contains a four-digit number punched in columns 1-4. The cards are first sorted according to the unit's digit. In the second pass, the cards are sorted according to the tens digit. In the third pass the cards are sorted according to the hundreds digit. In the fourth and last pass, the cards are sorted according to the thousands digit. For example, suppose cards are punched as shown in **Fig. 9.43.**

1	2	3	4	5	6	7
4348	2143	4361	5423	4538	2128	5438

Fig. 9.43 Punched card data

Input	Pocket 0	Pocket 1	Pocket 2	Pocket 3	Pocket 4	Pocket 5	Pocket 6	Pocket 7	Pocket 8	Pocket 9
4348									4348	
2143				2143						
4361		4361								
5423				5423						
4538									4538	
2128									2128	
5438									5438	

Fig. 9.43 (a) Pass 1 sort units digit

(i) *Pass 1 → The unit digits are sorted into pockets. The cards are collected pocket by pocket from pocket 9 to pocket 0. The cards are now re-input to the sorter.*

(ii) *Pass 2 → The tens digits are sorted into pockets. Again cards are collected pocket by pocket and re-input to the sorter.*

(iii) *Pass 3 → The 100th digits are sorted into pockets. Again cards are collected pocket by pocket and re-input to the sorter.*

(iv) *Pass 4 → The 1000's digits are sorted into pocket. Again cards are sorted pocket by pocket.*

When the cards are collected after 4th pass, the numbers are in the sorted order.

Input	Pocket 0	Pocket 1	Pocket 2	Pocket 3	Pocket 4	Pocket 5	Pocket 6	Pocket 7	Pocket 8	Pocket 9
4348					4348					
4538				4538						
2128			2128							
5438				5438						
2143					2143					
5423			5423							
4361							4361			

Fig. 9.43 (b) Pass 2 sort on 10th digit

Input	Pocket 0	Pocket 1	Pocket 2	Pocket 3	Pocket 4	Pocket 5	Pocket 6	Pocket 7	Pocket 8	Pocket 9
4361				4361						
4348				4338						
2143		2143								
4538						4538				
5438					5438					
2128		2128								
5423					5423					

Fig. 9.43 (c) Pass 3 sort on 100th digit

Input	Pocket 0	Pocket 1	Pocket 2	Pocket 3	Pocket 4	Pocket 5	Pocket 6	Pocket 7	Pocket 8	Pocket 9
4538					4538					
5438						5438				
5423						5423				
4361					4361					
4348					4348					
2143			2143							
2128			2128							

Fig. 9.43 (d) Pass 4 sort on 1000's digit

Now collecting the values of pockets from 9th to 0th then we get the list of array as shown in **Fig. 9.44.**

1	2	3	4	5	6	7
5438	5423	4538	4361	4348	2143	2128

Fig. 9.44 Sorted list using radix sort

Input	Pocket 0	Pocket 1	Pocket 2	Pocket 3	Pocket 4	Pocket 5	Pocket 6	Pocket 7	Pocket 8	Pocket 9
4348									4348	
2143				2143						
4361		4361								
5423				5423						
4538									4538	
2128									2128	
5438									5438	

Fig. 9.45 (a) Pass 1 sort units digit

Input	Pocket 0	Pocket 1	Pocket 2	Pocket 3	Pocket 4	Pocket 5	Pocket 6	Pocket 7	Pocket 8	Pocket 9
4361							4361			
2143					2143					
5423			5423							
4348					4348					
4538				4538						
2128			2128							
5438				5438						

Fig. 9.45 (b) Pass 2 sort on 10th digit

Input	Pocket 0	Pocket 1	Pocket 2	Pocket 3	Pocket 4	Pocket 5	Pocket 6	Pocket 7	Pocket 8	Pocket 9
5423					5423					
2128		2128								
4538						4538				
5438					5438					
2143		2143								
4348				4348						
4361				4361						

Fig. 9.45 (c) Pass 3 sort on 100th digit

Input	Pocket 0	Pocket 1	Pocket 2	Pocket 3	Pocket 4	Pocket 5	Pocket 6	Pocket 7	Pocket 8	Pocket 9
2128			2128							
2143			2143							
4348					4348					
4361					4361					
5423						5423				
5438						5438				
4538					4538					

Fig. 9.45 (d) Pass 4 sort on 1000's digit

From the result shown in **Fig. 9.44,** it is clear that the list is sorted in descending order.

If during the sorting operation one collects the pocket from 0th to 9th the result will come in ascending order. For example, **Fig. 9.45 (a-d)** illustrates the preceding statement.

Now collecting the values of pockets from 0th to 9th , we get the list of array as shown in **Fig. 9.46.**

1	2	3	4	5	6	7
2128	2143	4348	4361	4538	5423	5438

Fig. 9.46 Sorted list using radix sort

The result shown in **Fig. 9.46** denotes that the list is sorted in ascending order.

The pen paper method, which is shown in **Fig. 9.45 (a-d)** can be implemented on a computer. The sequential allocation of techniques is not practical in representing the pockets, since we do not know how many elements or records will occupy a particular pocket during a certain pass. The linked list allocation is used to resolve this uncertainty. Each pocket can be represented as a linked list **FIFO** queue. At the end of each pass, these queues can be easily combined in the proper order. If the maximum number of digits in an element is **m**, then **m** successive passes from the unit digit to the most significant digits are required in order to sort the number.

In general we can define an algorithm for radix sort as follows:

Step 1: Repeat through Step 6 for each digit in the key.
Step 2: Initialize the pockets.
Step 3: Repeat through Step 5 until end of the linked list.
Step 4: Obtain the next digit of the key.
Step 5: Insert the element in appropriate pocket.
Step 6: Combine the pockets to form a new linked list.

Suppose **rec** represents a list of **n** elements, i.e., $\mathbf{rec_1}$, $\mathbf{rec_2}$ **...** $\mathbf{rec_n}$ and **d** denotes the radix (For decimal number system, which is 10, for alphabets it is 26, for binary it is 2, for octal number system it is 8, etc.) and each element $\mathbf{rec_i}$ is represented by means of **m** digits.

$rec_i = d_{i\,1}\, d_{i\,2}\, d_{i\,3} \ldots d_{i\,m}.$

The radix sort algorithm requires **m** pass - the number of digits in each element. Pass **j** will compare each $\mathbf{d_{ij}}$ with each of the **d** digits. Hence, total number of comparisons (and in turn efficiency) is:

E (n) = d*m*n [Maximum value possible that is possible]

Where **d** and **m** are independent of **n**.

(i) Worst case : If n = m then $E(n) = d*n*n = d*n^2 \;\; O(n^2)$

(ii) Best case : $m = \log_d n$

$$E(n) = d*(\log_d n)*n$$
$$= O(n \log_d n)$$

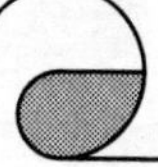

```
Large (rec)

Where rec → Represents address of the first element in the
linked list.

Step 1: [Initialization]
        p = 0      [is the temporary variable which keep the
                   value of the current node in the linked
                   list]
        save = rec [save is a pointer variable which points
                   to the address of the first element in
                   the list.
Step 2: Repeat through Step 3 while(save ≠ NULL)
Step 3: if (link[save] > p)
        (i)        p = link[save]
        (ii)       save = link[save]
step 4: Return (p)
```

Fig. 9.47 Algorithm to find largest number in the list

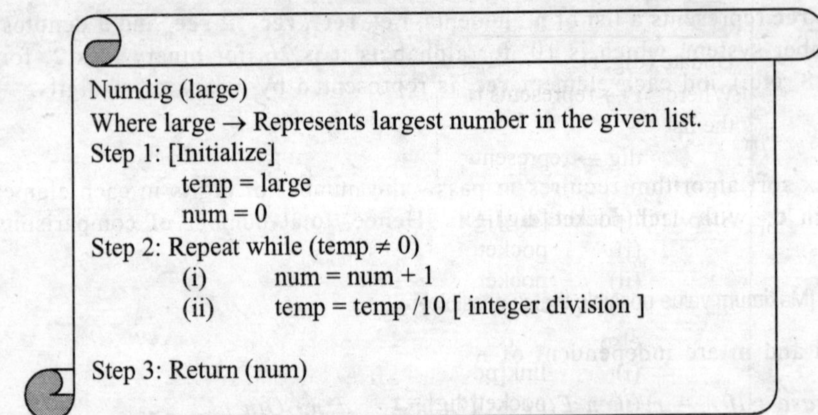

Numdig (large)
Where large → Represents largest number in the given list.
Step 1: [Initialize]
temp = large
num = 0
Step 2: Repeat while (temp ≠ 0)
(i) num = num + 1
(ii) temp = temp /10 [integer division]

Step 3: Return (num)

Fig. 9.48 Algorithm to find number of digits in the largest number in the given list

The sub-algorithms, which are necessary in the radix sort, are given in the **Fig. 9.47, Fig. 9.48, Fig. 9.49** and **Fig. 9.50.**

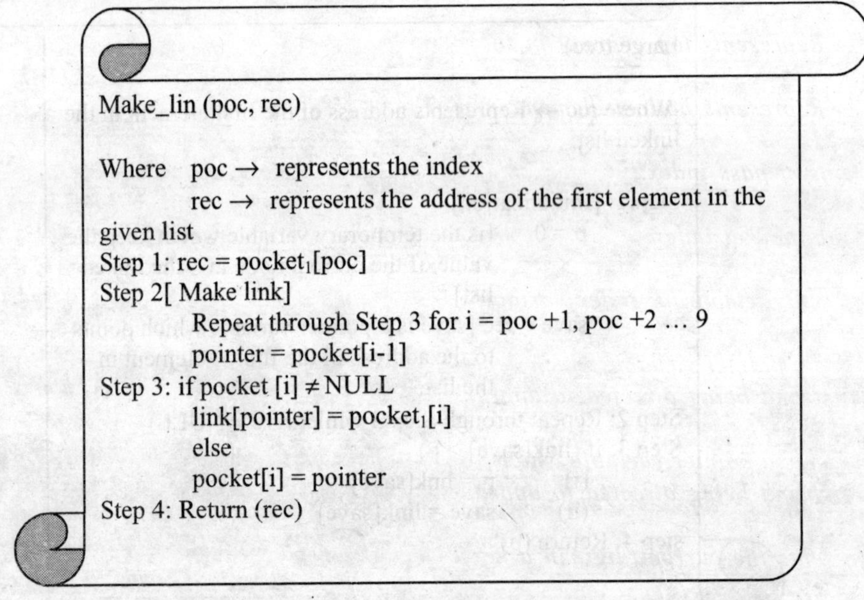

Make_lin (poc, rec)

Where poc → represents the index
rec → represents the address of the first element in the given list
Step 1: rec = $pocket_1$[poc]
Step 2[Make link]
Repeat through Step 3 for i = poc +1, poc +2 … 9
pointer = pocket[i-1]
Step 3: if pocket [i] ≠ NULL
link[pointer] = $pocket_1$[i]
else
pocket[i] = pointer
Step 4: Return (rec)

Fig. 9.49 Algorithm that make links elements during sorting

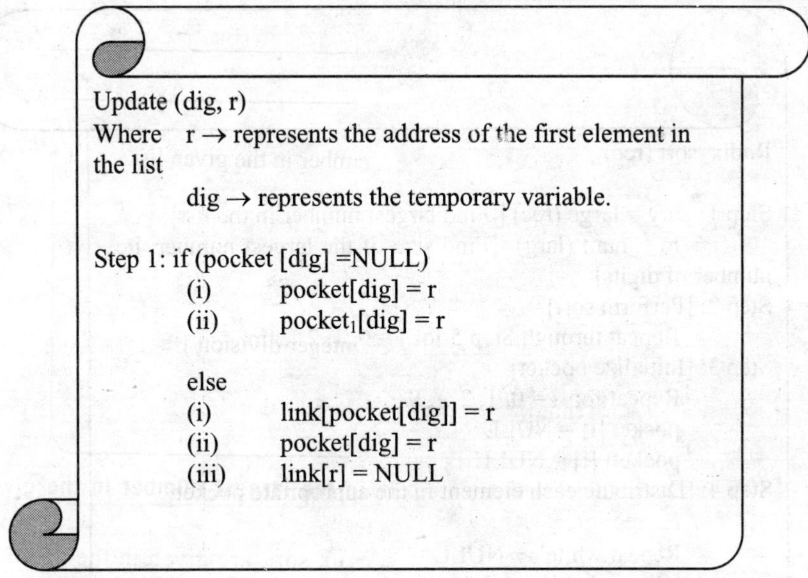
Update (dig, r)
Where r → represents the address of the first element in the list
dig → represents the temporary variable.

Step 1: if (pocket [dig] =NULL)
(i) pocket[dig] = r
(ii) $pocket_1$[dig] = r
else
(i) link[pocket[dig]] = r
(ii) pocket[dig] = r
(iii) link[r] = NULL

Fig. 9.50 Algorithm which updates the values of the pockets

pocket [i] → Represents top element in the ith pocket

$pocket_1$[i] → Represents bottom element in the ith pocket.

j → Represents j pass index.

i → Represents pocket index.

poc → Represents temporary index variable

r → Represents a pointer variable which denotes the address of the current element being examined in the list and being directed to appropriate pocket.

nex → Represents a pointer variable which denotes the address of the next element to be examined in the list and being directed to appropriate pocket.

dig → Represents the current digit in a key being examined.

```
Radix_sort (rec)

Step 1:  larg = large (rec) [ Find largest number in the list]
         m = num (larg)  [Find size of the largest number, i.e.,
number of digits]
Step 2: [Perform sort]
         Repeat through Step 5 for j = 0, 1, 2 … m
Step 3: [Initialize pocket]
         Repeat for  i = 0, 1, 2 … 9
         pocket [i] = NULL
         pocket1 [i] = NULL
Step 4: [Distribute each element in the appropriate pocket]
         r = rec
         Repeat while r ≠ NULL
         [Obtain jth digit of the key]
         dig = digit ( link[r], j)
         Update (dig, r)
         nex = link[r]
         r = nex
         if (r ≠ NULL)
         dig = digit(link[r], j)
         Update (dig, r)
Step 5: [Combine pockets]
         poc = 0
         Repeat while (pocket1 [poc] = NULL)
         poc = poc + 1
         rec = make_link(poc, rec)
Step 6 Return
```

Fig. 9.51 Algorithm for radix sort

The program segment **RADIX.C** implements the radix sort algorithm which is illustrated in **Fig. 9.51.**

```
// RADIX SORT
// RADIX.C

# include<iostream.h>
# include<malloc.h>
```

```
# include<stdlib.h>

struct node
{
      int data ;
      struct node *next;
};

typedef struct node node1;

class radix
{
public:
      node1 *first;
      node1 *pocket[100], *pocket1[100];
public:
      void create_node(node1 *, int);
      void display(node1 *);
      node1 *radix_sort(node1 *);
      int large(node1 * );
      int numdig(int );
      int digit(int , int);
      void update(int, node1 *);
      node1 *Make_link(int, node1 *);
};

// This function create nodes and take input data

void radix :: create_node(node1 *rec, int n)
{
      for( int i = 0 ; i< n; i++)
      {
            rec->next = (node1 *) malloc(sizeof(node1));
            cout<<"\n First node value:"<<i<<":";
            cin>>rec->data;
            rec = rec->next;

      }
      rec->next = NULL;
}

// Output Function

void radix ::  display(node1 * rec)
{
      while(rec)
```

```
    {
        cout<<" "<<rec->data;
        rec= rec->next;
    }
}

// This radix sort function

node1 * radix :: radix_sort(node1 *rec)
{
    int larg = large(rec);
    int m = numdig(larg);

    // These statements create pockets

    for(int k = 0 ; k < 10; k++)
    {
        pocket[k] = (node1 *)malloc(sizeof(node1));
        pocket1[k] = (node1 *)malloc(9*sizeof(node1));
    }

    // These statements initialize pockets

    for(int j = 1; j <= m ; j++)
    {
        for(int i = 0 ; i < 10 ; i++)
        {
            pocket[i] = NULL;
            pocket1[i] = NULL ;
        }

        node1 *r = rec ;
        while(r != NULL)
        {
            int dig = digit(r->data, j);
            node1 *nex = r->next ;
            update(dig,r);
            r = nex;
        }

        if(r!= NULL)
        {
            int dig = digit(r->data,j);
            update(dig,r);
        }
```

```
        int poc = 0 ;
        while(pocket1[poc] == NULL)
            poc ++;
        rec = Make_link(poc, rec);

        cout<<"\n Newly ordered list:\n";
        display(rec);
    }
    return(rec);
}

// This function finds largest number in the list

int radix :: large(node1 *rec)
{
    node1 *save ;
    int p = 0;
    save = rec ;
    while(save != NULL)
    {
        if(save ->data > p)
        {
            p = save->data;
        }
        save = save->next ;
    }

    cout <<"\n Largest element:"<<p;
    return(p);
}

// This function finds number digits in a number

int radix :: numdig(int large)
{
    int temp = large ;
    int num = 0 ;

    while(temp != 0)
    {
        ++num ;
        temp = temp/10 ;
    }

    cout <<"\n Number of digits of the number "<<large
      <<" is "<<num ;
```

```
    return(num);
}

// This function scarve a number into digits

int radix :: digit(int num, int j)
{
    int dig ;
    int temp = num ;

    for( int i = 0 ; i < j ; i++)
    {
        dig = temp % 10 ;
        temp = temp / 10 ;
    }
    cout<<"\n";
    cout <<j <<" digit of number "<<num <<" is "<<dig;
    return(dig);
}

// This function updates the pockets value

void radix :: update(int dig, node1 *r)
{
    if(pocket[dig] == NULL)
    {
        pocket[dig] = r ;
        pocket1[dig] = r ;
    }
    else
    {
        pocket[dig]->next = r ;
        pocket[dig] = r ;
    }
    r->next = NULL;
}

// This function create links between the nodes

node1* radix :: Make_link(int poc , node1 *rec)
{
    node1 *pointer;
    rec = pocket1[poc];
    for(int i = poc +1 ; i< 10 ; i++)
    {
        pointer = pocket[i-1];
```

```
        if(pocket[i] != NULL)
              pointer->next= pocket1[i];
        else
              pocket[i] = pointer ;
    }

    return(rec);
}

// Main function

void main()
{
    radix rad;
    node1 *start, *pointer;
    int number;

    cout<<"\n Input the elements of the list :\n";

    cout<<"\n Input the number of elements in the list:";
    cin>>number;

    start = (node1 *)malloc(sizeof(node1));

    rad.create_node(start, number);

    cout<<"\n Given list is as follows \n";
    rad.display(start);

    start = rad.radix_sort(start);

    cout<<"\n Sorted list is as follows:\n";
    rad.display (start);
}
```

9.11 RADIX EXCHANGE SORT

A considerably better distributive sort is the radix exchange sort, which is applicable when the keys are expressed in binary. Sorting is accomplished by considering groups with the some (M) first bits and ordering that group with respect to the (M+1st) bit. The ordering of a group on a given bit is accomplished by scanning down from the top of the group for a one bit and up from bottom for a zero bit, these two are exchanged and the sort continues. This algorithm requires the program to keep up with a large number of groups and coded in bad form, could require an additional table **n** long. However, with optimal coding it is possible to keep track of the groups by simply monitoring the top of the table and a list of break points, one for each bit of the keyword. Thus with 5-bit words a table of only 32 entries is required. For example, consider radix exchange sort shown in **Fig. 9.52.**

If the sort algorithm is programmed to quit sorting when a group contains only one item then the time required for the radix exchange sort is proportional to **n.log n** as compared to **n** $\log_p k$ (where **k** is the maximum key size and **p** is the radix) for the radix sort. Note that the radix exchange sort does not require extra table space for buckets.

Highlighted data show the interchange made there, order of collection is C1, C2, C3, C4, C5, C6, C7, C8, C9, C10, C11 and C12, i.e., 01, 02, 05, 09, 11, 13, 16, 19, 21, 26, 27, 31.

Decimal	Pass 1	Pass 2	Pass 3	Pass 4	Pass 5	
19	10011	01011	00010	00010	00001	C1
13	01101	01101	00001	00001	00010	C2
05	00101	00101	00101	00101	C3	
27	11011	01001	01001	01001	01001	C4
01	00001	00001	01101	01011	01011	C5
26	11010	00010	01011	01101	C6	
31	11111	11111	10101	10011	10000	C7
16	10000	10000	10000	10000	10011	C8
02	00010	11010	10011	10101	C9	
09	01001	11011	11011	11011	11011	11010 C10
11	01011	10011	11010	11010	11010	11011 C11
21	10101	10101	11111	11111	C12	

Fig. 9.52 radix exchange sort

9.12 HASHING

So far, we have succeeded in paring down our **O (n)** search to **O (n** $\log_2$ **n)** by keeping the list sorted sequentially with respect to the key value, i.e., the key in the first element is less than or equal to the key in the second element, which is less than the key in the third and so on. Can we do better than that? Is it possible to design a search of O (1), i.e., one that has a constant search time, no matter where the element is in the list?

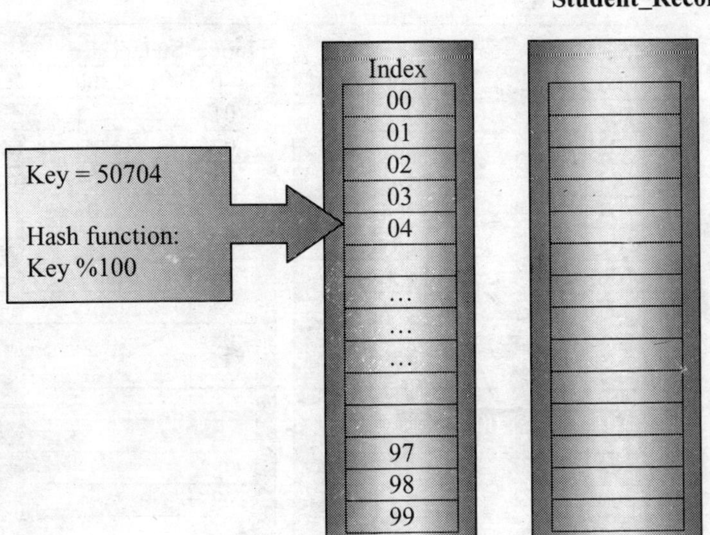

Fig. 9.53 Using a hash function to determine the location of the element in an array

For example, list of students of GBPEC institute. Each of the 100 students has an ID number in the range 0 to 99 and we want to access the student employee records by the key **STD_ID**. If we store the elements in an array that is indexed from 0 to 99, we can directly access any student's record through the array index. There is a one-to-one correspondence between the element keys and the array index, in effect the array index functions as the key of each element.

In practice, however, this perfect relationship between the key value and the location of an element is not easy to establish or maintain. Consider similar case, HNB Garhwal University that uses its students five-digit ID number as the primary key. Now the range of key values is from 00000 to 99999. Obviously it is impractical to set up an array of 100000 elements of which only 100 are needed, just to make sure that each student's element is in a perfectly unique and predictable location.

What if we keep the array size down to the size that we actually need (array of 100 elements) and just use the last two digits of the key to identify each student? For instance, the element of student 53374 is in **Student_Record[74]** and the element if the student 81235 is in **Student_Record[35].** Note that the elements are not sorted according to the value of the key as they were in our earlier discussion, the position of the student 81235's record precedes that of student 53374 in the array, even though the value of its key is larger. Instead, the elements are sorted with respect to some function of the key value.

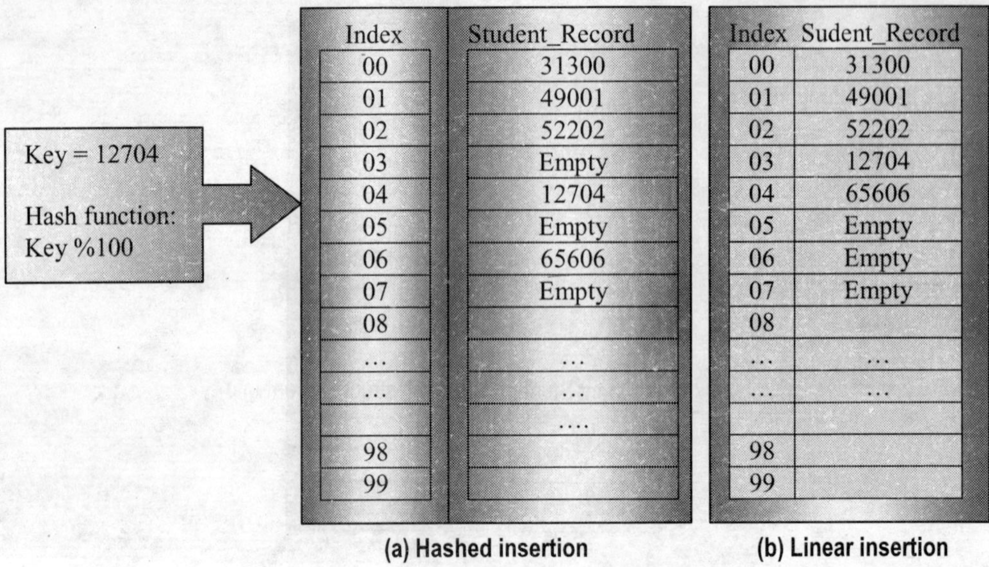

Fig. 9.54 Comparing hashed and sequential lists of identical elements

This function is called a hash function and the search technique we are using is called hashing. In the case of the student list above, the hash function is (key%100). 100 divides **STD_ID** the key and the remainder is used as an index into the array of students. The discussion is illustrated in **Fig. 9.53.** This function assumes that the array is indexed from 0 to 99 (MAX_INFO = 100).

The function to perform the conversion of key values to indexes is very simple. The hash function is defined as

```
int Hash(int Key)
{
    return (Key%100);
}
```

This function returns integer value between 0 and **MAX_INFO - 1.** Thus, we can say that a **hash** function used to manipulate the key of an element is a list to identify its location in the list. And **hashing** technique used for searching and accessing elements in a list in a relatively constant amount of time by manipulating the key to identify its location in the list.

This hash function has two uses. As we have seen, it is used as a method of accessing the list element. The result of the hash function tells one where to look for a particular element-information we need to access, modify or delete the element. For example, consider the following function that demonstrates the accessing of information from a list.

```
struct Student * Access_Record(int Key, struct Student Student_Record[]);
{
```

```
    int location;
    location = Hash(Key);
    return(Student_Record[location]);
}
```

There is second use of the hash function. It determines where in the array to store the element. If the student list elements were inserted into the list using an insert operation- into sequential array rooms or into rooms with their relative order determined by the key value- we could not use the hash function to retrieve them. We have to create a version of insert operation that puts each new record into the correct room according to the hash function. Here is a simple version of **Insert_Record(),** which assumes that the array room at the index returned from the hash function is not in use.

```
struct Student * Insert_Record(int Key, struct Student Student_Record[], struct Student Info);
{
    int location;
    location = Hash(Key);
    Student_Record[location] = Info;
    Length ++;
}
```

Fig. 9.54 illustrate an array, whose elements-records for the students with key values (unique ID numbers) 12704, 31300, 49001, 52202 and 65606-were added using **Insert_Record()** function. Note that this function does not fill the array positions sequentially. Because we have not yet inserted any elements whose keys produce the hash values 3 and 5, the array rooms 3 and 5 are logically "empty". In **Fig. 9.54 (b),** the same student records have been inserted into sorted list using linear insertion operation.

9.12.1 COLLISIONS

By now we are probably objecting to this scheme on the grounds that it does not guarantee unique hash locations. ID number 01234 and ID number 91234 both hash to the same location, **Student_Record[34].** The problem of avoiding these collisions is the challenge in designing a good hash function. A good hash function minimizes collisions by spreading the elements uniformly throughout the array. But minimization of collision is very difficult job.

Assuming that there are some collisions, where we want to store the elements that cause them? We will briefly describe several collisions handling methods.

9.12.2 LINEAR PROBING

A simple approach to resolving collisions is to store the colliding record (element) into the next available space. This technique is known as linear probing. Suppose in **Fig. 9.55** we want to add the student record (element) with the key ID number 77003. The function returns 3. But there is already a record stored in this array room, the record for student 50003. We increment location to 4 and examine the next array room. **Student_Record[4]** is also in use, so we increment location again. This time we find a room, i.e., empty, so we store the new record into **Student_Record[5].**

Linear probing resolves hash collision by sequential searching a hash table beginning at the location returned by the hash function. What happens if the key hashes to the last index in the array and that space is in use? We can consider array as a circular structure and continue looking for an empty room at the beginning of the array {Consider chapter 6 for circular queue}.

How do we know whether an array room is empty? We can initialize the array room to contain a special empty information, i.e., NULL ('\0') or if all students have nonnegative **STD_ID** keys, we can use -1 as the key value for an empty room. Now it is easy to tell if the room is free. We compare the value in the position to the empty value.

Here we define **Insert_Record()** function in another way, i.e., that use linear probing to find a place to store a new record. It assumes that there is room in the array for another record, i.e., a check has been made for is array full before the function is called.

```
struct Student * Insert_Record(int Key, struct Student Student_Record[], struct Student Info)
{
    int location;
    location = Hash(Key);

    while (Student_Record[location] != EmptyInfo)
    {
        location = (location+1) % MAX_INFO;
    }
    Student_Record[location = Info;
    Length ++;
}
```

To search for a record using this collision-handing technique, we perform the hash function on the key, then compare the desired key to the actual key in the record at the designated location. If the keys do not match, we use linear probing, beginning at the next room in array. Now we will give another version of **Access_Record ()** function that uses this approach. If the record is not found in the list, the outgoing parameter found is false and no record is return by the function.

```
struct Student * Access_Record(int Key, struct Student Student_Record[])
{
    int location;
    int Start_Loc;
    Flag = true;
    Start_Loc = Hash(Key);
    location = Start_Loc;

do
{
```

```
    if(Student_Record[location] !=Info || Student_Record[location] EmptyInfo)
        Flag = false;
    else
        location = (location+1) % MAX_INFO;
    } while(location != Start_Loc && Flag);
    Found = (Student_Record[location] == Info);
    If (found)
        Info = Student_Record[location];
}
```

9.12.3 DELETION

Order of insertion	Index	Student_Record
	00	Empty
	01	Record with key = 14001
	02	Empty
14001	03	Record with key = 50003
00104	04	Record with key = 00104
50003	05	Record with key = 77003
77003	06	Record with key = 42504
42504	07	Empty
33099	08	Empty
	...	...
...	...	...
...		....
	98	
	99	

Fig. 9.55 Hash table with linear probing

Collisions, however, complicate the matter. We can find the element using the same search approach as we used for **Access_Record()**. But when we locate the record in the hash table, we cannot merely replace the info with **EmptyInfo.** A review of **Access_Record ()** above shows the problem. In the loop, the detection of an empty room ends the search. If **Remove_Info()** "empties" the room occupied by a deleted record, we may terminate a subsequent search prematurely.

For example, in **Fig. 9.55,** suppose we remove the record with key 77003 by setting the array room 5 to **Empty_Info**. A subsequent search for the record with the key 42504 would begin at the hash location 4. The record in this room is not the one we are looking for, so we increment the hash location to 5. This room, which formerly was occupied by the record that we removed, is now empty, so we terminate the search. We have not really finished searching; however, the record that we are looking for is the next room.

One solution to this problem is to create a third constant value, **Removed_Record**, to use in rooms that were occupied by the deleted records. If a room contains **Removed_Record** it means that this room is currently free, but the room was previously occupied.

With this change we must modify both the insertion and accessing function operation, function to process rooms correctly. The insertion technique treats a room with **Removed_Record** and **Empty_Info** the same, the search for an available room for the new record ends. The **Empty_Info** halts the search in function **Access_Record()** but **Removed_Record** does not.

This solution corrects the search problem but generates another: after many deletions, the search path to a record may travel through many array rooms with **Removed_Record**. This may cause the efficiency of retrieving a record to deteriorate. These problems illustrate that hash tables, in the forms that we have studied so far, are not the most effective data structure for implementing lists whose elements may be deleted.

9.12.4 CLUSTERING

One problem with linear probing is that its results in a situation called clustering. A good hash function results in a uniform distribution of indexes throughout the array's index range. Initially, therefore, records are inserted throughout the array, each room equally likely to be filled. Over time, however, after a number of collisions have been resolved, the distribution of records in the array becomes less and less uniform. The records tend to cluster together, as multiple keys begin to complete for a single hash function. For example, consider the hash table given in **Fig. 9.55,** only a record whose key produces the hash value 8 would be inserted into array room 8. However, any records with keys that produces the hash values 3, 4, 5, 6 or 7 would be inserted into array room 7. That is array room 7 is five times as likely as array room 8 to be filled. Clustering results in inconsistent efficiency of insertion and retrieval operations.

9.12.5 REHASHING

The technique of linear probing discussed here is an example of collision resolution by rehashing. If the hash function produces a collision, the hash value is used as the input to rehash function to compute a new hash value. In the previous section, we added 1 to hash value that is we used the rehash function:

(Hash value + 1) % 100

For rehashing with linear probing we can use any function

(Hash value + constant) % array_size

as long as **constant** and **array_size** are relatively prime- that is the largest number that divides both of them evenly is 1. For instance, given the 100-rooms array in **Fig. 9.56,** we might use the constant 3 in the rehash function:

(Hash value + 3) % 100

Note 100 is not a prime number, 3 and 100 are relatively prime; they have no common factor larger than 1.

Suppose that we want to add a record with the key 14001 to the hash table in **Fig. 9.56.** The original hash function (Key %100) returns the hash value 1, but this array room is in use, it contains the record with key value 44001. To determine the next array room to try, we apply the rehash function using the results of the first hash function an input: (1+3) %100 = 4. The array room at index 4 is also in use, so we reapply the rehash function until we get an available room. Each time, we use the value computed from the previous rehash as input to the rehash function. The second rehash gives (4+3)%100 = 7; this room is in use. Third rehash gives (7+3)%100 = 10; the array room at index 10 is empty, so the new record is inserted there.

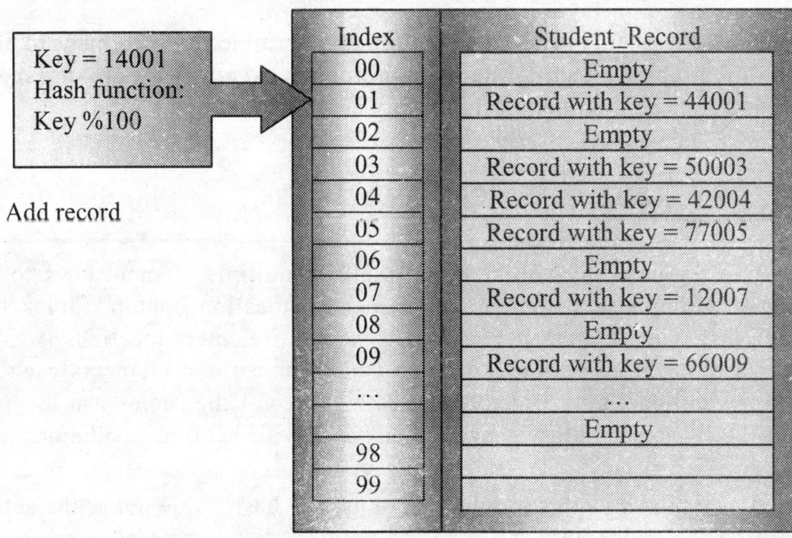

Fig. 9.56 Handling collisions with rehashing

Why the constant and array rooms must be relatively prime? For example, consider the rehash function

(Hash value +2) %100

We want to add the record with the key 14001 to the hash table shown in **Fig. 9.56,** the original hash function, Key %100, returns the hash value 1. This arrays room is already occupied. We resolve the collision by applying the rehash function above, examining successive odd-numbered indexes until a free room is found. What happens if all of the rooms with odd-numbered indexes are already in use? The search would fail-even though there are free rooms with even-numbered indexes. This rehash function does not cover the full index range of the array. However, if the constant and the number of array rooms are relatively prime, e.g. 3 and 100, the function produces successive rehashes that eventually cover every index in the array. Rehash functions that use linear probing do not eliminate clustering. For example, in **Fig. 9.56,** any record with a key value that produces the hash value 1, 4, 7 or 10 would be inserted into the room at index 10.

In linear probing, we add a constant usually 1, in each successive application of the rehash function. Another approach, called quadratic probing, makes the result of rehashing dependent on how many times the rehash function has been applied. In the ith rehash, the function is

(Hash_Value + i^2) % array_size

The first rehash adds 1 to **Hash_Value**, the second rehash adds 4, the third rehash adds 9 and so on. Quadratic probing reduces clustering, but it does not necessarily examine every room in the array. For example, if **array_size** is a power of 2 (e.g. 256, 512, 1024 or 2448), relatively few array rooms are examined. However, if **array_size** is a prime number of the **4*some_integer + 3,** quadratic probing does examine every room in the array.

A third approach uses a pseudo-random generator to determine the increment to **Hash_Value** in each application of the rehash function. Random probing is excellent for eliminating clustering, but it tends to be slower than the other techniques we have discussed.

9.12.6 BUCKET AND CHAINING

Another alternative for handling collisions is to allow multiple element keys to hash to the same location. One solution is to let each computed hash location contain rooms for multiple elements, rather than just a single element. Each of these multi-element locations is called bucket. **Fig. 9.57** illustrates a hash table with buckets that can contain three elements each. Using this approach, we can allow collisions to produce duplicate entries at the same hash location, up to a point. When the bucket becomes full, we must again deal with handling collisions.

Another solution, which avoids this problem, is to use the hash value not as the actual location of the element, but as the index into an array of pointers. Each pointer accesses a chain of elements that share the same hash location. **Fig. 9.58** illustrates this solution to the problem of collisions. Rather than rehashing, we simply allow both elements to share hash location 3. The entry in the array at this location contains a pointer to a linked list that includes both elements. To search for a given element, one first applies the hash function to the key and then searches the chain for the element. Searching is not eliminated, but it is limited to elements that actually share a hash location. In contrast, with linear probing one may have to search through many additional elements if the rooms following the hash location are filled with elements from collisions on other hash locations.

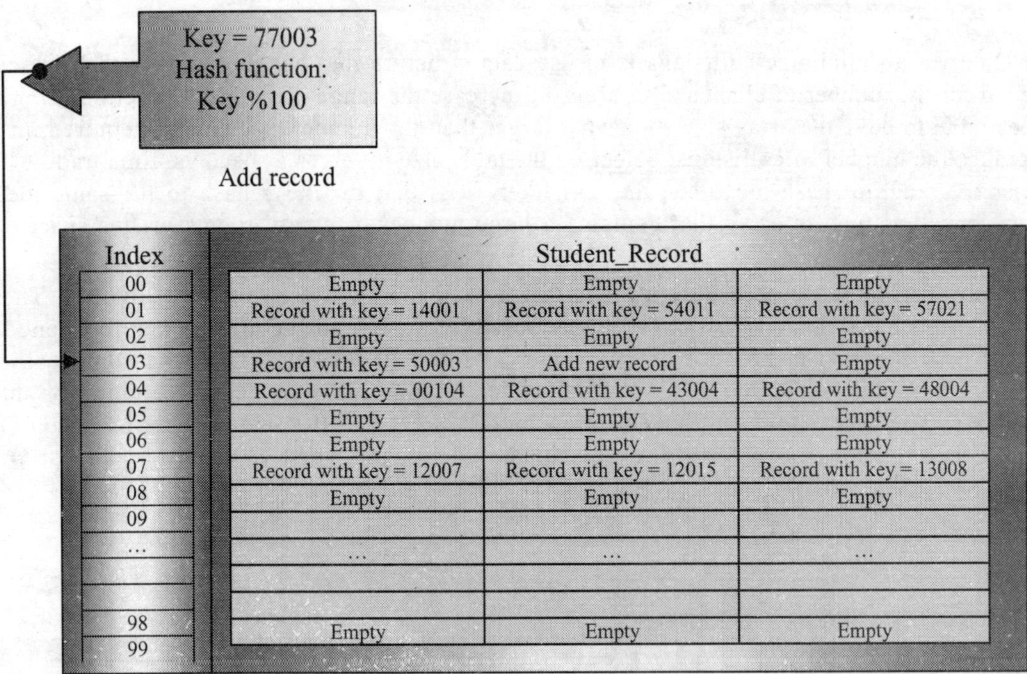

Fig. 9.57 Handling collisions with hashing with buckets

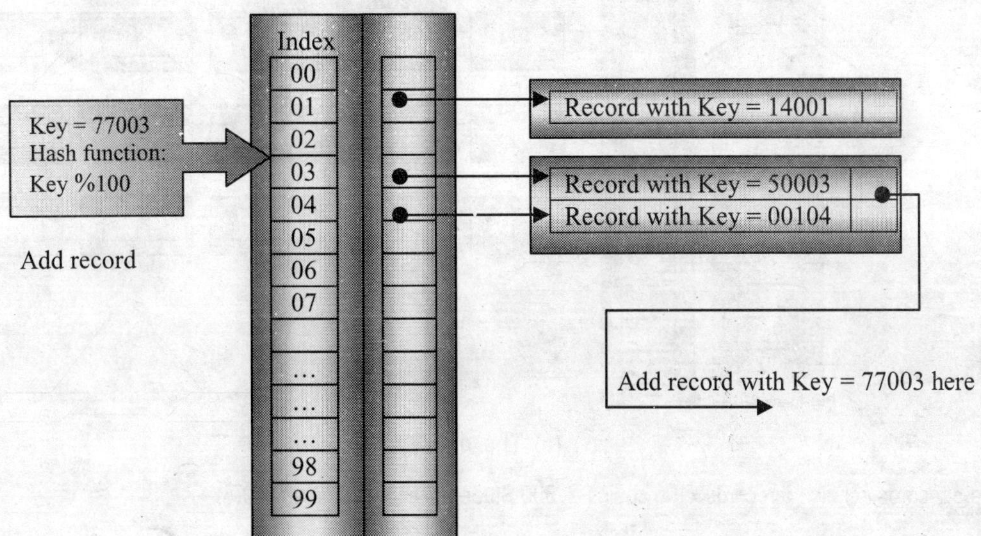

Fig. 9.58 Handling collisions by hashing with chaining

9.12.7 SELECTING GOOD HASH FUNCTION

One way to minimize collisions is to use data structure that has more space than is actually needed for the number of elements, in order to increase the range of the hash function. In practice it desirable to have the array size somewhat larger than the number of elements required, in order to reduce the number of collisions. Selecting the table size involves a space vs. time trade-off. The larger the range of hash locations, the less likely it is that two keys hash to the same location. However, allocating an array that contains a large number of empty rooms wastes space.

More important, one can design his/her own hash function to minimize collisions. The goal is to distribute the elements as uniformly as possible throughout the array. Therefore, one wants his/her hash function to produce unique values as often as possible. Once we admit collisions, we must introduce some sort of searching, either through array or chain searching or through rehashing. The access to each element is no longer direct and the search is no longer **O (1).** In fact, if the collisions cause very disproportionate chains, the worst case may be almost **O (n).**

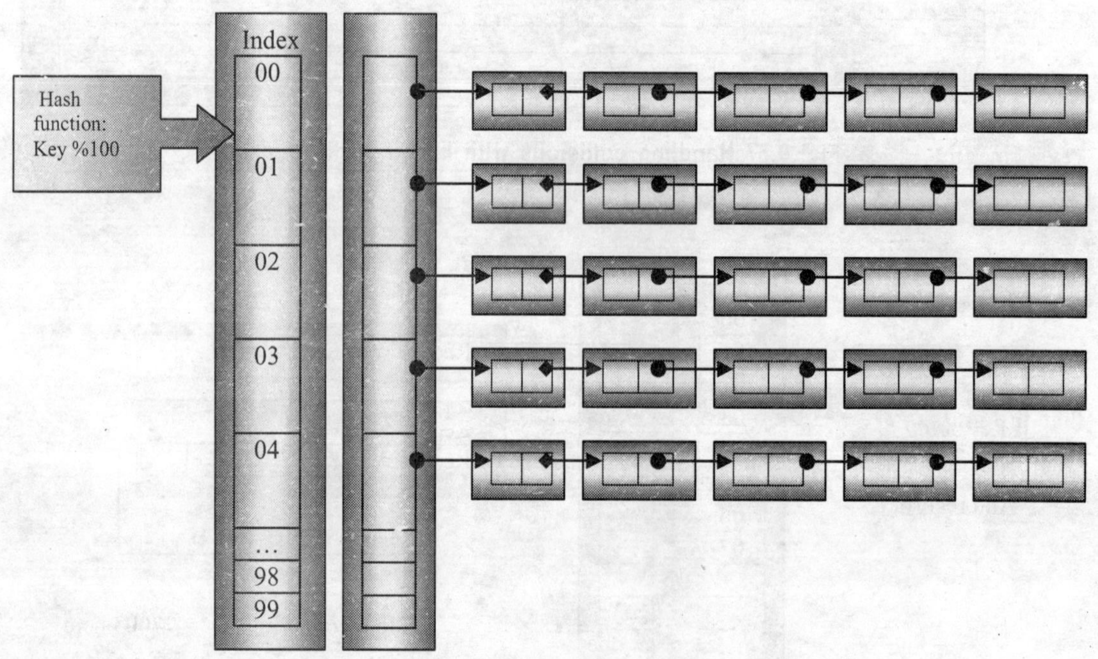

(a) The plan

Average 5 records / chain , 5 records x100 chains = 500 Students, expected search O(5)

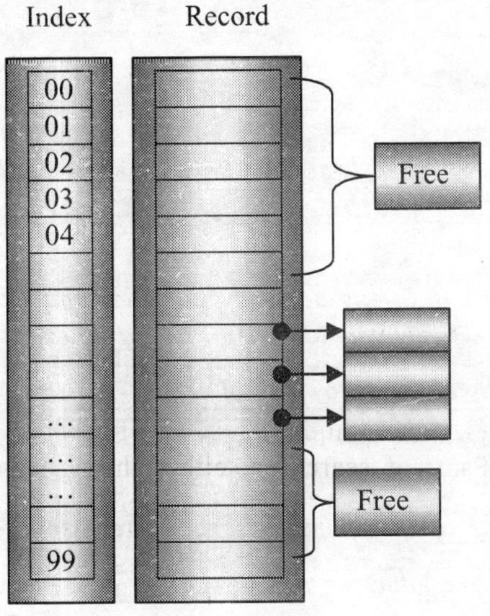

(b) The reality

Fig. 9.59 Hash scheme to handle student record

To avoid such a situation one needs to know something about the statistical distribution of keys. Imagine HNB Garhwal University whose student records are sorted according to a university ID six digits long. There are 500 students and we decide to use a chained approach to handling collisions. We set up 100 chains and use the hash function

STD_ID % 100

That is, we use the last two digits of the six-digit ID number as index. The planned hash scheme is shown in **Fig. 9.59 (a). Fig. 9.59 (b)** shows what happened when the hash scheme was implemented. How could the distribution of the elements have come out so skewed? It turns out that the university's ID number is a concatenation of three fields:

The hash scheme depended solely on the year student enrolled to produce hash values. Because the university was founded in 1917, all the elements were crowed very disproportionately into a small subset of the hash locations. A search for a student element, in this case is **O (n).** Although this is an exaggerated example, it illustrates the need to understand as completely as possible the domain and predicted values of keys in a hash scheme.

EXERCISE

*9.1 Suppose **String** is the following list of 14 alphabetic characters:*

DATASTRUCTURES

*Suppose the characters in **String** are to be sorted alphabetically. Use the quick sort algorithm to find the position of the first character **D**.*

*9.2 Suppose **Name** consists of the following list of names with **n = 5.***

Tom Boy Jadeja Sachin Sanath

*Find the number **C** of comparisons to sort **Name** using radix sort.*

*9.3 Suppose **S** consists of the following **n = 6** letters*

A B E H C L

*Find the number of comparisons to sort **S** using shell sort.*

9.4 Sort the following lists in ascending order using selection sort:

(i) 66, 77, 11, 88, 99, 22, 33, 44, 55, 77, 03, 04, 05
(ii) S, T, R, U, C, T, U, R, E, S, D, A, T, A

9.5 Sort the following lists in ascending order using insertion sort:

(i) 66, 77, 11, 88, 99, 22, 33, 44, 55, 77, 03, 04, 05
(ii) S, T, R, U, C, T, U, R, E, S, D, A, T, A

*9.6 Using the bubble sort algorithm, find the number **C** of comparisons and the number **I** of interchanges which alphabetize the **n= 10** letters in **STRUCTURES**.*

*9.7 Find the contents of the array **A** shown in **Fig. 9.60** after 3rd and 7th iterations if sorting is done by*

(i) bubble sort
(ii) shell sort
(iii) insertion sort
(iv) selection sort
(v) merge sort

53	17	20	33	28	14	29	15	77	24

Fig. 9.60 list in memory

9.8 *Show how the values in the array **A** shown in **Fig. 9.60** would have to be rearranged to satisfy **min** and **max** heap property. Sort the array using heap sort algorithm.*

9.9 *Sort the array **A** shown in **Fig. 9.60** using merge sort.*

9.10 *How many comparisons would be needed to sort a list of 50 elements using radix sort*

(i) in worst case
(ii) in the best case

9.11 *A sorting function is called to sort a list of 50 integers that have been read from a data file. If all 50 values are zero what would the execution requirement (in terms of big O) be if the sort used was*

(i) quick sort
(ii) bubble sort
(iii) selection sort
(iv) heap sort
(v) insertion sort
(vi) merge sort

9.12 *How many comparisons are required to sort an array of 50 elements using selection sort, if the original array values were already sorted?*

(i) 5000
(ii) 4950
(iii) 49
(iv) non of these

9.13 *A merge sort is used to sort an array of 1000 test scores in the descending order. Which of the following statement is true?*

(i) The sort is fasted if the original test scores are in order from smallest to largest.
(ii) The sort is fasted if the original test scores are in completely in random order.
(iii) The sort is fasted if the original test scores are in order from largest to smallest.
(iv) The sort is same, no matter what the order of the original elements.

9.14 *Which of the following sorts will take longest time to execute and which will take the shortest time?*

(i) merge sort
(ii) heap sort
(iii) selection sort
(iv) shell sort
(v) quick sort
(vi) insertion sort

*9.15 Fill in the **Table** shown in **Fig. 9.61,** showing the number of comparisons needed either to find the value or to determine that the value is not in the array, given the following values: 26, 15, 27, 12, 33, 95, 9, 5, 99, 14*

Value	Unsorted	Sorted, sequential search	Sorted, binary search	Binary search tree
15				
17				
14				
5				
99				
100				
0				

Fig. 9.61 Table

9.16 Apply selection sort algorithm to sort files in a directory?

*9.17 Does the tree shown in **Fig. 9.62** represent a heap or not? Discuss.*

9.18 Implement selection sort algorithm for linked lists. What is its complexity?

9.19 Implement bubble sort for doubly linked lists. What is its complexity?

9.20 Implement the insertion sort for linked lists. What is time complexity of this sort?

9.21 Implement merge sort algorithm to merge two linked lists. Sort the concatenated list. What is its time complexity?

9.22 Implement radix sort algorithm to sort files in a directory.

*9.23 Implement radix sort algorithm that sorts an array of **n** cells with values from 0 to **n-1** in place. Write a general radix sort algorithm for sorting strings using doubly linked list.*

*9.24 Create heap for the list of elements shown in **Fig. 9.63.***

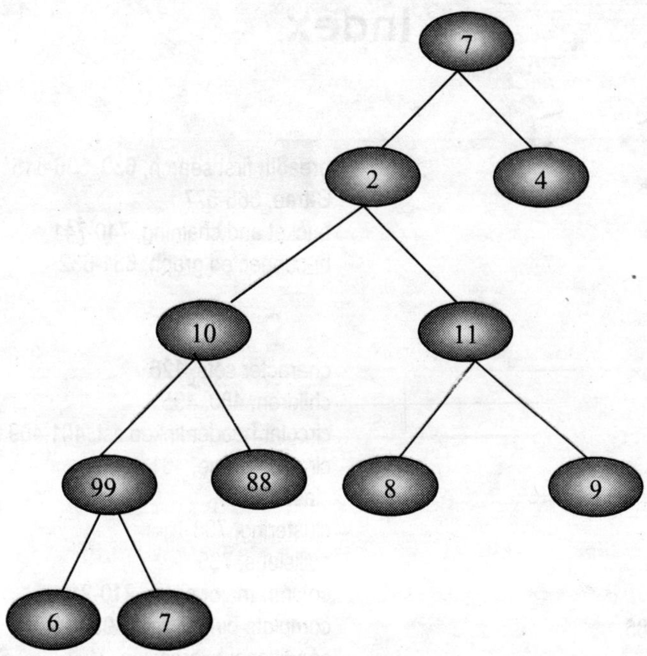

Fig. 9.62 Tree

Index	1	2	3	4	5	6	7	8	9	10
Values	97	22	43	100	34	97	81	10	44	41

Fig. 9.63 List of elements in memory

Index

A

algorithm, 79-80
analysis of algorithm, 80
    big-O notation, 83-84
    rate of growth, 80-81
    time, 81-83
AVL trees, 540-545
    height of, 555-556
    left high, 552-554
    right high, 551-552
Ackermann function, 93,97
Adel'son-vel'skill, G.M., 540
adjacency list, 629-630
adjacency matrix, 594-599
algebraic expression, 484-485
ancestor, 480
array, 84-85
    multidimensional, 206-207, 258-262
    one dimensional, 177-206
    two dimensional, 207-215
arithmetic operators with assignment, 8-9
associativity, 9-11

B

balanced binary tree, 540
    height, 540-545
    weight, 514-527
base address, 179-180
big-O notation, 83-84
binary search, 657-662
binary search tree, 528-532
binary tree, 482-495
application, 526-527
    complete, 495-500
    depth, 495-496
    expression, 484-485
    extended, 500
    height, 495-496
    representation, 500-505
    traversing, 506-514
branch, 480, 482
breadth first search, 630, 636-645
B-tree, 568-577
bucket and chaining, 740-741
bi-connected graph, 631-632

C

character sets, 126
children, 480, 495
circular header linked list, 401-409
circular queue, 461-470
class, 54-57
clustering, 738
collisions, 735
column-major order, 210-211
complete binary tree, 495-497
conditional expression, 11
constants, 1-3
    character, 2
    double, 2
    enumerated, 2
    float, 2
    integer, 2
    literal, 2
calloc, 33-37
const, 2
constructor, 59-60
critical node, 542-545
cut-vertex, 631-632

D

data structure, 84
    linear, 84-86, 176, 269, 421
    non-linear, 84, 86-87, 479, 587
decision table, 75
degree of a node (node & vertex), 480, 592, 500
deletion in doubly linked list, 368
    of a desired node, 369, 381-388
    of left most node, 369-374
    of right most node, 369, 374-380
deletion from array, 190-200
deletion in linked list, 304-305

of first node, 305-310
of last node, 305, 310-315
of a desired node, 305, 316-326
deletion in binary search tree, 532-540
deletion in B-tree, 573-577
D. Huffman, 517
delete, 38-39
depth, 481, 495-496
depth-first search, 630-636
deque, 470-472
descendent, 480
destructor, 59-61
digraph, 588-590
Dijkstra algorithm, 615-621
directed graph, 588-590
divide and conquer, 115-120
Donald Shell, 687
doubly linked list, 342-347
duplicates, 193-200
dynamic memory allocation, 32-37
data structure operations, 88
deletion, 88
insertion, 88
merging, 88
searching, 88
sorting, 88
traversing, 88

E

enumerated constants, 2, 4-5
escape sequences, 3-4
exponential, 97-102
extended binary tree, 500
external node (terminal node), 480, 514
external path length, 514-517

F

factorial, 91-94
father, 480
FCFS, 452
fibonacci sequence, 102-103
files and streams, 62-74
ifstream, 62-65
iostream, 62-65
istream, 62-65
istrstream, 62-65
ofstream, 62-65
ostream, 62-64
oststream, 62-64
flowchart, 75-78
FLOYD technique, 622-628
forest, 481-482
front, 453-473
function, 40-41
invocation, 41-43
prototyping, 47-49
structure, 52-53
termination, 43-45
overloading, 49-52
overhead, 120-121

G

Graph, 587-588
bi-connected, 631-632
directed, 588-590
edge, 588
loop, 590-591
mixed, 588-589
null, 591-592
path, 593
path matrix, 597-599, 622-628
undirected, 587-590
weighted, 590-591
multigraph, 589-590
graph representation, 594
matrix, 594-599
sequential, 594

graph traversal, 630
breadth first, 630, 636-645
depth first, 630-636

H

Hashing, 732-735
bucket and chaining, 740-741
clustering, 738
collisions, 735
deletion, 737-738
linear probing. 735-736
rehashing, 738-740
selection of good hash function, 742-743

header node, 394
header linked, 394
grounded, 394-401
circular, 394, 401-409
heap, 706-708
creation, 708-714
heap sort, 706-718
height of binary tree, 495-496
Huffman's, 516-525
algorithm, 516-525
code, 526-527
code tree, 526-527

I

input streams, 62
ifstream, 62-65
istream, 62-65
istrstream, 62-65
in-order
threading, 577-578
traversing, 509-510
in-degree, 592
index, 141
infix, 443-446
insertion
in a linked list, 282-303
in array, 183-189
in AVL tree, 545-551
in doubly linked list, 351-367
in multi-way tree, 569-573
insertion in doubly linked list, 351-352
first node, 352-358
a node at the end, 352, 359-365
at desired place, 352, 365-367
insertion in linked list, 282-283
as a first node, 282-288
as a last node, 282, 288-293
at specific location, 282, 293-303
insertion sort, 668-673
internal node (non-terminal), 480
isolated node, 591-592

L

labeled graph (weighted graph), 590-591
left sub-tree, 482-484
length
of path, 514-517
of string, 149-150
LIFO, 421
linear array, 84, 176
linear data structure, 84-86, 176, 269, 421
array, 84-85, 176-264
linked list, 85, 269-414
stack and queues, 86, 421-474
linear probing, 735-736
linear search, 652-656
linked list,
circular, 401-409
doubly, 342-347
header, 394-414
linear, 269-279
merging, 388-393
lower bound, 209

M

malloc, 33, 36-37
matrix, 207-211
addition, 216-220
adjacency, 594-599
inverse, 242-248
multiplication, 224-229
orthogonal, 233-238
path, 597-599, 622-628
rank, 251-257
singular, 238-242
sparse, 262-264
subtraction, 220-224
symmetric, 248-251
transpose, 230-233
weight, 622-624
memory allocation, 32-38
merge sort, 691-705
merging of two lists, 388-393
multi dimensional arrays, 258-262
multi-graph, 589-590

N

new, 38-40
node
terminal (external), 480
header, 394
non-terminal (internal), 480

isolated, 591-592
nonlinear data structure, 84, 479, 587
tree, 479-578
graph, 587-647
null, 591-592

O

output streams, 62
ofstream, 62-65
ostream, 62-64
ostrstream, 62-64
out-degree, 592 overflow, 11-12

P

parent node, 480
pop, 425-433
push, 425-433
parameter passing, 45
by reference, 46-47
by values, 45-46 path, 593
path length, 514-517
external, 514-517
weighted, 515-517
path matrix, 597-599, 622-628
pattern matching, 141-148, 158-173
peep, 434-438
pivot, 673-675
pointers, 19-24
array of, 24-27
double, 21-23
to structure, 28
polish notation, 443-444
infix, 443-446
prefix, 443
postfix, 443-452
polynomials, 409-414
representation, 409-410
addition, 412-414
precedence, 9-11
preorder traversing, 506-508
post order traversing, 510-511
priority queue, 472-474
prototype, 47-49

Q

queue, 452-474
priority, 472-474
circular, 461-470
double ended, 470-472
quick sort, 673-680

R

radix sort, 719-731
radix exchange sort, 731-732
rear, 453-474
recursion, 91-94
recursive process, 96
rehashing, 738-740
recursive algorithms
binary tree creation, 482-485
divide and conquer, 115-120
exponential power, 97-102
factorial, 91-94
fibonacci number, 102
greatest common divisor, 104
inorder, 509-510
post order, 510-511
preorder, 506-508
Towers of Hanoi, 105-114
right sub-tree, 482-483
root, 480
round robin, 452
row major order, 210-211

S

search
binary, 657-662
linear, 552-556
searching
in array, 201-206
in binary tree, 528-532
in linked list, 327-331
selection sort, 681-686
shortest path algorithm, 600-628
sibling, 480
sorting
bubble, 662-668
heap, 706-718
insertion, 668-673

merge, 691-705
quick, 673-680
radix, 719-731
radix exchange, 731-732
selection, 681-686
shell, 686-691
topological, 646-647
streams, 62-66
ifstream, 62-66
istream. 62-65
istrstream, 62-65
ostrstream, 62-64
ostream, 62-64
ofstream, 62-65
status bits, 66
stack, 421-422
stack representation, 423-424
array, 424-430
linked list, 424, 430-433
stack operation
peep, 434-438
pop, 425-433
push, 425-433
update, 438-442
string, 125-126
null string, 126
sub-string, 126, 140
string operation, 125, 139-140
concatenation, 148-149
indexing, 141-148
length, 126, 149-150
structure, 12-17
structure of string storage, 127
fixed length, 127-132
linked list, 139
variable length fixed maximum, 133-138
sub-tree, 480, 482-484
successor, 482-483
symmetric matrix, 248-251

T

ternary operator, 11
terminal node, 480
text editing, 150-151
deletion, 151, 153-158
insertion, 151-154
pattern matching, 158-173
text formatting, 150
threaded binary tree, 577-578
one way, 578
two way, 578
top of stack, 421-422
topological sorting, 646-647
towers of Hanoi, 105-114
traversing
binary tree, 506-514
doubly linked list, 347-351
linked list, 279-282
one dimensional array, 180-183
two dimensional, 211-215
tree, 479-482
2-tree, 500
binary, 482-495
binary search, 528-532
complete, 495-500
deletion, 532-540
depth, 481, 495-496
height, 481, 540-545
skewed, 503-504
threaded, 577-578
two-dimensional array, 211-215

U

union, 18-19
upper bound, 209

V

variable length string, 133-138

W

Warshall's algorithm, 600-614
weight, 591, 615-616, 622, 624
weight matrix, 622-624
weighted graph, 591, 615-617
weighted path length algorithm, 514-517
word, 125-126
word processing, 125